The Peaceful Settlement of International Disputes

Addressing not only inter-State dispute settlement but also the settlement of disputes involving non-State actors, *The Peaceful Settlement of International Disputes* offers a clear and systematic overview of the procedures for dispute settlement in international law.

In light of the diversification of dispute settlement procedures, traditional means of international dispute settlement are discussed alongside newly developing fields such as the dispute settlement system under the United Nations Convention on the Law of the Sea, the WTO dispute settlement systems, the peaceful settlement of international environmental disputes, intra-State disputes, mixed arbitration, the United Nations Compensation Commission and the World Bank Inspection Panel. Figures are used throughout the book to help the reader to better understand the procedures and institutions of international dispute settlement, and suggestions for further reading support exploration of relevant issues.

Suitable for postgraduate law and international relations students studying dispute settlement in international law and conflict resolution, this book helps students to easily grasp key concepts and issues.

YOSHIFUMI TANAKA is Professor of International Law at the Faculty of Law, University of Copenhagen. He has taught at several different universities and has published widely in the fields of peaceful settlement of international disputes, the law of the sea and international environmental law.

The Peaceful Settlement of International Disputes

Yoshifumi Tanaka
University of Copenhagen

CAMBRIDGE
UNIVERSITY PRESS

University Printing House, Cambridge CB2 8BS, United Kingdom

One Liberty Plaza, 20th Floor, New York, NY 10006, USA

477 Williamstown Road, Port Melbourne, VIC 3207, Australia

314-321, 3rd Floor, Plot 3, Splendor Forum, Jasola District Centre, New Delhi - 110025, India

79 Anson Road, #06-04/06, Singapore 079906

Cambridge University Press is part of the University of Cambridge.

It furthers the University's mission by disseminating knowledge in the pursuit of education, learning and research at the highest international levels of excellence.

www.cambridge.org
Information on this title: www.cambridge.org/9781107164277
DOI: 10.1017/9781316687062

© Yoshifumi Tanaka 2018

This publication is in copyright. Subject to statutory exception and to the provisions of relevant collective licensing agreements, no reproduction of any part may take place without the written permission of Cambridge University Press.

First published 2018

A catalogue record for this publication is available from the British Library

ISBN 978-1-107-16427-7 Hardback
ISBN 978-1-316-61588-1 Paperback

Cambridge University Press has no responsibility for the persistence or accuracy of URLs for external or third-party internet websites referred to in this publication, and does not guarantee that any content on such websites is, or will remain, accurate or appropriate.

Dedicated to my teachers,
Lucius Caflisch, Hugh Thirlway and Tetsuo Sato.

Nation will not take up sword against nation,
nor will they train for war any more.
Isaiah 2:4

Contents

List of Figures   *page* xiii
List of Tables   xiv
Preface   xv
Acknowledgements   xvii
List of Abbreviations   xviii
Table of Cases   xxi
Table of Treaties and Instruments   xxxiv

PART I FOUNDATION OF INTERNATIONAL DISPUTE SETTLEMENT   1

1 International Dispute Settlement in Perspective   3
1 Introduction   3
2 Obligation of Peaceful Settlement of International Disputes   5
3 The Concept of International Disputes in International Law   8
   3.1 Definition of International Disputes   8
   3.2 Identification of International Disputes   9
   3.3 The Distinction between Legal (Static) and Non-Legal (Dynamic) Disputes   14
   3.4 The Diversification of 'Disputes' in International Relations   17
4 Classification of Means of International Dispute Settlement   19
   4.1 Classification of Means of the Settlement of Inter-State Disputes   19
   4.2 Classification of Dispute Settlement Means in a Contemporary Context   23
5 Principal Features of the Dispute Settlement System in International Law   24
6 Conclusions   25

2 Negotiation, Good Offices and Mediation   28
1 Introduction   28
2 Negotiation and International Law   29
   2.1 The Relationship between Negotiation and International Law   29
   2.2 The Concept of Negotiation   30

3 Interaction between Negotiation and International Adjudication   31
   3.1 Pre-Adjudicative Stage   32
   3.2 During Adjudication   32
   3.3 Post-Adjudicative Stage   33
4 Obligation to Negotiate   37
5 Timeframe for Negotiations   40
6 Outcome of Negotiations   41
7 Good Offices   43
   7.1 General Considerations   43
   7.2 Process of Good Offices   43
   7.3 Functions and Practice of Good Offices   44
8 Mediation   45
   8.1 General Considerations   45
   8.2 Process of Mediation   46
   8.3 Practice of Mediation   47
   8.4 Limitations of Mediation and Good Offices   49
9 Conclusions   50

3 Inquiry and Conciliation   52
1 Introduction   52
2 Inquiry   53
   2.1 Functions of Inquiry   53
   2.2 Institution of Inquiry   54
   2.3 Case Study (1): Inquiry by Inquiry Commissions   56
   2.4 Case Study (2): Inquiry under the Auspices of International Organisations   62
3 Conciliation   65
   3.1 Typology of Conciliation   65
   3.2 Function of Conciliation   65
   3.3 Institutional Aspects of Conciliation   67
   3.4 Limits of Conciliation   69
4 Conclusions   71

4 International Dispute Settlement through the United Nations   73
1 Introduction   73
2 The Role of the Security Council in International Dispute Settlement   74
   2.1 Procedure of Dispute Settlement   74
   2.2 Activities of the UN Security Council   77
   2.3 Questions Associated with Veto   80
   2.4 Disqualification from Voting   82
   2.5 The Relationship between the Security Council and the International Court of Justice   84
3 The Role of the General Assembly in International Dispute Settlement   85
   3.1 Functions of the General Assembly   85
   3.2 Predominance of the Security Council over the General Assembly   87
4 The Role of the UN Secretary-General in International Dispute Settlement   88
   4.1 Activities of the UN Secretary-General   88
   4.2 Independence of the UN Secretary-General   95
5 The United Nations and Regional Arrangements   98
   5.1 Cooperation between the United Nations and Regional Arrangements   98
   5.2 Concurrence of Jurisdiction between the UN Security Council and Regional Organisations   99

5.3 Interaction between Regional Institutions and International Adjudication   100
5.4 Limits with Regional Organisations and Arrangements   101
6 Conclusions   102

5 Inter-State Arbitration   105
1 Introduction   105
2 Development of Inter-State Arbitration   107
3 The Selection of Arbitrators   109
   3.1 Disagreement with Regard to the Appointment of Arbitrators   109
   3.2 Independence and Impartiality of Arbitrators   111
4 Process of Arbitration   114
   4.1 Initiation of the Arbitration Process   114
   4.2 Scope of the Jurisdiction of an Arbitral Tribunal   116
   4.3 Applicable Law   117
5 Intervention by Third States   118
6 Effect of the Arbitral Award   119
   6.1 Implementation of the Arbitral Award   119
   6.2 Nullity of the Arbitral Award   121
7 Interpretation of the Arbitral Award   125
8 Conclusions   126

6 International Court of Justice (I): Organisation and Jurisdiction of the Court   128
1 Introduction   129
   1.1 The ICJ as a Principal Judicial Organ of the United Nations   129
   1.2 Importance of the ICJ in International Dispute Settlement   129
   1.3 Instruments Governing the ICJ   130
2 Parties before the ICJ   131
3 Organisation of the ICJ   132
   3.1 Election of Judges   132
   3.2 Independence and Impartiality of Judges   134
   3.3 A National Judge and Judge Ad Hoc   137
   3.4 Chambers of the ICJ   139
   3.5 The Registry   141
4 Contentious Jurisdiction of the ICJ   141
   4.1 General Considerations   141
   4.2 Special Agreement   142
   4.3 Compromissory Clause   144
   4.4 *Forum Prorogatum*   144
   4.5 Optional Clause   147
5 Reservations to the Optional Clause   149
   5.1 Principle of Reciprocity Concerning Reservations to the Optional Clause   149
   5.2 Reservations *Ratione Personae*   151
   5.3 Reservations *Ratione Temporis*   152
   5.4 Reservations *Ratione Materiae*   154
   5.5 The Validity of Automatic Reservation   157
   5.6 The Validity of Instantly Amendable Reservations   160
   5.7 Termination of Declarations   161

6 Advisory Jurisdiction   163
  6.1 Basics of an Advisory Opinion   163
  6.2 Procedure of Advisory Proceedings   166
  6.3 Admissibility of Request   167
  6.4 Effect of Advisory Opinion   170
7 Conclusions   171

7 International Court of Justice (II): Law and Procedure of the Court   175
1 Applicable Law   175
  1.1 General Considerations   175
  1.2 *Lex Lata* and *Lex Ferenda*   176
2 The Proceedings in Contentious Cases   178
  2.1 The Procedure in a Contentious Case   178
  2.2 The Principle *Ne Eat Iudex Ultra Petita Partium*   185
  2.3 Non-Appearance   187
3 Provisional Measures   190
  3.1 Purpose of Provisional Measures   190
  3.2 Requirements to Indicate Provisional Measures   191
  3.3 Provisional Measures and the Ceasing of Execution of Individuals   197
  3.4 Implementation of Provisional Measures   199
4 Preliminary Objections   200
  4.1 Procedural Issues   200
  4.2 The *Monetary Gold* Rule   202
  4.3 Admissibility of Disputes Involving Highly Political Issues   204
5 Intervention under Article 62 of the Court's Statute   205
  5.1 General Considerations   205
  5.2 The Concept of an Interest of a Legal Nature   206
  5.3 Jurisdictional Link   209
  5.4 Legal Effect of Judgments on an Intervener   210
6 Third State Intervention under Article 63 of the Court's Statute   211
7 Judgment of the ICJ   213
  7.1 *Res Judicata*   213
  7.2 Effect of Article 59 of the ICJ Statute   215
  7.3 Interpretation of Judgments   215
  7.4 Revision of Judgments   218
  7.5 Implementation of Judgments   221
8 Conclusions   222

PART II INTERNATIONAL DISPUTE SETTLEMENT IN PARTICULAR FIELDS   227

8 International Dispute Settlement in the UN Convention on the Law of the Sea   229
1 Introduction   229
2 Interlinkage between Voluntary and Compulsory Procedures of International Dispute Settlement   230
  2.1 The Interlinkage between Voluntary and Compulsory Procedures   230
  2.2 Conciliation   235

xi Contents

3 Compulsory Procedures of International Dispute Settlement   236
   3.1 Multiplicity of Forums: Montreux Formula   236
   3.2 Limitations and Exceptions to the Compulsory Procedures   237
4 International Tribunal for the Law of the Sea   243
   4.1 The Structure of ITLOS   243
   4.2 Jurisdiction of ITLOS   248
   4.3 Applicable Law   250
   4.4 Proceedings before ITLOS   251
   4.5 Preliminary Objections   252
   4.6 Provisional Measures   254
   4.7 Intervention   260
   4.8 Prompt Release Procedure   260
   4.9 Judgment   263
   4.10 Advisory Proceedings   264
5 Arbitration under the LOSC   268
   5.1 Annex VII Arbitral Tribunal under the LOSC   268
   5.2 Annex VIII Special Arbitral Tribunal   268
6 Fragmentation of International Law   269
7 Conclusions   271

9 The WTO Dispute Settlement System   275

1 Introduction   275
   1.1 International Dispute Settlement in GATT   275
   1.2 Principal Features of the WTO Dispute Settlement System   277
2 Basic Elements of the WTO Dispute Settlement System   279
   2.1 General Considerations   279
   2.2 The Dispute Settlement Body   280
   2.3 Access to the Dispute Settlement System of the WTO   281
   2.4 Causes of Action   282
   2.5 Applicable Law   284
3 Consultation   286
4 Good offices, Conciliation and Mediation   288
5 Panel Proceedings   289
   5.1 The Establishment of a Panel   289
   5.2 Composition and Terms of Reference of Panels   290
   5.3 Scope of Jurisdiction of WTO panels   291
   5.4 Panel Procedure   292
6 Appellate Review   295
7 Legal Effect of Reports of WTO Panels and the Appellate Body   296
8 Implementation of Rulings and Recommendations   298
   8.1 Remedies for Breach of WTO Law   298
   8.2 Compensation and Retaliation   299
9 Legal Nature of the WTO Panel Procedure   303
10 Arbitration   304
11 The WTO Dispute Settlement System and Developing States   305
   11.1 Consideration of Developing States in the DSU   305
   11.2 Practice of Developing States   307
12 Conclusions   308

10 Peaceful Settlement of International Environmental Disputes 311
1 Introduction 311
2 International Adjudication and the Settlement of International Environmental Disputes 312
   2.1 General Considerations 312
   2.2 The Role of Arbitration in the Settlement of International Environmental Disputes 314
   2.3 The Role Provisional Measures in Environmental Protection 318
   2.4 *Locus Standi* on the Basis of the Breach of Obligations *Erga Omnes Partes* 320
3 Fact-Finding by Treaty Commission 321
4 Non-Compliance Procedures 323
   4.1 General Considerations 323
   4.2 Triggering Non-Compliance Procedures 325
   4.3 Composition of Organs of Non-Compliance Procedures 327
   4.4 Functions of the Compliance/Implementation Committee 328
   4.5 Relationship between Non-Compliance Procedures and Dispute Settlement Procedures 329
5 Conclusions 332

11 Peaceful Settlement of Disputes Involving Non-State Actors 334
1 Introduction 334
2 Peaceful Settlement of Intra-State Disputes 335
   2.1 The Role of the United Nations in the Settlement of Intra-State Disputes 335
   2.2 Intra-State Arbitration: The *Abyei* Arbitration 343
3 Mixed Arbitration 346
   3.1 The International Centre for the Settlement of Investment Disputes (ICSID) 346
   3.2 The Iran-United States Claims Tribunal 352
4 United Nations Compensation Commission 355
   4.1 Outline of the UNCC 355
   4.2 The UNCC and Claims for Environmental Damage 358
5 Settlement of Disputes between an International Organisation and its Member States: Judicial Review 362
   5.1 General Considerations 362
   5.2 The *Lockerbie* Case 363
   5.3 Discussion 364
6 International Organisations and Individuals 367
   6.1 UN Internal Justice System 367
   6.2 Inspection Panel of the World Bank 368
7 Conclusions 376

12 The Quest for Peace in International Law 382
1 Introduction 382
2 Interlinkage between International Dispute Settlement and the Prohibition of the Threat or Use of Force 384
   2.1 The League of Nations 384
   2.2 The United Nations 387
3 Interlinkage between Disarmament and Peaceful Settlement of International Disputes 390
4 Looking Ahead 392

Index 396

Figures

Figure 1.1	Expansion of the scope of international disputes	*page* 17
Figure 1.2	Model 1	20
Figure 7.1	Process of proceedings of the ICJ	179
Figure 7.2	Intervention under Article 62 of the ICJ Statute	211
Figure 8.1	Chambers of ITLOS	245
Figure 8.2	Special Chambers	247
Figure 11.1	Total number of ICSID cases registered, by calendar year	347
Figure 11.2	The Panel process	371

Tables

Table 1.1	Model 2-A	page 21
Table 1.2	Model 2-B	22
Table 1.3	Model 3	23
Table 3.1	Examples of conciliation	69
Table 4.1	List of the Secretary-Generals of the United Nations	89
Table 5.1	Differences between arbitration and judicial settlement	106
Table 6.1	Geographical distribution of the judges of the ICJ	133
Table 6.2	Cases before an ad hoc chamber	140
Table 6.3	Modes to give a State's consent to the ICJ's jurisdiction	142
Table 6.4	List of cases submitted to the ICJ by special agreement	143
Table 6.5	Examples of the submission of application without jurisdictional basis	146
Table 6.6	Classification of reservations to declarations recognising the jurisdiction of the ICJ as compulsory	151
Table 6.7	UN organs and other international institutions entitled to ask the ICJ for an advisory opinion	164
Table 7.1	Examples of non-appearance before the ICJ	188
Table 7.2	Request for intervention under Article 62 of the ICJ Statute	207
Table 7.3	Request for intervention under Article 63 of the Statute of the PCIJ and of the ICJ	212
Table 7.4	Requests for interpretation of ICJ judgments	217
Table 8.1	Limitations and exceptions to the compulsory procedures	238
Table 8.2	Current composition of the members of ITLOS and the ICJ	244
Table 8.3	List of ITLOS cases concerning provisional measures	256
Table 8.4	List of prompt release cases	261
Table 8.5	Arbitration under Annex VII of the LOSC	269

Preface

Our time is characterised by various international disputes. Without the establishment of effective mechanisms for peacefully settling these disputes, it would be difficult to achieve sustainable peace in the international community. Hence peaceful settlement of international disputes should be a crucial subject in international relations.

The peaceful settlement of international disputes is interdisciplinary by nature and it can be approached from multiple disciplines. International law is one of the disciplines that provide an important insight into this subject. Indeed, the peaceful settlement of international disputes is one of the essential functions of international law. This book seeks to provide readers with a systematic overview of multiple means of international dispute settlement in international law. In so doing, this book attempts to consider the question regarding whether and to what extent international law can contribute to peacefully settling international disputes and achieving sustainable peace. In this regard, it must be stressed that development of procedures for the peaceful settlement of international disputes is a prerequisite to the achievement of sustainable peace in the international community.

This book is divided into two parts. Part I, which consists of Chapters 1 to 7, examines traditional means of the settlement of inter-State disputes. This Part examines both diplomatic and legal means of international dispute settlement: negotiation, good office, mediation, inquiry, conciliation, dispute settlement through the United Nations, inter-State arbitration and the International Court of Justice.

Part II, which consists of Chapters 8 to 12, deals with international dispute settlement systems in particular fields. This part addresses the dispute settlement system under the United Nations Convention on the Law of the Sea, the WTO dispute settlement system, the peaceful settlement of international environmental disputes and disputes involving non-State actors. Finally, the role of the peaceful settlement of international disputes is examined in a broad context focusing on the interaction between international dispute settlement, the principle of the non-use of force secured by the collective security system, and disarmament.

As the peaceful settlement of international disputes covers a considerably wide array of issues, it is highly difficult to make a detailed examination with regard to each and every issue of this subject in a single volume of moderate length. As an introduction to the general corpus of international law of the peaceful settlement of international disputes, this book has only the modest aim of examining the principal issues of the law succinctly. It does not discuss international commercial arbitration which is regulated by a distinct body of private law. Nor does it focus on human rights or international criminal courts and tribunals.

The manuscript of this book was completed in February 2017 at Copenhagen. All websites were current as of that date.

Acknowledgements

I would like to dedicate this book to three eminent professors of international law: Professor Hugh Thirlway and Professor Lucius Caflisch, both of the Graduate Institute of International Studies, Geneva (currently the Graduate Institute of International and Development Studies, Geneva), and Professor Tetsuo Sato of Hitotsubashi University, Tokyo. They were my supervisors when I was a graduate student in Geneva and Tokyo and I owe much to them.

I am grateful to the University of Copenhagen, Faculty of Law and its Library for its support in the completion of this book. I should like to express my sincere gratitude to Dr Michael Johnstone for proofreading some parts of my drafts. In addition, I appreciated very much the constructive comments I received from the anonymous reviewers, in particular, comments on Chapter 9 of this book. My thanks are also due to Marta Walkowiak and Valerie Appleby at Cambridge University Press for their warm and professional assistance and other Cambridge University Press staff. I thank Jeremy Langworthy for his thorough copy-editing.

Finally, I wish to express my special thanks to my wife, Akiko, for all her support and prayers throughout my study.

Abbreviations

ABC	Abyei Boundaries Commission
ACWL	Advisory Centre on WTO Law
AFDI	*Annuaire français de droit international*
AJIL	*American Journal of International Law*
BYIL	*British Year Book of International Law*
CERD	International Convention on the Elimination of All Forms of Racial Discrimination
CJIL	*Chinese Journal of International Law*
COP	Conference of the Parties
CSCE	Conference on Security and Cooperation Europe
DSB	Dispute Settlement Body
DSU	Understanding on Rules and Procedures Governing the Settlement of Disputes
EC	European Community
ECOWAS	Economic Community of West African States
EEZ	Exclusive Economic Zone
EJIL	*European Journal of International Law*
EU	European Union
FZ	Fishery Zone
GATT	General Agreement on Tariffs and Trade
GYIL	*German Yearbook of International Law*
ICAO	International Civil Aviation Organisation
ICISS	International Commission on Intervention and State Sovereignty
ICJ	International Court of Justice
ICLQ	*International and Comparative Law Quarterly*
ICSID	International Centre for the Settlement of Investment Disputes
IJMCL	*International Journal of Marine and Coastal Law*
ILC	International Law Commission

ILM	*International Legal Materials*	
	ILO	International Labour Organisation
	ILR	*International Law Reports*
	ITLOS	International Tribunal for the Law of the Sea
	LJIL	*Leiden Journal of International Law*
	LOSC	United Nations Convention on Law of the Sea
	MOP	Meeting of the Parties
	Max Planck Encyclopaedia	*Max Planck Encyclopaedia of Public International Law* (Oxford University Press, 2008–2011, online edition: www.mpepil.com)
	MINUSCA	United Nations Multidimensional Integrated Stabilization Mission in the Central African Republic
	MOU	Memorandum of Understanding
	MRR	Management Report and Recommendation in Response to the Inspection Panel Investigation Report
	NATO	North Atlantic Treaty Organisation
	NGO	Non-Governmental Organisation
	NILR	*Netherlands International Law Review*
	NJIL	*Nordic Journal of International Law*
	OAS	Organisation of American States
	OSPAR Convention	Convention for the Protection of the Marine Environment of the North-East Atlantic
	PCA	Permanent Court of Arbitration
	PCIJ	Permanent Court of International Justice
	RCADI	*Recueil des cours de l'Académie de droit international*
	RECIEL	Review of European, Comparative and International Environmental Law
	RGDIP	*Revue générale de droit international public*
	RIAA	*Reports of International Arbitral Awards*
	UN	United Nations
	UNAMET	United Nations Mission in East Timor
	UNAT	United Nations Appeals Tribunal
	UNCC	United Nations Compensation Commission
	UNCITRAL	United Nations Commission on International Trade Law
	UNCLOS	United Nations Conference on the Law of the Sea
	UNDT	United Nations Dispute Tribunal
	UNEF I	First United Nations Emergency Force in the Suez
	UNEP	United Nations Environment Programme
	UNOCI	United Nations Operation in Côte d'Ivoire
	UNOSOM II	United Nations Operation in Somalia II

UNPROFOR	United Nations Protection Force
UNTAC	United Nations Transitional Authority in Cambodia
UNTS	*United Nations Treaty Series*
WHO	World Health Organisation
WTO	World Trade Organisation
YILC	*Yearbook of International Law Commission*
ZaöRV	*Zeitschrift für ausländisches öffentliches Recht und Völkerrecht*

Table of Cases

Abyei Arbitration (The Government of Sudan v. the Sudan People's Liberation Movement/Army), 22 July 2009, available at: https://pca-cpa.org/en/cases 343
Access to Information under Article 9 of the OSPAR Convention (Ireland v. United Kingdom), available at: https://pca-cpa.org/en/cases 314
Accordance with international law of the unilateral declaration of independence in respect of Kosovo, Advisory Opinion of 22 July 2010, ICJ Reports 2010 165, 167
Advisory Opinion on the Effect of Award of Compensation Made by the United Nations Administrative Tribunal (1954) 135
Aegean Sea Continental Shelf (Greece v. Turkey), Request for the Indication of Interim Measures of Protection, Order of 11 September 1976, ICJ Reports 1976 189, 196
Aegean Sea Continental Shelf (Greece v. Turkey), Judgment of 19 December 1978, ICJ Reports 1978 32, 41, 143
Aerial Incident of 27 July 1955 (Israel v. Bulgaria), Judgment of 26 May 1959, ICJ Reports 1959 148, 160
Al-Jedda v. The United Kingdom, European Court of Human Rights, Application no. 27021/08, Judgment, 7 July 2011 366
Albania: Power Sector Generation and Restructuring Project (IDA Credit No. 3872-ALB), World Bank Inspection Panel, Investigation Report No. 49504-AL, 7 August 2009 376
Alleged Violations of Sovereign Rights and Maritime Spaces in the Caribbean Sea (Nicaragua v. Colombia), Preliminary Objections, Judgement of 17 March 2016 (not yet reported) 10, 11, 12, 213
Anglo-Iranian Oil Co. (United Kingdom v. Iran), Preliminary Objections, Judgment of 22 July 1952 ICJ Reports 1952 149, 150
Applicability of the Obligation to Arbitrate under Section 21 of the United Nations Headquarters Agreement of 26 June 1947, Advisory Opinion of 26 April 1988, ICJ Reports 1988 11

xxii Table of Cases

Application for Review of Judgment No. 273 of the United Nations Administrative Tribunal, Advisory Opinion, ICJ Reports 1982   165

Application for Revision and Interpretation of the Judgment of 24 February 1982 in the case concerning the Continental Shelf (Tunisia v. Libya), Judgment of 10 December 1985, ICJ Reports 1985   138, 216, 218, 219

Application for Revision of the Judgment delivered by the International Court of Justice (ICJ) on 23 May 2008 in the case concerning Sovereignty over Pedra Branca/Pulau Batu Puteh, Middle Rocks and South Ledge (Malaysia v. Singapore) (pending)   219

Application for Revision of the Judgment of 11 July 1996 in the case concerning Application of the Convention on the Prevention and Punishment of the Crime of Genocide (Bosnia and Herzegovina v. Yugoslavia), Preliminary Objections (Yugoslavia v. Bosnia and Herzegovina), Judgment of 3 February 2003, ICJ Reports 2003   135, 219, 220

Application for Revision of the Judgment of 11 September 1992 in the case concerning the Land, Island and Maritime Frontier Dispute (El Salvador v. Honduras: Nicaragua Intervening), Judgment of 18 December 2003, ICJ Reports 2003   208, 219

Application of the Convention on the Prevention and Punishment of the Crime of Genocide (Bosnia and Herzegovina v. Serbia and Montenegro), Request for the Indication of Provisional Measures, Order of 8 April 1993, ICJ Reports 1993   132, 135, 137, 180, 181, 394

Application of the Convention on the Prevention and Punishment of the Crime of Genocide (Bosnia and Herzegovina v. Serbia and Montenegro), Further Requests for the Indication of Provisional Measures, Order of 13 September 1993, ICJ Reports 1993   366

Application of the Convention on the Prevention and Punishment of the Crime of Genocide (Bosnia and Herzegovina v. Serbia and Montenegro), Preliminary Objections, Judgment of 11 July 1996, ICJ Reports 1996   201

Application of the Convention on the Prevention and Punishment of the Crime of Genocide (Bosnia and Herzegovina v. Serbia and Montenegro), Judgment of 26 February 2007, ICJ Reports 2007   200, 213, 219

Application of the Convention on the Prevention and Punishment of the Crime of Genocide (Croatia v. Serbia), Preliminary Objections, Judgment of 18 November 2008, ICJ Reports 2008   148

Application of the International Convention on the Elimination of All Forms of Racial Discrimination (Georgia v. Russian Federation), Request for the Indication of Provisional Measures, Order of 15 October 2008, ICJ Reports 2008   192

Application of the International Convention on the Elimination of All Forms of Racial Discrimination (Georgia v. Russian Federation), Preliminary Objection, Judgment of 1 April 2011, ICJ Reports 2011   10, 11, 12, 30, 32, 192, 199

ARA 'Libertad' (Argentina v. Ghana), ITLOS case No. 20, Provisional Measures, Order of 15 December 2012, ITLOS Reports 2012   231, 250, 257, 259

Arbitral Award case (Guinea-Bissau v. Senegal), 31 July 1989 20 RIAA   122
Arbitral Award of 31 July 1989 (Guinea-Bissau v. Senegal), Request for the Indication of Provisional Measures, Order of 2 March 1990, ICJ Reports 1990   194
Arbitral Award of 31 July 1989 (Guinea-Bissau v. Senegal), Judgment of 12 November 1991, ICJ Reports 1991   123, 138
Arbitral Award Made by the King of Spain on 23 December 1906 (Honduras v. Nicaragua), Judgment of 18 November 1960, ICJ Reports 1960   100, 120, 121, 137
Arbitration Between the Republic of Croatia and the Republic of Slovenia, Partial Award, 30 June 2016, available at: https://pca-cpa.org/en/cases   112
Arbitration Regarding the Iron Rhine Railway (Belgium v. Netherlands) (2005) 27 RIAA   314
'Arctic Sunrise' case (Netherlands v. Russian Federation), Provisional Measures (2013), ITLOS case No. 22, Order of 22 November 2013, ITLOS Reports 2013, 115, 252, 256
'Arctic Sunrise' Arbitration (Netherlands v. Russian Federation), Award on Jurisdiction, 26 November 2014 available at: https://pca-cpa.org/en/cases   240, 269
'Arctic Sunrise' Arbitration (Netherlands v. Russian Federation), Award on Merits, 14 August 2015, available at: https://pca-cpa.org/en/cases   115, 232, 251, 253, 259
Argentina-Chile Frontier Case, 9 December 1966, 16 RIAA   109
Armed Activities on the Territory of the Congo (Democratic Republic of the Congo v. Uganda), Provisional Measures, Order of 1 July 2000, ICJ Reports 2000   393
Armed Activities on the Territory of the Congo (Democratic Republic of the Congo v. Uganda), Judgment of 19 December 2005, ICJ Reports 2005   359, 394
Armed Activities on the Territory of the Congo (New Application: 2002) (Democratic Republic of the Congo v. Rwanda), Jurisdiction and Admissibility, Judgment of 3 February 2006, ICJ Reports 2006   10
Arrest Warrant of 11 April 2000 case (Democratic Republic of the Congo v. Belgium), Judgment of 14 February 2002, ICJ Reports 2002   12, 138
Atlanto-Scandian Herring Arbitration (Kingdom of Denmark in respect of the Faroe Islands v. European Union), terminated on 23 September 2014   269
Avena and Other Mexican Nationals (Mexico v. United States), Request for the Indication of Provisional Measures, Order of 5 February 2003   198
Award between the United States and the United Kingdom relating to the rights of jurisdiction of United States in the Bering's sea and the preservation of fur seals, 15 August 1893 (2008) 28 RIAA   108, 314
Barbados/Trinidad and Tobago case (2006) 27 RIAA   269
Barcelona Traction case (Belgium v. Spain) (1962)   137
Barcelona Traction, Light and Power Company, Limited (Belgium v. Spain) (New Application: 1962), Judgment of 5 February 1970, Second Phase, ICJ Reports 1970   320
Bay of Bengal Maritime Boundary Arbitration (Bangladesh v. India), Award, 7 July 2014, available at: https://pca-cpa.org/en/cases   269

Beagle Channel dispute (Argentina v. Chile), 18 February 1977, 21 RIAA, 35, 109, 116, 124, 134

Border and Transborder Armed Actions (Nicaragua v. Honduras), Judgment of 20 December 1988, Jurisdiction of the Court and Admissibility of the Application, ICJ Reports 1988 45, 201

Boundary case (Honduras v. Nicaragua), Award of 23 December 1906, RIAA 11 100, 121

British Guiana-Venezuela Boundary dispute (1897) 108

'*Camouco*' case (Panama v. France), 7 February 2000, ITLOS, case No. 5 (2000) 39 ILM 261, 262, 263

Certain Activities Carried Out by Nicaragua in the Border Area (Costa Rica v. Nicaragua), Provisional Measures, Order of 8 March 2011, ICJ Reports 2011(I) 192, 193, 196, 393, 394

Certain Activities Carried Out by Nicaragua in the Border Area (Costa Rica v. Nicaragua), Judgment, 16 December 2015, ICJ Reports 2015 34, 200

Certain Criminal Proceedings in France (Republic of the Congo v. France), Request for the Indication of a Provisional Measure, Order of 17 June 2003, ICJ Reports 2003 145, 196

Certain Expenses of the United Nations (Article 17, paragraph 2, of the Charter), Advisory Opinion of 20 July 1962, ICJ Reports 1962 167, 170, 171, 365, 366, 390

Certain Norwegian Loans (France v. Norway), Judgment of 6 July 1957, ICJ Reports 1957 150, 158, 159, 202

Certain Phosphate Lands in Nauru (Nauru v. Australia), Preliminary Objections, Judgment of 26 June 1992, ICJ Reports 1992 33, 154, 181, 203, 313

Certain Property (Liechtenstein v. Germany), Preliminary Objections, Judgment of 10 February 2005, ICJ Reports 2005 8, 11

Certain Questions of Mutual Assistance in Criminal Matters (Djibouti v. France), Judgment of 4 June 2008, ICJ Reports 2008 145, 146

Chad-Cameroon Petroleum and Pipeline Project (Loan No. 4558-CD); Petroleum Sector Management Capacity Building Project (Credit No. 3373-CD); and Management of the Petroleum Economy (Credit No. 3316-CD), World Bank Inspection Panel Report, 17 July 2002 376

Chagos Marine Protected Area Arbitration (Mauritius v. United Kingdom) Reasoned Decision on Challenge, 20 November 2011, available at: https://pca-cpa.org/en/cases 112, 113, 134

Chagos Marine Protected Area Arbitration (Mauritius v. United Kingdom), Award of 18 March 2015 231, 269

Chile – Taxes on Alcoholic Beverages, Arbitration under Article 21.3(c) of the Understanding on Rules and Procedures Governing the Settlement of Disputes, Award of the Arbitrator, WT/DS87/15, WT/DS110/14, 23 May 2000 298

City Oriente Limited v. Republic of Ecuador and Empresa Estatal Petróleos del Ecuador (Petroecuador) (ICSID case No. ARB/06/21), 19 November 2007 350

xxv Table of Cases

Conciliation between the Democratic Republic of Timor-Leste and the Commonwealth of Australia. Decision on Australia's Objections to Competence, 19 September 2016, available at https://pca-cpa.org/en/cases   232, 240, 241

Conditions of Admission of a State to Membership in the United Nations (Article 4 of the Charter), Advisory Opinion of 28 May 1948, ICJ Reports 1948   170

Conservation and Sustainable Exploitation of Swordfish Stocks in the South-Eastern Pacific Ocean (Chile v. European Community), ITLOS, case no. 7, Order to Suspend Proceedings 15 March 2001   248

Continental Shelf (Libya v. Malta), Application by Italy for Permission to Intervene, Judgment of 21 March 1984, ICJ Reports 1984   208, 210

Continental Shelf (Libya v. Malta), Judgment of 3 June 1985, ICJ Reports 1985   143, 186, 207, 209

Continental Shelf (Tunisia v. Libya), Application by Malta for Permission to Intervene, Judgment of 14 April 1981, ICJ Reports 1981   208, 209

Corfu Channel case (United Kingdom v. Albania), UN Security Council, 19 (1947). Resolution of 27 February 1947   79

Corfu Channel case (United Kingdom v. Albania), UN Security Council, 22 (1947). Resolution of 9 April 1947, S/324   77

Corfu Channel case (United Kingdom v. Albania), Preliminary Objection, Judgment of 25 March 1948, ICJ Reports 1948   131

Corfu Channel (United Kingdom v. Albania), Order of 17 December 1948, ICJ Reports 1948   183

Corfu Channel (United Kingdom v. Albania), Judgment of 9 April 1949, Merits, ICJ Reports 1949   394

Corfu Channel case (United Kingdom v. Albania), Judgment of 15 December 1949, Assessment of the amount of compensation due from the People's Republic of Albania to the United Kingdom of Great Britain and Northern Ireland, ICJ Reports 1949   145, 146, 176, 189, 202, 203, 214, 394

Delimitation of the Continental Shelf between Nicaragua and Colombia Beyond 200 Nautical Miles from the Nicaraguan Coast (Nicaragua v. Colombia) (not yet reported), Preliminary Objection, 17 March 2016   213

Delimitation of the Continental Shelf between the United Kingdom of Great Britain and Northern Ireland and the French Republic, Decision of 14 March 1978 (1980) 18 RIAA

Delimitation of the Maritime Boundary between Ghana and Côte d'Ivoire in the Atlantic Ocean (Ghana/Côte d'Ivoire), ITLOS case No. 23   248, 256

Delimitation of the Maritime Boundary in the Gulf of Maine Area (Canada v. United States), Order of 20 January 1982, Constitution of Chamber, ICJ Reports 1982   140, 143

Delimitation of the Maritime Boundary in the Gulf of Maine Area (Canada v. United States), Appointment of Expert, Order of 30 March 1984, ICJ Reports 1984   183

Dispute Concerning Delimitation of the Maritime Boundary between Bangladesh and Myanmar in the Bay of Bengal, Judgment (2012), ITLOS case No. 16, ITLOS Reports 2012, 269

Duzgit Integrity Arbitration (Malta v. São Tomé and Príncipe, pending)   251, 269

East Timor (Portugal v. Australia), Judgment of 30 June 1995, ICJ Reports 1995, p. 99   8, 9, 204

Electricity Company of Sofia and Bulgaria PCIJ, A/B 77 Judgment of 4 April 1939 (Preliminary Objection)   154

Enrica Lexie incident (Italy v. India), Request for the prescription of provisional measures, Order of 24 August 2015, ITLOS case No. 24   257, 258, 259

European Communities – Measures Affecting the Approval and Marketing of Biotech Products (EC – Approval and Marketing of Biotech Products), WT/DS291/R, WT/DS292/R, WT/DS293/R, 29 September 2006   285

European Communities – Measures Affecting Asbestos and Products Containing Asbestos, Appellate Body Report, WT/DS135/AB/R, adopted 5 April 2001   282, 284

European Communities – Measures Affecting the Importation of Certain Poultry Products, Appellate Body Report, WT/DS69/AB/R, adopted 23 July 1998   285

European Communities – Measures Concerning Meat and Meat Products (Hormones), Appellate Body Report. WT/DS26/13, WT/DS48/11, adopted 13 February 1998   302, 308

European Communities – Measures Concerning Meat and Meat Products (Hormones), Original Complaint by the United States – Recourse to Arbitration by the European Communities under Article 22.6 of the DSU, WT/DS26/ARB, 12 July 1999   303

European Communities – Regime for the Importation, Sale and Distribution of Bananas, Panel Reports, WT/DS27/R/ECU (Ecuador) / WT/DS27/R/GTM, WT/DS27/R/HND (Guatemala and Honduras) / WT/DS27/R/MEX (Mexico) / WT/DS27/R/USA (US), adopted 25 September 1997, as modified by Appellate Body Report WT/DS27/AB/R, DSR 1997:II, p. 695 to DSR 1997:III   290

European Communities – Regime for the Importation, Sale and Distribution of Bananas, Recourse to Arbitration by the European Communities under Article 22.6 of the DSU, Decision by the Arbitrators, WT/DS27/ARB, 9 April 1999   301

European Communities – Trade Description of Sardines, Appellate Body Report, WT/DS231/AB/R, adopted 23 October 2002   282

European Communities and Certain Member States – Appellate Body Report, Measures Affecting Trade in Large Civil Aircraft, WT/DS316/AB/R, adopted 1 June 2011   286

Factory at Chorzów case, Order of 21 November 1927, PCIJ Series A, No. 12   194

Fisheries Jurisdiction case (Germany v. Iceland), ICJ Reports 1972   191

Fisheries Jurisdiction case (Spain v. Canada), Jurisdiction of the Court, Judgment of 4 December 1998, ICJ Reports 1998   10, 150, 156, 239

Fisheries Jurisdiction case (United Kingdom v. Iceland), Interim Protection, Order of 17 August 1972, ICJ Reports 1972   190

Fisheries Jurisdiction case (United Kingdom v. Iceland), Judgment of 25 July 1974, ICJ Reports 1974   35, 36, 38, 177, 182, 188

Free Zones of Upper Savoy and the District of Gex, Order of 19 August 1929, PCIJ, Series A, No. 22   32

Frontier Dispute (Burkina Faso v. Republic of Mali), Request for the indication of Provisional Measures, Order of 10 January 1986, ICJ Reports 1986   140, 143, 199, 393, 394

Gabčíkovo-Nagymaros Project (Hungary v. Slovakia), Judgment of 25 September 1997, ICJ Reports 1997   143, 313

Grand Prince case (Belize v. France), Prompt Release (2001), ITLOS case No. 8,   261

Guinea/Guinea-Bissau case (1986) 25 ILM   134

Guyana/Suriname arbitral award, 17 September 2007, 30 RIAA   269, 395

Haya de la Torre (Colombia v. Peru), Judgment of 13 June 1951, ICJ Reports 1951, p. 83. In 3 January 1949   33

Honduras: Land Administration Project (IDA Credit 3858-HO), World Bank Inspection Panel, Investigation Report No. 39933-HN, 12 June 2007   376

'Hoshinmaru' case (Japan v. Russian Federation), Prompt Release (2007), ITLOS case No. 14, ITLOS Reports 2005–2008   261, 262, 263

Immunities and Criminal Proceedings (Equatorial Guinea v. France), Request for the Indication of Provisional Measures, 7 December 2016, ICJ Reports 2016 (not yet reported)   11, 192

Indus Waters Kishenganga arbitration (Pakistan v. India), PCA (2013) available at: https://pca-cpa.org/en/cases   314

Interhandel case (Switzerland v. USA), Judgment of 21 March 1959, ICJ Reports 1959   150, 158, 159, 202

Interpretation of the Greco-Turkish Agreement of 1 December 1926 (Final Protocol, Article IV), Advisory Opinion, 1928, PCIJ, Series B, No. 16   165

Interpretation of Judgments Nos. 7 and 8 (Factory at Chorzów), Judgment of 16 December 1927, PCIJ Series A, No. 13   213

Interpretation of Peace Treaties with Bulgaria, Hungary and Romania, First Phase, Advisory Opinion, 30 March 1950, ICJ Reports 1950   10

Interpretation of Peace Treaties with Bulgaria, Hungary and Romania, Advisory Opinion of 18 July 1950, ICJ Reports 1950   110, 167, 168

Japan – Measures Affecting Consumer Photographic Film and Paper, WT/DS44/R, adopted 22 April 1998   284

Japan – Taxes on Alcoholic Beverages, Appellate Body Report, WT/DS8/AB/R, WT/DS10/AB/R, WT/DS11/AB/R, adopted 1 November 1996   284, 297

Judgments of the Administrative Tribunal of the ILO upon Complaints Made against UNESCO, Advisory Opinion of 23 October 1956   181

'Juno Trader' case (Saint Vincent and the Grenadines v. Guinea-Bissau), Prompt Release (2004), ITLOS case No. 13, ITLOS Reports 2004   261, 263

Jurisdictional Immunities of the State (Germany v. Italy), Application by the Hellenic Republic for Permission to Intervene, ICJ Reports 2011   206

Jurisdictional Immunities of the State (Germany v. Italy: Greece intervening), Judgment of 3 February 2012, ICJ Reports 2012   34

Kasikili/Sedudu Island (Botswana v. Namibia), Judgment of 13 December 1999, ICJ Reports 1999   137

Lac Lanoux arbitration (France v. Spain) (1957) 12 RIAA   314

LaGrand (Germany v. United States), Request for the Indication of Provisional Measures, Order of 3 March 1999, ICJ Reports 1999   182, 192, 194, 197, 394

LaGrand (Germany v. United States), Judgment of 27 June 2001, ICJ Reports 2001   192, 198, 199, 200

Land and Maritime Boundary between Cameroon and Nigeria (Cameroon v. Nigeria: Equatorial Guinea intervening), Request for the Indication of Provisional Measures Order of 15 March 1996, ICJ Reports 1996   193, 195, 196, 393, 394

Land and Maritime Boundary between Cameroon and Nigeria (Cameroon v. Nigeria), Preliminary Objections, Judgment of 11 June 1998, ICJ Reports 1998   11, 14, 37

Land and Maritime Boundary between Cameroon and Nigeria (Cameroon v. Nigeria: Equatorial Guinea intervening), Order of 21 October 1999   206, 207

Land and Maritime Boundary between Cameroon and Nigeria (Cameroon v. Nigeria: Equatorial Guinea intervening), Judgment of 10 October 2002, ICJ Reports 2002   210, 215

Land, Island and Maritime Frontier Dispute (El Salvador v. Honduras: Nicaragua intervening), Order of 8 May 1987, Constitution of Chamber, ICJ Reports 1987   141

Land, Island and Maritime Frontier Dispute (El Salvador v. Honduras: Nicaragua intervening) Application by Nicaragua for Permission to Intervene, Judgment of 13 September 1990, ICJ Reports 1990   140, 144, 206, 207, 209, 210

Land Reclamation by Singapore in and Around the Straits of Johor (Malaysia v. Singapore), Provisional Measures, ITLOS case No. 12, Order of 8 Oct. 2013, ITLOS Reports 2003   36, 231, 257, 269, 319

Legal Consequences for States of the Continued Presence of South Africa in Namibia (South West Africa) notwithstanding Security Council Resolution 276 (1970), Advisory Opinion of 21 June 1971, ICJ Reports 1971   84, 135, 164, 165, 168, 365

Legal Consequences of the Construction of a Wall in the Occupied Palestinian Territory, Advisory Opinion of 9 July 2004, ICJ Reports 2004   87, 136, 170, 395

Legality of the Threat or Use of Nuclear Weapons, Advisory Opinion of 8 July 1996, ICJ Reports 1996   133, 163, 165, 167, 169, 267, 391, 395

Legality of the Use by a State of Nuclear Weapons in Armed Conflict, Advisory Opinion of 8 July 1996, ICJ Reports 1996   164, 165, 170

Legality of Use of Force (Serbia and Montenegro v. Belgium), Request for the Indication of Provisional Measures, Order of 2 June 1999, ICJ Reports 1999   11

M/V 'Louisa' case (Saint Vincent and the Grenadines v. Spain), Provisional Measures, Order of 23 December 2010, ITLOS case No. 18, ITLOS Reports 2008–2010   256, 258

M/V 'Louisa' case (Saint Vincent and the Grenadines v. Spain), Merits, Judgment of 28 May 2013, ITLOS case No. 18, ITLOS Reports 2013   237, 256

M/V 'Norstar' case (Panama v. Italy), ITLOS, Preliminary Objections, 4 November 2016, ITLOS case No. 25,   11, 231, 237, 253

M/V 'Saiga' case (Saint Vincent and the Grenadines v. Guinea), Prompt Release Judgment of 4 December 1998, ITLOS case No. 1, ITLOS Reports 1998 (1998) 37 ILM   261, 262

M/V 'Saiga' (No. 2) case (Saint Vincent and the Grenadines v. Guinea), Provisional Measures (1998), Merits (1999), ITLOS case No. 2 (1998) 37 ILM/(1999) 38 ILM   251, 252, 253, 256, 259, 269

M/V 'Virginia G' case (Panama v. Guinea-Bissau), Judgment (2014) ITLOS case No. 19, ITLOS Reports 2014   253, 269

Maritime Delimitation and Territorial Questions between Qatar and Bahrain (Qatar v. Bahrain), Jurisdiction and Admissibility, Judgment of 1 July 1994, ICJ Reports 1994,   42

Maritime Delimitation in the Area between Greenland and Jan Mayen (Denmark v. Norway), Judgment of 14 June 1993, ICJ Reports 1993   34, 69, 71

Maritime Delimitation in the Caribbean Sea and the Pacific Ocean (Costa Rica v Nicaragua), Order of 16 June 2016 (not yet reported)   183

Maritime Delimitation in the Indian Ocean (Somalia v. Kenya), Preliminary Objections, Judgment of 2 February 2016, ICJ Reports 2016 (not yet reported)   42, 155, 234

Mavromatis Palestine Concessions, Judgment No. 2, 1924, PCIJ, Series A, No. 2   8, 32, 40

Military and Paramilitary Activities in and against Nicaragua (Nicaragua v. United States of America), Provisional Measures, Order of 10 May 1984, ICJ Reports 1984   190, 394

Military and Paramilitary Activities in and against Nicaragua (Nicaragua v. United States of America), Declaration of Intervention of the Republic of El Salvador, Order of 4 October 1984, ICJ Reports 1984   211

Military and Paramilitary Activities in and against Nicaragua (Nicaragua v. United States of America), Jurisdiction of the Court and Admissibility of the Application, Judgment of 26 November 1984, ICJ Reports 1984   84, 148, 149, 150, 160, 161, 182, 199

Military and Paramilitary Activities in and against Nicaragua (Nicaragua v. United States of America), Judgment of 27 June 1986, Merits, ICJ Reports 1986   5, 6, 156, 181, 182, 187, 188, 189, 190, 204, 205, 222, 387

Monetary Gold Removed from Rome in 1943 (Italy v. France, United Kingdom and United States), Preliminary Question, Judgment of 15 June 1954, ICJ Reports 1954   131, 201, 202, 203, 313

'Monte Confurco' case (Seychelles v. France), ITLOS case No. 6, Judgment of 18 December 2000   261, 262, 263

MOX Plant case (Ireland v. United Kingdom), ITLOS case No. 10, Request for Provisional Measures, Order of 3 December 2001 (2002) 41 ILM   36, 231, 233, 255, 256, 257, 258, 259

MOX Plant case (Ireland v. United Kingdom), ITLOS case No. 10, Suspension of Proceedings on Jurisdiction and Merits and Request for Further Provisional Measures (2003) (case withdrawn 2008)   269, 318

Nada v. Switzerland, European Court of Human Rights, Grand Chamber, Application no. 10593/08, Judgment, 12 September 2012   366

North Sea Continental Shelf (Germany v. Netherlands) (Germany v. Denmark), Judgment of 20 February 1969, ICJ Reports 1969   28, 35, 36, 37, 131, 143

Northern Cameroons (Cameroon v. United Kingdom), Judgment of 2 December 1963, Preliminary Objections, ICJ Reports 1962   11, 205

Nottebohm (Liechtenstein v. Guatemala), Preliminary Objection, Judgment of 18 November 1953, ICJ Reports 1953   137, 142, 148

Nuclear Tests case (Australia v. France) (New Zealand v. France), Order of 22 June 1973, ICJ Reports 1973

Nuclear Tests case (Australia v. France) (New Zealand v. France), Judgment of 20 December 1974, ICJ Reports 1974   9, 38, 185, 186, 187, 189, 192, 204, 207, 211

Obligations concerning Negotiations relating to Cessation of the Nuclear Arms Race and to Nuclear Disarmament (Marshall Islands v. India), Judgment of 5 October 2016, Jurisdiction of the Court and admissibility of the application   13, 392

Obligations concerning Negotiations relating to Cessation of the Nuclear Arms Race and to Nuclear Disarmament (Marshall Islands v. Pakistan), Judgment of 5 October 2016, Jurisdiction of the Court and admissibility of the application (not yet reported)   137, 392

Obligations concerning Negotiations relating to Cessation of the Nuclear Arms Race and to Nuclear Disarmament (Marshall Islands v. United Kingdom), Judgment of 5 October 2016, Preliminary objections (not yet reported)   10, 13, 133, 391, 392

Oil Platforms (Iran v. USA), Judgment of 6 November 2003, ICJ Reports 2003   181, 182, 186, 394

Passage Through the Great Belt (Provisional Measures), ICJ Reports 1991   32, 196

Phosphates in Morocco case (Preliminary Objection), Judgment of 14 June 1938, PCIJ Series A/B No. 74, 1938   31

Prosecutor v. Duko Tadić a.k.a. 'Dule', case No. IT-94-1-AR 72, Decision of 2 October 1995 (1996) 35 ILM   18

Pulp Mills on the River Uruguay (Argentina v. Uruguay), Request for Provisional Measures, ICJ Reports 2007   195

Pulp Mills on the River Uruguay (Argentina v. Uruguay), Judgment of 20 April 2010, ICJ Reports 2010   38, 183, 184, 190

Question of the Delimitation of the Continental Shelf between Nicaragua and Colombia beyond 200 nautical miles from the Nicaraguan Coast (Nicaragua v. Colombia), Judgment of 17 March 2016, ICJ Reports 2016   133

Questions of Interpretation and Application of the 1971 Montreal Convention arising from the Aerial Incident at Lockerbie (Libya v. UK) (Libya v. USA), Provisional Measures, Order of 14 April 1992, ICJ Reports 1992   193, 363

Questions relating to the Obligation to Prosecute or Extradite (Belgium v. Senegal), Provisional Measures, Order of 28 May 2009, ICJ Reports 2009   12, 192, 193, 196

Questions relating to the Obligation to Prosecute or Extradite (Belgium v. Senegal), Judgment of 20 July 2012, Merits, ICJ Reports 2012   12, 321

Railway Traffic between Lithuania and Poland, Advisory Opinion, 1931, PCIJ, Series A/B, No. 42   30

'Rainbow Warrior' Arbitration (New Zealand v. France), Award of 30 April 1990, 20 RIAA   94

Reparation for Injuries Suffered in the Service of the United Nations, Advisory Opinion of 11 April 1949, ICJ Reports 1949   74, 171

Request for an advisory opinion submitted by the Sub-Regional Fisheries Commission (SRFC), ITLOS case No. 21, Advisory Opinion of 2 April 2015   266

Request for an Examination of the Situation in Accordance with Paragraph 63 of the Court's Judgment of 20 December 1974 in the Nuclear Tests (New Zealand v. France) case, Order of 22 September 1995, ICJ Reports 1995   138

Request for an Examination of the Situation in Accordance with Paragraph 63 of the Court's Judgment of 20 December 1974 in the Nuclear Tests (New Zealand v. France) Case, Order of 22 September 1995, Request for an examination of the situation – Request for the Indication of Provisional Measures, ICJ Reports 1995   207

Request for Interpretation of the Judgment of 20 November 1950 in the Asylum case (Colombia v. Peru), Judgment of 27 November 1950, ICJ Reports 1   33, 186, 216, 217

Request for Interpretation of the Judgment of 31 March 2004 in the case Concerning Avena and Other Mexican Nations (Mexico v. United States), Request for the Indication of Provisional Measures, Order of 16 July 2008, ICJ Reports 2008   198, 218

Request for Interpretation of the Judgment of 11 June 1998 in the case concerning the Land and Maritime Boundary between Cameroon and Nigeria (Nigeria v. Cameroon) (Preliminary Objections), Judgment of 25 March 1999   217

Request for Interpretation of the Judgment of 15 June 1962 in the case concerning the Temple of Preah Vihear (Cambodia v. Thailand) (Request for Interpretation), Request for the Indication of Provisional Measures, Order of 18 July 2011, ICJ Reports 2011   190, 192, 196, 199, 200, 216, 394

Request for Interpretation of the Judgment of 15 June 1962 in the case Concerning the Temple of Preah Vihear (Cambodia v. Thailand), Judgment of 11 November 2013, ICJ Reports 2013   5, 138, 216, 217

Reservations to the Convention on the Prevention and Punishment of the Crime of Genocide, Advisory Opinion of 28 May 1951, ICJ Reports 1951   164

Responsibilities and Obligations of States Sponsoring Persons and Entities with Respect to Activities in the Area, case No. 17, 1 February 2011   265

Right of Passage over Indian Territory (Portugal v. India), Preliminary Objections, Judgment of 26 November 1957, ICJ Reports 1957   152

Right of Passage over Indian Territory (Portugal v. India), Judgment of 12 April 160, Merits, ICJ Reports 1960   151, 153, 157, 160, 176

St Pierre and Miquelon case (1992) 31 ILM   117

Second stage of the proceedings between Eritrea and Yemen (Maritime Delimitation), 17 December 1999, 22 RIAA   118

South China Sea arbitration (Philippines v. China), PCA case No 2013-19, Award on Jurisdiction and Admissibility, 29 October 2015 available at: https://pca-cpa.org/en/cases   115, 118, 119, 232, 242, 250, 269, 271, 272, 315

South West Africa cases (Liberia v. South Africa) (Ethiopia v. South Africa), Judgment of 21 December 1962, Preliminary Objections ICJ Reports 1962   9, 10, 13, 31, 135, 176

Southern Bluefin Tuna case (New Zealand v. Japan; Australia v. Japan), ITLOS case No. 3 and 4, Request for Provisional Measures, Order of 27 August 1999 (1999) 38 ILM   36, 255, 256, 257, 258, 259, 269, 270, 271, 319

Southern Bluefin Tuna case (Australia and New Zealand v. Japan), Jurisdiction and Admissibility (2000), (2000) 39 ILM   270

Sovereignty over Pulau Ligitan and Pulau Sipadan (Indonesia v. Malaysia), Application to Intervene, Judgment, ICJ Reports 2001   210

Sovereignty over Pulau Ligitan and Pulau Sipadan (Indonesia v. Malaysia), Judgment of 17 December 2002, ICJ Reports 2002   138, 185, 206, 208

Status of Eastern Carelia, Advisory Opinion of 23 July 1923, PCIJ Ser. B, 1923, No. 5   7, 168

Territorial and Maritime Dispute (Nicaragua v. Colombia), Application to Intervene by Costa Rica, Judgment of 4 May 2011, ICJ Reports 2011   206, 207, 208, 210

Territorial and Maritime Dispute (Nicaragua v. Colombia), Application to Intervene by Honduras, Judgment of 4 May 2011, ICJ Reports 2011   207, 208

Territorial and Maritime Dispute (Nicaragua/Colombia), Judgment, ICJ Reports 2012   214

Territorial Sovereignty and Scope of the Dispute (Eritrea and Yemen), 9 October 1998, 22 RIAA   116

Tokios Tokelės v. Ukraine (ICSID case No. ARB/02/18), Order No. 1, 1 July 2003   350

'Tomimaru' case, Prompt Release, Judgment of 6 August 2007, ITLOS case No. 15 ITLOS Reports 2005-2008 261, 263

Trail Smelter case (United States v Canada), (1939) 33 AJIL / (1941) 35 AJIL   117, 314

United States – Anti-Dumping Act of 1916, Appellate Body Report, WT/DS136/AB/R, WT/DS162/AB/R, adopted 26 September 2000   292, 302

United States – Anti-Dumping Act of 1916, Original Complaint by the European Communities – Recourse to Arbitration by the United States under Article 22.6 of the DSU, Decision by Arbitrator, WT/DS136/ARB, 24 February 2004   302

United States – Certain Country of Origin Labelling (COOL) Requirements – Recourse to Article 22.6 of the DSU the United States, Decisions by Arbitrator, WT/DS384/ARB and Add.1 / WT/DS386/ARB and Add.1, circulated to WTO Members 7 December 2015   302

United States – Definitive Anti-Dumping and Countervailing Duties on Certain Products from China, Panel Report, WT/DS379/R, adopted 25 March 2011   285

United States – Definitive Safeguard Measures on Imports of Certain Steel Products, WT/DS248/R and Corr.1 / WT/DS249/R and Corr.1 / WT/DS251/R and Corr.1 / WT/DS252/R and Corr.1 / WT/DS253/R and Corr.1 / WT/DS254/R and Corr.1 / WT/DS258/R and Corr.1 / WT/DS259/R and Corr.1, adopted 10 December 2003   290

United States – Final Anti-Dumping Measures on Stainless Steel from Mexico, WT/DS344/AB/R, adopted 20 May 2008   297

United States – Import Prohibition of Certain Shrimp and Shrimp Products, Appellate Body Report, WT/DS58/AB/R, adopted 6 November 1998   281, 286, 314

United States – Imposition of Countervailing Duties on Certain Hot-Rolled Lead and Bismuth Carbon Steel Products Originating in the United Kingdom, Appellate Body Report, WT/DS138/AB/R, adopted 7 June 2000   281

United States – Sections 301–310 of the Trade Act 1974, Panel Report, WT/DS152/R, adopted 27 January 2000   281

United States – Standards for Reformulated and Conventional Gasoline, Appellate Body Report, WT/DS2/AB/R, adopted 20 May 1996   284

United States Diplomatic and Consular Staff in Tehran (United States of America v. Iran), Judgment of 24 May 1980, ICJ Reports 1980   16, 22, 32, 47, 84, 182, 188, 205

Vienna Convention on Consular Relations (Paraguay v. United States of America), Order of 9 April 1998, Request for the Indication of Provisional Measures, ICJ Reports 1998   197

Western Sahara, Advisory Opinion of 16 October 1975, ICJ Reports 1975   165, 168, 169

Whaling in the Antarctic (Australia v. Japan), Declaration of Intervention of New Zealand, Order of 6 February 2013, ICJ Reports 2013   212

Whaling in the Antarctic (Australia v. Japan, New Zealand Intervening), ICJ Reports 2014   156, 184, 212, 320

Yacretá Hydroelectric Project (Argentina v. Paraguay) World Bank case 7   375

Youssef Nada v. State Secretariat for Economic Affairs and Federal Department of Economic Affairs, Administrative Appeal Judgment, case No 1A 45/2007; ILDC 461(CH 2007); BGE 133 II 450, 14 November 2007   366

Table of Treaties and Instruments

Addis Ababa Agreement (1972)   343
Agreement between Australia and the Republic of Nauru for the Settlement of the Case in the International Court of Justice Concerning Certain Phosphate Lands in Nauru (1993)   33n
Agreement between Denmark and Norway (1995)   34
Agreement between France and Portugal with Respect to the Maritime Boundary between Guinea-Bissau and Senegal (1960)   122–3
  Article 3   122
Agreement Establishing the Advisory Centre on WTO Law (1999)   307–8
  Article 2(1)   308n
Agreement Establishing the World Trade Organization (1994) (WTO Agreement)   277, 304
  Preamble   277
  Article 2(2)   278n
  Article 2(4)   278n
  Article XIII(1)   277
  Annexes 1–3   277
  Annex 1A   278
  Annex 2   278
Agreement for Inquiry in the *Tubantia* Case (1921)   55n, 58
  Article 1   59n
  Article 2   59n
  Article 8   55n
Agreement Governing the Activities of States on the Moon and Other Celestial Bodies (1979)
  Article 15(2)   37
Agreement on a Comprehensive Political Settlement of the Cambodia Conflict (1991)   93
  Article 2(1)   93n

Agreement on Co-operation and Relationship between the United Nations and the
    International Tribunal for the Law of the Sea (1997)   243n
  Article 1(1)   243n
Agreement on the Privileges and Immunities of the International Atomic Energy
    Agency (1959)
  Section 34   171n
Agreement on the Privileges and Immunities of the International Tribunal for the Law
    of the Sea (1997)   245
Agreement on the Continental Shelf between Iceland and Jan Mayen (1981)   71
  Preamble   71n
  Article 1   71n
Agreement on Trade-Related Aspects of Intellectual Property Rights (1994) (TRIPS
    Agreement)   278n
  Article 64(2)–(3)   282n
Algiers Accords (General Declaration) (1981)   352
American Treaty on Pacific Settlement (Pact of Bogotá) (1948)   144
  Article I   387n
  Article XII   45n, 46, 46n
  Article XIII   47n
  Article XVI   67
  Article XXII   66
Anglo-American Mutual Aid Agreement (1942)   276
  Article VII   276
Antarctic Treaty (1959)
  Article IV   317
  Article IV(2)   6n
  Article VIII(2)   37
  Article XI   270
Arbitration Agreement between the Government of Sudan and the Sudan People's
    Liberation Movement/Army on Delimiting Abyei Area, 7 July 2008   344
  Article 2   344
  Article 3   345
  Article 5   344
  Article 9(3)   345
Atlantic Charter (1941)   276
Basel Convention on the Control of Transboundary Movements of Hazardous Wastes
    and their Disposal (1989)   324, 325, 328, 329
Boundary Treaty between Argentina and Chile (1881)   124
Bryan–Suarez Mujica Treaty (1914)   61
  Compromis, Article 4   61
Camp David Accord (1978)   47
Canada–United States Great Lakes Water Agreement (1972)   322

Cartagena Protocol on Biosafety to the Convention on Biological Diversity
 (2000)   323–4, 325
  Article 34   325n
Charter of the United Nations (1945) (UN Charter)   387, 390
  Article 2(3)   5, 7, 75, 387
  Article 2(4)   6, 75, 360, 387, 393
  Article 2(5)   90
  Article 4   81, 170
  Article 5   81
  Article 6   81, 83
  Article 10   85, 87
  Article 11(1)   390n
  Article 11(2)   85, 87
  Article 11(3)   75, 76, 85
  Article 12   38, 84, 85, 87n, 88, 389–90
  Article 12(1)   87, 88, 102
  Article 12(2)   87
  Article 14   87, 389–90
  Article 17(2)   170, 171
  Article 18(2)   86
  Article 25   79, 364
  Article 26   390n
  Article 27   80n
  Article 27(1)   80
  Article 27(2)   80
  Article 27(3)   80, 82, 83, 84, 86
  Article 28(1)   74n
  Article 32   86
  Articles 33–8   390n
  Article 33   77
  Article 33(1)   7, 74
  Article 33(2)   77
  Article 34   79, 85
  Article 35   74n, 75
  Article 35(1)   75, 76, 85
  Article 35(2)   75, 76, 85, 86
  Article 35(3)   87
  Article 36   76
  Article 36(1)   76, 77
  Article 36(2)   76n
  Article 36(3)   15n, 77
  Article 37(1)   74, 76, 77
  Article 37(2)   76, 77

Article 38   74, 76, 77
Article 39   18, 80, 83, 84, 388
Article 41   80, 388
Article 42   80, 388
Article 43   389
Article 47(1)   390n
Article 52   99
Article 52(1)   98
Article 52(2)   98
Article 52(3)   98
Article 53(1)   98
Article 54   98
Article 55   276
Articles 92-96   130
Article 92   129, 243n
Article 93(1)   129, 131
Article 93(2)   131
Article 94   264
Article 94(1)   221-2
Article 94(2)   83, 199, 221-2, 224
Article 96   164n, 165, 362
Article 96(1)   84, 87, 164, 165
Article 96(2)   164
Article 97   81, 88
Article 98   88
Article 99   75, 76, 88-9
Article 100(1)   95n
Article 103   193n, 364
Article 108   81
Chapters VI-VIII   81
Chapter VII   83
Chapter XIV   130
Chapter XVIII   129n
Chicago Convention on Use of Weapons against Civil Aircraft (1944)   63
    Article 3*bis*(a)   63
Comprehensive Nuclear Test Ban Treaty (1996)   391
Comprehensive Peace Agreement (2005)   344, 345
Convention on International Civil Aviation (1944)
    Article 88   222
Constitution of the International Labour Organization (1919)
    Article 33   222
Constitution of the World Health Organization (1946)
    Article 2   166

Convention against Transnational Organized Crime (2000)
  Article 35   192–3
  Article 35(2)   193
Convention for the Conservation of Southern Bluefin Tuna (1993)
  Article 16   270
  Article 16(1)   270
  Article 16(2)   270
Convention for the Protection of the Marine Environment of the North-East Atlantic (1992) (OSPAR Convention)   233, 329
  Article 22   329
  Article 23   327
Convention for the Suppression of Unlawful Acts against the Safety of Civil Aviation (1971) (Montreal Convention)   363
  Article 5(2)–(3)   363
  Article 7   363
  Article 8(3)   363
  Article 11   363
  Article 14   363
Convention on Access to Information, Public Participation in Decision-Making and Access to Justice in Environmental Matters (Aarhus Convention) (1998)   325, 326–7, 328, 329
  Article 15   325, 325n
Convention on Environmental Impact Assessment in a Transboundary Context (1991) (Espoo Convention)   319n, 331
  Article 1(vi)   319n
  Article 2(2)   331
  Article 3(7)   331
Convention on the Elimination of All Forms of Racial Discrimination (1965) (CERD)
  Article 11(1)   39
  Article 22   38–9, 192
Convention on the Prevention and Punishment of the Crime of Genocide (1948)
  Article IX   132
Convention on the Privileges and Immunities of the Specialized Agencies (1959)
  Section 32   171n
Convention on the Privileges and Immunities of the United Nations (1946)   362
  Article VIII, Section 30   170, 362n
Convention on the Settlement of Investment Disputes between States and Nations of Other States (1965) (ICSID Convention)   346–52
  Article 1(2)   347
  Article 2   347n
  Article 3   347n, 348n
  Article 5   348n
  Article 12   348n

Article 13   348n
Article 14(1)   348
Article 15(1)   348n
Article 25(1)   349
Article 25(2)   349n
Article 26   349n, 350
Article 27(1)   351
Article 31   348n
Article 37(2)(b)   348n
Article 40   348n
Article 42(1)   350
Article 42(2)   351
Article 42(3)   351
Article 47   350
Article 50   351n
Article 51(1)   352
Article 52   352
Article 52(1)   352
Article 53(1)   351
Article 54   351
Article 54(1)   351
Article 54(3)   351
Article 55   351
Article 57   348
Article 58   348n

Convention on the Transit Trade of Land-Locked States (1965)
Article 16(1)   40

Convention on Wetlands of International Importance especially as Waterfowl Habitat (Ramsar Convention) (1971)   325

Covenant of the League of Nations (1919)   386
Article 3(3)   87n
Article 4(4)   87n
Article 8   386
Article 8(1)   390
Article 11(1)   385
Article 12(1)   70, 385
Article 13   385
Article 13(1)   385
Article 13(2)   14, 70n, 386
Article 13(4)   385
Article 14   129, 163
Article 15(1)   70, 385
Article 15(6)   385
Article 15(7)   385

Article 15(9)   70, 87n
Article 15(10)   385
Article 19   389
Declaration of the Government of the Democratic and Popular Republic of Algeria Concerning the Settlement of Claims by the Government of the United States of America and the Government of the Islamic Republic of Iran (1981) (Claims Settlement Declaration)   352
   Article I   352
   Article II(1)   353n, 354n
   Article II(2)–(3)   354n
   Article III(1)   352
   Article III(2)   352n
   Article III(3)   353n
   Article III(4)   353n
   Article IV(1)   354
   Article V   354n
   Article VI(1)   352n
Draft Articles on Prevention of Transboundary Harm from Hazardous Activities (2001)   313n
Euratom Treaty (Treaty establishing the European Atomic Energy Community)   233
European Community (EC) Treaty (Treaty establishing the European Community)   233
   Article 226   233
European Convention for the Peaceful Settlement of Disputes (1957)
   Article 3   131
   Article 15   66
   Article 26   117n
Exchange of Notes Constituting an Agreement Modifying the Convention of 24 June 1901 between Denmark and the United Kingdom of Great Britain and Northern Ireland for regulating the Fisheries of their Respective Subjects Outside Territorial Waters in the Ocean Surrounding the Faroe Islands, 22 April 1955   59n
Exchange of Notes (with Annexed Map) Constituting an Agreement Replacing the Above-Mentioned Agreement of 22 April 1955, 27 April 1959   59
Gámez-Bonilla Treaty (1894)   121
   Article I   121
General Agreement on Tariffs and Trade (1947) (GATT)   276
   Article XX   286
   Article XXII   276
   Article XXIII   276
   Article XXIII(1)   277
   Article XXIII(2)   277
   Article XXV   276n
   Article XXV(1)   276n

General Agreement on Tariffs and Trade (1994) (GATT 1994)   278, 284
   Article XX   286, 313n
   Article XX(g)   313n
   Article XXII   282n
   Article XXIII   282n
   Article XXIII(1)   282
   Article XXIII(1)(b)   284
   Article XXIII(1)(c)   283
General Agreement on Trade in Services   278n
   Article XXIII(3)   282
Geneva General Act for the Pacific Settlement of International Disputes (1928)   70
   Article 1   70
   Article 17   70
   Article 20(1)   70
Hague Convention for the Pacific Settlement of International Disputes (1899)
      115, 211
   Article 3   43
   Article 6   43
   Article 8   45
   Articles 9–36   56, 57
   Articles 9–14   57
   Article 9   53n
   Article 14   52n
   Article 15   105
   Article 16   14
   Article 22   108n
   Article 23   108n
   Article 25   108n
   Article 28   108n
   Article 56   211n
Hague Convention for the Pacific Settlement of International Disputes (1907)   55, 57,
      115, 211
   Article 3   43
   Article 5   47n
   Article 6   43
   Article 8   45
   Article 9   53n
   Article 11   55n
   Article 36   55n
   Article 43   108n
   Article 44   108n
   Article 49   108n
   Article 84   211n
   Chapter III   58

ILC Draft Articles on Diplomatic Protection (2006)
   Article 18   252n
ILC Draft Articles on State Responsibility (2001)
   Article 48(1)   321
Indus Waters Treaty (1960)   49
   Annexure 5(4)(b)(ii)   106
Inter-American Treaty of Reciprocal Assistance (1947)   387
   Articles 1–2   387n
Inter-American Treaty on Good Offices and Mediation (1936)
   Article III   46n
International Convention for the Regulation of Whaling (1946)
   Article VIII   320
International Court of Justice Practice Directions (2001)
   Article XII   164n
International Court of Justice Rules of Court (1946)   139–40
   Article 24(2)   139
International Court of Justice Rules of Court (1972)
   Article 26(1)   140
International Court of Justice Rules of Court (1978)
   Article 9   184
   Article 15(1)   139n
   Article 16   139n
   Article 17(2)   139n, 140
   Article 17(3)   139n
   Article 18(1)   139n
   Article 22(1)   141n
   Article 23   141
   Article 26(1)(h)   141n
   Article 26(1)(n)   141n
   Article 34   114
   Article 38(1)   180n
   Article 38(2)   144, 180n
   Article 38(5)   145, 146
   Article 40(1)   180n
   Article 42   106n, 180
   Article 46(2)   180n
   Article 54(1)   181n
   Article 57   184
   Article 60(2)   181n
   Article 73(1)   190
   Article 74(1)   195
   Article 74(2)   195
   Article 75(1)   190, 200, 255

Article 76(1)   190
Article 78   200
Article 79(1)   201, 223
Article 79(3)   201n
Article 79(5)   201
Article 80(1)   180n
Article 80(2)   180n
Article 81(2)   206n
Article 84(1)   207n
Article 95(2)   185n
Article 98(2)   218n
Article 99–100   219n
Article 99(3)–(4)   220
Article 100(2)   216n, 221
Articles 102–9   164n
Article 102(2)   137
Article 102(3)   167
Israel–Egypt Peace Treaty (1979)   136
Kellog-Briand Pact (1928)   387
   Article I   387
   Article II   387
Kyoto Protocol to the United Nations Framework Convention on Climate Change (1997)   325
   Article 18   325n
Machakos Protocol (2002)   344
Model Rules on Arbitral Procedure (1958)   115
   Article 2(1)   115n
   Article 35   120, 120n
   Article 36(1)   120
Montreal Protocol on Substances that Deplete the Ozone Layer (1987)   323, 324–5, 328
   Article 2(9)(d)   325
   Article 8   324, 330
   Article 12(c)   326
North American Agreement on Environmental Cooperation (1993)   322
   Articles 14–15   322
North American Free Trade Agreement (NAFTA) (1992)   349
   Article 1131(1)   350n
Organisation of African Unity (OAU) Protocol (1964)
   Article XX   46n
Optional Protocol to the Vienna Convention Concerning Compulsory Settlement of Disputes (1958)   230
   Article I   192, 197–8

Paris Agreement with regard to the Restitution of Monetary Gold Found in Germany or in Third Countries   202
  Part III   202n
Permanent Court of Arbitration Optional Conciliation Rules (2012)
  Article 2(3)   65
  Article 7(1)   66
  Article 7(2)   66
  Article 14   66n
Permanent Court of Arbitration Optional Rules for Arbitrating Disputes between Two States (1992) (PCA Optional Rules)   112, 118
  Article 6(4)   111
  Article 33(1)   118n
PCA Optional Rules for Arbitrating Disputes between Two Parties of Which Only One is a State (1993)   344
Permanent Court of Arbitration Optional Rules for Fact-Finding Commission of Inquiry (1997) (PCA Optional Rules for Fact-Finding)
  Article 1(1)   54
  Article 5   54n
  Article 9(1)   54
  Article 9(2)   54
  Article 10   55
  Article 16(2)   55
Protocol Additional to the Geneva Conventions of 12 August 1949, and relating to the Protection of Victims of International Armed Conflicts (Protocol I), 8 June   1977
  Article 91   359n
Protocol for the Pacific Settlement of International Disputes (1924) (Geneva Protocol)   386
  Preamble   386
  Articles 2–4   386n
  Article 2   386
  Article 3   386
  Article 4   386
  Article 7   386n
  Article 10   386
Protocol on Environmental Protection to the Antarctic Treaty (1991)   316
  Article 7   317n
  Article 8   317n
  Article 11(3)   317
  Article 13   317n
  Article 15   317n
  Article 18   316, 317
  Article 19   317
  Article 19(1)   317

Article 19(3) 317n
Article 19(4) 317
Article 19(5) 317
Article 20(1) 317
Article 20(2) 317
Schedule
  Article 2(1) 317
  Article 6(1)(a) 317–18
  Article 6(1)(b) 317–18
  Article 6(2) 318n
  Article 7 318
  Article 10 317n
Protocol on the Resolution of Abyei Conflict (2004) (Abyei Protocol) 344
  Section 1.1.2 344
Protocol on Water and Health to the 1992 Convention on the Protection and Use of Transboundary Watercourses and International Lakes (1999) 325, 329
  Article 15 325n
Provisions for a Conference on Security and Cooperation in Europe (CSCE) Conciliation Commission (1992)
  Section VIII 66
  Section XII 66–7
  Section XIV 68–9
Regulations on the Procedure of International Conciliation (1961) 67
  Preamble 68n
  Article 1 53n
  Article 4 67
Revised General Act for the Pacific Settlement of International Disputes (1949) 115
  Article 15(1) 66
  Article 28 117
  Article 33(3) 68
Rome General Peace Accords (1992) (Rome Agreement) 49
Rome Statute for the Establishment of an International Criminal Court (1998)
  Article 36(8)(a) 132n
Rules of the International Tribunal for the Law of the Sea (1997) (ITLOS Rules)
  Article 24 315, 316
  Article 24(1) 315
  Article 24(2) 315
  Article 24(3) 316
  Article 28 248
  Article 29 247n
  Article 30 247
  Article 43 243n
  Article 89(4) 257

Article 89(5) 255
Article 91(2) 254n
Article 95 259
Article 95(1) 254n, 259
Article 97 252
Article 97(1) 252
Article 97(2) 252
Article 97(3) 252
Article 97(6) 252
Article 99 260n
Article 100 260n
Article 111(2)(b) 263n
Article 111(2)(c) 262, 263n
Article 112 248
Article 126 264
Article 127 264
Article 130 265n
Article 131(1) 266
Article 135(3) 265n
Article 138 266, 267
Article 138(3) 266n

Special Agreement between the Government of Canada and the Government of the United States of America to Submit to a Chamber of the International Court of Justice the Delimitation of the Maritime Boundary in the Gulf of Maine Area (1979) 140–41
Article I 140

Statute of the Administrative Tribunal of the International Labour Organization (1946)
Article XII(2) 170

Statute of the International Court of Justice (1945) (ICJ Statute)
Article 1 129n, 243n
Article 2 132, 134
Article 3(1) 132n
Articles 4–15 132
Article 4(1) 133
Article 5(2) 133n
Article 7(2) 133
Article 8 133
Article 9 132n
Article 10(1) 133n
Article 10(2) 133n
Article 10(3) 133n
Article 13(1) 132n
Article 16 114

Article 16(1)   134, 244
Article 16(2)   134
Article 17   114, 134n
Article 17(1)   134
Article 17(2)   134, 136
Article 20   134
Article 21   141
Article 21(1)   133
Article 22(1)   129n
Article 22(2)   133n
Article 24   114, 135
Article 24(1)   135
Article 25(3)   136, 185
Article 26   139
Article 26(1)   139
Article 26(2)   139, 140
Article 27   139n
Article 29   139
Article 30(2)   184
Article 31   137, 140, 167
Article 31(1)   137
Article 31(2)   137
Article 31(3)   137
Article 31(4)   139n
Article 31(5)   137n
Article 31(6)   137n
Article 32(1)   244
Article 33   129
Article 34(1)   131
Article 35   131
Article 35(1)   131
Article 35(2)   131, 132, 147
Article 35(3)   132
Article 36   15, 148n, 152
Article 36(1)   142, 197
Article 36(2)   101, 146, 147, 149n, 150, 152, 155, 157, 158–9, 162, 216, 233–4, 386
Article 36(3)   149
Article 36(4)   152
Article 36(5)   148
Article 36(6)   142
Article 38   117, 175
Article 38(1)   176, 284
Article 39(1)   178

Article 39(2)   179
Article 39(3)   179n
Article 40(1)   142, 180
Article 40(3)   106n
Article 41   191, 195, 196, 199, 222, 363, 364
Article 41(1)   190, 254, 255
Article 42(1)-(2)   180n
Article 43(1)   180
Article 46   181
Article 50   183, 316
Article 53   182, 189
Article 53(1)   189
Article 54(3)   184
Article 55(1)   185
Article 55(2)   133
Article 56(2)   185
Article 57   185
Article 58   185
Article 59   176, 210-11, 213, 215, 221, 297, 365
Article 60   185, 213-14, 216-18
Article 61   219n, 220
Article 61(1)   220
Article 61(2)   220
Article 61(4)   220
Article 61(5)   220
Article 62   118, 205-11, 223
Article 62(1)   206
Article 62(2)   207
Article 63   205-6, 211-12, 223
Article 63(1)   211
Article 63(2)   211, 212
Articles 65-8   164n
Article 65   165, 362
Article 65(1)   165, 167, 265
Article 65(2)   166n
Article 66   165
Article 66(1)   166
Article 68   166
Article 69   129
Statute of the International Tribunal for the Law of the Sea (1997) (ITLOS Statute)   243
   Article 1(2)   243n
   Article 2   243n, 244, 245
   Article 3(1)   243n

Article 4   244
Article 5(1)   244n
Article 7(1)   244
Article 8   114, 245
Article 10   245
Article 11   245
Article 12   244n
Article 13(1)   264n
Article 14   245
Article 15   247
Article 15(1)   247
Article 15(2)   247
Article 15(3)   248n
Article 15(5)   246n, 247
Article 17   265
Article 17(2)–(3)   245
Article 17(4)   245, 247
Article 17(6)   245n
Article 18(1)   244
Article 19(1)   243n
Article 20(2)   248
Articles 21–22   248
Article 21   249n, 266
Article 22   249n
Article 24   251
Article 25(1)   254
Article 25(2)   254, 255n
Article 28   252n
Article 29   263n
Article 30(1)   248n
Article 30(3)   264n
Article 31   260
Article 31(1)   260
Article 31(3)   260n
Article 32   260
Article 32(1)   260
Article 32(2)   260
Article 32(3)   260
Article 33   252, 264
Article 33(3)   264
Article 34   264n
Article 35(1)   245n
Article 35(2)   245

Article 35(3)　245n
　　Article 36(1)　246n
　　Article 36(2)　246n
　　Article 36(3)　246
　　Article 37　246n, 248
　　Article 38　250
　　Article 38(1)　284
　　Article 39　246, 264
　　Article 54(2)　251
Statute of the Permanent Court of International Justice (1920)
　　Article 36　15, 148
　　Article 36(2)　14–15, 149, 386
　　Article 63　211
Statute of the River Uruguay (1975)　38
　　Articles 7–12　38
　　Article 11　38
　　Article 12　38
　　Chapter XV　38
Statute of the United Nations Dispute Tribunal (2008)
　　Article 2　367n
　　Article 2(1)　368n
　　Article 3(1)　368n
　　Article 4(1)　367n, 368n
　　Article 10(1)　368n
　　Article 10(6)　368n
　　Article 10(9)　367n
　　Article 11(3)　367n
Treaty Banning Nuclear Weapon Tests in the Atmosphere, in Outer Space and Under Water (1963)　391n
Treaty between the Government of Canada and the Government of the United States of America to Submit to Binding Dispute Settlement the Delimitation of the Maritime Boundary in the Gulf of Maine Area (1979)　140
　　Article I　140n
　　Article II　141n
Treaty between the United States and Great Britain relating to Boundary Waters (1909)　321
　　Article IX　321–2
Treaty for Conciliation, Judicial Settlement and Arbitration between the UK and Switzerland (1965)　115
Treaty establishing the Organisation of Eastern Caribbean States (1981)
　　Article 14(1)　37
　　Article 14(2)　40
　　Annex A　40

Table of Treaties and Instruments

Treaty of Amity (1955)   186
  Article X   186
  Article X(1)   186
  Article XX(1)(d)   186–7
Treaty of Amity, Commerce and Navigation between Great Britain and the United States
    (1794) (Jay Treaty)   107
  Article 5   107
  Article 6   107
  Article 7   107
Treaty of Dorpat (1920)   168
  Article 10   168
  Article 11   168
Treaty of Peace and Friendship between Argentina and Chile (1984)   124
Treaty of Peace between Japan and Russia, signed at Portsmouth, 5 September
    1905   44
Treaty of Peace with Bulgaria (1947)   110
  Article 36   110n
Treaty of Peace with Hungary (1947)   110
  Article 40   110n
Treaty of Peace with Rumania (1947)   110
  Article 38   110n
Treaty of Versailles (1919)
  Article 435(2)   32n
Treaty of Washington (1871)
  Article VI   117n
Treaty on the Non-Proliferation of Nuclear Weapons (1968)   391
  Article VI   392
Treaty on the Prohibition of Nuclear Weapons (2017)   391
Understanding on Rules and Procedures Governing the Settlement of Disputes (1994)
    (DSU)   278, 284
  Article 1   285
  Article 1(1)   278n, 280, 291
  Article 2   285
  Article 2(1)   280
  Article 2(2)   280n
  Article 3(2)   278, 284, 291, 298
  Article 3(6)   287
  Article 3(7)   278, 286, 298, 301
  Article 3(8)   283n
  Article 4   287
  Article 4(1)   286–7
  Article 4(3)   287, 289n
  Article 4(4)   287

Article 4(6)   287n
Article 4(7)   287, 289n, 306
Article 4(8)   287n, 306
Article 4(10)   305
Article 5   288
Article 5(1)   288
Article 5(2)   288n
Article 5(3)   288n
Article 5(4)   288n
Article 5(5)   288n
Article 5(6)   288
Article 6(1)   289
Article 6(2)   289n, 291
Article 7   291
Article 7(1)   284
Article 8(1)   290
Article 8(2)   290
Article 8(3)   291
Article 8(4)   290n
Article 8(5)   290n
Article 8(6)   290
Article 8(7)   290
Article 8(9)   291
Article 8(10)   290, 306
Article 9(1)   290n
Article 9(2)   290n
Article 9(3)   290n
Article 10(2)   291, 293n
Article 10(3)   293
Article 11   281n, 284, 287, 292, 296
Article 12(6)   292n
Article 12(7)   288, 294n
Article 12(8)   294n
Article 12(9)   294n
Article 12(10)   306
Article 12(11)   306n
Article 13(1)   281
Article 14(1)–(2)   293
Article 15(1)   293n, 303
Article 15(2)   294n, 304
Article 15(3)   294n
Article 16(2)   295n
Article 16(3)   295

Article 16(4)   295n
Article 17   295
Article 17(1)   295n
Article 17(2)   295n
Article 17(3)   295
Article 17(4)   295, 296
Article 17(5)   280n, 296n
Article 17(6)   296n
Article 17(9)   281
Article 17(10)   296n
Article 17(14)   296n
Article 18(1)   293
Article 18(2)   293n
Article 19(1)   296n
Article 19(2)   285, 292n
Article 20   280n
Article 21   304
Article 21(1)   298
Article 21(2)   306
Article 21(3)   298n, 299
Article 21(3)(c)   303, 304, 305, 308n
Article 21(5)   299n
Article 21(6)   299
Article 21(7)   306
Article 21(8)   306
Article 22   299, 304
Article 22(1)   296, 299n, 301
Article 22(2)   299n, 300n, 303
Article 22(3)   300
Article 22(3)(a)   300n
Article 22(3)(b)   300n
Article 22(3)(c)   300n, 305
Article 22(4)   301n, 305
Article 22(5)   301n, 305n
Article 22(6)   300n, 301, 302, 303, 304, 305, 308n
Article 22(7)   304, 305
Article 23   278
Article 24   306
Article 24(1)   306
Article 24(2)   288, 306
Article 25   304, 305
Article 25(1)   304
Article 25(2)   304

Article 25(3)   304n, 305
Article 25(4)   304
Article 26(1)(a)   283
Article 26(1)(b)   297n
Article 27(2)   306, 307
Appendix 1   280
United Nations Convention against Torture and Other Cruel, Inhuman or Degrading Treatment or Punishment (1984)   321
Article 6(2)   321
Article 7(1)   321
United Nations Convention on Jurisdictional Immunities of States and their Property (2004)   41
Article 27(2)   41n
UN Convention on the Law of the Non-Navigational Uses of International Watercourses (1997)   322
Article 33(3)   322
Article 33(4)–(5)   323
Article 33(7)   323
Article 33(8)   323
Annex, Article 4(2)   111
United Nations Convention on the Law of the Sea (1982) (LOSC)   65, 229–74, 288
Article 15   240
Article 21   249n
Article 22   249n
Article 24   251
Article 73(2)   261
Article 74   71, 240, 241
Article 83   71, 240, 241
Article 87   253
Article 121   239n
Article 121(3)   239
Article 123   315
Article 153(1)   243n
Article 159(10)   265
Article 162(2)(v)   264
Article 165(2)(j)   264
Article 187   246, 248n
Article 187(b)(ii)   246n
Article 188(b)   245
Article 189   246n
Article 191   265, 267
Article 192   315
Article 194(1)   315

Article 194(5)   315
Article 206   315, 318
Article 216   261
Article 218   261
Article 219   261
Article 220(2)   261
Article 220(6)–(7)   261
Article 226(1)(b)   261
Article 226(1)(c)   261
Article 246   238, 240n
Article 246(5)   238
Article 246(6)   238
Article 253   238, 240n
Article 279   231n
Article 280   231n
Article 281   231, 232, 270, 271, 272
Article 281(1)   270
Article 282   231, 232, 233–4, 270
Article 283   231
Article 283(1)–(2)   31n
Article 283(2)   237
Article 284(1)   235
Article 284(2)–(3)   235n
Article 284(4)   235
Article 286   119, 236n, 242
Article 287   113, 119, 236n, 237, 242, 249, 250–1, 260, 262
Article 287(1)   236
Article 287(1)(a)   243n
Article 287(3)   236n
Article 287(4)   236
Article 287(5)   236
Article 288   248, 250
Article 288(1)   249–50, 268n
Article 288(2)   268n
Article 288(4)   237, 239n, 252
Article 290   254
Article 290(1)   254, 255
Article 290(3)   255
Article 290(5)   237, 254, 255, 256–7
Article 290(6)   254
Article 291   248n
Article 292   237n, 252, 260, 262
Article 292(1)   261n, 262

Article 292(2)   261
Article 293   268n
Article 293(1)   250
Article 293(2)   250
Article 294   239n
Article 294(1)   237
Article 294(3)   237
Article 295   253
Article 296   264
Article 297   237, 239, 240
Article 297(1)   237
Article 297(2)   238, 240
Article 297(2)(a)   238
Article 297(2)(a)(i)   240n
Article 297(2)(a)(ii)   240n
Article 297(2)(b)   238n
Article 297(3)   238, 240
Article 297(3)(a)   238, 239, 240n
Article 297(3)(b)   239
Article 297(3)(c)   239
Article 298   237, 240, 241
Article 298(1)   240, 241
Article 298(1)(a)(i)   241
Article 298(1)(a)(ii)   241n
Article 298(1)(a)(iii)   241n
Article 298(4)   240
Article 298(5)   240
Article 298(6)   240
Article 299   240
Part V   239
Part XI   245–6
  Section 5   230, 245
Part XV   249
  Sections 1–3   230
  Section 1   235
  Section 2   235, 270
  Section 3   235
Annex V   230, 241
  Article 3   235
  Article 4   67n
  Article 6   235
  Article 7   241
  Article 7(1)   241

Article 7(2)   68n, 235n, 239n
Article 8   68, 235
Article 9   68, 235n
Article 14   239
Section 1   235
Section 2   235
Annex VI   230
Article 21   250
Annex VII   114, 115, 230
Article 1   113, 119, 242, 268
Article 2   268
Article 2(1)   268n
Article 3   113
Article 3(e)   111, 113, 268
Article 9   252n
Annex VIII   106, 230
Articles 1–2   106n, 268n
Article 5(1)–(2)   269n
Article 5(3)   269n
United Nations Framework Convention on Climate Change (1992)
Article 14(6)   68
United Nations Model Rules for the Conciliation of Disputes between States (1995)   66
Article 7   66n
Article 8   67n
Article 21   68n
Article 25(1)   66
Article 26(1)   66n
Article 26(2)   67n
Article 27   67
Vienna Convention for the Protection of the Ozone Layer (1985)
Article 11   330
Article 11(5)   68
Vienna Convention on Consular Relations (1963)   192
Article 36(1)   198
Article 36(1)(b)   197
Vienna Convention on the Law of Treaties (1969)   65, 68, 284–6
Articles 31–3   285
Article 31(1)   284
Article 31(3)(c)   285–6, 285n
Article 32   284, 285
Article 66(b)   65
Paragraphs 4–5   66
Annex   67, 68n

Annex establishing Conciliation
  Paragraph 6   68n
Vienna Convention on the Law of Treaties between States and International Organizations or between International Organizations (1986)
  Article 66(2)(e)   171n
Vienna Convention on the Representation of States in their Relations with International Organisations of a Universal Character (1975)   41
  Article 85(1)   41n
Vienna Convention on Succession of States in respect of Treaties (1978)   41
  Article 42(1)   41n
Washington Agreement (1951)   101, 202
Washington Convention on International Trade in Endangered Species of Wild Fauna and Flora (CITES) (1973)   325

Foundation of International Dispute Settlement

OUTLINE OF PART I

1 International Dispute Settlement in Perspective 3
2 Negotiation, Good Offices and Mediation 28
3 Inquiry and Conciliation 52
4 International Dispute Settlement through the United Nations 73
5 Inter-State Arbitration 105
6 International Court of Justice (I): Organisation and Jurisdiction of the Court 128
7 International Court of Justice (II): Law and Procedure of the Court 175

International Dispute Settlement in Perspective

Main Issues

The settlement of disputes is one of the essential functions of law and this is equally true of international law. Indeed, the peaceful settlement of international disputes is a prerequisite to the maintenance of international peace and security. Furthermore, the establishment of mechanisms for settling international disputes is needed to secure the effectiveness of the international legal system. Peaceful settlement of international disputes thus occupies a central place within international law. As we shall discuss in this book, international law provides a range of means of international dispute settlement. They include negotiation, good offices, mediation, inquiry (fact-finding), conciliation, dispute settlement through international organisations, arbitration and judicial settlement. As a preliminary consideration, this chapter will discuss basic concepts and issues concerning peaceful settlement of international disputes in international law. The principal focus will be on the following issues:

(i) What is the obligation of peaceful settlement of international disputes?
(ii) What are international disputes in international law?
(iii) What is the principle of free choice of means?
(iv) What is the distinction between static and dynamic disputes?
(v) Should means of international dispute settlement differ according to the types of disputes?

1 INTRODUCTION

Whilst international disputes stem from a variety of factors, such as strategic, political, economic, cultural and religious factors, two elements in particular merit highlighting from the viewpoint of international law.

The first noteworthy element concerns the interpretation and application of rules of international law.[1] In the municipal legal system, basic functions of law – that is,

---

[1] L. Caflisch, 'Cent ans des règlement pacifique des différends interétatiques' (2001) 288 *RCADI*, pp. 257–61.

legislative, executive and judicial functions – are essentially monopolised by the State authority. In this sense, the municipal legal system can be regarded as a centralised legal system. Under this system, a dispute with regard to the interpretation and application of law is to be settled eventually by municipal courts. Jurisdiction of the municipal courts is obligatory in the sense that it does not rely on the consent of the parties of the litigation, and the decisions of the courts are enforced by the State authority. Thus the uniform interpretation and application of municipal law can be secured in the municipal legal system. In contrast, international law is considered as a decentralised legal system since there is no centralised authority which exercises legislative, executive and judicial functions. As there is no higher authority above individual States, rules of international law, customary or conventional, are interpreted and applied by States on their own. This is called auto-interpretation/auto-application. Normally States interpret rules of international law in such a way as to justify their policy. As a consequence, they may be interpreted in a different manner by different States. Yet the different interpretation and application of these rules are likely to create international disputes. These are in essence legal disputes. It can be said that the effectiveness of rules of international law relies essentially on the existence of mechanisms for settling international disputes with regard to the interpretation and application of these rules.[2]

The second noteworthy element relates to the antithesis between stability and change in international law. Once a rule of international law is established at a certain moment, the content of the rule is fixed in time. Thus the rule stabilises the legal order. Nevertheless, society, national or international, is constantly changing. Whilst the existing rules of international law may be advantageous to safeguard the interests of certain States, these rules may put other States at a disadvantage. As a consequence, a sharp tension is raised between States which have interests in maintaining the status quo and other States which demand a change of the status quo for their future development.[3] The tension is further intensified by uneven development and inequality of economic, military and political powers among States. Hence the antithesis between stability and change becomes a fundamental issue for international law.[4] Since there is no centralised machinery for peacefully changing the status quo in the international community, a change is often attempted by unilateral acts of a State or States. Yet, unilateral actions to change the status quo are likely to create international disputes. Here political or dynamic disputes may arise.[5]

Overall one can argue that fundamental causes of international disputes are deeply rooted in the decentralised system of international law and the international community. Hence disputes can be regarded as an inevitable part of international relations. In this regard, some argue that disputes have certain valuable characteristics because they aim to secure adjustments to the existing order and that this is necessary for the

---

[2] *Ibid.*, p. 261.
[3] See H. Morgenthau, *La notion du 'politique' et la théorie des différends internationaux* (Paris: Librairie du Recueil Sirey, 1933), pp. 70–3. For the purpose of this book, the status quo means the maintenance of the existing rules of international law and international order on the basis of the rules.
[4] J. L. Kunz, 'The Problem of Revision in International Law ("Peaceful Change")' (1939) 33 *AJIL*, pp. 38–40.
[5] See section 3.3 of this chapter.

development of any society.[6] In the international community which lacks a centralised organ performing the legislative function, a demand to change the status quo emerges via international disputes. In this sense, international disputes can be considered as a signal showing that the existing legal order is not satisfactory for some members of the international community.[7] Even so, it must always be remembered that international disputes may entail the risk of escalation endangering the international community as a whole.

Given that international disputes are inescapable in international relations, there is certainly a need to create effective mechanisms for peacefully resolving international disputes. Furthermore, as stated in the Report of the United Nations (UN) Secretary-General of 27 July 2015, the peaceful settlement of international disputes is essential to the maintenance of international peace and security and to promote the rule of law at the international level.[8] Thus the peaceful settlement of international disputes should be a crucial subject in international law. As a preliminary consideration, first, this chapter addresses the obligation of peaceful settlement of international disputes in international law (section 2). It then analyses the concept of international disputes in international law (section 3). Next, it moves on to examine the classification of various means of international dispute settlement (section 4). Finally, it discusses the principal features of the dispute settlement system in international law (section 5), before offering conclusions (section 6).

2 OBLIGATION OF PEACEFUL SETTLEMENT OF INTERNATIONAL DISPUTES

The obligation of peaceful settlement of international disputes is clearly embodied in Article 2(3) of the Charter of the United Nations (hereafter the UN Charter):[9]

> All Members shall settle their international disputes by peaceful means in such a manner that international peace and security, and justice, are not endangered.

Whilst the obligation under this provision is primarily incumbent upon members of the United Nations, it is binding on every State as a rule of customary international law.[10] This obligation is also to apply to the United Nations itself.[11] Subsequently the

---

[6] J. Collier and V. Lowe, *The Settlement of Disputes in International Law: Institutions and Procedures* (Oxford University Press, 2000), pp. 1–2.
[7] *Ibid.*, p. 2.
[8] UN General Assembly, Report of the UN Secretary-General, *Strengthening and Coordinating United Nations Rule of Law Activities*, A/70/206, 27 July 2015, p. 7, para. 21.
[9] 892 *UNTS*, p. 119. Entered into force 24 October 1945.
[10] *Case Concerning Military and Paramilitary Activities in and against Nicaragua* (Nicaragua v. United States of America), Judgment of 27 June 1986, ICJ Reports 1986, p. 145, para. 290. See also *Request for Interpretation of the Judgment of 15 June 1962 in the Case Concerning the Temple of Preah Vihear* (Cambodia v. Thailand), Judgment of 11 November 2013, ICJ Reports 2013, para. 105.
[11] B. Simma, D.-E. Khan, G. Nolte and A. Paulus (eds.), *The Charter of the United Nations: A Commentary* (hereafter *A Commentary*), 3rd edn, Vol. I (Oxford University Press, 2012), p. 188.

obligation of peaceful settlement of international disputes is confirmed in multiple international instruments, such as the 1970 Friendly Relations Declaration,[12] the 1982 Manila Declaration,[13] and the 2012 Declaration on the Rule of Law.[14]

The obligation of peaceful settlement of international disputes means that States must settle disputes by peaceful means, not coercive means. It is not suggested that all international disputes must be resolved immediately. In appropriate circumstances, wisdom may require parties to freeze disputes and maintain the status quo. The 1959 Antarctic Treaty that freezes claims to territorial sovereignty over Antarctica is a case in point.[15] However, it must be remembered that freezing of international disputes is only possible as long as all parties in dispute agree to do so. In addition, absence of solution must not constitute a threat to the maintenance of international peace and security.[16]

It is important to note that the obligation of peaceful settlement of international disputes is closely linked to the outlawry of war and the prohibition of the use or threat of force in international law. In fact, if States can freely recourse to war to resolve a dispute, the obligation of peaceful settlement of international disputes will become meaningless. At present, the use or threat of force is prohibited in international law. Under Article 2(4) of the UN Charter:

> All Members shall refrain in their international relations from the threat or use of force against the territorial integrity or political independence of any state, or in any other manner inconsistent with the Purposes of the United Nations.[17]

The International Court of Justice (ICJ), in the 1986 *Nicaragua* case (Merits), confirmed the customary law nature of the principle of non-use of force expressed in Article 2(4) of the UN Charter.[18] As the use of force is prohibited in international law, it is logical that all disputes must be settled in a peaceful manner. In this sense, the obligation of peaceful settlement of international disputes can be thought to be the corollary of the prohibition of the use of force in international law.[19]

---

[12] *Declaration on Principles of International Law Concerning Friendly Relations and Co-operation Among States in Accordance with the Charter of the United Nations*, Annex to the UN General Assembly Resolution 2625(XXV), 24 October 1970.

[13] UN General Assembly Resolution 37/10. *Manila Declaration on the Peaceful Settlement of International Disputes*, A/RES/37/2, 15 November 1982, Section I, para. 2.

[14] UN General Assembly Resolution, 67/1. *Declaration of the High-level Meeting of the General Assembly on the Rule of Law at the National and International Level*, A/RES/67/1, 30 November 2012, para. 4.

[15] Article IV(2). Text in: 402 *UNTS*, p. 71. Entered into force 23 June 1961.

[16] A. Pellet, 'Peaceful Settlement of International Disputes' in *Max Planck Encyclopaedia*, para. 5.

[17] For a detailed analysis of Article 2(4), see *A Commentary*, Vol. I, pp. 200–34.

[18] *Military and Paramilitary Activities in and against Nicaragua* (Nicaragua v. United States of America), Judgment of 27 June 1986, Merits, ICJ Reports 1986, p. 100, para. 190. According to the ICJ, the principle of non-use of force includes the prohibition of the threat of force. *Ibid.*, p. 118, para. 227.

[19] D. W. Bowett, 'Contemporary Developments in Legal Techniques in the Settlement of Disputes' (1983-II) 169 *RCADI*, p. 177; P.-M. Dupuy and Y. Kerbrat, *Droit international public*, 12th edn (Paris: Dalloz, 2014), p. 613. See also Chapter 12, section 1 of this book.

7 International Dispute Settlement in Perspective

A catalogue of means of international dispute settlement is provided in Article 33(1) of the UN Charter:

> The parties to any dispute, the continuance of which is likely to endanger the maintenance of international peace and security, shall, first of all, seek a solution by negotiation, enquiry, mediation, conciliation, arbitration, judicial settlement, resort to regional agencies or arrangements, or other peaceful means of their own choice.

This provision calls for three comments.

First, taken literally, this provision seems to apply only to disputes 'the continuance of which is likely to endanger the maintenance of international peace and security'. However, this is not the case and all disputes must be settled peacefully in international law.[20]

Second, Article 33(1) of the UN Charter is not an exhaustive list of means of dispute settlement. In fact, Article 33(1) goes on to add 'other peaceful means of their own choice'. It seems to follow that the means of dispute settlement are not limited to the methods clearly mentioned in that provision.[21] Indeed, the Manila Declaration adds good offices as a means of dispute settlement, although Article 33(1) makes no reference to good offices.[22] States are also free to combine means of dispute settlement or create an original technique for dispute settlement.[23]

Third, as shown in the phrase 'their own choice', the choice of dispute settlement means relies on the consent of the parties in dispute. This is called the principle of free choice of means. According to the advisory opinion of the *Status of Eastern Carelia* case:

> It is well established in international law that no State can, without its consent, be compelled to submit its disputes with other States either to mediation or to arbitration, or to any other kind of pacific settlement.[24]

The Friendly Relations Declaration also confirms this principle, stating that: 'International disputes shall be settled on the basis of the sovereign equality of States and in accordance with *the principle of free choice of means*.'[25]

The obligations set out in Articles 2(3) and 33(1) of the UN Charter are regarded as an obligation of conduct and there is no obligation to reach a specific result.[26] Even

---

[20] J. Verhoeven, *Droit international public* (Brussels: Larcier, 2000), p. 694; the Manila Declaration, para. I(2). See also Friendly Relations Declaration.
[21] José Antonio Pastor Ridruejo, 'Le droit international à la veille du vingt et unième siècle: normes, faits et valeurs: Cours général de droit international public' (hereafter 'Cours général') (1998) 274 *RCADI*, p. 99; Caflisch, 'Cent ans', p. 274.   [22] Section I, para. 5.
[23] Verhoeven, *Droit international public*, p. 696.
[24] *Status of Eastern Carelia*, Advisory Opinion of 23 July 1923, PCIJ Ser. B, 1923, No. 5, p. 27.
[25] Emphasis added. See also Section I, para. 3, of the Manila Declaration.
[26] *A Commentary*, Vol. I, p. 190; R. Kolb, *The International Court of Justice* (Oxford: Hart Publishing 2013), p. 23; Pellet, 'Peaceful Settlement', para. 16.

so, it must be noted that peaceful settlement of international disputes is governed by the principle of good faith.[27] In the event of failure to reach a solution by any one of the means of dispute settlement, the State Parties to an international dispute are under the duty to 'continue to seek a settlement of the dispute by other peaceful means agreed upon by them'.[28]

3 THE CONCEPT OF INTERNATIONAL DISPUTES IN INTERNATIONAL LAW

3.1 Definition of International Disputes

An often quoted definition of international disputes is that stated in the *Mavromatis* judgment of 1924 by the Permanent Court of International Justice (PCIJ):[29]

> [A] disagreement over a point of law or fact, a conflict of legal views or of interests between two persons.[30]

The *Mavromatis* formula and its variations have been repeatedly confirmed in the ICJ jurisprudence.[31]

However, the time-honoured formula appears to be too broad in its scope in the sense that it includes 'conflict of interests' in the category of disputes. If there are always differences of interests behind international disputes, a mere disagreement of interests does not automatically create a dispute in a legal sense.[32] For example, an exporting country of petrol usually attempts to export it at a high price, while an importing country of petrol has an interest in buying it at a low price. Here there is a difference concerning economic interests between States. Nonetheless, this is not a dispute in international law, unless

---

[27] Manila Declaration, Section I, para. 5. See also Section I, para. 11. For a comprehensive analysis of the principle of good faith in international law, see R. Kolb, *La bonne foi en droit international public: contribution à l'étude des principes généraux de droit* (Paris: PUF, 2000). See in particular, pp. 579 *et seq*. See also United Nations, *Handbook on the Peaceful Settlement of Disputes between States* (New York: United Nations, 1992), p. 6.

[28] The second principle of the Friendly Relation Declaration; Section I, para. 7 of the Manila Declaration; *A Commentary*, Vol. I, p. 1075.

[29] Generally on this issue, see R. Jennings, 'Reflections on the Term "Dispute"' in R. St. J. Macdonald (ed.), *Essays in Honour of Wang Tieya* (Dordrecht: Nijhoff, 1994), pp. 401–5; C. Schreuer, 'What Is a Legal Dispute?' in I. Buffard, J. Crawford, A. Pellet and S. Wittich (eds.), *International Law between Universalism and Fragmentation, Festschrift in Honour of Gerhard Hafiner* (Leiden: Nijhoff, 2008), pp. 959–79; R. Kolb, 'Note sur certaines caractéristiques du différend international' (2004) *The Global Community: Yearbook of International Law and Jurisprudence*, pp. 227–42; Kolb, *The International Court of Justice*, pp. 300 *et seq*.

[30] *Mavromatis Palestine Concessions*, Judgment No. 2, 1924, PCIJ, Series A, No. 2, p. 11.

[31] For instance, see *Case Concerning East Timor* (Portugal v. Australia), Judgment of 30 June 1995, ICJ Reports 1995, p. 99, para. 22; *Case Concerning Certain Property* (Liechtenstein v. Germany), Preliminary Objections, Judgment of 10 February 2005, p. 18, para. 24. See also Kolb, *The International Court of Justice*, p. 302.

[32] Kolb, *The International Court of Justice*, p. 306.

9 International Dispute Settlement in Perspective

there is an obligation to fix the price of petrol.[33] In this respect, the ICJ in the *South West Africa* case stated that:

> [I]t is not sufficient for one party to a contentious case to assert that a dispute exists with the other party. A mere assertion is not sufficient to prove the existence of a dispute any more than a mere denial of the existence of the dispute proves its non-existence. *Nor is it adequate to show that the interests of the two parties to such a case are in conflict. It must be shown that the claim of one party is positively opposed by the other.*[34]

Further, conceptually distinction should be made between disputes and conflicts, even though the term 'dispute' and 'conflict' are often used interchangeably. Whilst conflicts are often unfocused and general in their nature, disputes are formulated by way of claims and counterclaims or denials, focusing on specific issues. For the purpose of this book, a general state of hostility or a wider antagonism between States should be called international 'conflict',[35] whilst the term international 'dispute' in the traditional sense signifies a specific disagreement between subjects of international law concerning a matter of fact, law or policy in which a claim of one party is positively opposed by the other.[36] A dispute always arises from a conflict, while the existence of a conflict does not always lead to a dispute. When submitting an international dispute to an international court, a party or parties in dispute must extrapolate relevant elements from a conflict and convert them into a dispute which is relevant to examination by the court. International courts and tribunals can settle only legal aspects of an international 'conflict'. Hence the judicial settlement of an international dispute does not mean that all aspects of an international conflict are resolved.

3.2 Identification of International Disputes

3.2.1 Criteria for Identifying International Disputes

In reality, it is not infrequent that one of the parties in dispute declines to admit the existence of an international dispute in international adjudication.[37] In this case, a dispute arises with regard to the existence of a dispute. As the ICJ ruled in the 1974 *Nuclear Tests* case, 'the existence of a dispute is the primary condition for the Court to

---

[33] P. Cahier, 'Changements et continuité du droit international: Cours général de droit international public' (1985-VI) 195 *RCADI*, pp. 329–30.

[34] Emphasis added. *South West Africa* cases (Liberia v. South Africa) (Ethiopia v. South Africa), Judgment of 21 December 1962, Preliminary Objections, ICJ Reports 1962, p. 328. This view was echoed by the Court in the *East Timor* case, ICJ Reports 1995, p. 100, para. 22.

[35] Morgenthau called such a wider antagonism 'tensions' which must be distinct from 'disputes' focusing on a clearly defined single issue. Morgenthau, *La Notion du 'politique'*, p. 78. Charles de Visscher also took a similar view. Charles de Visscher, *Theory and Reality in Public International Law*, Revised edn (trans. P. E. Corbett) (Princeton University Press, 1968), p. 353.

[36] This definition is based on that proposed by J. G. Merrills, *International Dispute Settlement*, 6th edn (Cambridge University Press, 2017), p. 1. Concerning the distinction between conflicts and disputes, see Collier and Lowe, *The Settlement of Disputes*, p. 1.

[37] Generally on this issue, see S. Yee, 'A Proposal for Formalizing the "No Case Exists" Objections Procedure at the International Court of Justice' (2005) 4 *CJIL*, pp. 393–416.

exercise its judicial function'.[38] Thus whether an international dispute exists between the parties should be an important question in judicial proceedings. As stated by the ICJ in the 1998 *Fisheries Jurisdiction* case between Spain and Canada, 'it is for the Applicant, in its Application, to present to the Court the dispute with which it wishes to seise the Court and to set out the claims which it is submitting to it'.[39] In the Court's view:

> Whether there exists an international dispute is a matter for objective determination. The mere denial of the existence of a dispute [by a State] does not prove its non-existence.[40]

Whilst the evaluation of the existence of a dispute is context-specific, the ICJ jurisprudence appears to reveal some key elements of deciding the existence of a dispute. These elements can be summarised as follows:

(i) The Court's determination of the existence of a dispute is a matter of substance, not a question of form or procedure.[41]
(ii) As the ICJ stated in the *South West Africa* case, it must be shown that the claim of one party is positively opposed by the other.[42] In this regard, the Court, in the 2016 *Nicaragua/Colombia* case, took the view that: '[A]lthough a formal diplomatic protest may be an important step to bring a claim of one party to the attention of the other, such a formal protest is not a necessary condition [for the existence of a dispute].'[43] If one of the parties maintains the application of a treaty and the other denies it, the difference of the views concerning the applicability of the treaty alone is not adequate to confirm the existence of a dispute. The ICJ is required to ascertain whether the matters claimed before the Court, such as alleged breaches of the treaty or acts

---

[38] The *Nuclear Tests* case (Australia v. France) (New Zealand v. France), Judgment of 20 December, ICJ Reports 1974, pp. 270–1, para. 55.
[39] *Fisheries Jurisdiction* case (Spain v. Canada), Jurisdiction of the Court, Judgment of 4 December, ICJ Reports 1998, p. 447, para. 29.
[40] *Interpretation of Peace Treaties with Bulgaria, Hungary and Romania, First Phase*, Advisory Opinion, 30 March 1950, ICJ Reports 1950, p. 74.
[41] *Obligations concerning Negotiations relating to Cessation of the Nuclear Arms Race and to Nuclear Disarmament* (Marshall Islands v. United Kingdom), Judgment of 5 October 2016, Preliminary Objections (not yet reported), para. 38; *Application of the International Convention on the Elimination of All Forms of Racial Discrimination* (Georgia v. Russian Federation), Preliminary Objection, Judgment of 1 April 2011, ICJ Reports 2011, p. 84, para. 30.
[42] *South West Africa* case (Ethiopia v. South Africa; Liberia v. South Africa), Preliminary Objections, Judgment of 21 December 1962, ICJ Reports 1962, p. 328. See also *Armed Activities on the Territory of the Congo (New Application: 2002)* (Democratic Republic of the Congo v. Rwanda), Jurisdiction and Admissibility, Judgment of 3 February 2006, ICJ Reports 2006, p. 40, para. 90. Judge Owada, in the 2011 *Georgia/Russia* case, argued that a party must show that there exists a situation in which the claim advanced by the Applicant party is positively met with *an attitude of opposition*. Separate Opinion of Judge Owada in *Application of the International Convention on the Elimination of All Forms of Racial Discrimination* (Georgia v. Russian Federation) (hereafter the *Georgia/Russia* case), Preliminary Objections, Judgment of 1 April 2011, ICJ Reports 2011, p. 174, para. 12.
[43] *Alleged Violations of Sovereign Rights and Maritime Spaces in the Caribbean Sea* (Nicaragua v. Colombia), Preliminary Objections, Judgment of 17 March 2016 (not yet reported), para. 72.

complained of by the applicant, are capable of falling within the provisions of that instrument to determine the existence of a dispute.[44]

(iii) According to the Court in the *Georgia/Russia* case, '[t]he existence of a dispute may be inferred from the failure of a State to respond to a claim in circumstances where a response is called for'.[45] It would seem to follow that failure to respond to the demands of one of the parties to a dispute does not automatically preclude the existence of a dispute.[46] Furthermore, the ICJ, in the 2016 *Nicaragua/Colombia* judgment (preliminary objection), took the view that the fact that the parties remained open to a dialogue does not by itself prove that there existed no dispute between them concerning the subject matter of the dispute.[47]

(iv) As the ICJ observed in the *Georgia/Russia* case, '[w]hile the existence of a dispute and the undertaking of negotiations are distinct as a matter of principle, the negotiations may help demonstrate the existence of the dispute and delineate its subject-matter'.[48]

(v) Dispute must clearly specify issues between the parties. A hypothetical dispute or a question *in abstracto* cannot be regarded as a dispute capable of judicial settlement.[49] As stated in the *Northern Cameroons* judgment, the Court 'may pronounce judgment only in connection with concrete cases where there exists at the time of the adjudication an actual controversy involving a conflict of legal interests between the parties'.[50] However, it is not suggested that actual or concrete damage is required to establish the existence of a dispute. In the *Headquarters Agreement* case, for instance, the United States made clear that it would not take actions to close the PLO Mission to the United Nations,[51] although the United States had passed legislation designed to lead to the closure of the Mission.[52] The United States thus argued that

---

[44] *Legality of Use of Force* (Serbia and Montenegro v. Belgium), Request for the Indication of Provisional Measures, Order of 2 June 1999, ICJ Reports 1999, p. 137, para. 38; *Immunities and Criminal Proceedings* (Equatorial Guinea v. France), Request for the Indication of Provisional Measures, 7 December 2016, ICJ Reports 2016 (not yet reported), para. 47.

[45] The *Georgia/Russia* case, Preliminary Objection, ICJ Reports 2011, p. 84, para. 30. See also *Applicability of the Obligation to Arbitrate under Section 21 of the United Nations Headquarters Agreement of 26 June 1947*, Advisory Opinion of 26 April 1988, ICJ Reports 1988, p. 28, para. 38; *Land and Maritime Boundary between Cameroon and Nigeria* (Cameroon v. Nigeria) (hereafter the *Cameroon/Nigeria* case), Preliminary Objections, Judgment of 11 June 1998, ICJ Reports 1998, p. 315, para. 89. The ICJ's view was echoed by ITLOS. See The *M/V 'Norstar'* case (Panama v. Italy), Preliminary Objections, 4 November 2016, ITLOS case No. 25, para. 101.

[46] Schreuer, 'What Is a Legal Dispute?', pp. 964–5.

[47] The 2016 *Nicaragua/Colombia* case (Preliminary Objections), para. 69.

[48] The *Georgia/Russia* case, Preliminary Objection, ICJ Reports 2011, p. 84, para. 30. Yet, Judge ad hoc Fleischhauer, in the *Certain Property* case, expressed his misgivings that if the Court regards negotiations over a contentious issue as evidence of the existence of a dispute, this could have negative effects on the readiness of States to engage in attempts at peaceful settlement of disputes. Declaration of Judge ad hoc Fleischhauer, *Certain Property* (Liechtenstein v. Germany), Preliminary Objections, Judgment of 10 February 2005, ICJ Reports 2005, p. 69. See also H. Thirlway, *The International Court of Justice* (Oxford University Press, 2016), p. 54.

[49] Schreuer, 'What Is a Legal Dispute?', pp. 970–1.

[50] *Northern Cameroons* (Cameroon v. United Kingdom), Judgment of 2 December 1963, Preliminary Objections, ICJ Reports 1962, pp. 33–4.

[51] ICJ Reports 1988, p. 29, para. 39.   [52] *Ibid.*, pp. 15–19, paras. 9–15.

there was no dispute between the United Nations and itself.[53] Nonetheless, the Court was not persuaded by this argument. According to the Court:

> While the existence of a dispute does presuppose a claim arising out of the behaviour of or a decision by one of the parties, it in no way requires that any contested decision must already have been carried into effect. What is more, a dispute may arise even if the party in question gives an assurance that no measure of execution will be taken until ordered by decision of the domestic courts.[54]

In addition, the ICJ ruled, in the *Arrest Warrant* case, that Belgium had violated international law by issuing against the incumbent Foreign Minister of the Democratic Republic of the Congo the arrest warrant of 11 April 2000 and its international circulation, even though no arrest had ever taken place under the arrest warrant.[55]

(vi) As the ICJ stated in the *Belgium/Senegal* case, the 'dispute must *in principle* exist at the time the Application is submitted to the Court'.[56] According to the Court, '*[i]n principle*, the critical date for determining the existence of a dispute is the date on which the application is submitted to the Court'.[57] The term 'in principle' seems to allow for some nuance when determining the existence of a dispute on the date the case is referred to it.[58]

3.2.2 Case Study

In some cases, the existence of a particular dispute constitutes a debatable issue. An eminent example is the *Georgia/Russia* case. In this case, a contentious issue arose whether there was a dispute between the parties with regard to violations of the 1965 Convention on the Elimination of All Forms of Racial Discrimination.[59] While, at the stage of the proceedings of provisional measures, the majority opinion of the Court found that a dispute with regard to the 1965 Convention existed between the parties,[60] seven judges, in their Joint Dissenting Opinion, denied the existence of the dispute.[61] The voting record, eight votes versus seven, suggests that the decision of the Court in this matter was highly controversial. The existence of a dispute was also at issue at the stage of the proceedings concerning preliminary objections put forward by the Russian Federation. Again, the Russian Federation claimed

---

[53] *Ibid.*, p. 29, para. 39.   [54] *Ibid.*, p. 30, para. 42.
[55] *Arrest Warrant of 11 April 2000* (hereafter the *Arrest Warrant* case) (Democratic Republic of the Congo v. Belgium), Judgment of 14 February 2002, ICJ Reports 2002, p. 33, para. 78(2).
[56] Emphasis added. *Questions relating to the Obligation to Prosecute or Extradite* (Belgium v. Senegal), Judgment of 20 July 2012, Merits, ICJ Reports 2012, p. 442, para. 46. The *dictum* was repeatedly confirmed by the Court.
[57] The 2016 *Nicaragua/Colombia* case (Preliminary Objections), para. 25.
[58] In this regard, Kolb argued that while there must at least be the beginnings of a dispute before the parties seise the Court, the definitive dispute can crystallise later in the course of the proceedings. Kolb, *The International Court of Justice*, p. 315.
[59] Text in: 660 *UNTS*, p. 195. Entered into force 4 January 1969.
[60] The *Georgia/Russia* case, Request for the Indication of Provisional Measures, Order of 15 October 2008, ICJ Reports 2008, p. 387, para. 112.
[61] Joint Dissenting Opinion of Vice-President Al Khasawneh and Judges Ranjeva, Shi, Koroma, Tomka, Bennouna and Skotnikov, *ibid.*, pp. 400 *et seq.*

that there was no dispute between the parties respecting the interpretation or application of the 1965 International Convention on the Elimination of All Forms of Racial Discrimination (CERD) at the date Georgia filed its application. In this regard, the Court observed that the Georgian claims of 9 to 12 August 2008 expressly referred to alleged ethnic cleansing by Russian forces. It thus concluded that the exchanges between the Georgian and Russian representatives in the Security Council on 10 August 2008, the claims made by the Georgian President on 9 and 11 August and the response on 12 August by the Russian Foreign Minister established that by the day on which Georgia submitted its application, there was a dispute between Georgia and the Russian Federation about the latter's compliance with its obligations under CERD as invoked by Georgia in this case.[62]

By contrast, the Court, in the 2016 *Marshall Islands/United Kingdom* case, has dismissed a case on the ground that no dispute existed between the applicant and the respondent prior to the filing of the application instituting proceedings.[63] This case, which relates to the alleged breach of treaty and customary obligations concerning nuclear disarmament by the United Kingdom, was determined, after eight votes to eight, by the President's casting vote. As shown in the voting record, opinions of the members of the Court were sharply divided with regard to the existence of a dispute. The most debatable issue in this case pertains to the validity of a requirement of the respondent's awareness. In this regard, the ICJ held that:

> [A] dispute exists when it is demonstrated, on the basis of the evidence, that the respondent was aware, or could not have been unaware, that its views were 'positively opposed' by the applicant.[64]

However, some members of the Court questioned the validity of the awareness test since this is a new requirement that cannot be found in the case law of the Court.[65] In this

---

[62] The *Georgia/Russia* case, Preliminary Objection, ICJ Reports 2011, p. 120, para. 113. Yet, the Court's approach was criticised by Judge Owada. According to the learned judge, the Court's approach 'amounts to suggesting that in order to establish the existence of a dispute between the parties the Applicant is required *to establish a positive act of manifestation of opposition* from the Respondent'(emphasis original). In the view of Judge Owada, however, such a high threshold was not contained in the *dictum* of the *South West Africa* cases. Separate Opinion of Judge Owada, pp. 174-5, paras. 11-13.

[63] *Obligations concerning Negotiations relating to Cessation of the Nuclear Arms Race and to Nuclear Disarmament* (Marshall Islands v. United Kingdom), Preliminary Objections, Judgment of 5 October 2016, ICJ Reports 2016 (not yet reported), para. 59. For the same reason, the ICJ also dismissed the cases between Marshall Islands on the one hand and India and Pakistan on the other hand. *Obligations concerning Negotiations relating to Cessation of the Nuclear Arms Race and to Nuclear Disarmament* (Marshall Islands v. Pakistan), Judgment of 5 October 2016, Jurisdiction of the Court and admissibility of the application; *Obligations concerning Negotiations relating to Cessation of the Nuclear Arms Race and to Nuclear Disarmament* (Marshall Islands v. India), Judgment of 5 October 2016, Jurisdiction of the Court and admissibility of the application.

[64] *Obligations concerning Negotiations relating to Cessation of the Nuclear Arms Race and to Nuclear Disarmament* (Marshall Islands v. United Kingdom), Preliminary Objections, Judgment of 5 October 2016, ICJ Reports 2016 (not yet reported), para. 41. Judge Owada further elaborated the element of the respondent's awareness. Separate Opinion of Judge Owada, *ibid.*, paras. 3-14.

[65] Separate Opinion of Judge Sebutinde, *ibid.*, paras. 15 and 30-3; Dissenting Opinion of Judge Robinson, *ibid.*, para. 4; Dissenting Opinion of Judge Crawford, *ibid.*, para. 1; Dissenting Opinion of Judge Bennouna; Dissenting Opinion of Judge Cançado Trindade, *ibid.*, para. 14; Dissenting Opinion of Judge ad hoc Medjaoui, paras. 26-31.

regard, Judge Crawford stated that: 'At no point did the Court say that awareness was a legal requirement.'[66] In fact, traditionally the ICJ took a flexible approach when deciding the existence of a dispute and its jurisdiction to deal with a particular case.[67] Thus some doubts could be expressed regarding whether the judgment deviated from the judicial flexibility in the ICJ jurisprudence.[68] Furthermore, as the Court itself ruled in the 1998 *Cameroon/Nigeria* case, there is no requirement for formal notification.[69] In the *Marshall Islands/United Kingdom* case, the Court offered no persuasive reason why it must deviate from its case law by applying an overly formalistic approach. In light of the sharp criticisms from the members of the Court, whether the awareness test can be generalised needs careful consideration.

3.3 The Distinction between Legal (Static) and Non-Legal (Dynamic) Disputes

The next issue concerns the distinction between legal or static disputes and non-legal or dynamic disputes.[70] The distinction between legal and non-legal disputes can be found in various treaties. By way of example, Article 16 of the 1899 Hague Convention recognised that:

> *In questions of a legal nature*, and especially in the interpretation or application of International Conventions, arbitration is recognized by the Signatory Powers as the most effective, and at the same time the most equitable, means of settling disputes which diplomacy has failed to settle.[71]

The distinction between legal and political disputes was also reflected in Article 13(2) of the Covenant of the League of Nations:[72]

> Disputes as to the interpretation of a treaty, as to any question of international law, as to the existence of any fact which if established would constitute a breach of any international obligation, or as to the extent and nature of the reparation to be made for any such breach, are declared to be among those which are generally suitable for submission to arbitration or judicial settlement.

Furthermore, Article 36(2) of the Statute of the Permanent Court of International Justice enumerated legal disputes, providing that any State signatory to the Protocol establishing the Court may recognise in advance the jurisdiction of the Court, in relation to any

---

[66] Dissenting Opinion of Judge Crawford, *ibid.*, para. 4.   [67] *Ibid.*, paras. 7–10.
[68] See, for instance, Separate Opinion of Judge Sebutinde, *ibid.*, para. 1.
[69] *Land and Maritime Boundary between Cameroon and Nigeria* (Cameroon v. Nigeria: Equatorial Guinea intervening), Judgment of 11 June 1998, Preliminary Objections, ICJ Reports 1998, p. 297, para. 39.
[70] Generally on this issue, see A. Beirlaen, 'La Distinction entre les différends juridiques et les différends politiques dans la pratique des organisations internationales' (1975) 11 *RBDI*, pp. 405–41.
[71] Emphasis added. The electronic text of the Convention is available at: http://avalon.law.yale.edu/19th_century/hague01.asp. Entered into force 4 September 1900.
[72] The electronic text of the League Covenant is available at: http://avalon.law.yale.edu/20th_century/leagcov.asp. Entered into force 10 January 1920.

Member of the League or State accepting the same obligation 'in all or any of the classes of legal disputes concerning: (a) the interpretation of a treaty; (b) any question of international law; (c) the existence of any fact which if established would constitute a breach of any international obligation; (d) the extent and nature of the reparation to be made for any such breach'.[73] This provision is basically succeeded in Article 36 of the Statute of the ICJ.[74] The question of interest here concerns a criterion for distinguishing legal disputes from non-legal disputes. In this regard, three views can be identified.

On the first view, legal and non-legal disputes are distinguished according to the importance of the disputes. According to this view, important disputes are regarded as political disputes and less important disputes are considered as legal disputes. Nonetheless, the concept of importance is too subjective to be useful. Further, this view is not in conformity with judicial practice. In fact, experience has shown that disputes of highly political importance had also been settled by judicial means.[75] The mere fact that a certain dispute is important does not provide a reason for considering it as non-justiciable.

According to the second view, legal disputes should be distinct from non-legal disputes according to the existence or non-existence of rules of international law applicable to the disputes. Under this hypothesis, legal disputes are disputes to which there are rules of international law applicable. If there is no rule applicable to the dispute, the dispute should be regarded as a non-legal one. However, the existence of relevant rules of international law can be determined only after examining the dispute before international courts. Accordingly, it seems logically impossible to decide *a priori* whether a dispute is regarded as a legal dispute or a non-legal dispute. Further, even if relevant rules applicable to the dispute do not exist, it is not impossible for an international court to determine the dispute on the basis of the fundamental principles of international law. In this case, it is also possible for the international court to decline the claim of a disputing party because of the absence of relevant rules of international law. This is a judicial decision by the court. In this sense, as a matter of theory, one can argue that there is no dispute which cannot be legally determined by international courts and tribunals.[76] Accordingly, the second view of law cannot provide a valid criterion in this matter.

On the third view, a legal dispute is one where parties claim rights on the basis of the existing rules of international law. By contrast, a non-legal dispute arises out of claims to alter the existing rule of the law. It follows that the distinction between legal and non-legal disputes must be based on the claims of the disputing parties, not the nature of the disputes. According to Lauterpacht, 'it is the refusal of the State to submit the dispute to judicial settlement, and not the intrinsic nature of the controversy, which

---

[73] The electronic text is available at: www.refworld.org/docid/40421d5e4.html.
[74] See also Article 36(3) of the UN Charter.
[75] H. Lauterpacht, *The Function of Law in the International Community* (Oxford University Press, 2011), pp. 153–61.
[76] J. Combacau and S. Sur, *Droit international public*, 10th edn (Paris: Montchrestien, 2012), p. 557; T. Sogawa, *International Law IV* (in Japanese) (Tokyo: Hosei Daigaku Tsushin Kyoikubu, 1950), p. 226.

makes it political'; accordingly, 'the only decisive test of the justiciability of the dispute is the willingness of the disputants to submit the conflict to the arbitrament of law'.[77] It may be said that the third view represents the majority opinion.[78] Whilst disputes arising from claims to alter the status quo are normally called political disputes, following Kunz, it may be relevant to call them 'dynamic disputes' in light of its dynamism in changing the status quo.[79] By contrast, legal disputes can be called 'static disputes' in the sense that the disputing parties attempt to settle the dispute by an independent and impartial third party, such as a judicial body, within the framework of the existing rules of international law.

In reality, however, it is less easy to distinguish the two types of disputes since States often present multiple reasons, including both legal and non-legal reasoning, to justify their claim at the same time.[80] Normally international disputes can be regarded as hybrid disputes that have both legal and non-legal dimensions. As a matter of theory, all international disputes can be determined by an international court or tribunal if it can establish jurisdiction to deal with the disputes.[81] However, the point at issue is whether non-legal or dynamic disputes can be effectively settled through international adjudication. As E. H. Carr stated, '[t]he essence of a political dispute is the demand that the relevant legal rule, though admittedly applicable, shall not be applied'.[82] Accordingly, it seems unrealistic to consider that dynamic disputes can be effectively settled by international courts and tribunals applying the existing rules of the law.[83] Further, the settlement of dynamic disputes is closely linked to peaceful change of international law.[84] However, a court, national or international, is the product and the mouthpiece of law and the revision of the existing rules or status quo is not within the domain of the courts but within the realm of politics.[85] Even if the interpretation of rules of international law by an international court or tribunal may change over time, this does not mean that the court or tribunal is entitled to change the rules. As the demand to alter the status quo relates to the overall development of a State or States in the future, the change of the status quo can be made only by States on the basis of political decisions.[86] Therefore, it may have to be accepted that international adjudication contains

---

[77] Lauterpacht, *The Function of Law*, p. 172.   [78] Caflisch, 'Cent ans', p. 266.
[79] J. L. Kunz, 'The Law of Nations, Static and Dynamic' (1933) 27 *AJIL*, pp. 634–5. In Japan, Takeo Sogawa clarified the distinction between dynamic disputes and static disputes. Sogawa, *International Law IV*, p. 228; S. Oda and Y. Ishimoto (eds.), *Sogawa Takeo Ronbunshu: Kokusaiho to Senso Ihoka (Collected Papers of Takeo Sogawa: International Law and Outlawry of War)* (in Japanese) (Tokyo: Sinzansha, 2004), pp. 71–2.
[80] Caflisch, 'Cens ans', p. 267.
[81] This view was supported by the ICJ stated in the *Tehran Hostage* case. *United States Diplomatic and Consular Staff in Tehran* (United States of America v. Iran), Judgment of 24 May 1980, ICJ Reports 1980, p. 20, para. 37.
[82] E. H. Carr, *The Twenty Years' Crisis 1919–1939: An Introduction to the Study of International Relations* (Reprint, Perennial, 2001), p. 203.
[83] *Ibid*. See also J. L. Brierly, *The Basis of Obligation in International Law and Other Papers* (Oxford, Clarendon Press, 1958), p. 103.
[84] Kunz, 'The Law of Nations', pp. 649–50. Generally on peaceful change, see de Visscher, *Theory and Reality*, pp. 333–49; H. Owada, 'Peaceful Change' in *Max Planck Encyclopaedia*.
[85] Kunz, 'The Problem of Revision', p. 50.   [86] Sogawa, *International Law IV*, p. 231.

17 International Dispute Settlement in Perspective

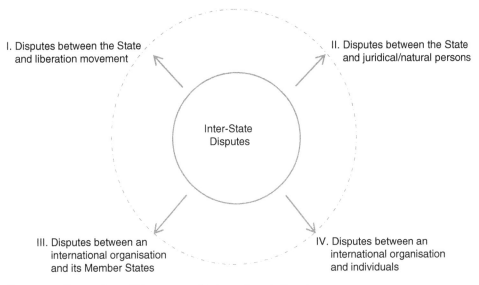

Figure 1.1 Expansion of the scope of international disputes

an inherent limitation concerning the settlement of dynamic disputes;[87] and that in essence, dynamic disputes would be better settled by political authority.

3.4 The Diversification of 'Disputes' in International Relations

The scope of international disputes is not static, but changes over time. Traditionally the primary focus of international law has been on the settlement of *inter-State* disputes. Given that the State remains the primary actor in international relations and inter-State disputes can directly affect international peace and security, peaceful settlement of inter-State disputes will in no way lose its importance. At present, however, the emergence of non-State actors in international relations presents novel challenges with regard to the settlement of international disputes between two parties of which at least one party is a non-State actor. In a broad perspective, four types of disputes involving non-State actors can be identified (see Figure 1.1):

(i) intra-State dispute between the government and a liberation movement
(ii) dispute between States and natural/juridical persons
(iii) dispute between an international organisation and its Member States
(iv) dispute between an international organisation and individuals.

---

[87] It is not suggested that international courts cannot render a judgment with regard to dynamic disputes. From a formalistic viewpoint, all international disputes can be decided judicially. Where a dynamic dispute was submitted before an international court, it would render a judgment in favour of the status quo. Yet it is open to debate whether the judgment will bring an effective settlement of the dispute. Kunz, 'The Problem of Revision', p. 44. Concerning limitations of the judicial function, see H. J. Morgenthau, *Politics Among Nations: The Struggle for Power and Peace*, 7th edn (revised by K. W. Thompson and W. D. Clinton) (Boston: McGraw Hill Higher Education, 2005), pp. 446–54.

First, as the UN Secretary-General Boutros Boutros-Ghali observed in his report, *Supplement to an Agenda for Peace*, 'so many of today's conflicts are within States rather than between States'.[88] The intra-State disputes often escalate to guerrilla wars fought not only by regular armies but also by militias and armed civilians with little discipline and with ill-defined chains of command.[89] In fact, internal armed conflicts have been the predominant mode of warfare since the mid 1950s, while inter-State armed conflicts have remained at a relatively low level since the end of World War II.[90] With time intra-State disputes are likely to be internationalised and can be a threat to peace under Article 39 of the UN Charter. In this regard, the Appeals Chamber of the International Criminal Tribunal of the former Yugoslavia, in the *Tadić* case, held that:

> [T]here is a common understanding, manifested by the 'subsequent practice' of the membership of the United Nations at large, that the 'threat to the peace' of Article 39 may include, as one of its species, internal armed conflicts.[91]

In fact, the Security Council concerned that the continuation of the fighting in Yugoslavia which was causing a heavy loss of human life and material damage constituted a threat to international peace and security.[92] It also determined that the situation in Bosnia and Herzegovina and in other parts of the former Socialist Federal Republic of Yugoslavia constituted a threat to international peace and security.[93] Furthermore, the UN Security Council, in its Resolution 788, determined that the deterioration of the situation in Liberia constituted a threat to international peace and security.[94] Likewise the Security Council, in its Resolution 929, determined that the magnitude of the humanitarian crisis in Rwanda constituted a threat to peace and security in the region.[95] As shown by these examples, intra-State disputes can be said to have elements of international character.

Second, the settlement of disputes between the State and natural/juridical persons attract growing attention. A typical example in this matter is the settlement of investor-State disputes. Furthermore, as exemplified by the Iran-United States Claims Tribunal and UN Compensation Commission, the settlement of disputes between the State and natural/juridical persons can be at issue in the peace process between hostile States.[96]

Third, development of international organisations is a remarkable feature of international law after World War II. While international organisations perform valuable roles in international relations, their increasing activities may create disputes between an

---

[88] *Supplement to an Agenda for Peace: Position Paper of the Secretary-General on the Occasion of the Fiftieth Anniversary of the United Nations*, A/50/60, S/1995/1, 25 January 1995, p. 3, para. 10.
[89] *Ibid.*, p. 5, para. 12.
[90] M. G. Marshall and B. R. Cole, *Global Report 2014: Conflict, Governance and State Fragility* (Centre for Systemic Peace, 2014), pp. 11–13.
[91] *The Prosecutor v. Duko Tadić aka 'Dule'*, Case No. IT-94-1-AR 72, Decision of 2 October 1995; (1996) 35 *ILM*, p. 43, para. 30.
[92] UN Security Council Resolution 713 (1991) of 25 September 1991, preambular para. 4.
[93] UN Security Council Resolution 757 (1992) of 30 May 1992, preambular para. 17.
[94] UN Security Council, Resolution 788 (1992), S/RES/788, 19 November 1992, preambular para. 5.
[95] UN Security Council Resolution 929 (1994), S/RES/929 (1994), 22 June 1994, preambular para. 10.
[96] See Chapter 11, sections 3 and 4 of this book.

19 International Dispute Settlement in Perspective

international organisation and its Member States. As typically shown in the *Lockerbie* case, for instance, the validity of the UN Security Council resolution may be disputed by its Member States.[97] Furthermore, in the context of the exploration and exploitation of mineral resources in the deep sea-bed beyond the limits of national jurisdiction, a dispute may arise between the International Sea-Bed Authority and sponsoring States. In this case, the Sea-Bed Disputes Chamber of the International Tribunal for the Law of the Sea (ITLOS) is empowered to deal with a dispute between the International Sea-Bed Authority on the one hand and States and non-State actors on the other hand.[98]

Fourth, the proliferation of international organisations creates at least two types of dispute. The first relates to disputes between an international organisation and its staff and the second pertains to remedies for individuals affected by projects financed by a multilateral financial institution. The first type of dispute constitutes internal disputes within an international organisation. As for the second type of dispute, a particular issue arises as to how it is possible for individuals or people to bring their claims against an international organisation where its activity has an adverse impact on them. In this regard, inspection procedures set out in multilateral financial institutions, such as the World Bank Inspection Panel, merits discussion.[99] Overall it can be observed that the scope of disputes is expanding, while inter-State disputes are at the heart of international dispute settlement in international law.

4 CLASSIFICATION OF MEANS OF INTERNATIONAL DISPUTE SETTLEMENT

4.1 Classification of Means of the Settlement of Inter-State Disputes

4.1.1 Model 1: A Single Model

International law governing the peaceful settlement of international disputes is not just a random collection of multiple dispute settlement means, but constitutes a system. To understand the structure of the system, this section discusses a classification of traditional means of the settlement of inter-State disputes. In this regard, two models can be presented: a single model and a dual model.

According to the first model, dispute settlement means can be considered as the development from subjective means to more objective means.[100] This may be called a single model (see Figure 1.2). Negotiation can be viewed as the most subjective means of dispute settlement because it purports to settle a dispute by the parties to the dispute acting on their own, without the involvement of any third party. In appropriate circumstances, a third party may be involved in the process of negotiations by offering good offices or mediation. To some extent, the subjective nature of negotiation may be mitigated by the involvement of a third party. The degree of objectivity in international dispute settlement is further enhanced by resorting to inquiry and conciliation because international disputes are to be settled by a third commission which is composed of individuals independent

---

[97] See Chapter 11, section 5 of this book.
[98] See Chapter 8, section 4.1.2 of this book.
[99] See Chapter 11, section 6.2 of this book.
[100] Sogawa, *International Law IV*, p. 218.

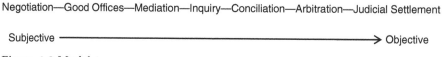

Figure 1.2 Model 1

from the disputing parties. Yet, the outcome of inquiry and conciliation is not binding upon the disputing parties and they have no obligation to accept the solutions.

The objectivity of dispute settlement is eventually secured by international adjudication. The latter can be divided into two rubrics: arbitration and judicial settlement. Arbitration is carried out by arbitrators selected by the disputing parties in an ad hoc manner. To this extent, there is still scope for subjective elements of the disputing parties to come into play in the selection of arbitrators. Judicial settlement signifies the settlement of international disputes by the permanent international court whose members are in principle elected in advance on the basis of rules of international law. According to this model, judicial settlement is the most objective means of dispute settlement. Nonetheless, this model is open to criticisms in two respects.

First, this model implicitly presupposes that ideally all disputes should be resolved by judicial settlement eventually. In this sense, it represents the supremacy of judicial means and introduces a hierarchy between dispute settlement means. However, it is open to debate whether judicial settlement can always be considered as the best means of international dispute settlement. Even in the municipal legal system, many disputes are settled by alternative dispute resolution processes, i.e. dispute settlement other than adjudication. In the international community, diplomatic means is a normal mode of dispute settlement.[101] Hence the supremacy of judicial means is unfounded in international relations.

Second, the single model seems to ignore the difference in the nature of international disputes. An appropriate means of international dispute settlement differs according to the nature of international disputes. Hence there is a need to explore another model of international dispute settlement.

4.1.2 Model 2: A Dual Model

According to the dual model, the means of dispute settlement in international law can be divided into two categories according to either the criterion of dispute settlement and the nature of dispute settlement means (Model 2-A) or the nature of disputes (Model 2-B).

Under Model 2-A, various means of dispute settlement are divided into two categories, namely, the diplomatic methods and the legal or judicial methods (see Table 1.1). This is an orthodox view and the distinction is supported by many writers.[102] The diplomatic

---

[101] Verhoeven, *Droit international public*, p. 705.
[102] See for instance, J. Merrills, 'The Means of Dispute Settlement' in E. D. Evans (ed.), *International Law*, 4th edn (Oxford University Press, 2014), pp. 564 *et seq.*; M. N. Shaw, *International Law*, 7th edn (Cambridge University Press, 2014), pp. 735 *et seq.*; A. Cassese, *International Law*, 2nd edn (Oxford University Press, 2005), p. 279; Nguyen Quoc Dinh, P. Daillier, M. Forteau and A. Pellet, *Droit international public*, 8th edn (Paris, LGDJ, 2009), p. 921; Dupuy and Kerbrat, *Droit international public*, p. 615; Ridruejo, 'Le Droit international', pp. 97–102; Caflisch, 'Cent ans', p. 274; G. Abi-Saab, 'Cours général de droit international public' (1987-VII) 207 *RCADI*, p. 232; Combacau and Sur, *Droit international public*, pp. 562 and 569.

21 International Dispute Settlement in Perspective

TABLE 1.1 MODEL 2-A

Diplomatic Means		Legal Means
A. Direct Diplomatic Means Negotiation		A. Arbitration (ad hoc)
B. Diplomatic Means with the Involvement of a Third Party		B. Judicial settlement (permanent)
Good offices	Conciliation	
Mediation	Settlement through international	
Inquiry	organisations	

means of dispute settlement refer to methods which are not based on rules of international law and the outcome is not binding upon the parties to a dispute. These means include: negotiation, good offices, mediation, inquiry, conciliation and dispute settlement through international organisations.

The diplomatic means can be divided into two subcategories. The first subcategory contains negotiation carried out only by the parties to a dispute (non-third-party diplomatic means). The second subcategory is diplomatic means in which a third party is involved (third-party diplomatic means). This subcategory contains good offices, mediation, inquiry, conciliation and dispute settlement through international organisations. With some exceptions, decisions of international organisations are not binding upon the Member States. When decisions of an organ are binding on the Member States, the binding nature is already provided in the constitutive instrument, and the Member State gives their consent in advance by ratifying the instrument. Thus dispute settlement through international organisations can be viewed as a variation of diplomatic means of peaceful settlement of international disputes.[103] There is no hierarchy or chronological order among diplomatic means, whilst normally negotiation is a point of departure.

The legal means of dispute settlement concerns the methods on the basis of rules of international law. Legal means contain arbitration and judicial settlement. Unlike diplomatic means, the outcome of legal methods is binding upon the disputing parties. As will be examined,[104] however, international adjudication relies on consent of the parties in dispute. Therefore, there is no guarantee that the disputing parties can reach an agreement to submit their dispute to an international court or tribunal.

Under this model, there is no hierarchy between means of international dispute settlement, and the different types of dispute settlement methods coexist at the same time. The parties to a dispute can freely choose or combine relevant means with a view to

---

[103] Caflisch, 'Cent ans', p. 283. Dupuy and Kerbrat also discuss dispute settlement through international organisations under the rubric of 'dispute settlement and multilateral diplomacy'. Dupuy and Kerbrat, *Droit international public*, pp. 618 *et seq*. Indeed, dispute settlement by international organisations, such as the United Nations, can be considered as an institutional procedure of mediation which is adjunct to negotiations. Therefore, it can be considered that negotiations, along with good offices and mediation, have an affinity with dispute settlement through international organisations.
[104] See Chapters 5 and 6 of this book.

TABLE 1.2 MODEL 2-B

Dynamic Means of Dispute Settlement	Static Means of Dispute Settlement
Negotiation	Inquiry
Good offices	Conciliation
Mediation	Arbitration
Settlement through international organisations	Judicial settlement

better resolve the dispute. As normally an international dispute is multifaceted and contains both legal and political elements, the settlement of international disputes often requires both legal and political process. Thus the interlinkage between diplomatic and legal means is crucial in the overall settlement of international disputes.[105]

According to Model 2-B, the means of dispute settlement can be divided into two categories, namely static means of dispute settlement and dynamic means of dispute settlement (see Table 1.2).[106] Static means of dispute settlement seek to settle disputes by an impartial commission or a judicial body which is composed of individuals, independent from the parties in dispute on the basis of the existing rules of international law. Inquiry, conciliation, arbitration and judicial settlement fall within the scope of static means of dispute settlement since these organs consists of independent individuals and have no political authority to change the existing rules of the law. By contrast, dynamic means of dispute settlement is the method which seeks to settle international disputes by political authority. Dispute settlement through international organisations, such as the United Nations, is a case in point.

Strictly speaking, negotiation is regarded as an unspecialised means that can be used in the settlement of both static and dynamic disputes.[107] Considering that negotiation is a political process by nature, however, negotiation can be thought to perform a valuable role particularly in the settlement of non-legal or dynamic disputes. This would hold particularly true when a great power is involved in a negotiation process. In light of the essentially political nature, it might not be unreasonable to consider negotiation, along with good offices and mediations, as a sort of dynamic means of international dispute settlement.

It is not suggested that the static means have no relevance to the settlement of dynamic disputes. If the parties in dispute could agree to separate legal issues from political context (de-politicisation), it may be possible to refer only legal issues of the dispute to arbitration or judicial settlement. Indeed, as the ICJ stated in the *Tehran Hostage* case, 'the resolution of such legal questions by the Court may be an important, and sometimes decisive, factor in promoting the peaceful settlement of the dispute'.[108]

---

[105] See Chapter 2, section 3; Chapter 4, section 5.3 of this book.
[106] The dichotomy of static and dynamic means of international dispute settlement was presented by Takeo Sogawa in Japan. Sogawa, *International Law IV*, pp. 231–2. This approach was supported by Y. Matsui et al., *International Law* (in Japanese), 5th edn (Tokyo, Yuhikaku), pp. 262–4.
[107] Sogawa, *International Law IV*, p. 233.   [108] The *Tehran Hostage* case, ICJ Reports 1980, p. 22, para. 40.

TABLE 1.3 MODEL 3

Non-adjudicative Means	Adjudicative or Quasi-adjudicative Means
1. Negotiation, good offices, mediation	1. Arbitration
	(i) Inter-State arbitration
	(ii) Intra-State arbitration
	(iii) Mixed Arbitration
2. Fact-finding and conciliation	2. Judicial settlement
3. Settlement through international organisations	3. *Sui generis* dispute settlement system
4. Non-compliance procedures	

4.2 Classification of Dispute Settlement Means in a Contemporary Context

In addition to traditional means of the settlement of inter-State disputes, presently particular means and procedures of the settlement of disputes involving non-State actors are developing. Alternative dispute resolution, such as non-compliance procedures, is also becoming crucial.[109] Hence there is a need to consider the classification of multiple means of the settlement of both inter-State disputes and disputes involving non-State actors.

In a broad perspective, international law of peaceful settlement of international disputes should be considered as a dual system that consists of both non-adjudicative and adjudicative/quasi-adjudicative means (see Table 1.3). Even in the municipal legal system, the majority of disputes are settled outside the court room and settlement by adjudication remains rather exception. The same is particularly true in the international legal system where jurisdiction of international courts and tribunals relies on the consent of parties in dispute. In the international legal system, it would be no exaggeration to say that a considerable majority of disputes are settled by using non-adjudicative means, namely negotiation, good offices, mediation, fact-finding, conciliation, settlement through international organisation, and non-compliance procedures. Fact-finding in this context is broader than the traditional ones and it comprises not only inquiry in inter-State disputes but also the United Nations Compensation Commission and the World Bank Inspection Panel.[110] Non-compliance procedures enshrined in multilateral treaties can also be included within the scope of non-adjudicative means, even though, strictly speaking, these procedures are not a means of dispute settlement, but a means to prevent the breach of treaty obligations and disputes in this matter.[111] Thus the scope of non-adjudicative means in the settlement of international disputes in a contemporary context is broader than traditional diplomatic means of the settlement of inter-State disputes.

Adjudicative or quasi-adjudicative means comprise: inter-State arbitration, intra-State arbitration, mixed arbitration, judicial settlement and *sui generis* dispute settlement

---

[109] See Chapter 10, section 4 of this book.
[110] Some argue that the World Bank Inspection Panel performs a quasi-judicial function. However, the World Bank regarded the Inspection Panel as an impartial fact-finding body. This issue will be discussed in Chapter 11, section 6.2 of this book.
[111] Non-compliance procedures will be discussed in Chapter 10, section 4.

systems, such as the World Trade Organisation (WTO) dispute settlement system. Unlike traditional legal means of the settlement of inter-State disputes, various types of arbitration as well as *sui generis* dispute settlement systems are included in this category. In this sense, the scope of adjudicative/non-adjudicative means is also broader than traditional legal means of inter-State disputes.

5 PRINCIPAL FEATURES OF THE DISPUTE SETTLEMENT SYSTEM IN INTERNATIONAL LAW

On the basis of the above considerations, it is necessary to overview the principal features of the dispute settlement system in international law. The system is characterised by four elements that are interlinked: its consent-based nature, its non-hierarchical nature, its flexibility and its evolutionary nature.

First, the international dispute settlement system can be considered as a consent-based system in the sense that it relies on consent of the parties in dispute. In fact, international courts and tribunals have no compulsory jurisdiction, unless States expressly accept jurisdiction of the courts or tribunals. The consent-based nature can be viewed as a corollary of the decentralised nature of international law and community.

Second, there is no hierarchy between the non-adjudicative and adjudicative/quasi-adjudicative means of international dispute settlement. Nor is there any hierarchy among various dispute settlement means. While States can freely decide an order in the application of multiple dispute settlement means, this does not mean that one means prevails over other means. Thus the international dispute settlement system in international law can be regarded a non-hierarchical system.

Third, in accordance with the principle of free choice of means, States can freely select relevant means and, if necessary, different means of dispute settlement can be combined. In this sense, the dispute settlement system in international law is flexible by nature. Given that legal or adjudicative means can resolve only legal issues, it must be supplemented by non-adjudicative means in order to resolve disputes in a comprehensive manner. Conversely, judicial decision on the core legal issue can facilitate the political process of international dispute settlement. Hence adjudicative and non-adjudicative means need to be integrally interlinked in the overall settlement of international disputes. It is also to be noted that international disputes may evolve over time.[112] Accordingly, different means of international dispute settlement will be needed according to different phases of international disputes.

Fourth, the international dispute settlement system in international law is not static but changes as time goes by. It is likely that particular procedures of dispute settlement may evolve in a particular field of international law. Procedural rules of international courts and tribunals also evolve to address new issues of international dispute settlement. In this sense, the international dispute settlement system can be said to be evolutionary by nature.

---

[112] For a various model of dispute, see O. Ramsbotham, T. Woodhouse and H. Miall, *Contemporary Conflict Resolution: The Prevention, Management and Transformation of Deadly Conflicts*, 3rd edn (Cambridge: Polity, 2011), pp. 10 *et seq.*

6 CONCLUSIONS

The principal points discussed in this chapter can be summarised as follows.

(i) In international law, all States are under the obligation to settle international disputes by using peaceful means in accordance with the principle of free choice of means. Thus examination of rules and procedures of the peaceful settlement of international disputes should be a crucial subject in international law.

(ii) The identification of the existence of international disputes is a point of departure for the peaceful settlement of these disputes. As an international court has no jurisdiction if there is no dispute between the parties, the existence of a dispute between the parties becomes an important issue in international adjudication. However, the existence of an international dispute is not self-evident. More often than not, the existence of a dispute itself is denied by one of the disputing parties. In this case, the existence of a dispute is objectively determined by an international court.

(iii) The scope of international disputes may change over time. Traditionally the principal focus of international law was on the settlement of inter-State disputes. In light of the increasing activities of non-State actors in international relations, however, growing attention is paid to the settlement of international disputes between two parties of which one party is a non-State actor. Thus there is a need to explore procedures for the settlement of both inter-State disputes and disputes involving non-State actors.

(iv) At present, dispute settlement means are increasingly diverse in international law. Relevant means of international dispute settlement differ according to the types of disputes. In broad terms, the international law of peaceful settlement of international disputes can be considered as a dual system comprising both non-adjudicative and adjudicative/quasi-adjudicative means. The dispute settlement system in international law is characterised by four elements: its consent-based nature, its non-hierarchical nature, its flexibility and its evolutionary nature.

(v) As international disputes are multifaceted, there is no guarantee that all aspects of disputes can be settled by using only one means. In this regard, it must be noted that the function of international adjudication is limited to the settlement of legal issues. Hence the interlinkage between adjudicative and non-adjudicative means of international dispute settlement is crucial in the overall settlement of international disputes.

FURTHER READING

Textbooks and Monographs

J. Bercovitch and R. Jackson, *Conflict Resolution in the Twenty-first Century: Principles, Methods and Approaches* (The University of Michigan Press, 2009).

D. W. Bowett, 'Contemporary Developments in Legal Techniques in the Settlement of Disputes' (1983) 180 *RCADI*, pp. 169–235.

L. Caflisch, 'Cent ans de règlement pacifique des différends interétatiques' (2001) 288 *RCADI*, pp. 245–467.

J. Collier and V. Lowe, *The Settlement of Disputes in International Law: Institutions and Procedures* (Oxford University Press, 1999).

C. Giorgetti (ed.), *The Rules, Practice and Jurisprudence of International Courts and Tribunals* (Leiden: Nijhoff, 2013).

C. Hauss, *International Conflict Resolution*, 2nd edn (New York: Continuum, 2010).

J. G. Merrills, *International Dispute Settlement*, 6th edn (Cambridge University Press, 2017).

J. S. Nye Jr and D. A. Welch, *Understanding Global Conflict and Cooperation: Introduction to Theory and History*, 9th edn (Essex: Pearson, 2014).

F. Orrego Vicuña, *International Dispute Settlement in an Evolving Global Society: Constitutionalisation, Accessibility, Privatization* (Cambridge University Press, 2004).

O. Ramsbotham, T. Woodhouse and H. Miall, *Contemporary Conflict Resolution: The Prevention, Management and Transformation of Deadly Conflicts*, 4th edn (Cambridge: Polity, 2016).

C. Romano, K. J. Alter, and Y. Shany (eds.), *The Oxford Handbook of International Adjudication* (Oxford University Press, 2014).

United Nations, *Handbook on the Peaceful Settlement of Disputes between States* (New York, United Nations, 1992).

J. H. W. Verzijl, *International Law in Historical Perspective, Part VIII. Inter-State Disputes and Their Settlement* (Leyden: Sijthoff, 1976).

Articles

I. Brownlie, 'The Peaceful Settlement of International Disputes' (2009) 8 *Chinese Journal of International Law*, pp. 267–83.

J. Crawford, 'Continuity and Discontinuity in International Dispute Settlement: An Inaugural Lecture' (2010) 1 *Journal of International Dispute Settlement*, pp. 3–24.

M. Mendelson, 'International Dispute Settlement: Developments and Challenges' (2008) 61 *Revue Hellénique de Droit International*, pp. 463–75.

J. G. Merrills, 'The Mosaic of International Dispute Settlement Procedures: Complementary or Contradictory?' (2007) 54 *NILR*, pp. 361–93.

Collections of Documents

M. E. O'Connell, *International Dispute Resolution: Cases and Materials*, 2nd edn (Durham: Carolina Academic Press, 2012).

K. Oellers-Frahm and A. Zimmermann (eds.), *Dispute Settlement in Public International Law*, 2nd edn, 2 vols. (Berlin: Springer, 2001).

Christian J. Tams and Antonios Tzanakopoulos (eds.), *The Settlement of International Disputes: Basic Documents* (Oxford: Hart Publishing, 2012).

Anthologies and Encyclopaedias

R. Bernhardt (ed.), *Encyclopaedia of Public International Law: Settlement of Disputes*, Vol. I, 1981.

Laurence Boisson de Chazournes, M. Kohen and J. E. Viñuales (eds.), *Diplomatic and Judicial Means of Dispute Settlement* (Leiden: Nijhoff, 2013).

D. French, M. Saul and N. D. White (eds.), *International Law and Dispute Settlement: New Problems and Techniques* (Oxford: Hart Publishing, 2010).

H. Miall, T. Woodhouse, O. Ramsbotham and C. Mitchell, *The Contemporary Conflict Resolution Reader* (Cambridge: Polity, 2015).

M. E. O'Connell (ed.), *International Dispute Settlement* (Aldershot: Ashgate, 2003).

R. Wolfrum and I. Gätzschmann (eds.), *International Dispute Settlement: Room for Innovations?* (Berlin: Springer, 2012).

Journals

There are several journals focusing particularly on international dispute settlement, such as: *Leiden Journal of International Law, Journal of International Dispute Settlement, The Law and Practice of International Courts and Tribunals* and *ICSID Review*.

Websites

Court of Justice of the European Union: http://curia.europa.eu/
International Court of Justice: www.icj-cij.org/en
International Tribunal for the Law of the Sea: www.itlos.org/
Permanent Court of Arbitration: www.pca-cpa.org
United Nations: www.un.org
WTO: www.wto.org/english/tratop_e/dispu_e/dispu_e.htm#disputes

Negotiation, Good Offices and Mediation

Main Issues

Given that the majority of disputes are resolved through negotiation in practice, negotiation can be considered as the fundamental means for settling international disputes. Hence it seems appropriate to commence our examination with negotiation. Good offices and mediation may be said to be an adjunct to negotiation since these means aim to facilitate dispute settlement through negotiation between the parties in dispute. Accordingly, it is necessary to examine these means of dispute settlement in connection with negotiation. In this regard, it is important to note that negotiation and legal means of international dispute settlement, namely international adjudication, are not mutually exclusive but complementary. Thus particular attention must be paid to interaction between negotiation and international adjudication. This chapter will focus particularly on the following issues:

(i) Why should negotiation be examined in international law?
(ii) What are the principal features and functions of negotiation in the field of international dispute settlement?
(iii) What is the interrelationship between negotiation and international adjudication?
(iv) If an international dispute cannot be settled through negotiation, what is the next step to be taken?
(v) What is the role of good offices and mediation and what are their limitations?

1 INTRODUCTION

It is generally recognised that the majority of international disputes are settled by negotiations. In some cases, negotiations may be the only and final means of settling international disputes. Therefore, it would be no exaggeration to say that negotiation is the fundamental means of international dispute settlement.[1] In reality, however, it is not infrequent that direct negotiation encounters serious difficulties or even deadlock due to the adamant

---

[1] The *North Sea Continental Shelf* cases, ICJ Reports 1969, p. 47, para. 86.

attitude of parties in dispute. In this case, involvement of a third party may be needed with a view to making concessions or breaking stalemate in negotiations.

The degree of involvement of the third party varies on a case-by-case basis. Where the involvement of the third party is limited to providing an additional channel of communication, such an intermediary is considered to be offering 'good offices'. Where a third party takes a more active role by making proposals, such an act is called 'mediation'. Good offices can be said to be a modest mode of assistance by a third party, whilst mediation is an active mode of intervention by the third party.

In summary, the difference between good offices and mediation lies in the degree of involvement of the third party. In practice, the distinction between good offices and mediation may not be clear-cut since the degree of the third party's involvement may vary over time.[2] In any case good offices and mediation can be considered as an adjunct to negotiation.[3]

Against that background, first, this chapter discusses the position of negotiation in international law (section 2). It then analyses the interaction between negotiation and international adjudication (section 3). Next, it moves on to examine obligation to negotiate (section 4), the timeframe of negotiation (section 5), and the outcome of negotiations (section 6). This chapter further addresses the issues of good offices (section 7) and mediation (section 8), respectively. Finally, conclusions are presented in section 9.

2 NEGOTIATION AND INTERNATIONAL LAW

2.1 The Relationship Between Negotiation and International Law

Some argue that negotiation is a matter of politics, not law. If so, why should we examine negotiation in the context of international law? In approaching this question, four points must be noted.

First, the behaviour of States is constrained by international law and negotiation is no exception. In fact, the *Principles and Guidelines for International Negotiations* (hereafter the UN Guidelines for Negotiations), which were adopted by the UN General Assembly in 1998, confirm that 'in their negotiations States should be guided by the relevant principles and rules of international law'.[4]

Second, at present, the ever-expanding body of international law covers almost all areas of international relations. Accordingly, international law constitutes one of the important elements that must be taken into consideration in the process of negotiations. Indeed, the advantage of a legal basis in the negotiation process is clear. Related to this, it is to be noted that the function of international law is not limited to determining the legality of the behaviour of States. It also operates as a medium to facilitate

---

[2] J. Combacau and S. Sur, *Droit international public*, 10th edn (Paris: Montchrestien, 2012), p. 566.
[3] J. Merrills, *International Dispute Settlement*, 6th edn (Cambridge University Press, 2017), p. 26; S. M. A. Salman, 'Good Offices and Mediation and International Water Disputes' in The International Bureau of the Permanent Court of Arbitration, *Resolution of International Water Disputes* (The Hague: Kluwer, 2003), pp. 175-6.
[4] UN General Assembly Resolution, 8 December 1998, A/RES/53/101.

communication between States by providing a common language.[5] Hence negotiations should not and cannot be totally detached from international law.[6]

Third, some treaties provide an obligation to negotiate as a precondition to resorting to other means of dispute settlement, including judicial settlement.[7] In this case, the existence of negotiations between parties in dispute constitutes a condition for an international court or tribunal to establish its jurisdiction. As will be seen,[8] the existence of negotiations is to be determined by an international court or tribunal in a particular case.

Lastly, in appropriate circumstances, an international court or tribunal may order the parties in dispute to negotiate on the basis of its decision. In this case, the disputing parties are required to negotiate in accordance with the decision of the court. This is called 'judicially directed negotiation'. Negotiation may also be needed in order to implement decisions of international courts. Thus negotiation and judicial settlement are intimately intertwined in international dispute settlement. In light of the four points mentioned above, there are good reasons to argue that negotiation as a means of dispute settlement must be examined in conjunction with international law.

2.2 The Concept of Negotiation

Whilst negotiation is an elusive concept, the ICJ in the 2011 *Georgia/Russia* case clarified to some extent the concept of negotiations.[9] Three points in particular merit highlighting.

First, negotiations must be distinct from mere protests or disputations. Negotiation entails more than the plain opposition of legal views or interests between two parties, or the existence of a series of accusations and rebuttals, or even the exchange of claims and directly opposed counterclaims.

Second, negotiation requires, at the very least, a genuine attempt by one of the disputing parties to engage in discussion with the other disputing party with a view to resolving the dispute,[10] even though an obligation to negotiate does not imply an obligation to reach agreement.[11]

Third, to meet the precondition of negotiation in the compromissory clause of a treaty, these negotiations must relate to the subject matter of the treaty containing the compromissory clause. In other words, the subject matter of the negotiations must relate to the subject matter of the dispute which must concern the substantive obligations contained in the treaty in question.[12]

---

[5] Y. Onuma, 'International Law in and with International Politics: The Function of International Law in International Society' (2003) 14 *EJIL*, pp. 130–4; R. Higgins, 'The Place of International Law in the Settlement of Disputes by the Security Council' (1970) 64 *AJIL*, p. 3.

[6] M. Lachs, 'International Law, Mediation and Negotiation' in A. Samuel (ed.), *Multilateral Negotiation and Mediation: Instruments and Methods* (New York: International Peace Academy, 1985), p. 192 (reproduced in E. O'Connell (ed.), *International Dispute Settlement* (Aldershot: Ashgate, 2003)).

[7] United Nations, *Handbook on the Peaceful Settlement of Disputes between States* (New York: United Nations, 1992), p. 9, para. 21.

[8] See section 4 of this chapter.

[9] *Case Concerning Application of the International Convention on the Elimination of All Forms of Racial Discrimination* (Georgia v. Russian Federation) (hereafter the *Georgia/Russia* case), Preliminary Objections, Judgment of 1 April 2011, ICJ Reports 2011, pp. 132–3, paras. 157–61.

[10] *Case Concerning Application of the International Convention on the Elimination of All Forms of Racial Discrimination* (Georgia v. Russian Federation) (hereafter the *Georgia/Russia* case), Preliminary Objections, Judgment of 1 April 2011, ICJ Reports 2011, p. 132, para. 157.

[11] *Railway Traffic between Lithuania and Poland*, Advisory Opinion, 1931, PCIJ, Series A/B, No. 42, p. 116

[12] The *Georgia/Russia* case, ICJ Reports 2011, p. 133, para. 161.

According to the ICJ, 'the precondition of negotiation is met only when there has been a failure of negotiations, or when negotiations have become futile or deadlocked'.[13] Ascertainment of whether negotiations have taken place and whether they have failed or become futile or deadlocked are essentially questions of fact for consideration in each case. When considering this issue, substance of negotiation is more important than form.[14]

In fact, negotiation varies in form. Bilateral negotiation is directly performed by duly appointed representatives or delegations of parties to a dispute or through written correspondence. If negotiation through established machinery proves unproductive, summit diplomacy between heads of State or foreign ministers may be employed in order to attempt to break the deadlock.[15] Furthermore, the ICJ in the 1962 *South West Africa* case stressed the importance of parliamentary diplomacy.[16] Nowadays negotiations can be conducted in multiple ways owing to the development of communication technology.[17]

Some legal instruments refer to 'exchanges of views'.[18] Exchanges of views are closely linked to negotiation or consultation. Hence, in the broad sense, exchanges of views can be considered as a variation of negotiation or consultation. However, warning (i.e. a threat by one party to invoke certain measures to settle a dispute) is distinct from negotiation since, as Judge Cheng stated in the *Phosphates in Morocco* case, '[i]t is the essence of negotiations to discuss some question with a view to settling it, whereas warning is merely the intimation of a will to do certain things ... on certain contingencies'.[19]

3 INTERACTION BETWEEN NEGOTIATION AND INTERNATIONAL ADJUDICATION

As negotiation and international adjudication are not mutually exclusive, consideration must be given to interaction between negotiation and international adjudication. Negotiation performs an important role at three distinct stages of international adjudication.[20]

---

[13] *Ibid.*, para. 159.   [14] *Ibid.*, para. 160.
[15] For a close analysis of summits, see G. R. Berridge, *Diplomacy: Theory and Practice*, 4th edn (Basingstoke: Palgrave Macmillan, 2010), pp. 161–78.
[16] *South West Africa* (Ethiopia v. South Africa; Liberia v. South Africa), Judgment of 21 December 1962, ICJ Reports 1962, p. 346. This case related to the continued existence of the Mandate for South West Africa and the duties and performance of South Africa as mandatory thereunder. Ethiopia and Liberia asked the ICJ to declare, *inter alia*, that South Africa had the duty to cease the practice of apartheid in the Territory of South West Africa.
[17] K. Hakapää, 'Negotiation' in *Max Planck Encyclopaedia*, para. 2. For an analysis of the impact of communication technologies upon diplomatic negotiation, see C. Archetti, 'The Impact of New Media on Diplomatic Practice: An Evolutionary Model of Change' (2012) 7 *The Hague Journal of Diplomacy*, pp. 181–206.
[18] See, for instance, Article 283(1) and (2) of the UN Convention on the Law of the Sea (hereafter the LOSC). 1833 *UNTS*, p. 3. Entered into force on 16 November 1994.
[19] Separate Opinion of Mr Cheng Tien-His in the *Phosphates in Morocco* case (Preliminary Objection), Judgment of 14 June 1938, PCIJ Series A/B No. 74, 1938, p. 39.
[20] See G. Abi-Saab, 'Negotiation and Adjudication: Complementarity and Dissonance' in L. Boisson de Chazournes, M. G. Kohen and H. E. Viñuales (eds.), *Diplomatic and Judicial Means of Dispute Settlement* (Leiden: Nijhoff, 2013), pp. 327–33. See also M. G. Kohen, 'Interaction between Diplomatic and Judicial Means at the Initiation of Proceedings', *ibid.*, pp. 13–24; L. Reed, 'Observations on the Relationship between Diplomatic and Judicial Means of Dispute Settlement', *ibid.*, pp. 291–305.

3.1 Pre-Adjudicative Stage

At the pre-adjudicative stage, negotiation contributes to indicating the limit of consent given by States.[21] Negotiation may also help demonstrate the existence of the dispute and delineate its subject matter.[22] In relation to this, the PCIJ, in the *Mavrommatis* case, stated that 'before a dispute can be made the subject of an action in law, its subject-matter should have been clearly defined by means of diplomatic negotiations'.[23] In addition, negotiation encourages the parties to attempt to settle their dispute by mutual agreement, thus avoiding recourse to binding third-party adjudication.

3.2 During Adjudication

Negotiation can continue in parallel with international adjudication. As the PCIJ stated in its order in the case of the *Free Zones of Upper Savoy and the District of Gex*, the judicial settlement of international disputes 'is simply an alternative to the direct and friendly settlement of such disputes between the parties'.[24] One can thus argue that an ongoing negotiation process does not preclude resort to judicial means of dispute settlement. In this regard, the *dictum* of the ICJ, in the *Aegean Sea Continental Shelf* case, deserves quoting:

> The jurisprudence of the Court provides various examples of cases in which negotiations and recourse to judicial settlement have been pursued in *pari passu*. Several cases, the most recent being that concerning the Trial of Pakistani Prisoners of War (I.C.J. Reports 1973, p. 347), show that judicial proceedings may be discontinued when such negotiations result in the settlement of the dispute. Consequently, the fact that negotiations are being actively pursued during the present proceedings is not, legally, any obstacle to the exercise by the Court of its judicial function.[25]

This *dictum* was confirmed by the 1980 *Tehran Hostage* judgment.[26]

In some cases, the ICJ 'welcomed' negotiations between the parties in dispute. For example, the Court, in the *Passage through the Great Belt* case, stated that: '[P]ending a decision of the Court on the merits, any negotiation between the Parties with a view to achieving a direct and friendly settlement is to be welcomed.'[27] However, Judge Oda, in the same case, questioned the role of negotiations pending a decision of the Court.

---

[21] The *Georgia/Russia* case, Preliminary Objections, ICJ Report 2011, p. 124, para. 131.
[22] *Ibid.*, p. 84, para. 30.
[23] *Mavrommatis Palestine Concessions*, Judgment No. 2, 1924, PCIJ, Series A, No. 2, p. 15.
[24] *Free Zones of Upper Savoy and the District of Gex*, Order of 19 August 1929, PCIJ, Series A, No. 22, p. 13. This case related to the interpretation of Article 435(2) of the Treaty of Versailles concerning the free zones of Upper Savoy and the Gex district.
[25] *Aegean Sea Continental Shelf* (Greece v. Turkey), Judgment of 19 December 1978, ICJ Reports 1978, p. 12, para. 29.
[26] *United States Diplomatic and Consular Staff in Tehran* (United States of America v. Iran), Judgment of 24 May 1980, ICJ Reports 1980, p. 23, para. 43. See also section 8.3.1 of this chapter.
[27] *Passage through the Great Belt* (Finland v. Denmark), Order of 29 July 1991, Request for the Indication of Provisional Measures, ICJ Reports 1991, p. 20, para. 35. See also Separate Opinion of Judge Broms, *ibid.*, p. 39. See also Declaration of Judge Tarassov, *ibid.*, p. 24. The *Great Belt* case concerned the legality of the construction of a fixed bridge over the Great Belt by Denmark.

According to the learned judge, 'if negotiations could lead to a solution of their dispute, recourse to the judicial process would not have been necessary. ... Moreover, if what the Court wishes to encourage is that the Parties should negotiate as to their respective attitudes or conduct pending judgment of the merits, it should be obvious that neither side will be willing to risk prejudicing its case by making concessions.'[28] Despite Judge Oda's concern, the *Passage through the Great Belt* case was eventually settled by agreement between the disputing parties.[29]

Another example in this matter is provided by the *Certain Phosphate Lands in Nauru* case. After the judgment on the preliminary objections,[30] negotiations took place between Australia and Nauru during 1992 and 1993, while proceedings of the merits were being followed. In 1993, the two parties concluded an agreement to settle the dispute[31] and agreed to discontinue the proceedings and the case was removed from the Court's list.

3.3 Post-Adjudicative Stage

3.3.1 General Considerations

At the post-adjudicative stage, negotiation may be needed to effectuate a judgment given by an international court or tribunal. In this regard, four points can be made.

First, in some cases, negotiation may be needed to implement a judgment at the post-adjudicative phase.[32] A case in point are the *Asylum* and *Haya de la Torre* disputes between Colombia and Peru. The ICJ, in the 1951 *Haya de la Torre* case, held that:

> It is unable to give any practical advice as to the various courses which might be followed with a view to terminating the asylum, since, by doing so, it would depart from its judicial function. But it can be assumed that the Parties, now that their mutual legal relations have been made clear, will be able to find a practical and satisfactory solution by seeking guidance from those considerations of courtesy and good-neighbourliness which, in matters of asylum, have always held a prominent place in the relations between the Latin-American republics.[33]

---

[28] Separate Opinion of Judge Oda, *ibid.*, p. 26.
[29] On 3 September 1992, only one week before the oral hearings were to open before the Court, Denmark and Finland agreed to settle the dispute. Denmark agreed to pay a sum of 90 million Danish kroner (around 15 million US dollars), and Finland agreed to withdraw its application. M. Koskenniemi, 'Case Concerning Passage through the Great Belt' (1996) 27 *ODIL*, pp. 274-9. See also by the same writer, 'Introductory Note' (1993) 32 *ILM*, p. 103.
[30] *Certain Phosphate Lands in Nauru* (Nauru v. Australia), Preliminary Objections, Judgment of 26 June 1992, ICJ Reports 1992, p. 240. For this case, see Chapter 7, section 4.2.
[31] Agreement between Australia and the Republic of Nauru for the Settlement of the Case in the International Court of Justice Concerning Certain Phosphate Lands in Nauru (1993) 32 ILM, pp. 1474-5. See also Background/Content Summary, *ibid.*, pp. 1471-3.
[32] For a detailed examination of this subject, see L. Boisson de Chazournes and A. Angelini, 'After "The Court Rose": The Rise of Diplomatic Means to Implement the Pronouncements of the International Court of Justice' (2012) 11 *The Law and Practice of International Courts and Tribunals*, pp. 1-46.
[33] *Haya de la Torre* (Colombia v. Peru), Judgment of 13 June 1951, ICJ Reports 1951, p. 83. On 3 January 1949, the Colombian ambassador in Lima granted asylum to M. Victor Raúl Haya de la Torre, head of a political party in Peru. In the *Haya de la Torre* case, Colombia asked the ICJ to declare that in executing the judgment of 20 November 1950, it was not bound to deliver M. Haya de la Torre to the Peruvian authorities.

Nonetheless, the parties still disagreed on its interpretation, and negotiations went on unsuccessfully. As a consequence, they could not find a practical solution of the dispute. Thus, on 18 November 1953, Colombia brought the case to the attention of the Inter-American Peace Commission. It was on 22 March 1954 when the disputing parties eventually reached a compromise in an agreement concluded in Bogotá. Almost three years had passed from the ICJ judgment of 1951 to the termination of the asylum of Haya de la Torre.[34]

Second, the manner of the implementation of a judgment can be changed by agreement between the parties in dispute. An interesting example is furnished by the *Greenland/Jan Mayen* case between Denmark and Norway.[35] In the Agreement of 18 December 1995 drawing the delimitation lines between FZs and the continental shelf, the parties adjusted three of four points indicated by the ICJ.[36] In so doing, the parties partly modified the ICJ judgment of 1993 by agreement at the post-adjudicative phase. The *Greenland/Jan Mayen* case seems to suggest that negotiation at the post-adjudicative phase may influence the manner of the implementation of the Court's judgment.

Third, negotiation may be needed to determine the amount of compensation for the material damage caused by breaches of obligations by the respondent State. The 2015 *Costa Rica/Nicaragua* case is an example. In this case, the ICJ ruled that Costa Rica is entitled to receive compensation for the material damage caused by those breaches of obligations by Nicaragua that have been ascertained by the Court. In this regard, the Court opined that: '[T]he Parties should engage in negotiation in order to reach an agreement on these issues.'[37] It went to add that: '[I]f they fail to reach such an agreement within 12 months of the date of the present judgment, the Court will, at the request of either Party, determine the amount of compensation on the basis of further written pleadings limited to this issue.'[38]

Fourth, in addition to a judgment rendered by an international court or tribunal, further negotiation may be needed to fully settle a particular dispute. An example is provided by the 2012 *Jurisdictional Immunities of the State* case between Germany and Italy. In this case, the ICJ rejected Italy's argument that Germany could be refused immunity. However, the Court was aware that its judgment might preclude judicial redress for the Italian nationals concerned. It thus stated that the claims arising from the treatment of the Italian military internees, together with other claims of Italian nationals which have allegedly not been settled, 'could be the subject of further negotiation involving the two States concerned with a view to resolving the issue'.[39] This statement seems to suggest that compensation for the

---

[34] C. Schulte, *Compliance with Decisions of the International Court of Justice* (Oxford University Press, 2004), pp. 107–9.

[35] Maritime Delimitation in the Area between Greenland and Jan Mayen (Denmark v. Norway), Judgment of 14 June 1993, ICJ Reports 1993, p. 38. This case related to the delimitation of the fishery zone and continental shelf in the region between Greenland and Jan Mayen.

[36] Schulte, *Compliance*, pp. 223–4; Report by Anderson in J. I. Charney and L. M. Alexander (eds.), *International Maritime Boundaries*, Vol. II (Dordrecht: Nijhoff, 1993), p. 2519.

[37] *Certain Activities Carried Out by Nicaragua in the Border Area* (Costa Rica v. Nicaragua), Judgment, 16 December 2015, ICJ Reports 2015, para. 142.

[38] Ibid.

[39] *Jurisdictional Immunities of the State* (Germany v. Italy: Greece intervening), Judgment of 3 February 2012, ICJ Reports 2012, p. 144, para. 104. Germany requested the ICJ to declare that by allowing civil claims based on violations of international humanitarian law by the German Reich during World War II from September 1943 to May 1945, to be brought against the Federal Republic of Germany, Italy violated the obligations with regard to the jurisdictional immunity which the Federal Republic of Germany enjoys under international law. *Ibid.*, p. 107, para. 15.

various groups of victims, which was the root cause of the dispute between Germany and Italy, should be settled through negotiation.

Lastly, in the case of non-compliance with judgments rendered by international courts, further negotiation would be needed to settle the international dispute concerned. The award in the *Beagle Channel* dispute between Argentina and Chile is a case in point. Although the arbitral tribunal rendered an award on this case, the Government of Argentina declared a nullity of the award. This dispute was eventually resolved after mediation by the Holy See.[40]

3.3.2 Judicially Directed Negotiation

In some cases, the ICJ directed parties in dispute to carry out negotiation on the basis of its decision. This is called judicially directed negotiation. The 1969 *North Sea Continental Shelf* cases are a case in point. In this case, Denmark and the Netherlands requested the Court to decide the principles and rules of international law applicable to the delimitation of the continental shelf between the two kingdoms and the Federal Republic of Germany. The Court held that 'delimitation is to be effected by agreement in accordance with equitable principles, and taking account of all relevant circumstances'.[41] Related to this, the Court specified several factors to be taken into account in the course of the negotiations.[42] After the judgment, the parties renegotiated and two bilateral agreements delimitating the continental shelves were initialled on October 1970. The continental shelf disputes between the three States were finally settled by the ratification of the two agreements on 7 December 1972.[43]

Another example is provided by the *Fishery Jurisdiction* case of 1974. A central issue in this case related to the validity of the 50-mile exclusive fishing zone of Iceland. The ICJ ruled that a unilateral extension of the exclusive fishing rights of Iceland to 50 nautical miles from the baselines were not opposable to the United Kingdom,[44] while accepting Iceland's preferential rights in the adjacent waters.[45] At the same time, it held that Iceland and the UK were under mutual obligations to undertake negotiations in good faith for the equitable solution of their differences concerning their respective fishery rights in the area concerned.[46] In the operative part of the judgment, the Court enumerated relevant factors which must be taken into account in these negotiations.[47] According to the Court, to direct the disputing parties to negotiation is a proper exercise of the judicial function in this case.[48]

---

[40] The *Beagle Channel* dispute will be discussed in Chapter 5, section 6.2.3 of this book.
[41] *North Sea Continental Shelf* (Federal Republic of Germany/Netherlands) (Federal Republic of Germany/Denmark) (hereafter the *North Sea Continental Shelf* cases), Judgment of 20 February 1969, ICJ Reports 1969, p. 53, para. 101(C).
[42] *Ibid.*, p. 54, para. 101(D).
[43] For a detailed analysis of the negotiation process following the 1969 *North Sea Continental Shelf* judgment, see A. G. Oude Elferink, *The Delimitation of the Continental Shelf between Denmark, Germany and the Netherlands: Arguing Law, Practicing Politics?* (Cambridge University Press, 2013), pp. 342 *et seq.*
[44] *Fisheries Jurisdiction* (United Kingdom of Great Britain and Northern Ireland v. Iceland), Judgment of 25 July 1974, ICJ Reports 1974, p. 34, para. 79(1).
[45] *Ibid.*, p. 29, para. 68.   [46] *Ibid.*, p. 34, para. 79(3).   [47] *Ibid.*, p. 34, para. 79(4).   [48] *Ibid.*, p. 32, para. 75.

In some cases, the ITLOS prescribed provisional measures to order the disputing parties to enter into or resume negotiation. In the 1999 *Southern Bluefin Tuna* cases, for instance, the Tribunal prescribed a provisional measure requiring that: 'Australia, Japan and New Zealand should resume negotiations without delay with a view to reaching agreement on measures for the conservation and management of southern bluefin tuna.'[49] In the *MOX Plant* case, it prescribed provisional measures requiring Ireland and the United Kingdom to enter into consultation in order to (a) exchange information with regard to possible consequences for the Irish Sea arising out of the commissioning of the MOX plant, (b) monitor risks or the effects of the operation of the MOX plant for the Irish Sea and (c) devise, as appropriate, measures to prevent pollution of the marine environment which might result from the operation of the MOX plant.[50] In the *Case Concerning Land Reclamation* between Malaysia and Singapore, the Tribunal prescribed a provisional measure ordering Malaysia and Singapore to enter into consultation forthwith in order to establish promptly a group of independent experts with a mandate to conduct a study over a period of one year to determine the effects of Singapore's land reclamation and to propose measures to deal with any adverse effects of such land reclamation.[51]

Judicially directed negotiation requires two observations. First, a judgment to direct negotiation seeks to facilitate negotiation to find a solution between the parties in dispute by determining core legal issues in a particular case. In the *North Sea Continental Shelf* cases, for instance, the hard-core issue in negotiations (i.e. the obligatory nature of the equidistance method in continental shelf delimitation) was resolved by the Court. The decision of the Court greatly facilitated the negotiations between the three States and they successfully concluded treaties drawing the continental shelf boundaries.

Second, certain types of disputes are hard to fully settle by an international court or tribunal. An example is provided by disputes concerning equitable shares of marine living resources. Equitable shares of these resources need to be determined on the basis of detailed scientific knowledge and data. As the ICJ observed in the *Fishery Jurisdiction* case, the relevant information and expertise would be mainly in the possession of the parties in dispute. Accordingly, the Court would meet with difficulties if it were itself to attempt to lay down a precise scheme for an equitable adjustment of the rights of the disputing parties.[52] According to Judge Dillard, '[t]he Court's role is best limited to providing legal guide-lines which may *facilitate* the establishment of the system and in the event of a subsequent dispute, to help redress disturbances to it'.[53]

---

[49] The *Southern Bluefin Tuna* case, ITLOS Case No. 3 and 4, Request for Provisional Measures, Order of 27 August 1999, para. 90. The order is available at: www.itlos.org/index.php?id=35. For this case, see Chapter 10, section 2.3 of this book.
[50] The *MOX Plant* case, ITLOS Case No. 10, Request for Provisional Measures, Order of 3 December 2001, para. 89(1). For this case, see Chapter 10, section 2.3 of this book.
[51] *Case Concerning Land Reclamation*, Provisional Measures, ITLOS Case No. 12, Order of 8 October 2003, ITLOS Reports 2003, p. 28, para. 106(1)(a)(i). Further, see Chapter 10, section 2.3 of this book.
[52] The *Fisheries Jurisdiction* case, ICJ Reports 1974, pp. 31–2, para. 73.
[53] Emphasis original. Separate Opinion of Judge Dillard, *ibid.*, p. 71.

4 OBLIGATION TO NEGOTIATE

This section discusses the obligation to negotiate in international law. As negotiation is one of the various means of dispute settlement, States have free recourse to an appropriate method of their own choice. Hence, in the absence of a treaty obligation to negotiate or a decision of an international court to negotiate, there is no general duty to attempt to settle international disputes by negotiation.[54] In relation to this, the ICJ, in the *Cameroon/Nigeria* case (preliminary objections), held that:

> Neither in the Charter nor otherwise in international law is any general rule to be found to the effect that the exhaustion of diplomatic negotiations constitutes a precondition for a matter to be referred to the Court.[55]

When an obligation to negotiation is provided in a treaty, however, obviously the contracting parties to the treaty are required to negotiate. In practice, many treaties place an explicit obligation upon the contracting parties to carry out negotiation where a dispute is raised between the parties. Under Article 14(1) of the 1981 Treaty establishing the Organisation of Eastern Caribbean States,[56] for instance, '[a]ny dispute that may arise between two or more of the Member States regarding the interpretation and application of this Treaty shall, upon the request of any of them, be amicably resolved by direct agreement'. Article 8(2) of the 1959 Antarctic Treaty requires that the contracting parties concerned in any case of dispute with regard to the exercise of jurisdiction in Antarctica shall immediately consult together with a view to reaching a mutually acceptable solution. Article 15(2) of the 1979 Agreement Governing the Activities of States on the Moon and Other Celestial Bodies also provides an obligation to enter into consultation without delay.[57]

Negotiations must be carried out meaningfully in good faith. This point was amplified by the ICJ in the *North Sea Continental Shelf* cases. In the words of the Court,

> [T]he parties are under an obligation to enter into negotiations with a view to arriving at an agreement, and not merely to go through a formal process of negotiation as a sort of prior condition for the automatic application of a certain method of delimitation in the absence of agreement; they are under an obligation so to conduct themselves that the negotiations are meaningful, which will not be the case when either of them insists upon its own position without contemplating any modification of it.[58]

---

[54] C. M. Fombad, 'Consultation and Negotiation in the Pacific Settlement of International Disputes' (1989) 1 *African Journal of International and Comparative Law*, pp. 709–11; Kohen, 'Interaction', p. 23; Ph. Gautier, 'Settlement of Disputes' in D. Attard, M. Fitzmaurice and N. Gutiérrez (eds.), *The IMLI Manual on International Maritime Law, Vol. I: The Law of the Sea* (Oxford University Press, 2014), p. 541.

[55] *Land and Maritime Boundary between Cameroon and Nigeria* (Cameroon v. Nigeria: Equatorial Guinea intervening), Preliminary Objections, Judgment of 11 June 1998, ICJ Reports 1998, p. 303, para. 56.

[56] English text in: 1338 *UNTS*, p. 98. Entered into force 2 July 1981.

[57] English text in: 1363 *UNTS*, p. 22. Entered into force 11 July 1984.

[58] The *North Sea Continental Shelf* cases, ICJ Reports 1969, p. 47, para. 85.

The ICJ, in the *Fishery Jurisdiction* judgment, also stressed the principle of good faith in negotiation.[59] Given that, as the ICJ stated in the 1974 *Nuclear Test* case, the principle of good faith is one of the fundamental principles governing the creation and performance of legal obligations, whatever their source,[60] it is natural that negotiation is governed by this principle.

In the ICJ jurisprudence, an obligation to negotiate was at issue in the 2010 *Pulp Mills on the River Uruguay* case between Argentina and Uruguay. Article 12 of the 1975 Statute of the River Uruguay holds that: 'Should the parties fail to reach agreement within 180 days following the notification referred to in Article 11, the procedure indicated in Chapter XV shall be followed.'[61] Articles 7 to 11 further provide the cooperation mechanism, including the obligation of notification. In this regard, the ICJ held that:

> [B]y authorising the construction of the mills and the port terminal at Fray Bentos before the expiration of the period of negotiation, Uruguay failed to comply with the obligation to negotiate laid down by Article 12 of the Statute. Consequently, Uruguay disregarded the whole of the co-operation mechanism provided for in Articles 7 to 12 of the 1975 Statute.[62]

Some treaties oblige the parties to negotiate before resorting to dispute settlement by a third party, including international courts and tribunals. In this case, negotiation between the parties in dispute constitutes a precondition for resorting to international courts and tribunals and, thus, the existence of negotiation constitutes a key issue in establishing the jurisdiction of an international court. An interesting example in this regard is provided by the *Georgia/Russia* case. While Georgia instituted proceedings against the Russian Federation in accordance with Article 22 of CERD,[63] this provision provides for negotiation as a precondition for referring a dispute to the ICJ.[64] In the proceedings of provisional measures, the Russian Federation argued that: '[T]here has never been the slightest negotiation between the Parties on the interpretation or application of the Convention on the elimination of racial discrimination.' It thus asserted that the Court had no jurisdiction because the preconditions in Article 22 had not been met.[65] In

---

[59] ICJ Reports 1974, p. 33, para. 78.
[60] *Nuclear Tests* (Australia v. France), Judgment of 20 December 1974, ICJ Reports 1974, p. 268, para. 46. For a comprehensive study of the principle of good faith, see R. Kolb, *La Bonne Foi en droit international public: Contribution à l'étude des principes généraux de droit* (Paris: PUF, 2000).
[61] English text in: 1295 *UNTS*, p. 339. Entered into force 18 September 1976.
[62] *Pulp Mills on the River Uruguay* (Argentina v. Uruguay), Judgment of 20 April 2010, ICJ Reports 2010, pp. 67–8, para. 149. This case dealt with a dispute concerning the breach, allegedly committed by Uruguay, of obligations under the Statute of the River Uruguay that arose out of construction of two pulp mills on the River Uruguay.
[63] English text in: 660 *UNTS*, p. 212. Entered into force 4 January 1969.
[64] Article 22 provides that: 'Any dispute between two or more States Parties with respect to the interpretation or application of this Convention, which is not settled by negotiation or by the procedures expressly provided for in this Convention, shall, at the request of any of the parties to the dispute, be referred to the International Court of Justice for decision, unless the disputants agree to another mode of settlement.'
[65] The *Georgia/Russia* case, ICJ Reports 2008, p. 383, para. 102.

this regard, the Court ruled that issues relating to the CERD had been raised in bilateral contacts between the parties and that these issues had manifestly not been resolved by negotiation prior to the filing of the application. According to the Court, in several representations to the UN Security Council in the days before the filing of the application, those same issues were raised by Georgia and commented upon by the Russian Federation. The Court thus held that it had *prima facie* jurisdiction under Article 22 of the 1965 Convention.[66]

Nonetheless, seven judges, in their Joint Dissenting Opinion, questioned the interpretation of the majority opinion, and argued that the Court's interpretation would amount to denying any legal effect of the provision.[67] According to the seven dissenters, 'it is not sufficient that there have been contact between the parties; these contacts must have been regarding the subject of the dispute, either the interpretation or application of the Convention'.[68] These judges thus concluded that the very substance of the CERD was never debated between the parties before the filing of a claim before the Court.[69] Article 11(1) of the CERD provides that: 'If a State Party considers that another State Party is not giving effect to the provisions of this Convention, it may bring the matter to the attention of the Committee [Committee on the Elimination of Racial Discrimination].' As the Court itself noted, however, 'neither Party claims that the issues in dispute have been brought to the attention of the Committee'.[70]

Subsequently the Russian Federation raised preliminary objections contesting the jurisdiction of the ICJ. A pivotal issue in this regard was whether or not a precondition to refer a dispute to the Court under Article 22 of the CERD (i.e. negotiations) existed between the parties. Here the Court ruled that the concept of negotiations requires, at the very least, 'a genuine attempt by one of the disputing parties to engage in discussions with the other disputing party, with a view to resolving the dispute'.[71] It went on to add that according to the ICJ Jurisprudence, 'the precondition of negotiation is met only when there has been a failure of negotiations, or when negotiations have become futile or deadlocked'.[72]

The Court noted that a dispute between Georgia and the Russian Federation falling within the ambit of CERD arose only in the period immediately before the filing of the application.[73] Having examined the relevant evidence, the Court concluded that:

> [T]he facts in the record show that, between 9 August and 12 August 2008, Georgia did not attempt to negotiate CERD-related matters with the Russian Federation, and that, consequently, Georgia and the Russian Federation did not engage in negotiations with respect to the latter's compliance with its substantive obligations under CERD.[74]

---

[66] *Ibid.*, pp. 388, paras. 115–17.
[67] Joint Dissenting Opinion of Vice-President Al Khasawneh and Judges Ranjeva, Shi, Koroma, Tomka, Bennouna and Skotnikov, p. 402, paras. 12.
[68] *Ibid.*, pp. 403–4, para. 15.   [69] *Ibid.*, p. 402, para. 12.
[70] Order, *ibid.*, p. 388, para. 116.
[71] The *Georgia/Russia* case, Preliminary Objections, ICJ Reports 2011, p. 132, para. 157.
[72] *Ibid.*, p. 133, para. 159.   [73] *Ibid.*, p. 135, para. 167.   [74] *Ibid.*, pp. 139–40, para. 182.

Hence it upheld, by ten votes to six, the second preliminary objection raised by the Russian Federation, and found, by ten votes to six, that it had no jurisdiction to entertain the application filed by Georgia.[75] The *Georgia/Russia* case thus demonstrated that the interpretation of the obligation to negotiate significantly affects the establishment of the jurisdiction of the ICJ.

5 TIMEFRAME FOR NEGOTIATIONS

In the situation where negotiations have taken place but failed to yield a solution, are the disputing parties obliged to continue negotiations?[76] In this regard, the PCIJ, in the *Mavrommatis* case, held that:

> Negotiations do not of necessity always presuppose a more or less lengthy series of notes and despatches; it may suffice that a discussion should have been commenced, and this discussion may have been very short; this will be the case if a dead lock is reached, or if finally a point is reached at which one of the Parties definitely declares himself unable, or refuses, to give way, and there can therefore be no doubt that *the dispute cannot be settled by negotiation.*[77]

However, it is not easy to objectively decide the question whether the dispute cannot be settled by negotiation. A possible solution on this matter may be to set out a clear time limit for the completion of the negotiation process.[78] In fact, several treaties provide a timeframe for negotiations. For instance, Article 14(2) of the 1981 Treaty establishing the Organisation of Eastern Caribbean States provides that:

> If the dispute is not resolved within three months of the date on which the request referred to in the preceding paragraph has been made, any party to the dispute may submit it to the conciliation procedure provided for in Annex A to this Treaty by submitting a request to that effect to the Director-General of the Organisation and informing the other party or parties to the dispute of the request.

Under Article 16(1) of the 1965 Convention on the Transit Trade of Land-locked States,

> Any dispute which may arise with respect to the interpretation or application of the provisions of this Convention which is not settled by negotiation or by other peaceful means of settlement within a period of nine months shall, at the request of either party, be settled by arbitration.[79]

---

[75] *Ibid.*, p. 141, para. 187(2).
[76] United Nations, *Handbook*, p. 15, para. 50.
[77] Emphasis original. *Mavrommatis Palestine Concessions*, Judgment of 30 August 1924, PCIJ, Series A, No. 2, p. 13.
[78] United Nations, *Handbook*, pp. 15–16, para. 51.
[79] Entered into force 9 June 1967. The electronic text is available at: www.jus.uio.no/english/services/library/treaties/09/9-04/land-locked-states.xml.

A similar provision can be found in the 1975 Vienna Convention on the Representation of States in their Relations with International Organisations of a Universal Character,[80] the 1978 Vienna Convention on Succession of States in respect of Treaties[81] and the 2004 United Nations Convention on Jurisdictional Immunities of States and their Property.[82]

6 OUTCOME OF NEGOTIATIONS

When negotiations are successful, the parties normally issue an instrument reflecting the terms of the agreement arrived at. This document may be a comprehensive agreement, a joint statement, communiqué, memorandum or declaration.[83] Where negotiations have resulted in the conclusion of a treaty, namely a binding legal instrument, no serious problem will arise. In the case of a joint statement or communiqué, however, a dispute may arise with regard to the nature of the instrument. An illustrative example is provided by the *Aegean Sea Continental Shelf* case between Greece and Turkey.[84] In this case, a dispute was raised as to the legal significance of the Brussels Communiqué, which was a joint communiqué issued to the press by the Prime Ministers of Greece and Turkey on 31 May 1975.[85]

The interpretation of this communiqué was sharply divided between the parties. Whilst Greece considered that this instrument was an agreement to refer the continental shelf dispute to the ICJ, Turkey denied the legally binding nature of the communiqué. Thus the Court examined the Brussels Communiqué in the context in which the meeting of 31 May 1975 took place and the Communiqué was drawn up. According to the Court, there was no evidence that Turkey was ready to contemplate, not a joint submission of the dispute to the Court, but a general acceptance of the Court's jurisdiction with respect to it. The general position taken up by Turkey in Court in the previous diplomatic exchanges was that it was ready to consider *a joint submission of the dispute to the Court by means of a special agreement*. This construction was further supported by the subsequent practice of the parties. The Court thus concluded that the Brussels Communiqué was not intended to constitute an immediate commitment by the Greek and Turkish Prime Ministers to accept unconditionally the unilateral submission of the present dispute to the Court and that it did not furnish a valid basis for establishing the Court's jurisdiction to entertain the application filed by Greece on 10 August 1976.[86]

---

[80] Article 85(1). Doc.A/CONF.67/16. Not yet entered into force. The electronic text is available at: http://legal.un.org/ilc/texts/instruments/english/conventions/5_1_1975.pdf.
[81] Article 42(1). Entered into force 6 November 1996. Text in: 1946 *UNTS*, p. 3.
[82] Article 27(2). Not yet entered into force. UN General Assembly, *United Nations Convention on Jurisdictional Immunities of States and Their Property*, 2 December 2004, A/RES/59/38, available at: www.unhcr.org/refworld/docid/4280737b4.html.
[83] United Nations, *Handbook*, p. 21, para. 68.
[84] *Aegean Sea Continental Shelf* (Greece v. Turkey), Judgment of 19 December 1978, Jurisdiction of the Court, ICJ Reports 1978, p. 3.   [85] *Ibid.*, pp. 39–40, para. 97.
[86] *Ibid.*, pp. 43–4, paras. 104–7.

A contrasting example is provided by the *Maritime Delimitation and Territorial Questions* case between Qatar and Bahrain (Jurisdiction and Admissibility). In this case, a question arose whether the Minutes of a meeting of the Cooperation Council of Arab States, held in December 1990, constituted an agreement between Qatar and Bahrain which conferred a basis of jurisdiction to the ICJ. Whilst Qatar considered that the 1990 Minutes enabled Qatar to seise the Court unilaterally, Bahrain maintained that it did not constitute a legally binding instrument. In this regard, the Court held that the Minutes were not a simple record of a meeting, but created rights and obligations in international law for the parties. It thus concluded that the Minutes constituted an international agreement.[87] In order to avoid possible disputes with regard to the nature of a joint communiqué, there will be a need for the relevant parties to clarify the nature of their statements which inform the public of the outcome of negotiations.

A similar issue arises with regard to the legal status of the Memorandum of Understanding (MOU). One may take the 2016 *Somalia/Kenya* case (preliminary objections) as an example. On 7 April 2009, the Government of Kenya and the Transitional Federal Government of Somalia signed a MOU in respect of submissions on the outer limits of the continental shelf beyond 200 nautical miles to the Commission on the Limits of the Continental Shelf. When Somalia submitted a maritime delimitation dispute with Kenya to the ICJ, a question was raised with regard to the legal status of the MOU. In light of the express provision of the MOU that it shall enter into force upon signature and the terms of the authorisation given to the Somali Minister, the Court, in its judgment, concluded that the MOU is a valid treaty that entered into force upon signature.[88]

If the negotiations are unsuccessful, the parties may choose to adjourn the negotiation process *sine die* ('without a day') or to issue a communiqué recording the failure of the negotiations. As demonstrated in the Falklands/Malvinas dispute, lack of progress in negotiation may encourage the use of force by eliminating alternatives of peaceful settlement of disputes.[89] Since the coercive method of dispute settlement is no longer acceptable in international law, however, parties to a dispute are required to make an effort to resolve the dispute by resorting to other peaceful methods of dispute settlement.[90] Hence it is important to establish alternative mechanisms of international dispute settlement after the failure of negotiations. In fact, the dispute settlement clauses of many multilateral treaties provide that a dispute which cannot be settled by negotiation is to be submitted to another peaceful settlement procedure.[91] Furthermore, as will be seen next, the assistance of a third party offering good offices and mediation is also useful to break deadlock and facilitate peaceful settlement of international disputes.

---

[87] *Maritime Delimitation and Territorial Questions between Qatar and Bahrain* (Qatar v. Bahrain), Jurisdiction and Admissibility, Judgment of 1 July 1994, ICJ Reports 1994, p. 121, para. 25.
[88] *Maritime Delimitation in the Indian Ocean* (Somalia v. Kenya), Preliminary Objections, Judgment of 2 February 2016, ICJ Reports 2016 (not yet reported), para. 50.
[89] Merrills, *International Dispute Settlement*, pp. 23–4.
[90] See the Manila Declaration, Section I, para. 7.   [91] United Nations, *Handbook*, p. 21, paras. 70 *et seq.*

7 GOOD OFFICES

7.1 General Considerations

Good offices are a procedure in which a third party seeks to facilitate efforts towards a peaceful settlement of disputes between parties by providing them with a channel of communication. Good offices may be performed by a single State or a group of States, or by non-State actors, such as international institutions and individuals acting independently. As provided in Article 3 of the 1899 Hague Convention, the exercise of the right to offer good offices or mediation 'can never be regarded by either of the parties in dispute as an unfriendly act'.[92] At the same time, it has to be stressed that an offer of good offices is subject to acceptance of all the parties to the dispute.[93] This is a corollary of the principle of the free choice of means and the outcome of the process depends entirely upon the attitude of the parties to the dispute. In this regard, Article 6 of the 1899 and 1907 Hague Conventions makes clear that the results of good offices 'have exclusively the character of advice and never have binding force'.

Normally good offices involve no more than helping to bring the parties in dispute into direct negotiations. However, the role of a third party exercising good offices may change over time and involvement of the third party may be deepened according to the developments of the events concerning the dispute. Hence the distinction between good offices and mediation is thin in practice.[94]

7.2 Process of Good Offices

The procedures of good offices rest essentially on the goodwill of the parties in dispute.[95] Hence the confidence of the parties in dispute in a third party offering good offices is a key element to create a successful outcome. Experience demonstrates that the permanent neutral State is especially in a favoured position to exercise good offices. For instance, historically Switzerland has played a significant role in good offices and mediation. Good offices, along with mediation, may also be exercised by a politically leading State[96] and a political organ, such as the United Nations.

Good offices may be set in motion either upon the initiative of a third party, or by an invitation of all the parties to the dispute in an ad hoc manner. Good offices may also be resorted to in accordance with the provisions of a treaty. In either case, good offices cannot be exercised without the consent of the parties in dispute.

Good offices may be performed by establishing contact with the parties in dispute through informal meetings with each party. In so doing, the third party exercising good offices may transmit to the parties each other's position relating to the dispute. Where direct negotiation between the parties in dispute has been interrupted, good offices may be exercised by visiting the capitals of the disputing parties, or by

---

[92] See also Article 3 of the 1907 Hague Convention.   [93] United Nations, *Handbook*, p. 33, para. 101.
[94] *Ibid.*, pp. 33–4, para. 103; R. R. Probst, '"Good Offices" in International Relations in the Light of Swiss Practice and Experience' (1975-III) 146 *RCADI*, p. 227.
[95] *Ibid.*, p. 228.   [96] *Ibid.*, p. 237.

requesting the disputing parties to send representatives to a meeting with the third party offering good offices together with representatives of another party to the dispute, or alone at a certain location.[97] In any case it is important that good offices should be invoked in a timely manner with a view to preventing further deterioration of disputes.[98]

7.3 Functions and Practice of Good Offices

As noted, the primary function of good offices is to assist the parties in dispute with a view to facilitating negotiations in the settlement of international disputes. An illustrative example is furnished by good offices skilfully exercised by Switzerland in the Franco-Algerian conflict in 1960–2. Since the Algerian uprising against French domination had become critical, Switzerland offered good offices with a view to facilitating official French–Algerian negotiations. In the final phase of the negotiation in March 1962, which was held in Evian on the French side of Lake Leman, the independence of Algeria was accepted. In this phase also, Switzerland continued to play a valuable role in assuring the security of the Algerian delegation whose headquarters were on the Swiss side of Lake Leman, in organising its transport to the meeting place on French territory; in providing the necessary means of communication and information; and in endeavouring to promote an atmosphere of confidence between the two parties. Finally both sides expressly voiced their gratitude for the valuable role of Switzerland.[99]

Good offices can also contribute to prevent further deterioration of international disputes. The preventive function of good offices is confirmed in the 1988 Manila Declaration as follows:

> [T]he Security Council should consider sending, at an early stage, fact-finding or good offices missions or establishing appropriate forms of United Nations presence, including observers and peace-keeping operations, as a means of preventing the further deterioration of the dispute or situation in the areas concerned.

In the situation where an armed conflict has already taken place, good offices may be tendered in order to halt or scale down hostilities. An example is the good offices offered by the American President Theodore Roosevelt in concluding the Russo-Japanese War that broke out in 1904. In 1905, Roosevelt performed good offices and called upon the two belligerents to enter into direct negotiations in order to end the war. As a result, on 5 September 1905, the peace treaty was signed at Portsmouth.[100] It is also well known that France exercised its good offices in relation to the Viet Nam War with a view to facilitating

---

[97] United Nations, *Handbook*, p. 39, paras. 118–19.   [98] *Ibid.*, p. 36, para. 108.
[99] Probst, 'Good Offices', pp. 263–4.
[100] Treaty of Peace between Japan and Russia, signed at Portsmouth, 5 September 1905. The text in: 199 *The Consolidated Treaty Series*, p. 144. Further, see Y. Matsui, 'Modern Japan, War and International Law' in N. Ando (ed.), *Japan and International Law: Past, Present and Future* (The Hague: Kluwer, 1999), pp. 17–18; United States, Department of States, Office of Historian, 'The Treaty of Portsmouth and the Russo-Japanese War, 1904–1905', available at: https://history.state.gov/milestones/1899-1913/portsmouth-treaty.

peace negotiations between the United States and Viet Nam.[101] In addition, there are many instances where an organ of the United Nations has tendered good offices.[102]

8 MEDIATION

8.1 General Considerations

Mediation is a process whereby a third party actively assists two or more parties in dispute, with their consent, to develop a mutually acceptable solution in the settlement of an international dispute by offering its own proposals.[103] By offering mediation, a third party intervenes in the negotiation process between parties to a dispute with a view to reconciling the claims of the contending parties and to advance his own proposals aimed at a mutually acceptable compromise solution. The ICJ formulated mediation as 'third States, on their own initiative, endeavoured to bring together the viewpoints of the States concerned by making specific proposals to them'.[104] The importance of mediation in the peaceful settlement of international disputes was acknowledged by UN General Assembly Resolution 70/304 of 2016.[105]

Mediation can also contribute to prevent further deterioration of disputes which may disrupt good relationships between relevant parties. In this regard, UN General Assembly Resolution 65/283 of 2011 recognised 'the useful role that mediation can play in preventing disputes from escalating into conflicts and conflicts from escalating further, as well as in advancing the resolution of conflicts'.[106]

Credible mediation must fulfil several conditions. In this regard, UN General Assembly Resolution 70/304 highlighted, *inter alia*, the following conditions for effective mediation:

(i) national ownership
(ii) the consent of parties to a particular dispute or conflict
(iii) respect for national sovereignty
(iv) the impartiality of the mediators
(v) their compliance with agreed mandates
(vi) compliance with obligations of States and other relevant actors under international law, including applicable treaties

---

[101] L. Caflisch, 'Cent ans des règlement pacifique des différends interétatiques' (2001) 288 *RCADI*, p. 277; United Nations, *Handbook*, p. 37, para. 111. See also, P. Isoart, 'L'Accord de Paris sur la cessation de la guerre et le rétablissement de la paix au Sud-Vietnam' (1972) 18 *AFDI*, pp. 101–21; J. Charpentier, 'Pratique française concernant le droit international', *ibid.*, pp. 995–6.
[102] United Nations, *Handbook*, p. 37, para. 112; Chapter 4, sections 2.2, 3.1 and 4.1.5 of this book.
[103] United Nations, *Guidance for Effective Mediation* (New York: United Nations, 2012), p. 4. This document was issued as an annex to the report of the Secretary-General on *Strengthening the Role of Mediation in the Peaceful Settlement of Disputes, Conflict Prevention and Resolution* (A/66/811, 25 June 2012). See also Berridge, *Diplomacy*, p. 236; Article XII of the 1948 Pact of Bogotá.
[104] *Border and Transborder Armed Actions* (Nicaragua v. Honduras), Judgment of 20 December 1988, Jurisdiction of the Court and Admissibility of the Application, ICJ Reports 1988, p. 99, para. 75.
[105] UN General Assembly Resolution, *Strengthening the Role of Mediation in the Peaceful Settlement of Disputes, Conflict Prevention and Resolution*, A/RES/70/304, 26 September 2016, para. 2.
[106] UN General Assembly Resolution, *Strengthening the Role of Mediation in the Peaceful Settlement of Disputes, Conflict Prevention and Resolution*, A/RES/65/283, 22 June 2011, p. 2, Preamble para. 12. See also Article 8 of the Hague Convention.

46 Foundation of International Dispute Settlement

(vii) the operational preparedness, including process and substantive expertise, of the mediators

(viii) coherence, coordination and complementarity of mediation efforts.[107]

Mediation, if successful, is likely to result in a compromised solution which offers something to each party in dispute. Indeed, to make concessions through a mediator may be politically easier than direct concession to the other disputant.[108]

8.2 Process of Mediation

Mediation may be set in motion upon the initiative of a third party, such as a single State, a group of States, or non-State actors such as international institutions, non-governmental organisations (NGOs) or a prominent individual. In any case the consent of all the parties to a dispute is needed to initiate mediation. Some treaties make clear that the mediator or mediators are to be chosen by mutual consent of the parties.[109] Thus confidence in the mediator from the parties in dispute constitutes an important element for successful mediation. In this regard, impartiality of the mediator is crucial to obtain and keep their confidence.[110] The requirement of impartiality is particularly important when the International Committee of the Red Cross or the UN Secretary-General exercises mediation.[111] Furthermore, the mediator's influence or effective power relative to the disputing parties is a crucial element in selecting a qualified mediator. The mediator's influence may be economic, political and even spiritual. In the case of a dispute between two Catholic States, for instance, the Holy See may have an important role to play as a mediator. The 1978 *Beagle Channel* dispute between Argentina and Chile is a case in point.[112]

While specific activities of mediation vary according to the nature of disputes as well as with the passage of time, these activities may include communication, clarification of issues, drafting of proposals, search for areas of agreement between the disputing parties, and elaboration of arrangements etc.[113] The political sensitivity of the mediation process requires informality and confidentiality. These elements are highlighted in the Pact of Bogotá, by providing in Article XII that:

> The functions of the mediator or mediators shall be to assist the parties in the settlement of controversies in the simplest and most direct manner, avoiding formalities and seeking an acceptable solution. No report shall be made by the mediator and, so far as he is concerned, the proceedings shall be wholly confidential.

---

[107] UN General Assembly Resolution, A/RES/70/304, para. 4.
[108] Salman, 'Good Offices and Mediation', p. 199.
[109] See, for instance, the 1936 Inter-American Treaty on Good Offices and Mediation (Article III), the 1948 Pact of Bogotá (Article XII) and the 1964 OAU Protocol (Article XX).
[110] Berridge, *Diplomacy*, p. 246.
[111] However, impartiality is not synonymous with neutrality in values. For instance, the UN Secretary-General must uphold principles and values embodied in the UN Charter when offering mediation.
[112] See Chapter 5, section 6.2 of this book.   [113] United Nations, *Handbook*, p. 42, para. 130.

47   Negotiation, Good Offices and Mediation

In fact, even *post factum* the parties in dispute and mediation are often reluctant to place on record all the details and nuances of the procedure they went through.[114]

As international disputes continue, possibly over years, the role of the mediator will remain crucial.[115] Continuous involvement will enhance personal trust between the disputing parties and the mediator and reduce the risk of false expectations being generated. In order to maintain constant efforts, the mediator should have a strong incentive to obtain a settlement of the dispute concerned.[116] There is also a need to maintain coherence and consistency. At the same time, the views and needs of the parties in dispute and other stakeholders must be adequately reflected in the mediation process.

Final results of mediation may be embodied in an agreement, a protocol, a declaration, a communiqué, an exchange of letters or a gentleman's agreement signed or certificated by a mediator or mediators. Where the parties to a dispute do not accept the proposals made by the mediator, the mediation process terminates.[117] Like other diplomatic means of dispute settlement, the outcome of mediation (i.e. proposals made by the mediator) are not binding upon the parties to a dispute. Even so, political pressure upon disputing States cannot be denied and a proposed solution can sometimes be imposed. In this regard, care should be taken in noting that a third party exercising good offices or mediation does not always act with pure charity, and undertakes mediation for its own political purpose.[118] The offer of good offices or mediation does not guarantee the impartiality of the solution.

8.3 Practice of Mediation

Mediation can be furnished by State(s), whether acting singly or collectively, and non-State actors, such as international institutions, NGOs and individuals.

8.3.1 Mediation by State(s)

Great powers may be involved in international disputes as mediators owing to their influence and a wide range of strategies. An example in this regard is the United States mediation between Egypt and Israel at Camp David. US President Carter's mediation resulted in an agreement, and eventually a peace treaty (i.e. the Camp David Accord) was signed between Egypt and Israel on 17 September 1978.[119] Mediation can also be furnished by a small or middle-sized State. An often quoted example of this type of mediation is Algeria's mediation in the *Diplomatic Hostages* dispute of 1980. This dispute involved occupation of the US Embassy in Tehran by Iranians. At approximately 10.30 a.m. on 4 November 1979, during the course of a demonstration of approximately 3,000 persons, the US Embassy compound in Tehran was overrun by a strongly armed group of several hundred people. The invading group occupied the Chancery building as well as other buildings. In the course

---

[114] *Ibid.*, para. 131.
[115] Some treaties set up a clear timeframe. See, for instance, Article XIII of the 1948 Pact of Bogotá.
[116] Berridge, *Diplomacy*, pp. 247-9.
[117] See Article 5 of the 1907 Hague Convention.   [118] Caflisch, 'Cens ans', pp. 280-1.
[119] J. Bercovitch and R. Jackson, *Conflict Resolution in the Twenty-First Century: Principles, Methods and Approaches* (University of Michigan Press, 2009), pp. 39-40; T. Princen, 'Camp David: Problem-Solving or Power Politics as Usual?' (1991) 28 *Journal of Peace Research*, pp. 57-69.

of the attack, all the diplomatic and consular personnel and other persons present in the premises were seized as hostages, and detained in the Embassy compound. Subsequently other US personnel and one US private citizen seized elsewhere in Tehran were brought to the compound and added to the number of hostages. Algeria then pursued a combined good offices and mediation role in the settlement of the dispute. After some very complex negotiations over Iranian assets in the United States, the dispute was eventually settled. The settlement enhanced Algeria's reputation in the eyes of Americans as well as resolving a crisis which could have led to war between a superpower and a Muslim State. Algeria also exercised mediation in incidents concerning the Iran–Iraq dispute of 1975.[120] Algeria's mediation demonstrates that relatively small States can mediate in international disputes involving far larger States than themselves.[121]

Mediation can be offered by two or more parties simultaneously without attempting to coordinate their activities or with coordination of their activities. Where third parties coordinate their actions, it is sometimes described as 'collective mediation' and the coordinating body involved as a 'contact group'. A case in point is the Contact Group on Bosnia, consisting of France, Germany, Italy, the Russian Federation, the United Kingdom and the United States. It was created in April 1994 and was revived in an attempt to deal with the Kosovo crisis in 1999. When only two parties are involved in mediation, such as the original UN/EU mission to broker a settlement in Bosnia, it may be called 'joint mediation'.[122]

8.3.2 Mediation by Non-State Actors

Non-State actors can also be important mediators. Related to this, it is of particular interest to note that the Mediation Support Unit was established at the United Nations in 2006. This Unit provides advisory, financial and logistical support to peace processes and works to strengthen the mediation capacity of regional and subregional organisations. It also serves as a repository of mediation knowledge, policy and guidance, lessons learned and best practices.[123] Furthermore, the Standby Team of Mediation Experts was established as a service of the Mediation Support Unit in March 2008. It is a specialised resource that seeks to provide expert advice to senior UN officials or other partners, upon request, either by deploying in person to the field or by providing advice remotely.[124]

Furthermore, the UN Secretary-General has repeatedly performed good offices and mediations.[125] By way of example, it is widely known that in 1982, the UN Secretary-General, Pérez de Cuéllar, undertook good offices in the Falklands/Malvinas dispute.[126] An increasing number of regional international organisations are also seeking to enhance their own mediation capacities.[127] In relation to this, one may note with interest that the Organisation of American States and the United Nations have concluded

---

[120] Merrills, *International Dispute Settlement*, p. 28.   [121] Berridge, *Diplomacy*, p. 240.
[122] Ibid., pp. 243–5.
[123] See http://peacemaker.un.org/mediation-support; www.un.org/undpa/en/diplomacy-mediation.
[124] See http://peacemaker.un.org/mediation-support/stand-by-team.
[125] See Chapter 4, section 4.1 of this book.
[126] UN Security Council Resolution 505 (1982) of 26 May 1982, paras. 2 and 4 of the operative part.
[127] Bercovitch and Jackson, *Conflict Resolution*, pp. 40–1.

a joint mediation partnership.[128] In addition, the International Committee of the Red Cross regularly intervenes where armed conflicts or the treatment of detainees raise humanitarian issues.

In the particular context of international water disputes, the World Bank is influential as a mediator since the development of water management plans relies on loans from the Bank.[129] An illustrative example is provided by the World Bank's good offices and mediation served for the settlement of the Indus Water dispute between India and Pakistan.[130] After nine years of negotiations, on 19 September 1960, the Indus Waters Treaty was signed by India and Pakistan and the World Bank also became a signatory of the treaty because it accepted a wide range of responsibilities in the implementation of the arrangements agreed under its terms. Thus the mediation efforts of the World Bank successfully resolved the Indus water dispute.

In appropriate circumstances, private individuals or NGOs may be engaged in mediations in an unofficial capacity. The activities of private and unofficial actors are sometimes called Track II diplomacy, comparing it to Track I diplomacy carried out by official, diplomatic and governmental actors.[131] At present, non-official actors are becoming an increasingly important facet of mediations. In fact, notably, there are many secular NGOs dedicated to dispute prevention and resolutions. Examples may include the Carter Centre, set up by former US President Jimmy Carter, and Conciliation Resources in London.[132] Further, religious bodies may perform a valuable role as a mediator. An illustrative example is provided by the role of Sant'Egidio, the Rome-based religious group, in the ending of the civil war in Mozambique in the early 1990s. The mediation of Sant'Egidio resulted in the signing of the Rome Agreement in October 1992.[133]

8.4 Limitations of Mediation and Good Offices

Whist mediation and good offices have a valuable role to play in peaceful settlement of international disputes, these means include some limitations. Three points in particular merit highlighting.

First, there is no guarantee that a third party can offer good offices or meditation in a timely manner. In the case of disputes between the major powers, in particular, it seems difficult to find a qualified third party offering mediation since any third States might regard themselves as unqualified to act as the mediator because of their limited influence or power.[134]

---

[128] Report of the UN Secretary-General, *Preventive Diplomacy*, UN Document S/2011/552, p. 3, available at: http://peacemaker.un.org/resources/key-un-documents.
[129] This issue will be discussed in Chapter 10.
[130] For an analysis of the Indus Water dispute, see S. M. A. Salman, 'Mediation of International Water Dispute: the Indus, the Jordan, and the Nile Basins Interventions' in L. Boisson de Chazournes, C. Leb and M. Tignino, *International Law and Fresh Water: The Multiple Challenges* (Cheltenham: Edward Elgar Publishing, 2013), pp. 369 *et seq.*; Salman, 'Good Offices and Mediation', pp. 183 *et seq.*; S. C. McCaffrey, *The Law of International Watercourses*, 2nd edn (Oxford University Press, 2007), pp. 289 *et seq.*
[131] Bercovitch and Jackson, *Conflict Resolution*, pp. 137–50.
[132] Berridge, *Diplomacy*, p. 243.   [133] *Ibid.*; Bercovitch and Jackson, *Conflict Resolution*, pp. 142–3.
[134] Merrills, *International Dispute Settlement*, p. 29.

Second, mediation is not always an attractive means of dispute settlement for parties in dispute since, by accepting mediation, they acknowledge that the dispute is a legitimate matter of international concern. As in the case of South Africa in the apartheid era, where a question of international accountability lies at the heart of the controversy, mediation will be difficult to operate.

Third, in certain circumstances, the parties in dispute may not give consent to mediation or good offices. If consent was given, it may not always translate into full commitment to the mediation process.[135] For instance, an offer of good offices or mediation by a third party would not be acceptable in domains of vital importance for States, such as disarmament and arms control.[136] Where a government believes either that it can win the dispute, or that the time to make concessions has not yet arrived, it is unlikely that the government will accept an offer of mediation. In fact, the Soviet Union refused to accept the mediation of the UN Secretary-General following its intervention in Hungary in 1956.[137] It seems probable that mediation becomes ineffective in situations where any solution would require one side to abandon its main objective and receive little in return. The Gulf War of 1991 is a case in point. Following Iraq's invasion of Kuwait in August 1990 and the imposition of sanctions by the UN Security Council, the Secretary-General, France, the Soviet Union and a number of others made attempts to bring about a peaceful solution but in vain, essentially because a key demand was that Iraq should withdraw from Kuwait and not be rewarded for its aggression.[138]

9 CONCLUSIONS

This chapter examined three diplomatic means of international dispute settlement: negotiation, good offices and mediation. The matters considered in this chapter allow the following conclusions.

(i) Even though negotiation is in essence a political process, it cannot be completely detached from international law since it is governed by basic principles of the law, such as principles of sovereign equality, non-intervention, prohibition of the threat or use of force, and good faith. International law can provide a common language facilitating communication and legitimise the claims of the parties in dispute. Hence international law constitutes an important element in the negotiation process.

(ii) While there is no obligation to negotiate in customary international law, in many treaties negotiation is provided as a precondition to recourse to judicial settlement. In this case, the existence of prior negotiation is a prerequisite to establish the jurisdiction of an international court or tribunal.

(iii) Negotiation and judicial settlement are not mutually exclusive, but are closely interlinked. At the pre-adjudicative stage, negotiation can contribute to identifying

---

[135] UN, *Guidance for Effective Mediation*, p. 8.
[136] Lachs, 'International Law, Mediation and Negotiation', p. 194.
[137] Merrills, *International Dispute Settlement*, p. 30.   [138] *Ibid.*, p. 39.

the existence of a dispute and its subject matter. Negotiation can continue during international adjudication. In some cases, the ICJ has ordered the disputing parties to re-negotiate after clarifying relevant rules of international law or elements to be taken into account. In so doing, the Court can contribute to facilitating the negotiation process. The interaction between negotiation and international adjudication is important to effectively settle international disputes.

(iv) The essential function of good offices and mediation is to facilitate dispute settlement through negotiations between the parties in dispute. Good offices and mediation are subject to the consent of the parties to a dispute. The outcome of good offices and mediation is not binding on the parties in dispute. The effectiveness of good offices and mediation rests on the goodwill of the disputing parties. Overall good offices and mediation can be considered adjunct to negotiations.

FURTHER READING

Negotiation

G. R. Berridge, *Diplomacy: Theory and Practice*, 4th edn (Palgrave Macmillan, 2010).

F. O. Hampson, C. A. Crocker and P. R. Aall, 'Negotiation and International Conflict' in C. Webel and J. Galtung (eds.), *Handbook of Peace and Conflict Studies* (London: Routledge, 2007), pp. 35–50.

V. Lowe, 'The Interplay between Negotiation and Litigation in International Dispute Settlement' in T. M. Ndiaye and R. Wolfrum (eds.), *Law of the Sea, Environmental Law and Settlement of Disputes, Liber Amicorum Judge Thomas A. Mensah* (Leiden: Nijhoff, 2007), pp. 235–47.

A. Plantey, *International Negotiation in the Twenty-First Century*, trans. F. Meadows (Abingdon: Routledge-Cavendish, 2007).

M. Weibel, 'The Diplomatic Channel' in J. Crawford, A. Pellet, S. Olleson and K. Parlett (eds.), *The Law of International Responsibility* (Oxford University Press, 2010), pp. 1085–97.

Good Offices and Mediation

J. Bercovitch (ed.), *Studies in International Mediation* (Basingstoke: Palgrave Macmillan, 2002).

S. Horowitz, 'Mediation' in C. Webel and J. Galtung (eds.), *Handbook of Peace and Conflict Studies* (London: Routledge, 2007), pp. 51–63.

R. R. Probst, *'Good Offices' in the Light of Swiss International Practice and Experience* (Dordrecht: Nijhoff, 1989).

S. M. A. Salman, 'Good Offices and Mediation and International Water Disputes' in The International Bureau of the Permanent Court of Arbitration, *Resolution of International Water Disputes* (The Hague: Kluwer, 2003), pp. 155–99.

United Nations, *Guidance for Effective Mediation* (New York: United Nations, 2012).

3

Inquiry and Conciliation

Main Issues

Both inquiry and conciliation constitute a diplomatic means of international dispute settlement. Inquiry aims to elucidate the issues of facts underlying an international dispute by an inquiry commission, while conciliation seeks to investigate matters of fact and relevant issues and present specific solutions to the dispute by a conciliation commission. Inquiry and conciliation are carried out by impartial and independent individuals. The outcome is not binding upon the parties in dispute. This chapter will review procedures of inquiry and conciliation focusing particularly on the following issues:

(i) What are the principal features of inquiry and conciliation?
(ii) What is the role of inquiry in peaceful settlement of international disputes and what are its limitations?
(iii) What are the functions of conciliation in peaceful settlement of international disputes?
(iv) While conciliation procedures have been enshrined in many treaties, the actual use of conciliation is very limited. Why is the practice of conciliation so limited?

1 INTRODUCTION

International disputes often arise from disagreements with regard to some issues of fact. Where the root causes of an international dispute rest on disagreements concerning a matter of fact, an objective assessment of points of fact by a third party can significantly contribute to reducing the risks of stalemate or the escalation of the dispute. The arrangement for fact-finding is called 'inquiry' or 'fact-finding'.[1] Inquiry can be defined as a specific institutional arrangement to elucidate the issues of fact underlying international disputes by an independent and impartial commission. Like other diplomatic means of international dispute settlement, the outcome of inquiry is not binding upon the parties in dispute.[2]

---

[1] The terms 'fact-finding' and 'inquiry' are synonymous and interchangeable.
[2] See, for instance, Article 14 of the 1899 Hague Convention for the Pacific Settlement of International Disputes.

According to the Regulations on the Procedure of International Conciliation, adopted by the *Institute de droit international* in 1961, conciliation is defined as:

> A method for the settlement of international disputes of any nature according to which a Commission set up by the Parties, either on a permanent or an ad hoc basis to deal with a dispute proceeds to the impartial examination of the dispute and attempts to define the terms of a settlement susceptible of being accepted by them, or of affording the Parties with a view to its settlement, such aid as they may have requested.[3]

Conciliation seeks not only to undertake objective investigation but also to provide a solution susceptible of being accepted by parties in dispute. Like inquiry, conciliation is carried out by a commission which is composed of independent and impartial individuals. A conciliation commission issues a final report in the form of non-binding recommendations to the parties in dispute. First, this chapter examines inquiry, focusing on specific examples in section 2. It then discusses the issues of conciliation in section 3. Finally conclusions are presented in section 4.

2 INQUIRY

2.1 Functions of Inquiry

Inquiry was for the first time provided in the 1899 Hague Convention for the Pacific Settlement of International Disputes (hereafter the 1899 Hague Convention) after the *Maine* incident of 15 February 1898. This disaster involved a destruction of the US battleship *Maine*, which was at anchor in Havana harbour, by an explosion killing 259 of her officers and crew. Although, for the investigation of the incident, two rival commissions of inquiry were held by Spain and the United States, they reached difference conclusions with regard to the facts. After the incident, serious attention was devoted to the issue of fact-finding in the 1899 Hague Conference.[4] The delegates to the Conference eventually agreed to establish an International Commission of Inquiry and procedures for establishing the commission were provided in the 1899 Hague Convention.

As noted, the primary role of inquiry is to facilitate the settlement of international disputes by elucidating issues of facts underlying international disputes.[5] The role of inquiry is increasingly important in the settlement of international disputes involving scientific and technical matters, such as international water disputes.[6] Inquiry can also contribute to the prevention of international disputes. In this respect, UN General Assembly Resolution 1967 (XVIII) of 16 December 1963 acknowledges that:

---

[3] Article 1 of the Regulations on the procedure of International Conciliation, Session de Salzbourg, 1961, available at: www.idi-iil.org/idiF/resolutionsF/1961_salz_02_fr.pdf.
[4] J. G. Merrills, *International Dispute Settlement*, 6th edn (Cambridge University Press, 2017), p. 44.
[5] See Article 9 of the 1899 and 1907 Hague Conventions.
[6] This issue will be discussed in Chapter 10, section 3 of this book.

54 Foundation of International Dispute Settlement

> [A]n important contribution to the peaceful settlement of disputes and to the *prevention of such disputes* could be made by providing for impartial fact-finding within the framework of international organisations and in bilateral and multinational conventions.[7]

The independence and impartiality of an inquiry commission are a prerequisite to ensure the objectiveness of the assessment.[8] The requirements of independence and impartiality are explicitly provided in Article 1(1) of the 1997 Permanent Court of Arbitration Optional Rules for Fact-Finding Commission of Inquiry (PCA Optional Rules):

> These Rules shall apply when the parties have agreed to have recourse to a Fact-finding Commission of Inquiry ('Commission') pursuant to the Permanent Court of Arbitration ('PCA') Optional Rules for Fact-finding Commissions of Inquiry, to establish, by means of *an impartial and independent* investigation, facts with respect to which there is a difference of opinion between them.[9]

Another important condition for inquiry is cooperation of the parties in dispute. In this regard, Article 9(1) of the PCA Optional Rules for Fact-Finding obliges the parties to 'cooperate with the Commission in good faith' and to 'comply with requests by the Commission to submit written materials, provide evidence and attend meetings'. Article 9(2) further requires the parties to 'undertake to make use of all means at their disposal to insure the appearance of witnesses and experts before the Commission'.

2.2 Institution of Inquiry

Inquiry may be set in motion by mutual consent of the parties to a dispute in an ad hoc manner. In this case, the composition of a commission of inquiry is to be determined by the parties to a dispute also in an ad hoc manner. Some treaties, such as the Bryan treaties, provide for the establishment of a permanent commission of inquiry whose jurisdiction is to be accepted in advance by the States Parties to the treaty in question. In this case, inquiry may be initiated in accordance with the terms of an applicable treaty establishing inquiry as a means of handling this category of dispute. The jurisdiction of such an inquiry commission may be invoked without further agreement between the parties in dispute, or may be subject to a special agreement between the disputing parties.[10] An inquiry commission may also be instituted by international institutions, such as the United Nations and the Council of the International Civil Aviation Organisation (ICAO).[11]

---

[7] Emphasis added. UN General Assembly Resolution, 1967(XVIII). *Question of Methods of Fact-Finding*, A/RES/18/1967, para. 5 of the Preamble.

[8] In the case of frontier disputes, however, there are bilateral treaties providing that an inquiry is to be carried out directly between the local frontier officials of the State Parties to such a dispute, without involving a third party. United Nations, *Handbook on the Peaceful Settlement of Disputes between States* (New York: United Nations, 1992), p. 29, paras. 88–9.

[9] Emphasis added. See also Article 5. Text in: C. J. Tams and A. Tzanakopoulos (eds.), *The Settlement of International Disputes: Basic Documents (hereafter Basic Documents)* (Oxford: Hart Publishing, 2012), p. 87.

[10] *Ibid.*, pp. 27–8, para. 84.   [11] See section 2.4 of this chapter.

While normally an inquiry is carried out by a commission or a panel composed of a group of people, it may also be undertaken by one person alone. For instance, the UN Secretary-General may appoint a special representative or a mission to carry out an inquiry in a certain situation or events. It is generally understood that the individuals to be appointed to a commission of inquiry should be specialists in the matters likely to come up in the investigation in question.[12]

Usually commissions for inquiry enjoy a certain degree of freedom in settling the rules of procedure. For example, the Exchange of Notes Constituting an Agreement in the *Red Crusader* case of 1961 provided that: 'The Commission shall, subject to the provisions of the Agreement, determine its own procedure and all questions affecting the conduct of the investigation.'[13] If the parties agree, the provisions of the 1907 Hague Convention may be made applicable to the commission concerning all points not specifically covered by the agreement on the setting up of the inquiry commission.[14] The *Tavignano* inquiry of 1913 was a case in point.[15]

The proceedings of the fact-finding are confidential. Under Article 10 of the Optional Rules:

> Unless the parties agree otherwise, or unless disclosure is required by the law applicable to a party, the members of the Commission and the parties shall keep confidential all matters relating to the fact-finding proceedings, including the investigations, hearings, deliberations and findings of the Commission. Unless the parties agree otherwise, the Commission shall meet *in camera*.

The seat of inquiry is to be selected by agreement between the parties in dispute. For instance, an inquiry commission into the *Dogger Bank* incident between Great Britain and Russia sat at Paris, the capital city of a third State.[16] In some cases, the seat of inquiry is left open and the inquiry commission is to determine the country wherein it would sit, taking account of the greater facilities for the investigation.[17] Concerning financial arrangements, usually equal sharing of the expenses is the rule. For example, the 1907 Hague Convention stipulates that each party pays its own expenses and an equal share of the expenses incurred by the commission.[18] This is echoed by Article 16(2) of the PCA Optional Rules for Fact-Finding.

---

[12] United Nations, *Handbook*, pp. 31–2, para. 97.
[13] Exchange of notes constituting an agreement establishing a Commission of Enquiry to investigate certain incidents affecting the British trawler *Red Crusader*. London, 15 November 1961, subpara. c (i). Text in 420 UNTS, p. 67.
[14] The electronic text of the 1907 Hague Convention is available at: http://avalon.law.yale.edu/20th_century/pacific.asp. Entered into force 26 January 1910.
[15] Article 8 of the Agreement for Inquiry. The *Tavignano, Camouna an Gaulois* Cases, in J. B. Scott (ed.), *The Hague Court Reports Comprising the Awards, Accompanied by Syllabi, the Agreements for Arbitration, and Other Documents in Each Case submitted to the Permanent Court of Arbitration and to Commissions of Inquiry under the Provisions of the Convention of 1899 and 1907 for the Pacific Settlement of International Disputes* (hereafter *The Hague Court Reports*) (New York: Oxford University Press, 1916), pp. 418–19. A similar provision can be seen in the 1921 Agreement for Inquiry in the *Tubantia* case. Article 8. Scott, *The Hague Court Reports* (1932 edn), pp. 144–5.
[16] Article V of the Agreement of submission in the *Dogger Bank* Incident between Great Britain and Russia. The text was reproduced in Tams and Tzanakopoulos, *Basic Documents*, p. 92.
[17] United Nations, *Handbook*, p. 31, para. 93. See also Article 11 of the 1907 Hague Convention.
[18] Article 36. See also United Nations, *Handbook*, p. 32, para. 98.

As noted, the outcome of an inquiry is a non-binding report. However, it is possible that, as in the *Tiger* case of 1917, parties to the dispute agree in advance to accept the report of the commission as binding.[19]

2.3 Case Study (1): Inquiry by Inquiry Commissions

2.3.1 The *Dogger Bank* Inquiry (1904)

On the basis of the above consideration, this section examines some examples of inquiry. The first instance to be discussed is the *Dogger Bank* incident of 1904.[20] This incident took place during the Russo-Japanese War. During the night of 21-22 October 1904, the Russian Baltic Fleet, commanded by Admiral Rojdestvensky and bound for Pacific, encountered some thirty British trawlers fishing in the Dogger Bank in the North Sea. Admiral Rojdestvensky suspected that the fleet was being attacked by Japanese torpedo boats and, thus, fired upon a flotilla of British fishing vessels. Two fishermen were killed and others were injured; one of the trawlers sank and five others were damaged.

While Great Britain demanded from Russia an official apology, Russia claimed that the action had been provoked by Japanese torpedo boats and that the commander of the fleet could not be punished. Prompted by the good offices offered by France, the parties agreed to establish an International Commission of Inquiry sitting in Paris which was composed of five senior naval offices from each of the two parties, France, the United States and Austria-Hungary. The commission was charged with fact-finding in accordance with Articles 9-36 of the 1899 Hague Convention. Specifically the tasks of the commission were:

- to elucidate by means of an impartial and conscientious investigation the question of fact connected with the incident which occurred during the night of 21/22 October 1904, in the North Sea
- to determine where the responsibility lay and the degree of blame attaching to the subjects of the two High Contracting Parties or to the subjects of other countries in the event of their responsibility being established by the inquiry.

The majority of the commissioners considered that there were no Japanese torpedo boats either among the trawlers or anywhere near and that the opening fire by the Russian fleet could not be justified.[21] The majority of the commissioners also expressed the opinion that the responsibility for this action and the results of the opening fire were to be attributed to Admiral Rojdestvensky.[22] At the same time, the commissioners declared that their findings were not of a nature to cast any discredit upon the military qualities or the humanity of Admiral Rojdestvensky, or of the personnel of his squadron.[23] In light of this finding,

---

[19] See section 2.3.2 of this chapter. See also Chapter 8, section 5.2 of this book.
[20] For the text of the Agreement of Submission and the Report of the Commission, see (1908) 2 *AJIL*, pp. 929 *et seq.* For the *Dogger Bank* incident, see T. H. Irmscher, 'Dogger Bank Incident (1904)' in *Max Planck Encyclopaedia*; R. D. N. Lebow, 'Accidents and Crises: The Dogger Bank Affair' (1978) 31 *Naval War College Review*, pp. 66-75.
[21] (1908) 2 *AJIL*, p. 935.   [22] *Ibid.*, p. 934.   [23] *Ibid.*, p. 936.

Great Britain ceased insisting upon the punishment of Rojestvensky, and Russia paid £65,000 in compensation to the victims of the incident and the families of the dead men.

The *Dogger Bank* incident exemplified the value of international inquiry commissions as instruments of dispute settlement. It also demonstrated that inquiry can be employed in cases in which 'honour' and 'essential interests' were involved. Yet, it cannot pass unnoticed that the commission had to spend precious time deciding upon its rules of procedure. In response, the 1907 Hague Convention further elaborated skeletal provisions of the 1899 Convention (Articles 9–14) to included more detailed procedural provisions (Articles 9–36). The new procedure on inquiry was used in the *Tavignano* case (1912), the *Tiger* case (1918) and the *Tubania* case (1922), which will be examined below.

2.3.2 Inquiry Under the 1907 Hague Convention

Under the 1907 Hague Convention, three inquiries were carried out. The first instance related to the *Tavignano, Camouna* and *Gaulois* cases (hereafter the *Tavignano* case).[24] This involved a series of incidents off the Tunisian coast during the Turco-Italian war of 1911–12. On 25 January 1912, the French mail steamer *Tavignano* was seized by the Italian torpedo boat *Fulmine* off the coast of Tunis and conducted to Tripoli under suspicion of having on board contraband of war. The suspicion proved to be unwarranted and the vessel was released on the following day. On the same date, the two Tunisian mahones (flat-bottomed sailing vessels formerly used by the Turks), *Camouna* and *Gaulois*, were fired upon by the Italian torpedo boat *Canopo* in the same waters.

The French Government claimed indemnities for these acts from the Italian Government on the ground that the three vessels (i.e. the *Tavignano, Camouna* and *Gaulois*) were in Tunisian territorial waters when challenged by the Italian warships, and that these vessels were not subject to either attack or capture under international law. However, the Italian Government claimed that since the acts complained took place on the high seas, no rule of international law had been violated. A crucial issue thus arose with regard to the location of the incident. In accordance with the 1907 Hague Convention, France and Italy agreed to submit the case to an International Commission of Inquiry, composed of three naval officers.[25]

In its report unanimously adopted on 23 July 1912, the commission concluded that: 'The evidence and documents presented are not of a nature to permit of determination of the exact geographical points where occurred the various acts which have been submitted to inquiry, but simply of the zones in which they occurred, it being impossible to decide upon an exact point in the zones.'[26] Concerning the pursuit of the mahones, the commission determined three points specified in latitudes and longitudes, which were the centres of inexact circles each of a half-mile radius. With regard to the location where the *Tavignano* was stopped, however, the commission merely identified the area of a rectilinear quadrilateral set off by four apexes, specified in latitudes and longitudes.[27]

---

[24] Scott, *The Hague Court Reports* (1916), pp. 413 *et seq.* For a closer analysis of this case, see Nissim Bar-Yaacov, *The Handling of International Disputes by Means of Inquiry* (Oxford University Press, 1972), pp. 142 *et seq.* See also Merrills, *International Dispute Settlement*, pp. 46–9.
[25] Agreements signed 15 April and 20 May 1912. Reproduced in Scott, *The Hague Court Reports* (1916), p. 417.
[26] *Ibid.*, p. 414.   [27] *Ibid.*

It made no reference to territorial waters in the whole report. The crucial question thus remained undecided.[28]

Following the report, the French Government claimed that the Italian Government must express its regrets concerning the *Tavignano* and must pay small reparation for the mahones but in vain. On 8 November 1912, the two governments thus signed a *compromis* of arbitration to deal with the case. Under Article 2 of the *compromis*, in everything concerning the questions of fact raised by the two incidents, the Arbitral Tribunal was to make use of the report presented by the commission. Before the case could be heard, however, the case was settled out of court when the Italian Government agreed to pay the sum of 5,000 francs for this purpose.[29]

The second instance under the 1907 Hague Convention was the *Tiger* case of 1917.[30] This case related to an incident which took place off the northern coast of Spain during World War I. On 7 May 1917, a German submarine pursued and sank the Norwegian vessel, the *Tiger*, on the grounds that it was carrying contraband of war destined for Germany's enemies. Spain and Norway were neutral in the war. Whereas Spain claimed that the incident took place in its territorial waters, Germany maintained that it had taken place on the high seas. As in the *Tavignano* incident, the crucial question concerned the location of the incident. After a series of diplomatic exchanges, Spain and Germany agreed to submit the dispute to a Commission of Inquiry under the 1907 Hague Convention. The commission was composed of three naval officers and its task was to answer the question as to whether the *Tiger* was pursued and sunk by a German submarine within or outside the zone of 3 miles from the Spanish coast. After having six meetings between 1 and 8 November 1919, the commission concluded that the *Tiger* was pursued and arrested by a German submarine within the zone of 3 sea-miles off the Spanish coast, whereas the vessel was sunk outside that zone.[31] Spain and Germany accepted the binding effect of the commission's report.[32] Thus the *Tiger* inquiry has proved the possibility of a definitive settlement of a dispute by means of inquiry.[33]

The third instance of inquiry was the 1922 *Tubantia* case between Germany and the Netherlands. This case also related to the sinking of a neutral merchant vessel by a German submarine during World War I.[34] On 16 March 1916, the Dutch steamer *Tubantia* was sunk by a torpedo a few hours out from Amsterdam. The torpedo was identified as German, belonging to U-boat 13. The Netherlands claimed that the submarine was responsible for the loss of the steamer, while Germany maintained that the torpedo had been launched at a British vessel ten days earlier. After prolonged negotiations, in September 1916, the two governments agreed to submit the case to an International Commission of Inquiry in accordance with Chapter III of the 1907 Hague Convention and, on 30 March 1921, an Agreement for Inquiry was signed by the two governments in Berlin.

---

[28] Bar-Yaacov, *The Handling of International Disputes*, p. 151.   [29] *Ibid.*, pp. 151–2.
[30] Concerning this case in some detail, see *ibid.*, pp. 156–70.   [31] *Ibid.*, p. 167.
[32] *Ibid.*, pp. 160, 167–8.   [33] *Ibid.*, p. 167.
[34] Concerning this case, see *ibid.*, pp. 171–9; Scott, *The Hague Court Reports* (1932), pp. 135 *et seq.*

The task of the International Commission of Inquiry was to ascertain the cause of the sinking of the Dutch steamer *Tubantia* on 16 March 1916.[35] The commission was composed of five members, consisting of naval officers from Denmark, Sweden, the Netherlands and Germany.[36] Unlike the *Tavignano* and *Tiger* Commissions, this commission also included a Swiss jurist to act as as president. Notably, the proceedings of the *Tubanita* inquiry have many features in common with judicial proceedings, such as the exchange of memorials and counter-memorials before the sitting of the Commission and the cross-examination of witnesses.[37] After weighing all the evidence, on 27 February 1922, the report of the commission concluded that the *Tubantia* had been sunk by the explosion of a torpedo launched by a German submarine. However, the question of determining whether the torpedoing took place knowingly or as the result of an error of the commander of the submarine remained in suspense. It had not been possible to determine whether the loss of the *Tubantia* was due to it having struck a spent torpedo that had remained floating on the surface of the water.[38] Germany accepted the conclusions of the report and paid an indemnity in the amount of 6.5 million Dutch florins.[39] Thus the *Tubanita* inquiry definitively settled the dispute.

2.3.3 The *Red Crusader* Incident (1961)

The 1961 *Red Crusader* case between the United Kingdom and Denmark is a leading case of inquiry after World War II.[40] The *Red Crusader* incident took place in the waters off the Faroe Islands. These waters were a traditional fishing area for British trawlers. Although originally fishing limits around the Faroes were 3 miles measured from straight baselines,[41] the Faroes unilaterally proclaimed a 12-mile limit in 1958. In the face of British objections, however, a 6-plus-6-mile solution was formulated. In accordance with the Exchange of Notes Constituting Agreement between Denmark and the United Kingdom of 27 April 1959,[42] an inner belt of 6 miles off the islands was reserved for local fishermen, while British trawlers were allowed to fish in the outer 6-mile belt except for certain areas in defined periods. The limit of inner 6 miles was referred to as the 'blue line'.

On 29 May 1961, the Danish fisheries protection vessel, the *Niels Ebbesen*, encountered the British trawler *Red Crusader* close to the Faroe Islands, and the Danish commander ordered it to stop, accusing the trawler of illegal fishing inside the exclusive Danish fishery zone (FZ). Nonetheless, the British trawler ignored signals to stop given by searchlight and siren until a blank 40 mm shell was fired across her bow. The Danish authorities then put an officer and sailor on board the *Red Crusader* and ordered her to follow the *Niels Ebbesen* in

---

[35] Article 1 of the Agreement for Inquiry.   [36] Article 2 of the Agreement for Inquiry.
[37] Bar-Yaacov, *The Handling of International Disputes*, pp. 178–9.
[38] Scott, *The Hague Court Reports* (1932), p. 143.
[39] Bar-Yaacov, *The Handling of International Disputes*, p. 177.
[40] *The Red Crusader*, Commission of Inquiry (Denmark v. United Kingdom), 23 March 1962 (1967) 35 *ILR*, pp. 485 et seq. For an outline and commentary of the incident, see J. Polakiewicz, 'Red Crusader Incident' in R. Bernhardt (ed.), *Encyclopaedia of International Law*, Vol. IV (Amsterdam: North-Holland, 2000), p. 63; X. H. Oyarce, 'Red Crusader Incident (1961)' in *Max Planck Encyclopaedia*.
[41] Exchange of Notes Constituting an Agreement Modifying the Convention of 24 June 1901 between Denmark and the United Kingdom of Great Britain and Northern Ireland for regulating the Fisheries of their Respective Subjects Outside Territorial Waters in the Ocean Surrounding the Faroe Islands, 22 April 1955, 213 *UNTS*, p. 318.
[42] The Exchange of Notes (with Annexed Map) Constituting an Agreement Replacing the Above-Mentioned Agreement of 22 April 1955, 27 April 1959, 337 UNTS, p. 416.

order to have the matter examined and tried by a Faroese court. While underway, however, the *Red Crusader* suddenly changed course and tried to escape. The boarding guards were secluded. The *Niels Ebbesen* took up pursuit, and, after firing several warning shots without result, the frigate opened fire with solid shot. The *Red Crusader* suffered damage to its prow, the radar scanner, mast and lights, but escaped and reached the high seas. Between the Faroes and the Orkneys, the two ships met two British naval vessels. One of them interposed itself between the *Red Crusader* and the *Niels Ebbesen*, thereby, despite Danish protests, permitting the *Red Crusader* to escape and return to Aberdeen.

By virtue of an Exchange of Notes of 15 November 1961, a Commission of Inquiry was established in order to investigate certain incidents relating to this arrest and to subsequent events. The commission was constituted on 21 November 1961 at The Hague with neutral members only – namely Professor Charles de Visscher as president and Professor André Gros and Captain C. Moolenburgh as members. The commission was requested to investigate and report to the two governments: (1) the facts leading up to the arrest of the *Red Crusader*, (2) events between the arrest of the *Red Crusader* and the meeting with the British naval vessels and (3) facts and incidents from that moment up to the arrival of the *Red Crusader* in Aberdeen. On 23 March 1962, the commission rendered its report.

With respect to the first issue, the commission found that no proof of fishing inside the blue line has been be established, in spite of the fact that the *Red Crusader* was inside the inner 6-mile belt from about 21.00 hours until 21.14 hours on 29 May 1961 with her gear not stowed.[43]

Concerning the second issue, the commission stated that the firing of solid gun-shots exceeded legitimate use of armed force on two counts: (a) firing without warning of solid gun-shot; (b) creating danger to human life on board the *Red Crusader* without proved necessity. The escape of the *Red Crusader* was considered to be in flagrant violation of the order received and obeyed. However, this and the seclusion of the boarding party could not justify the violent Danish response.[44]

Finally, as for the third issue, the commission considered that British naval vessels made every effort to avoid any recourse to violence.[45] Denmark withdrew part of its charges during the proceedings. Both governments accepted the findings of the commission as final and withdrew their respective claims.

2.3.4 The *Letelier and Moffitt* Inquiry (1991)

The *Letelier and Moffitt* case was the only inquiry by a commission established by one of the Bryan treaties.[46] On 21 September 1976, Mr Orlando Letelier, a former Foreign Minister of Chile, was killed in Washington DC when a bomb which had been planted

---

[43] *The Red Crusader*, p. 495.   [44] *Ibid.*, p. 499.
[45] *Ibid.*, p. 500.
[46] *Letelier and Moffitt*, Chile-United States of America International Commission (1992) 88 *ILR*, pp. 727 et seq. For a commentary of this case, see H. D. Collums, 'The Letelier Case: Foreign Sovereign Liability for Acts of Political Assassination' (1980–1) 21 *Virginia Journal of International Law*, pp. 251–68; E. H. Singer, 'Terrorism, Extradition, and FSIA Relief: the Letelier Case' (1986) 19 *Vanderbilt Journal of Transnational Law*, pp. 57–82; S. Schmahl, 'Letelier and Moffitt Claim' in *Max Planck Encyclopaedia*; J. Merrills, *International Dispute Settlement*, 6th edn (Cambridge University Press, 2017), pp. 54–6.

in his car exploded. The explosion also killed an American lady, Mrs Ronni Moffitt, and seriously injured her husband, Mr Michael Moffitt, both of whom had been travelling in the car with Mr Letelier. Thus Mr Moffitt, Mr Letelier's estate and various relatives of the two persons killed brought an action for damages against the Republic of Chile in the United States District Court, District of Columbia, alleging that the Republic of Chile had been responsible for the two killings. In 1980, the District Court denied sovereign immunity of Chile and subsequently gave judgment in default against Chile, awarding the plaintiffs approximately US$5 million. Yet, this judgment was not satisfied. Further, an attempt to obtain execution against the assets of the Chilean national airline was rejected by the United States Court of Appeals.

In 1988, the US Government made an international claim against the Government of Chile concerning the killing of Mr Letelier and Mrs Moffitt and the injuries to Mr Moffitt, subsequently invoking the 1914 Bryan–Suarez Mujica Treaty. Although the Government of Chile denied responsibility for the incident, it expressed its willingness to make an *ex gratia* payment to the US Government to be received on behalf of the families of the victims. On 11 June 1990, the two States concluded an agreement under which Chile agreed to make an *ex gratia* payment. The amount of this payment was to be determined by the commission established under the 1914 Treaty, and this was to be the sole question decided by the commission.[47] Thus, the five-member commission was established pursuant to the *compromis* appended to the Agreement. The members were: Judge Aguilar Mawdsley of the ICJ, from Guyana, as president; Sir John Freeland, the British member of the European Court of Human Rights; Professor Francisco Orrego Vicuña, a distinguished Latin American lawyer; and a national from each of the parties.[48] In accordance with the *compromis*, the commission was to determine the amount of the payment to be made by the Government of Chile 'in accordance with applicable principles of international law, as though liability were established'.[49] On 11 January 1991, the commission unanimously determined that Chile should pay to the United States a total of US$2,611,892.[50] The parties had already undertaken to treat the commission's decision as binding and within a month of the ruling, Chile agreed to pay the total sum warded.

2.3.5 Summary

Two comments can be made on the basis of the above survey. First, the *Tubantia* and *Red Crusader* Commissions and the *Letelier and Moffitt* Commission were close to arbitration. Indeed, a majority of the *Red Crusader* Commission were jurists as were all the members of the *Letelier and Moffitt* Commission. Furthermore, the report of the *Red Crusader* Commission went beyond its prescribed fact-finding mission and passed a judgment on the validity of the behaviour of the parties involved. In particular, the findings of the commission that the subsequent firing 'exceeded legitimate use of armed force' were clearly a legal ruling. It can be said that overall the findings of the commission were an

---

[47] *Letelier and Moffitt*, pp. 727–8.   [48] *Ibid.*, p. 731.
[49] Article 4 of the *Compromis, ibid.*   [50] *Ibid.*, p. 737, para. 43.

62 Foundation of International Dispute Settlement

essentially judicial operation.[51] Likewise the *Letelier and Moffitt* Commission examined the question by applying principles of international law, and the decision of the commission included several important legal rulings, such as the application of the *dictum* of the *Chorzow Factory* case. In addition, the Separate Opinion of Professor Orrego Vicuña explicitly demonstrated that numerous legal questions were in issue in the decision. All in all, the precedents appear to suggest that inquiry may be close to arbitration, beyond its fact-finding task.

Second, there is no guarantee that the outcome of an inquiry will be smoothly accepted and a final solution agreed expeditiously between the disputing parties. In the *Red Crusader* incident, for instance, it took almost a year to agree upon a settlement after the proceedings of the inquiry were completed. In this regard, it is difficult to disagree with Merrills, stating that: '[A] binding arbitration award, specifying damages or some other remedy, might have provided a more expeditious solution.'[52] Hence there is a reasonable concern that dispute settlements may be delayed because further negotiations may be required in order to find a solution on the basis of the report of the inquiry commission.

2.4 Case Study (2): Inquiry under the Auspices of International Organisations

2.4.1 Inquiry into KE007 Incident

Inquiry is positively reappraised and utilised by international organisations. An illustrative example may be the KE007 inquiry conducted by the ICAO.[53] The KE007 incident involved the shooting down of a South Korean jumbo jet over Soviet territory. On 31 August 1983, a Korean Airline Boeing 747, designated KE007, departed from John F. Kennedy International Airport, New York, United States, on a one-stop scheduled flight for Kimpo International Airport, Seoul, in the Republic of Korea. The en-route stop occurred at Anchorage International Airport, Alaska, United States. On departing Anchorage, the flight had 269 persons on board including 240 passengers. Soon after its departure from Anchorage, KE007 began deviating to the right (north) of its assigned direct route to Bethel. This deviation resulted in its 500-km penetration into sovereign USSR airspace overlying portions of the Kamchatka Peninsula and Sakhalin Island and their surrounding territorial waters. At about 18.20 hours when it was in the vicinity of Sakhalin Island, USSR, the flight was intercepted by military aircraft operated by the USSR. At 18.27 hours, the aircraft was hit by at least one of two air-to-air missiles fired from one of the USSR interceptor aircraft. As a direct result of the missile attack, KE007 crashed and sank into the Sea of Japan south-west of Sakhalin Island. There were no survivors.[54]

In 1983, the Council of the ICAO set up an inquiry by its Secretary-General into the destruction of Korean Airlines Boeing 747. Whereas the Soviet Union did not cooperate with the investigation, the Commission of Inquiry revealed sixteen points.[55] In particular, it found that the USSR authorities assumed that KE007 was an 'intelligence' aircraft

---

[51] Merrills, *International Dispute Settlement*, p. 52.   [52] *Ibid.*, p. 53.
[53] (1984) 23 *ILM*, pp. 864 *et seq.*   [54] *Ibid.*, p. 865.
[55] *Ibid.*, pp. 908–9.

and they did not make exhaustive efforts to identify the aircraft through in-flight visual observation.[56]

Subsequently, in May 1984, the ICAO Assembly adopted an amendment to the Chicago Convention on Use of Weapons against Civil Aircraft. Newly inserted Article 3*bis*(a) of the Chicago Convention provides that:

> The Contracting States recognise that every State must refrain from resorting to the use of weapons against civil aircraft in flight and that, in case of interception, the lives of persons on board and the safety of aircraft must not be endangered.[57]

Following the emergence of new evidence, the investigation was resumed in December 1992. In June 1993, the ICAO released a report on the completion of the fact-finding investigation into the shooting down of a Korean Airline Boeing 747 on 31 August 1983. The report concluded that the tract deviation of KE007 was due to the crew's failure.[58]

2.4.2 Inquiries Into the *Mavi Marmara* Incident

Another example is provided by the *Mavi Marmara* incident in May 2010.[59] The *Mavi Marmara* was a vessel flying the flag of Comoros and carried activists as well as a cargo of humanitarian supplies. Its aim was to deliver aid to Gaza and to breach Israel's naval blockade of Gaza.[60] On 31 May 2010, Israeli zodiac boats made a first attempt to board the *Mavi Marmara*, which was still on the high seas, from the sea shortly before 04.30 hours but in vain. Just minutes after the unsuccessful attempt to board, the Israeli forces landed soldiers on the *Mavi Marmara* from three helicopters. Israeli soldiers fired live ammunition at passengers, resulting in nine civilian deaths (Turkish citizens) and a large number of injuries.[61] On 31 May 2010, the *Mavi Marmara* was captured and diverted to the Israeli port of Ashodod where those aboard were detained.[62] This incident caused tension between Turkey and Israel.

On 2 August 2010, the UN Secretary-General established a Panel of Inquiry in respect of this incident. Its report concluded that Israel's naval blockade was legal but the loss of life and injuries resulting from the use of force by Israeli forces was unacceptable.[63] At the same

---

[56] *Ibid.*, p. 909.
[57] The Convention on International Civil Aviation. Signed in 1944. Entered into force 4 April 1947. English text in: 15 *UNTS*, p. 296. The electronic text is available at: www.icao.int/publications/Documents/7300_cons.pdf.
[58] *ICAO News Release*, PIO 8/93.
[59] Related to this, the *Dignity* incident of 30 December 2008 may also be noted. The *Dignity*, carrying medical volunteers and supplies, was forcefully interdicted by an Israeli patrol boast 90 miles off Gaza. E. Papastavridis, *The Interception of Vessels on the High Seas: Contemporary Challenges to the Legal Order of the Oceans* (Oxford: Hart Publishing 2013), p. 94.
[60] UN Security Council S/PV.6325, 31 May 2010, p. 2. On 3 January 2009, Israel declared a naval blockade on the coast of the Gaza Strip. Human Rights Council, Report of the International fact-Finding Mission to Investigate Violations of International Law, Including International Humanitarian and Human Rights Law, Resulting from the Israeli Attacks on the Flotilla of Ships Carrying Humanitarian Assistance, 27 September 2010, A/HRC/15/21, pp. 8–9, para. 34.
[61] *Ibid.*, pp. 29–30. One victim possessed dual nationality of Turkey and the United States.
[62] For the facts of the *Mavi Marmara* incident, *ibid.*, pp. 25–35, paras. 112–61; D. Guilfoyle, 'The Mavi Marmara Incident and Blockade in Armed Conflict' (2011) 81 *BYIL*, pp. 172–5.
[63] *Report of the Secretary-General's Panel of Inquiry on the 31 May 2010 Flotilla Incident*, September 2011, paras. 81 and 134.

64 Foundation of International Dispute Settlement

time, the UN Human Rights Council decided to carry out an investigation on the incident. Unlike the Report of the Secretary-General's Panel of Inquiry, the Report of the Human Rights Council concluded that: 'Principally, the action of the Israel Defence Force in intercepting the *Mavi Marmara* on the high seas in the circumstances and for the reasons given was clearly unlawful.'[64] It also stated that the conduct of the Israel Defence Force toward the flotilla passengers was disproportionate and constituted a 'grave violation of human rights law and international humanitarian law'.[65]

2.4.3 Inquiry Into Malaysia Airlines MH17

A more recent example is provided by the inquiry on the crash of Malaysia Airlines in 2014. On 17 July 2014, the Malaysia Airlines flight NM17 was shot down over Donetsk Oblast, the eastern part of Ukraine where there was an ongoing armed conflict and all 298 occupants lost their lives. On 21 July 2014, the UN Security Council unanimously adopted Resolution 2166 and expressed its support for efforts to establish a full, thorough and independent international investigation into the incident in accordance with international civil aviation guidelines.[66] It also demanded that all military activities, including by armed militia groups, be immediately ceased in the immediate area surrounding the crash site to allow for security and safety of the international investigation and that all States and actors in the region cooperate fully in relation to the international investigation of the incident.[67] The Dutch Safety Board has investigated the causes of the MH17 crash and concluded, in October 2015, that:

> At 13.20:03 hours (15.20:03 CET) a warhead detonated outside and above the left hand side of the cockpit of flight MH17. It was a 9N314 M warhead carried on the 9M38-series of missiles as installed on the Buk surface-to-air missile system.[68]

However, the Board did not answer the question of who was responsible for the crash since to provide that answer is the task of the criminal investigation.[69]

2.4.4 Summary

On the basis of the above cursory survey, two points can be made. First, the cooperation of relevant States is a prerequisite to effectively carry out an inquiry. As in the case of the KE007 incident, an unwillingness of a key party can prevent the establishment of an inquiry commission since the consent of the parties in dispute is required. In such a case, investigation by an international organisation may come into play.

---

[64] A/HRC/15/21, p. 53, para. 262.   [65] *Ibid.*, para. 264.
[66] UN Security Council Resolution, S/RES/2166 (2014) 21 July 2014, para. 3.
[67] *Ibid.*, paras. 7 and 9.
[68] The Dutch Safety Board, *Crash of Malaysia Airlines Flight MH17, Hrabove, Ukraine, 17 July 2014* (The Hague: The Dutch Safety Board, 2015), p. 253.
[69] *Ibid.*, p. 7.

Second, as shown in the *Mavi Marmara* incident, more than one inquiry can be carried out by different bodies at the same time. In this case, there is the risk that they may reach different conclusions. In reality, the two reports on the *Mavi Marmara* incident expressed different views with regard to the legality of the action of the Israel Defence Force.

3 CONCILIATION

3.1 Typology of Conciliation

In broad terms, two types of conciliation can be identified: optional conciliation and compulsory conciliation. The optional conciliation procedure may be set in motion by mutual consent of the States Parties to an international dispute on an ad hoc basis, relying upon a treaty in force between them. By way of example, Article 2(3) of the Permanent Court of Arbitration Optional Conciliation Rules (hereafter PCA Optional Conciliation Rules) lays down that: 'If the other party rejects the invitation, there will be no conciliation proceedings.'[70]

In contrast, the compulsory conciliation procedure is set in motion through an independent compulsory process on the basis of the request of only one party to a dispute. The case in point is the 1969 Vienna Convention on the Law of Treaties. Article 66(b) of the Convention provides that:

> Any one of the parties to a dispute concerning the application or the interpretation of any of the other articles in Part V of the present Convention may set in motion the procedure specified in the Annex to the Convention [Conciliation] by submitting a request to that effect to the Secretary-General of the United Nations.

If the resort to conciliation is compulsory, however, the outcome of the conciliation remains non-binding, unless parties agree otherwise. As will be discussed in Chapter 8, compulsory conciliation is also set out in the United Nations Convention on Law of the Sea (LOSC).[71]

3.2 Function of Conciliation

3.2.1 Dual Function of Conciliation

Conciliation performs a dual function: (i) To investigate and elucidate the issues of facts, and (ii) to facilitate the settlement of disputes by suggesting mutually acceptable solutions to the parties in dispute.[72] The dual function of the conciliation was clearly stated

---

[70] Available at: www.pca-cpa.org/showpage.asp?pag_id=1188. Reproduced in Tams and Tzanakopoulos, *Basic Documents*, p. 104.
[71] See Chapter 8, section 2.3 of this book.   [72] United Nations, *Handbook*, pp. 46–7, paras. 144–5.

in Article 15(1) of the 1949 Revised Geneva General Act for the Pacific Settlement of International Disputes as follows:

> The task of the Conciliation Commission shall be to elucidate the questions in dispute, to collect with that object all necessary information by means of enquiry or otherwise, and to endeavour to bring the parties to an agreement. It may, after the case has been examined, inform the parties of the terms of settlement which seem suitable to it, and lay down the period within which they are to make their decision.

A similar provision can be seen in Article 15 of the 1957 European Convention for the Peaceful Settlement of Disputes, Article 22 of the 1948 Pact of Bogotá and paragraphs 4 and 5 of the 1969 Vienna Convention on the Law of Treaties.

3.2.2 Requirements for Conciliation

Three requirements must be met to secure the effectiveness of conciliation: independence and impartiality of conciliation commission, confidentiality and non-aggravation of the situation.

Independence and impartiality are crucial to secure confidence of the parties in a conciliation commission. In this regard, the United Nations Model Rules for the Conciliation of Disputes between States adopted in 1995 (hereafter the 1995 UN Model Rules) makes clear that: 'The commission, acting *independently* and *impartially*, shall endeavour to assist the parties in reaching an amicable settlement of the dispute.'[73] Under Article 7(1) of the PCA Optional Conciliation Rules, '[t]he conciliator assists the parties in an independent and impartial manner in their attempt to reach an amicable settlement of their dispute.'[74] Article 7(2) of the rules further provides that: 'The conciliator will be guided by principles of objectivity, fairness and justice ... .'

The second requirement is confidentiality. Confidentiality is stressed by the 1995 UN Model Rules, providing in Article 25(1) that:

> The commission's meetings shall be closed. The parties and the members and expert advisers of the commission, the agents and counsel of the parties, and the secretary and the secretariat staff, shall maintain strictly the *confidentiality* of any documents or statements, or any communication concerning the progress of the proceedings unless their disclosure has been approved by both parties in advance.[75]

Confidentiality of conciliation is explicitly provided in some treaties. For instance, Section XII of the 1992 Provisions for a Conference on Security and Cooperation Europe (CSCE) Conciliation Commission holds that: 'Any measures recommended under Section VIII, and any information and comments provided to the Commission by the parties in confidence,

---

[73] Emphasis added. Article 7. A/RES/50/50. Adopted on 11 December 1995. Reproduced in Tams and Tzanakopoulos, *Basic Documents*, p. 98.
[74] Emphasis added.
[75] Emphasis added. See also Article 26(1) of the 1995 UN Model Rules; Article 14 of PCA Optional Conciliation Rules.

will remain confidential unless the parties agree otherwise.'[76] However, the parties may make available to the public all or some of the documents or authorise the publication of all or some of those documents by mutual agreement.[77]

Third, during the process of the conciliation, the parties in dispute are required not to aggravate the situation. In this respect, Article 16 of the 1948 Pact of Bogotá makes clear that: 'Once the request to convoke the Commission [of Investigation and Conciliation] has been received, the controversy between the parties shall immediately be suspended, and the parties shall refrain from any act that might make conciliation more difficult.' This obligation is also echoed by Article 27 of the 1995 UN Model Rules.

3.3 Institutional Aspects of Conciliation

Normally a conciliation commission is composed of three or five members.[78] While the modes of selecting conciliators vary according to treaties, usually each party to a dispute appoints either one of the three conciliators or two of the five conciliators. The third or the fifth conciliator is then appointed by a joint decision of the two parties to the dispute or by a joint decision of either the two or the four conciliators already appointed by the parties.[79] Under the traditional conciliation, composition of a conciliation committee is largely left in the hands of the parties in dispute. Under this system, however, considerable difficulties arise where one of the disputing parties declines to respond to the invitation of the other party to constitute a conciliation commission. The disagreement prevents the completion of the composition of a commission. To avoid such a situation, some treaties permit a third party, such as the UN Secretary-General, to undertake the constitution of the commission.[80] Annex of the 1969 Vienna Convention on the Law of Treaties is an example.[81]

In most of the treaties, the conciliation commission is empowered to determine its own procedure.[82] The Regulation on the Procedure of International Conciliation adopted by *Institut de droit international* further elaborates the procedure by stating in Article 4 that:

> At its first meeting, the Commission will name its secretary and, taking account of such circumstances, among others, as the time which may have been granted to it for the completion of its task, will determine the method for proceeding to the examination of the affair, whether, in particular, the Parties should be invited to present written pleadings, and in what order and with what time-limits such pleadings must be presented, as well as the time and the place where the agents and counsel will, should occasion arise, be heard.

---

[76] Adopted on 15 December 1992. Reproduced in Tams and Tzanakopoulos, *Basic Documents*, p. 131.
[77] Article 26(2) of the 1995 UN Model Rules.
[78] It is also possible to refer a dispute to a sole conciliation. In 1977, for instance, Kenya, Uganda and Tanzania asked the Swiss diplomat, Dr Victor Umbricht, to make proposals for the distribution of the assets of the former East African Community and he made a vital contribution to the settlement of the dispute. Merrills, *International Dispute Settlement*, pp. 68–9. For a detailed examination of this case, see V. Umbricht, 'Principle of International Mediation: The Case of the East African Community' (1984) 187 *RCADI*, pp. 307–89.
[79] United Nations, *Handbook*, p. 49, para. 150.
[80] *Ibid.*, p. 50, para. 153.   [81] Text in: 1155 *UNTS*, p. 331. Entered into force 27 January 1980.
[82] See Article 8 of the UN Model Rules, Article 4 of Annex V of the LOSC. See also, United Nations, *Handbook*, pp. 51–2, paras. 156–8.

An ad hoc commission may meet at the place selected by the parties in dispute or by its chairman as may be agreed. In such cases, the venue of the commission could be the alternate capitals of the parties to the dispute or other places within their territories or in a neutral place in a third State. The Permanent Conciliation Commission may normally use their designated seats, while they are free if appropriate to meet at another place.

Conciliation should be expected to reach its desired result within a reasonable time. Treaties set out various time limits within which a conciliation commission is expected to conclude its work. Whilst a six-month duration was common in earlier multilateral treaties, a twelve-month duration can be seen in recent multilateral treaties due to the influence of the Vienna Convention on the Law of Treaties.[83] The question of termination of conciliation was not addressed by the earlier multilateral treaties. However, the LOSC makes clear this point, by providing in Article 8 of Annex V that:

> The conciliation proceedings are terminated when a settlement has been reached, when the parties have accepted or one party has rejected the recommendations of the report by written notification addressed to the Secretary-General of the United Nations, or when a period of three months has expired from the date of transmission of the report to the parties.

Normally expenses for conciliation shall be divided equally.[84] By way of example, Article 9 of Annex V of the LOSC stipulates that: 'The fees and expenses of the commission shall be borne by the parties to the dispute.'

As noted, the report of the conciliation commission is not binding upon the parties in dispute.[85] However, it is not suggested that the recommendation of a conciliation committee has no normative force. Article 33(3) of the 1949 Revised General Act obliges the parties to undertake to abstain from all measures likely to react prejudicially upon the arrangements proposed by the conciliation commission and, in general, to abstain from any sort of action whatsoever which may aggravate or extend the dispute.[86] Some treaties require the parties to consider recommendations of a conciliation commission in good faith. For instance, Article 11(5) of the 1985 Vienna Convention for the Protection of the Ozone Layer provides that: 'The Commission shall render a final and recommendatory award, which the parties shall consider in good faith.'[87] A similar obligation can be seen in Article 14(6) of the 1992 Framework Convention on Climate Change.[88] The States Parties may accept recommendations of conciliation as binding. For instance, Section XIV of the Provisions for a CSCE Conciliation Commission provides that: 'A participating State may at any time, whether before or after a dispute has been referred to the Commission,

---

[83] United Nations, *Handbook*, p. 52, para. 159. The first sentence of para. 6 of Annex to the Vienna Convention provides that: 'The Commission shall report within twelve months of its constitution.'
[84] United Nations, *Handbook*, p. 53, para. 161.
[85] See LOSC, Article 7(2) of the Annex V; para. 6 of Annex establishing Conciliation, the 1969 Vienna Convention on the Law of Treaties; and Preamble of the Regulations on the Procedure of International Conciliation adopted by the *Institut de droit international*.
[86] English text in: 71 *UNTS*, p. 102. Entered into force 20 September 1950.
[87] English text in: 1513 *UNTS*, p. 324. Entered into force 22 September 1988.
[88] English text in: 1771 *UNTS*, p. 165. Entered into force 21 March 1994. See also Article 21 of the UN Model Rules.

TABLE 3.1 EXAMPLES OF CONCILIATION

Before World War II

The 1929 Chaco Commission, which examined an outbreak of fighting at Fort Vanguardia on the border between Bolivia and Paraguay

The 1931 Germano-Lithuanian Commission, which concerned the expulsion of five Germans from Memel

The 1934 Belgium-Luxembourg Commission, which examined a dispute over contraband traffic

The 1938 Denmark and Lithuania Commission relating to the construction of a railway

After World War II

The 1947 Franco-Siamese Conciliation Commission with regard to frontier dispute

The 1952 Belgian-Danish Commission which was asked to examine the circumstances in which two Danish merchant ships had been evacuated from Antwerp when Belgium was overrun by the Germans in 1940

The 1955 Franco-Swiss Commission which was requested to examine who should pay the cost concerning the internment of Polish soldiers in Switzerland

The 1956 Italo-Swiss Commission which was set up to examine the exemption of Swiss nationals from a special Italian property tax

The 1956 Italo-Greece Commission which examined a dispute concerning the torpedoing of the Greek ship *Roula* by an Italian submarine off the coast of Crete in August 1940

The 1958 Franco-Moroccan Commission which was asked to investigate the French authorities' diversion of an aircraft carrying Ben Bella and four other leaders of the Algerian revolt from Morocco to Tunis

The 1977 East African Community conciliation by Dr Victor Umbricht with regard to the distribution of the assets of the former East African Community

The 1981 Conciliation Commission between Norway and Iceland in the Jan Mayen dispute

The Conciliation between the Democratic Republic of Timor-Leste and the Commonwealth of Australia (pending)

---

declare, either generally or in relation to a particular dispute, that it will accept as binding, on condition of reciprocity, any terms of settlement proposed by the Commission.'

3.4 Limits of Conciliation

Whereas to date more than 200 bilateral treaties addressing conciliation procedures have been concluded, the record of the conciliation is hardly impressive. Before World War II, there were only a few instances where the procedure of conciliation was successfully applied, and they were not, it seemed, serious disputes. The number of conciliations after World War II also remains modest (see Table 3.1).[89] Given that there are more than 200

---

[89] Merrills, *International Dispute Settlement*, pp. 64–74. The list is non-exhaustive.

bilateral treaties and various multilateral instruments with similar provisions concerning conciliation,[90] it may have to be accepted that conciliation has not been as widely used as its promoters expected. Here the question arises why the conciliation procedure failed to become an attractive option for major disputes between States. In approaching this question, there is a need to examine the original nature of conciliation.

A prototype of conciliation can be found in the Covenant of the League of Nations. Under Articles 12(1) and 15(1) of the League Covenant, any dispute likely to lead to a rupture must be submitted to arbitration, judicial settlement and inquiry by the Council. It follows that these disputes are concentrated on the League Council, unless these are submitted to arbitration or judicial settlement. The Council may also refer the dispute to the Assembly pursuant to Article 15(9) of the League Covenant. It was clear that the settlement of international disputes through the Council or the Assembly of the League of Nations would be under the strong influence of great powers. By criticising the highly political nature of the dispute settlement mechanisms, some States, such as Norway and Sweden, campaigned for the establishment of a conciliation commission composed of impartial individuals. The League of Nations thus adopted a resolution recommending Member States to conclude agreements providing for the submission of disputes to impartial conciliation commissions in 1922.[91] The conciliation set out by individual agreements was essentially characterised as a non-political and decentralised means of international dispute settlement. The institution of conciliation showed a sharp contrast to dispute settlement through the global political organ (i.e. the League of Nations). Given that under the League system, legal disputes were to be submitted to judicial settlement,[92] it can be reasonably presumed that conciliation was to be used to settle non-legal or political disputes.

The role of conciliation was clarified in the 1928 Geneva General Act for the Pacific Settlement of International Disputes. Under Article 1, '[d]isputes of every kind between two or more Parties to the present General Act which it has not been possible to settle by diplomacy shall ... be submitted, ... to the procedure of conciliation'. Under Article 20(1), '[n]otwithsanding the provisions of Article 1, disputes of the kind referred to in Article 17 [disputes concerning the parties' rights] arising between parties who have acceded to the obligations contained in the present chapter [judicial settlement] shall only be subject to the procedure of conciliation if the parties so agree'. It can be seen that under the Geneva General Act, disputes concerning the parties' rights or legal disputes were supposed to be settled by judicial settlement, while the conciliation procedure was to apply to the settlement of non-legal disputes.

In summary, the institution of conciliation was developed as a means to settle non-legal disputes which were not submitted to arbitration or judicial settlement. Yet, it is debatable whether conciliation is well-placed to settle non-legal or political disputes. In essence, conciliation aims at the settlement of international disputes by an independent and impartial committee. Given that non-legal disputes often involve politically sensitive issues, it is unlikely that States would leave the settlement of these disputes to a conciliation

---

[90] *Ibid.*, pp. 84–5.
[91] *Ibid.*, p. 59; T. Sogawa, *International Law IV* (in Japanese) (Tokyo: Hoseidaigaku Tsushin Kyoikubu, 1950), pp. 242–4.
[92] See Article 13(2) of the League Covenant.

committee which is composed of independent and impartial individuals. This is particularly true in the settlement of dynamic disputes that demand a change of the status quo. However, a conciliation committee has no authority to change the status quo. Nor does it have any political authority to back up its proposals. Accordingly, non-legal disputes can hardly be settled by independent and impartial individuals who lack any political authority. Here we can find an inherent limitation with conciliation.[93]

However, it is not suggested that conciliation is less important in the peaceful settlement of international disputes. It may not be impossible to submit one aspect of a dynamic dispute to a conciliation commission by 'de-politicising' the dispute. Furthermore, conciliation may be useful in the situation where the parties in dispute desire an equitable compromise, although the dispute in question essentially concerns legal issues. An example is provided by the 1981 Norway and Jan Mayen conciliation concerning the delimitation of the continental shelf between Iceland and Jan Mayen.[94] In this case, the Conciliation Commission examined various issues of international law, such as status of islands, Articles 74 and 83 of the LOSC and the concept of natural prolongation. The commission concluded that it should take into account both the fact that agreement by Iceland and Norway on Iceland's 200-mile economic zone has already given Iceland a considerable area beyond the median line and the fact that the uncertainties with respect to the resources potential of the area create a need for further research and exploration. Thus rather than propose a demarcation line for continental shelf different from the economic zone line, the commission recommended that cooperative arrangements should be established in a joint development agreement covering substantially all of the area offering any significant prospect of hydrocarbon production.[95] This recommendation was accepted by the parties and the joint development scheme was set out in the 1981 Agreement on the Continental Shelf between Iceland and Jan Mayen. It is noteworthy that the Conciliation Commission successfully settled the dispute by proposing flexible solutions, whilst it examined legal issues at the same time. The Iceland–Jan Mayen conciliation seems to demonstrate the value of conciliation which can perform the dual function – namely the examination of legal issues and the recommendation of a flexible solution.

4 CONCLUSIONS

This chapter examined two diplomatic means of international dispute settlement: inquiry and conciliation. The matters considered in this chapter can be summarised in four points.

(i) Normally clarification of a disputed fact constitutes a point of departure in the settlement of international disputes. Thus the objective assessment of the issues of facts by inquiry is useful in the settlement of international disputes, in particular,

---

[93] Sogawa, *International Law*, pp. 255–6; T. Sogawa (S. Oda and Y. Ishimoto eds.), *International Law and Outlawry of War* (in Japanese) (Tokyo: Shinzansha, 2004), pp. 92–100.

[94] (1981) 20 *ILM*, pp. 797–842. See also R. Churchill, 'Maritime Delimitation in the Jan Mayen' (1985) 9 *Marine Policy*, pp. 16–38.

[95] *Jan Mayen* conciliation, pp. 825–6. See also the Preamble of the 1981 Agreement on the Continental Shelf between Iceland and J. I. Charney and L. M. Alexander (eds.), *International Maritime Boundaries*, Vol. II (Dordrecht: Nijhoff, 1993), p. 1762. Article 1 of the Agreement provides that the delimitation line between the Parties' parts of the continental shelf in the area between Iceland and Jan Mayen shall coincide with the delimitation line for the Parties' economic zones.

disputes involving technical and factual issues. Inquiry may be set in motion by mutual consent of the parties to a dispute in an ad hoc manner or on the initiative of an international organisation.

(ii) As demonstrated by the *Red Crusader* Commission as well as the *Letelier and Moffitt* Commission, inquiry may be close to arbitration in practice. Unlike arbitration, however, the report of an inquiry commission is not binding, unless the parties in dispute agree otherwise.

(iii) Conciliation performs a dual function: elucidation of the issues of facts and presentation of mutually acceptable solutions to facilitate the settlement of international disputes. Like inquiry, the independence and impartiality of members of a conciliation commission are essential elements.

(iv) A conciliation commission which consists of independent and impartial individuals has no political authority to implement its proposed solution. Nor does the conciliation commission have the power to change the status quo on the basis of its political authority. Accordingly, dynamic disputes that demand the change of the status quo cannot be effectively settled by conciliation. However, conciliation may have a useful part to play in the situation where a static/legal dispute was raised but the parties in dispute prefer a flexible solution to a legally binding solution.

FURTHER READING

N. Bar-Yaacov, *The Handling of International Disputes by Means of Inquiry* (London: Oxford University Press, 1974).

J.-P. Cot, *International Conciliation* (London: Europa, 1972).

R. Donner, 'The Procedure of International Conciliation: Some Historical Aspects' (1999) 1 *Journal of the History of International Law*, pp. 103–24.

S. M. G. Koopmans, *Diplomatic Dispute Settlement: The Use of Inter-State Conciliation* (The Hague: T. M. C. Asser Press, 2008).

R. M. Mosk, 'The Role of Facts in International Dispute Resolution' (2003) 304 *RCADI*, pp. 9–180.

4

International Dispute Settlement through the United Nations

Main Issues

The role of international institutions is increasingly important in various fields of international relations and this is equally true in the peaceful settlement of international disputes. In particular, the role of the United Nations is crucial owing to its universal membership and its political authority. Here consideration must be given to the role of the Security Council, General Assembly and the Secretary-General in international dispute settlement. The interrelationship between the United Nations and regional international institutions also merits discussion. This chapter will seek to examine the principal issues of international dispute settlement through the United Nations, focusing particularly on the following issues:

(i) What is the procedure for international dispute settlement in the UN Security Council?
(ii) What are the role of and limitation with the UN Security Council in peaceful settlement of international disputes?
(iii) What is the role of the UN General Assembly in international dispute settlement?
(iv) What are the conditions for enhancing the role of the UN Secretary-General in international dispute settlement?
(v) What is the interrelationship between the United Nations and regional international institutions?

1 INTRODUCTION

The United Nations is a global international organisation established in 1945. It is characterised by three principal features: universal membership, independence and permanent nature.[1] As a universal institution, the United Nations can provide a global forum for discussing the settlement of specific disputes. As an independent organisation, the United

---

[1] For an analysis of the drafting history of the UN Charter, see B. Simma *et al.* (eds.), *The Charter of the United Nations: A Commentary* (hereafter *A Commentary*), 3rd edn, Vol. I (Oxford University Press, 2012), pp. 1–23.

Nations can address international disputes as a third party. As a permanent international institution, the United Nations can continuously and consistently address international disputes.[2] Since the United Nations is a political institution,[3] however, its politics – in particular, politics of the permanent members of the Security Council – inevitably affect the commitments of the Organisation in international dispute settlement.

This chapter examines the role of the three organs of the United Nations in peaceful settlement of international disputes: the Security Council (section 2), the General Assembly (section 3) and the UN Secretary-General (section 4).[4] This chapter also discusses the relationship between the United Nations and regional organisations in section 5. Finally conclusions are presented in section 6.

2 THE ROLE OF THE SECURITY COUNCIL IN INTERNATIONAL DISPUTE SETTLEMENT

2.1 Procedure of Dispute Settlement

The procedure for peaceful settlement of international disputes is set out under Chapter VI of the UN Charter. In broad terms, the procedure of the UN Security Council can be divided into three stages: (i) submission of a dispute, (ii) adoption of agenda and discussion and (iii) determination of specific measures.[5]

2.2.1 Step 1: Submission of a Dispute

Dispute settlement procedures under Chapter VI of the UN Charter are set in motion by referring a dispute to the Security Council. International disputes can be referred to the Council by (i) the parties to a dispute or (ii) by other parties (i.e. non-disputing parties).

As for (i), should the parties to a dispute which is likely to endanger the maintenance of international peace and security fail to settle it by peaceful means of dispute settlement, they are obliged to refer a dispute to the Security Council pursuant to Article 37(1) of the UN Charter. The reference under this provision is obligatory. It follows that one of the parties to a dispute can unilaterally refer the dispute to the Security Council, if the other fails to fulfil its reference obligation.[6] Literally Article 37(1) applies only to a dispute in the sense of Article 33(1), not to situations which are likely to endanger the maintenance of international peace and security.[7] Under Article 38 of the UN Charter, all the parties to

---

[2] See Article 28(1) of the UN Charter.
[3] *Reparation for Injuries Suffered in the Service of the United Nations*, Advisory Opinion of 11 April 1949, ICJ Reports 1949, p. 179.
[4] Enforcement action under Chapter VII of the UN Charter falls outside the scope of this chapter since it is distinct from peaceful settlement of international disputes under Chapter VI. The ICJ will be discussed in Chapters 6 and 7 of this book.
[5] T. Sato, *The Law of International Organisations* (in Japanese) (Tokyo: Yuhikaku, 2005), pp. 265 *et seq.*
[6] *A Commentary*, Vol. I, p. 1150. In reality, it is rare that States refer a dispute which is likely to endanger the maintenance of international peace and security to the Security Council. The one and only submission under Article 37(1) of the UN Charter concerned a dispute between Egypt and the United Kingdom which was submitted by Egypt on 8 July 1947. Article 35 of the UN Charter was also mentioned at the same time. *Ibid.*, p. 1152.
[7] *Ibid.*, p. 1149.

any dispute may request that the Security Council make recommendations to the parties with a view to a pacific settlement of the dispute. A non-Member of the United Nations may also bring to the attention of the Security Council or of the General Assembly any dispute to which it is a party if it accepts in advance, for the purposes of the dispute, the obligations of pacific settlement provided in the present Charter by virtue of Article 35(2) of the UN Charter. Such obligations include the obligation of peaceful settlement of international disputes set out in Article 2(3) and Chapter VI and the prohibition of threat or use of force under Article 2(4) of the UN Charter. The initiative of non-Member States on the basis of this provision is limited and, between 1946 and 1980, this provision has been used in only four cases.[8] In addition, the Republic of Korea (South Korea) invoked this provision in the Korean Air Lines Flight KE007 case (1983) and the Korean Air Flight 858 case (1988). After that, disputes and situations were referred to the Security Council by Member States only.[9] Given that few non-Member States of the United Nations are left, this provision seems to be obsolete.[10]

As for (ii), a dispute may also be submitted to the Security Council by a third State, the General Assembly or the Secretary-General. First, under Article 35(1) of the UN Charter, *any Member of the United Nations* may bring any dispute, or any *situation* of the nature which might lead to international friction or give rise to a dispute, to the attention of the Security Council or of the General Assembly. The appeal to the Security Council or the General Assembly under this provision is voluntary.[11] Unlike the General Assembly which meets, as a rule, only in annual sessions, the Security Council is always available. In this regard, the supremacy of the Security Council as addressee of the power of initiative under Article 35 is clear.[12] Article 35(1) is of particular importance because it is the sole legal basis which allows any Member State to address the Security Council or General Assembly immediately.[13] It appears that the concept of 'situation' is broader than that of 'dispute'. It seems to follow that Members of the United Nations may bring less serious disputes than those that endanger the maintenance of international peace and security to the Security Council. In practice, the Member States tend to bring only 'situations' or 'questions' to the attention of the Security Council, avoiding the designation of a matter as a 'dispute'.[14]

Second, the General Assembly is empowered to call the attention of the Security Council to *situations* which are likely to endanger international peace and security under Article 11(3). The concept of situations is broader than that of disputes.

Third, the UN Secretary-General may also bring to the attention of the Security Council any matter which in his opinion may threaten the maintenance of international peace and security in accordance with Article 99. While there is no clear definition of the term 'matter', this term can be regarded as a broad concept comprising both situation and dispute.[15]

---

[8] Siam (1946), Hyderabad (1948), Tunisia (1952) and Kuwait (1961). *Ibid.*, p. 1114. [9] *Ibid.*
[10] R. Kolb, *The International Court of Justice* (Oxford: Hart Publishing, 2013), p. 30.
[11] *A Commentary*, p. 1152. [12] *Ibid.*, pp. 1110–11.
[13] *Ibid.*, p. 1113. Yet it is very rare that Article 35 is cited in submissions to the Security Council. *Ibid.*, p. 1111.
[14] *Ibid.*, p. 1112. [15] Sato, *The Law of International Organisations*, p. 267.

2.2.2 Step 2: Adoption of Agenda and the Examination of a Dispute

Should a dispute, a situation or a matter be referred to the Security Council, the Security Council is to determine whether it should discuss these issues. The decision is a procedural matter and is not subject to veto.

First, should the parties in dispute refer a dispute to the Security Council in accordance with Article 37(1), the Council is to determine, *inter alia*, whether the continuance of the dispute is in fact likely to endanger the maintenance of international peace and security, whether peaceful settlement of disputes has been exhausted, or whether the dispute is essentially within the domestic jurisdiction of any State.[16] A decision of the Security Council in this matter is regarded as a procedural matter. Should a dispute be submitted to the Security Council in accordance with Article 38 or Article 35(2), the Security Council is to examine the existence of the request of all the parties to the dispute or the acceptance of the obligation of the pacific settlement of international disputes.

Second, should a third party refer a dispute to the Security Council pursuant to Articles 35(1), 11(3) and 99 of the UN Charter, the Security Council is to determine whether the continuance of the dispute is likely to endanger the maintenance of international peace and security. It then decides whether the dispute should be a subject of its discussion.

2.2.3 Step 3: Determination of Specific Measures

Where a dispute becomes a subject for discussion, the Security Council is to take the specific measures necessary for dispute settlement. The Security Council resolutions adopted under Chapter VI of the UN Charter are only recommendatory.[17] Even so, in light of their membership status and their duty to cooperate, Member States to whom such recommendations are addressed are obliged to consider them in good faith.[18]

First, should the parties to a dispute refer the dispute to the Security Council and if the Security Council deems that the continuance of the *dispute* is likely to endanger the maintenance of international peace and security, it *shall* decide whether to take action under Article 36 or to recommend such terms of settlement as it may consider appropriate.[19] As shown in the term 'shall', this is mandatory for the Council. Yet the application of Article 37(2) is limited to the dispute, precluding situations. The fact that the same dispute is being dealt with by the UN General Assembly or is pending before the ICJ does not prevent the Security Council from recommending appropriate measures in accordance with Article 37(2).[20] Where the Security Council recommends 'appropriate procedures or methods of adjustment' under Article 36(1), it shall take into consideration any procedures for the settlement of the dispute which have already been adopted by the parties.[21] The Security

---

[16] In contrast to Article 36(1) of the UN Charter, the Security Council is not empowered to intervene in a dispute *ex officio* under Article 37(2). It can exercise its extended recommendatory powers only upon reference by at least one of the parties. *A Commentary*, p. 1154. See also p. 1152.
[17] M. Shaw, *International Law*, 7th edn (Cambridge University Press, 2014), p. 886; Sato, *The Law of International Organisations*, pp. 268-9.
[18] *A Commentary*, p. 1144.   [19] Article 37(2) of the UN Charter.
[20] *A Commentary*, p. 1159.
[21] Article 36(2). The distinction between 'the appropriate procedures or methods of adjustment' (Article 36(1)) and 'terms of settlement' (Article 37(2)) is not always clear in practice. United Nations, *Handbook*, p. 117, para. 328.

Council should also take into consideration that legal disputes should as a general rule be referred to the ICJ under Article 36(3). The Security Council accordingly recommended that the United Kingdom and Albanian Governments should immediately refer the *Corfu Channel* dispute to the ICJ.[22] Furthermore, the UN Security Council invited the parties in the *Aegean Sea Continental Shelf* dispute to continue to take into account the resort to appropriate judicial means – in particular, the ICJ.[23]

If all the parties to any dispute so request, the Security Council *may* make recommendations to the parties with a view to a pacific settlement of the dispute pursuant to Article 38 of the UN Charter. Given that the words 'any dispute' include disputes which do not yet endanger the maintenance of international peace and security, this provision can be said to extend the power of the Security Council.[24] As the word 'may' signifies, however, this is not obligatory for the Security Council. Like those under Articles 36(1) and 37(2) of the UN Charter, recommendations of the Security Council under Article 38 are not legally binding.[25] Even though Article 38 is significant in the sense that it permits the parties to refer a dispute to the Security Council before it has escalated into a danger for international peace and security, to this day, Article 38 has remained a dead letter.[26] In summary, the Security Council is only allowed to recommend the substance of a dispute (i.e. the terms of settlement) either according to Article 37(2) when the parties to the dispute have referred the matter to the Council pursuant to Article 37(1) or at any time when all the parties so request under Article 38 of the UN Charter.[27]

Second, should any dispute or any situation be referred to the Security Council by any Member of the United Nations, the Council shall, 'when it deems necessary', call upon the parties to settle their dispute by pacific means in accordance with Article 33(2) of the UN Charter. The qualification by the words, 'when it deems necessary', seems to signify that the Security Council is vested with discretion to determine whether it should request to the parties to resolve the dispute by pacific means. Such an appeal is not binding upon the parties to a dispute.[28] Furthermore, the Security Council may, 'at any stage of a dispute of the nature referred to in Article 33 or of a situation of like nature', recommend appropriate procedures or methods of adjustment by virtue of Article 36(1). This provision is important since it allows the Security Council to deal with a dispute on its own initiative. Unlike Article 37(2), Article 36(1) does not allow the Security Council to recommend 'such terms of settlement' as it may consider appropriate. Whilst the Security Council often calls for the parties in dispute to resort to various peaceful means, normally the Council does not explicitly refer to specific provisions of the UN Charter.

2.2 Activities of the UN Security Council

While the Security Council's commitments in international dispute settlement vary in specific contexts, in particular, three types of activities merit highlighting: (i) calling for negotiations, (ii) good offices and mediation and (iii) inquiry.

---

[22] UN Security Council, 22 (1947). Resolution of 9 April 1947, S/324.
[23] UN Security Council Resolution 395 (1976) of 25 August 1976, para. 4 of the operative part.
[24] *A Commentary*, p. 1162. Yet Article 38 does not apply to 'situations'. *Ibid.*, p. 1165.
[25] *Ibid.*, p. 1168.   [26] *Ibid.*, p. 1163.   [27] *Ibid.*, p. 1133.   [28] *Ibid.*, pp. 1083–4.

First, the simplest commitment of the Security Council is to call for the parties in dispute to enter into negotiations. The situation in Cyprus is an example. In the Resolution 353 of 20 July 1974, the UN Security Council called upon Greece, Turkey and the United Kingdom to enter into negotiations without delay for the restoration of peace in the area and constitutional government in Cyprus and to keep the Secretary-General informed.[29] In dealing with the Iranian question of 1946, the UN Security Council requested the Soviet Union and Iran to inform the Council of any results achieved in negotiations.[30]

Second, on many occasions, the Security Council set up a special committee to tender good offices. To address the Indonesia question, for instance, the Security Council resolved to tender good offices to the parties in order to assist in the peaceful settlement of disputes concerning hostilities between the armed forces of the Netherlands and Indonesia. In this regard, the Council expressed its readiness, if the parties so requested, to assist in the settlement through a committee of the Council consisting of three members of the Council, each party selecting one, and the third to be designated by the two so elected.[31] The Council then requested the Committee of Good Offices to assist the parties in reaching agreement on an arrangement which would ensure the observance of the ceasefire resolution.[32] Furthermore, in 1958, a good offices mission, constituted by the Security Council as well as the United States and the United Kingdom, assisted towards the settlement of the Tunisian question between France and Tunisia.[33]

The Security Council has also frequently requested that the UN Secretary-General intervene to facilitate negotiations between the parties in dispute. In 1956, for instance, good offices of the UN Secretary-General on behalf of the Security Council were used in the Palestine question to secure compliance with the armistice agreement.[34] In 1982, the Security Council requested the UN Secretary-General to undertake a renewed mission of good offices in the *Falklands/Malvinas* dispute. It also requested the UN Secretary-General to enter into contact immediately with the parties with a view to negotiating mutually acceptable terms for a ceasefire.[35] In the case of the Iran–Iraq War, the Security Council requested that the UN Secretary-General dispatch a team of UN observers to verify, confirm and supervise the ceasefire and withdrawal of all forces. It also required the Secretary-General to explore the question of entrusting an impartial body with inquiring into responsibility for the conflict and to report to the Council.[36] After Iraq's invasion of Kuwait in 1990, the Security Council reposed its trust in the Secretary-General to make available his good offices and to report to the Security Council on the results of good offices and diplomatic efforts.[37] It further requested the Secretary-General, in the context of the continued exercise of his good

---

[29] UN Security Council, Resolution 353 (1974) of 20 July 1974, para. 5 of the operative part.
[30] UN Security Council, 2 (1946). Resolution of 30 January 1946.
[31] UN Security Council, 31 (1947). Resolution of 25 August 1947, S/525, II; United Nations, *Repertoire of the Practice of the Security Council, Supplement 1946–1951* (New York: United Nations, 1954), pp. 317, 415–16.
[32] UN Security Council, 36 (1947). Resolution of 1 November 1947, S/597, paras. 1–2 of the operative part.
[33] United Nations, *Repertoire of the Practice of the Security Council, Supplement 1956–1958* (New York: United Nations, 1959), pp. 137–8.
[34] *Ibid.*, pp. 14–15.
[35] UN Security Council Resolution 505 (1982) of 26 May 1982, paras. 2 and 4 of the operative part.
[36] UN Security Council Resolution 598 (1987) of 20 July 1987, paras. 2 and 6 of the operative part.
[37] UN Security Council, Resolution 674 (1990) of 29 October 1990, paras. 12–13.

offices, to seek, *inter alia*, to ensure food, water and basic services necessary to the protection and well-being of Kuwaiti nationals and to the diplomatic and consular missions in Kuwait and the evacuation of third-State nationals.[38] However, the Secretary-General was essentially relegated to the sidelines because the crisis was acted on by a few States willing to use force under US command in Operation Desert Storm.[39]

Third, under Article 34, the Security Council may investigate any dispute, or any situation which might lead to international friction or give rise to a dispute, in order to determine whether the continuance of the dispute or situation is likely to endanger the maintenance of international peace and security.[40] As the permissive wording of the provision 'may' suggests, the Security Council has discretion on this matter. If a decision to investigate is made under Article 34, the States concerned are obliged to accept and carry out this decision and to permit the entry of an investigative subsidiary organ into their territories since a decision under Article 34 has binding effect in the sense of Article 25 of the UN Charter.[41] The decision in this matter is a non-procedural matter and is subject to veto.[42]

The UN Security Council established a commission of inquiry with an explicit reference to Article 34 of the UN Charter only in two cases. The first case concerned the Greek Frontier Incidents Question. In 1946, the Security Council 'under Article 34 of the Charter' established a Commission of Investigation to ascertain the facts relating to the alleged border violations along the frontier between Greece on the one hand and Albania, Bulgaria and Yugoslavia on the other.[43] The second case related to the India–Pakistan Question concerning the legal status of Kashmir. In 1948, the Security Council Resolution 39 established the United Nations Commission for India and Pakistan which was composed of representatives of three Members of the United Nations. The commission was invested with a dual function to investigate the facts pursuant to Article 34 and to exercise any mediatory influence likely to smooth away difficulties.[44]

In other cases, the Security Council ordered investigations but not explicitly based on Article 34. In 1947, for instance, the Security Council established a fact-finding subcommittee to investigate evidence relating to the *Corfu Channel* incident between the United Kingdom and Albania.[45] In 1979, the UN Security Council established a commission consisting of three members of the Security Council to examine the situation relating to settlements in the Arab territories occupied since 1967, including

---

[38] *Ibid.*, para. 7.
[39] T. M. Franck, 'The Secretary-General's Role in Conflict Resolution: Past, Present and Pure Conjecture' (1995) 6 *EJIL*, p. 372.
[40] The Security Council also possesses implied powers to acquire information by means of investigations for purposes other than those mentioned in Article 34. *A Commentary*, p. 1088.
[41] *Ibid.*, p. 1103. According to *A Commentary*, the legally binding effect of the decision to investigate respecting the States concerned follows from the functional nexus between the competence to investigate under Article 34 and the primary responsibility for the maintenance of international peace and security conferred on the Security Council. *Ibid.*, p. 1104.
[42] *Ibid.*, pp. 1100–1. Veto will be discussed later.
[43] UN Security Council, 15 (1946). Resolution 15 of 19 December 1946, S/339.
[44] UN Security Council, 39 (1948). Resolution of 20 January 1948, S/654. Yet the Security Council failed to bring about a permanent settlement of the dispute. On this issue, see S. Subbiah, 'Security Council Mediation and the Kashmir Dispute: Reflections on Its Failures and Possibilities for Renewal' (2004) 27 *Boston College International and Comparative Law Review*, pp. 173–85.
[45] UN Security Council, 19 (1947). Resolution of 27 February 1947.

80 Foundation of International Dispute Settlement

Jerusalem.[46] In 1981, the Security Council sent a fact-finding mission to the Seychelles to investigate the involvement of mercenaries in an invasion.[47] In 2014, the Security Council stressed the need for a full, thorough and independent international investigation into the downing of a civil aircraft on an international flight, Malaysia Airlines flight MH17 in Donetsk Oblast, Ukraine. It thus called on all States and actors in the region to cooperate fully in relation to the international investigation of the incident.[48]

In addition, the Security Council can request the Secretary-General to collect and analyse relevant information. In the Security Council Resolution 1584 concerning Côte d'Ivoire, for instance, the Security Council requested the Secretary-General to create the Group of Experts to examine and analyse information gathered by the United Nations Operation in Côte d'Ivoire (UNOCI) and the French forces and to gather and analyse all relevant information in that country.[49]

A dispute or situation which leads to an actual 'threat to the peace, breach of the peace, or act of aggression' under Article 39 activates the action of the Security Council under Chapter VII of the UN Charter. Specifically the Security Council may decide measures not involving the use of armed force and it may call upon the Members of the United Nations to apply such measures under Article 41. If the measures provided for in Article 41 would be inadequate or have proved to be inadequate, the Security Council may take military action as may be necessary to maintain or restore international peace and security in accordance with Article 42. Thus the functions of the Security Council in the field of international dispute settlement are complemented by the enforcement power.[50]

2.3 Questions Associated With Veto

Even though the Security Council can perform multiple roles in international dispute settlement, its function is compromised by the right of veto of the permanent members of the Security Council. Under Article 27(1) of the UN Charter, each member of the Security Council shall have one vote. Decisions of the Security Council on procedural matters shall be made by an affirmative vote of nine members pursuant to Article 27(2). Concerning all other questions (i.e. non-procedural matters) an affirmative vote of all permanent members of the Council is required under Article 27(3). The negative vote of a permanent member is called a veto.[51] The abstention of a permanent member is not considered as

---

[46] UN Security Council Resolution 446 (1979) of 22 March 1979, para. 4 of the operative part.
[47] UN Security Council Resolution 496 (1981) of 15 December 1981, para. 3 of the operative part. For other examples, see *A Commentary*, p. 1092.
[48] UN Security Council Resolution 2166 (2014), S/RES/2166 (2014), 21 July 2014, para. 9 of the operative part. See also Chapter 3, section 2.4.2 of this book.
[49] UN Security Council Resolution 1584(2005), 1 February 2005, S/RES/1584(2005), para. 7. This resolution was adopted under Chapter VII of the UN Charter.
[50] J. Merrills, *International Dispute Settlement*, 6th edn (Cambridge University Press, 2017), pp. 236–7.
[51] Veto means in Latin 'I prohibit', 'I oppose'. R. Kolb, *An Introduction to the Law of the United Nations* (Oxford: Hart Publishing, 2010), p. 135. For an analysis of the veto, see D. E. Lee, 'The Genesis of the Veto' (1947) 1 *International Organization*, pp. 33–42; T. Schindlmayr, 'Obstructing the Security Council: The Use of the Veto in the Twentieth Century' (2001) 3 *Journal of the History and International Law*, pp. 218–34; B. Fassbender, 'Veto' in *Max Planck Encyclopaedia*; B. Conforti and C. Focarellui, *The Law and Practice of the United Nations*, 4th edn (Leiden: Nijhoff, 2010), pp. 76–88. For a detailed analysis of Article 27 of the UN Charter, see A. Zimmermann, 'Voting Article 27' in *A Commentary*, pp. 871 *et seq*.

a veto and it does not affect the decision of the Security Council. Veto supposes that a decision could have been adopted if no permanent member had voted against it. Where a decision has not been adopted because it falls short of the required majority, the negative votes of the permanent members are not counted as a veto. It is generally understood that non-procedural matters include:[52]

- admission of any State to membership in the United Nations (Article 4)
- suspension of the rights and privileges of membership (Article 5)
- expulsion from the United Nations (Article 6)
- appointment of the Secretary-General (Article 97)
- amendments to the UN Charter (Article 108)
- recommendations or decisions under Chapters VI, VII and VIII.

A prior decision on whether a matter is procedural or not is considered as a non-procedural matter and is subject to veto. This is called a 'double veto'.[53] The double veto can be regarded as an additional mechanism for safeguarding the veto power.[54]

It is arguable that great powers should be given weighted power, status and responsibility due to their ability. However, there appears to be some scope to reconsider the question whether recommendations under Chapter VI concerning peaceful settlement of international disputes should fall within the scope of non-procedural matters. The San Francisco Declaration explained the wide scope of non-procedural matters on the basis of the theory of 'a chain of events'. This chain of events begins when the Council decides to make an investigation, or determines that the time has come to call upon States to settle their differences, or makes recommendations to the parties. 'After investigation', the Declaration continues, 'the Council must determine whether the continuance of the situation or dispute would be likely to endanger international peace and security. If it so determines, the Council would be under obligation to take further steps.'[55] Yet, there is the risk that a veto of any decisions concerning Chapter VI may paralyse procedures for international dispute settlement by the Security Council.

While enforcement measures under Chapter VII of the UN Charter may require the concurrence of the permanent members of the Security Council due to the primary responsibility of great powers in the maintenance of international peace and security, some doubts could be expressed regarding whether the same could apply to the procedures for peaceful settlement of international disputes under Chapter VI. This is particularly true in the interdependent world where many of the small and medium States are intimately aligned with one or the other of the great powers that dominate the international scene.

[52] Sato, *The Law of International Organisations*, p. 184; Kolb, *An Introduction*, p. 137.
[53] Generally on this issue, see L. Gross, 'The Double Veto and the Four-Power Statement on Voting in the Security Council' (1953) 67 *Harvard Law Review*, pp. 251–80; Yuen-Li Liang, 'Notes on Legal Questions Concerning the United Nations: The So-Called "Double Veto"' (1949) 43 *AJIL*, pp. 134–44.
[54] I. L. Claude, Jr, *Swords into Plowshares: The Problems and Progress of International Organization*, 4th edn (New York: Random House, 1971), p. 142. The question of the double veto was raised with regard to the Spanish question (1946), Albania's application for membership of the United Nations (1946), the border incidents between Greece and her northern neighbouring States (1947) and seizure of power by the Communists in Czechoslovakia (1948). Gross, 'The Double Veto', pp. 270–1.
[55] *The United Nations Conference on International Organization, San Francisco, California, April 25 to June 26, 1945, Selected Documents* (Washington DC: US Gov't Print Office, 1946), p. 753, I, para. 5.

Because of the veto, it is unlikely to take action against any State closely aligned with one of the permanent members of the Council.

To prevent abuse of veto, the concept of 'the responsibility not to veto' is advocated by some commentators. According to the International Commission on Intervention and State Sovereignty (ICISS), this concept means that: 'The Permanent Five members of the Security Council should agree not to apply their veto power, in matters where their vital state interests are not involved, to obstruct the passage of resolutions authorizing military intervention for human protection purposes for which there is otherwise majority support.'[56] Notably, UN Secretary-General Ban Ki-moon urged the permanent members to 'refrain from employing or threatening to employ the veto in situations of manifest failure to meet obligations relating to the responsibility to protect' in situations of genocide, war crimes, ethnic cleansing and crimes against humanity.[57] Yet, it is uncertain whether the concept of the responsibility not to veto would be established as a norm in light of the absence of consent of the permanent members of the Security Council. Critics also express their misgivings that this concept lowers the threshold for military intervention.[58]

Some States thus explored a different option. In the draft resolution of 2012 prepared as part of the follow-up to the outcome of the Millennium Summit, five States – Costa Rica, Jordan, Liechtenstein, Singapore and Switzerland – called for the permanent member of the Security Council to provide a public explanation for any use of the veto, in particular with regard to its consistency with the purposes and principles of the UN Charter and applicable international law.[59] They also recommended that the permanent members refrain from using a veto to block Council action aimed at preventing or ending genocide, war crimes and crimes against humanity.[60] However, the draft resolution was subsequently withdrawn due to the pressure of the permanent members of the Security Council.[61]

2.4 Disqualification from Voting

When considering the voting system in the Security Council, Article 27(3) of the UN Charter merits particular note. The second part of this provision provides that: '[I]n decisions under Chapter VI, and under paragraph 3 of Article 52, a party to a dispute shall abstain from voting.' Article 27(3) is said to lay down the principle of *nemo judex in re sua* (nobody is

---

[56] ICISS, *The Responsibility to Protect* (Ottawa: International Development Research Centre, 2001), p. XVIII, available at: http://responsibilitytoprotect.org/ICISS%20Report.pdf. Generally on this idea, see A. Blätter and P. D. Williams, 'The Responsibility Not to Veto' (2011) 3 *Global Responsibility to Protect*, pp. 301–22; T. Reinold, 'The "Responsibility Not to Veto", Secondary Rules, and the Rule of Law' (2014) 6 *Global Responsibility to Protect*, pp. 269–94.
[57] UN General Assembly, Report of the UN Secretary-General, *Implementing the Responsibility to Protect*, A/63/677, 12 January 2009, p. 27, para. 61. See also UN General Assembly Resolution, 60/1. 2005 World Summit Outcome, A/RES/60/1, 24 October 2005, p. 30, para. 139.
[58] I. Marboe, 'R2P and the "Abusive" Veto: The Leal Nature of R2P and Its Consequences for the Security Council and Its Members' (2011) 16 *Austrian Review of International and European Law*, p. 133; D. H. Levine, 'Some Concerns about "The Responsibility Not to Veto"' (2011) 3 *Global Responsibility to Protect*, pp. 323–45.
[59] Revised Draft Resolution, Enhancing the Accountability, Transparency and Effectiveness of the Security Council, A/66/L.42/Rev.2, 15 May 2012, para. 19. These States are called 'Small 5' or 'S-5'.
[60] *Ibid.*, para. 20.
[61] GA/11234, 16 May 2012, available at: www.un.org/press/en/2012/ga11234.doc.htm. See also, www.swissinfo.ch/eng/security-council-reform_swiss-withdraw-un-draft-resolution/32719648; Marboe, 'R2P and the "Abusive" Veto', p. 133.

the judge in his own matter).⁶² Under this provision, in so far as the decisions under Chapter VI are concerned, a permanent member of the Security Council is required to abstain from voting in a matter which involves a dispute to which it is a party. However, resolutions concerning enforcement action under Chapter VII and those which affect membership status under Article 6 are excluded from its sphere of application. The Security Council's recommendations or decisions taken under Article 94(2) concerning the implementation of ICJ judgments also fall outside scope of Article 27(3) and the right of veto applies for these decisions. Accordingly, it is impossible for the Security Council to take action against a permanent member that refuses to comply with the judgment of the ICJ.⁶³

Literally the disqualification from voting under Article 27(3) does not apply to a 'situation'. Yet, the distinction between 'dispute' and 'situation' is difficult to make in practice.⁶⁴ Hence a member of the Security Council can always vote in decisions by regarding any 'dispute' as a 'situation'. Furthermore, as Article 27(3) does not apply to decisions under Chapter VII, it is necessary to determine whether a given Security Council decision was taken under Chapter VII or rather under Chapter VI. However, the determination might prove difficult where the Security Council has not made a formal determination under Article 39 of the UN Charter.⁶⁵ In certain circumstances, it is also less easy to identify the scope of 'a party to a dispute'.⁶⁶ In light of the above reasons, the practical application of Article 27(3) appears to encounter considerable difficulties.

In reality, the disqualification from voting under Article 27(3) has been rarely used. In the Suez Crisis of 1951, for instance, Israel brought a complaint before the Security Council, denouncing the Egyptian measure aimed at blocking the Suez Canal to ships directed toward Israeli ports. Before Israel appealed to the Council, several States, including three permanent members of the Council (i.e. the United States, the United Kingdom and France) as well as two non-permanent members in 1951 (i.e. the Netherlands and Turkey), had lodged protests against Egypt. When a draft resolution which urged Egypt to lift the restrictive measures on Suez traffic was proposed in the Council, the Egyptian representative raised the question of the applicability of the last part of Article 27(3) and claimed that the five States mentioned above had an obligation to abstain from the vote. After a heated discussion, the Council decided that the obligation did not exist.⁶⁷ Furthermore, while the Soviet Union cast a veto at the end of a debate on her invasion of Czechoslovakia, her right to do so was not challenged.⁶⁸ More recently, the Russian Federation exercised veto to the draft resolution tabled by forty-two States on 15 March 2014 with regard to Russia's annexation of the province of Crimea. It is arguable that the draft resolution would fall under Article 27(3) of the UN Charter. Yet, no States raised the issue of the applicability of the duty to abstain under the last part of this provision.⁶⁹

---

⁶² Zimmermann, 'Voting Article 27', p. 919.
⁶³ *Ibid.*, pp. 920 *et seq.*; Conforti and Focarelli, *The Law and Practice*, p. 89.
⁶⁴ *Ibid.*, p. 93.   ⁶⁵ Zimmermann, 'Voting Article 27', p. 920.
⁶⁶ R. Higgins, 'The Place of International Law in the Settlement of Disputes by the Security Council' (1970) 64 *AJIL*, p. 2.
⁶⁷ Conforti and Focarelli, *The Law and Practice*, p. 91.   ⁶⁸ Higgins, 'The Place of International Law', p. 2.
⁶⁹ E. Milano, 'Russia's Veto in the Security Council: Whither the Duty to Abstain under Art. 27(3) of the UN Charter?' (2015) 75 *ZaöRV*, pp. 215–31.

2.5 The Relationship between the Security Council and the International Court of Justice

The interrelationship between the UN Security Council and the ICJ should be an important issue when considering the interplay between political and judicial organs in the settlement of international disputes.[70] The interaction of the two organs must be examined in three respects.

First, the Security Council may request the ICJ to give an advisory opinion on any legal question under Article 96(1) of the UN Charter. Here an issue arises whether or not, for the Security Council, the decision to make a request would fall within the scope of non-procedural matters under Article 27(3) of the UN Charter. In practice, only one advisory opinion was requested by the Security Council[71] and, in this case, the majority required in Article 27(3) of the Charter had been reached. Thus difficulties have not arisen in practice.[72]

Second, it is possible that one dispute is submitted to the Security Council and the ICJ at the same time. In the 1984 *Nicaragua* case, the Court took the position that 'the fact that a matter is before the Security Council should not prevent it being dealt with by the Court and that both proceedings could be pursued *pari passu*';[73] and that 'even after a determination under Article 39, there is no necessary inconsistency between Security Council action and adjudication by the Court'.[74] The Court thus ruled that:

> While in Article 12 there is a provision for a clear demarcation of functions between the General Assembly and the Security Council, in respect of any dispute or situation ... there is no similar provision anywhere in the Charter with respect to the Security Council and the Court. The Council has functions of a political nature assigned to it, whereas the Court exercises purely judicial functions. Both organs can therefore perform their separate but complementary functions with respect to the same events.[75]

This view was echoed by the Court in the *Tehran Hostage* case.[76]

Third, a more contentious issue is whether or not the Court can review the legality of resolutions adopted by the UN Security Council. This issue will be discussed in Chapter 11, section 5.

---

[70] Generally on this issue, see R. Kolb, *Ius contra bellum: Le droit international relatif au maintien de la paix*, 2nd edn (Brussels: Bruylant, 2009), pp. 199–204.
[71] *Legal Consequences for States of the Continued Presence of South Africa in Namibia (South West Africa) notwithstanding Security Council Resolution 276 (1970)*, Advisory Opinion of 21 June 1971, ICJ Reports 1971, p. 16. The advisory jurisdiction of the ICJ will be discussed in Chapter 6, section 6 of this book.
[72] *Ibid.*, p. 22, para. 22; *A Commentary*, p. 1980.
[73] The *Nicaragua* case, Jurisdiction and Admissibility, ICJ Reports 1984, p. 433, para. 93.
[74] *Ibid.*, p. 432, para. 90.   [75] *Ibid.*, pp. 434–5, para. 95.
[76] *Case Concerning United States Diplomatic and Consular Staff in Tehran* (United States of America v. Iran), Judgment of 24 May 1980, ICJ Reports 1980, pp. 21–2, para. 40.

3 THE ROLE OF THE GENERAL ASSEMBLY IN INTERNATIONAL DISPUTE SETTLEMENT

3.1 Functions of the General Assembly

The General Assembly consists of all the Members of the United Nations. The role of the General Assembly is crucial in the situation where the Security Council has failed to take effective actions because of the use of the veto. Under Article 10 of the UN Charter, the General Assembly 'may discuss any questions or any matters within the scope of the present Charter, and, except as provided in Article 12 of the UN Charter, may make recommendations to the Members of the United Nations or to the Security Council or to both on any such questions or matters'. Article 11(2) of the UN Charter enables the General Assembly to discuss any questions relating to the maintenance of international peace and security brought before it by any Member of the United Nations, or by the Security Council or by a State which is not a Member of the United Nations in accordance with Article 35(2) of the UN Charter, and to make recommendations with regard to any such questions to the State or States concerned or to the Security Council or to both.[77]

Unlike Article 34 of the UN Charter, no mention was made of the General Assembly's power to investigate. However, the 1988 Declaration on the Prevention and Removal of Disputes explicitly stated that:

> If a dispute or situation has been brought before it, the General Assembly should consider, including in its recommendations making more use of fact-finding capabilities, in accordance with Article 11 and subject to Article 12 of the Charter.[78]

The 1991 Declaration on Fact-Finding also confirmed that 'fact-finding missions may be undertaken by the Security Council, the General Assembly and the Secretary-General'.[79]

Under Article 35(1) of the UN Charter, any Member of the United Nations may bring any dispute, or any situation of the nature referred to in Article 34, to the attention of the General Assembly. A non-Member State of the United Nations may also bring to the attention of the General Assembly any dispute to which it is a party if it accepts in advance, for the purposes of the dispute, the obligations of pacific settlement provided in the present

---

[77] According to the General Assembly Resolution 377(V) of 1950 (Uniting for Peace Resolution), if the Security Council, because of lack of unanimity of the permanent members, fails to exercise its primary responsibility for the maintenance of international peace and security in any case where there appears to be a threat to the peace, breach of the peace or act of aggression, the General Assembly shall consider the matter immediately with a view to making *appropriate recommendations* to Members for collective measures, including in the case of a breach of the peace or act of aggression *the use of armed force when necessary*, to maintain or restore international peace and security. The General Assembly, Resolution 377(V), *Uniting for Peace*, 3 November 1950, para. A-1.

[78] UN General Assembly, *Declaration on the Prevention and Removal of Disputes and Situations which May Threaten International Peace and Security and on the Role of the United Nations in this Field* (hereafter the 1988 *Declaration on the Prevention and Removal of Disputes*), A/RES/43/51, 5 December 1988, para. 1(18).

[79] UN General Assembly, *Declaration on Fact-Finding by the United Nations in the Field of the Maintenance of International Peace and Security*, A/RES/46/59, 9 December 1991, para. II-7.

Charter by virtue of Article 35(2). There is no provision analogous to Article 32 that applies to the General Assembly. Thus, unlike the Security Council, if a non-Member of the United Nations is a party to a dispute, that State is not invited to participate in the discussion relating to the dispute in the General Assembly.[80]

Decisions of the General Assembly on important questions shall be made by a two-thirds majority of the Members present and voting pursuant to Article 18(2) of the UN Charter. There is no veto in the General Assembly. Although no provision analogous to Article 27(3) of the UN Charter excluding the parties to a dispute from voting applies to the procedure in the General Assembly,[81] this will not create a serious problem in light of the large number of Member States participating in the voting in the General Assembly.

The General Assembly has adopted various resolutions dealing with international disputes. In 1948, for instance, the General Assembly empowered a United Nations Mediator in Palestine to use his good offices with the local and community authorities in Palestine.[82] In pursuance of the General Assembly Resolution of 14 May 1948, Count Folke Bernadotte, President of the Swedish Red Cross, was appointed as United Nations Mediator in Palestine on 20 May 1948.[83] On 1 February 1951, the General Assembly established a Good Offices Committee to explore the possibility of ceasing aggression in Korea.[84] Furthermore, the General Assembly requested the Secretary-General to seek the release of eleven American air crew held by China in 1954.[85] When dealing with the question of East Timor, the General Assembly requested the Secretary-General to initiate consultation with all parties directly concerned with a view to exploring avenues for achieving a comprehensive settlement of the problem.[86] More generally the General Assembly adopted a resolution on strengthening the role of mediation in 2011.[87]

The recent situation concerning Ukraine was a major challenge not only to the Security Council but also to the General Assembly. In this regard, the General Assembly Resolution called upon all States to desist and refrain from actions aimed at the partial or total disruption of the national unity and territorial integrity of Ukraine and urged all parties to pursue immediately the peaceful resolution of the situation through direct political dialogue. It also called upon all States, international organisations and specialised agencies not to recognise any alteration of the status of the Autonomous Republic of Crimea and the city of Sevastopol.[88]

---

[80] H. Kelsen, *The Law of the United Nations: A Critical Analysis of Its Fundamental Problems* (New York: Frederick A. Praeger, Inc., 1950) (reprinted, New Jersey: The Lawbook Exchange, Ltd, 2011), p. 460.

[81] Ibid.

[82] UN General Assembly, *Appointment and Terms of Reference of a United Nations Mediator in Palestine*, A/RES/186 (S-2), 14 May 1948, para. 1(a).

[83] Unfortunately Count Bernadotte was assassinated in Jerusalem on 17 September 1948. Subsequently, this incident led to the ICJ's advisory opinion in the *Reparation for Injuries* case.

[84] UN General Assembly, *Intervention of the Central People's Government of the People's Republic of China in Korea*, A/RES/498(V), 1 February 1951.

[85] UN General Assembly Resolution 906(IX). *Complaint of Detention and Imprisonment of United Nations Military Personnel in violation of the Korean Armistice Agreement*, 10 December 1954, para. 3. This affair will be discussed in section 4.2.

[86] UN General Assembly Resolution 37/30, *Question of East Timor*, 23 November 1982, para. 1.

[87] UN General Assembly, *Strengthening the Role of Mediation in the Peaceful Settlement of Disputes, Conflict Prevention and Resolution*, A/RES/65/283, 22 June 2011.

[88] UN General Assembly Resolution, *Territorial Integrity of Ukraine*, A/RES/68/262, 27 March 2014, paras. 2, 3 and 6.

In addition, the General Assembly is empowered to request the ICJ to give an advisory opinion on any legal question in accordance with Article 96(1) of the UN Charter. In fact, the majority of advisory opinions were requested by the General Assembly.[89]

3.2 Predominance of the Security Council over the General Assembly

In the League of Nations, the Assembly and the Council have the same power to deal with any matter within the sphere of action of the League or affecting the peace of the world.[90] By contrast, the UN Charter provides the predominance of the Security Council over the General Assembly with respect to the maintenance of international peace and security, by stipulating in Article 12(1) of the UN Charter that:

> While the Security Council is exercising in respect of any dispute or situation the functions assigned to it in the present Charter, the General Assembly shall not make any recommendation with regard to that dispute or situation unless the Security Council so requests.

The essence of this provision is confirmed in Articles 10, 11(2), 14 and 35(3) of the UN Charter. Article 12(1) aims to avoid unnecessary overlap over functions of the General Assembly and the Security Council, and the adoption of opposing resolutions with regard to the same dispute or situation. To this end, Article 12(2) requires the Secretary-General to notify the General Assembly of any matters relative to the maintenance of international peace and security which are being dealt with by the Security Council or which the Security Council ceases to deal with.

In the early practice of the United Nations, both the General Assembly and the Security Council interpreted and applied Article 12(1) in a strict manner. As a consequence, the General Assembly could not make a recommendation on a question concerning the maintenance of international peace and security while the matter remained on the Council's agenda. The Council, on a number of occasions, deleted items from its agenda in order to enable the Assembly to deliberate on them.[91]

However, the interpretation of Article 12(1) has evolved over time and the limitation embodied in this provision was progressively relaxed because it became apparent that the Security Council failed to exercise its function properly due to veto.[92] For instance, the General Assembly deemed itself entitled in 1961 to adopt recommendations in the matter of the Congo (resolutions 1955(XV) and 1600(XVI)) and in 1963 in respect of the Portuguese colonies (Resolution 1913(XVIII)), while those cases still appeared on the Council's agenda. In this regard, the ICJ, in the *Wall* case,[93] observed that:

---

[89] *A Commentary*, pp. 1984-5. [90] Articles 3(3), 4(4) and 15(9) of the Covenant of the League of Nations.
[91] *Legal Consequences of the Construction of a Wall in the Occupied Palestinian Territory*, Advisory Opinion of 9 July 2004, ICJ Reports 2004, p. 149, para. 27.
[92] For an analysis of practice concerning Article 12, see United Nations, *Repertory of Practice of United Nations Organs, Article 12*, available at: http://legal.un.org/repertory/art12.shtml.
[93] The UN General Assembly, in Resolution ES-10114 of 8 December 2003 at its Tenth Emergency Special Session, requested the ICJ to give an advisory opinion with regard to the legal consequences arising from the construction of the wall being built by Israel, the occupying power, in the Occupied Palestinian Territory. ICJ Reports 2004, p. 141, para. 1. The Court gave its advisory opinion in 2004.

> [T]here has been an increasing tendency over time for the General Assembly and the Security Council to deal in parallel with the same matter concerning the maintenance of international peace and security ... It is often the case that, while the Security Council has tended to focus on the aspects of such matters related to international peace and security, the General Assembly has taken a broader view, considering also their humanitarian, social and economic aspects.[94]

In the Court's view, 'the accepted practice of the General Assembly, as it has evolved, is consistent with Article 12, paragraph 1, of the Charter'.[95] Article 12 provides an interesting example of the evolutionary interpretation of the UN Charter through subsequent practice of the United Nations. One can argue that the General Assembly may adopt similar resolutions as the Security Council concerning the same issue, even though it cannot adopt resolutions which are contrary to resolutions of the Security Council.[96]

4 THE ROLE OF THE UN SECRETARY-GENERAL IN INTERNATIONAL DISPUTE SETTLEMENT

4.1 Activities of the UN Secretary-General

4.1.1 General Considerations

The role of the UN Secretary-General is highly diverse, ranging from the day-to-day administration to preventive diplomacy and overseeing the work of the UN peacekeeping forces (see Table 4.1).[97] Nevertheless, the UN Charter contains only succinct and general provisions concerning the UN Secretary-General. Under Article 97 of the UN Charter, the UN Secretary-General shall be the chief administrative officer of the Organisation. Article 98 of the UN Charter establishes the duty of the Secretary-General not only to act in that capacity, but also to perform such other functions as are entrusted to him by the other principal organs. Under the same provision, the Secretary-General is obliged to make an annual report to the General Assembly on the work of the United Nations pursuant to Article 98. In that document, where appropriate the Secretary-General can suggest means by which the functions of the United Nations may be improved in the field of peaceful settlement of international disputes.[98]

Under Article 99 of the UN Charter, the Secretary-General may bring to the attention of the Security Council any matter which in his opinion may threaten the maintenance of international peace and security. Whilst the power given to the Secretary-General under this provision has been used mainly in the field of the maintenance of peace and security, the Secretary-General can also use the power for the purposes of peaceful settlement of

---

[94] *Ibid.*, pp. 149–50, para. 27.
[95] *Ibid.*, p. 150, para. 28. See also *Accordance with International Law of the Unilateral Declaration of Independence in respect of Kosovo*, Advisory Opinion of 22 July 2010, ICJ Reports 2010, p. 421, para. 44.
[96] Sato, *The Law of International Organisations*, p. 273; *A Commentary*, pp. 519–20.
[97] J. M. Hanhimäki, *The United Nations: A Very Short Introduction* (Oxford University Press, 2008), p. 36.
[98] United Nations, *Handbook*, p. 130, para. 372.

TABLE 4.1 LIST OF THE SECRETARY-GENERALS OF THE UNITED NATIONS

1. Trygve Lie (Norway), Term of Office: 1946–52
2. Dag Hammarskjöld (Sweden), Term of Office: 1953–61
3. U Thant (Myanmar/Burma), Term of Office: 1961–71
4. Kurt Waldheim (Austria), Term of Office: 1972–81
5. Javier Pérez de Cuéllar (Peru), Term of Office: 1982–91
6. Boutros Boutros-Ghali (Egypt), Term of Office: 1992–6
7. Kofi A. Annan (Ghana), Term of Office: 1997–2006
8. Ban Ki-moon (Republic of Korea), Term of Office: 2007–16
9. António Guterres (Portugal), Term of Office: 2017–

international disputes.[99] Although it is uncommon that Article 99 is expressly invoked, on many occasions the Secretary-General's actions have implicitly relied on this provision.[100] Among various ancillary powers of the UN Secretary-General under Article 99,[101] five functions in particular merit highlighting.

4.1.2 Preventive Diplomacy

Preventive diplomacy is action to prevent disputes from arising between parties, to prevent existing disputes from escalating into conflicts and to limit the spread of the latter when they occur.[102] The UN Secretary-General has a great role to play in preventive diplomacy.[103] Originally preventive diplomacy was advocated by the UN Secretary-General Dag Hammarskjöld as a means for containment of the Cold War.[104] Subsequently the importance of preventive diplomacy has been stressed by his successors. For instance, Boutros Boutros-Ghali stated that the Secretary-General 'is most effective when engaged in the quiet practice of preventive diplomacy'.[105] Kofi Annan also stressed that: 'Preventive diplomacy is an important part of my responsibilities, pursued through persuasion, confidence-building and information-sharing to find solutions to difficult problems at a very early stage.'[106]

---

[99] *Ibid.*, pp. 130–1, para. 373.
[100] According to *A Commentary*, there were only two occasions where Article 99 was explicitly invoked: the 1960 Congo crisis (Dag Hammarskjöld) and the 1979 Tehran Hostage case (Kurt Waldheim). *A Commentary*, pp. 2014–15.
[101] *A Commentary* enumerates six powers of the UN Secretary-General: fact-finding, appointment of a special representative, good offices, submitting drafts, political pressure, and norm entrepreneur and trigger. *A Commentary*, pp. 2012–14.
[102] Boutros Boutros-Ghali, *An Agenda For Peace*, 2nd edn (New York: United Nations, 1995), p. 45, para. 20.
[103] Generally on preventive diplomacy, see J. Bercovitch and R. Jackson, *Conflict Resolution in the Twenty-First Century: Principles, Methods and Approaches* (University of Michigan Press, 2009), pp. 87–100.
[104] Claude, Jr, *Swords into Plowshares*, p. 313.
[105] Boutros Boutros-Ghali, 'Global Leadership after the Cold War' (1996) March/April, *Foreign Affairs*, p. 91.
[106] United Nations General Assembly/Security Council, Report of the Secretary-General, *Prevention of Armed Conflict*, A/55/985, S/2001/574, 7 June 2001, p. 15, para. 52. See also Boutros-Ghali, *An Agenda for Peace*, p. 46, para. 23.

The 2011 Report of the UN Secretary-General, titled *Preventive Diplomacy: Delivering Results*, enumerated key elements of successful preventive diplomacy:

(i) early warning which leads to early action
(ii) flexibility taking into account local preferences
(iii) enhancement of partnerships between the United Nations and other regional organisations
(iv) sustainability
(v) evaluation to monitor outcomes
(vi) continued financial resources.[107]

Preventive diplomacy is also carried out by States, regional international institutions and NGOs.[108] Related to this, the 2011 Report indicated that closer cooperation between the United Nations and regional organizations such as the African Union and the Council of the Wise of the Economic Community of West African States (ECOWAS), both of which operate early-warning systems, had ensured more and better data.[109]

4.1.3 Fact-Finding

The second function relates to fact-finding.[110] In this regard, there was an early constitutional controversy as to whether the Secretary-General may himself establish a fact-finding mission, or whether this can be done only upon authorisation by the Security Council. This question was resolved in favour of the Secretary-General so to act. In fact, the 1988 Declaration requires the Secretary-General to consider making full use of fact-finding capabilities with the consent of the host State.[111] The 1991 Declaration on Fact-Finding also calls for the Secretary-General to pay special attention to using the United Nations' fact-finding capabilities at an early stage in order to contribute to the prevention of disputes and situations.[112] The instrument also requires the Secretary-General, on his own initiative or at the request of the State concerned, to consider undertaking a fact-finding mission when a dispute or a situation exists.[113] To this end, the Secretary-General is required to prepare and update lists of experts in various fields who would be available for fact-finding missions.[114]

The 2000 Report of the Panel on United Nations Peace Operations (hereafter the Brahimi Report) also supported 'the Secretary-General's more frequent use of fact-finding missions to areas of tension, and stresses Member States' obligations, under Article 2(5) of the Charter, to give "every assistance" to such activities of the United Nations'.[115] For

---

[107] UN Document S/2011/552, 26 August 2011, pp. 19–22, paras. 44–64.
[108] M. S. Lund, 'Early Warning and Preventive Diplomacy' in D. Druckman and P. F. Diehl, *Conflict Resolution*, Vol. III (London: Sage Publications, 2006), p. 6.
[109] UN Document S/2011/552, 26 August 2011, p. 19, para. 45.
[110] Generally on this issue, see M. C. Bourloyannis, 'Fact-Finding by the Secretary-General of the United Nations' (1989–90) 22 *New York University Journal of International Law*, pp. 641–69.
[111] The 1988 *Declaration on the Prevention and Removal of Disputes*, para. 22.
[112] *Declaration on Fact-Finding by the United Nations in the Field of the Maintenance of International Peace and Security*, A/RES/46/59, 9 December 1991, para. 12.
[113] *Ibid.*, para. 13   [114] *Ibid.*, para. 14.
[115] *Report of the Panel on United Nations Peace Operations (Brahimi Report)*, A/53/305-S/2000/809, 21 August 2000, p. 54, 1(b).

instance, the UN Secretary-General has on his own initiative sent fact-finding missions, *inter alia*, to enquire into the incident which occurred on 10 October 1984 in the camp for Iraqi prisoners of war at Gorgan, Iran[116] and to investigate allegations of chemical-weapons use in the 1986 conflict between Iran and Iraq.[117]

4.1.4 Organisation of Peacekeeping Operations

Peacekeeping is the deployment of a United Nations presence in the field, hitherto with the consent of all the parties concerned, normally involving United Nations military and/or police personnel and frequently civilians as well. Peacekeeping is a technique that expands the possibilities for both the prevention of conflict and the making of peace.[118] The UN Secretary-General is involved in the organisation and arrangements of UN peacekeeping operations.

It is common knowledge that UN Secretary-General Dag Hammarskjöld, together with Lester Pearson, Canadian Secretary of State for External Affairs, proposed a peacekeeping operation as a means of securing the withdrawal of British, French and Israeli forces from Egypt during the Suez crisis of 1956. In this regard, UN General Assembly Resolution 998 requested, as a matter of urgency, the Secretary-General to submit to it within forty-eight hours a plan for the setting up of an emergency international United Nations Force to secure and supervise the cessation of hostilities.[119] Resolution 999 further authorised the Secretary-General immediately to arrange with the parties concerned for the implementation of the ceasefire and the halting of the movement of military forces and arms into the area.[120] Thus the UN Emergency Force (UNEF I), which can be said to be the first true peacekeeping operation, was established. UNEF I provided the model for traditional peacekeeping operations.[121]

In the Congo crisis of 1960, UN Security Council Resolution 143 authorised the Secretary-General to take the necessary steps, in consultation with the Government of the Republic of Congo, to provide that government with such military assistance as may be necessary.[122] To address the Cyprus question, the Security Council, in its Resolution 186, recommended the creation of a United Nations Peacekeeping Force in Cyprus and the composition and size of the Force should be established by the Secretary-General, in consultation with the Governments of Cyprus, Greece, Turkey and the United Kingdom.[123]

More recently, in April 2014, UN Security Council Resolution 2149 decided to establish the United Nations Multidimensional Integrated Stabilization Mission in the Central African Republic (MINUSCA) for an initial twelve-month period until 30 April 2015.[124]

---

[116] *Report of a Mission Dispatched by the UN Secretary-General, Prisoners of War in Iran and Iraq*, UN Doc. S/16962, 22 February 1985.
[117] *Report of a Mission Dispatched by the UN Secretary-General to Investigate Allegations of the Use of Chemical Weapons in the Conflict Between the Islamic Republic of Iran and Iraq*, UN Doc. S/17911, 12 March 1986, and S/20134, 19 August 1988.
[118] Boutros-Ghali, *An Agenda For Peace*, p. 45, para. 20.
[119] UN General Assembly Resolution 998 (ES-I), 4 November 1956.
[120] UN General Assembly Resolution 999 (ES-I), 4 November 1956, para. 2.
[121] See also Chapter 11, section 2.1.2.
[122] UN Security Council Resolution 143 (1960), S/4387, 14 July 1960, para. 2.
[123] UN Security Council, 186 (1964). Resolution of 4 March 1964, S/5575, para. 4.
[124] UN Security Council Resolution 2149 (2014), S/RES/2149(2014), 10 April 2014, para. 18.

It authorised the Secretary-General to deploy to MINUSCA, before 15 September 2014, such military enablers as may be necessary in order to bolster MINUSCA's military and police components. It also requested the Secretary-General to take all possible steps to accelerate the deployments of MINUSCA's civilian and military capabilities in the Central African Republic.[125]

4.1.5 Good Offices and Mediation

The UN Secretary-General's good offices and mediation also merit mention. In his report of 2005, UN Secretary-General Kofi Annan stressed the importance of good offices:

> Although it is difficult to demonstrate, the United Nations has almost certainly prevented many wars by using the Secretary-General's 'good offices' to help resolve conflicts peacefully.[126]

He thus urged Member States to allocate additional resources to the Secretary-General for his good offices function.[127] Furthermore, in 2016, the UN General Assembly requested 'the Secretary-General to continue to offer his good offices, in accordance with the UN Charter and relevant UN resolutions'.[128] The UN Secretary-General's good offices and mediation can derive from resolutions of the Security Council, resolutions of the General Assembly, the Secretary-General's inherent powers and by agreement of disputing parties. Yet the source of authorisation is not always clear in practice.

On various occasions, the UN Secretary-General has tendered good offices and mediation.[129] In September 1946, for instance, good offices were for the first time tendered by UN Secretary-General Trygve Lie to investigate alleged infiltration across Greece's northern border. He also stepped forward with detailed solutions to the Berlin crisis and proposed talks on the Korean War.[130] Subsequently the UN Secretary-General has been mandated to act as a mediator in the Cyprus Conflict, the Middle East, the situation between Iraq and Iran and the situation in Sudan (Darfur).[131]

In the Suez Crisis of 1956, Dag Hammarskjöld called Foreign Ministers of the United Kingdom, France and Egypt into private consultation in his office to see if some agreement could be reached. After four-day consultations, six principles were accepted and the principles were reported to the Security Council on 12 October 1956.[132] On 29 October 1956, however, Israeli forces launched their attack across Egypt's Sinai peninsula and,

---

[125] Ibid., paras. 23–4.
[126] Report of the Secretary-General, *In Larger Freedom: Towards Development, Security and Human Rights for All*, A/59/2005, 21 March 2005, p. 30, para. 108.
[127] Ibid.
[128] UN General Assembly Resolution, *Strengthening the Role of Mediation in the Peaceful Settlement of Disputes, Conflict Prevention and Resolution*, A/RES/70/304, 26 September 2016, para. 14.
[129] For a detailed examination on the UN Secretary-General's Good Offices, see T. M. Franck, *Fairness in International Law and Institutions* (Oxford University Press, 1995), pp. 173–217.
[130] *A Commentary*, p. 2013.   [131] Ibid., p. 1078.
[132] B. Urquhart, *Hammarskjöld* (New York: W. W. Norton and Company, 1994), pp. 165–8.

subsequently, British and French troops also invaded Egypt.[133] As a consequence, the agreed principles were ignored by these States and the UN Secretary-General's good offices failed to prevent the armed conflict. Even so, it must be remembered that his continuous efforts in the Suez Crisis led to the genesis of the traditional model of the United Nations peacekeeping (i.e. UNEF I).

What is of particular interest in this context concerns the interlinkage between the UN Secretary-General's good offices and subsequent peacekeeping of the United Nations. By way of illustration, the situation of Cambodia merits mention. After its invasion by Viet Nam in December 1978, the UN General Assembly expressed its great concern about the armed conflict in Cambodia. It thus requested the UN Secretary-General to exercise his good offices in order to contribute to a peaceful solution of the problem.[134] The Secretary-General exercised his good offices over the years and his proposals gave momentum to the negotiations between parties involved. In October 1991, the parties reached an Agreement which provided for the establishment of the United Nations Transitional Authority in Cambodia (UNTAC) under the direct responsibility of the UN Secretary-General.[135] Unlike traditional peacekeeping, UNTAC performed an unprecedentedly comprehensive supervisory and administrative role in Cambodia, including supervision of ceasefire and administrative structures, disarmament and organisation of the conduct of free and fair elections.[136] In this sense, UNTAC can be regarded as multidimensional peacekeeping.

Furthermore, some consideration must be given to a series of good offices tendered by the UN Secretary-General with regard to the East Timor situation. Although East Timor was administered by Portugal, Portugal withdrew after civil war. Indonesia then intervened militarily and integrated East Timor as its twenty-seventh province in 1976. However, the United Nations never accepted the integration.[137] Against that background, the UN Secretary-General, Pérez de Cuéllar initiated consultation with all parties concerned to settle the question of East Timor according to the General Assembly's request of 1982.[138] Since then, at the request of the General Assembly, successive Secretaries-General held regular talks with Indonesia and Portugal with a view to resolving the status of the territory. For instance, the UN Secretary-General Boutros Boutros-Ghali stated, in his report, that he had continued to provided his good offices 'in search for a just, comprehensive and internationally acceptable solution to the question of East Timor'.[139]

---

[133] For the Suez Crisis, see M. Fröhlich, 'The "Suez Story": Dag Hammarskjöld, the United Nations and the Creation of UN Peacekeeping' in C. Stahn and H. Melber (eds.), *Peace Diplomacy, Global Justice and International Agency: Rethinking Human Security and Ethics in the Spirit of Dag Hammarskjöld* (Cambridge University Press, 2014), pp. 305–40.

[134] UN General Assembly Resolution 34/22. The situation in Kampuchea, 14 November 1979, para. 11.

[135] Agreement on a Comprehensive Political Settlement of the Cambodia Conflict, Article 2(1), available at: www.usip.org/sites/default/files/file/resources/collections/peace_agreements/agree_comppol_10231991.pdf.

[136] Further, see www.un.org/en/peacekeeping/missions/past/untac.htm.

[137] Further, see East Timor – UNTAET Chronology, available at: www.un.org/en/peacekeeping/missions/past/etimor/Untaetchrono.html. See also East Timor – UNTAET Background, available at: www.un.org/en/peacekeeping/missions/past/etimor/UntaetB.htm.

[138] UN General Assembly Resolution 37/30, Question of East Timor, 23 November 1982, para. 1.

[139] Report of the Secretary-General on the Work of the Organisation, A/49/1, 2 September 1994, p. 66, para. 505. However, Indonesia has not indicated any interest in negotiating the question of the status of East Timor. Franck, 'The Secretary-General's Role', p. 374.

In June 1998, Indonesia proposed autonomy for East Timor within Indonesia. Although the proposal was rejected by East Timorese resistance leaders, from August to October 1998, the UN Secretary-General Kofi Annan and the Foreign Ministers of Indonesia and Portugal held in-depth discussions on Indonesia's proposals.

In May 1999, the two governments reached a set of agreements and entrusted the UN Secretary-General with organising a 'popular consultation' in order to ascertain whether the East Timorese people accepted or rejected a special autonomy for East Timor within the unitary Republic of Indonesia.[140] Thus the Security Council authorised the establishment of the United Nations Mission in East Timor (UNAMET) to 'organise and conduct a popular consultation, scheduled for 8 August 1999'.[141] UNAMET exercised all legislative and executive authority, including the administration of justice in East Timor. UNAMET can be viewed as another example of multidimensional peacekeeping. The proposed autonomy was rejected and East Timor eventually became independent in 2002.

4.1.6 Ruling of Disputes

The Secretary-General may be asked to rule on problems arising from a dispute between States. The *'Rainbow Warrior'* affair between France and New Zealand is a case in point. This affair concerns the destruction of the British-registered vessel, *'Rainbow Warrior'*, in Auckland Harbour, New Zealand. In order to protest about a new series of nuclear tests planned by France in 1985, Greenpeace sent its vessel, *'Rainbow Warrior'*, to Auckland. On 10 July 1985, the vessel was sunk at its moorings in Auckland Harbour as a result of extensive damage caused by two high-explosive devices and one person, a Netherlands citizen, was killed. On 12 July 1985, two agents of the French Directorate General of External Security (DGSE) were interviewed by the New Zealand Police and subsequently arrested and prosecuted. Although initially France denied any involvement in this affair, it confirmed that the *'Rainbow Warrior'* had been sunk by agents of the DGSE under orders.

On 4 November 1985, the two agents pleaded guilty in the District Court in Auckland to charges of manslaughter and wilful damage to a ship by means of an explosive. On 22 November 1985, the agents, Alain Mafart and Dominique Prieur, were sentenced by the Chief Justice of New Zealand to a term of ten years' imprisonment.[142] Subsequently bilateral efforts to find a solution to the problems arising from the *'Rainbow Warrior'* affair were undertaken. However, as France began impeding New Zealand imports early in 1986, New Zealand suspended negotiations in protest at continued economic sanctions by France. Following an appeal by Ruud Lubbers, President of the European Council of Ministers and Prime Minister of the Netherlands, in June 1986, the two governments formally approached the Secretary-General and referred to him all the problems between

---

[140] See East Timor – UNTAET Chronology; East Timor – UNTAET Background.
[141] UN Security Council Resolution 1246(1999), S/RES/1246 (1999), 11 June 1999, para. 1.
[142] Concerning the facts of this affair, see Pugh, 'Legal Aspects', pp. 656–8. For the facts and claims of the parties, see 'Memorandum of the Government of New Zealand to the Secretary-General of the United Nations', 19 *RIAA*, pp. 201–7; 'Memorandum of the Government of the French Republic to the Secretary-General of the United Nations', *ibid.*, pp. 207–12. The two Memoranda were submitted pursuant to the agreement of 19 June 1986 between New Zealand and France.

them arising from the *'Rainbow Warrior'* affair for a ruling which both sides agreed to abide by.

On 6 July 1986, the Secretary-General ruled, *inter alia*, that:

(i) The Prime Minister of France should convey to the Prime Minister of New Zealand a formal and unqualified apology for the attack, contrary to international law.
(ii) The French Government should pay the sum of US$7 million to the Government of New Zealand as compensation for all the damage it had suffered.
(iii) The two French agents should be transferred to a French military facility on the isolated island of Hao in French Polynesia for a period of three years.
(iv) Any dispute concerning the interpretation or application of the agreements concluded as a result of the ruling should be submitted to an arbitral tribunal.[143]

Although the two agents were sent to the island of Hao in accordance with the Secretary-General's ruling, later the French Government returned them to metropolitan France before the expiry of the stipulated three-year period of isolation. Thus a further dispute was raised between France and New Zealand. In 1990, the dispute was eventually settled by arbitration.[144]

4.2 Independence of the UN Secretary-General

The independence of the UN Secretary-General and the staff is considered a prerequisite to effectively perform their functions.[145] The importance of independence of the Secretary-General was highlighted by Dag Hammarskjöld during his initiative in obtaining the release of American aircrew imprisoned by China. During the Korean War, American aircraft had been shot down and aircrew had been held by Beijing. In this instance, the UN General Assembly Resolution of 10 December 1954 requested of the Secretary-General the following tasks:

- to seek the release of these eleven United Nations Command personnel and all other captured personnel of the United Nations Command still detained
- to make, by the means most appropriate in his judgment, continuing and unremitting efforts to this end and to report progress to all members on or before 31 December 1954.[146]

---

[143] *Ibid.*, pp. 213–15. Scholarly opinions were divided on the subject of the nature of the ruling of the UN Secretary-General in the *'Rainbow Warrior'* case. Merrills and Pugh seem to consider the role of the Secretary-General as arbitration, French writers appear to regard it as mediation. Merrills, *International Dispute Settlement*, pp. 91 and 108; M. Pugh, 'Legal Aspects of the Rainbow Warrior Affair' (1987) 36 *ICLQ*, p. 657 and p. 663; Ngyen Quoc Dinh *et al.*, *Droit International Public*, 8th edn (Paris: LGDJ, 2009), p. 949.
[144] Award of 30 April 1990, 20 *RIAA*, p. 215. The Arbitral Tribunal declared that the French Republic committed a material and continuing breach of its obligations to New Zealand because it failed to order the return of Major Mafart to the island of Hao as from 12 February 1988, although it did not breach its obligation to New Zealand by removing Major Mafart from the island of Hao on 13 December 1987. The Tribunal also declared that the French Republic committed a material breach of its obligations to New Zealand by removing Captain Prieur from the island of Hao on 5 and 6 May 1988. *Ibid.*, p. 275. For a commentary on this award, see J. S. Davidson, 'The Rainbow Warrior Arbitration Concerning the Treatment of the French Agents Mafart and Prieur' (1991) 40 *ICLQ*, pp. 446–57.
[145] See Article 100(1) of the UN Charter.
[146] UN General Assembly, 906(IX). *Complaint of Detention and Imprisonment of United Nations Military Personnel in Violation of the Korean Armistice Agreement*, Resolution 906 of 10 December 1954, paras. 3 and 4. See also section 3.1 of this chapter.

At the first formal meeting with Chou En-Lai, Prime Minister and Minister for Foreign Affairs of the People's Republic of China, Hammarskjöld expressed the view that in fulfilling his obligation to reduce international tensions anywhere in the world, the Secretary-General did not work for any one nation or even for a majority of nations as expressed in a vote in the General Assembly, but under his constitutional responsibility for the general purposes set out in the UN Charter.[147] According to Hammarskjöld, if the Secretary-General's diplomatic functions derive from resolutions of the Security Council or General Assembly, the legal basis for the actions of the Secretary-General rests with the UN Charter. This view is known as the 'Peking formula'.[148]

As shown in this formula, the independence of the UN Secretary-General can be regarded as an essential element for his successful commitment to peaceful settlement of international disputes.[149] Independence does not mean isolation, however. For instance, support of public opinion as a living force in international affairs constitutes an important element for effective performance of his functions in international dispute settlement. It is also important to retain the confidence of the principal organs of the United Nations and major States in order to perform his diplomatic functions effectively.[150] Related to this, the Brahimi Report states that: 'For preventive initiatives to reduce tension and avert conflict, the Secretary-General needs clear, strong and sustained political support from Member States.'[151] Three observations can be made here.

First, in the situation where a determined great power opposes commitments of the United Nations in the settlement of international disputes, functions of the UN Secretary-General as well as the United Nations are likely to be paralysed. One might take the Hungarian uprising of 1956 as an example.[152] On 25 October 1956, Soviet forces penetrated Hungary. The Soviet Union further developed its invasion and, on 4 November 1956, Soviet forces launched a major attack on Hungary with a view to crushing the spontaneous national uprising in a quest for democratisation. The Hungarian Prime Minister, Imre Nagy, requested the UN Secretary-General to put on the agenda of the General Assembly the question of Hungary.[153] Nonetheless, the Secretary-General as well as other organs of the United Nations was unable to take effective measures to prevent the Soviet invasion of Hungary. The Security Council decided to call an emergency special session of the General Assembly as provided in General Assembly Resolution 377 A(V) of 3 November 1950, and the matter was passed on to the Assembly.[154] However, the Soviet

---

[147] Urquhart, *Hammarskjöld*, p. 105.
[148] *Ibid.*, p. 495. After difficult negotiations, the airmen were eventually released. For the 'Peking formula', see also A. O'Donoghue, 'Breaking Free: Dag Hammarskjöld, Good Offices and Heads of International Organisations' in C. Stahn and H. Melber (eds.), *Peace Diplomacy, Global Justice and International Agency: Rethinking Human Security and Ethics in the Spirit of Dag Hammarskjöld* (Cambridge University Press, 2014), pp. 354-6.
[149] In this regard, the UN Secretary-General Boutros Boutros-Ghali clearly stated that: 'If one word above all is to characterise the role of the secretary-general, it is independence.' Boutros-Ghali, 'Global Leadership', p. 98.
[150] Franck, 'The Secretary-General's Role', pp. 381-2. [151] *The Brahimi Report*, pp. viii and 1, para. 3.
[152] Generally on this subject, see Urquhart, *Hammarskjöld*, pp. 231-48.
[153] UN Document A/3251, *Hungary: Request for the Inclusion of an Additional item in the Agenda of the General Assembly*, 1 November 1956.
[154] UN Security Council, Resolution of 4 November 1956, S/3733.

Union were strongly opposed to any Assembly discussion with regard to the situation of Hungary. In addition, the United States was not prepared to engage deeply in this matter. As a consequence, the UN Secretary-General proved to have little practical influence on the Hungarian affair and the Hungarian revolution was eventually defeated by the Soviet Union.

Second, generally legal authority arising from UN Security Council or General Assembly resolutions will provide strong support for the Secretary-General in the effective performance of his good offices or mediation.[155] In the case where a resolution provides a large discretion to the Secretary-General, he will be able to perform his function in a flexible manner. Yet a vague resolution can be used as a camouflage for Member States not to take specific actions to resolve international disputes, by centralising all responsibilities on the Secretary-General. The UN General Assembly Resolution 1004 (ES-II) with regard to the situation of Hungary, adopted on 4 November 1956, may be a case in point. This resolution contained no specific measures to be taken by the General Assembly, and merely requested the Secretary-General 'as soon as possible to suggest methods to bring an end to the foreign intervention in Hungary in accordance with the Principles of the Charter of the United Nations'.[156] As Thomas Frank rightly stated, however, the Secretary-General 'should never be used as a "black hole" down which to drop issues some members wish to forget'.[157]

Third, in the situation where the Security Council decides to take a clear and uncompromised position, it is hard for the Secretary-General to assume an independent mediating role. In the Iraqi invasion of Kuwait, for instance, the UN Secretary-General could do little more than act as an emissary for the Security Council which had already demanded that Iraq withdraw immediately and unconditionally all its forces to the positions in which they were located on 1 August 1990[158] and decided to impose sanctions upon Iraq.[159] In this instance, the Secretary-General could not invoke the 'Peking formula' and his role was limited to negotiating within the extent of those essentially non-negotiable terms.[160] In the *Lockerbie* case, the Security Council requested the Secretary-General to seek the cooperation of the Libyan Government to provide a full and effective response to requests by the United Kingdom, France and the United States for extradition of the suspects of the destruction of Pan Am Flight 103 and Union de Transport Aériens Flight 772.[161] The Secretary-General was asked to act under the term of paragraph 4 of Resolution 731 and not as a mediator between the Security Council and the Libyan authorities.[162] In this case, it appeared that his role was limited to being the Council's letter carrier.[163]

---

[155] Hammarskjöld gave considerable importance to the grant of authority enabling him to enter into negotiations. O. Schachter, 'Dag Hammarskjöld and the Relation of Law to Politics' (1962) 56 *AJIL*, p. 6.
[156] UN General Assembly, Resolution 1004 (ES-II), para. 4 of the operative part.
[157] Franck, 'The Secretary-General's Role', p. 374.
[158] UN Security Council Resolution 660 (1990) of 2 August 1990, para. 2.
[159] UN Security Council Resolution 661 (1990) of 6 August 1990, paras. 3–4.
[160] Franck, 'The Secretary-General's Role', p. 372.
[161] UN Security Council Resolution 731 (1992) of 21 January 1992, para. 4.
[162] Report by the Secretary-General Pursuant to Paragraph 4 of Security Council Resolution 731 (1992), S/23574, 11 February 1992, p. 1.
[163] Franck, 'The Secretary-General's Role', p. 373.

5 THE UNITED NATIONS AND REGIONAL ARRANGEMENTS

5.1 Cooperation between the United Nations and Regional Arrangements

Regional organisations and arrangements can perform a valuable role in peaceful settlement of international disputes. In fact, the Security Council encouraged the peaceful settlement of local disputes through regional arrangements in accordance with Chapter VIII of the Charter.[164] The relationship between the United Nations and regional organisations differs at the stage of peaceful settlement of international disputes and that of enforcement action. At the latter stage, the United Nations predominates over regional organisations by virtue of Article 53(1) of the UN Charter.[165] In contrast, in the field of peaceful settlement of international disputes, the UN Charter appears to give regional arrangements or agencies a certain degree of autonomy under Article 52(1) of the UN Charter. The Members of the United Nations entering into regional arrangements or constituting such agencies are required to make every effort to achieve pacific settlement of local disputes through such regional arrangements or by such regional agencies before referring them to the Security Council in accordance with Article 52(2) of the UN Charter. Article 52(3) requires the Security Council to 'encourage the development of pacific settlement of local disputes through such regional arrangements or by such regional agencies either on the initiative of the states concerned or by reference from the Security Council'. This provision is supported by the 1988 Declaration, which requires the Security Council as well as the General Assembly to consider encouraging and, where appropriate, endorsing efforts at the regional level by the States concerned or by regional arrangements or agencies to prevent or remove a dispute or situation in the region concerned.[166] In any case the Security Council should be kept informed of such activities in accordance with Article 54.

The importance of collaboration between the United Nations and regional arrangements was affirmed by the *Agenda for Peace*:

> [R]egional arrangements or agencies in many cases possess a potential that should be utilised in serving the functions covered in this report: preventive diplomacy, peacekeeping, peacemaking and post-conflict peacebuilding. Under the Charter, the Security Council has and will continue to have primary responsibility for maintaining international peace and security, but regional action as a matter of decentralisation, delegation and cooperation with United Nations efforts could not only lighten the burden of the Council but also contribute to a deeper sense of participation, consensus and democratisation in international affairs.[167]

---

[164] Statement by the President of the Security Council, S/PRST/2011/18, 22 September 2011, p. 2.
[165] For instance, the question whether enforcement action includes non-military measures or peacekeeping operations remains a matter for discussion.
[166] The 1988 *Declaration on the Prevention and Removal of Disputes*, paras. 13 and 17.
[167] Boutros-Ghali, *An Agenda for Peace*, p. 64, para. 64.

While cooperation between the United Nations and regional organisations takes various forms, five fields in particular are highlighted by the UN Secretary-General in his *Supplement to an Agenda for Peace*. They can be summarised as follows:[168]

(i) *Consultation*: Consultation seeks to exchange views on conflicts that both the United Nations and the regional organisation may be trying to solve.
(ii) *Diplomatic support*: The regional organisation supports peacemaking activities of the United Nations by diplomatic initiatives and/or by providing technical input. An example is support by the Organisation for Security and Cooperation in Europe (OSCE) on constitutional issues relating to Abkhazia.
(iii) *Operational support*: An example is the provision by the North Atlantic Treaty Organisation (NATO) of air power to support the United Nations Protection Force (UNPROFOR) in the former Yugoslavia.
(iv) *Co-deployment*: Co-deployment of field mission may herald a new division of labour between the United Nations and regional organisation, under which the regional organisation carries the main burden, while a small United Nations operation supports it and verifies whether it is functioning properly. An example is United Nations field missions deployed in conjunction with ECOWAS in Liberia and with the Commonwealth of Independent States (CIS) in Georgia.
(v) *Joint operations*: The United Nations Mission in Haiti is a case in point. The staffing, direction and financing of the mission were shared between the United Nations and the Organisation of American States (OAS).

5.2 Concurrence of Jurisdiction between the UN Security Council and Regional Organisations

The relationship between the UN Security Council and regional organisations is not always cooperative but a conflict of jurisdiction may arise between the two organs. One might take the Guatemalan affair of June 1954 as an example. In 1953, the United States decided that the regime of Guatemalan President Jacobo Arbenz Guzmán, who had been in power since March 1951, must end. On 18 June 1954, a US-trained Guatemalan exile, Colonel Castillo Armas, invaded Guatemala from Honduras with a force of 150 men. Even though the Government of Guatemala requested an urgent meeting of the Security Council on 19 June, Henry Cabot Lodge Jr, representative of the United States to the United Nations and President of the Security Council for June, maintained that the obvious procedure was for the matter to be referred to the OAS. According to Lodge, recourse to the regional organisation was even compulsory under Article 52 of the UN Charter.[169]

On 20 June 1954, the Security Council adopted a resolution calling for 'the immediate termination of any action likely to cause bloodshed' and requesting 'all Members of the United Nations to abstain, in the spirit of the Charter, from rendering assistance to

---
[168] *Supplement to an Agenda for Peace: Position Paper of the Secretary-General on the Occasion of the Fiftieth Anniversary of the United Nations*, A/50/60, S/1995/1, 25 January 1995, pp. 20–1, para. 86.
[169] Urquhart, *Hammarskjöld*, pp. 88–90.

any such action'.¹⁷⁰ Nevertheless, this resolution was not complied with. The Guatemalan Government once again asked for a further meeting at the Security Council. Yet the Council was slow to move because the United States attempted to deter further involvement of the Security Council on this matter. When the Council finally met on 25 June, Lodge opposed its consideration of the Guatemalan dispute until the matter had first been dealt with by the OAS. Thus he opposed the adoption of the agenda at the Security Council.¹⁷¹ His position was supported by the Council and the agenda was rejected by a narrow vote of four in favour and five against, with France and the United Kingdom abstaining.¹⁷² The Arbenx Government eventually fell on 27 June.¹⁷³ It is arguable that under the UN Charter, settlement through regional organisations and arrangements should be tried first. However, this does not mean that the Security Council cannot deal with a dispute or situation since the Security Council has the primary responsibility for the maintenance of international peace and security. After the event, the UN Secretary-General Hammarskjöld expressed the following view, which merits recording:

> [T]he importance of regional arrangements in the maintenance of peace is fully recognised in the Charter and the appropriate use of such arrangements is encouraged. But in those cases where resort to such arrangements is chosen in the first instance, that choice should not be permitted to cast any doubt on the ultimate responsibility of the United Nations.¹⁷⁴

5.3 Interaction between Regional Institutions and International Adjudication

As mentioned earlier,¹⁷⁵ the interaction between diplomatic and legal means is of particular importance in the overall settlement of international disputes. In this regard, the role of regional institutions as facilitator of judicial settlement of international disputes merits discussion.¹⁷⁶ One may take the role of the OAS in the 1960 *Arbitral Award made by the King of Spain on 23 December 1906* as an example.¹⁷⁷ The dispute concerned the validity of an arbitral award made by the King of Spain concerning a territorial dispute between Nicaragua and Honduras.¹⁷⁸ King Alfonso XII delivered the award with terms favourable to Honduras on 23 December 1906,¹⁷⁹ but Nicaragua challenged its validity from 19 March 1912.¹⁸⁰ Faced with the prospect of an armed conflict, the Council of the OAS, at

---

[170] UN Security Council Resolution of 20 June 1954, S/3237.
[171] Security Council Official records, 676th Meeting, 25 June 1954, S/PV.676, p. 30, para. 178.
[172] *Ibid.*, p. 34, para. 195.   [173] Urquhart, *Hammarskjöld*, pp. 91–2.
[174] Annual Report of the Secretary-General on the Work of the Organization 1 July 1953–20 June 1954, General Assembly Official Records, Ninth Session, Supplement No. 1, A/2663, p. xi. See also Urquhart, *Hammarskjöld*, pp. 93–4.
[175] See Chapter 1, section 4.1.2.
[176] On this issue, see Merrills, *International Dispute Settlement*, pp. 293 *et seq.*
[177] For a detailed analysis of this subject, see C. Schulte, *Compliance with Decisions of the International Court of Justice* (Oxford University Press, 2004), pp. 126–32.
[178] See Chapter 5, section 6.2.1.
[179] *The Boundary Case between Honduras and Nicaragua*, 23 December 1906, RIAA 11, 101–17.
[180] *Arbitral Award Made by the King of Spain on 23 December 1906* (Honduras v. Nicaragua), Judgment of 18 November 1960, ICJ Reports 1960, pp. 202–3.

Honduras's request, appointed an investigating committee and issued a report suggesting the ICJ as an appropriate forum to settle the dispute. To this end, an ad hoc committee appointed by the OAS Council drafted a proposal for an agreement to submit the case before the ICJ.[181] On 21 July 1957, the two parties reached an agreement to submit the dispute with respect to the arbitral award handed down by the King of Spain to the ICJ owing to the assistance of the OAS acting as a consultative body.[182] On 1 July 1958, Honduras instituted proceedings against Nicaragua before the Court with regard to the validity of the arbitral award made by the King of Spain on the basis of the Washington Agreement and Article 36(2) of the ICJ Statute. Thus, the OAS assisted the parties to refer the dispute to the ICJ.

In 1960, the Court, by fourteen votes to one, found that the award made by the King of Spain on 23 December 1906 was valid and binding and that Nicaragua was under an obligation to give effect to it.[183] Yet the implementation of the judgment was not easy since Nicaragua had to withdraw from an inhabited area which it had been occupying for several decades. Faced with practical difficulties in implementing the ICJ judgment, the Inter-American Peace Committee offered assistance to the parties. In particular, it settled the issues of demarcation and undertook a final inspection of the boundary markers. In July 1963, nearly three years after the judgment of the Court, the dispute over the arbitral award was eventually settled.[184] Thus the Inter-American Peace Committee performed an important role in facilitating cooperation between the disputing parties in the implementation of the ICJ judgment.

5.4 Limits with Regional Organisations and Arrangements

Despite the positive role of regional organisations and arrangements in international dispute settlement, it cannot pass unnoticed that regional arrangements have some limitations.[185]

First, international disputes are often inter-regional. In the Falkland/Malvinas dispute between the United Kingdom and Argentina, for instance, the United Kingdom was a Member State of the EEC, while Argentina was a member of the OAS. Thus the efforts to settle the dispute by these organisations could achieve little success.

Second, there is no guarantee that Member States of a regional arrangement always share common interests and loyalties. Revolutions, civil wars and other disruptive events within States may divide the membership of a regional arrangement. The division of Member States will seriously deter regional initiatives in dispute settlement. In fact, the effectiveness of the League of Arab States has been severely hampered by divisions among Member States. On the Israel–Palestine issue, for instance, Egypt and Jordan have reached peace agreements with Israel, whilst most Arab States are still technically at war with Israel.[186]

---

[181] Schulte, *Compliance*, p. 127. [182] ICJ Reports 1960, p. 203. [183] *Ibid.*, p. 217.
[184] C. Schulte, *Compliance*, pp. 129–1. See also J. G. Merrills, 'The International Court of Justice and the Adjudication of Territorial and Boundary Disputes' (2000) 13 *Leiden Journal of International Law*, p. 899.
[185] Merrills, *International Dispute Settlement*, pp. 290 *et seq.*
[186] M. Rishmawi and M. Comandulli, 'League of Arab States (LAS)' in *Max Planck Encyclopaedia*, para. 64.

Third, usually regional arrangements are largely dependent on the willingness of Member States to provide the appropriate resources necessary for a given operation. It follows that available resources are a key element for regional arrangements to commit to international dispute settlement. The combination of a small budget and limited personnel may restrict the activities of a regional arrangement in this field.

6 CONCLUSIONS

This chapter examined the role of the three organs of the United Nations in this field: the Security Council, General Assembly and Secretary-General. The matters considered in this chapter lead to the following conclusions.

(i) The UN Security Council performs multiple functions relating to international dispute settlement, such as calling for negotiations between parties to a dispute, tendering good offices and mediation, and inquiry. The functions of the Security Council are complemented by the enforcement power under Chapter VII of the UN Charter. Nonetheless, the functions of the Security Council are often prevented by the veto system. Even though the veto system is not without merit, it entails the risk of deterring effective action of the Security Council, including the settlement of international disputes through the Council.

(ii) The General Assembly has a wide range of powers to discuss and recommend measures for peaceful settlement of international disputes. The role of the General Assembly in this field is of particular importance where the Security Council has failed to take effective actions because of the use of the veto. Even though, under Article 12(1) of the UN Charter, the Security Council predominates over the General Assembly with respect to the maintenance of international peace and security, the interpretation of this provision has been relaxed over time.

(iii) The UN Secretary-General performs a wide range of activities relating to international dispute settlement. These activities include:

- good offices and mediation
- inquiry
- preventive diplomacy
- organisation of peacekeeping operations
- ruling on international disputes.

The independence of the UN Secretary-General is thought to be a key element for his successful commitment to international dispute settlement. In addition, public opinion as a living force and the confidence of the principal organs of the United Nations and major States are regarded as important elements with a view to performing his functions effectively.

(iv) Regional arrangements and agencies also perform a valuable role in the peaceful settlement of international disputes. In this regard, cooperation and coordination between the United Nations and regional institutions are important particularly in the following

fields: consultation, diplomatic support, operational support, co-deployment and joint operations.
(v) On the other hand, regional organisations and arrangements are not free from difficulty in at least these four respects:

- the intra-regional nature of international disputes
- division among the Member States
- lack of goodwill of Member States
- use of a regional arrangement by a major power as a pretext for taking no action.

Even though the role of regional organisations in international dispute settlement is important, the capacity of these organisations varies considerably.[187] Therefore, it can be considered that the role of the United Nations in this field cannot be completely replaced by the regional organisations.

FURTHER READING

Dispute Settlement System in the United Nations

M. Brus, S. Muller and S. Wiemers, *The United Nations Decade of International Law: Reflections on International Dispute Settlement* (Dordrecht: Nijhoff, 1991).

R. Higgins, 'The Place of International Law in the Settlement of Disputes by the Security Council' (1970) 64 *AJIL*, pp. 1–18.

C. Peck, *The United Nations as a Dispute Settlement System: Improving Mechanisms for the Prevention and Resolution of Conflict* (The Hague: Kluwer, 1996).

S. R. Ratner, 'Image and Reality in the UN's Peaceful Settlement of Disputes' (1995) 6 *EJIL*, pp. 426–44.

UN Secretary-General

K. A. Annan and S. Chesterman, *Secretary or General?: The UN Secretary-General in World Politics* (Cambridge University Press, 2007).

S. Ask and A. Mark-Jungkvist (eds.), *The Adventure of Peace: Dag Hammarskjöld and the Future of the United Nations* (New York: Palgrave Macmillan, 2006).

T. M. Franck, *Fairness in International Law and Institutions* (Oxford University Press, 1995), pp. 173–217.

'The Secretary-General's Role in Conflict Resolution: Past, Present and Pure Conjecture' (1995) 6 *EJIL*, pp. 360–87.

B. Rivlin and L. Gordenker (eds.), *The Challenging Role of the UN Secretary-General: Making 'The Most Impossible Job in the World' Possible* (Westport: Praeger, 1993).

O. Schachter, 'Dag Hammarskjöld and the Relation of Law to Politics' (1962) 56 *AJIL*, pp. 1–8.

C. Stahn and H. Melber (eds.), *Peace Diplomacy, Global Justice and International Agency: Rethinking Human Security and Ethics in the Spirit of Dag Hammarskjöld* (Cambridge University Press, 2014).

[187] *Ibid.*, p. 21, para. 87.

E. Stein, 'Mr. Hammarskjöld, the Charter Law and the Future Role of the United Nations Secretary General' (1962) 56 *AJIL*, pp. 9–32.

B. Urquhart, *Hammarskjöld* (New York: W. W. Norton and Company, 1994).

M. Virally, 'Le Testament politique de Dag Hammarskjöld' (1961) 7 *AFDI*, pp. 355–80.

Regional Institutions and Arrangements

Since many studies have been published with regard to various regional institutions and arrangements, only recent monographs will be listed here.

A. M. Arnull, *The European Union and Its Court of Justice*, 2nd edn (Oxford University Press, 2006).

S. Blockmans, J. Wouters and T. Ruys (eds.), *The European Union and Peacebuilding: Policy and Legal Aspects* (The Hague: T. M. C. Asser Press, 2010).

L. Boisson de Chazournes, 'Les Relations entre organisations régionales et organisations universelles' (2010) 347 *RCADI*, pp. 79–406.

M. Herz, *Organisation of American States (OAS)* (London: Routledge, 2010).

B. Horwitz, *The Transformation of the Organisation of American States: A Multilateral Framework for Regional Governance* (London: Anthem Press, 2010).

Inter-State Arbitration

Main Issues

Arbitration is one of the legal means of international disputes. An arbitral tribunal is established in an ad hoc manner on the basis of the consent of the parties in dispute and its decisions are binding upon the litigating parties. Arbitration is flexible compared to standing international courts and tribunals in the sense that the parties to a dispute can retain considerable control over the process of arbitration. Among various types of arbitration, this chapter will focus on *inter-State* arbitration. In particular, the following issues will be examined:

(i) What are the principal features of inter-State arbitration?
(ii) What are the problems associated with the selection of arbitrators?
(iii) What is the standard to determine the independence and impartiality of arbitrators?
(iv) What are the reasons that may deprive the validity of an arbitral award?
(v) What is the advantage of arbitration and what are its limitations?

1 INTRODUCTION

As provided in Article 15 of the 1899 Convention for the Pacific Settlement of International Disputes, '[i]nternational arbitration has for its object the settlement of differences between States by judges of their own choice, and on the basis of respect for law'. While, at present, multiple types of arbitration exist in the international community, this chapter will focus on inter-State arbitration.[1]

Like judicial settlement, the results of arbitration are legally binding upon the parties to the dispute. In this regard, arbitration is distinguished from diplomatic means of international dispute settlement. However, arbitration is distinct from judicial settlement in five respects (see Table 5.1).

(i) *A composition of arbitral tribunals*: While judicial settlement concerns international dispute settlement by pre-constituted international courts and tribunals, arbitrators are to be chosen by parties to a dispute on a case-by-case basis.[2] Accordingly, the

---

[1] Other types of arbitration, i.e. mixed arbitration and intra-State arbitration, will be considered in Chapter 11.
[2] United Nations, *Handbook on the Peaceful Settlement of Disputes between States* (New York: United Nations, 1992), p. 55, para. 170.

TABLE 5.1 DIFFERENCES BETWEEN ARBITRATION AND JUDICIAL SETTLEMENT

	Arbitration	Judicial Settlement (ICJ)
Organ	Ad hoc	Permanent
Judges	Selected by the parties in dispute	Pre-determined
Applicable Law	Rules adopted by the parties	International Law
Procedure	Determined by the parties	Established by the courts
Submission of disputes	Consent of the parties	Consent of the parties
Publicity	May be secret	Public
Outcome	Binding upon the parties	Binding upon the parties

parties in dispute can control the composition of an arbitral tribunal. This procedure contributes to strengthening the confidence of the parties.[3] Normally an arbitral tribunal is composed of three or five or, at most, seven members. The relatively small size of the arbitral organ makes the arbitration procedure simple and speedy. The preference for a more restricted tribunal might also have an advantage in case of more technical disputes.[4]

Where appropriate, an expert in a non-legal field, such as a scientist or an engineer, may be appointed as an arbitrator. An example is provided by the special arbitration set out under Annex VIII of the LOSC. The Annex VIII arbitral tribunal deals with disputes relating to fisheries, marine environmental protection, marine scientific research and it is composed of experts in these fields.[5] To take another example, under paragraph 4(b)(ii) of Annexure G of the 1960 Indus Water Treaty, one of the arbitrators is to be a 'highly qualified' engineer. The appointment of a scientist or an engineer as an arbitrator is thought to be relevant particularly in arbitration concerning environmental or international water disputes.[6]

(ii) *The applicable law*: In the case of judicial settlement, international courts and tribunals are in principle called upon to render the judgment on the basis of international law. In the case of arbitration, however, the parties may require an arbitral tribunal to apply specific rules which are not necessarily binding rules of international law, while normally international law is applied in arbitration.

(iii) *Procedure*: In the case of arbitration, the parties may agree procedures necessary for arbitration in a flexible manner, whilst procedures for judicial settlement are pre-determined.

(iv) *Publicity*: Unlike the ICJ,[7] the proceedings before the arbitral tribunal are not public, unless the parties in dispute agree otherwise. Pleadings and oral statements can also

---

[3] Permanent Court of Arbitration (PCA), Circular Note of the Secretary General (1960) 54 *AJIL*, p. 934.
[4] *Ibid.*, p. 935.   [5] LOSC, Articles 1 and 2 of Annex VIII.
[6] See also Chapter 10, section 2.2 of this book.
[7] In the case of the ICJ, secrecy is precluded by the ICJ Statute and Rules of Court. Article 40(3) of the ICJ Statute and Article 42 of the Rules of Court.

be confidential. Thus the parties to a dispute can take positions in the pleadings and oral statements without concern that these may be later cited by third States as evidence of State practice.

(v) *Speed of the proceedings*: Normally arbitration will take less time than a case before the ICJ.[8] Speedy settlement of international disputes is an advantage of arbitration. A short period of the proceedings before an arbitral tribunal may reduce the cost of litigation.

Noting the above points, this chapter will examine the law and procedure of inter-State arbitration. First, this chapter reviews development of inter-State arbitration in section 2. It then examines the issues of the selection of arbitrators in section 3. Next, this chapter outlines the process of arbitration in section 4. Furthermore, intervention by third States and effects of the arbitral award are examined in sections 5 and 6, respectively. Finally, this chapter addresses the interpretation of the arbitral award in section 7, before presenting conclusions in section 8.

2 DEVELOPMENT OF INTER-STATE ARBITRATION

As a preliminary consideration, it is necessary to briefly outline the development of arbitration.[9] The antecedents of arbitration are said to be detected in the practice of ancient Greece and certain European polities during the Middle Ages. However interesting the facts may be, examples of arbitration in the Middle Ages differed from contemporary arbitration for the modern state had not emerged at that time.[10]

It has been generally considered that the origin of modern arbitration dated back to the 1794 Treaty of Amity, Commerce and Navigation between Great Britain and the United States (the Jay Treaty).[11] The treaty set up three arbitral commissions, namely the St Croix River Commission (Article 5), the British Debts Commission (Article 6) and the Maritime Claims Commission (Article 7) and their decisions were considered as final and conclusive. In particular, the Maritime Claims Commission managed to deliver a large number of awards. The Jay Treaty can be said to mark a landmark in the development of international arbitration in modern times.[12] At that time, however, arbitral commissions were still considered as the extension of diplomacy because they consisted exclusively of the disputing parties' nationals.[13]

---

[8] PCA, Circular Note, p. 937.
[9] Generally on this subject, see C. Gray and B. Kingsbury, 'Developments in Dispute Settlement: Inter-State Arbitration Since 1945' (1992) 63 *BYIL*, pp. 97–134; L. Simpson and H. Fox, *Arbitration: Law and Practice* (London: Stevens and Sons Limited, 1959), pp. 1 *et seq.*; J. Collier and V. Lowe, *The Settlement of Disputes in International Law: Institutions and Procedures* (Oxford University Press, 2000), pp. 31–35.
[10] C. H. Brower II, 'Arbitration' in *Max Planck Encyclopaedia*, paras. 10–11.
[11] The text of the Jay Treaty is available at: http://avalon.law.yale.edu/18th_century/jay.asp. It was partly reproduced in: C. J. Tams and A. Tzanakopoulos (eds.), *The Settlement of International Disputes: Basic Documents* (Oxford: Hart Publishing, 2012), p. 1. John Jay was the first Chief Justice of the United States Supreme Court and former Secretary of Foreign Affairs. K. S. Ziegler, 'Jay Treaty (1794)' in *Max Planck Encyclopaedia*, para. 1.
[12] *Ibid.*, paras. 9 and 15.
[13] Collier and Lowe, *The Settlement of Disputes*, p. 32; Brower II, 'Arbitration', para. 18.

The more decisive step toward the modern form of arbitration was taken in the *Alabama Claims* case of 1872.[14] This case related to Great Britain's responsibilities as a neutral during the American Civil War.[15] The *Alabama* was built in Birkenhead under the misleading name *Enrica*. The *Enrica* sailed from Liverpool for the Azores where it received coal, guns, ammunition, uniforms and supplies. It changed its name to *Alabama* and sailed to attack US vessels. She burned or sank sixty-four US vessels before she was herself sunk in June 1864 near Cherbourg. The United States complained that Great Britain had violated its neutrality by allowing ships to be built and sold to the Confederate States.

The British and American Governments established a five-member Arbitral Tribunal, including two national members. The Arbitral Tribunal followed a strictly judicial procedure and issued a reasoned award.[16] The arbitration resulted in an award against Great Britain of US$15,500,000 in gold. The award was duly honoured and the *Alabama Claims* dispute was successfully resolved by the arbitration. The success of the *Alabama Claims* arbitration was followed in subsequent disputes, such as the *Bering Sea Fur Seal* case (1893) and the *British Guiana–Venezuela Boundary* dispute (1897). It also inspired the States represented at the 1899 Hague Peace Conference to adopt a Convention on dispute settlement which established a Permanent Court of Arbitration (PCA).

The establishment of the PCA under the 1899 Hague Convention marked a landmark in the development of arbitration in international law. The seat of the PCA is at The Hague.[17] The PCA embraces three bodies: a panel of members, an International Bureau, and an Administrative Council. Concerning the panel of members, the 1899 Hague Convention allowed parties to nominate a maximum of four persons 'of known competency in questions of international law, of the highest moral reputation and disposed to accept the duties of Arbitrator'. The persons thus selected are to be inscribed, as Members of the Court, in a list which shall be notified by the International Bureau to all the Signatory Powers. Such persons are nominated for terms of six years.[18] An International Bureau, established at The Hague, serves as record office for the Court. This Bureau is the channel for communications relative to the meetings of the Court.[19] A Permanent Administrative Council which is composed of the Diplomatic Representatives of the Signatory Powers accredited to The Hague and of the Netherlands Minister for Foreign Affairs as President has the direction and control of the International Bureau.[20]

In summary, the PCA was little more than a panel of names from which arbitrators may be selected when the occasion arises. Therefore, some argue that the name of the *Permanent* Court of Arbitration is a misnomer.[21] According to a survey, the PCA dealt with

---

[14] J. B. Moore, *History and Digest of the International Arbitrations to Which the United States Has Been a Party*, Vol. I (Washington: Government Printing Office, 1898), pp. 495 *et seq.* See also, T. W. Balch, *The Alabama Arbitration* (Philadelphia, 1900); T. Bingham, 'The Alabama Claims Arbitration' (2005) 54 *ICLQ*, pp. 1–25; by the same writer, 'Alabama Arbitration' in *Max Planck Encyclopaedia*; A. Cook, *The 'Alabama' Claims* (Ithaca: Cornell University Press, 1975); A. Clapham, *Brierly's Law of Nations*, 7th edn (Oxford University Press, 2012), pp. 410–13.

[15] In May 1861, the British Government recognised the Confederates as belligerents and declared British neutrality.

[16] J. G. Merrills, *International Dispute Settlement*, 6th edn (Cambridge University Press, 2017), p. 91.

[17] Article 25 of the 1899 Hague Convention; Article 43 of the 1907 Hague Convention.

[18] Article 23 of the 1899 Hague Convention; Article 44 of the 1907 Hague Convention.

[19] Article 22 of the 1899 Hague Convention; Article 43 of the 1907 Hague Convention.

[20] Article 28 of the 1899 Hague Convention; Article 49 of the 1907 Hague Convention.

[21] M. O. Hudson, 'The Permanent Court of Arbitration' (1933) 27 *AJIL*, p. 445.

only eight cases between 1899 and 1907,[22] and fourteen cases between 1908 and 1923.[23] It can be observed that the activities of the PCA remained modest before World War II.

In the 1990s, several reforms were made with a view to more activating the PCA.[24] For instance, a series of optional rules were adopted.[25] Those optional rules provide a guideline for States respecting the referral of international disputes to arbitration. Furthermore, a Financial Assistant Fund was established in order to facilitate the recourse to arbitration or other means of settlement. Terms of reference are specified in *Permanent Court of Arbitration Financial Assistance Fund for Settlement of International Disputes: Terms of Reference and Guidelines* approved by the Administrative Council on 11 December 1995.[26] Moreover, the interlinkage between the PCA and other international organs was strengthened. For instance, the PCA concluded an exchange of letters between the Secretary-General and the Registrar of ITLOS concerning cooperation between two institutions on relevant legal and administrative matters in December 2005.[27] In many cases, the PCA is acting as registry in arbitration under Annex VII of the LOSC.[28]

3 THE SELECTION OF ARBITRATORS

3.1 Disagreement with Regard to the Appointment of Arbitrators

The State Parties to a specific dispute can freely determine the composition of an arbitration tribunal, unless their treaty obligations provide otherwise. While there were some cases where a sole arbitrator was appointed,[29] at present, the practice of arbitration by only one arbitrator has become less common and, more often than not, an arbitral tribunal consists of three or five members.[30]

---

[22] These cases were: Mexico/USA (14 October 1902), France, Germany, Great Britain/Japan (22 May 1905), Germany, Great Britain, Italy/Venezuela (22 February 1904), France/Guatemala (25 April 1904), the Netherlands/Portugal (25 June 1914), France/Great Britain (8 August 1905), Norway/Sweden (23 October 1909), and France/Germany (22 May 1909). A. M. Stuyt, *Survey of International Arbitrations 1974-1989* (Dordrecht: Nijhoff, 1990), pp. 205, 253, 261, 276, 281-2, 293-4.

[23] These cases were: Great Britain/USA (7 September 1910), USA/Venezuela (25 October 1910), Italy/Peru (3 May 1902), Russia/Turkey (11 November 1912), France/Great Britain (24 February 1911), France/Italy (6 May 1913), France/Italy (6 May 1913), France/Italy (3 May 1913), France, Great Britain, Spain/Portugal (2 and 4 September 1920), France/Peru (11 October 1921), Norway/USA (13 October 1922), the Netherlands/USA (4 April 1928), France/ Great Britain (9 June 1931), and Sweden/USA (18 July 1932). *Ibid.*, pp. 296-7, 305, 307, 310, 313-15, 320, 325, 347, 381, 406, 409. See also L. Caflisch, 'Cent ans de règlement pacifique des différends interétatiques' (2001) 288 *RCADI*, p. 315.

[24] See B. E. Shifman, 'The Revitalization of the Permanent Court of Arbitration' (1995) 23 *International Journal of Legal Information*, pp. 284-92; by the same writer, 'The Permanent Court of Arbitration: Recent Development' (1995) 8 *LJIL*, pp. 193-202; S. Muller and W. Mus, 'The Flame Rekindled' (1993) 6 *LJIL*, pp. 203-14; J. L. Bleich, 'A New Direction for the PCA: The Work of the Expert Group' (1993) 6 *LJIL*, pp. 215-40.

[25] The electronic texts of the documents are available at the homepage of the Permanent Court of Arbitration: www.pca-cpa.org/.

[26] This document is available at the homepage of the Permanent Court of Arbitration: www.pca-cpa.org/.

[27] *105th Annual Report of the Permanent Court of Arbitration* (2005), p. 6, para. 53.

[28] For the Annex VII Arbitral Tribunal of the LOSC, see Chapter 8, section 5.1 of this book.

[29] In the *Argentina-Chile Frontier* case of 1966, Queen Elizabeth II was appointed as a sole arbitrator, but actually the Arbitral Tribunal composed of three members was established under the direction of the Queen. 9 December 1966, 16 *RIAA*, p. 109. The same was true in the *Beagle Channel* arbitration of 1977. In this case, Queen Elizabeth II was appointed as a sole arbitrator and, then, the Arbitral Tribunal composed of five judges of the ICJ was established under the direction of the Queen. 18 February 1977, 21 *RIAA*, p. 53.

[30] For various formulae of the selection of arbitration, see Caflisch, 'Cent ans de règlement pacifique des différends interétatiques', pp. 368-77.

When parties in dispute could agree the composition of an arbitral tribunal, no serious legal issue arises. Where there is no agreement in the appointment of either the third or the fifth member or one of the parties to a dispute has not appointed its member of the arbitral tribunal, however, the establishment of an arbitral tribunal encounters considerable difficulty. In reality, this question was raised in the 1950 *Peace Treaties* case (second phase).[31] In April 1949, the question of the observance of human rights in Bulgaria and Hungary was referred to the UN General Assembly. The latter adopted a resolution in which it expressed its deep concern at the grave accusations made against the Governments of Bulgaria and Hungary in this connection, and drew their attention to their obligations under the 1947 Peace Treaties which they had signed with the Allied and Associated Powers (i.e. the United States and the United Kingdom).

The 1947 Peace Treaties contained a provision concerning peaceful settlement of international disputes as follows:

> Any such dispute not resolved by them within a period of two months shall, unless the parties to the dispute mutually agree upon another means of settlement, be referred at the request of either party to the dispute to a Commission composed of one representative of each party and a third member selected by mutual agreement of the two parties from nationals of a third country. Should two parties fail to agree within a period of one month upon the appointment of the third member, the Secretary-General of the United Nations may be requested by either party to make the appointment.[32]

The United States and the United Kingdom required that a Treaty Commission be established on the basis of this clause. Nonetheless, the Governments of Bulgaria, Hungary and Romania had refused to designate their representatives to the Treaty Commissions for the settlement of disputes, arguing that there was no dispute. The UN General Assembly thus requested the ICJ to answer, *inter alia*, the following question:

> III. If one party fails to appoint a representative to a Treaty Commission under the Treaties of Peace with Bulgaria, Hungary and Rumania where that party is obliged to appoint a representative to the Treaty Commission, is the Secretary-General of the United Nations authorised to appoint the third member of the Commission upon the request of the other party to a dispute according to the provisions of the respective Treaties?[33]

In this regard, the Court held that: 'While the text in its literal sense does not completely exclude the possibility of the appointment of the third member before the

---

[31] *Interpretation of Peace Treaties with Bulgaria, Hungary and Romania*, Advisory Opinion of 18 July 1950, ICJ Reports 1950, p. 221. For a commentary of this case, see K. S. Carlston, 'Interpretation of Peace Treaties with Bulgaria, Hungary, and Rumania, Advisory Opinions of the International Court of Justice' (1950) 44 *AJIL*, pp. 728–37; A. Jakab, 'Peace Treaties with Bulgaria, Hungary, and Romania, Interpretation of (Advisory Opinions)' in *Max Planck Encyclopaedia*.

[32] Articles 36, 40 and 38, respectively, of the Peace Treaties with Bulgaria, Hungary and Romania, ICJ Reports 1950, p. 226.

[33] *Ibid.*

appointment of both national Commissioners it is nevertheless true that according to the natural and ordinary meaning of the terms it was intended that the appointment of both the national Commissioners should precede that of the third member.'[34] According to the Court, the Secretary-General's power to appoint a third member is derived solely from the agreement of the parties as expressed in the disputes clause of the treaties. Thus 'by its very nature such a clause must be strictly construed and can be applied only in the case expressly provided for therein'.[35] Furthermore, the appointment of a third member by the Secretary-General would result only in the constitution of a two-member commission. In the view of the Court, however, '[a] Commission consisting of two members is not the kind of commission for which the Treaties have provided'.[36]

In conclusion, the Court decided, eleven votes to two, to answer Question III in the negative. As a consequence, there were no procedural means to review the breach of human rights and fundamental freedoms as guaranteed by the peace treaties by the named three States. The *Peace Treaties* case demonstrated that a refusal by one State to appoint its arbitrator deters the initiation of arbitration. As Judge Read stated, however, this situation would allow a defaulting party to disregard with impunity most of the substantive treaty provisions.[37] A possible solution in this matter may be that a third party is to appoint the second member, when one of the parties has refused to appoint its own member. This solution is adopted by, for example, Article 4(2) of Annex to the 1997 UN Convention on the Law of the Non-Navigational Uses of International Watercourses.[38] Article 3(e) of Annex VII of the LOSC also provides a similar procedure.[39]

3.2 Independence and Impartiality of Arbitrators

Under Article 6(4) of the 1992 PCA Optional Rules:

> In making the appointment, the appointing authority shall have regard to such considerations as are likely to secure the appointment of *an independent and impartial* arbitrator and shall take into account as well the advisability of appointing an arbitrator of a nationality other than the nationalities of the parties.[40]

As stated in the provision, independence and impartiality can be regarded as key requirements when appointing arbitrators. In fact, an absence of independence and impartiality may lead to the loss of confidence of the parties and undermine the validity of arbitration.

---

[34] Second Phase, ICJ Reports 1950, p. 227.   [35] *Ibid*.   [36] *Ibid*., p. 228.
[37] Dissenting Opinion of Judge Read, *ibid*., p. 245.
[38] Article 4(2) of Annex to the 1997 UN Convention provides that: 'If one of the parties to the dispute does not appoint an arbitrator within two months of receipt of the request, the other party may inform the President of the International Court of Justice, who shall make the designation within a further two-month period.' Under the 1997 Convention, the arbitral tribunal shall consist of three members.
[39] See Chapter 8, section 5.1 of this book.   [40] Emphasis added.

When considering this subject, two cases merit discussion: the *Croatia/Slovenia* arbitration (Partial Award)[41] and *Chagos Marine Protected Area* arbitration.[42]

3.2.1 The *Croatia/Slovenia* Arbitration (Partial Award)

A pivotal issue in the *Croatia/Slovenia* arbitration was whether the breach of independence and impartiality by an arbitrator prevents continuation of the arbitral proceedings. The territorial and maritime dispute between Croatia and Slovenia was submitted to arbitration under the arbitration agreement of 4 November 2009. On 22 July 2015, Serbian and Croatian newspapers reported that telephone conversations between Dr Jernej Sekolec, the arbitrator originally appointed by Slovenia in the present proceedings, and one of the Agents designated by Slovenia, Ms Drenik, had been intercepted. In the course of these conversations, Dr Sekolec reportedly disclosed confidential information about the Tribunal's deliberations to Ms Drenik. Following the press reports, both Dr Sekolec and Ms Drenik resigned from their functions, as arbitrator and as Agent, in the present proceedings.[43] Shortly afterwards, the arbitrator originally appointed by Croatia, Professor Budislav Vukas, also resigned.[44] Subsequently, the Tribunal was recomposed on 25 September 2015.[45] The incident gave rise to significant disagreement between the parties as to how to proceed with the arbitration. Whereas Croatia requested the Tribunal to discontinue the arbitral proceedings, Slovenia asked the Tribunal to complete its mandate as envisaged by the arbitration agreement.[46]

The Tribunal stressed that the PCA Optional Rules extended the same high standard of impartiality or independence to all arbitrators, regardless of their method of appointment. According to the Tribunal, there was no doubt that Dr Sekolec and Ms Drenik acted in blatant violation of provisions concerning impartiality and independence.[47] However, the enquiry was whether, as alleged by Croatia, the proceedings before the Tribunal could not go further because of the breaches. In this regard, the Tribunal stated that it had not only the power but also the duty to settle the land and maritime dispute which was submitted to it after lengthy and difficult negotiations between the two countries under the auspices of the European Union and that it had the duty to safeguard the 'integrity of the arbitral process' and to stop that process if it could not ensure that integrity.[48] It then highlighted three principal elements. First, no doubt had been expressed on the impartiality or independence of the three remaining arbitrators or of the two new ones and, thus, the Tribunal was properly recomposed.[49] Second, since Dr Sekolec and Professor Vukas have resigned as arbitrators, their views expressed in prior deliberation meetings are of no relevance

---

[41] Arbitration between the Republic of Croatia and the Republic of Slovenia, Partial Award, 30 June 2016, available at: https://pca-cpa.org/en/cases.
[42] *Chagos Marine Protected Area* arbitration (Mauritius v United Kingdom), available at: https://pca-cpa.org/en/cases. For a commentary of this decision, see R. Churchill, 'Dispute Settlement in the Law of the Sea: Survey for 2011' (2012) 27 *IJMCL*, pp. 542–5; I. Papanicolopulu, 'Submission to Arbitration of the Dispute on the Marine Protected Area around the Chagos Archipelago' (2011) 26 *IJMCL*, pp. 667–78.
[43] The *Croatia/Slovenia* arbitration, paras. 38 and 41.
[44] *Ibid.*, para. 43. [45] *Ibid.*, para. 49. [46] *Ibid.*, paras. 6–7. [47] *Ibid.*, para. 175.
[48] *Ibid.*, para. 183. [49] *Ibid.*, para. 186.

for the work of the Tribunal in its current composition.[50] Third, in order to put to rest the question of any procedural disadvantage to Croatia resulting from the actions of Dr Sekolec, the Tribunal would be ready to consider reopening the oral phase of the case and to give each party a further opportunity to express its views concerning what it regards as the most important facts and arguments. In so doing, the procedural balance between the parties was secured.[51]

In conclusion, the Tribunal held that there was no obstacle to the continuation of the proceedings under the arbitral agreement.[52] It further ruled that the breaches of the arbitration agreement by Slovenia did not render the continuation of the proceedings impossible.[53] The Tribunal thus unanimously decided that the arbitration agreement remained in force and that the arbitral proceedings should continue.[54]

3.2.2 The *Chagos Marine Protected Area* Arbitration

Furthermore, the standard for determining the independency and impartiality must be examined. This issue was discussed in the *Chagos Marine Protected Area* arbitration. This case concerned the legality of a 200-nautical mile Marine Protected Area (MPA) around the Chagos Archipelago on 1 April 2010. In order to obtain an authoritative and legally binding declaration regarding the legality of the MPA, on 20 December 2010, Mauritius commenced arbitration proceedings against the United Kingdom pursuant to Article 287 of the LOSC and in accordance with Article 1 of Annex VII of the LOSC.[55] The PCA acted as Registry in this case.[56]

The members of the Tribunal were appointed in accordance with LOSC Article 3 of Annex VII. Whilst Mauritius appointed Judge Rüdiger Wolfrum, a German national, the United Kingdom appointed Judge Sir Christopher Greenwood, a British national.[57] The three remaining arbitrators were appointed by the President of ITLOS pursuant to LOSC Annex VII, Article 3(e). These arbitrators were Judge James Kateka, a Tanzanian national; Judge Albert Hoffmann, a South African national; and Professor Ivan Shearer, an Autralian national as President of the Tribunal. It followed that all three judges came from States bordering the Indian Ocean.[58]

However, Mauritius claimed that the appointment of Judge Greenwood as an arbitrator was incompatible with the principle of independence and impartiality because of the 'long-standing' and 'close working' character of the relationship between Judge Greenwood and the Government of the United Kingdom. In this regard, Mauritius claimed the application of the 'Appearance of Bias Standard' which was codified in the International Bar Association Guidelines on Conflicts of Interests in International Arbitration (hereafter the IBA Guidelines). It argued that the Appearance of Bias Standard

---

[50] *Ibid.*, para. 193.   [51] *Ibid.*, para. 194.   [52] *Ibid.*, para. 196.   [53] *Ibid.*, para. 225.
[54] *Ibid.*, para. 231.   [55] Reasoned Decision on Challenge, p. 1, para. 4.
[56] *Ibid.*, p. 1, para. 9.   [57] *Ibid.*, paras. 5–6.
[58] *Ibid.*, para. 8; Churchill, 'Survey for 2011', p. 542.

reflected in the IBA Guidelines is a universal standard and a general principle of law.[59] In light of the Standard, Mauritius advocated that: '[T]he proper inquiry is not whether actual bias or dependence upon a party exists, but instead, whether there is an appearance of bias or lack of independence [or impartiality].'[60] This can be called the Appearance of Bias Standard.

However, the United Kingdom rejected the validity of the Appearance of Bias Standard and claimed the application of the Specific Prior Involvement Standard on the basis of Articles 16, 17 and 24 of the ICJ Statute, Article 34 of the Rules of Court, Article 8 of the Statute of ITLOS, and the practice of these two international courts and of inter-State arbitral tribunals under Annex VII of the LOSC. According to 'the Involvement of the Very Subject Matter Standard', 'the arbitrator must not have had any involvement with the actual dispute that is before the arbitral tribunal'.[61]

The Arbitral Tribunal, in its Reasoned Decision on Challenge of 30 November 2011, did not consider that principles and rules relating to arbitrators, developed in the context of international commercial arbitration and arbitration regarding investment disputes, are applicable to inter-State disputes.[62] In the view of the Tribunal, the law applicable to the present arbitration is that to be found in Annex VII of the LOSC, supplemented by the law and practice of international courts and tribunals in inter-State cases.[63] Thus the Arbitral Tribunal was not convinced that the Appearance of Bias Standard as presented by Mauritius and derived from private law sources was of direct application in the present case.[64] According the Arbitral Tribunal, 'a party challenging an arbitrator must demonstrate and prove that, applying the standards applicable to inter-State cases, there are justifiable grounds for doubting the independence and impartiality of that arbitrator in a particular case'.[65] In light of the standard as well as the practice of the ICJ, the Tribunal concluded that Judge Greenwood's prior activities as counsel were not such as to give rise to justifiable doubts as to his independence or impartiality.[66]

4 PROCESS OF ARBITRATION

4.1 Initiation of the Arbitration Process

Mutual consent of the parties to a dispute provides a foundation of arbitration. The parties in dispute may refer an international dispute to arbitration by three ways: dispute settlement treaties, a compromissory clause, and a *compromis*.

First, the State Parties may agree to submit all or special categories of future dispute to arbitration in multilateral or bilateral treaties entirely devoted to the peaceful settlement

---

[59] Reasoned Decision on Challenge, p. 8, para. 46 and p. 10, para. 58.
[60] Ibid., p. 7, para. 43. Related to this, Mauritius referred to Judge Mensah's statement concerning the practice of ITLOS. Ibid., p. 14, para. 77.
[61] Ibid., p. 9, para. 53. In this regard, the United Kingdom referred to the statement of Judge Guillaume with regard to the practice of the ICJ. Ibid., p. 30, para. 164. This statement will be referred to in section 3.2 of Chapter 6.
[62] Ibid., p. 28, para. 156.   [63] Ibid., p. 30, para. 165.   [64] Ibid., p. 31, paras. 168–9.
[65] Ibid., p. 31, para. 166.   [66] Ibid., p. 32, para. 173; p. 34, paras. 183–4.

of international disputes. Such treaties are commonly called 'dispute settlement treaties'. Examples include the 1899 and 1907 Hague Conventions for the Pacific Settlement of International Disputes and the 1949 Revised General Act. An example of a bilateral treaty wholly devoted to the peaceful settlement of disputes is provided by the 1965 Treaty for Conciliation, Judicial Settlement and Arbitration between the UK and Switzerland.[67]

Second, the parties to a dispute may agree to submit all or part of their future disputes regarding that treaty to arbitration by a compromissory clause (*clause compromissoire*) in a treaty. A compromissory clause is a provision which provides for the settlement by arbitration of all or part of the disputes which may arise in regard to the interpretation or application of that treaty. Given that the compromissory clauses generally lack specificity concerning the rules of establishment and operation of the tribunal, the parties usually need to conclude a special agreement, i.e. *compromis* when submitting a dispute to arbitration.[68]

Third, the parties to a dispute may agree to submit disputes to arbitration by a special agreement or *compromis* after the occurrence of the dispute. The term *compromis* refers to an agreement for the immediate reference of a specific dispute to settlement by a judicial or arbitral body. In other words, *compromis* means the ad hoc treaty instrument directed to the settlement of a specific existing dispute.[69] According to the Model Rules on Arbitral Procedure prepared by the International Law Commission (ILC) in 1958, a *compromis* shall specify, as a minimum:

(a) the undertaking to arbitrate according to which the dispute is to be submitted to the arbitrators
(b) the subject matter of the dispute and, if possible, the points on which the parties are or are not agreed
(c) the method of constituting the tribunal and the number of arbitrators.[70]

Normally arbitration does not encounter the problems with non-appearance. Where an international dispute was submitted to an arbitral tribunal as an obligation set out in a treaty, however, non-appearance of one of the disputing parties may be at issue. In the *'Arctic Sunrise'* case, for instance, the Russian Federation did not appear before the Annex VII Arbitral Tribunal under the LOSC.[71] Similarly, China refused to appear before the Annex VII Arbitral Tribunal in the *South China Sea* arbitration between the Philippines and China.[72] However, it must be stressed that non-appearance of one of the disputing parties does not constitute a bar to the judicial proceedings and that the eventual judgment is binding upon the non-appearing parties.[73]

---

[67] English text in: 605 *UNTS*, p. 206; (1965) 4 *ILM*, pp. 943–56. Entered into force 9 February 1967.
[68] United Nations, *Handbook*, pp. 57–8, paras. 174–5.
[69] H. Thirlway, 'Compromis' in *Max Planck Encyclopaedia*, paras. 1 and 4.   [70] Article 2(1).
[71] See Chapter 8, section 4.4 of this book.
[72] Y. Tanaka, 'Reflections on the Philippines/China Arbitration: Award on Jurisdiction and Admissibility' (2016) 15 *The Law and Practice of International Courts and Tribunals*, pp. 307–11.
[73] G. Fitzmaurice, 'The Problem of the "Non-Appearing" Defendant Government' (1980) 51 *BYIL*, p. 98; H. Thirlway, *The Law and Procedure of the International Court of Justice: Fifty Years of Jurisprudence*, Vol. II (Oxford University Press, 2013), p. 1824. See also Chapter 8, section 4.4 of this book.

4.2 Scope of the Jurisdiction of an Arbitral Tribunal

The subject matter of the dispute is a key element for determining the scope of the jurisdiction of an arbitral tribunal. By defining the scope of issues narrowly in a *compromis*, the parties in dispute can prevent an investigation of wider questions which might create more problems than it would resolve, or exclude from arbitration particular issues for which negotiation or some other means of settlement is considered more appropriate. However, an extremely narrow formulation creates considerable difficulties for an arbitral tribunal in the process of arbitration. An illustrative example is the 1988 *Taba* arbitration which concerned the location of certain pillars marking an international boundary between Egypt and Israel. In this arbitration, these two States set out their respective submissions in an appendix to the *compromis* and asked the Tribunal to decide the location of the pillars in dispute.[74] In an annex to the agreement, these States stated that:

> 5. The Tribunal is not authorized to establish a location of a boundary pillar other than a location advanced by Egypt or by Israel and recorded in Appendix A. The Tribunal also is not authorized to address the location of boundary pillars other than those specified in paragraph 1.[75]

It followed that the Tribunal could only choose between the rival locations put forward by the parties and could not select a different solution. This type of formula creates a problem if neither party can make out a persuasive case.

In some cases, the parties to a dispute failed to reach an agreement in formulating issues to be submitted to an arbitral tribunal in a *compromis*. The 1977 *Beagle Channel* dispute is a case in point. In this case, Chile and Argentina were unable to formulate a mutually acceptable formulation for the *compromis*. Thus two different versions of the question were provided in the *compromis*, and referred both to the Tribunal for decision.[76] In this regard, the Court of Arbitration considered that the two different approaches adopted by the parties (i.e. the 'maritime' (Argentina) and the 'territorial' (Chile)) appeared to the Court to lead to much the same thing since title to territory automatically involves jurisdiction over the appurtenant waters and continental shelf and adjacent submarine areas.[77] It thus determined the boundary within the Beagle Channel and recognised the sovereignty of Chile over the disputed islands of Picton, Lennox and Nueva.[78]

A similar problem was raised in the 1998 *Eritrea/Yemen* arbitration. In this case, Eritrea and Yemen could not reach an agreement with regard to the question as to whether certain islands fell within the scope of the arbitration.[79] Thus the two parties left the question for the Tribunal itself to determine the scope of the dispute, taking into account 'the

---

[74] *Case Concerning the location of boundary markers in Taba between Egypt and Israel*, 29 September 1988, 20 *RIAA*, p. 1.
[75] *Ibid.*, p. 114.   [76] Article I of the arbitration agreement of 22 July 1971, 21 *RIAA*, p. 65.
[77] *Ibid.*, p. 80, para. 6.
[78] *Ibid.*, pp. 189–90, para. 176. See also section 6.4 of this chapter.
[79] *Territorial Sovereignty and Scope of the Dispute (Eritrea and Yemen)*, 9 October 1998, 22 *RIAA*, p. 231, para. 74.

respective positions of the two Parties'.[80] Concerning the question of the scope of the dispute, the Arbitral Tribunal preferred the view of Eritrea and accordingly made an award on sovereignty in respect of all the islands and islets with respect to which the parties had put forward conflicting claims, which include Jabal al-Tayr and the Zubayr group, as well as the Hancocks and the Mohabbakahs.[81]

In the 1977 *Anglo-French Continental Shelf* case, a question was raised as to whether the Arbitral Tribunal had jurisdiction to draw a delimitation line in a territorial sea between the Channel Islands and the coasts of Normandy and Brittany. Since this would be go beyond the terms of *compromis* which the United Kingdom and France were evidently unwilling to extend, the Court decided that a delimitation of this area was outside its competence and must be left for the parties themselves to determine.[82]

In the 1992 *St Pierre and Miquelon* arbitration, France sought a delimitation of the continental shelf appertaining to islands situated off the Canadian coast. Related to this, it also asked the Arbitral Tribunal to determine their entitlement beyond the 200-mile limit. Nonetheless the Arbitral Tribunal held that this would involve determining France's rights vis-à-vis the international community which was not a party to the arbitration. It therefore decided that it had no jurisdiction to extend its ruling in the way questioned.[83]

4.3 Applicable Law

As explained earlier, the parties before an arbitral tribunal may agree to apply specific rules other than rules of international law, although many arbitration agreements specifically stipulate international law as the applicable law. In the *Alabama* arbitration, for instance, the parties instructed the Tribunal to apply a particular set of rules concerning neutrality which the British Government did not consider to represent rules of international law at the time the claims arose.[84] In the *Trail Smelter* arbitration, the parties instructed the Tribunal to apply 'the law and practice followed in dealing with cognate questions in the United States of America as well as international law and practice, and shall give consideration to the desire of the High Contracting Parties to reach a solution just to all parties concerned'.[85]

However, a question arises where there is no agreement concerning the applicable law. In this regard, Article 28 of the 1949 Revised General Act for the Pacific Settlement of International Disputes provides that:

> If nothing is laid down in the special agreement or no special agreement has been made, the Tribunal shall apply the rules in regard to the substance of the dispute enumerated in Article 38 of the Statute of the International Court of Justice. In so far as there exists no such rule applicable to the dispute, the Tribunal shall decide *ex aequo et bono*.[86]

---

[80] Article 2(2) of arbitration agreement of 3 October 1996, 22 *RIAA*, p. 216.   [81] *Ibid.*, p. 234, para. 90.
[82] 18 *RIAA* p. 24, paras. 20–1.   [83] 21 *RIAA* p. 292, paras. 78–9.
[84] Article VI of the 1871 Treaty of Washington. Article VI specified three rules applicable to this case. The electronic text of the treaty is available at: www.marshall.edu/special-collections/css_alabama/pdf/treaty_washington.pdf. See also Clapham, *Brierly's Law of Nations*, p. 412; Bingham, 'Alabama Arbitration', para. 7.
[85] Article IV of the Special Agreement. *Trail Smelter case* (United States v Canada) (1950) 3 *RIAA*, p. 1908.
[86] See also Article 26 of the 1957 European Convention for the Peaceful Settlement of Disputes.

The 1992 Permanent Court of Arbitration Optional Rules for Arbitrating Disputes between Two States (hereafter the 1992 PCA Optional Rules) also contain a similar provision.[87]

In the *Taba* arbitration, the *compromis* contained no reference at all to the applicable law, but merely asked the Tribunal to decide the location of the boundary pillars 'of the recognised international boundary'. The Arbitral Tribunal thus assumed that the decision was to be decided on the basis of international law.[88]

5 INTERVENTION BY THIRD STATES

The *Projet de règlement pour la procédure arbitrale internationale* adopted by the *Institut de droit international* took the position that a third party's intervention is admissible only with the consent of the parties that concluded the *compromis*.[89] A commentary on Article 62 of the ICJ Statute echoed this view, stating that: 'Generally, provisions for arbitral procedures provide for intervention only with the parties' consent.'[90] Furthermore, Brownlie clearly stated that: 'Arbitration is litigation in conditions of privacy; no third-party intervention is possible.'[91] In summary, there may be room for the view that where there is no provision permitting intervention by a third party in the rules of procedure, a request for intervention in the arbitral proceedings can be accepted only with consent of the original parties.

In practice, arbitral tribunals appear to take a flexible approach to the admissibility of third-party intervention in arbitral proceedings. In the *Eritrea/Yemen* arbitration (the Second Phase), for instance, the Kingdom of Saudi Arabia had written to the Registrar of the Tribunal on 31 August 1997 pointing out that its boundaries with Yemen were disputed, without attempting to intervene in the arbitral proceedings. It also suggested that the Tribunal should restrict its decision to areas 'that do not extend north of the latitude of the most northern point on Jabal al-Tayr Island'.[92] Saudi Arabia's claim was taken into account by the Tribunal, stating that: 'Reference has been made above to the need not to extend the boundary to areas that might involve third parties.'[93]

Another example in this regard is the position of Viet Nam in the *South China Sea* arbitration. Even though Viet Nam has not applied to intervene in the proceedings of the arbitration, it sent a series of Notes Verbales to the Tribunal and actively expressed its view with regard to substantive issues in the *South China Sea* arbitration. The Arbitral Tribunal took the position that it would address the permissibility of Viet Nam's intervention in

---

[87] See Article 33(1). This document was reproduced in C. J. Tams and A. Tzanakopoulos (eds.), *The Settlement of International Disputes: Basic Documents* (Oxford: Hart Publishing, 2012), p. 205.
[88] Merrills, *International Dispute Settlement*, p. 100.
[89] Institut de droit international, *Projet de règlement pour la procédure arbitrale internationale*, Session de La Haye, 1875, Article 16, available at: www.justitiaetpace.org/idiF/resolutionsF/1875_haye_01_fr.pdf.
[90] C. Chinkin, 'Article 62' in A. Zimmermann et al. (eds.), *The Statute of the International Court of Justice: A Commentary*, 2nd edn (Oxford University Press, 2012), p. 1568.
[91] I. Brownlie, 'The Peaceful Settlement of International Disputes' (2009) 8 *CJIL*, p. 277.
[92] *Second Stage of the Proceedings between Eritrea and Yemen* (Maritime Delimitation), 17 December 1999, 22 RIAA, p. 344, para. 44.
[93] *Ibid.*, p. 372, para. 164. See also S. Yee, 'Intervention in an Arbitral Proceedings under Annex VII to the UNCLOS?' (2015) 14 *CJIL*, p. 98, footnote 45.

the proceedings only when Viet Nam made a formal application of such intervention.[94] However, it relied on Viet Nam's claim when considering whether any third parties are indispensable to the proceedings. In fact, 'in light of Viet Nam's own stance with respect to the proceedings', the Tribunal found that Viet Nam was not an indispensable third party and that its absence as a party did not preclude the Tribunal from proceeding with the arbitration.[95] The *South China Sea* arbitration appears to suggest that a third party's claim can be taken into account by an arbitral tribunal, even if that party did not officially intervene in the proceedings.

6 EFFECT OF THE ARBITRAL AWARD

6.1 Implementation of the Arbitral Award

Arbitral awards can be reasonably expected to be implemented since States normally prefer to end a dispute rather than incur the political costs which would follow from refusing to accept a decision.[96] Yet, one cannot completely deny the risk that an arbitral award is not implemented by one of the parties in dispute. In this regard, two points can be made.

First, where a dispute was unilaterally referred to arbitration, there is the risk that one of the disputing parties categorically denies the validity of arbitration as a whole and refuses to implement the award. The *South China Sea* arbitration is a case in point. On 22 January 2013, the Philippines initiated arbitration proceedings against People's Republic of China in accordance with Articles 286 and 287 of the LOSC and Article 1 of Annex VII of the Convention. On 19 February 2013, however, China presented a Note Verbale to the Department of Foreign Affairs of the Philippines, rejecting the arbitration.[97] After the deliberation of the *South China Sea* arbitral award on 12 July 2016, the Chinese Ministry of Foreign Affairs issued the statement on the award and solemnly declared that: '[T]he award is null and void and has no binding force. China neither accepts nor recognizes it.'[98] This view was confirmed by a white paper published by China's State Council Information Office, which stated that: 'China does not accept or recognize those awards. China opposes and will never accept any claim or action based on those awards.'[99] It is beyond serious argument that the mere declaration of non-acceptance of an arbitral award does not deprive the arbitral award of validity. Even if an arbitral award cannot be implemented because of the refusal of one of the disputing parties, this does not mean that the award will lose its effect. The award provides a precedent with regard to the interpretation and application of relevant rules of international law.

---

[94] PCA Case No. 2013-19, the *South China Sea* arbitration (Jurisdiction and Admissibility), 29 October 2015, p. 73, para. 186, available at: https://pca-cpa.org/en/cases.
[95] *Ibid*, p. 74, para. 187.
[96] Merrills, *International Dispute Settlement*, p. 114.
[97] PCA Case No. 2013-19, the *South China Sea* arbitration (Jurisdiction and Admissibility), 29 October 2015, p. 15, para. 27.
[98] Statement of the Ministry of Foreign Affairs of the People's Republic of China on the Award of 12 July 2016 of the Arbitral Tribunal in the South China Sea Arbitration Established at the Request of the Republic of the Philippines, available at: www.chinese-embassy.org.uk/eng/zgyw/t1379492.htm.
[99] 'China Adheres to the Position of Settling through Negotiation the Relevant Disputes between China and the Philippines in the South China Sea', 13 July 2016, para. 120, available at: www.fmprc.gov.cn/mfa_eng/zxxx_662805/t1380615.shtml.

Second, if disputing parties agreed to refer their dispute to arbitration, one of the parties may subsequently claim a nullity of an arbitral award. In Latin America, for instance, arbitration was accepted as a means of the settlement of disputes, including even territorial issues, in many treaties concluded between the mid nineteenth and early twentieth centuries. In some cases, however, the validity of arbitral award was disputed.[100] Here an issue arises with regard to nullity of the arbitral award.

In this regard, Vattel stated, in his time-honoured publication, *Le Droit des gens*, that arbitral awards had no effect if there were 'manifest injustice' of the award, *ultra vires* decisions, and obvious partiality of the arbitrators.[101] The Resolution of *Institut de droit international* of 1875 enumerated three elements – namely, the excess of jurisdiction, corruption and essential error – as reasons that deprive the arbitral award of validity.[102] Under Article 35 of the Model Rules, the validity of an award may be challenged by either party on one or more of the following grounds:

(a) that the tribunal has exceeded its powers
(b) that there was corruption on the part of a member of the tribunal
(c) that there has been a failure to state the reasons for the award or a serious departure from a fundamental rule of procedure
(d) that the undertaking to arbitrate or the *compromis* is a nullity.

Item (a) concerns *excès de pouvoir*, which means the transgression committed by a competent tribunal of the legal framework of its mission. *Excès de pouvoir* can be committed by international judges through acts or omissions. If an international court failed to adjudicate on a point referred to in the *compromis*, there is *excès de pouvoir infra petita*.[103]

When the validity of an arbitral award was disputed by one of the parties, two possible solutions exist. The first solution is the referral of the dispute to the ICJ. In this regard, Article 36(1) of the Model Rules stipulates that: 'If, within three months of the date on which the validity of the award is contested, the parties have not agreed on another tribunal, the International Court of Justice shall be competent to declare the total or partial nullity of the award on the application of either party.' In fact, the validity of an arbitral

---

[100] See Dissenting Opinion of Judge Urrutia Holguín in *Case Concerning the Arbitral Award made by the King of Spain on 23 December 1906* (Honduras v Nicaragua) (hereinafter the *King of Spain* case), Judgment of 18 November 1960, ICJ Reports 1960, pp. 223–6.
[101] Emmerich de Vattel, *The Law of Nations; or Principles of the Law of Nature, Applied to the Conduct and Affairs of Nations and Sovereigns*, trans Joseph Chitty (Philadelphia: T. and J. W. Johnson and Co., Law Booksellers, 1853), pp. 277–8, section 329. See also L. Caflisch, 'Vattel and the Peaceful Settlement of International Disputes' in V. Chetail and P. Haggenmacher (eds.), *Vattel's International Law in a XXIst Century Perspective* (Leiden: Nijhoff, 2011), p. 264.
[102] Institut de droit international, Session de La Haye (1875), *Projet de règlement pour la procedure arbitrale international*, Article 27. Nicaragua, in its counter-memorial, relied on this provision. Counter-memorial submitted by the Government of Nicaragua, pp. 165–7, paras. 84–91.
[103] Joint Dissenting Opinion of Judges Aguilar Mawdsley and Ranjeva in the *1989 Arbitral Award* case, ICJ Reports 1991, p. 129, para. 23.

award was discussed before the ICJ in two cases: the *King of Spain*[104] and *Arbitral Award of 31 July 1989*.[105] The second solution is to settle the dispute through good offices or mediation by a third party. The *Beagle Channel* dispute is an example. The next section will examine the cases concerning the nullity of the arbitral award.

6.2 Nullity of the Arbitral Award

6.2.1 Case Concerning the Arbitral Award Made by the King of Spain on 23 December 1906 (Honduras/Nicaragua)

A leading case on this subject is the *King of Spain* case between Honduras and Nicaragua. On 7 October 1894, Honduras and Nicaragua concluded the Gámez-Bonilla Treaty in order to demarcate the boundary line between the two republics.[106] Although the Mixed Boundary Commission established by Article I of the treaty succeeded in determining the boundary from the Pacific Coast to the *Portillo de Teotecacinte*, it was unable to agree on the boundary from that point to the Atlantic Coast.[107] With regard to the latter section of the boundary, the King of Spain, Alphonse XIII, handed down an arbitral award on 23 December 1906.[108] In a Note dated 19 March 1912, however, Nicaragua challenged the validity and binding character of the award. As a consequence, a dispute arose with regard to the award. Honduras and Nicaragua attempted to settle the dispute by direct negotiation or through the good offices or mediation of other states but to no avail. On 21 July 1957, the two parties reached an agreement to submit the dispute to the ICJ.[109]

On 1 July 1958, Honduras instituted proceedings against Nicaragua before the ICJ with regard to a dispute concerning the arbitral award made by the King of Spain.[110] By this application Honduras requested the Court to declare, *inter alia*, that Nicaragua was under an obligation to give effect to the award. By contrast, Nicaragua solicited the Court to adjudge and declare that the decision given by the King of Spain on 23 December 1906 did not possess the character of a binding arbitral award and that the arbitral decision was incapable of being executed by reason of its omissions, contradictions and obscurities.[111] In this regard, Nicaragua invoked three reasons which deprived the award made by the King of Spain of validity: (i) excess of jurisdiction; (ii) essential error; and (iii) lack or inadequacy of reasons in support of the conclusions arrived at by the arbitrator.[112]

---

[104] For a commentary on this case, see Y. Tanaka, 'Case Concerning the Arbitral Award Made by the King of Spain on 23 December 1906 (Honduras v Nicaragua), 1960' in J.-M. Sorel and P. W. Almeida (eds.), *Latin America and the International Court of Justice: Contributions to International Law* (London: Routledge, 2016), pp. 262–72.
[105] *Arbitral Award of 31 July 1989* (Guinea-Bissau v Senegal), Judgment of 12 November 1991, ICJ Reports 1991, p. 53.
[106] The *King of Spain* case, p. 199.   [107] *Ibid.*, p. 202.
[108] *Ibid.* See also *The Boundary Case between Honduras and Nicaragua*, 23 December 1906, RIAA 11, pp. 101–17.
[109] The *King of Spain* case, p. 203. See also C. Schulte, *Compliance with Decisions of the International Court of Justice* (Oxford University Press, 2004), p. 127.
[110] The *King of Spain* case, pp. 194–5.   [111] *Ibid.*, pp. 204–5.   [112] *Ibid.*, p. 210.

In considering the nullity of the arbitral award, an issue arose as to what extent the Court should examine the substance of the arbitral award made by the King of Spain. As the Court rightly observed, the award was not subject to appeal. The Court was called upon to only decide whether the award was proved to be null and with having no effect, not to pronounce on whether the award should be right or wrong.[113] Hence the Court focused on the question whether the award relied on 'historical and legal considerations' or whether it dealt with all relevant considerations 'in logical order'. For the Court, the *manner* of the examination of relevant materials was of utmost importance in the award. In this regard, notably, the Court referred to 'convincing reason' or 'precise indication of essential error' as the criterion for determining the nullity of arbitral award.[114] In conclusion, the Court dismissed all of the allegations of Nicaragua and found that, by fourteen votes to one, that the award made by the King of Spain on 23 December 1906 was valid and binding and that Nicaragua was under an obligation to give effect to it.[115] The *King of Spain* judgment requires three comments.

First, the ICJ stressed the conduct of Nicaragua as evidence that Nicaragua accepted the validity of the arbitral award made by the King of Spain. According to the Court's approach, the conduct of parties to a dispute constitutes a key element when considering the validity of arbitral awards.

Second, it must be stressed that the ICJ is not a Court of Appeal of arbitration and that its task was limited to examining whether the award issued on 23 December 1906 was proved to be a nullity, thereby having no effect. In examining the nullity of arbitral awards, however, it was necessary for the Court to evaluate the substance of the award. In this regard, the Court took a formalistic approach by focusing on the *manner* of the examination of relevant materials in the award.

Third, the Court, in the *King of Spain* judgment, referred to 'convincing reason' or 'precise indication of essential error' as the criterion for determining the nullity of arbitral award. It appears that the ICJ set out a high standard in this matter. According to the standard, it would be difficult to prove that the arbitrator committed an essential error. In light of the limited amount of case law in this matter, whether the criterion can be generalised needs careful consideration.

6.2.2 The *Arbitral Award* Case (Guinea-Bissau/Senegal)

Another leading case is the *Arbitral Award* case between Guinea-Bissau and Senegal. By Article 3 of an arbitration agreement of 12 March 1985, Guinea-Bissau and Senegal had requested the Arbitral Tribunal to determine whether an Agreement of 1960 between France and Portugal with respect to the maritime boundary had the force of law in relations between Guinea-Bissau and Senegal.[116] In the event of a negative response to that question, the Arbitral Tribunal was to proceed to draw maritime delimitation lines between Guinea-Bissau and Senegal *de novo*.

---

[113] *Ibid.*, p. 214.   [114] *Ibid.*, p. 215.
[115] *Ibid.*, p. 217. For an analysis of the *King of Spain* case, see Y. Tanaka, 'Case Concerning the Arbitral Award Made by the King of Spain on 23 December 1906', pp. 262–72.
[116] At that time, Senegal was a French dependent territory and Guinea-Bissau was a Portuguese colony.

On 31 July 1989, the Arbitral Tribunal ruled, two votes to one, that the 1960 Agreement was binding on the parties so far as concerned the maritime zones – namely, the territorial sea, the contiguous zone and the continental shelf – but that it did not establish a boundary in relation to areas that at that time were not known to exist – namely, the exclusive economic zone (EEZ) or the fisheries zone. In light of this 'positive' response to the first question, the Tribunal did not proceed to draw a new maritime boundary for the EEZ. Nor did it indicate that the latter must follow the established line of the continental shelf.[117] The President of the Arbitral Tribunal, Mr Barberis, who had voted with the majority, appended a declaration, whilst Mr Bedjaoui appended a dissenting opinion.[118] Guinea-Bissau disputed the validity of the award of 31 July 1989 and asked the ICJ to declare that the award is null and void.[119] In particular, two issues arose in this case.

The first issue concerned President Barberis's declaration in the arbitral award. While accepting that the 1960 Agreement did not have the force of law with respect to the waters of the EEZ or the FZ, he stated, in his declaration, that: '[T]he Tribunal would have been competent to delimit the waters of the exclusive economic zone or the fishery zone between the two countries. The Tribunal thus could have settled the whole of the dispute.'[120] In this regard, Guinea-Bissau argued that President Barberis's declaration contradicted and invalidated his vote, thus leaving the award unsupported by a real majority.[121] However, the Court considered that President Barberis's declaration contained no contradiction with that of the award. According to the Court, even if there had been any contradiction between the view expressed by President Barberis and that stated in the award, such contradiction could not prevail over the position which President Barberis had taken when voting for the award. In agreeing to the award, he definitively agreed to the decisions.[122] The Court thus unanimously rejected the submission of Guinea-Bissau concerning the non-existence of the arbitral award given on 31 July 1989.[123]

Second, Guinea-Bissau claimed that the award was absolutely null and void, as the Tribunal failed to reply to the second question raised by the arbitration agreement.[124] However, the Court was not persuaded by this claim since the agreement between the two states made an answer to the second question conditional on a negative answer to the first. In the Court's view, having given an affirmative answer to the first question, the Arbitral Tribunal found as a consequence that it did not have to reply to the second question.[125] Thus, by eleven votes to four, the Court rejected the submission of Guinea-Bissau that the arbitral award of 31 July 1989 was absolutely null and void.[126]

---

[117] 31 July 1989, 20 *RIAA*, p. 153, para. 88. The members of the Arbitral Tribunal were: Julio A. Barberis (president), André Gros, and Mohammed Bedjaoui. Bedjaoui voted against the award.
[118] Mr Bedjaoui, in his dissenting opinion annexed to the award of 31 July 1989, questioned the existence of a majority considering the declaration of the President of the Arbitral Tribunal. *Ibid*., pp. 212–13, para. 161.
[119] *Arbitral Award of 31 July 1989* (Guinea-Bissau v Senegal), Judgment of 12 November 1991, ICJ Reports 1991, p. 56, para. 10.
[120] *Ibid*., pp. 60–1, para. 19.   [121] *Ibid*., p. 64, para. 30; p. 56, para. 10.   [122] *Ibid*., p. 64, paras. 31–3.
[123] *Ibid*., p. 75, para. 69(1).   [124] *Ibid*., p. 56, para. 10.
[125] *Ibid*., p. 68, para. 43; p. 73, para. 60.
[126] *Ibid*., p. 75, para. 69(2). However, some members of the Court dissented to the majority opinion. See Dissenting Opinion of Judge Thierry, *ibid*., pp. 178–9; Joint Dissenting Opinion of Judges Aguilar Mawdsley and Ranjeva, *ibid*., p. 129, paras. 24–5.

6.2.3 The *Beagle Channel* Arbitration (Argentina/Chile)

Good offices or mediation can provide an alternative solution to a dispute concerning the validity of arbitral award. A case in point is the 1978 *Beagle Channel* dispute between Argentina and Chile.[127] This dispute involved sovereignty over three islands – Picton, Nueva and Lennox – and the maritime boundary along the Beagle Channel between Argentina and Chile at the southernmost tip of South America. There was disagreement between Argentina and Chile with regard to their entire boundary along the southern extent of South America and sovereignty over Patagonia and the groups of islands and straits at the very south of the continent. Negotiations in the 1870s resulted in the 1881 Boundary Treaty between the two countries. Nonetheless, its interpretation was subsequently disputed by Argentina several times. In the 1960s, negotiations failed and the dispute was submitted to arbitration by the British Crown in 1971. In February 1977, an arbitral tribunal rendered an award, giving all three disputed islands to Chile and tracing a maritime boundary by a median line through the Beagle Channel. Yet, the arbitration award of 1977 was rejected on 25 January 1978 by the Argentina Government, claiming it was a nullity. While Chile suggested taking the matter to the ICJ, Argentina refused to do so. Both sides sent troops to the border.[128]

Faced with the tense situation, on 22 December 1978, Pope John Paul II offered mediation through his special envoy Cardinal Antonio Samoré and both States accepted the offer. On 12 December 1980, the Pope proposed a settlement.[129] This was not accepted by Argentina, however.

After the Falklands/Malvinas war with the United Kingdom, the political situation of Argentina dramatically changed and democratically elected President Raúl Alfonsin took office on 10 December 1983. The relationship between Chile and Argentina improved quickly and, on 23 January 1984, the Joint Declaration of Peace and Friendship between Argentina and Chile was signed.[130] Subsequently, Vatican Secretary of State Cardinal Agostino Casaroli resumed mediation efforts and presented a final proposal to the parties in June 1984. They agreed to the proposal and the Treaty of Peace and Friendship was signed on 29 November 1984 at the Vatican City.[131] Overall the *Beagle Channel* dispute was eventually settled by mediation of the Holy See. This instance appears to suggest that in certain circumstances, an international dispute may not be settled by arbitration alone and that further diplomatic efforts may be needed to finally achieve a settlement.

---

[127] For a commentary on the *Beagle Channel* dispute, see in particular, T. Princen, 'International Mediation: The View from the Vatican: Lessons from Mediating the Beagle Channel Dispute' (1987) 3 *Negotiation Journal*, pp. 347–66; L. A. de La Fayette, 'Beagle Channel Dispute' in *Max Planck Encyclopaedia*.
[128] *Ibid.*, paras. 24–5.
[129] Papal Proposal in the Beagle Channel Dispute Proposal of the Mediator, 12 December 1980, reproduced in J. I. Charney and L. M. Alexander (eds.), *International Maritime Boundaries*, Vol. I (Dordrecht: Nijhoff, 1993), pp. 731–5.
[130] Reproduced *ibid.*, pp. 735–6.
[131] Entered into force 2 May 1985. For the text of the treaty, see *ibid.*, pp. 736–55.

7 INTERPRETATION OF THE ARBITRAL AWARD

After an arbitral award is rendered, a dispute may arise with regard to its interpretation. The *Anglo-French Continental Shelf* arbitration is an example.[132] On 18 July 1977, the Court of Arbitration delivered its decision concerning the delimitation of the continental shelf between the United Kingdom and France. Subsequently, a serious disagreement arose relating to the tracing of a maritime boundary in a chart. As a consequence, on 17 October 1977, an application concerning the meaning and the scope of the decision of 30 June 1977 was submitted by the United Kingdom to the Court of Arbitration on the basis of Article 19(2) of the arbitration agreement of 10 July 1975.[133]

The delimitation lines determined by the Arbitral Court are straight lines drawn on a Standard Mercator chart. In the Atlantic sector, the delimitation line decided by the Court is a line drawn mid-way between two equidistance lines, the first of which does not use the Scilly Isles as a basepoint and the second of which does so use it. Nevertheless, an equidistance line developed on a Standard Mercator chart based on plane geometry and disregarding the curvature of the earth, and an equidistance line traced on a Transverse Mercator chart taking into account the curvature of the earth, do not coincide.

The United Kingdom asserted that, as a result of the scale distortions inherent in charts drawn on the Mercator projection, the line drawn on a Standard Mercator chart does not represent the line lying mid-way between true equidistance lines based on Ushant and the Scilly Isles and on Ushant and Land's End, respectively. In fact, the United Kingdom observed that the true bisector line would lie approximately 4 nautical miles to the south of the line traced by the Court's expert on the chart.[134] Although a small deviation of the boundary line may have a minor effect over a short distance, it would be magnified the greater the distance the boundary continues out from the shore. In this connection, the United Kingdom recalled that that distance was approximately 170 miles.[135] The discrepancy resulting from the distorting effect on the Mercator projection was unacceptable to the United Kingdom. By contrast, France argued that the distortions on a Mercator chart remain sufficiently slight. In the view of France, a boundary was sufficiently close to half-way and was in perfect accord with the Court's reasoning in paragraphs 249–51 of the award.[136]

An important factor in this dispute related to the nature of the charts generally used in the delimitation of maritime boundaries and the extent of the use of Transverse Mercator charts in hydrographic departments. In this respect, the United Kingdom considered the Transverse Mercator to be in general use.[137] By contrast, the French Government argued that the use of navigational charts, which were universally based on the Mercator projection, was extremely general and that the Transverse Mercator was by no means

---

[132] Case Concerning the Delimitation of the Continental Shelf between the United Kingdom of Great Britain and Northern Ireland and the French Republic, Decision of 14 March 1978 (1980) 18 *RIAA*, p. 271.
[133] Article 10(2) of the arbitration agreement provided that '[E]ither Party may, within three months of the rendering of the Decision, refer to the Court any dispute between the parties as to the meaning and scope of the Decision.' *Ibid.*, p. 279, para. 17.
[134] *Ibid.*, p. 302, para. 40.   [135] *Ibid.*, p. 311, para. 67.   [136] *Ibid.*, pp. 302–3, para. 42.
[137] *Ibid.*, p. 307, para. 55.

universally used and any particular quality in this projection did not render it superior to other projections.[138]

The Court rejected the argument of the United Kingdom, stating that:

> The information available to the Court, as already indicated, does not appear to it to establish that the delimitation of maritime boundaries by a loxodrome line on a standard navigational chart based on Mercator projection without correction for scale error is either inadmissible in law or as yet so outmoded in practice as to make its use open, in general, to challenge.[139]

It thus concluded that: '[T]he techniques used in the calculation of the half-effect boundary may not be considered as incompatible with the method for its delimitation laid down in paragraphs 251, 253 and 254 of its Decision of 30 June 1977.'[140]

8 CONCLUSIONS

Owing to its flexibility, inter-State arbitration can have a useful role to play in peaceful settlement of international disputes. The discussion in this chapter can be summarised in four points.

(i) A distinctive feature of arbitration is that the parties in dispute can retain control over the whole process of arbitration, *inter alia*:

- the composition of the arbitral tribunal
- the procedural arrangements, including the location of an arbitral tribunal
- applicable law.

Further, the proceedings before the arbitral tribunal will not be public, if the parties so wish. In these respects, arbitration is distinguished from judicial settlement through permanent international courts and tribunals.

(ii) Although flexibility is an advantage of arbitration, it also creates some weaknesses. As demonstrated in the 1950 *Peace Treaties* case, for instance, one of the disputing parties may impede the process of arbitration by refusing the appointment of arbitrator(s). In order to prevent this situation, some treaties provide a procedure whereby a third party appoints an arbitrator where one of the disputing parties refuses to do so. Furthermore, owing to its ad hoc nature, arbitration is not well-placed to develop case law, compared to judicial settlement.

(iii) Even though an arbitral award is binding upon the parties involved, further dispute may arise with regard to the validity of the arbitral award. In this case, two solutions exist. One is to refer the dispute to the ICJ, while another is to settle the dispute through negotiation, where appropriate, with good offices or mediation of a third party. If a dispute concerning the nullity of an arbitral award is referred to the ICJ, the

---

[138] *Ibid.*, p. 309, paras. 61–2. [139] *Ibid.*, p. 328, para. 111. [140] *Ibid.*, pp. 328–9, para. 111.

Court's role is limited to ascertaining whether there are reasons which may deprive the validity of an arbitral award.

(iv) In examining the nullity of arbitral awards, the Court in the *King of Spain* case referred to 'convincing reason' or 'precise indication of essential error' as the criterion for determining the nullity of an arbitral award. In light of an the limited amount of case law in this matter, however, whether the criterion can be generalised needs careful consideration.

FURTHER READING

M. J. P. A. François, 'La Cour permanente d'arbitrage, son origine, sa jurisprudence, son avenir' (1955-I) 87 *RCADI*, pp. 457-553.

C. Gray and B. Kingsbury, 'Developments in Dispute Settlement: Inter-State Arbitration Since 1945' (1993) 63 *BYIL*, pp. 97-134.

P. Hamilton, et al. (eds.), *The Permanent Court of Arbitration: International Arbitration and Dispute Resolution: Summaries of Awards, Settlement Agreements and Reports* (The Hague: Kluwer, 1999).

H. M. Holtzmann, 'Some Reflections on the Nature of Arbitration' (1993) 6 *LJIL*, pp. 265-77.

H. M. Holtzman and E. Kristjansdottir (eds.), *International Mass Claims Processes Legal and Practical Perspectives* (Oxford University Press, 2007).

T. Van den Hout, 'La Cour permanente d'arbitrage: un état des lieux' (2008) 135 *Journal du droit international*, pp. 733-51.

H. Jonkman, 'The Role of the Permanent Court of Arbitration in International Dispute Resolution' (2000) 279 *RCADI*, pp. 9-49.

G. Keutgen, 'Cour permanente d'arbitrage: règlement pour l'arbitrage des différends relatifs aux ressources naturelles et/ou à l'environnement' (2001) 78 *RGDIP*, pp. 385-6.

M. C. W. Pinto, 'Structure, Process, Outcome: Thoughts on the "Essence" of International Arbitration' (1993) 6 *LJIL*, pp. 241-64.

S. Rosenne, 'The International Court of Justice and International Arbitration' (1993) 6 *LJIL*, pp. 297-322.

'Some Thoughts on International Arbitration Today' (1993) 27 *Israel Law Review*, pp. 447-459.

The International Bureau of the Permanent Court of Arbitration (ed.), *Redressing Injustices Through Mass Claims Processes: Innovative Responses to Unique Challenges* (Oxford University Press, 2006).

6

International Court of Justice (I): Organisation and Jurisdiction of the Court

Main Issues

The ICJ is a permanent court which is empowered to exercise contentious jurisdiction to decide inter-State disputes on the basis of the consent of the State Parties to the case and to give advisory opinions to the UN organs and specialised agencies. Decisions of the Court are binding on the parties with regard to the case. The jurisdiction of the ICJ is general in the sense that it can deal with all kinds of legal dispute between States. The ICJ thus provides an important insight into judicial settlement in international law. Chapter 6, along with Chapter 7, will seek to examine principal issues concerning the law and procedure of the ICJ. Following the Introduction (section 1), Chapter 6 will address the issues of the organisation and jurisdiction of the ICJ: parties before the ICJ (section 2), organisation of the ICJ (section 3), contentious jurisdiction of the ICJ (section 4), reservations to the optional clause (section 5), and advisory proceedings (section 6). In particular, the following issues will be discussed:

(i) What is the composition of the ICJ?
(ii) How is it possible to secure independence and impartiality of judges of the ICJ?
(iii) Is the institution of a judge ad hoc contrary to the requirement of independence and impartiality?
(iv) What are the modes of giving a State's consent to the jurisdiction of the ICJ?
(v) What is the function of reservations to the optional clause?
(vi) Are 'automatic reservations' (or 'self-judging reservations') valid in international law?
(vii) What are the problems with 'instantly changeable reservations'?
(viii) What is the function of advisory jurisdiction of the ICJ?

1 INTRODUCTION

1.1 The ICJ as a Principal Judicial Organ of the United Nations

The ICJ was established by the Charter of the United Nations as the successor to the PCIJ.[1] The ICJ came into existence with the election of its first judges in February 1946.[2] The seat of the Court is established at The Hague, the Netherlands.[3] In contrast to the PCIJ, which was not an organ of the League of Nations, the ICJ is the principal judicial organ of the United Nations.[4] As an organ of the United Nations, the ICJ is supposed to contribute to achieving purposes and principles of the organisation by its strictly judicial activity. The ICJ is closely linked to the United Nations in three respects.

First, the UN Charter and the Statute of the ICJ were adopted at the same time and the Statute is an integral part of the Charter. In this regard, Article 92 of the UN Charter makes clear that the Court 'shall function in accordance with the annexed Statute which is based upon the Statute of the Permanent Court of International Justice and forms an integral part of the present Charter'. Amendments to the Court's Statute are to be effected by the same procedure as is provided by the UN Charter for amendments to that Charter.[5]

Second, as provided in Article 93(1) of the UN Charter, '[a]ll Members of the United Nations are *ipso facto* parties to the Statute of the International Court of Justice'. Accordingly, the membership of the United Nations overlaps parties to the ICJ Statute.

Third, the expenses of the Court are to be borne by the United Nations in such a manner as shall be decided by the General Assembly under Article 33 of the ICJ Statute.[6]

1.2 Importance of the ICJ in International Dispute Settlement

Given that a majority of international disputes are settled through negotiations, the role of judicial settlement seems to remain comparatively modest in international dispute settlement.[7] However, it is not suggested that the ICJ performs merely a marginal role in this field. Rather, the Court's role is crucial for at least four reasons.

First, the ICJ as a judicial organ is not affected by differences in political, economical and military powers between States. Hence the Court should be a useful means of international dispute settlement, particularly for smaller States. It seems symbolic that Libya submitted the dispute concerning *Lockerbie* to the ICJ, whilst the United Kingdom and the United States referred this dispute to the Security Council.

---

[1] The PCIJ was set up under Article 14 of the League of Nations in 1921.
[2] H. Thirlway, *The International Court of Justice* (Oxford University Press, 2016), p. 3. For the background of the establishment of the ICJ, see R. Kolb, *The Elgar Companion to the International Court of Justice* (Cheltenham: Edward Elgar Publishing, 2014), pp. 22 *et seq*.
[3] Article 22(1) of the Statute of the International Court of Justice. The electronic text of the Statute is available at: www.icj-cij.org/documents/index.php?p1=4&p2=2&p3=0. For a detailed survey of the Statute of the ICJ, see A. Zimmermann *et al.* (eds.), *The Statute of the International Court of Justice: A Commentary*, 2nd edn (Oxford University Press, 2012) (hereafter *A Commentary*).
[4] Article 92 of the UN Charter. See also Article 1 of the Statute of the Court. However, its status as the 'principal judicial organ' of the United Nations must not be taken to mean that the ICJ enjoys priority as a forum for dispute settlement.
[5] Article 69 of the ICJ Statute. See also Chapter 18 of the UN Charter.
[6] Further, see Thirlway, *The International Court of Justice* (2016), pp. 4–6.
[7] See Chapter 2, section 1 of this book.

Second, the ICJ is the only court with a general jurisdiction at the global level. Therefore, it can deal with all types of inter-State disputes, if the jurisdiction can be established.

Third, even though, unlike municipal courts in common law system, the ICJ does not adopt the principle of binding precedents, it is an established convention that the Court refers to its previous decisions to secure a sufficient degree of continuity and predictability in its jurisprudence.[8] The ICJ as a permanent court can better contribute to development of rules of international law to a far higher degree than ad hoc tribunals through its case law.[9]

Fourth, it is generally recognised that the decisions of the ICJ have authority over the interpretation and application of rules of international law. The Court's interpretation of rules of law may influence the behaviour of States, even though its decisions are binding only upon the parties in respect of the case. In addition, the Court has been able to supplement the work of the ILC by identifying the existence of a rule of customary international law or the customary-law status of a rule embodied in a treaty.

At present, the calendar of the Court is increasingly busy. The average number of pending cases each year has increased exponentially over the preceding five decades, from three cases through the 1960s, to less than five through the 1980s, thirteen during the 1990s, and an average of over twenty pending cases each year over the last decade.[10] This factual situation seems to exemplify the usefulness of the Court in peaceful settlement of international disputes, whilst there are signs of an overload.[11]

1.3 Instruments Governing the ICJ

The ICJ is governed by four instruments: (i) the UN Charter, (ii) the Statute of the ICJ, (iii) the Rules of Court and (iv) the Practice Directions.[12] Chapter XIV of the UN Charter, containing Articles 92, 93, 94, 95 and 96, is devoted to the ICJ. The ICJ Statute, annexed to the UN Charter, contains detailed rules concerning the law and procedure of the Court. The ICJ Statute is not only binding on the Court but also on parties before the Court. Particular parties before the Court may not derogate from the Statute by agreement between them. In this sense, the ICJ Statute is imperative by nature.[13] The Rules of Court, initially adopted on 6 May 1946, provide detailed procedures of the ICJ with regard to, *inter alia*, the organisation and members of the Court, the Registry, contentious cases and advisory proceedings. Subsequently the rules were provisionally revised in 1972 and, then, revised in depth on 1 July 1978.

---

[8] Generally on this issue, see G. Guillaume, 'The Use of Precedent by International Judges and Arbitrators' (2011) 2 *Journal of International Dispute Settlement*, pp. 5–23. See also Thirlway, *The International Court of Justice*, p. 138.

[9] For a classical study on this subject, see Sir Hersch Lauterpacht, *The Development of International Law by the International Court* (Cambridge: Grotius, 1982). See also C. J. Tams and J. Sloan (eds.), *The Development of International Law by the International Court of Justice* (Oxford University Press, 2013).

[10] Speech by H. E. Judge Hisashi Owada, President of the International Court of Justice, to the Sixth Committee of the General Assembly, 30 October 2009, p. 1, available at: www.icj-cij.org/presscom/files/4/15744 .pdf.

[11] H. Thirlway, 'The International Court of Justice' in M. D. Evans (ed.), *International Law*, 4th edn (Oxford University Press, 2014), p. 614.

[12] Further, see Kolb, *The Elgar Companion*, pp. 63 *et seq.*

[13] *Ibid.*, pp. 96–7.

The main purpose of the Practice Directions is to speed up and simplify procedures of the ICJ in light of its increasing contentious workload. The initial Practice Directions were issued on 31 October 2001 and entered into force immediately.[14] They are the result of the Court's ongoing review of its working methods and they do not alter the Rules of Court, but are additional thereto. In summary, a triple hierarchy of sources exists: the ICJ Statute, Rules of Court and Practice Directions.[15]

2 PARTIES BEFORE THE ICJ

Under Article 34(1) of the ICJ Statute, only States may be parties in cases before the Court. Neither individuals, international organisations nor component States of federations can be a party. To be a party to a particular case, a State must be one of those to which the Court is open or having access to the Court pursuant to Article 35 of the ICJ Statute. Under Article 35(1) of the Statute, the Court is open to the States Parties to the present Statute and any such State can submit disputes to the Court. As noted, all members of the United Nations are *ipso facto* parties to the Statute of the ICJ by virtue of Article 93(1) of the UN Charter. A State which is not a Member of the UN may also become a party to the Statute of the ICJ subject to conditions to be determined in each case by the General Assembly upon the recommendation of the Security Council in conformity with Article 93(2) of the Charter. As will be discussed in section 4, however, the mere fact that a State has become a party to the Statute of the Court does not give the Court jurisdiction to adjudicate on a particular dispute to which that State is a party. The parties in dispute must agree to the Court exercising its jurisdiction relating to that dispute since the consent of parties to a dispute provides a foundation of the jurisdiction of the Court.

The Court is also open to any other State which is not a party to the ICJ Statute under certain conditions by virtue of Article 35(2) of the Court's Statute.[16] In the 1954 *Monetary Gold* case, for example, the Italian Government, which was a non-party to the ICJ Statute, expressly gave the undertakings required by the Security Council resolution with regard to the particular dispute.[17] In the 1969 *North Sea Continental Shelf* cases, the Federal Republic of Germany declared acceptance of the jurisdiction of the ICJ on 29 April 1961 in conformity with Article 3 of the European Convention for the Peaceful Settlement of Disputes and the Security Council Resolution of 15 October 1946.[18] In the 1949 *Corfu Channel* case, Albania's letter of 2 July 1947, which accepted the recommendation of the Security Council of 1947, was considered as a voluntary and indisputable acceptance of the Court's jurisdiction.[19]

---

[14] Practice Directions as amended on 20 January 2009 and 21 March 2013 are available at the website of the ICJ. See www.icj-cij.org/documents/index.php?p1=4&p2=4&p3=0.
[15] Kolb, *The Elgar Companion*, p. 92.
[16] Such conditions were specified in Resolution 9 (1946) of the Security Council of the United Nations, 15 October 1946.
[17] *Monetary Gold Removed from Rome in 1943* (Italy v. France, United Kingdom of Great Britain and Northern Ireland and United States of America), Preliminary Question, Judgment of 15 June 1954, ICJ Reports 1954, pp. 21–2.
[18] Special Agreement of 2 February 1967, available at: www.icj-cij.org/docket/files/51/9329.pdf.
[19] *Corfu Channel* case (United Kingdom of Great Britain and Northern Ireland v. Albania), Preliminary Objection, Judgment of 25 March 1948, ICJ Reports 1948, p. 27.

In the *Genocide* case, a question was raised whether or not the respondent State (i.e. Yugoslavia (Serbia and Montenegro)), can be regarded as a Member of the United Nations. Without giving an answer to this question, the Court considered that proceedings may validly be instituted on the basis of the Genocide Convention that Bosnia-Herzegovina and Yugoslavia had ratified, and independently of the conditions laid down by the Security Council in its Resolution 9 of 1946. In this regard, the Court took the view that Article IX of the Genocide Convention relied on by Bosnia-Herzegovina in this case could be regarded *prima facie* as a special provision contained in a treaty in force referred to in Article 35(2) of the ICJ Statute.[20] When a State which is not a Member of the United Nations is a party to a case, the Court shall fix the amount which that party is to contribute towards the expenses of the Court pursuant to Article 35(3) of the ICJ Statute.

3 ORGANISATION OF THE ICJ

3.1 Election of Judges

The Court shall consist of fifteen members, no two of whom may be nationals of the same State.[21] Under Article 2 of the ICJ Statute, the Court shall be composed of a body of independent judges, elected regardless of their nationality from among persons of high moral character, who possess the qualifications required in their respective countries for appointment to the highest judicial offices, or are jurisconsults of recognised competence in international law. The members of the Court are to be elected for nine years and may be re-elected.[22] Five judges are elected every three years. At every election, the electors shall bear in mind not only that the persons to be elected should individually possess the qualifications required, but also that in the body as a whole the representation of the forms of civilization and of the principal legal systems of the world should be assured.[23] This requirement is of particular importance to secure fairness and authority of the ICJ as a 'World Court'. The current geographical distribution of judges is summarised in Table 6.1.[24] Unlike the International Criminal Court,[25] there is no requirement for securing a fair representation of gender.

The procedure of election of the judges is set out by Articles 4–15 of the ICJ Statute. The members of the Court shall be elected by the General Assembly and by the Security Council from a list of persons nominated by the national groups in the Permanent

---

[20] *Application of the Convention on the Prevention and Punishment of the Crime of Genocide* (Bosnia and Herzegovina v. Serbia and Montenegro) (hereafter the *Crime of Genocide* case), Request for the Indication of Provisional Measures, Order of 8 April 1993, ICJ Reports 1993, p. 14, para. 19.
[21] Article 3(1) of the ICJ Statute.   [22] Article 13(1) of the ICJ Statute.   [23] Article 9 of the ICJ Statute.
[24] The list of current members of the Court is available at: www.icj-cij.org/court/index.php?p1=1&p2=2&p3=1.
[25] Article 36(8)(a) of the Rome Statute for the Establishment of an International Criminal Court requires that: 'The States Parties shall, in the selection of judges, take into account the need, within the membership of the Court, for: … (iii) A fair representation of female and male judges.' Text in: 2187 *UNTS*, p. 3. Entered into force 1 July 2002.

TABLE 6.1 GEOGRAPHICAL DISTRIBUTION OF THE JUDGES OF THE ICJ

West Europe and others	Eastern Europe	Asia	Africa	Latin America
5	2	3	3	2

Court of Arbitration pursuant to Article 4(1) of the ICJ Statute. No group may nominate more than four persons, not more than two of whom shall be of their own nationality.[26] The Secretary-General shall prepare a list in alphabetical order of all the persons thus nominated. The Secretary-General is to submit this list to the General Assembly and to the Security Council in accordance with Article 7(2) of the ICJ Statute. The General Assembly and the Security Council shall proceed independently of one another to elect the members of the Court pursuant to Article 8 of the Court's Statute. The election is not subject to veto of permanent members of the Council.[27] Those candidates who obtain an absolute majority of votes in the General Assembly and in the Security Council shall be considered as elected.[28] In the event of more than one national of the same State obtaining an absolute majority of the votes both of the General Assembly and of the Security Council, the oldest of these only shall be considered.[29] In practice, national candidates of the permanent members of the Security Council have constantly been elected.[30]

The Court shall elect its President and Vice-President for three years and they may be re-elected in accordance with Article 21(1) of the ICJ Statute. The President and the Registrar shall reside at the seat of the Court.[31] Whilst all questions shall be decided by a majority of the judges present, in the event of an equality of votes, the President or the judge who acts in his place shall have a casting vote under Article 55(2) of the Court's Statute. The casting vote of the President was exercised in the 1966 *South West Africa* case,[32] the advisory opinion on the 1996 *Legality of the Use of Nuclear Weapons* case,[33] the 2016 *Nicaragua/Colombia* case concerning the question of the delimitation of the continental shelf beyond 200 nautical miles (preliminary objections)[34] and the 2016 *Marshall Islands/United Kingdom* case.[35]

---

[26] Article 5(2) of the ICJ Statute.
[27] Article 10(2) of the ICJ Statute
[28] Article 10(1) of the ICJ Statute.
[29] Article 10(3) of the ICJ Statute.
[30] Thirlway, *The International Court of Justice* (2016), p. 4.
[31] Article 22(2) of the ICJ Statute.
[32] *South West Africa* (Ethiopia v. South Africa) (Liberia v. South Africa), Judgment of 18 July 1966, Second Phase, ICJ Reports 1966, p. 51, para. 100.
[33] *Legality of the Threat or Use of Nuclear Weapons*, Advisory Opinion of 8 July 1996, ICJ Reports 1996, p. 266, para. 105(2)(E).
[34] *Question of the Delimitation of the Continental Shelf between Nicaragua and Colombia beyond 200 Nautical Miles from the Nicaraguan Coast* (Nicaragua v. Colombia), Judgment of 17 March 2016, ICJ Reports 2016, para. 126(1)(b) and (2)(b).
[35] *Obligations concerning Negotiations relating to Cessation of the Nuclear Arms Race and to Nuclear Disarmament* (Marshall Islands v. United Kingdom), Preliminary Objections, Judgment of 5 October 2016, ICJ Reports 2016 (not yet reported), para. 59. See also Chapter 1, section 3.2 of this book.

3.2 Independence and Impartiality of Judges

Independence and impartiality of the judges who compose the Court are a prerequisite to secure the authority of its decisions. These elements are also essential to obtain the confidence of States.[36] The requirement of independence is clearly provided in Article 2 of the ICJ Statute: 'The Court shall be composed of a body of *independent* judges, elected regardless of their nationality from among persons of high moral character ... '.[37] The judges of the Court can be considered as independent, so long as there is no external source of control or political influence which prevents them from acting in an autonomous fashion.[38]

The requirement of impartiality is provided in Article 20 of the ICJ Statute: 'Every member of the Court shall, before taking up his duties, make a solemn declaration in open court that he will exercise his powers impartially and conscientiously.' Yet, the concept of impartiality is not wholly unambiguous and the impartiality of judges may be a matter of controversy in a particular case. In considering this issue, the following provisions of the ICJ Statute merit attention.

First, under Article 16(1) of the ICJ Statute, no member of the Court may exercise any political or administrative function or engage in any other occupation of a professional nature.[39] Any doubt on this point shall be settled by the decision of the Court in accordance with Article 16(2) of the ICJ Statute.[40]

Second, Article 17(1) of the ICJ Statute prohibits the members of the Court to act as agent, counsel or advocate in any case. Furthermore, as provided in Article 17(2) of the Statute, '[n]o member may participate in the decision of any case in which he has previously taken part as agent, counsel, or advocate for one of the parties, or as a member of a national or international court, or of a commission of inquiry, or in any other capacity'. It follows that no judge, whether regular or ad hoc, can sit in a particular case if he or she has been involved previously with the very subject matter of that case.[41] In this regard, Judge Gilbert Guillaume, a former ICJ President, stated that:

---

[36] J. D. Morley, 'Relative Incompatibility of Functions in the International Court' (1970) 19 *ICLQ*, p. 316. On this issue, see also, *Institut de droit international*, Resolution: The Position of the International Judge, 9 September 2011; International Law Association, The Burgh House Principles on the Independence of the International Judiciary.

[37] Emphasis added.

[38] C. Brown, 'Legal Norms to Promote the Independence and Accountability of International Tribunals' (2003) 2 *The Law and Practice of International Courts and Tribunals*, pp. 75 and 84.

[39] This rule does not apply to judges ad hoc.

[40] It is generally agreed that judges of the ICJ may be arbitrators. In fact, all members of the Arbitral Tribunal in the *Beagle Channel* arbitration – Sir Gerald Fitzmaurice (President), André Gros, Sture Petrén, Charles Onyeama, Hardy C. Dillard – were judges of the ICJ. Furthermore, two members of the Arbitral Court – Sir Humphrey Waldock and André Gros – were appointed as an arbitrator in the 1977 *Anglo-French Continental Shelf* arbitration. In the 1985 *Guinea/Guinea-Bissau* arbitration, all members of the Arbitral Tribunal – Manfred Lack (President), Keba Mbaye and Mohamed Bedjaoui – were judges of the ICJ. Judges of the ICJ may also engage in academic activities. S. Oda (with H. Sakai and K. Tanaka), *International Court of Justice*, Updated edition (in Japanese) (Tokyo: Nihon Hyoronsha, 2011), pp. 131–2.

[41] See *In the Matter of Arbitration before an Arbitral Tribunal Constituted under Annex VII of the 1982 United Nations Convention on the Law of the Sea between the Republic of Mauritius and the United Kingdom of Great Britain and Northern Ireland*, Reasoned Decision on Challenge, 20 November 2011, p. 26, para. 143; Practice Direction VII. For practice of the ICJ concerning Article 17, see Morley, 'Relative Incompatibility', pp. 316 *et seq.*; P. Couvreur, 'Article 17' in *A Commentary*, pp. 372–85. See also, H. Thirlway, *The Law and Procedure of the International Court of Justice: Fifty Years of Jurisprudence*, Vol. I (Oxford University Press, 2013), pp. 896 *et seq.*; Vol. II, pp. 1753 *et seq.*

[T]he practice of the Permanent Court of International Justice and that of the present Court is clear: a member of the Court or an ad hoc judge having had in the past close relations with one of the Parties to the dispute need not for that reason alone be disqualified. ... On the other hand, it is prohibited for a member of the Court or an ad hoc judge to sit in a case if he had, in one way or another, been previously involved with the very subject matter of the case.[42]

Third, under Article 24 of the ICJ Statute:

1. If, for some special reason, a member of the Court considers that he should not take part in the decision of a particular case, he shall so inform the President.
2. If the President considers that for some special reason one of the members of the Court should not sit in a particular case, he shall give him notice accordingly.
3. If in any such case the member of the Court and the President disagree, the matter shall be settled by the decision of the Court.

In the 1954 *Advisory Opinion on the Effect of Award of Compensation Made by the United Nations Administrative Tribunal*, Judge Basdevant, referring expressly to Article 24, considered that there were certain considerations of a personal nature which made it incumbent upon him not to take part in the case.[43] In the *South West Africa* case, the Australian President, Sir Percy Spender, instructed the Pakistan national, Sir Mohammed Zafrullah Kahn, not to sit.[44] Furthermore, two members of the Court, Judges Fleischhauer and Higgins, having previously dealt, in their respective capacities as Legal Counsel of the United Nations and Member of the United Nations Human Rights Committee, with certain matters likely to be material to the present case, did not sit in the preliminary objections phase of the *Case Concerning Application of the Convention on the Prevention and Punishment of the Crime of Genocide*.[45] Likewise, three Members of the Court, Judges Fleischhauer, Higgins and Kooijmans, have considered that they should not take part in the decision of the *Case Concerning Application for Revision of the Judgment of 11 July 1996 in the Case Concerning Application of the Convention on the Prevention and Punishment of the Crime of Genocide* in accordance with Article 24(1) of the ICJ Statute.[46]

In some cases, one of the parties in dispute opposed certain judges' participation in a particular case. In the *Namibia* advisory opinion of 1971, for instance, the Government of South Africa had taken objection to the participation of three members of the Court in the proceedings: Sir Mohammed (Pakistan), the President of the ICJ; and Judges Padilla

---

[42] Quoted in: Reasoned Decision on Challenge, 20 November 2011, p. 30, para. 164.
[43] His daughter, Madame Bastid, was the President of the Administrative Tribunal of the United Nations. Sir Robert Jennings, 'Article 24' in *A Commentary*, p. 459.
[44] Morley, 'Relative Incompatibility', p. 326; J. Collier and V. Lowe, *The Settlement of Disputes in International Law: Institutions and Procedures* (Oxford University Press, 1999), p. 130.
[45] The *Crime of Genocide* case, CR 96/5, p. 6.
[46] *Application for Revision of the Judgment of 11 July 1996 in the Case Concerning Application of the Convention on the Prevention and Punishment of the Crime of Genocide* (Bosnia and Herzegovina v. Yugoslavia), Preliminary Objections (Yugoslavia v. Bosnia and Herzegovina), CR 2002/40, p. 8.

Nervo (Mexican) and Morozov (the Soviet Union). Its objections were based on statements made or other participation by the members concerned in their former capacity as representatives of their governments in United Nations organs which were dealing with matters concerning South West Africa. After careful examination of each case, in each of them the Court reached the conclusion that the participation of the member concerned in his former capacity as representative of his government did not attract the application of Article 17(2) of the ICJ Statute.[47]

In the *Wall* case, the Government of Israel opposed the participation of Judge Elaraby (Egypt) in the proceedings of the advisory opinion on the ground that he had previously played an active, official and public role as an advocate for a cause that was in contention in that case.[48] In this regard, the Government of Israel referred not only to Judge Elaraby's participation in the Tenth Emergency Special Session of the General Assembly but also to his previous activities as principal Legal Adviser to the Egyptian Ministry of Foreign Affairs, and as Legal Adviser to the Egyptian Delegation to the Camp David Middle East Peace Conference of 1978, and his involvement in initiatives following the signing of the Israel–Egypt Peace Treaty in 1979. The Israeli Government further cited the published report of an interview given by Judge Elaraby to an Egyptian newspaper in August 2001 which reported his view on questions concerning Israel. The Israeli Government thus claimed that Judge Elaraby has been actively engaged in opposition to Israel including matters which went directly to aspects of the questions before the Court.[49]

However, the Court was not persuaded by Israel's argument. According to the Court, the activities of Judge Elaraby were performed in his capacity of a diplomatic representative of his country, most of them many years before the question of the construction of a wall in the occupied Palestinian territory arose. Furthermore, that question was not an issue in the Tenth Emergency Special Session of the General Assembly until after Judge Elaraby had ceased to participate in that Session as representative of Egypt. According to the Court, in the newspaper interview of August 2001, Judge Elaraby expressed no opinion on the question put in the present case. The Court thus decided that the matters brought to the attention of the Court by the Government of Israel were not such as to preclude Judge Elaraby from participating in the present case.[50]

Where a judge or judges were disqualified, they are not replaced by others and the ICJ will simply sit as a restricted composition. Under Article 25(3) of the ICJ Statute, a quorum of nine judges shall suffice to constitute the Court. The ICJ has never encountered a problem concerning the quorum.[51]

---

[47] *Legal Consequences for States of the Continued Presence of South Africa in Namibia (South West Africa) notwithstanding Security Council Resolution 276 (1970)*, Advisory Opinion of 21 June 1971, ICJ Reports 1971, p. 18, para. 9. But four judges voted against Judge Morozov's participation in the proceedings. Order No. 3 of 26 January 1971, *ibid.*, p. 10. See also Kolb, *The Elgar Companion*, pp. 118–19.

[48] Thirlway, *The Law and Procedure*, Vol. II, pp. 1753–7.

[49] *Legal Consequences of the Construction of a Wall in the Occupied Palestinian Territory*, Order of 30 January 2004, ICJ Reports 2004, pp. 4–5, paras. 4–5.

[50] *Ibid.*, p. 5, para. 8. However, Judge Burgenthal dissented the majority opinion. Dissenting Opinion of Judge Burgenthal, *ibid.*, pp. 7–10.

[51] Kolb, *The Elgar Companion*, p. 120.

3.3 A National Judge and Judge Ad Hoc

Judges of the nationality of each of the parties shall retain their right to sit in the case before the Court under Article 31(1) of the ICJ Statute.[52] The participation of a national judge is defended on the ground that it will be useful to ensure that the case presented by his or her country is fully understood, while (s)he is required to act impartially.[53]

The Court frequently includes no national judge of one or both parties to a case in the bench. In this case, a question arises as to how it is possible to ensure the equality of the parties to the dispute. If the Court includes a judge of the nationality of only one of the parties, there are two options. The first option is to require the judge belonging to the nationality of a party to retire from the case and the second option is to appoint a judge ad hoc to sit. The PCIJ and the ICJ adopted the second option. Under Article 31(2) of the ICJ Statute, if the Court includes upon the bench a judge of the nationality of one of the parties, any other party may choose a person to sit as judge. If the Court includes upon the bench no judge of the nationality of the parties, each of these parties may proceed to choose a judge to sit by virtue of Article 31(3) of the ICJ Statute. The judge under Article 31(2) and (3) is called a judge ad hoc. As shown by the term 'may', a party in dispute remains free to choose whether or not it exercises the right to appoint a judge ad hoc.[54]

Like the regular judge, a judge ad hoc is required to be a person of high moral character and to possess similar qualifications to those required by the regular judge.[55] Should there be several parties in the same interest, they shall, for the purpose of the preceding provisions, be reckoned as one party only.[56] Any doubt upon this point shall be settled by the decision of the Court.[57] Article 31 of the ICJ Statute also applies to an advisory opinion by virtue of Article 102(2) of the Rules of Court. Judges ad hoc are not restricted only to the nationals of the parties in dispute.[58]

According to Lauterpacht, who sat on the bench as a judge ad hoc in the *Crime of Genocide* case, a judge ad hoc has the special obligation to 'endeavour to ensure that, so far as is reasonable, every relevant argument in favour of the party that has appointed him has been fully appreciated in the course of collegial consideration and, ultimately, is

---

[52] Article 31(1) of the ICJ Statute.
[53] Thirlway, 'International Court of Justice', p. 592.
[54] By way of example, in the *Kasikili/Sedudu Island* case, neither Botswana nor Namibia had appointed a judge ad hoc. *Kasikili/Sedudu Island* (Botswana/Namibia), Judgment of 13 December 1999, ICJ Reports 1999, p. 1045. In the *Marshall Islands/Pakistan* case, Pakistan did not exercise its right to choose a judge ad hoc, while the Marshall Islands appointed a judge ad hoc. *Obligations concerning Negotiations relating to Cessation of the Nuclear Arms Race and to Nuclear Disarmament* (Marshall Islands v. Pakistan), Judgment of 5 October 2016, Jurisdiction of the Court and admissibility of the application (not yet reported), para. 3.
[55] Article 31(6) of the ICJ Statute.
[56] Thirlway, *Law and Procedure*, Vol. II, pp. 1744-8. See also Thirlway, *The International Court of Justice*, pp. 15-19.
[57] Article 31(5) of the ICJ Statute.
[58] In the *Nottebohm* case, for instance, Liechtenstein appointed P. Guggenheim, a Swiss. In the *Case Concerning Arbitral Award Made by the King of Spain on 23 December of 1906*, Honduras appointed R. Ago, an Italian and Nicaragua appointed F. Urrutia Holguin, a Colombian. In the *Barcelona Traction* case of 1962, Belgium appointed W. Riphagen, a Dutch, while Spain appointed E. C. Armandugon, a Uruguayan. D. D. Nsereko, 'The International Court, Impartiality and Judge ad hoc' (1973) 13 *Indian Journal of Internationl Law*, p. 214.

reflected – though not necessarily accepted – in any separate or dissenting opinion that he may write'.[59] Specifically, judges ad hoc are expected to ensure:

- that the parties are equally represented
- that the main forms of civilisation will always be represented on the Court
- that a person knowledgeable in the national legal systems and philosophies of the parties will be available to acquaint the Court with them, explain their positions in the case and help in drawing up the awards in a way understandable to them
- that, by so doing, a judge ad hoc may enhance the parties' confidence in the Court.[60]

However, the institution of judges ad hoc creates particular sensitivity associated with the requirements of impartiality and independence. For instance, Sir Gerald Fitzmaurice criticised the institution of judges ad hoc since the primary loyalty of a judge ad hoc is to the State which appointed him, while that of regular judges is for the Court.[61] Sir Hersch Lauterpacht also argued that: 'The interests of the parties must be represented and defended by advocates and counsel – not by Judges pledged by their oath to the duty of impartiality.'[62]

It is true that in many if not most cases, judges ad hoc voted in favour of the State that appointed them.[63] Given the large difference in number between the regular judges and a judge ad hoc, however, there would be little risk that the outcome of the judgment would be changed by a judge ad hoc and they do little harm. In addition, psychological interest for the State which nominated the judge ad hoc cannot be underestimated since, owing to the presence of a judge ad hoc, in those cases where there is a judge having the

---

[59] Separate Opinion of Judge Lauterpacht in the *Crime of Genocide* case, Order of 13 September 1993, ICJ Reports 1993, p. 409, para. 6. This view was echoed by Dissenting Opinion of Judge ad hoc Franck, *Sovereignty over Pulau Ligitan and Pulau Sipadan* (Indonesia v. Malaysia), Judgment of 17 December 2002, ICJ Reports 2002, pp. 693–4, para. 9; Separate Opinion of Judge ad hoc Bula-Bula, *Arrest Warrant of 11 April 2000* (Democratic Republic of the Congo v. Belgium), Judgment of 14 February 2002, ICJ Reports 2002, p. 101, para. 3; Dissenting Opinion of Judge ad hoc Sir Geoffrey Palmer, *Request for an Examination of the Situation in Accordance with Paragraph 63 of the Court's Judgment of 20 December 1974 in the Nuclear Tests* (New Zealand v. France) case, Order of 22 September 1995, ICJ Reports 1995, pp. 420–1, para. 118.
[60] Nsereko, 'The International Court, Impartiality and Judge ad hoc', p. 222.
[61] Observations of M. Gerald-Gray Fitzmaurice (1954-I) 45 *Annuaire de l'Institut de droit international*, p. 445.
[62] Observations of Mr H. Lauterpacht (1954-I) 45 *Annuaire de l'Institut de droit international*, p. 534.
[63] In some cases, however, judges ad hoc did not support the positions of the States that appointed them. For example, Judge ad hoc Bastid, appointed by Tunisia, voted against the position of Tunisia in the Application for Revision and Interpretation of the Judgment of 24 February 1982 in the *Case Concerning the Continental Shelf*, as did all the members of the Court. *Application for Revision and Interpretation of the Judgment of 24 February 1982 in the Case Concerning the Continental Shelf (Tunisia/Libyan Arab Jamahiriya)* (Tunisia v. Libyan Arab Jamahiriya), Judgment of 10 December 1985, ICJ Reports 1985, p. 229, para. 69(A) and (C). Judge ad hoc Thierry, appointed by Guinea-Bissau, voted against one of the positions of Guinea-Bissau in the case of the Arbitral Award of 31 July 1989. *Arbitral Award of 31 July 1989* (Guinea-Bissau v. Senegal), Judgment of 12 November 1991, ICJ Reports 1991, p. 75, para. 69(1). In the 2013 *Preah Vihear* case, Judge ad hoc Cot, appointed by Thailand, voted for the unanimous judgment which admitted Cambodia's request for the interpretation of the 1962 judgment, whilst Thailand claimed that the request was inadmissible. *Request for Interpretation of the Judgment of 15 June 1962 in the Case Concerning the Temple of Preah Vihear* (Cambodia v. Thailand), Judgment of 11 November 2013, ICJ Reports 2013, para. 108. See also Declaration of Judge ad hoc Cot, *ibid.*, p. 350. Further, see G. H. Hernández, *The International Court of Justice and the Judicial Function* (Oxford University Press, 2014), p. 152; Kolb, *The Elgar Companion*, pp. 113–14.

nationality of one of the parties on the Court, the other party needs not feel itself to be in a weaker position.[64] It may be said that the *raison d'être* of a judge ad hoc is to provide an important link between the parties and the Court.[65]

3.4 Chambers of the ICJ

Cases are heard by the full Court unless the parties to a case request that the case be heard by a Chamber. The ICJ embraces three Chambers under the ICJ Statute: (i) the Chamber of Summary Procedure, (ii) the Special Chamber and (iii) an ad hoc Chamber. A judgment given by any of the Chambers provided for in Articles 26 and 29 shall be considered as rendered by the Court.[66]

First, Chamber of Summary Procedure is to be established with a view to securing the speedy dispatch of business under Article 29 of the ICJ Statute. This Chamber is composed of five judges. The President and Vice-President of the Court are to be the members of the Chamber *ex officio*.[67] The President shall request one or, if necessary, two of the members of the Court forming the Chamber to give place to the members of the Court of the nationality of the parties concerned.[68] This Chamber was used only once in the period of the PCIJ, that was the Treaty of Neuilly case of 1924.[69]

Second, the Special Chamber is established for dealing with particular categories of cases, for example, labour cases and cases relating to transit and communications pursuant to Article 26(1) of the ICJ Statute.[70] In 1993, the Court created a Chamber for Environmental Matters and it was periodically reconstituted until 2006. Yet, no State ever requested that a case be dealt with by it. The Court thus decided not to hold elections for a bench for this Chamber in 2006.

Third, an ad hoc Chamber can be established in accordance with Article 26(2) of the ICJ Statute. The number of judges to constitute such a Chamber shall be determined by the Court with the approval of the parties.[71] When the parties have agreed, the President shall ascertain their view regarding the composition of the Chamber, and shall report to the Court accordingly.[72] When the Court has determined, with the approval of the parties, the number of members who are to constitute the Chamber, it shall proceed to their election by secret ballot.[73] The list of the cases before an ad hoc Chamber is summarised in Table 6.2.

An issue to be examined in this context concerns the selection of the members of an ad hoc Chamber.[74] Originally Article 24(2) the 1946 Rules of Court provided that the members of all Chambers shall be elected by the Court, by secret ballot, and by an absolute

---

[64] G. Guillaume, 'Some Thoughts on the Independence of International Judges Vis-à-Vis States' (2003) 2 *The Law and Practice of International Courts and Tribunal*, p. 164.
[65] J. G. Merrills, *International Dispute Settlement*, 6th edn (Cambridge University Press, 2017), p. 146. See also Kolb, *The Elgar Companion*, p. 111.
[66] Article 27 of the ICJ Statute.   [67] Article 15(1) of the Rules of Court.
[68] Article 31(4) of the ICJ Statute.   [69] Judgment of 12 September 1924.
[70] See also Article 16 of the Rules of Court.   [71] Article 26(2) of the ICJ Statute.
[72] Article 17(2) of the Rules of Court.
[73] Articles 17(3) and 18(1) of the Rules of Court.
[74] On this issue, see Thirlway, *The Law and Procedure*, Vol. I, pp. 902 *et seq*.

TABLE 6.2 CASES BEFORE AN AD HOC CHAMBER

Year of creation	Case
1982	The *Gulf of Main* case (Canada/USA)
1985	The *Frontier Dispute* case (Burkina Faso/Republic of Mali)
1987	The *Elettronica Sicula S.p.A. (ELSI)* case (United States of America v. Italy)
1987	The *Land, Island and Maritime Frontier Dispute* case (El Salvador/Honduras: Nicaragua intervening)
2002	The *Frontier Dispute* case (Benin/Niger)
2002	The *Application for Revision of the Judgment of 11 September 1992 in the Case Concerning the Land, Island and Maritime Frontier Dispute* (El Salvador/Honduras: Nicaragua intervening)

majority of votes. The 1946 Rules contained no provision taking the parties' request into account. However, the provision was replaced by Article 26(1) of the Rules of 1972, which provided that when the Court decides to form a Chamber to deal with a particular case, the President is required to *consult* the agents of the parties regarding the composition of the Chamber, and shall report to the Court accordingly. As a consequence, the will of the parties would be reflected in selecting the members of the Chamber. Although the term 'consult' in Article 26(1) of the 1972 Rules was replaced by the term 'ascertain' in Article 17(2) of the 1978 Rules of Court, the effect of this provision appears to be essentially the same as that of Article 26(1) of the 1972 Rules. If the President's requirement to 'ascertain' the parties' views regarding the composition of the Chamber is meant to signal to the parties that they should propose names of judges, there is the risk that the Court is to be dictated by the parties in the election of the Chamber.[75]

The procedure for ad hoc Chamber was used, for the first time, in the *Gulf of Maine* case between Canada and the United States.[76] In the treaty of 1979, Canada and the United States agreed to submit the Gulf of Maine dispute concerning the maritime boundary to a Chamber of the ICJ.[77] Article I of the Special Agreement provided that the dispute was to be submitted to a Chamber of the ICJ, composed of five persons, to be constituted after consultation with the parties, pursuant to Articles 26(2) and 31 of the ICJ Statute.[78] In this regard, Canada and the United States made clear that unless their wishes as to the composition of the Court were carried out, they would withdraw the case and refer the

---

[75] S. Oda, 'Further Thoughts on the Chambers Procedure of the International Court of Justice' (1988) 82 *AJIL*, p. 556.

[76] Generally on this issue, see E. McWhinney, 'Special Chambers within the International Court of Justice: The Preliminary, Procedural Aspect of the Gulf of Maine Case' (1985-6) 12 *Syracuse Journal of International Law and Commerce*, pp. 1–14.

[77] Article I of the 1979 Treaty between the Government of Canada and the Government of the United States of America to Submit to Binding Dispute Settlement the Delimitation of the Maritime Boundary in the Gulf of Maine Area.

[78] Special Agreement between the Government of Canada and the Government of the United States of America to Submit to a Chamber of the International Court of Justice the Delimitation of the Maritime Boundary in the Gulf of Maine Area.

dispute to arbitration.[79] As Judge Morozov stated, this was some kind of 'ultimatum'.[80] In the words of Judge Oda, the ICJ 'has approved the composition of the Chamber entirely in accordance with the latest wishes of the Parties'.[81]

In practice, it seems unlikely that the Court will ignore the parties' wishes since they are at liberty to go elsewhere, such as an arbitral tribunal, if dissatisfied.[82] Yet, the imposition of a particular composition may deprive the Court of its freedom of choice of judges.[83] Furthermore, this approach may result in its regionalisation by depriving the Court of its essential characteristic of universality.[84] In fact, all the members of the ad hoc Chamber in the *Gulf of Maine* case were from Western Europe and North America.[85]

3.5 Registry

The Court is to appoint its Registrar in accordance with Article 21 of the ICJ Statute. The Registrar shall be elected for a term of seven years and may be re-elected.[86] Furthermore, the Court is to elect a Deputy-Registrar.[87] The Registrar is the regular channel of communication to and from the Court. The registry and the Registrar perform multiple functions, such as judicial, diplomatic, administrative and language functions.[88] The Registrar signs all judgments, advisory opinions and orders of the Court, and the minutes referred to in subparagraph (f).[89] In addition, the Registrar is to have custody of the seals and stamps of the Court, the archives of the Court, and such other archives as may be entrusted to the Court.[90]

4 CONTENTIOUS JURISDICTION OF THE ICJ

4.1 General Considerations

The 'jurisdiction' of a court or a tribunal signifies the power to decide a dispute in accordance with law.[91] The exercise of jurisdiction of the ICJ must rest on the consent of States and no State is bound to submit its disputes with other States to the Court without its consent. This is a corollary of the principle of free choice of means. It is generally recognised

---

[79] Article II of the 1979 Treaty.
[80] *Delimitation of the Maritime Boundary in the Gulf of Maine Area* (Canada/United States of America), Order of 20 January 1982, Constitution of Chamber, Dissenting Opinion of Judge Morozov, ICJ Reports 1982, p. 11.
[81] Declaration of Judge Oda in the *Gulf of Maine* case, ICJ Reports 1982, p. 10.
[82] Declaration of Judge Oda in *Land, Island and Maritime Frontier Dispute* (El Salvador/Honduras: Nicaragua intervening), Order of 8 May 1987, Constitution of Chamber, ICJ Reports 1987, p. 13; Jiménez de Aréchaga, 'The Amendments to the Rules of Procedure of the International Court of Justice' (1973) 67 *AJIL*, p. 3.
[83] Dissenting Opinion of Judge El-Khani, *Land, Island and Maritime Frontier Dispute* (El Salvador/Honduras: Nicaragua intervening), Order of 8 May 1987, Constitution of Chamber, ICJ Reports 1987, p. 12.
[84] *Ibid.* See also Oda, 'Further Thoughts on the Chambers Procedure', pp. 557–8.
[85] McWhinney, 'Special Chambers', pp. 7–11.   [86] Rules of Court, Article 22(1).
[87] Rules of Court, Article 23.
[88] Kolb, *The Elgar Companion*, pp. 162–4; Thirlway, *The International Court of Justice*, pp. 21–3.
[89] Article 26(1)(h) of the Rules of Court.   [90] Article 26(1)(n) of the Rules of Court.
[91] Thirlway, *The International Court of Justice*, p. 35.

TABLE 6.3 MODES TO GIVE A STATE'S CONSENT TO THE ICJ'S JURISDICTION

Before the dispute arises	After the dispute arises
The optional clause	A compromissory clause in a treaty
A Special Agreement	Forum prorogatum

that an international court or tribunal has the power to decide on the existence and extent of its own jurisdiction concerning any dispute before it.[92] This is called the principle of *la compétence de la compétence*. This principle is explicitly provided in Article 36(6) of the Statute of the Court.[93] However, there is no presumption that jurisdiction exists or that jurisdiction does not exist.[94]

As will be discussed next, a State's consent can be given via four different ways: (i) a special agreement, (ii) a compromissory clause in a treaty, (iii) *forum prorogatum* and (iv) the optional clause (see Table 6.3).

4.2 Special Agreement

The commonly used method of consenting to the exercise of the ICJ's jurisdiction is special agreement which is concluded after a dispute arises. Under Article 36(1) of the ICJ Statute, the jurisdiction of the Court comprises all cases which the parties refer to it. Cases may be brought before the Court by the notification of the special agreement pursuant to Article 40(1) of the Statute of the Court. While the other three modes concern unilateral submission of contentious cases to the Court, the special agreement relates to a joint referral of a dispute to the Court. In this case, parties to a dispute mutually recognise the existence of the dispute by concluding special agreement.

Normally no jurisdictional problems will be raised in a case brought before the Court by special agreement. As they have the specific willingness to settle their dispute by judicial settlement, it can be reasonably expected that the parties in dispute will appear before the Court and will implement the decision of the Court.[95] Thus some argue that joint referral of a dispute to the Court may be regarded as an ideal in the contentious proceedings of the Court.[96] In reality, however, referrals of disputes to the Court by special agreement are not too numerous (see Table 6.4).[97] In addition, a special agreement is not totally free from controversy.

---

[92] *Ibid.*, p. 38. See also *Nottebohm* (Liechtenstein v. Guatemala), Preliminary Objection, Judgment of 18 November 1953, ICJ Reports 1953, p. 119.

[93] Article 36(6) stipulates that: 'In the event of a dispute as to whether the Court has jurisdiction, the matter shall be settled by the decision of the Court.'

[94] Thirlway, *The International Court of Justice*, p. 39.

[95] S. Oda, 'The Compulsory Jurisdiction of the International Court of Justice: A Myth? A Statistical Analysis of Contentious Cases' (2000) 49 *ICLQ*, p. 262. See also p. 257.   [96] *Ibid.*, p. 34.

[97] After 2010, no joint referral case exists. See also M. Kawano, 'The Role of Judicial Procedures in the Process of the Pacific Settlement of International Disputes' (2009) 346 *RCADI*, pp. 461–2.

TABLE 6.4 LIST OF CASES SUBMITTED TO THE ICJ BY SPECIAL AGREEMENT

1949	Asylum (Colombia v. Peru)
1950	Haya de la Torre (Colombia v. Peru)
1951	Manquiers et Ecrehos (France v. United Kingdom)
1957	Sovereignty over Certain Frontier Land (Belgium v. Netherlands)
1967	North Sea Continental Shelf (Federal Republic of Germany v. Netherlands) North Sea Continental Shelf (Federal Republic of Germany v. Denmark)
1978	Continental Shelf (Tunisia v. Libyan Arab Jamahiriya)
1981	Delimitation of the Maritime Boundary in the Gulf of Maine Area (Canada v. USA)
1982	Continental Shelf (Libyan Arab Jamahiriya v. Malta)
1983	Frontier Dispute (Burkina Faso v. Republic of Mali)
1986	Land, Island and Maritime Frontier Dispute (El Salvador v. Honduras: Nicaragua intervening)
1990	Territorial Dispute (Libyan Arab Jamahiriya v. Chad)
1993	Gabčíkovo-Nagymaros Project (Hungary v. Slovakia)
1996	Kasikili/Sedudu Island (Botswana v. Namibia)
1998	Sovereignty over Pulau Ligitan and Pulau Sipadan (Indonesia v. Malaysia)
2002	Frontier Dispute (Benin v. Niger)
2003	Sovereignty over Pedra Branca/Pulau Batu Putech, Middle Rocks and South Ledge (Malaysia v. Singapore)
2010	Frontier Dispute (Burkina Faso v. Niger)

First, the existence of a special agreement may be a matter of dispute between the parties. The *Aegean Sea Continental Shelf* case is a case in point.[98] As already discussed,[99] whereas the Turkish Government argued that a joint communiqué (i.e. the Brussels Communiqué of 31 May 1975), did not amount to an agreement under international law, the Greek Government maintained that the joint communiqué may constitute such an agreement.[100] In this regard, the ICJ ruled that the Joint Communiqué did not constitute an immediate commitment by the Greek and Turkish Prime Ministers to accept unconditionally the unilateral submission of the present disputes to the Court.[101]

Second, a question may arise with regard to the interpretation of a special agreement. In the *Libya/Malta* case, for instance, there was a divergence of opinions between the parties concerning the scope of the task to be performed by the Court embodied in the Special

---

[98] *Aegean Sea Continental Shelf* (Greece v. Turkey), Judgment of 19 December 1978, Jurisdiction of the Court, ICJ Reports 1978, p. 3.   [99] Chapter 2, section 6 of this book.
[100] ICJ Reports 1978, p. 39, para. 95.   [101] *Ibid.*, p. 44, para. 107.

Agreement.[102] Malta wished the Court to be asked to draw the delimitation line, whereas Libya wanted it to be requested only to pronounce on the principles and rules of international law applicable and it would not accept that the line itself should be drawn by the Court.[103] In this regard, the Court considered that since it was required to decide how in practice the principles and rules of international law can be applied in order that the parties may delimit the continental shelf by agreement 'without difficulty', this necessarily entailed the indication by the Court of the method or methods which it considers to result from the proper application of the appropriate rules and principles. The Court thus held that it was not apparent how this operation could be performed unless that result took the form of at least an approximate line which could be illustrated on a map.[104]

In the *El Salvador/Honduras* case, there was a fundamental disagreement between the parties as to whether or not the Special Agreement empowered or required the Chamber of the ICJ to delimit a maritime boundary, either within or without the Gulf.[105] Whereas El Salvador claimed that the Chamber has no jurisdiction to effect any delimitation of the maritime spaces, Honduras sought the delimitation of the maritime boundary inside and outside the Gulf of Fonseca. After the examination of the text of the Agreement, the Chamber of the ICJ concluded that no indication of a common intention to obtain a maritime delimitation by the Chamber could be derived from the text as it stands.[106]

4.3 Compromissory Clause

A dispute can be referred to the ICJ on the basis of a compromissory clause – that is to say, a clause in a treaty providing that all disputes relating to the application or interpretation of the treaty may be brought by one or the other party before the Court by unilateral application.[107] According to a survey, presently some 300 bilateral or multilateral treaties provide for compulsory recourse to the ICJ in the resolution of disputes concerning the application and interpretation of the treaty in question.[108] The 1948 American Treaty on Pacific Settlement (Pact of Bogotá) is a well-known example.

4.4 *Forum Prorogatum*

Under Article 38(2) of the 1978 Rules of Court, the application shall specify 'as far as possible' the legal grounds upon which the jurisdiction of the Court is said to be based. The qualification 'as far as possible' appears to imply that the specification of the legal basis

---

[102] *Continental Shelf* (Libyan Arab Jamahiriya/Malta), Judgment of 3 June 1985, ICJ Reports 1985, p. 13.
[103] *Ibid.*, p. 23, para. 18.   [104] *Ibid.*, p. 24, para. 19.
[105] *Land, Island and Maritime Frontier Dispute* (El Salvador/Honduras: Nicaragua intervening), Judgment of 11 September 1992, ICJ Reports 1992, p. 351.
[106] *Ibid.*, pp. 582–5, paras. 372–8.
[107] Thirlway, 'The International Court of Justice', pp. 597–8.
[108] Speech by H. E. Judge Hisashi Owada to the Sixth Committee of the General Assembly, 30 October 2009, p. 4. See also S. Oda, 'The International Court of Justice Viewed From the Bench (1976–1993)' (1993-VII) 244 *RCADI*, pp. 36–7. It must be noted that in most cases the parties are allowed to make reservations concerning the compromissory clauses. *Ibid.*, p. 37.

of the jurisdiction of the Court is not absolutely required in the application instituting the proceedings before the Court. Under Article 38(5) of the Rules of Court:

> When the applicant State proposes to found the jurisdiction of the Court upon a consent thereto yet to be given or manifested by the State against which such application is made, the application shall be transmitted to that State. It shall not however be entered in the General List, nor any action be taken in the proceedings, unless and until the State against which such application is made consents to the Court's jurisdiction for the purposes of the case.

This provision was introduced by the Court into its 1978 Rules. According to the Court, '[t]he purpose of this amendment was to allow a State which proposes to found the jurisdiction of the Court to entertain a case upon a consent thereto yet to be given or manifested by another State to file an application setting out its claims and inviting the latter to consent to the Court dealing with them, without prejudice to the rules governing the sound administration of justice'.[109] It follows that the consent of a State to the ICJ's jurisdiction may be established by means of acts subsequent to the initiation of proceedings. This system is called *forum prorogatum*. According to this system, even in a situation where there is no basis of jurisdiction of the Court, an applicant State brings a case against other States with a legitimate expectation that the respondent State may consent to proceed with the case. The State which is asked to consent to the Court's jurisdiction to settle a dispute is completely free to respond as it sees fit.[110]

The first example of *forum prorogatum* is the 1949 *Corfu Channel* case. In this case, the United Kingdom unilaterally submitted an application before the Court on the basis of the recommendation of the Security Council. Albania then accepted jurisdiction of the Court to this case. The Court thus decided that it had jurisdiction in this case. Subsequently, the *forum prorogatum* route has occasionally been used. In reality, however, the acceptance of the Court's jurisdiction by respondent on the basis of *forum prorpgatum* remains very rare (see Table 6.5).

One can find two recent, highly unusual examples of *forum prorogatum*. The first example is the *Case Concerning Certain Criminal Proceedings in France* between Republic of Congo and France. In this case, the applicant (i.e. the Republic of Congo) did not in its application invoke any provisions relied on as affording a basis on which the jurisdiction of the Court might be established, but it proposed to found the jurisdiction of the Court upon a consent thereto yet to be given by France, as contemplated by Article 38(5) of the Rules of Court. By letter dated 8 April 2003 from the Minister for Foreign Affairs of France, France consented explicitly to the jurisdiction of the Court to entertain the application on the basis of that text.[111] However, subsequently the case was removed from the General List at the request of the Republic of Congo.[112]

---

[109] *Case Concerning Certain Questions of Mutual Assistance in Criminal Matters* (Djibouti v. France) (hereafter the *Djibouti/France* case), Judgment of 4 June 2008, ICJ Reports 2008, p. 204, para. 63.
[110] *Ibid.*, p. 205, para. 63.
[111] Letter from the Minister for Foreign Affairs of the French Republic (Consent to the Jurisdiction of the Court to Entertain the Application Pursuant to Article 38, para. 5, of the Rules of Court) 8 April 2003.
[112] Order dated 16 November 2010, Removal from the List, ICJ Reports 2010, p. 635.

TABLE 6.5 EXAMPLES OF THE SUBMISSION OF APPLICATION WITHOUT JURISDICTIONAL BASIS

1. The *Corfu Channel* case (UK v. Albania)→Judgment (1949).
2. Treatment in Hungary of Aircraft and Crew of the United States of America (USA v. Hungary)→Order (1954): Removed from the list.
3. Treatment in Hungary of Aircraft and Crew of United States of America (USA v. USSR)→Order (1954): Removed from the list.
4. Aerial Incident of 10 March 1953 (USA v. Czechoslovakia)→Order (1956): Removed from the list.
5. Antarctica (UK v. Argentina, Chile)→Order (1956): Removed from the list.
6. Aerial Incident of 7 October 1952 (USA v. USSR)→Order (1956): Removed from the list.
7. Aerial Incident of 4 September 1954 (USA v. USSR)→Order (1958): Removed from the list.
8. Aerial Incident of 7 November 1954 (USA v. USSR)→Order (1959): Removed from the list.
9. *Case Concerning Certain Criminal Proceedings in France* (Republic of Congo v. France)→France accepted the Court's jurisdiction, but, later, the case was removed from the list at the request of Congo.
10. *Case Concerning Certain Questions of Mutual Assistance in Criminal Matters* (Djibouti v. France)→Judgment (2008).
11. *Obligations concerning Negotiations relating to Cessation of the Nuclear Arms Race and to Nuclear Disarmament* (Marshall Islands v. China, the Democratic People's Republic of Korea, France, Israel, the Russian Federation and the United States)→Not entered in the Court's General List

The second example is the *Case Concerning Certain Questions of Mutual Assistance in Criminal Matters* between Djibouti and France. On 9 January 2006, the Republic of Djibouti instituted proceedings against France in respect of a dispute concerning France's violation of the 1986 Convention on Mutual Assistance in Criminal Matters between Djibouti and France. In the absence of a declaration by France accepting the compulsory jurisdiction of the Court under Article 36(2) of the ICJ Statute or of a compromissory clause contained in a treaty between the parties and applicable in the present dispute, Djibouti sought to base the Court's jurisdiction on Article 38(5) of the Rules of Court. By its letter of 25 July 2006, France consented to the Court's jurisdiction solely on the basis of Article 38(5). According to France, this consent is valid only for the purposes of the case.[113] This was the first time it fell to the Court to decide the merits of a dispute brought before it by an application based on Article 38(5) of the Rules of Court.[114] As the ICJ pointedly observed, where jurisdiction is based on *forum prorogatum*, great care must be taken regarding the scope of the consent as circumscribed by the responding State.[115] In particular, the consent allowing for the Court to assume jurisdiction must be certain.[116]

---

[113] The *Djibouti/France* case, ICJ Reports 2008, p. 198, para. 39; p. 209, para. 77.
[114] *Ibid.*, p. 204, para. 63.   [115] *Ibid.*, p. 211, para. 87.   [116] *Ibid.*, p. 204, para. 62.

The heart of the matter respecting *forum prorogatum* is the scope of the subject of the dispute before the Court. If the respondent consents to the Court's jurisdiction, it is for it to specify the aspects of the dispute which it agrees to submit to the judgment of the Court.[117] Accordingly, when consent is given *post hoc*, a State may well give only partial consent, and in so doing narrow the jurisdiction of the Court by comparison with what had been contemplated in the application.[118]

In the *Djibouti/France* case, France has taken the view that it had only accepted the Court's jurisdiction over the stated subject matter of the case which was to be found, and only to be found, in paragraph 2 of the application. However, the ICJ took the position that if a section entitled 'subject of the dispute' did not entirely circumscribe the extent of the issues intended to be brought before the Court, the subject matter of the dispute may be discerned from a reading of the whole application. According to the Court, 'the subject of the dispute was not to be determined exclusively by reference to matters set out under the relevant section heading of the Application'.[119] It thus ruled that the consent of the respondent is not limited to the 'subject of the dispute' as described in paragraph 2 of the application.[120] As stated by Judge Tomka, however, greater importance should have been given to the precise terms of the application in light of legal security.[121] Overall great caution is necessary when having recourse to *forum prorogatum* since it may open the door to abuse of the judicial procedure, merely making a gesture of deference to the judicial settlement of disputes.[122]

4.5 Optional Clause

The fourth and important method of conferring the jurisdiction to the Court involves the 'optional clause' enshrined in Article 36(2) of the ICJ Statute, which deserves quoting in full:[123]

> The States Parties to the present Statute may at any time declare that they recognize as compulsory *ipso facto* and without special agreement, in relation to any other State accepting the same obligation, the jurisdiction of the Court in all legal disputes concerning:
>
> (a) the interpretation of a treaty;
> (b) any question of international law;
> (c) the existence of any fact which, if established, would constitute a breach of an international obligation;
> (d) the nature or extent of the reparation to be made for the breach of an international obligation.

---

[117] *Ibid.*, p. 205, para. 63.   [118] *Ibid.*, p. 206, para. 66.   [119] *Ibid.*, p. 207, para. 70.
[120] *Ibid.*, p. 210, para. 83.
[121] Separate Opinion of Judge Tomka, *ibid.*, p. 275, para. 25.
[122] S. Yee, 'Forum Prorogatum Returns to the International Court of Justice' (2003) 16 *Leiden Journal of International Law*, p. 706; Oda, 'International Court of Justice', p. 47.
[123] Article 36(2) of the ICJ Statute inherited the same provision (Article 36(2)) of the Statute of the PCIJ. For a legislative history of the optional clause, see Oda, 'International Court of Justice', p. 39.

The intended effect of the optional clause is that those States that were ready to accept jurisdiction of the Court could do so among themselves. Accordingly, should States A and B accept the optional clause, jurisdiction of the Court is to be established between these States through this clause and State A can unilaterally submit a dispute with State B to the Court. In addition, under Article 36(5) of the ICJ Statute, '[d]eclarations made under Article 36 of the Statute of the Permanent Court of International Justice and which are still in force shall be deemed, as between the parties to the present Statute, to be acceptances of the compulsory jurisdiction of the International Court of Justice for the period which they still have to run and in accordance with their terms'.[124]

A State cannot withdraw a declaration after the Court has been seised of a case so as to deprive it of jurisdiction. Nor can the Court, once seised of a case, be deprived of jurisdiction by expiration of a declaration by lapse of time. This is the so-called *Nottebohm* rule because it was specified in the *Nottebohm* case between Liechtenstein and Guatemala.[125] The key passage of this case deserves quoting:

> Once the Court has been regularly seized, the Court must exercise its powers, as these are defined in the Statute. After that, the expiry of the period fixed for one of the Declaration on which the Application was founded is an event which is unrelated to the exercise of the powers conferred on the Court by the Statute, which the Court must exercise whenever it has been regularly seised and whenever it has not been shown, on some other ground, that it lacks jurisdiction or that the claim is inadmissible.[126]

The Court thus held that: '[T]he subsequent lapse of the Declaration, by reason of the expiry of the period or by denunciation, cannot deprive the Court of the jurisdiction already established.'[127] The *Nottebohm* rule was confirmed by the Court in the 2008 *Genocide Convention* case between Croatia and Serbia, stating that: '[T]he removal, after an application has been filed, of an element on which the Court's jurisdiction is dependent does not and cannot have any retroactive effect.'[128]

The acceptance of the optional clause is a unilateral act which creates a series of bilateral engagements with other States accepting the same obligation of compulsory jurisdiction.[129] The mutual obligations arise at the time the second declaration is made, even though the declaration has not been communicated to the other contending State.[130]

---

[124] The effect of Article 36(5) was at issue in the *Aerial Incident of 27 July 1955*. In this case, the majority opinion of the ICJ upheld Bulgaria's preliminary objection that its declaration to accept the Court's jurisdiction made in 1921 had ceased to be in force in 1946. *Aerial Incident of 27 July 1955* (Israel v. Bulgaria), Judgment of 26 May 1959, ICJ Reports 1959, pp. 144–5.

[125] The *Nottebohm* case concerned the legality of measures taken by Guatemala's against Nottebohm during World War II. On 17 December 1951, Liechtenstein referred the case against Guatemala to the ICJ on the basis of Article 36 of the ICJ Statute. Concerning the facts, see memorial submitted by the Government of the Principality of Liechtenstein, pp. 24–32.

[126] *Nottebohm*, Preliminary Objection, ICJ Reports 1953, p. 122.   [127] *Ibid.*, p. 123.

[128] *Application of the Convention on the Prevention and Punishment of the Crime of Genocide* (Croatia v. Serbia), Preliminary Objections, Judgment of 18 November 2008, ICJ Reports 2008, p. 438, para. 80.

[129] The *Nicaragua* case, Jurisdiction of the Court and Admissibility of the Application, Judgment of 26 November 1984, ICJ Reports 1984, p. 418, para. 60.

[130] Collier and Lowe, *The Settlement of Disputes*, pp. 140–1.

As at 2016, some seventy-two of the parties to the ICJ Statute had deposited with the UN Secretary-General a declaration of acceptance of the optional clause.[131] The percentage of acceptances of the optional clause was merely around 37.3 per cent. Furthermore, as will be discussed next, most of the declarations accepting the optional clause are qualified by reservations.[132] In addition, not infrequently States withdrew their declaration of accepting the compulsory jurisdiction of the Court when the Court gave judgments unfavourable to them. For instance, after having indicated provisional measures in the *Anglo-Iranian Oil Co.* case, Iran denounced its declaration of accepting the Court's jurisdiction.[133] Although the ICJ, in the 1984 *Nicaragua* case, established its jurisdiction,[134] the United States did not appear before the Court in the proceedings of the merits of the case. In 1985, the United States withdrew its declaration accepting the Court's jurisdiction.[135]

5 RESERVATIONS TO THE OPTIONAL CLAUSE

5.1 Principle of Reciprocity Concerning Reservations to the Optional Clause

When the Statute of the PCIJ was first drafted in 1920, reservations to the acceptance of compulsory jurisdiction of the Court were not anticipated. In response to questions concerning the legality of a reservation to the declaration of accepting the Court's jurisdiction, however, the Assembly of the League of Nations took the view in 1924 that the terms of Article 36(2) of the Statute of the PCIJ were sufficiently wide to permit States to make reservations to the declaration with a view to promoting acceptance of the Court's jurisdiction. This view was echoed by the resolution of the Assembly of the League of Nations in 1928. In the 1930s, it became common practice for States to make various reservations when accepting the compulsory jurisdiction of the Court,[136] and the practice has been succeeded in the ICJ.

Under Article 36(3) of the ICJ Statute, the declarations to accept the compulsory jurisdiction of the Court may be made unconditionally or on condition of reciprocity on the part of several or certain States, or for a certain time. In the words of the Court:

> Declaration of acceptance of the compulsory jurisdiction of the Court is facultative, unilateral engagements that States are absolutely free to make or not to make. In making the declaration a State is equally free either to do so unconditionally and without limit of time for its duration, or to qualify it with conditions or reservations.[137]

States which accept the jurisdiction of the Court under the optional clause do so only 'in relation to any other state accepting the same obligation'.[138] It follows that if the claimant State

---

[131] The data is available at: www.icj-cij.org/jurisdiction/index.php?p1=5&p2=1&p3=3. The United Kingdom is the only permanent member of the Security Council to have issued a declaration of acceptance.
[132] See section 7 of this chapter.   [133] (1951–2) 6 *ICJ Yearbook*, p. 184.
[134] ICJ Reports 1984, p. 442, para. 113.   [135] (1985–6) 40 *ICJ Yearbook*, p. 60.
[136] Oda, 'The International Court of Justice', p. 41.
[137] The *Nicaragua* case, ICJ Reports 1984, p. 418, para. 59.
[138] Article 36(2) of the ICJ Statute.

has accepted the optional clause subject to reservations, the defendant State can rely upon the claimant State's reservations by way of reciprocity. As the Court stated in the *Interhandel* case, '[r]eciprocity in the case of Declarations accepting the compulsory jurisdiction of the Court enables a Party to invoke a reservation to that acceptance which it has not expressed in its own Declaration but which the other Party has expressed in its Declaration'.[139]

In accordance with the principle of reciprocity, the scope of the jurisdiction of the Court is defined by the narrower of the two acceptances. In this regard, the Court, in the *Anglo-Iranian Oil Co.* case, ruled that: 'As the Iranian Declaration is more limited in scope than the United Kingdom Declaration, it is the Iranian Declaration on which the Court must base itself.'[140] Likewise, it found, in the *Norwegian Loans* case, that:

> A comparison between the two Declarations shows that the French Declaration accepts the Court's jurisdiction within narrower limits than the Norwegian Declaration; consequently, the common will of the Parties, which is the basis of the Court's jurisdiction, exists within these narrower limits indicated by the French reservation.[141]

The principle of reciprocity to reservations becomes applicable to the parties to a dispute on the day of application. Accordingly, one of the parties in dispute cannot invoke another party's reservations before the referral of the dispute to the Court.[142] In addition, the principle of reciprocity is not applicable to the duration of the optional clause. According to the ICJ, '[t]he notion of reciprocity is concerned with the scope and substance of the commitments entered into, including reservations, and not with the formal conditions of their creation, duration and extinction'.[143]

A reservation to an optional clause should be interpreted in a manner compatible with the effect sought by the reserving State.[144] In this regard, the Court stated that:

> All elements in a declaration under Article 36, paragraph 2, of the Statute which, read together, comprise the acceptance by the declarant State of the Court's jurisdiction, are to be interpreted as a unity, applying the same legal principles of interpretation throughout.[145]

In practice, the effect of reservations to the optional clause can be a matter of debate in the case law of the ICJ. The following sections turn to an examination of some typical examples of reservations to the optional clause. These reservations can be divided into three principal categories: reservations *ratione personae*, reservations *ratione temporis* and reservations *ratione materiae* (see Table 6.6).

---

[139] *Interhandel* case (Switzerland v. USA), Judgment of 21 March 1959, ICJ Reports 1959, p. 23.
[140] *Anglo-Iranian Oil Co.* (United Kingdom v. Iran), Preliminary Objections, Judgment of 22 July 1952, ICJ Reports 1952, p. 103.
[141] *Case of Certain Norwegian Loans* (France v. Norway), Judgment of 6 July 1957, ICJ Reports 1957, p. 23.
[142] See the *Nicaragua* case, ICJ Reports 1984, Jurisdiction and Admissibility, p. 420, para. 64.
[143] *Ibid.*, p. 419, para. 62.
[144] *Fisheries Jurisdiction* (Spain v. Canada), Jurisdiction of the Court, Judgment, ICJ Reports 1998, p. 455, para. 52.
[145] *Ibid.*, p. 453, para. 44.

TABLE 6.6 CLASSIFICATION OF RESERVATIONS TO DECLARATIONS RECOGNISING THE JURISDICTION OF THE ICJ AS COMPULSORY

Reservations *ratione personae*	Reservations *ratione temporis*	Reservations *ratione materiae*
• Non-existence of diplomatic relations	• Limitation of time scope	• Existence of agreed means
		• Disputes concerning multilateral treaty
• Certain group or region	• Particular period of national history	• Specific subjects
		• Domestic jurisdiction
• Time	• Events prior to the declaration	• Automatic reservations

5.2 Reservations *Ratione Personae*

Reservations *ratione personae* aim to preclude litigation of dispute with specific categories of States. The scope of States which are precluded from litigation before the ICJ may be determined on the basis of (i) non-existence of diplomatic relations, (ii) members of a certain group or region and (iii) a time element.

The first type of reservations *ratione personae* can be seen in the declaration made by Djibouti in 2005. It precludes disputes with the government of any State with which, on the date of an application to bring a dispute before the Court, the Government of Djibouti has no diplomatic relations or which has not been recognised by the Government of Djibouti. The Israeli Declaration of 1956, amended in 1984, excluded any dispute between the State of Israel and any other State whether or not a Member of the United Nations which does not recognise Israel or which refuses to establish or to maintain normal diplomatic relations with Israel and the absence or breach of normal relations precedes the dispute and exists independently of that dispute.[146]

The best example of the second type of reservations *ratione personae* may be the reservation excluding disputes with a member of the Commonwealth of Nations.[147] The declaration made by Barbados in 1980 excluded 'disputes with the Government of any other country which is a member of the Commonwealth of Nations, all of which disputes shall be settled in such manner as the parties have agreed or shall agree'. Similar declarations were made by Canada (1994), Gambia (1966), India (1974), Kenya (1965), Malta (1966), Mauritius (1968), and the United Kingdom (2014).

The third type of reservation *ratione personae* aims to prevent so-called 'surprise applications'. The validity of the surprise application was at issue in the *Right of Passage* case

---

[146] (1983–4) 38 *ICJ Yearbook*, pp. 70–1. The declaration of Israel was withdrawn on 21 November 1985. (1985–6) 40 ICJ Yearbook, p. 60.

[147] The Commonwealth is defined as 'a voluntary association of independent States most of which are former British colonies'. C. Steinorth, 'Commonwealth' in *Max Planck Encyclopaedia*, para. 1.

of 1960 between Portugal and India.[148] In this case, Portugal had been filed against India only three days after the latter had deposited its declaration under Article 36(2) of the Court's Statute. India disputed the jurisdiction of the ICJ on the ground that the application violated the equality, mutuality and reciprocity to which India was entitled under the optional clause because it had been filed before copies of the Portuguese declaration could have been transmitted by the Secretary-General to the other parties to the Statute in accordance with Article 36(4). However, the Court dismissed the preliminary objection of India. According to the Court, the legal effect of a declaration of acceptance does not depend upon subsequent action or inaction of the Secretary-General. Furthermore, Article 36 provides for no additional requirement, for instance, that the information transmitted by the Secretary-General must reach the parties to the Statute, or that some period must elapse subsequent to the deposit of the declaration before it can become effective.[149] In the view of the Court, '[a] State accepting the jurisdiction of the Court must expect that an Application may be filed against it before the Court by a new declarant State on the same day on which the State deposits with the Secretary-General its Declaration of Acceptance'.[150]

The Court's decision in the *Right of Passage* case exemplified the vulnerability of States that have made declarations under the optional clause and the tactical advantage enjoyed by those that have not. Many States thus made reservations with a view to preventing surprise applications. By way of example, the declaration of the United Kingdom precludes:

> any dispute in respect of which any other Party to the dispute has accepted the compulsory jurisdiction of the International Court of Justice only in relation to or for the purpose of the dispute; or where the acceptance of the Court's compulsory jurisdiction on behalf of any other Party to the dispute was deposited or ratified less than twelve months prior to the filing of the application bringing the dispute before the Court.

This reservation was incorporated in many declarations, such as Australia (2002), Bulgaria (1992), Cyprus (2002), India (1974), Japan (2015), Nigeria (1998), the Philippines (1972), Poland (1996), Portugal (2005) and Spain (1990).

5.3 Reservations *Ratione Temporis*

Reservations *ratione temporis* seek to limit the time scope of the application of the optional clause. Three types of reservations *ratione temporis* exist.

A first type seeks to limit the time scope of the acceptance of the optional clause with regard to disputes arising from a certain date. For instance, the 1956 declaration of the

---

[148] *Right of Passage over Indian Territory* (Portugal v. India) (hereafter the *Right of Passage* case), Judgment of 12 April 1960, Merits, ICJ Reports 1960, p. 6. This case concerned Portugal's right of passage through the territory of India in order to ensure communications between its territory of Daman (coastal Daman) and its enclaved territories of Dadra and Nagar-Aveli. *Ibid.*, p. 10.
[149] The *Right of Passage* case, Preliminary Objections, Judgment of 26 November 1957, ICJ Reports 1957, pp. 146–7.
[150] *Ibid.*, p. 146.

Netherlands is limited to disputes which may arise after 5 August 1921. The declaration of the United Kingdom limits its acceptance of the compulsory jurisdiction of the ICJ over disputes arising after 1 January 1984. On 24 October 2001, Nicaragua made a reservation not to accept the jurisdiction of the Court 'in relation to any matter or claim based on interpretations of treaties or arbitral awards that were signed and ratified or made, respectively, prior to 31 December 1901'. The declaration made by Portugal in 2005 precludes any dispute arising before 26 April 1974 or concerning situations or facts prior to that date. The declaration of Sweden is limited to disputes which may arise with regard to situations or facts subsequent to 6 April 1947.

A second type of reservations *ratione temporis* aims to avoid litigation relating to a particular period of national history. For instance, the Israeli declaration of 1956 excluded disputes arising out of events occurring between 15 May 1948 and 20 July 1949, the period of the war of independence.[151]

A third type of reservations *ratione temporis* seeks to ensure that only events subsequent to the declaration are subject to the Court's compulsory jurisdiction. Frequently the date of the declaration becomes the cut-off point. For instance, the declaration of Barbados accepts the compulsory jurisdiction of the ICJ over 'all disputes arising after the declaration is made'. Senegal made a similar declaration in 1985. The use of this type of limitation *ratione temporis* has the effect of restricting the scope of compulsory jurisdiction of the Court. This is particularly true in the situation where a State makes a fresh declaration and uses the date of the declaration as the critical date. For example, Canada terminated its declaration of 1985 and made its new declaration in 1994, using the date of the declaration as the cut-off date. The effect was to reduce the period subject to the compulsory jurisdiction of the Court by around nine years.

To apply the reservation *ratione temporis*, the critical date of a dispute – that is, the date when a dispute was raised – is of central importance. In this regard, the 'double exclusion formula' is in issue.[152] This formula precludes disputes prior to the date of the declaration and disputes arisen out of facts or situations prior to the same date. The declaration made by Portugal in 2005 is a case in point. It precludes 'any dispute, unless it refers to territorial titles or rights or to sovereign rights or jurisdiction, arising before 26 April 1974 or concerning situations or facts prior to that date'. A similar declaration was made by Spain in 1990.

When the double exclusion formula is incorporated into declarations of States, the Court is required to ascertain both the date of the dispute and the facts or situations from which it arose. A leading case on this matter is the *Right of Passage* case. By the terms of the declaration made by India on 28 February 1940, India accepted the jurisdiction of the Court 'over all disputes arising after February 5th, 1930, with regard to situations or facts subsequent to the same date'. India contended that claims relating to the passage were raised by Portugal before 5 February 1930 and that the situation to which the titles invoked by Portugal refer was repeatedly the subject of difficulties prior to 5 February 1930. It thus contended that the present dispute had not satisfied either of the two conditions stated

---

[151] (1983–4) 38 *ICJ Yearbook*, pp. 70–71.
[152] This is the term of Meron. T. Meron, 'Israel's Acceptance of the Compulsory Jurisdiction of the International Court of Justice' (1969) 4 *Israel Law Review*, p. 327.

and, thus, the Court had no jurisdiction to deal with this case. Referring to the *Electricity Company of Sofia and Bulgaria*, however, the Court drew a distinction between 'the situations or facts which constitute the source of the rights claimed by one of the Parties' and 'the situations or facts which are the source of the dispute'. According to the Court, '[o]nly the latter are to be taken into account for the purpose of applying the Declaration accepting the jurisdiction of the Court'.[153] The Court eventually rejected the preliminary objection of India since it was only in 1954 that a controversy as to the title of Portugal concerning the right of passage to go into the enclaved territories was raised.[154]

5.4 Reservations *Ratione Materiae*

Reservations *ratione materiae* aim to exclude from the Court's jurisdiction certain categories of disputes. As there are many variations in this matter, only some noteworthy examples can be presented here.

5.4.1 Reservations Excluding From the Court's Jurisdiction Disputes for Which Some Other Means of Peaceful Settlement has been Agreed or Shall be Agreed

This type of reservation seeks to preclude disputes wheret the parties have already agreed to employ other means of dispute settlement before a case is to be referred to the Court. For instance, Suriname reserves 'disputes in respect of which the parties, excluding the jurisdiction of the International Court of Justice, have agreed to settlement by means of arbitration, mediation or other methods of conciliation and accommodation'. Furthermore, Australia reserves 'any dispute in regard to which the parties thereto have agreed *or shall agree* to have recourse to some other method of peaceful settlement'. The words in italics allow a State to use an alternative procedure of dispute settlement after a case has been referred to the Court. The main effect of all reservations of this type is to discourage another State from taking a case to the Court in violation of an agreement to use some other means of settlement.[155] Given that the parties in dispute can freely discontinue proceedings before the Court and employ another procedure at any time, however, this part of the reservation seems to be rather deceptive.[156] In any case, the reservation *ratione materiae*, with some differences of wording, has been incorporated in many declarations.[157] The legal effect of this type of reservation was at issue in two cases before the ICJ.

The first instance is the 1992 *Certain Phosphate Lands in Nauru* case. On 19 May 1992, Nauru instituted proceedings against Australia concerning a dispute over the

---

[153] The *Right of Passage* case, Judgment of 12 April, ICJ Reports 1960, p. 35.   [154] *Ibid.*, pp. 35–6.
[155] Merrills, 'The Optional Clause Revisited', p. 225.   [156] *Ibid.*
[157] Examples include: Austria (1971), Barbados (1980), Botswana (1970), Cambodia (1957), Canada (1994), Cote d'Ivoire (2001), Djibouti (2005), Estonia (1991), Gambia (1966), Germany (2008), Republic of Guinea (1998), Honduras (1986), Hungary (1992), India (1974), Japan (2007), Kenya (1965), Lesotho (2000), Liberia (1952), Lithuania (2012), Luxembourg (1930), Madagascar (1992), Malawi (1966), Malta (1966), Marshall Islands (2013), Mauritius (1968), the Netherlands (1956), New Zealand (1977), Nigeria (1998), Pakistan (1960), Peru (2003), the Philippines (1972), Portugal (2005), Senegal (1985), Slovakia (2004), Spain (1990), Sudan (1958), Swaziland (1969) and the United Kingdom (2014).

rehabilitation of certain phosphate lands in Nauru worked out before Nauruan independence on the basis of Article 36(2) of the ICJ Statute. The declaration of Nauru stipulates that its acceptance of the Court's jurisdiction does not extend to 'any dispute with respect to which there exists a dispute settlement mechanism under an agreement between the Republic of Nauru and another State'. Likewise the declaration of Australia specifies that it 'does not apply to any dispute in regard to which the parties thereto have agreed or shall agree to have recourse to some other method of peaceful settlement'.[158] In this regard, Australia contended that Nauru was placed under the Trusteeship System by a Trusteeship Agreement approved by the General Assembly on 1 November 1947, and that any dispute which arose in the course of the Trusteeship between 'the Administering Authority and the indigenous inhabitants' fell within the exclusive jurisdiction of the United Nations Trusteeship Council and General Assembly. It thus maintained that Australia and Nauru had agreed 'to have recourse to some other method of peaceful settlement' within the meaning of the reservation in Australia's declaration, and that consequently the Court lacked jurisdiction to deal with Nauru's application.[159] However, the Court unanimously rejected the argument of Australia on the ground that no such agreement whereby the two States undertook to settle their dispute relating to rehabilitation of the phosphate lands by resorting to an agreed procedure other than recourse to the Court has been pleaded or shown to exist.[160]

The second instance is the 2016 *Somalia/Kenya* case (preliminary objections). On 28 August 2014, Somalia instituted proceedings against Kenya concerning a maritime delimitation dispute on the basis of Article 36(2) of the ICJ Statute.[161] However, Kenya raised a preliminary objection to the jurisdiction of the Court since Kenya's declaration acceptancing the jurisdiction of the Court precluded disputes 'in regard to which the parties to the dispute have agreed or shall agree to have recourse to some other method or methods of settlement'.[162] In this regard, a question was raised regarding whether the parties, in the MOU signed by the Government of Kenya and the Transitional Federal Government of the Somali Republic on 7 April 2009, agreed on a method of settlement of their delimitation dispute other than by way of proceedings before the Court. A central issue concerned the interpretation of paragraph 6 of the MOU. In light of the text of the MOU as a whole, the object and purpose of the MOU, and in its context, the Court did not consider that the text of the sixth paragraph could have been intended to establish a method of dispute settlement in relation to the delimitation of the maritime boundary between the parties. It thus rejected the preliminary objection raised by Kenya.[163]

---

[158] *Case Concerning Certain Phosphate Lands in Nauru* (Nauru v. Australia) Preliminary Objections, Judgment of 26 June 1992, ICJ Reports 1992, p. 245, para. 8.
[159] *Ibid.*, p. 246, paras. 9-10.   [160] *Ibid.*, pp. 246-7, para. 11.
[161] *Maritime Delimitation in the Indian Ocean* (Somalia v. Kenya), Preliminary Objections, Judgment of 2 February 2016, ICJ Reports 2016 (not yet reported), para. 1.
[162] Preliminary Objections of Kenya, 7 October 2015, p. 63, paras. 140 *et seq.*
[163] The Somalia/Kenya case (preliminary objections), ICJ Reports 2016 (not yet reported), para. 98.

5.4.2 Reservations Excluding Disputes Arising Under a Multilateral Treaty

Some States made reservations excluding disputes arising under a multilateral treaty.[164] This type of reservation may give rise to a difficult issue respecting applicable law to a case before the Court. An illustrative example is provided by the 1986 *Nicaragua* case (Merits).

When the United States accepted the Optional Clause in 1946, its declaration featured a novel reservation covering 'disputes arising under a multilateral treaty unless (1) all parties to the treaty affected by the decision are also parties to the case before the Court, or (2) the United States of America specially agrees to jurisdiction'. In this case, the United States claimed that whilst Nicaragua relied in its application on four multilateral treaties, the Court lacked jurisdiction over the dispute as various parties to those treaties would be affected by the decision and yet were not parties to the case. In this regard, the Court took the view that: '[C]ustomary international law continues to exist and to apply, separately from international treaty law, even where the two categories of law have an identical content.'[165] It thus decided that it should exercise the jurisdiction to deal with this case on the basis of customary international law.[166] As a consequence, the United States reservation in question seemed to have had little, if any, effect on the outcome of the case. Yet, the Court's approach in the *Nicaragua* case cannot always minimise the legal effect of the multilateral treaties reservation since the purpose of concluding treaties may be to change the obligations of a State under customary law.[167]

5.4.3 Reservations Precluding Specific Subject Matters of Disputes

This type of reservation aims to prevent the referral of particular subjects of contentious cases before the Court. By way of illustration, Japan precludes 'any dispute arising out of, concerning, or relating to research on, or conservation, management or exploitation of, living resources of the sea' from the ICJ's jurisdiction.[168] Given that the reservation was made after the *Whaling in the Antarctic* judgment of 2014, it can be reasonably presumed that the reservation seeks to prevent any litigation with regard to scientific whaling conducted by Japan.

The effect of this type of reservation *ratione materiae* was tested in the 1998 *Fishery Jurisdiction* case between Spain and Canada. This dispute related to the arrest of the *Estai*, a fishing vessel flying the Spanish flag and manned by a Spanish crew, by the Canadian Authority some 245 miles from the Canadian coast in 1995.[169] While, on 10 May 1994, Canada accepted the compulsory jurisdiction of the ICJ, it precluded 'disputes arising out of or concerning conservation and management measures taken by Canada with respect to vessels fishing in the NAFO Regulatory Area'.[170] After examining the nature

---

[164] See, for instance, declarations of India (1974), Malta (1966), Pakistan (1960) and the Philippines (1972).
[165] The *Nicaragua* case, Merits, Judgment of 27 June 1986, ICJ Reports 1986, p. 96, para. 179.
[166] *Ibid.*, pp. 93–7, paras. 175–82.
[167] Merrills, 'The Optional Clause Revisited', pp. 231–2.
[168] Declaration made by Japan on 6 October 2015.
[169] *Fisheries Jurisdiction* (Spain v. Canada), Jurisdiction of the Court, Judgment of 4 December, ICJ Reports 1998, p. 432. The point of arrest was in Division 3L of the NAFO Regulatory Area (Grand Banks area).
[170] *Ibid.*, p. 439, para. 14.

of the dispute between Spain and Canada, the Court held that the dispute submitted to it by Spain comes within the terms of the reservation contained in paragraph 2(d) of the Canadian declaration of 10 May 1994.[171] It thus concluded that it had no jurisdiction to adjudicate upon this dispute.[172] However, five members of the Court, including the judge ad hoc, voted against the judgment.[173] The *Fishery Jurisdiction* judgment gave rise to the question as to whether the credibility of the optional clause system might not be damaged where a State can freely exempt from that system certain specific actions it intends to take because it may be incompatible with the existing rules of international law.[174]

5.4.4 Reservations Precluding Disputes That Fall Within the Scope of Domestic Jurisdiction

Lastly, some mention must be made of limitation *ratione materiae* concerning domestic jurisdiction. This type of reservation aims to exclude from the Court's jurisdiction of disputes which are 'within the domestic jurisdiction' of those States. For instance, the declaration of Canada excludes 'disputes with regard to questions which by international law fall exclusively within the jurisdiction of Canada'. This type of reservation was incorporated in many declarations accepting the optional clause.[175] Theoretically, however, this reservation is unnecessary since the jurisdiction of the Court under Article 36(2) of the Statute is limited to the four classes of legal disputes listed in it, all of which concern questions of international law.[176]

In appropriate circumstances, the Court can join a preliminary objection on the basis of the domestic jurisdiction reservation on the ground that that objection is not preliminary by nature. In this case, the domestic jurisdiction reservation does not constitute a bar to the jurisdiction of the Court. In fact, the ICJ, in the *Right of Passage* case, ruled that it was not possible to pronounce upon the preliminary objection concerning domestic jurisdiction raised by India at this stage without prejudging the merits and that it decided to join that objection to the merits.[177]

5.5 The Validity of Automatic Reservation

Perhaps the most contentious issue concerning reservations may be the validity of 'automatic' or 'self-judging' reservations. This particular type of reservation can be seen in the United States declaration of 14 August 1946 and its variations upon it. In the Declaration of 1946, the United States Government made a reservation which stated that:

---

[171] *Ibid.*, p. 467, para. 87.
[172] *Ibid.*, p. 468, para. 89.
[173] See Dissenting Opinion of Judge Ranjeva, *ibid.*, p. 553, para. 1; Dissenting Opinion of Judge Bedjaoui, *ibid.*, p. 533, para. 43. See also P. Weil, 'Le Principe de la jurisdiction consensuelle à l'épreuve du feu: à propos de l'arrêt de la Cour internationale de Justice dans l'affaire de la competence en matière de pêcheries (Espagne c. Canada)' in C. A. Armas Barea *et al.* (eds.), *Liber Amicorum 'Im Memoriam' of Judge José Maria Ruda* (The Hague: Kluwer, 2000), pp. 157–78.
[174] In this regard, see P. Kooijmans, 'The ICJ in the 21st Century: Judicial Restraint, Judicial Activism, or Proactive Judicial Policy' (2007) 56 *ICLQ*, p. 747.
[175] These declarations include: Barbados (1980), Botswana (1970), Cambodia (1957), Cote d'Ivoire (2001), Cyprus (2002), Djibouti (2005), Gambia (1966), Republic of Guinea (1998), Honduras (1986), India (1974), Kenya (1965), Liberia (1952), Madagascar (1992), Malta (1966), Mauritius (1968), Nigeria (1998), Pakistan (1960), Poland (1996), Senegal (1985), Slovakia (2004) and Swaziland (1969).
[176] Merrills, 'The Optional Clause Revisited', p. 238; Alexandrov, 'Accepting the Compulsory Jurisdiction', pp. 112–13. See also Collier and Lowe, *The Settlement of Disputes*, p. 143.
[177] The *Right of Passage* case, Preliminary Objections, ICJ Reports 1957, p. 150.

> Provided, that this declaration shall not apply to ... b. disputes with regard to matters which are essentially within the domestic jurisdiction of the United States of America as determined by the United States of America.

This reservation is sometimes called as the 'Connally Amendment', since it was introduced by the US Senator Connally. Subsequently, the same reservation was made by several countries, such as France (withdrawn in 1974), Liberia, Malawi, Mexico, the Philippines and Sudan. The automatic or self-judging reservation excludes matters within the domestic jurisdiction of the reserving State *as determined by the reserving State*. It would enable the reserving State to declare, even after the Court had been seised of a dispute on the basis of the optional clause declaration, that the dispute was a matter of domestic jurisdiction, and that the Court had therefore no jurisdiction.[178]

The validity of the automatic reservation was at issue in the 1957 *Norwegian Loans* case between France and Norway. This case concerned a long-standing dispute concerning the payment of various Norwegian loans issued in France.[179] Although France instituted an application against Norway on the basis of Article 36(2) of the Statute of the Court in 1955, Norway raised four preliminary objections. The first objection, which consisted of two parts, is relevant here. First, according to the Norwegian Government, the subject of the dispute was within the exclusive domain of the municipal law of Norway. Second, the Norwegian Government relied upon the reservation in the French Declaration concerning differences relating to matters which are essentially within the national jurisdiction as understood by the French Government.[180]

The French Declaration of 1 March 1949 contained the following reservation:

> This declaration does not apply to differences relating to matters which are essentially within the national jurisdiction as understood by the Government of the French Republic.[181]

In this regard, the Court took the view that the Norwegian Government was entitled, by virtue of the condition of reciprocity, to invoke the reservation contained in the French Declaration, and this reservation excluded from the jurisdiction of the Court the dispute which has been referred to it by the Application of the French Government. The Court thus found that it was without jurisdiction in this case. It seemed to follow that the Court accepted the application of the French reservation, even though it did not examine the validity of the reservation.[182]

Nonetheless, the validity of the French reservation was challenged by some members of the Court. In the *Norwegian Loans* and *Interhandel* cases, for instance, Judge Sir Hersch Lauterpacht questioned the validity of the French reservation for two main reasons. First, the French reservation was contrary to the fundamental principle of *la compétence de la*

---
[178] Thirlway, 'The International Court of Justice', p. 600.
[179] *Certain Norwegian Loans* (France v. Norway), Judgment of 6 July 1957, ICJ Reports 1957, pp. 18–20.
[180] *Ibid.*, p. 21.   [181] *Ibid.*, p. 23.   [182] *Ibid.*, pp. 26–7.

compétence provided in Article 36(6) of the Statute of the Court.[183] Second, the 'automatic reservation' is invalid as lacking in the essential condition of validity of a legal instrument since it leaves to the party making the declaration the right to determine the extent and the very existence of its obligation. According to Judge Lauterpacht, an instrument in which a party is entitled to determine the existence of its obligation is not a valid and enforceable legal instrument of which a court of law can take cognizance.[184]

Should the automatic reservations be invalid, a further question arises as to whether or not the automatic reservation makes the declaration to accept the optional clause invalid as a whole. Opinions of the members of the Court were divided in this matter. Judge Lauterpacht, in the *Norwegian Loans* case, considered that the acceptance of France as a whole must be held to be invalid.[185] This view was echoed by Judge Spender in the *Interhandel* case.[186] In contrast, when examining the validity of the automatic reservation made by the United States in the *Interhandel* case, Judge Klaestad took the view that the invalidity of the US automatic reservation does not necessarily imply that it is impossible for the Court to give effect to the other parts of the Declaration of Acceptance which are in conformity with the Statute.[187] Likewise Judge Armand-Ugon, in the *Interhandel* case, considered that the American automatic reservation could be separated from the rest of the acceptance and that the acceptance of the Court's jurisdiction by the United States was not altogether without value.[188] In practice, States have treated States making automatic reservation as parties to the optional clause, and no State has objected to the making of an automatic reservation.[189]

However, the question whether there is no limit to the automatic reservation needs further consideration. In the *Norwegian Loans* case, Norway took the position that: '[S]hould a Government seek to rely upon it with a view to denying the jurisdiction of the Court in a case which manifestly did not involve a "matter which is essentially within the national jurisdiction" it would be committing an *abuse de droit* which would not prevent the Court from acting.'[190] Judge Read supported this position:

> [T]he respondent State, in invoking the [automatic] reservation, must establish that there is a genuine understanding, i.e. that the circumstances are such that it would be reasonably possible to reach the understanding that the dispute was essentially national. Whether the circumstances are such is not a matter for decision by a respondent government, but by the Court.[191]

---

[183] Separate Opinion of Judge Sir Hersch Lauterpacht, *ibid.*, p. 44. See also Dissenting Opinion of Judge Sir Hersch Lauterpacht, ICJ Reports 1959, p. 104.
[184] Separate Opinion of Judge Sir Hersch Lauterpacht, ICJ Reports 1957, p. 48. See also Dissenting Opinion of Judge Guerrero, *ibid.*, p. 69.
[185] Separate Opinion of Judge Sir Hersch Lauterpacht, *ibid.*, pp. 57–8.
[186] Separate Opinion of Judge Sir Percy Spender, ICJ Reports 1959, p. 57.
[187] Dissenting Opinion of Judge Klaestad, *ibid.*, pp. 77–8.
[188] Dissenting Opinion of Judge Armand-Ugon, *ibid.*, pp. 93–4.
[189] See J. Crawford, 'The Legal Effect of Automatic Reservations to the Jurisdiction of the International Court' (1979) 50 *BYIL*, p. 81.
[190] Dissenting Opinion of Judge Read, ICJ Reports 1957, p. 94; Preliminary Objections submitted by the Government of the Kingdom of Norway, 20 April 1956, p. 131, para. 26.
[191] Dissenting Opinion of Judge Read, ICJ Reports 1957, p. 94.

Further, in the *Aerial Incident of 27 July 1955* between the United States and Bulgaria, Bulgaria relied on the United States' automatic reservation on the basis of reciprocity. However, the United States maintained that: 'Where a subject matter is quite evidently one of international concern, and has so been treated by the parties to the suit, it is not open to either of them to determine that the matter lies essentially within domestic jurisdiction.'[192] This statement is noteworthy as the United States admitted the limit of the automatic reservation.

Related to this, it may be relevant to recall that in the *Nicaragua* case (Jurisdiction and Admissibility), the United States did not resort to its automatic reservation, even though it raised several preliminary objections to the Court's jurisdiction. While the reason remains a matter of speculation, it seems difficult to argue that military and paramilitary activities in a foreign State (Nicaragua) could fall within the scope of domestic jurisdiction of the United States. In light of the principle of good faith and the prohibition of abuse of rights in international law, it appears reasonable to argue that the State cannot invoke the automatic reservation if the subject of a dispute manifestly falls outside the scope of the national jurisdiction.[193]

5.6 Validity of Instantly Amendable Reservations

Another type of reservation that needs further consideration is the 'instantly amendable reservation'. According to this reservation, a State accepting the jurisdiction of the ICJ can immediately change the scope of its acceptance in this matter. For example, the declaration of Ireland (2011) reserves 'the right at any time, by means of a notification addressed to the Secretary-General of the United Nations and with effect from the date of such notification, either to amend or withdraw the present Declaration'.[194]

The validity of this reservation was at issue in the *Right of Passage* case.[195] In this case, Portugal, in its Declaration of 1955, reserved 'the right to exclude from the scope of the present declaration, at any time during its validity, any given category or categories of disputes, by notifying the Secretary-General of the United Nations and with effect from the moment of such notification'.[196] India disputed the validity of the Portuguese Declaration of 1955 on the basis that this reservation was incompatible with the object and purpose of the optional clause.[197] According to India, this reservation introduced into the declaration a degree of uncertainty as to reciprocal rights and obligations which

---

[192] Observations and Submissions of the Government of the United States of America on the Preliminary Objection of the Government of the People's Republic of Bulgaria, February 1960, p. 305. Later, this case was removed from the list of the ICJ. Correspondence, 28 October 1957-13 June 1960, p. 677; Order of 30 May 1960 Removal from the list. ICJ Reports 1960, pp. 146-8.

[193] T. Sugihara, *Kokusai Saiban no Kenkyu* (A Study of International Adjudication) (in Japanese) (Tokyo: Yuhikaku, 1986), pp. 164-6.

[194] The same type of reservation was made by several States, including: Canada (1944), Cyprus (2002), Honduras (1986), Kenya (1965), Malawi (1966), Malta (1966), Marshall Islands (2013), Portugal (2005), Senegal (1985) and the United Kingdom (2014).

[195] For the validity of this type of reservations see *ibid.*, pp. 167-9; C. H. M. Waldock, 'Decline of the Optional Clause' (1955-6) 32 *BYIL*, pp. 275-6.

[196] *Right of Passage over Indian Territory* (Portugal v. India), Preliminary Objections, Judgment of 26 November 1957, ICJ Reports 1957, p. 141. [197] *Ibid.*

deprives the acceptance of the compulsory jurisdiction of the Court of all practical value.[198] Yet, the Court was not persuaded by India's argument. According to the Court, when a case is submitted to the Court, it is always possible to ascertain the reciprocal obligations of the parties in accordance with their respective declarations. For the Court, the degree of uncertainty resulting from Portugal's reservation is substantially the same as that created by the right claimed by many signatories of the optional clause to terminate their declarations of acceptance by simple notification without any obligatory period of notice. Furthermore, the Court considered that it was clear that any reservation notified by Portugal in pursuance of its reservation became automatically operative against it in relation to other signatories of the optional clause. Hence it accepted the validity of the Portugal's reservation.[199]

However, a State that makes an instantly amendable reservation can at any time escape from a future litigation against that State by notifying the Secretary-General of the exclusion of a particular matter from its declaration, as soon as that State sees the possibility of litigation against it. Accordingly, as Woldock stated, this form of reservation renders the acceptance of compulsory jurisdiction of the Court completely illusory.[200] Moreover, unlike automatic reservation, other States cannot invoke instantly amendable reservations on the basis of reciprocity. In addition, the instantly amendable reservation undermines the purpose of the optional clause to much the same extent as a provision whereby a declaration is made immediately terminable by notice to the Secretary-General.[201] It can be considered that instantly amendable reservations make the scope of the acceptance of the ICJ's compulsory jurisdiction highly uncertain.

5.7 Termination of Declarations

The declarations accepting the optional clause include various conditions concerning the duration of the acceptance of the optional clause. Whilst these conditions vary according to the declarations, four principal types can be presented.

5.7.1 Declarations Which Contain no Reference to Termination

Examples of this type of declarations include: Botswana (1970), Commonwealth of Dominica (2006), Cote d'Ivoire (2001), Dominican Republic (1924), Egypt (1957), Estonia (1991), Georgia (1995), Haiti (1921), Malawi (1966), Nicaragua (1921), Panama (1921), Paraguay (1996), Senegal (1985), Togo (1979), Uganda (1963) and Uruguay (1921).

Where a declaration of a State contains no reference to termination, an issue arises as to whether the declaration can be instantly terminated. A leading case in this matter is the 1984 *Nicaragua* case. Whilst the declaration of the United States contained six months' notice proviso for terminating the acceptance of the jurisdiction of the Court, the declaration of Nicaragua made no reference to duration of acceptance. The United States thus claimed that the Nicaraguan 1929 Declaration, being of undefined duration, was liable

---

[198] *Ibid.*, pp. 141–3. [199] *Ibid.*, pp. 143–4.
[200] Waldock, 'Decline of the Optional Clause', p. 275. [201] *Ibid.*, p. 276.

to immediate termination, without previous notice and that therefore Nicaragua had not accepted 'the same obligation' as itself for the purposes of Article 36(2) of the Court's Statute and consequently may not rely on the six months' notice proviso against the United States.[202] This claim purported to deprive the Court of jurisdiction in the *Nicaragua* case, by ignoring the requirement of six months' notice for terminating the declaration since it was anticipated that proceedings were imminent. Nevertheless, the Court did not accept the immediate termination of the declaration of the United States. In the words of the Court:

> [T]he right of immediate termination of declarations with indefinite duration is far from established. It appears from the requirements of good faith that they should be treated, by analogy, according to the law of treaties, which requires a reasonable time for withdrawal from or termination of treaties that contain no provision regarding the duration of their validity.[203]

5.7.2 Declaration Which Defines a Specific Period of Time for Acceptance

There are two types of declaration that define a specific period of time for acceptance. The first represents declarations which fix a certain period of time and no more. For example, Nauru's declaration is limited to five years. The second concerns declarations which define a fixed period and are automatically renewed unless notice is given not less than six months before the termination of the period. For instance, Denmark accepted the Court's jurisdiction for a period of five years from 10 December 1956 and thereafter for further periods of five years, if this declaration is not denounced by notice of not less than six months before the expiration of any five-year period. Finland (1958), the Netherlands (1956), Norway (1996) and Sweden (1957) made similar declarations. As a variation, the declaration of Costa Rica (1973) states that: 'This Declaration shall be valid for a period of five years and shall be understood to be tacitly renewed for like periods, unless denounced before the expiration of the said period.' The 1971 declaration of Austria states that: 'This Declaration shall remain in force for a period of five years and thereafter until it will be terminated or modified by a written declaration.' A similar declaration was made by Belgium (1958), Cambodia (1957), Cameroon (1994), Djibouti (2005), Greece (1994) and Liberia (1952).

5.7.3 Declarations to be Terminated on Notification After a Certain Period of Time

The third type of declaration is those which can be terminated on notification after a six-month or one-year period of advance notice. For example, the declaration of Liechtenstein (1950) states that the present declaration shall take effect from the date on which the principality becomes a party to the Statute and shall have effect as long as the

---

[202] The *Nicaragua* case, Jurisdiction and Admissibility, ICJ Reports 1984, p. 419, para. 62.
[203] *Ibid.*, p. 420, para. 63. However, Judge Oda criticised the Court's view. Separate Opinion of Judge Oda, *ibid.*, p. 510.

declaration has not been revoked subject to one year's notice. Switzerland (1948) made a similar declaration. Likewise, the declaration of Mexico (1947) shall be binding for a period of five years as from 1 March 1947 and after that date shall continue in force until six months after the Mexican Government gives notice of denunciation. A similar condition is incorporated in the declarations of Bulgaria (1992, six months' notice), New Zealand (1977, six months' notice), Guinea-Bissau (1989, six months' notice), Hungary (1992, six months' notice) and Suriname (1987, one year's notice).

5.7.4 Declarations Which can be Instantly Terminated on Notification

Quite a few declarations state that the acceptance of the jurisdiction of the ICJ can be instantly terminated on notification.[204] These declarations can be called 'instantly terminable declarations'. By way of example, the declaration of Portugal (2005) states that the Portuguese Republic recognises the jurisdiction of the Court as compulsory *ipso facto* and without special agreement 'until such time as notice may be given to terminate the acceptance'. A State which made the instantly terminable declaration enjoys a considerable advantage over those which did not since that State can avoid defending a case by terminating its acceptance as soon as litigation is threatened. Given that these declarations entail the serious risk of undermining the jurisdiction of the Court,[205] the validity of instant termination of declarations needs careful consideration.[206]

6 ADVISORY JURISDICTION

6.1 Basics of an Advisory Opinion

Advisory opinions of the ICJ are defined as 'judicial statements on legal questions submitted to the Court by organs of the UN and other international legal bodies so authorised'.[207] The advisory function was already provided by Article 14 of the League Covenant to the PCIJ[208] and it was subsequently succeeded by the ICJ. As the ICJ stated in its advisory opinion concerning the *Legality of the Threat or Use of Nuclear Weapons*, the purpose of the Court's advisory function is not to settle disputes between States, but to furnish legal advice to the relevant organs and institutions which may request an advisory

---

[204] Examples include: Australia (2002), Barbados (1980), Canada (1994), Cyprus (2002), Democratic Republic of Congo (1989), Gambia (1966), Germany (2008), Honduras (1986), India (1974), Ireland (2011), Kenya (1965), Lesotho (2000), Lithuania (2012), Malta (1966), Madagascar (1992), Marshall Islands (2013), Mauritius (1968), Nigeria (1998), Pakistan (1960), Peru (2003), the Philippines (1972), Poland (1996), Portugal (2005), Republic of Guinea (1998), Slovakia (2004), Somalia (1963), Sudan (1958), Swaziland (1969), Timor-Leste (2012) and the United Kingdom (2014).
[205] Merrills, 'The Optional Clause Revisited', p. 204.
[206] Further, see R. Kolb, 'La Denunciation avec effet immediate de declarations facultatives établissant la competence de la court internationale de justice' in M. G. Kohen (ed.), *Promoting Justice, Human Rights and Conflict Resolution through International Law, Liber Amicorum Lucius Caflisch* (Leiden: Brill, 2007), pp. 875–90.
[207] K. Oellers-Frahm, 'Article 96' in B. Simma, D.-E. Khan, G. Nolte and A. Paulus (eds.), *The Charter of the United Nations: A Commentary*, Vol. II (Oxford University Press, 2012), p. 1976.
[208] Article 14 of the League Covenant stipulated that: 'The Court may also give an advisory opinion upon any dispute or question referred to it by the Council or by the Assembly.'

164 Foundation of International Dispute Settlement

TABLE 6.7 UN ORGANS AND OTHER INTERNATIONAL INSTITUTIONS ENTITLED TO ASK THE ICJ FOR AN ADVISORY OPINION*

UN organs

The Security Council, the General Assembly, the Economic and Social Council, the Trusteeship Council (suspended), the Interim Committee of the General Assembly and the Committee on Applications for Review of Administrative Tribunals Judgments (until 1995).

Other international institutions

ILO, FAO, UNESCO, WHO, IBRD, IFC, IDA, IMF, ICAO, ITU, WMO, IMO, WIPO, IFAD, UNIDO and IAEA.

* ICJ, *The International Court of Justice*, 6th edition (The Hague: ICJ, 2013), p. 83. Curiously UPU is not included in specialised agencies which may request for advisory opinions.

opinion.[209] To date, the ICJ has given some twenty-two advisory opinions during the last seventy years. The advisory function of the Court is enshrined in four instruments: the UN Charter,[210] the ICJ Statute,[211] the Rules of Court[212] and the Practice Directions.[213]

The procedure for advisory proceedings is open only to authorised international organs and institutions. Under Article 96(1) of the UN Charter, the General Assembly and the Security Council are entitled to request the Court to give an advisory opinion on any legal question.[214] This power is facultative, not obligatory. Further, other UN organs and specialised agencies, which may at any time be so authorised by the General Assembly, may request advisory opinions of the Court on legal questions arising within the scope of their activities in accordance with Article 96(2) of the UN Charter (see Table 6.7).

According to the Court, three conditions must be satisfied in order to find the jurisdiction of the Court when a request for an advisory opinion is submitted to it by a specialised agency:

(i) The agency requesting the opinion must be duly authorised, under the Charter, to request opinions from the Court.
(ii) The opinion requested must be on a legal question.
(iii) This question must be one arising within the scope of the activities of the requesting agency.[215]

The *dictum* of the Court calls for three comments.

---

[209] *Legality of the Threat or Use of Nuclear Weapons*, Advisory Opinion of 8 July 1996, ICJ Reports 1996, p. 236, para. 15. See also *Reservations to the Convention on the Prevention and Punishment of the Crime of Genocide*, Advisory Opinion of 28 May 1951, ICJ Reports 1951, p. 19; *Legal Consequences for States of the Continued Presence of South Africa in Namibia (South West Africa) notwithstanding Security Council Resolution 276 (1970)*, ICJ Reports 1971, p. 24.
[210] Article 96. [211] Articles 65-68. [212] Articles 102-109. [213] Article XII.
[214] See also Chapter 4, sections 2.5 and 3.1 of this book.
[215] *Legality of the Use by a State of Nuclear Weapons in Armed Conflict*, Advisory Opinion of 8 July 1996, ICJ Reports 1996, pp. 71-2, para. 10.

First, the organ requesting an advisory opinion 'has the right to decide for itself on the usefulness of an opinion in the light of its own needs' and 'it is not for the Court itself to purport to decide whether or not an advisory opinion is needed' by the organ for the performance of its function.[216] States are not empowered by the Statute of the Court to ask an advisory opinion to the Court, although States may participate in the advisory proceedings in accordance with the ICJ Statute.[217]

Second, it is for the Court to satisfy that the question on which it is requested to give its opinion is a 'legal question' within the meaning of Article 96 of the UN Charter and Article 65 of the Statute.[218] The term 'any legal question' under Article 96(1) can be understood as meaning any question of international law.[219] In reality, any legal question may include some issues of facts. In this regard, the Court took the view that: '[A] mixed question of law and fact is none the less a legal question within the meaning of Article 96, paragraph 1, of the Charter and Article 65, paragraph 1, of the Statute.'[220] Considering that the ICJ has an inherent power to interpret the meaning and scope of the question requested for an advisory opinion, the question can be reformulated by the Court. As the Court itself observed,[221] in some cases, the Court has departed from the language of the question put to it where the question was not adequately formulated,[222] or it has clarified the question before giving its opinion where the question asked was vague.[223]

Third, organs of the United Nations and other specialised agencies can seek advisory opinion only on legal questions 'within the scope of activities', not on any question under the UN Charter.[224] This requirement is called the principle of speciality. According to the principle of speciality, international organisations 'are invested by the States which create them with powers, the limits of which are a function of the common interests whose promotion those States entrust to them'.[225] The application of the principle of speciality constituted the main issue in the advisory opinion of 8 July 1996 concerning the *Legality of the Use by a State of Nuclear Weapons in Armed Conflict*. A crucial issue in this case was whether or not the World Health

---

[216] *Legality of the Threat or Use of Nuclear Weapons*, ICJ Reports 1996, p. 237, para. 16.
[217] See Article 66 of the ICJ Statute.
[218] *Accordance with international law of the unilateral declaration of independence in respect of Kosovo (Request for Advisory Opinion)* (hereafter *Kosovo Advisory Opinion*), Advisory Opinion of 22 July 2010, ICJ Reports 2010, p. 414, para. 25.
[219] Kolb, *The International Court of Justice*, p. 1040.
[220] *Western Sahara*, Advisory Opinion of 16 October 1975, ICJ Reports 1975, p. 19, para. 17. See also *Legal Consequences for States of the Continued Presence of South Africa in Namibia (South West Africa) notwithstanding Security Council Resolution 276 (1970)*, ICJ Reports 1971, p. 27, para. 40.
[221] *Kosovo Advisory Opinion*, ICJ Reports 2010, p. 423, para. 50.
[222] *Interpretation of the Greco-Turkish Agreement of 1 December 1926 (Final Protocol, Article IV)*, Advisory Opinion, 1928, PCIJ, Series B, No. 16, pp. 14–16.
[223] *Application for Review of Judgment No. 273 of the United Nations Administrative Tribunal*, Advisory Opinion, ICJ Reports 1982, pp. 348–50, paras. 46–8.
[224] Kolb, *The International Court of Justice*, p. 1022.
[225] *Legality of the Use by a State of Nuclear Weapons in Armed Conflict*, Advisory Opinion of 8 July 1996, ICJ Reports 1996, p. 78, para. 25. For a commentary on this case, see, for instance, C. F. Amerasinghe, 'The Advisory Opinion of the International Court of Justice in the WHO Nuclear Weapons Case: A Critique' (1997) 10 *Leiden Journal of International Law*, pp. 523–9; J. Klabbers, 'Global Governance before the ICJ: Re-reading the WHO Opinion' (2009) 13 *Max Planck Yearbook of United Nations Law*, pp. 1–28.

Organisation (WHO) has jurisdiction to address the legality of the use of nuclear weapons. According to the Court:

> [T]he WHO Constitution can only be interpreted, as far as the powers conferred upon that Organisation are concerned, by taking due account not only of the general principle of speciality, but also of the logic of the overall system contemplated by the Charter.[226]

The functions attributed to the WHO are listed in twenty-two subparagraphs in Article 2 of its constitution. In this regard, the Court considered that: 'None of these subparagraph [(a)–(v) in Article 2 of its Constitution] expressly refers to the legality of any activity hazardous to health and that none of the functions of the WHO is dependent upon the legality of the situation upon which it must act.'[227] In the Court's view, 'to ascribe to the WHO the competence to address the legality of the use of nuclear weapons ... would be tantamount to disregarding the principle of speciality'.[228] Hence the Court considered that the question raised in the request for an advisory opinion submitted to it by the WHO did not arise 'within the scope of [the] activities' of the WHO.[229] In conclusion, the Court, by eleven votes to three, found that it was not able to give the advisory opinion requested by the WHO.[230] In the ICJ jurisprudence, this is the only case where the ICJ declined to give an advisory opinion.

6.2 Procedure of Advisory Proceedings

An advisory opinion must be requested by means of a written request containing an exact statement of the question upon which an opinion is requested and accompanied by all documents likely to throw light upon the question.[231] The Registrar notifies the request for an advisory opinion to all States entitled to appear before the Court.[232] These States and international organisations considered by the Court as likely to be able to furnish information on the question may present to the Court written statements within a time limit fixed by the Court and may also participate in the oral proceedings.[233] The procedure for advisory cases, as for contentious cases, is divided into written and oral phases, though the Court has exercised the power to dispense with oral proceedings where it has seen fit to do so. The decision of the Court is produced by a deliberation process identical to that adopted for judicial cases and closely resembles the judgment.[234]

A particular issue to be examined in this context concerns the appointment of judge ad hoc in advisory proceedings.[235] In this regard, Article 68 of the ICJ Statute stipulates that:

---

[226] ICJ Reports 1996, p. 80, para. 26.   [227] Ibid., pp. 75–6, para. 20.   [228] Ibid., p. 79, para. 25.
[229] Ibid., p. 81, para. 26.
[230] Ibid., p. 84, para. 32. However, Judges Shahabuddeen, Weeramantry and Koroma appended dissenting opinions.
[231] Article 65(2) of the ICJ Statute.   [232] Article 66(1) of the ICJ Statute.
[233] Article 66(2) of the ICJ Statute.
[234] Oda, *The International Court of Justice*, p. 95.
[235] Thirlway, 'The International Court of Justice', p. 613.

> In the exercise of its advisory functions the Court shall further be guided by the provisions of the present Statute which apply in contentious cases to the extent to which it recognizes them to be applicable.

Under Article 102(3) of the Rules of Court, Article 31 of the Statute relating to judge ad hoc shall apply, as also the provisions of these rules concerning the application of that Article, when an advisory opinion is requested upon a legal question actually pending between two or more States. It seems that the appointment of judge ad hoc in advisory proceedings is context-specific. In the *Namibia* case, for instance, South Africa was not permitted to appoint a judge ad hoc since the requested opinion did not relate to a legal question actually pending between two or more States.[236] In the *Western Sahara* case, Morocco was permitted to appoint a judge ad hoc, but Mauritania was not because there was a legal dispute between Morocco and Spain, while there was no dispute involving Mauritania.[237]

6.3 Admissibility of Request

6.3.1 General Considerations

Under Article 65(1) of the ICJ Statute, '[t]he Court may give an advisory opinion on any legal question at the request of whatever body may be authorized by or in accordance with the Charter of the United Nations'. It has been submitted that as shown by the term 'may', the Court has discretion to decide whether or not to respond to a request for an advisory opinion.[238] In this regard, the Court, in its advisory opinion of 1962, stated that:

> The power granted is of a discretionary character. ... [E]ven if the question is a legal one, which the Court is undoubtedly competent to answer, it may nonetheless decline to do so.[239]

The Court in the advisory opinion concerning the *Legality of the Threat or use of Nuclear Weapons* reiterated that: '[T]he Statute leaves a discretion as to whether or not it will give an advisory opinion that has been requested of it, once it has established its competence to do so.'[240] However, it is mindful of the fact that its answer to a request for an advisory opinion 'represents its participation in the activities of the Organization [the United Nations], and, in principle, should not be refused'.[241] In this regard, the ICJ, in the *Western Sahara* case, took the position that: '[O]nly "compelling reasons" should lead it to refuse

---

[236] ICJ Reports 1971, pp. 24–7, paras. 32–9.   [237] ICJ Reports 1975, pp. 15–16, para. 9.
[238] For a critique of the idea of the discretionary power of the Court, see *ibid.*, pp. 1091 *et seq.*; R. Kolb, 'De la prétendu discrétion de la cour internationale de justice de refuser de donner un avis consultatif' in L. Boisson de Chazournes and V. Gowlland-Debbas (eds.), *The International Legal System in Quest of Equity and Universality, Liber Amicorm George Abi-Saab* (The Hague: Kluwer, 2001), pp. 609–27.
[239] *Certain Expenses of the United Nations (Article 17, paragraph 2, of the Charter)*, Advisory Opinion of 20 July 1962, ICJ Reports 1962, p. 155. This view was echoed in the advisory opinion of 1975. *Western Sahara*, Advisory Opinion of 16 October 1975, ICJ Reports 1975, p. 21, para. 23.
[240] ICJ Reports 1996, pp. 234–5, para. 14.
[241] *Interpretation of Peace Treaties with Bulgaria, Hungary and Romania*, Advisory Opinion of 30 March 1950 (first phase), ICJ Reports 1950, p. 71. See also *Accordance with international law of the unilateral declaration of independence in respect of Kosovo*, ICJ Reports 2010, p. 416, paras. 29–31.

to give a requested advisory opinion ... .'[242] In practice, the discretionary power on the basis of 'compelling reasons' has never been exercised by the ICJ. Since the threshold of 'compelling reasons' is very high, the scope of so-called 'discretion' of the Court is in fact minimised.[243] In considering compelling reasons, two issues merit special mention: lack of consent of an interested State and the highly political nature of the question.

6.3.2 Lack of Consent of States

Where a request for an advisory opinion relating to a pending dispute between States was made, an issue arises whether the Court can give its opinion without consent of the disputing parties. The leading case on this matter is the 1923 *Eastern Carelia* case. In 1917, a war broke out between Finland and the Soviet Government and, later, a peace treaty was concluded between the two parties (Treaty of Dorpat) in 1920. Articles 10 and 11 of the treaty contained provisions concerning 'autonomy' of Eastern Carelia and those provisions were complemented by a declaration made by the Soviet Government on this matter. After the entry into force of the Treaty of Dorpat on 1 January 1921, however, a dispute was raised between Finland and the Soviet Government as to the interpretation and legal effect of Articles 10 and 11 of the treaty as well as of the declaration. Finland thus submitted the matter to the Council of the League of Nations, and the Council requested an advisory opinion from the PCIJ on this subject. Russia was neither a member of the League of Nations nor a party to the Statute of the PCIJ, and refused to take part in the proceedings before the Court. In the view of the Court, '[t]he question put to the Court is not one of abstract law, but concerns directly the main point of the controversy between Finland and Russia' and '[a]nswering the question would be substantially equivalent to deciding the dispute between the parties'.[244] However, this would be contrary to the principle in international law that 'no State can, without its consent, be compelled to submit its disputes with other States either to mediation or to arbitration, or to any other kind of pacific settlement'.[245] The PCIJ thus declined to render an advisory opinion.

Nonetheless, the *dictum* of the *Eastern Carelia* case was qualified by the ICJ in the *Interpretation of Peace Treaties* case, stating that:

> The consent of States, parties to a dispute, is the basis of the Court's jurisdiction in contentious cases. The situation is different in regard to advisory proceedings even where the Request for an Opinion relates to a legal question actually pending between States. The Court's reply is only of an advisory character: as such, it has no binding force. It follows that no State, whether a Member of the United Nations or not, can prevent the giving of an Advisory Opinion which the United Nations considers to be desirable in order to obtain enlightenment as to the course of action it should take.[246]

---

[242] *Western Sahara*, ICJ Reports 1975, p. 21, para. 23. For a list of possible arguments which endeavour to persuade the ICJ not to give an advisory opinion, see Kolb, *The International Court of Justice*, p. 1082.
[243] See also *ibid.*, pp. 1088 *et seq*.
[244] *Status of Eastern Carelia*, Advisory Opinion of 23 Jully 1923, PCIJ, Series B, No. 5, pp. 28–9.
[245] *Ibid.*, p. 27.
[246] Emphasis added. ICJ Reports 1950, p. 71. See Separate Opinion of Judge De Castro in *Legal Consequences for States of the Continued Presence of South Africa in Namibia (South West Africa) notwithstanding Security Council Resolution 276 (1970)*, ICJ Reports 1971, p. 172.

On the other hand, the Court, in the *Western Sahara* case, stated that:

> [L]ack of consent might constitute a ground for declining to give the opinion requested if, in the circumstances of a given case, considerations of judicial propriety should oblige the Court to refuse an opinion. In short, the consent of an interested State continues to be relevant, not for the Court's competence, but for the appreciation of the propriety of giving an opinion.[247]

It went on to add that: 'In certain circumstances, therefore, the lack of consent of an interested State may render the giving of an advisory opinion incompatible with the Court's judicial character.'[248] The *dictum* of the Court seems to suggest that consent of interested States remains pertinent, not for the existence of jurisdiction but as an element of judicial propriety.[249] In any case, to this day, there is no case where a request for an advisory opinion was rejected by the ICJ because of the lack of consent of States.[250]

6.3.3 Highly Political Nature of the Question

A further issue to be considered is whether the request of an advisory opinion should be declined in light of its highly political nature.[251] This issue was raised in the advisory opinion concerning the *Legality of the Threat or Use of Nuclear Weapons*.[252] In this case, Judge Oda took the view that: 'I have no doubt that the request was prepared and drafted – not in order to ascertain the status of existing international law on the subject but to try to promote the total elimination of nuclear weapons – that is to say, with highly *political* motives.'[253] The learned judge thus stated that: 'Under the circumstances and considering the discretionary competence of the Court in declining to render an advisory opinion, the Court should, in my view, for the reason of judicial propriety, have dismissed the request raised under Resolution 49/75 K.'[254]

Judge Oda's view was not supported by the Court, however. According to the Court, '[t]he question put to the Court by the General Assembly is indeed a legal one, since the Court is asked to rule on the compatibility of the threat or use of nuclear weapons with the relevant principles and rules of international law'.[255] Furthermore, 'the political nature of the motives which may be said to have inspired the request and the political implications that the opinion given might have are of no relevance in the establishment of its

---

[247] ICJ Reports 1975, p. 25, para. 32.   [248] *Ibid.*, para. 33.
[249] Thirlway, *The Law and Procedure*, Vol. I, p. 843.
[250] Thirlway, 'The International Court of Justice', p. 612.
[251] See also Chapter 7, section 4.3 of this book.
[252] *Legality of the Threat or Use of Nuclear Weapons*, Advisory Opinion of 8 July 1996, ICJ Reports 1996, p. 226. The UN General Assembly, in its Resolution 49/75K of 15 December 1994, requested the ICJ to give an advisory opinion with regard to the following question: 'Is the threat or use of nuclear weapons in any circumstance permitted under international law?' In 1996, the Court gave its advisory opinion on this subject.
[253] Dissenting Opinion of Judge Oda in *ibid.*, p. 368, para. 44.
[254] *Ibid.*, p. 372, para. 52.
[255] Advisory Opinion, *ibid.*, p. 234, para. 13.

jurisdiction to give such an opinion'.[256] In the *Wall* case, the Court reiterated its view, stating that it 'cannot accept the view ... that it has no jurisdiction because of the "political" character of the question posed'.[257]

The ICJ's view was in line with the precedents on this matter. In the advisory opinion concerning *Conditions of Admission of a State to Membership in the United Nations (Article 4 of the Charter)*, for instance, the Court expressed the view that: 'It is not concerned with the motives which may have inspired this request ... .'[258] It took a similar position in the advisory opinion concerning *Certain Expenses of the United Nations (Article 17, paragraph 2, of the Charter)*.[259] Although, in the *Namibia* advisory opinion, South Africa contended that the Court should not exercise its advisory jurisdiction because of political pressure to which the Court has been or might be subjected, the Court dismissed this claim since it is 'an organ which, in that capacity, acts only on the basis of the law, independently of all outside influence or interventions whatsoever, in the exercise of the judicial function entrusted to it alone by the Charter and its Statute'.[260] In light of the jurisprudence of the Court, one can argue that its highly political nature is not regarded as a compelling reason to decline the request for an advisory opinion.

6.4 Effect of Advisory Opinion

An advisory opinion is only advisory and, thus, it does not have *res judicata*.[261] Even so, advisory opinions of the ICJ carry authority with regard to the interpretation and application of constitutive instruments of the international institutions, including the UN Charter and the requesting organ must duly take account of the opinion. Where a requesting organ adopts a legal solution to the point of law decided by the Court's advisory opinion, the organ will be obliged to accept the point as an authoritative conclusion.[262] Furthermore, if a State seeks to advocate an interpretation contrary to an advisory opinion of the Court, it will be in a weak position. Thus an advisory opinion of the Court can be used to bring pressure to bear on a particular State to comply with the general view of States on a legal question. Examples in this matter are provided by the *Namibia* and *Wall* cases.[263]

Some agreements accept in advance the binding nature of an advisory opinion.[264] For example, Article 8, Section 30, of the 1946 Convention on the Privileges and Immunities of the United Nations provides that: 'The opinion given by the Court shall be accepted as decisive by the parties.'[265] Likewise, Article XII(2) of the 1946 Statute of the Administrative

---

[256] *Ibid*. The Court expressed the same view in the advisory opinion requested by the WHO concerning the *Legality of the use by a State of Nuclear Weapons in Armed Conflict*, ICJ Reports 1996, p. 74, para. 17.
[257] *Legal Consequences of the Construction of a Wall in the Occupied Palestinian Territory*, Advisory Opinion of 9 July 2004, ICJ Reports 2004, p. 155, para. 41.
[258] *Conditions of Admission of a State to Membership in the United Nations (Article 4 of the Charter)*, Advisory Opinion of 28 May 1948, ICJ Reports 1948, p. 61.
[259] *Certain Expenses of the United Nations (Article 17, paragraph 2, of the Charter)*, Advisory Opinion of 20 July 1962, ICJ Reports 1962, pp. 155-6.
[260] ICJ Reports 1971, p. 23, paras. 27-9.
[261] *Res judicata* will be discussed in Chapter 7, section 7.1.
[262] Kolb, *The International Court of Justice*, pp. 1097-8; Kolb, *The Elgar Companion*, p. 277.
[263] Thirlway, *The International Court of Justice* (2016), p. 139.
[264] Oellers-Frahm, 'Article 96', p. 1987.
[265] 1 *UNTS*, p. 15. Entered into force 17 September 1946.

Tribunal of the International Labour Organization makes clear that: 'The opinion given by the Court [the ICJ] shall be binding.'[266] It can be said that the essentially non-binding character of an advisory opinion is not an obstacle to conclude an agreement of this kind.[267]

Furthermore, the Court's advisory opinion can contribute to development of rules of international law, including institutional law of the United Nations.[268] By way of example, the ICJ, in the *Reparation* case, accepted the implied power of the United Nations.[269] Furthermore, the Court, in the advisory opinion concerning the *Certain Expenses*, ruled that the expenditures relating to peacekeeping operations constituted 'expenses of the Organization' within the meaning of Article 17(2) of the UN Charter.[270] These advisory opinions marked an important landmark in the development of UN law.

7 CONCLUSIONS

The practice of the ICJ mirrors the role – and limitations – of international adjudication in peaceful settlement of international disputes. Principal points discussed in this chapter can be summarised as follows:

(i) The validity of the composition of the ICJ constitutes an important element to maintain the authority of the Court. To secure the validity of the Court, two requirements are crucial: 'the representation of the forms of civilization and of the principal legal systems of the world' and 'independence and impartiality of judges'.

(ii) The jurisdiction of the ICJ rests on the consent of the parties to a case. This is the fundamental principle governing the establishment of the Court's jurisdiction. The consent to accept the Court's jurisdiction can be expressed by four modes:
- special agreement
- compromissory clauses
- optional clause
- *forum prorogatum*.

While referral of a case to the Court on the basis of a special agreement may be desirable, the number of examples of this mode remains rather modest. In light of the risk of abuse of judicial procedure and uncertainty of the scope of the consent of the parties, great caution is needed in recourse to *forum prorogatum*. In addition, the number of States accepting the optional clause remains modest. Overall there is

---

[266] The text is available at: www.ilo.org/public/english/tribunal/about/statute.htm. Other examples include: Section 32 of Convention on the Privileges and Immunities of the Specialized Agencies; Section 34 of Agreement on the Privileges and Immunities of the International Atomic Energy Agency; Article 66(2)(e) of the Vienna Convention on the Law of Treaties between States and International Organisations or between International Organizations.
[267] Thirlway, 'The International Court of Justice', p. 611.
[268] Kolb, *The International Court of Justice*, p. 1099.
[269] *Reparation for Injuries Suffered in the Service of the United Nations*, Advisory Opinion of 11 April 1949, ICJ Reports 1949, p. 182.
[270] *Certain Expenses of the United Nations (Article 17, paragraph 2, of the Charter)*, Advisory Opinion of 20 July 1962, ICJ Reports 1962, pp. 179–80.

no significant change with regard to the acceptance of the compulsory jurisdiction of the Court.

(iii) Reservations to the optional clause are regarded as a device to reconcile the requirement for the universality of the Court's jurisdiction with the safeguard of the State's sovereignty. In reality, many States make a variety of reservations to the optional clause. These reservations are divided into three types: reservations *ratione personae*, reservations *ratione temporis* and reservations *ratione materiae*. Some types of reservation, such as automatic reservations, entail the serious risk of undermining the jurisdiction of the ICJ.

(iv) An advisory opinion of the Court seeks to provide legal assistance to the relevant organs and institutions which may request it, by clarifying the judicial aspects of activities of relevant international institutions. Only authorised international organs and institutions can request an advisory opinion from the ICJ. In this regard, the principle of speciality is of particular importance. The Court is to give its advisory opinion unless there are 'compelling reasons' to decline the request. The threshold of 'compelling reasons' is very high in ICJ jurisprudence and, in practice, there is little scope for 'discretion' of the Court in this matter. While advisory opinions are not binding, they carry authority and affect various activities of international institutions and the development of international law.

FURTHER READING

General

P. W. Almeida and J.-M. Sorel (eds.), *Latin America and the International Court of Justice: Contributions to International Law* (London: Routledge, 2016).

M. S. M. Amr, *The Role of the International Court of Justice as the Principal Judicial Organ of the United Nations* (The Hague: Kluwer, 2003).

P. Couvreur, *The International Court of Justice and the Effectiveness of International Law* (Leiden: Nijhoff, 2016).

S. Forlati, *The International Court of Justice: An Arbitral Tribunal or a Judicial Body?* (Berlin: Springer, 2014).

G. I. Hernández, *International Court of Justice and the Judicial Function* (Oxford University Press, 2014).

ICJ, *The International Court of Justice*, 6th edn (The Hague: ICJ, 2014).

M. Kawano, 'The Role of Judicial Procedures in the Process of the Pacific Settlement of International Disputes' (2009) 346 *RCADI*, pp. 9–474.

R. Kolb, *The International Court of Justice* (Oxford: Hart Publishing, 2013).

The Elgar Companion to the International Court of Justice (Cheltenham: Edward Elgar Publishing, 2014).

S. Oda, 'The International Court of Justice Viewed from the Bench 1976–1993' (1993) 244 *RCADI*, pp. 9–190.

C. Peck and R. Lee (eds.), *Increasing the Effectiveness of the International Court of Justice* (The Hague: Kluwer, 1997).

J. J. Quintana, *Litigation at the International Court of Justice: Practice and Procedure* (Leiden: Nijhoff, 2015).

S. Rosenne, *The Law and Practice of the International Court, 1920–1996* (The Hague: Nijhoff, 1997).

S. Rosenne, *The World Court: What it is and How it Works* (Dordrecht: Nijhoff, 1995).

H. Thirlway, 'The International Court of Justice 1989–2009: At the Heart of the Dispute Settlement System?' (2010) 57 *NILR*, pp. 347–95.

Law and Procedure of the International Court of Justice: Fifty Years of Jurisprudence, 2 vols. (Oxford University Press, 2013).

The International Court of Justice (Oxford University Press, 2016).

A. M. Weisburd, *Failings of the International Court of Justice* (Oxford University Press, 2016).

A. Zimmermann et al. (eds.), *The Statute of the International Court of Justice: A Commentary*, 2nd edn (Oxford University Press, 2012).

Judges of the Court

H. R. Fabri and J.-M. Sorel, *Indépendance et impartialité des juges internationaux* (Paris: Pedone, 2010).

R. Mackenzie et al., *Selecting International Judges: Principle, Process and Politics* (Oxford University Press, 2010).

J. Malenovský, 'L'indépendance des juges internationaux' (2010) 349 *RCADI*, pp. 9–276.

D. Terris, C. P. R. Romano and L. Swigart, *The International Judge: An Introduction to the Men and Women Who Decide the World's Cases* (Oxford University Press, 2007).

Jurisdiction of the Court

G. Abi-Saab, 'On Discretion: Reflections on the Nature of the Consultative Function of the International Court of Justice' in L. Boisson de Chazournes and P. Sands (eds.), *International Law, the International Court of Justice and Nuclear Weapons* (Cambridge University Press, 1999), pp. 36–50.

R. Ago, '"Binding" Advisory Opinions of the International Court of Justice' (1991) 85 *AJIL*, pp. 439–51.

S. A. Alexandrov, 'Accepting the Compulsory Jurisdiction of the International Court of Justice with Reservations: An Overview of Practice with a Focus on Recent Trends and Cases' (2001) 14 *LJIL*, pp. 89–124.

M. Aljaghoub, *The Advisory Function of the International Court of Justice 1946–2005* (Berlin: Springer, 2006).

A. Aust, 'Advisory opinions' (2010) 1 *Journal of International Dispute Settlement*, pp. 123–51.

C. N. Brower and P. H. F. Bekker, 'Understanding "Binding" Advisory Opinions of the International Court of Justice' in N. Ando, E. McWhinney and R. Wolfrum (eds.), *Liber Amicorum Judge Shigeru Oda* (The Hague: Kluwer, 2002), pp. 351–68.

C. J. Greenwood, 'Judicial Integrity and the Advisory Jurisdiction of the International Court of Justice' in G. Gaja and J. G. Stoutenburg (eds.), *Enhancing the Rule of Law Through the International Court of Justice* (Leiden: Nijhoff, 2014), pp. 63–73.

Sir R. Jennings, 'Recent Cases on "Automatic" Reservations to the Optional Clause' (1958) 7 *ICLQ*, pp. 349–66.

V. Lamm, *Compulsory Jurisdiction in the International Law* (Cheltenham: Edward Elgar Publishing, 2014).

J. G. Merrills, 'The Optional Clause Revisited' (1993) 64 *BYIL*, pp. 197–244.

'Does the Optional Clause still Matter?' in K. H. Kaikobad and M. Bohlander (eds.), *International Law and Power: Perspectives on Legal Order and Justice, Essays in Honour of Colin Warbrick* (Leiden: Nijhoff, 2009), pp. 431–54.

M. Milanovic and M. Wood, *The Law and Politics of the Kosovo Advisory Opinion* (Oxford University Press, 2015).

S. Oda, 'The Compulsory Jurisdiction of the International Court of Justice: A Myth? A Statistical Analysis of Contentious Cases' (2000) 49 *ICLQ*, pp. 251–77.

G. Törber, *The Contractual Nature of the Optional Clause* (Oxford: Hart Publishing, 2015).

M. Wood, 'Advisory Jurisdiction: Lessons from Recent Practice' in H. P. Hestemeyer (ed.), *Coexistence, Cooperation and Solidarity: Liber Amicorum Rüdiger Wolfrum*, Vol. II (Leiden: Nijhoff, 2012), pp. 1833–49.

7

International Court of Justice (II): Law and Procedure of the Court

Main Issues

Rules of procedure of the ICJ evolve over time. In particular, rules concerning preliminary objections, provisional measures, and third-party intervention have been developed through its jurisprudence. Thus there is a need to review the Court's practice to understand rules of procedure of the Court. As a permanent court having general jurisdiction, the practice of the Court also provides an insight into development of the law of international adjudication. Following Chapter 6, this chapter will seek to address the law and procedure of the ICJ with regard to: the applicable law (section 1), proceedings of the Court (section 2), provisional measures (section 3), preliminary objections (section 4), third-party interventions (sections 5 and 6) and judgment (section 7). Particular focus will be on the following issues:

(i) What is the distinction between *lex lata* and *lex ferenda* and what is the impact of *lex ferenda* on the decision of the Court?
(ii) What is the process of the proceedings of the Court?
(iii) What are the requirements for the Court to indicate provisional measures?
(iv) What are the preliminary objections?
(v) How is it possible to safeguard legal interests of the third party in judicial process of the Court?
(vi) What is the legal effect of the Court's judgments?

1 APPLICABLE LAW

1.1 General Considerations

It is relevant to commence our examination with the law applied by the Court.[1] The key provision in this matter is Article 38 of the ICJ Statute:[2]

---

[1] Generally on this issue, see also H. Thirlway, *The International Court of Justice* (Oxford University Press, 2016), pp. 27–33.
[2] A detailed examination of sources of international law is outside the scope of this chapter. For a recent monograph on sources of international law, see H. Thirlway, *The Sources of International Law* (Oxford University Press, 2014).

> 1. The Court, whose function is to decide in accordance with international law such disputes as are submitted to it, shall apply:
>   a. international conventions, whether general or particular, establishing rules expressly recognized by the contesting states;
>   b. international custom, as evidence of a general practice accepted as law;
>   c. the general principles of law recognized by civilized nations;
>   d. subject to the provisions of Article 59, judicial decisions and the teachings of the most highly qualified publicists of the various nations, as subsidiary means for the determination of rules of law.
> 2. This provision shall not prejudice the power of the Court to decide a case *ex aequo et bono*, if the parties agree thereto.

To this day, there is no case that was determined on the basis of *ex aequo et bono*. Nor has the ICJ based a decision entirely and directly on general principles of law.[3]

While treaties are binding only upon the parties to them, it is widely accepted that rules of general customary law are binding upon all States in the international community.[4] In some cases, application of special or local customary law, which is applicable only within a defined group of States, is also at issue. The well-known example of local customary law may be the practice of diplomatic asylum in Latin America. As the ICJ stated in the *Right of Passage over Indian Territory* case,[5] a special or local customary law may also exist between only two States.

1.2 *Lex Lata* and *Lex Ferenda*

According to legal orthodoxy, only *lex lata*, i.e. law which has been made or positive law, can be applied to disputes before the ICJ. Indeed, if the distinction between *lex lata* and *lex ferenda* (law which ought to be made, i.e. developing or embryonic law) is not preserved, international law cannot survive as a normative system.[6] The ICJ has stressed the distinction on various occasions. In the 1966 *South West Africa* case, for instance, the Court stated that:

> As is implied by the opening phrase of Article 38, paragraph 1, of its Statute, the Court is not a legislative body. Its duty is to apply the law as it finds it, not to make it.[7]

---

[3] According to Thirlway, the only possible candidate may be the *Corfu Channel* judgment that referred to 'certain general and well-recognised principles' including 'elementary considerations of humanity'. *Ibid.*, p. 93.
[4] *North Sea Continental Shelf* (Federal Republic of Germany/Denmark) (Federal Republic of Germany/Netherlands), Judgment of 20 February 1969, ICJ Reports 1969, pp. 38–9, para. 63.
[5] ICJ Reports 1960, p. 39.
[6] H. Bull, *The Anarchical Society: A Study of Order in World Politics*, 3rd edn (Hampshire: Palgrave, 2002), p. 153.
[7] *South West Africa* (Liberia v. South Africa), Judgment of 18 July 1966, Second Phase, ICJ Reports 1966, p. 48, para. 89. See also p. 34, para. 49. See also *Legality of the Threat or Use of Nuclear Weapons*, Advisory Opinion of 8 July 1996, ICJ Reports 1996, p. 237, para. 18.

No serious question will arise in relation to the distinction between *lex lata* and *lex ferenda* where *lex lata* is well established in international law. When an existing rule of customary law is being replaced by an emergent customary law (*lex ferenda*) and the application of such a rule of customary law is at issue in the international courts and tribunals, however, a difficult question arises whether and to what degree an element of *lex ferenda* should be taken into consideration in the judicial process. The ICJ encountered this question in the 1974 *Fishery Jurisdiction* case between the United Kingdom and Iceland, and between the Federal Republic of Germany and Iceland, respectively.[8]

In the 1974 *Fishery Jurisdiction* case, the opinions of the members of the Court were sharply divided with regard to the consideration of *lex ferenda* in the judicial process. The principal subject of this case related to the validity of the Iceland's claim to a 50-mile exclusive fisheries zone.[9] In its memorial, the United Kingdom asserted that the Icelandic claim was 'contrary to the established law and relied upon a view of the law which was *de lege ferenda*'.[10] Although Iceland disputed the Court's jurisdiction and did not appear before the Court, the Prime Minister of Iceland took the view that a 12-mile limit was no longer a customary international law owing to the fact that at least twenty States had a wider limit than 12 miles, some of them even 200 nautical miles.[11] It was becoming apparent that, at that time, the validity of existing rules of law of the sea were strongly challenged by developing States and that *de lege ferenda* in relation to the EEZ up to 200 nautical miles from the baselines was being rapidly formulated at the Third United Nations Conference on the Law of the Sea (UNCLOS III).[12]

The Court, for its part, refuted to apply *lex ferenda*:

> The possibility of the law changing is ever present: but that cannot relieve the Court from its obligation to render a judgment on the basis of the law as it exists at the time of its decision.[13]

However, the Court did not totally 'brush aside' the consideration of an element of *lex ferenda*, even though it rejected the application of *lex ferenda*.[14] In the operative part

---

[8] *Fisheries Jurisdiction* (United Kingdom of Great Britain and Northern Ireland v. Iceland), Merits, Judgment of 25 July 1974, ICJ Reports 1974, p. 3; *Fisheries Jurisdiction* (Federal Republic of Germany v. Iceland), Merits, Judgment of 25 July 1974, ICJ Reports 1974, p. 175. As the Court's decision in each case is essentially very similar, all references to its judgment as well as Opinions of Judges will be quoted from the *Fishery Jurisdiction* judgment between the United Kingdom and Iceland.

[9] R. Churchill, 'The Fisheries Jurisdiction Cases: The Contribution of the International Court of Justice to the Debate on Coastal States' Fisheries Rights' (1975) 24 *ICLQ*, p. 85; ICJ Reports 1974, p. 6.

[10] Memorial on the merits submitted by the United Kingdom, p. 370, para. 296.

[11] *Ibid.*, pp. 353-4, para. 245.

[12] M. Virally, 'A propos de la "lex ferenda"' in *Le Droit international en devenir: essais écrits au fil des ans* (Paris: PUF, 1990), p. 222; José Antonio Pastor Ridruejo, 'Le Droit international à la veille du vingt et unième siècle: normes, faits et valeurs: Cours général de droit international public' (1998) 274 *RCADI*, pp. 45-6.

[13] Judgment, ICJ Reports 1974, p. 19, para. 40. See also pp. 23-4, para. 53; Dissenting Opinion of Judge Gros, *ibid.*, p. 135; Dissenting Opinion of Judge Petrén, *ibid.*, pp. 156-8.

[14] Indeed, several members of the Court argued that *lex ferenda* should be taken into account in the process of judicial reasoning. Joint Separate Opinion of Judges Foster, Bengzon, Jiménez de Aréchaga, Nagendra Singh and Ruda, *ibid.*, p. 48, para. 12.

of the judgment of 1974, the Court, by ten votes to four, held that the Regulations of Iceland concerning the 50-nautical-mile exclusive fishing zone were not opposable to the Government of the United Kingdom.[15] Thus, the Court did not generally find that the 50-mile exclusive fishing zone of Iceland was contrary to existing customary international law.

Given that the Court ruled that the concept of a 12-mile exclusive FZ had crystallised as customary law,[16] it can be presumed that an exclusive FZ beyond 12 miles was not generally recognised.[17] The Court also found that the concept of preferential rights of the coastal States became customary law and that this concept was not compatible with the exclusion of all fishing activities of other States.[18] The Court's findings did seem to suggest that a 50-mile exclusive FZ would be at variance with customary international law or *lex lata*.[19] Nonetheless, the Court avoided pronouncing on the illegality of Iceland's claim for its exclusive FZ in a general manner. As Judge Ignacio-Pinto stated, '[t]he Court has deliberately evaded the question which was placed squarely before it in this case, namely, whether Iceland's claims are in accordance with rules of international law'.[20]

The above analysis seems to demonstrate that the Court did not mechanically apply the *lex lata* to the *Fishery Jurisdiction* dispute. Where an existing rule of customary law is significantly changing owing to a developing law or *lex ferenda* and the change is irreversible, the Court's decisions on the basis of the mechanical application of *lex lata* would be of little effect in practice. In this situation, there is a need for the Court to mitigate the rigid application of *lex lata* by taking a newly developing law into account. Hence an element of *lex ferenda* can potentially affect the *manner* of the application of *lex lata*.[21]

2 THE PROCEEDINGS IN CONTENTIOUS CASES

2.1 The Procedure in a Contentious Case

2.1.1 Outline of the Procedure

Above all, this section overviews the procedure in a contentious case. As provided in Article 39(1) of the ICJ Statute, '[t]he official language of the Court shall be English and French'. The parties to a dispute may agree to conduct the case wholly in one of the two official languages by virtue of Article 39(1). In the absence of an agreement as to

---

[15] Judgment, *ibid.*, p. 34, para. 79(1).   [16] *Ibid.*, p. 23, para. 52.
[17] Churchill, 'The Fisheries Jurisdiction Cases', p. 90.   [18] Judgment, ICJ Reports 1974, p. 27, para. 62.
[19] See Dissenting Opinion of Judge Onyeama, *ibid.*, p. 171, para. 17; Churchill, 'The Fisheries Jurisdiction Cases', p. 88; C. P. R. Romano, *The Peaceful Settlement of International Environmental Disputes: A Pragmatic Approach* (The Hague: Kluwer, 2000), pp. 169–70.
[20] Declaration of Judge Ignacio-Pinto, ICJ Reports 1974, p. 36. See also Separate Opinion of Judge Dillard, *ibid.*, p. 56; Joint Separate Opinion of Judges Foster, Bengzon, Jiménez de Aréchaga, Nagendra Singh and Ruda, *ibid.*, p. 45, para. 1.
[21] Further, see Y. Tanaka, 'Rethinking *Lex Ferenda* in International Adjudication' (2008) 51 *GYIL*, p. 482.

International Court of Justice (II)

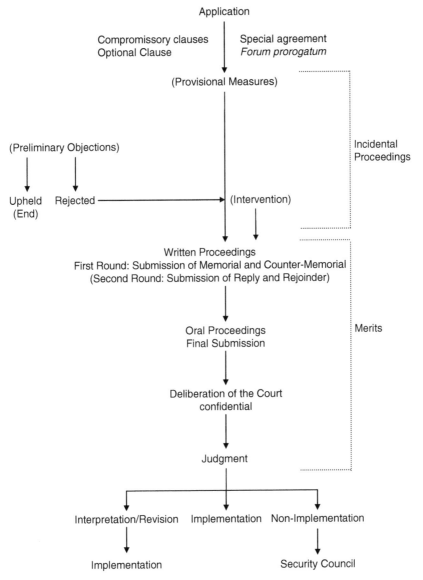

Figure 7.1 Process of proceedings of the ICJ

Note: Matters within parentheses are not always raised in the proceedings.

which language shall be employed, each party may, in the pleadings, use the language which it prefers in accordance with Article 39(2). In principle, all documents submitted to the Court are to be translated by the Registry or the party submitting into the other language.[22] Likewise, in principle, all speeches in the Court must be made in one of the official languages.[23]

---

[22] Thirlway, *The International Court of Justice* (2016), p. 8.
[23] Under Article 39(3) of the ICJ Statute, however, the Court is empowered to, at the request of any party, authorise a language other than French or English to be used by that party.

The process of the proceedings in contentious cases is shown in Figure 7.1.[24] Cases are brought before the Court either by the notification of the special agreement or by a written application addressed to the Registrar pursuant to Article 40(1) of the ICJ Statute.[25] The Registrar is to transmit copies of any application or notification of a special agreement instituting proceedings before the Court to (a) the UN Secretary-General, (b) the Members of the United Nations and (c) other States entitled to appear before the Court pursuant to Article 42 of the Rules of Court. This will enable relevant States to be aware of the existence and nature of the proceedings.[26] The parties shall be represented by agents, and they may have assistance of counsel or advocates before the Court.[27] In principle, all steps on behalf of the parties after proceedings have been instituted shall be taken by agents.[28] Under Article 43(1) of the ICJ Statute, the procedure shall consist of two parts: written and oral.

In the case of unilateral application, the parties exchange written pleadings. The applicant submits a memorial and the respondent files a counter-memorial. In some cases, they are followed by a reply (applicant) and a rejoinder (respondent).[29] Where a dispute was referred to the Court by a special agreement, the number and order of the pleadings are governed by the provisions of the agreement, unless the Court decides otherwise. If the special agreement contains no such provision, and if the parties have not subsequently agreed on the number and order of pleadings, they shall each file a memorial and counter-memorial, within the same time limits.[30]

The respondent State can make a counterclaim in the counter-memorial.[31] In addition to a request that the principal claim be dismissed, a counterclaim further seeks to take the offensive. According to the ICJ, the thrust of a counterclaim is 'to widen the original subject matter of the dispute by pursuing objectives other than the mere dismissal of the claim of the Applicant in the main proceedings – for example, that a finding be made against the Applicant' and 'in this respect, the counterclaim is distinguishable from a defence on the merits'.[32] The counterclaim must be 'within the jurisdiction of the Court' and it must be 'directly connected with the subject-matter of the claim of the other party'.[33] The Court must satisfy itself as to its jurisdiction over the counterclaim.[34]

---

[24] For a detailed analysis of the proceedings of the Court, see H. Thirlway, 'The Drafting of ICJ Decisions: Some Personal Recollections and Observations' (2006) 5 *Chinese Journal of International Law*, pp. 15–28; R. Kolb, *The Elgar Companion to the International Court of Justice* (Cheltenham: Edward Elgar Publishing, 2014), pp. 299 *et seq.*

[25] See also Article 38(1) and (2) of the Rules of Court.

[26] Thirlway, *The International Court of Justice* (2016), p. 89.

[27] Article 42(1) and (2) of the ICJ Statute.   [28] Article 40(1) of the Rules of Court.

[29] A Reply and a Rejoinder are now exceptional. H. Thirlway, 'The International Court of Justice' in M. D. Evans, *International Law*, 4th edn (Oxford University Press, 2014), p. 593.

[30] Article 46(2) of the Rules of Court.   [31] Article 80(2) of the Rules of Court.

[32] *Application of the Convention on the Prevention and Punishment of the Crime of Genocide* (Bosnia and Herzegovina v. Serbia and Montenegro), Counterclaims, Order of 17 December 1997, ICJ Reports 1997, p. 256, para. 27.

[33] Article 80(1) of the Rules of Court.

[34] R. Kolb, *The International Court of Justice* (Oxford: Hart Publishing, 2013), p. 663. Further, see Thirlway, *The International Court of Justice* (2016), pp. 94–7.

Upon the closure of the written proceedings, the case is ready for hearing (i.e. oral proceedings).[35] Under Article 46 of the ICJ Statute, '[t]he hearing in Court shall be public, unless the Court shall decide otherwise, or unless the parties demand that the public be not admitted'. The oral argument is an essential part of the adversarial system of trial.[36] Counsel must speak in one of the two official languages of the Court, French or English. At the conclusion of the last statement made by a party at the hearing, its agent, without recapitulation of the arguments, is to read that party's final submissions.[37] Importantly, as the Court stated in the *Oil Platforms* case, '[i]t is well established in the Court's jurisprudence that the parties to a case cannot in the course of proceedings "transform the dispute brought before the Court into a dispute that would be a different nature"'.[38] The *dictum* also applies to the case of counterclaims.[39]

2.1.2 Equality of the Parties

The equality of the parties is a fundamental principle of judicial proceedings in general and the ICJ is no exception.[40] As the ICJ stated in the *Nicaragua* case, 'the equality of the parties to the dispute must remain the basic principle for the Court'.[41] The principle of the equality of the parties requires that the same and equal rights and opportunities must be given to both parties in dispute in proceedings of the Court, such as the same number of written pleadings and the same amount of time to present their written and oral proceedings. The structure of the proceedings must be adversarial to secure the equality of arms. Owing to this principle, the most powerful State is in no better position than the smallest State in proceedings of the ICJ.

The Court has shown some flexibility with regard to the equality of the parties at the stage of the proceedings of provisional measures. For instance, the Court, in the *Application of the Convention on the Prevention and Punishment of the Crime of Genocide*, accepted a series of documents filed by Bosnia-Herzegovina on the eve of, and even during, the oral proceedings as 'observations', taking account of the urgency of the matter and other particular circumstances. However, the Court expressed its misgivings that the late submission of documents 'is difficult to reconcile with an orderly progress of the procedure before the Court, and with respect for the principle of equality of the Parties'.[42]

---

[35] Article 54(1) of the Rules of Court. Under the ICJ Statute and Rules of Court, 'pleadings' refers solely to the written arguments of the parties, not to the speeches made by the Agent and Council at the hearings, which are properly referred to as 'oral argument'. Subsection 3 of the Rules of Court refers to 'the oral proceedings'. Thirlway, 'The Drafting of ICJ Decisions', p. 16, footnote 2.

[36] Sir Robert Jennings, 'The Role of the International Court of Justice' (1997) 68 *BYIL*, p. 14.

[37] Article 60(2) of the Rules of Court.

[38] *Case Concerning Oil Platforms* (Iran v. USA), Judgment of 6 November 2003, ICJ Reports 2003, p. 213, para. 117. See also *Certain Phosphate Lands in Nauru* (Nauru v. Australia), Preliminary Objections, Judgment of 26 June 1992, ICJ Reports 1992, p. 265, para. 63.

[39] The *Oil Platform* case, ICJ Reports 2003, p. 213, para. 117.

[40] Kolb, *The Elgar Companion*, p. 216. Further, see Kolb, *The International Court of Justice*, pp. 1119 *et seq*.

[41] *Military and Paramilitary Activities in and against Nicaragua* (Nicaragua v. United States of America), Judgment of 27 June 1986, ICJ Reports 1986, p. 26, para. 31. See also *Judgments of the Administrative Tribunal of the ILO upon Complaints Made against UNESCO*, Advisory Opinion of 23 October 1956, p. 86.

[42] *Application of the Convention on the Prevention and Punishment of the Crime of Genocide* (Bosnia and Herzegovina v. Serbia and Montenegro), Order of 13 September 1993. Further Requests for the Indication of Provisional Measures, ICJ Reports 1993, pp. 336–7, para. 21.

Furthermore, as will be seen,[43] the United States was not given an opportunity to present its view at the stage of the proceedings of provisional measures in the *LaGrand* case.

2.1.3 The Burden of Proof

Apart from the procedural rules on the form and the timing for the submission of evidence, the ICJ Statute and the Rules of Court contains no guidance concerning the exclusion of evidence.[44] Accordingly, the ICJ has a wide discretion in the assessment of the evidence. As the Court stated in the *Nicaragua* case, 'within the limits of its Statute and Rules, it [the Court] has freedom in estimating the value of the various elements of evidence'.[45] The procedures and rules on evidence seem to be less developed[46] and it is difficult to identify any established standard of proof of evidence in the jurisprudence of the ICJ.[47]

A standard of proof may be a debatable issue in a particular case. The *Oil Platforms* case is an example. After examining whether the United States had discharged the burden of proof that the USS *Samuel B. Roberts* was the victim of a mine laid by Iran, the ICJ held that the evidence submitted by the United States was 'highly suggestive, but not conclusive'.[48] However, the Court's view was criticised by Judge Higgins since 'it is impossible to know, in the absence of any articulated standard or further explanation, why the Court reached this conclusion'.[49]

The general rule of the burden of proof can be summarised in the maxim *onus probandi incumbit actori*, which means that 'the actor bears the burden of proof'. In the words of the Court in the *Nicaragua* case, '[u]ltimately ... it is the litigant seeking to establish a fact who bears the burden of proving it'.[50] The application of the burden of proof rule is limited to questions of fact and this rule does not apply to questions of law because the Court knows the law.[51] Furthermore, as the Court stated in the *Fisheries Jurisdiction* case, 'there is no burden of proof to be discharged in the matter of jurisdiction'.[52] It can be considered that there is no burden of proof with regard to matters of public knowledge or to undisputed facts.[53] In the *Hostage* case, for instance, the ICJ noted that: 'The essential facts of the present case are, for the most part, matters of public knowledge';[54] and that the facts alleged before the Court by the United States were not denied by the Iranian Government.[55] It thus ruled that, within the meaning of Article 53 of the Statute, the allegations of fact on which the United States bases its claims in the present case were well founded.[56]

---

[43] See section 3.3 of this chapter.
[44] R. Wolfrum and M. Möldner, 'International Courts and Tribunals, Evidence' in *Max Planck Encyclopaedia*, para. 58.
[45] ICJ Reports 1986, p. 40, para. 60.
[46] Separate Opinion of Judge Owada in the *Oil Platforms* case, ICJ Reports 2003, p. 322, para. 52.
[47] Kolb, *The Elgar Companion*, p. 251.   [48] The *Oil Platforms* case, ICJ Reports 2003, p. 195, para. 71.
[49] Separate Opinion of Judge Higgins, *ibid.*, p. 235, para. 36. See also Separate Opinion of Judge Buergenthal, *ibid.*, p. 288, para. 44.
[50] ICJ Reports 1984, p. 437, para. 101.   [51] Kolb, *The Elgar Companion*, p. 237.
[52] *Fisheries Jurisdiction* (Spain v. Canada), Judgment of 4 December 1998, ICJ Reports 1998, p. 450, para. 38.
[53] Kolb, *The Elgar Companion*, p. 240.
[54] *United States Diplomatic and Consular Staff in Tehran* (United States of America v. Iran), Judgment of 24 May 1980, ICJ Reports 1980, p. 9, para. 12.
[55] *Ibid.*, p. 10, para. 13.   [56] *Ibid.*

2.1.4 Experts

In relation to the assessment of evidence, some mention must be made of the role of experts in judicial proceedings before the ICJ.[57] Here five categories of experts can be identified: (i) court-appointed experts, (ii) party-appointed experts, (iii) expert counsel, (iv) invisible experts and (v) assessors.[58]

(i) *Court-appointed experts*: In accordance with Article 50 of the ICJ Statute, '[t]he Court may, at any time, entrust any individual, body, bureau, commission, or other organization that it may select, with the task of carrying out an enquiry or giving an expert opinion'. In the *Corfu Channel* case, for example, the Court appointed experts since it was necessary to obtain an expert opinion with regard to certain points contested between the parties.[59] The Court, in its judgment of 1949, stated that it 'cannot fail to give great weight to the opinion of the Experts who examined the locality in a manner giving every guarantee of correct and impartial information'.[60] In the *Gulf of Maine* case, the ICJ, upon a joint request of the parties, appointed an expert using its powers under Article 50 of the Statute.[61] Recently it appointed experts in the *Costa Rica/Nicaragua* case concerning maritime delimitation.[62] However, generally the Court has refrained from appointing experts.[63] Related to this, the Court, in the *Pulp Mills* case, declared that:

> [I]t is the responsibility of the Court, after having given careful consideration to all the evidence placed before it by the Parties, to determine which facts must be considered relevant, to assess their probative value, and to draw conclusions from them as appropriate.[64]

However, a question arises whether the Court as a judicial body is well-placed to tackle complex scientific issues. In this regard, Judges Al-Khasawneh and Simma, in the *Pulp Mills* case, expressed their misgivings that: 'The Court on its own is not in a position adequately to assess and weigh complex scientific evidence of the type presented by the Parties.'[65] In response, the use of scientific experts is worth considering in the settlement of disputes involving scientific and technical aspects.

---

[57] Generally on this issue, see D. Peat, 'The Use of Court-Appointed Experts by the International Court of Justice' (2014) 84 *BYIL*, pp. 271–303; C. E. Foster, 'New Clothes for the Emperor? Consultation of Experts by the International Court of Justice' (2014) 5 *Journal of International Dispute Settlement*, pp. 139–73.

[58] L. C. Lima, 'The Evidential Weight of Experts before the ICJ: Reflections on the Whaling in the Antarctic Case' (2015) 6 *Journal of International Dispute Settlement*, p. 628.

[59] *Corfu Channel* (United Kingdom of Great Britain and Northern Ireland v. Albania), Order of 17 December 1948, ICJ Reports 1948, p. 124.

[60] Judgment of 9 April 1949, ICJ Reports 1949, p. 21.

[61] *Delimitation of the Maritime Boundary in the Gulf of Maine Area* (Canada/United States of America), Appointment of Expert, Order of 30 March 1984, ICJ Reports 1984, p. 165.

[62] *Maritime Delimitation in the Caribbean Sea and the Pacific Ocean* (Costa Rica v. Nicaragua), Order of 16 June 2016 (not yet reported), available at: www.icj-cij.org/homepage/index.php.

[63] Kolb, *The Elgar Companion*, p. 78.

[64] *Pulp Mills on the River Uruguay* (Argentina v. Uruguay), Judgment of 20 April 2010, ICJ Reports 2010, p. 72, para. 168.

[65] Joint Dissenting Opinion of Judges Al-Khasawneh and Simma, *ibid.*, p. 110, para. 4.

(ii) *Party-appointed experts*: Under Article 57 of the Rules of Court, the parties can appoint experts. The role of the party-appointed experts was noteworthy in the 2014 *Whaling in the Antarctic* case. In this case, both Japan and Australia called experts at the hearings. In the *Whaling in the Antarctic* judgment, the experts' views were often quoted by the Court when examining key points.[66] In this case, the Court seemed to attach particular importance to the fact that the experts called by the disputing parties agreed or to the fact that the opinion of one expert was not contested by a party.[67]

(iii) *Expert counsel*: It is not uncommon at the oral hearing for experts to appear before the Court as counsel of a party in dispute. However, the Court has been critical of the use of experts as counsel. In this regard, the Court, in the *Pulp Mills* case, stated that:

> [T]hose persons who provide evidence before the Court based on their scientific or technical knowledge and on their personal experience should testify before the Court as experts, witnesses or in some cases in both capacities, rather than counsel, so that they may be submitted to questioning by the other party as well as by the Court.[68]

(iv) *Invisible experts*: The Court has made recourse to the internal 'phantom experts' or 'invisible experts' in particular cases, such as maritime delimitation cases. The existence of this type of expert is not well known and the experts' conclusions would never be made public. In this regard, Judges Simma and Al-Khazawneh, in their Joint Dissenting Opinion in the *Pulp Mills* case, expressed their misgivings that the recourse to the invisible experts would deprive the Court of transparency, openness, procedural fairness and the ability for the parties to comment upon or otherwise assist the Court in understanding the evidence before it.[69]

(v) *Assessors*: Under Article 9 of the Rules of Court, '[t]he Court may, either *proprio motu* or upon a request made not later than the closure of the written proceedings, decide, for the purpose of a contentious case or request for advisory opinion, to appoint assessors to sit with it without the right to vote'.[70] Yet the difference between assessors and experts appointed by the Court remains less clear. To this day, no request or proposal for the appointment of assessors has been made before the PCIJ or ICJ.[71]

2.1.5 Decisions of the Court

Decisions of the Court are a production of the collective work of the bench and all judges, including dissenters, are to participate in the drafting process.[72] As provided in Article 54(3) of the ICJ Statute, '[t]he deliberations of the Court shall take place in

---

[66] M. Fitzmaurice, *Whaling and International Law* (Cambridge University Press, 2015), pp. 99–102.
[67] Lima, 'The Evidential Weight of Experts', p. 633.
[68] ICJ Reports 2010, p. 72, para. 167.
[69] Joint Dissenting Opinion of Judges Simma and Al-Khazawneh in the *Pulp Mills* case, *ibid.*, p. 114, para. 14. See also B. Simma, 'The International Court of Justice and Scientific Expertise' (2012) 106 *Proceedings of the Annual Meeting of American Society of International Law*, p. 231.
[70] See also Article 30(2) of the ICJ Statute.
[71] H. Thirlway, 'Article 30' in A. Zimmermann et al. (eds.), *The Statute of the International Court of Justice: A Commentary*, 2nd edn (Oxford University Press, 2012) (hereafter *A Commentary*), p. 528.
[72] The same is equally true of advisory opinions.

private and remain secret'.[73] All questions are to be decided by a majority of the judges present under Article 55(1) of the ICJ Statute. The quorum (i.e. the minimum number of judges required to constitute the Court) is nine.[74] Abstention is not permitted.[75] Under Article 56 (2) of the Statute, the judgment shall contain the names of the judges who have taken part in the question. The judgment shall be signed by the President and by the Registrar. It shall be read in open court, due notice having been given to the agents in accordance with Article 58. The judgment is final and without appeal in accordance with Article 60.

Under Article 57 of the ICJ Statute, '[i]f the judgment does not represent in whole or in part the unanimous opinion of the judges, any judge shall be entitled to deliver a separate opinion'.[76] A judge who agrees with the conclusion of the Court, but for different reasons, or who prefers to give his own reasoning, may a separate opinion,[77] while a judge who is against the majority opinion may deliver a dissenting opinion. A declaration is a very brief statement in which the judge succinctly expresses his or her disagreement or difference with the majority opinion.

In some cases, the voting by a judge in the judgment may seem to differ from his or her view expressed in a separate opinion. For instance, there may be the situation where a judge, in his or her separate opinion, expresses the view which is against the majority opinion, even though the judge voted in favour to the conclusion of the Court. Even so, the separate opinion has no legal effect to alter the voting record and the position of the judge is to be determined by the voting.

Separate and dissenting opinions contribute to illuminating the meaning of the judgment and enhance the transparency and the quality of the judgment of the Court since the majority opinions are required to address different views expressed in separate and dissenting opinions. Dissenting opinions also assure the losing party that its arguments were considered extensively by the entire Court.[78] Yet, too many separate and dissenting opinions may give rise to a question to what extent the judgment reflected the 'majority' opinion.

2.2 The Principle *Ne Eat Iudex Ultra Petita Partium*

This is a convenient point to mention the principle *ne eat iudex ultra petita partium* (shortened as the *ne ultra petita* or *non ultra petita* ('not beyond what is asked for') principle). This principle signifies that the judge may not award beyond the demands

---

[73] The *Nuclear Test* cases are the only known example of this rule being violated. See Declaration of President Lacks, ICJ Reports 1974, p. 273. See also Thirlway, *The International Court of Justice* (2016), p. 125.
[74] Article 25(3) of the ICJ Statute.
[75] Resolution Concerning the Internal Judicial Practice of the Court, Article 8(v).
[76] See also Article 95(2) of the Rules of Court. For an analysis of the function and limitations of separate and dissenting opinions, see Kolb, *The International Court of Justice*, pp. 1011–18.
[77] G. Fitzmaurice, *The Law and Procedure of the International Court of Justice*, Vol. I (Cambridge University Press, 1986), p. 2.
[78] See Dissenting Opinion of Judge ad hoc Franck, *Sovereignty over Pulau Ligitan and Pulau Sipadan* (Indonesia v. Malaysia), Judgment of 17 December 2002, ICJ Reports 2002, p. 694, para. 11.

of the parties.⁷⁹ The ICJ, in the *Asylum* case (Request for Interpretation), affirmed this principle:

> [O]ne must bear in mind the principle that it is the duty of the Court not only to reply to the questions as stated in the final submissions of the parties, but also to abstain from deciding points not included in those submissions.⁸⁰

According to Fitzmaurice:

> The *non ultra petita* rule is not only an inevitable corollary – indeed, virtually a part of the general principle of the consent of the parties as the basis of international jurisdiction – it is also a necessary rule, for without it the consent principle itself could constantly be circumvented.⁸¹

Since the true *petium* (i.e. subject matter) is not always clear, the subject matter of a particular dispute is to be ascertained by the Court. This point was affirmed by the Court in the *Nuclear Tests* cases:

> It has never been contested that the Court is entitled to interpret the submissions of the parties, and in fact is bound to do so; this is one of the attributes of its judicial functions.⁸²

The application of the *ne ultra petita* principle was at issue in the *Oil Platforms* case. In this application of 1992, Iran contended, *inter alia*, that in attacking and destroying on 19 October 1987 and 18 April 1988 Iran's oil platforms, the United States breached its obligation to Iran under Article X(1) of the 1955 Treaty of Amity.⁸³ The Court noted that the United States had relied on Article XX(1)(d) of the treaty as determinative of the question of the existence of a breach of its obligations under Article X.⁸⁴ It thus decided to examine first the application of Article XX(1)(d) of the 1955 Treaty, in light of international law on the use of force in self-defence.⁸⁵ The Court eventually concluded in its *dispositif* that the actions of the United States against Iran could not be justified under Article XX(1)(d) of the treaty.⁸⁶ However, the ICJ's approach was not free from controversy. According

---

[79] A. X. Fellmeth and M. Horwitz, *Guide to Latin in International Law* (Oxford University Press, 2009), p. 191. Further, see Kolb, *The Elgar Companion*, pp. 226 et seq.

[80] *Request for Interpretation of the Judgment of 20 November 1950 in the Asylum Case* (Colombia v. Peru), Judgment of 27 November 1950, ICJ Reports 1950, p. 402. See also *Continental Shelf* (Libyan Arab Jamahiriya/Malta), Judgment of 3 June 1985, ICJ Reports 1985, p. 23, para. 19.

[81] G. Fizmaurice, *The Law and Procedure of the International Court of Justice*, Vol. II (Cambridge University Press, 1993), p. 529.

[82] *Nuclear Tests* (Australia v. France) (New Zealand v. France), Judgment of 20 December 1974, ICJ Reports 1974, p. 262, para. 29; p. 466, para. 30.

[83] The *Oil Platforms* case, ICJ Reports 2003, p. 173, para. 20.

[84] *Ibid.*, p. 178, para; 32.   [85] *Ibid.*, p. 183, paras. 43–4.   [86] *Ibid.*, p. 218, para. 125(1).

to Higgins, 'at no time, from beginning to end, has there been a request for any finding under Article XX, paragraph 1(d)'.[87] In the view of the learned judge, the Court seemed to be endeavouring to fall within the *ultra petita* jurisprudence by emphasising the desirability of a finding on Article XX(1)(d).[88] Yet, invocations of the original dispute and importance of subject matter cannot serve to transform a contingent defence into a subject matter that is 'desirable' to deal with in the text of the judgment and in the *dispositif*. Judge Higgins eventually concluded that: 'The Court has thus not shown anything that falls within any qualification to the *non ultra petita* rule.'[89]

The *ne ultra petita* principle is subject to some limitations.[90] First, the Court is not bound by the parties' legal argument and can freely rely on its decision on whatever legal and factual basis since the law is the matter of the Court (*jura novit curia*).[91] In the words of the Court, 'the principle *jura novit curia* signifies that the Court is not solely dependent on the argument of the parties before it with respect to the applicable law'.[92]

Second, the principle does not apply to the Court's jurisdiction and admissibility of a particular case because these matters must be objectively determined by the Court itself. The existence of a dispute is also to be determined by the Court.[93]

Third, the *ne ultra petita* principle does not apply to incidental proceedings. For instance, as will be discussed in section 3 of this chapter, the Court can indicate provisional measures *proprio motu*. These measures may differ from the measures requested by a party in dispute.

2.3 Non-Appearance

It is not infrequent that one of the parties in dispute refuses to appear before an international court (see Table 7.1). In default cases, the ICJ merely expressed its 'regret' with regard to the non-cooperation of the non-appearing party. In the *Nicaragua* case (Merits), for instance, the United States declined to participate in the proceedings of the merits after jurisdiction of the Court was established. Yet, the Court merely stated that:

> When a State named as party to proceedings before the Court decides not to appear in the proceedings, or not to defend its case, the Court usually expresses regret, because such a decision obviously has a negative impact on the sound administration of justice .... In the present case, the Court regrets even more deeply the decision of the respondent State not to participate in the present phase of the proceedings ....[94]

---

[87] Separate Opinion of Judge Higgins, *ibid.*, p. 228, para. 12.   [88] *Ibid.*, p. 229, para. 16.
[89] *Ibid.*, p. 231, paras. 23–4. See also Separate Opinion of Judge Buergenthal, *ibid.*, p. 271, paras. 4 *et seq*.
[90] Kolb, *The Elgar Companion*, pp. 230–2.
[91] Further, see A. Orakhelashvili, 'The International Court and "Its Freedom to Select the Ground Upon Which It will Base Its Judgment"' (2007) 56 *ICLQ*, pp. 171–84.
[92] The *Nicaragua* case, ICJ Reports 1986, p. 24, para. 29.   [93] See Chapter 1, section 3.2 of this book.
[94] The *Nicaragua* case, ICJ Reports 1986, p. 23, para. 27. See also the *Nuclear Tests* case, Judgment of 20 December 1974, ICJ Reports 1974, p. 257, para. 15 (Australia v. France); p. 461, para. 15 (Australia v. New Zealand).

TABLE 7.1 EXAMPLES OF NON-APPEARANCE BEFORE THE ICJ

Case	Parties	Non-Appearance Party
The *Fishery Jurisdiction* case (1974)	UK, FRG/Iceland	Iceland
The *Nuclear Tests* case (1974)	France/Australia, New Zealand	France
The *Trial of Pakistani Prisoners of War* case (1973)	Pakistan/India	India
The *Aegean Sea* case (1976)	Greece/Turkey	Turkey
The *Hostage* case (1980)	USA/Iran	Iran
The *Nicaragua* case (1986)	Nicaragua/USA	USA

The tone of the term 'regret' does not seem to suggest that the Court determined a breach of an obligation of the State to participate in the judicial proceedings. It seems difficult to affirm the obligation to participate in the proceedings of the Court under the ICJ Statute.[95]

Non-appearance of a respondent State has a negative impact on the sound administration of justice.[96] In the event of default by one party, the appearing State is placed in an unfavourable position since that State cannot know what arguments it has to meet because of the absence of the respondent State.[97] At the same time, the non-appearing State also puts an international court in a difficult position owing to the lack of information. Furthermore, the non-appearing State is likely to ignore the decision of the Court.[98] In fact the absent respondent States did not implement judgments in the *Fishery Jurisdiction*, *Teheran Hostages* and *Nicaragua* cases. However, it has to be stressed that the eventual judgment will be binding upon the non-appearing parties.[99]

It is well established that non-appearance of one of the disputing parties does not constitute a bar to the judicial proceedings. In the words of the ICJ:

> [T]he non-participation of a party in the proceedings at any stage of the case cannot, in any circumstances, affect the validity of its judgment. Nor does such validity depend upon the acceptance of that judgment by one party.[100]

---

[95] Thirlway, *The Law and Procedure*, Vol. I, pp. 998; T. Sugihara, *Kokusai Shiho Saiban Seido* (The Institution of the International Court of Justice) (Tokyo: Yuhikaku, 1996), pp. 228–9. See also Dissenting Opinion of Judge Gros in the *Nuclear Tests* case, Order of 22 June 1973, ICJ Reports 1973, pp. 116 and 118 (Australia v. France); pp. 151 and 153 (New Zealand v. France).
[96] The *Nicaragua* case, ICJ Reports 1986, p. 23, para. 27.
[97] Argument by Mr O'Connell in the *Aegean Sea Continental Shelf* case, Oral Arguments on Jurisdiction, 19 December 1978, CR 1978, p. 318.
[98] L. Caflisch, 'Cent ans de règlement pacifique des différends interétatiques' (2001) 288 *RCADI*, p. 353.
[99] Thirlway, *The Law and Procedure*, Vol. II, p. 1824.
[100] The *Nicaragua* case, ICJ Reports 1986, p. 23, para. 27.

Under Article 53(1) of the ICJ Statute, '[w]henever one of the parties does not appear before the Court, or fails to defend its case, the other party may call upon the Court to decide in favour of its claim'.[101] Given that there is no obligation to appear before the Court, however, Article 53 of the ICJ Statute should not be interpreted as giving disadvantage or penalty to a non-appearing State.[102]

More often than not, the non-appearing State indirectly defends its case and 'responds' to the allegations made against it, but does so by means of a variety of unorthodox 'backstairs' or side wind methods which avoid entering a formal 'appearance' in the case.[103] The question of interest here is how the 'backstairs' communication should be treated. The ICJ's practice shows that normally the Court has taken account of informal communications.[104] In the *Aegean Continental Shelf* case, for instance, Turkey submitted the 'Observations of the Turkish Government on the request of the Government of Greece for provisional measures dated 10 August 1976',[105] even though it refused to appear before the Court. In this regard, the Court explicitly stated that: '[H]aving regard to the position taken by the Turkish Government in its observations communicated to the Court on 26 August 1976 ... it is necessary to resolve first of all the question of the Court's jurisdiction with respect to the case.'[106] In the *Nicaragua* case, the Court considered that: '[I]t is valuable for the Court to know the views of both parties in whatever form those views may have been expressed.'[107] Furthermore, the Court in the *Nuclear Tests* case based its decision on a public statement by the French Government, which had not been submitted before it by any formal means.[108] In the words of Judge ad hoc Barwick, '[t]hose contents and that of the French *White Paper* on Nuclear Tests, published but not communicated to the Court during the hearing of the case, have in fact been fully considered'.[109]

As the ICJ stated in the *Nicaragua* case, however, 'the Court cannot by its own enquiries entirely make up for the absence of one of the Parties'.[110] The Court is not compelled to examine their accuracy in all their details for this might in certain unopposed cases prove impossible in practice. Accordingly, as the Court stated in the *Corfu Channel* case, '[i]t is sufficient for the Court to convince itself by such methods as it considers suitable that the

---

[101] Article 53 is not applied in proceedings on requests for advisory opinions. H. Thirlway, *The Law and Procedure of the International Court of Justice: Fifty Years of Jurisprudence*, Vol. I (Oxford University Press, 2013), p. 995. In addition, some argue that Article 53 does not apply to the proceedings at the stage of provisional measures. Sugihara, *Kokusai Shiho*, p. 227. Sugihara also argues that Article 53(1) does not apply to the procedure for examining the jurisdiction of the Court. Ibid.

[102] Thirlway, *The Law and Procedure*, Vol. I, p. 1006.

[103] The ICJ, in the *Nicaragua* case, stated that: 'Though formally absent from the proceedings, the party in question frequently submits to the Court letters and documents, in ways and by means not contemplated by the Rules.' ICJ Reports 1986, p. 25, para. 31. See also Thirlway, *The Law and Procedure*, Vol. I, p. 1003; Caflisch, 'Cent ans', p. 353.

[104] Yet, the ICJ's approach has been challenged by writers since the non-appearing State is placed in a more advantageous position than that of an appearing party at least in some respects.

[105] *Aegean Sea Continental Shelf* (Greece v. Turkey), Request for the Indication of Interim Measures of Protection, Order of 11 September 1976, ICJ Reports 1976, p. 5, para. 7.

[106] Ibid, p. 13, para. 45. See also ICJ Reports 1978, p. 20, para. 46.

[107] ICJ Reports 1986, p. 25, para. 31.   [108] Thirlway, *The Law and Procedure*, Vol. I, p. 1005.

[109] Dissenting Opinion of Judge Sir Garfield Barwick, ICJ Reports 1974, p. 401.

[110] ICJ Reports 1986, p. 25, para. 30.

submissions are well founded'.[111] As a consequence, the decision of an international court or tribunal may be unfavourable to a defaulting party. However, this must be regarded as an inevitable consequence of its failure to plead during the judicial proceedings.[112]

3 PROVISIONAL MEASURES

3.1 Purpose of Provisional Measures

The purpose of provisional measures ('*mesures conservatoires*' in French) is to preserve the respective rights of the disputing parties pending the final decision of a court and to ensure effectiveness of its judgment and judicial functions.[113] The power to indicate provisional measures is expressly conferred to the ICJ by Article 41(1) of the Statute of the Court:

> The Court shall have the power to indicate, if it considers that circumstances so require, any provisional measures which ought to be taken to preserve the respective rights of either party.[114]

Notably this provision refers to the preservation of 'rights of *either* party', not merely rights of the applicant State.[115] Under Article 73(1) of the Rules of Court, 'A written request for the indication of provisional measures may be made by a party at any time during the course of the proceedings in the case in connection with which the request is made.' The ICJ may also decide *proprio motu* to examine the *possibility* of provisional measures by virtue of Article 75(1) of the Rules of Court.[116] The Court has never yet used this power.[117]

Under Article 76(1) of the Rules of Court, '[a]t the request of a party, the Court may, at any time before the final judgment in the case, revoke or modify any decision concerning provisional measures if, in its opinion, some change in the situation justifies such revocation or modification'.[118] This provision signifies that provisional measures indicated by the Court have no force of *res judicata*.[119]

---

[111] *Corfu Channel* (United Kingdom of Great Britain and Northern Ireland v. Albania), Assessment of the amount of compensation due from the People's Republic of Albania to the United Kingdom of Great Britain and Northern Ireland, Judgment of 15 December 1949, ICJ Reports, p. 248.
[112] See Dissenting Opinion of Judge Jennings in the *Nicaragua* case, ICJ Reports 1986, p. 544.
[113] See, for instance, *Request for Interpretation of the Judgment of 15 June 1962 in the Case Concerning the Temple of Preah Vihear* (Cambodia v. Thailand) (hereafter the *Temple of Preah Vihear* case (Request for Interpretation)), Request for the Indication of Provisional Measures, Order of 18 July 2011, ICJ Reports 2011, p. 545, para. 33; The *Nicaragua* case, Order of 10 May 1984, ICJ Reports 1984, p. 182, para. 32; Separate Opinion of President Jiménez de Aréchaga, ICJ Reports 1976, p. 15. See also Kolb, *The International Court of Justice*, p. 616.
[114] Some commentators argue that the institution of provisional measures is essential to any judicial process. See C. Brown, *A Common Law of International Adjudication* (Cambridge University Press, 2007), pp. 128–33; Fitzmaurice, *The Law and Procedure*, Vol. II, p. 542. Oda and Sugihara took a similar view. Oda, *The International Court of Justice*, p. 70; Sugihara, *Kokusai Shiho*, p. 269.
[115] Thirlway, *The International Court of Justice* (2016), p. 157. See also the *Pulp Mills* case, Request for the Indication of Provisional Measures, Order of 23 January 2007, ICJ Reports 2007, pp. 10–11, paras. 29–30.
[116] Article 75(1) stipulates that: 'The Court may at any time decide to examine *proprio motu* whether the circumstances of the case require the indication of provisional measures which ought to be taken or complied with by any or all of the parties.' In this regard, see Thirlway, *The International Court of Justice* (2016), p. 154.
[117] *Ibid.*, p. 153. See also Thirlway, *The Law and Procedure*, Vol. I, pp. 953–6; Vol. II, pp. 1804–6.
[118] See also the *Fisheries Jurisdiction* case (United Kingdom v. Iceland), Interim Protection, Order of 17 August 1972, ICJ Reports 1972, p. 18.
[119] For *res judicata*, see section 7.1 of this chapter.

3.2 Requirements to Indicate Provisional Measures

Whether to indicate provisional measures is a matter within the discretion of the Court. The requirements for the Court to indicate provisional measures have evolved over the years through its jurisprudence.[120] The following requirements must be fulfilled to indicate provisional measures.

3.2.1 *Prima Facie* Jurisdiction

The first requirement for the indication of provisional measures is the existence of *prima facie* jurisdiction over the merits of a specific case.[121] Since the institution of provisional measures seeks to safeguard the respective rights of the parties concerning the subject of a specific case, there must be a possibility of delivering a judgment on the merits. At the stage of the proceedings of provisional measures, however, the Court cannot make a detailed examination concerning the substantive validity of claims of a party in dispute and the basis of jurisdiction because it is constrained by considerations of urgency and the material available for decision is less complete. The Court thus confines itself to confirming *prima facie* jurisdiction at the stage of the proceedings of provisional measures. In this regard, the Court, in the *Fisheries Jurisdiction* case, held that:

> Whereas on a request for provisional measures the Court need not, before indicating them, finally satisfy itself that it has jurisdiction on the merits of the case, yet it ought not to act under Article 41 of the Statute if the absence of jurisdiction on the merits is manifest.[122]

It then ruled that:

> Whereas the above-cited provision in an instrument emanating from both Parties to the dispute appears, prima facie, to afford a possible basis on which the jurisdiction of the Court might be founded.[123]

---

[120] R. Higgins, 'Interim Measures for the Protection of Human Rights' (1997) 36 *Columbia Journal of Transnational Law*, p. 108. See also Thirlway, *The International Court of Justice* (2016), pp. 154–63.

[121] Further, see S. Rosenne, 'Provisional Measures and *Prima Facie* Jurisdiction Revisited' in N. Ando, E. McWhinney and R. Wolfrum (eds.), *Liber Amicorum Judge Shigeru Oda* (The Hague: Kluwer, 2002), pp. 515–44; C. Dominicé, 'La Compétence "prima facie" de la Cour internationale de Justice aux fins d'indication de measures conservatoires', *ibid.*, pp. 383–95.

[122] *Fisheries Jurisdiction* (United Kingdom v. Iceland), Order of 17 August 1972, Provisional Measures, ICJ Reports 1972, p. 15, para. 15; *Fisheries Jurisdiction* (Federal Republic of Germany v. Iceland), ICJ Reports 1972, p. 33, para. 16.

[123] ICJ Reports 1972, p. 16, para. 17 (United Kingdom v. Iceland); ICJ Reports 1972, p. 34, para. 18 (Federal Republic of Germany v. Iceland). 'The above-cited provision', as used in this passage, refers to the penultimate paragraph of the Exchange of Notes between the Governments of Iceland and of the United Kingdom dated 11 March 1961 and paragraph 5 of the Exchange of Notes between the Governments of Iceland and of the Federal Republic dated 19 July 1961, respectively.

In successive cases the Court has essentially maintained the standard formula.[124] The *prima facie* jurisdiction calls for three brief comments.

First, as the ICJ repeatedly confirms, the establishment of *prima facie* jurisdiction does not mean that the Court has definitive jurisdiction to entertain the merits of a specific case. In this regard, the Court, in recent cases, has included a standard paragraph which states that: 'Whereas the Court need not satisfy itself in a definitive manner that it has jurisdiction as regards the merits of the case.'[125]

Second, once the Court has confirmed *prima facie* jurisdiction at the stage of a request for provisional measures in a specific case, it can be reasonably presumed that it would enter into the merits of the case. This is not always true, however. In the *Georgia/Russia* case of 2008, the Court held that it had *prima facie* jurisdiction to order provisional measures.[126] At the stage of preliminary objections, however, the Court concluded that it had no jurisdiction to deal with the case between Georgia and the Russian Federation due to the lack of negotiations which constitutes a precondition for the seisin of the Court under Article 22 of the Convention on the Elimination of All Forms of Racial Discrimination (CERD).[127]

Third, as stated by the Court in the 1974 *Nuclear Tests* cases, the existence of a dispute is the primary condition for the Court to exercise its judicial function.[128] In proceedings for provisional measures, the existence of a dispute is thought to constitute a necessary condition for the Court to have *prima facie* jurisdiction. By way of example, the Court, in the *LaGrand* case, confirmed the *prima facie* existence of a dispute with regard to the application of the Convention within the meaning of Article I of the Optional Protocol concerning the Compulsory Settlement of Disputes, which accompanies the Vienna Convention on Consular Relations.[129] In the 2011 *Temple of Preah Vihear* order, the Court held that a difference of opinion *appears* to exist between the parties in several respects.[130] Yet it remains obscure to what degree the standard for identifying the *prima facie* existence of a dispute differs from the standard for definitively determining the existence of the dispute. In the 2016 *Immunities and Criminal Proceedings* case, Equatorial Guinea invoked Article 35 of the Convention against Transnational Organised Crime as one of the bases of the jurisdiction of the

---

[124] Yet Thirlway has suggested that in the series of cases brought by Yugoslavia against the Member States of NATO concerning the use of force on Yugoslav territory, the Court took a more demanding approach to the question of jurisdiction. Thirlway, *The Law and Procedure*, Vol. I, pp. 934–5.

[125] *Certain Activities Carried Out by Nicaragua in the Border Area* (Costa Rica v. Nicaragua), Order of 8 March 2011, ICJ Reports 2011, pp. 17–18, para. 49; *Questions relating to the Obligation to Prosecute or Extradite (Belgium v. Senegal)*, Provisional Measures, Order of 28 May 2009, ICJ Reports 2009, p. 147, para. 40.

[126] *Case Concerning Application of the International Convention on the Elimination of All Forms of Racial Discrimination* (Georgia v. Russian Federation) (hereafter the *Georgia/Russia* case), Request for the Indication of Provisional Measures, Order of 15 October 2008, ICJ Reports 2008, p. 388, para. 117.

[127] The *Georgia/Russia* case, Preliminary Objections, Judgment of 1 April 2011, ICJ Reports 2011, pp. 139–40, paras. 182–4.

[128] The *Nuclear Tests* case (Australia v. France), ICJ Reports 1974, pp. 270–1, para. 55.

[129] *LaGrand* (Germany v. USA) (hereafter the *LaGrand* case), Request for the Indication of Provisional Measures, Order of 3 March 1999, ICJ Reports 1999, p. 14, para. 17.

[130] ICJ Reports 2011, p. 544, para. 31.

Court.[131] However, the ICJ found that, *prima facie*, a dispute capable of falling within the provisions of the Convention did not exist between the parties and that it did not have *prima facie* jurisdiction under Article 35(2) of the Convention.[132]

Fourth, in certain circumstances, an issue arises whether the Court must also consider *prima facie* admissibility. As some leading commentators suggest, the Court should not indicate provisional measures if there was a real possibility of a finding of inadmissibility.[133] In this regard, the Court in the *Cameroon/Nigeria* case held that:

> Whereas without ruling on the question whether, faced with a request for the indication of provisional measures, the Court must, before deciding whether or not to indicate such measures, ensure that the Application of which it is seised is admissible prima facie, it considers that, in this case, the consolidated Application of Cameroon does not appear prima facie to be inadmissible in the light of the preliminary objections raised by Nigeria.[134]

3.2.2 Plausible Character of the Alleged Rights in the Principal Request

The second condition for provisional measures is the plausible character of the alleged rights in the principal request. Until recently, the Court has not explicitly examined the plausibility of the alleged rights in the principal request as a distinct condition for provisional measures.[135] Yet, the Court in its order in the *Belgium/Senegal* case referred to the plausibility test, stating that: '[T]he power of the Court to indicate provisional measures should be exercised only if the Court is satisfied that the rights asserted by a party are at least plausible.'[136] In the *Belgium/Senegal* case, the plausibility test was discussed in connection with the link between the right to be protected and the measures requested. In the *Costa Rica/Nicaragua* case of 2011, however, this element was explicitly considered

---

[131] *Immunities and Criminal Proceedings* (Equatorial Guinea v. France), Request for the Indication of Provisional Measures, 7 December 2016, ICJ Reports 2016 (not yet reported), para. 32.
[132] *Ibid.*, para. 50.
[133] Thirlway, *The Law and Procedure*, Vol. I, p. 936; Kolb, *The International Court of Justice*, pp. 624–5.
[134] *Land and Maritime Boundary between Cameroon and Nigeria* (Cameroon v. Nigeria: Equatorial Guinea intervening), Request for the Indication of Provisional Measures Order of 15 March 1996, ICJ Reports 1996, p. 21, para. 33.
[135] Sugihara, *Kokusai Shiho*, p. 282. See also J. Sztucki, *Interim Measures in the Hague Court* (Deventer: Kluwer, 1983), pp. 123 and 259. An exceptional case may be the *Lockerbie* case. After the proceedings had been instituted, the UN Security Council adopted a resolution under Chapter VII of the UN Charter calling upon Libya to surrender two Libyan nationals who had been charged with responsibility for the destruction of the PanAm flight. The Court held that under Article 103 of the UN Charter, the obligations of the parties under the Charter prevail over their obligations under any other international agreement, including the Montreal Convention. Thus, the ICJ declined the Libya's request for the indication of provisional measures on the ground that the rights claimed by Libya under the Montreal Convention cannot be regarded as appropriate for protection by the indication of provisional measures. *Questions of Interpretation and Application of the 1971 Montreal Convention arising from the Aerial Incident at Lockerbie* (Libya v. UK) (Libya v. USA), Provisional Measures, Order of 14 April 1992, ICJ Reports 1992, p. 15, paras. 39–40; pp. 126–7, paras. 42–3.
[136] *Questions relating to the Obligation to Prosecute or Extradite* (Belgium v. Senegal), Provisional Measures, Order of 28 May 2009, ICJ Reports 2009, p. 151, para. 57.

as a distinct requirement for indicating provisional measures. In this regard, the Court stated that:

> [F]or the purposes of considering the request for the indication of provisional measures, the Court needs only to decide whether the rights claimed by the Applicant on the merits, and for which it is seeking protection, are plausible.[137]

The Court, in its jurisprudence, did not clarify the standard for the plausibility test. The vagueness of the test may entail the risk of undermining predictability of an order of the Court with regard to provisional measures.[138]

As stressed by the PCIJ in the *Factory at Chorzów* case,[139] provisional measures must be distinct from interim judgments. Yet, the examination of the plausibility of the alleged rights at the stage of provisional measures may run the risk of dealing with matters which should be examined at the stage of the merits and, consequently, the order of provisional measures may close to the interim judgment. If this is the case, there is the risk that the plausibility test may make the distinction between provisional measures and pre-judgment obscure.[140]

3.2.3 Link Between the Alleged Rights and the Measures Requested

As explained earlier, the purpose of provisional measures is to preserve the rights which are in dispute. Accordingly, these measures are essentially ancillary to the main claim, and they must relate to the rights which are the subject of dispute in judicial proceedings. It follows that provisional measures cannot be used to deal with issues which are not the subject of the main dispute and must not go beyond what is required to preserve the parties' respective rights in relation to the case.[141] An illustrative example is the *Arbitral Award of 31 July 1989*. In its order of 1990, the ICJ declined to indicate provisional measures since 'the alleged rights sought to be made the subject of provisional measures are not the subject of the proceedings before the Court on the merits of the case'.[142]

The question of interest here is whether non-aggravation measures must be linked to the protection of the alleged rights in the principal request before the Court. On this issue,

---

[137] *Certain Activities carried out by Nicaragua in the Border Area* (Costa Rica v. Nicaragua) (hereafter the *Costa Rica/Nicaragua* case), Provisional Measures, Order of 8 March 2011, ICJ Reports 2011, ICJ Reports 2011, p. 19, para. 57.

[138] Separate Opinion of Judge Koroma in the *Costa Rica/Nicaragua* case, ICJ Reports 2011, p. 31, paras. 7–8.

[139] The PCIJ stated that: 'Considering that the request of the German Government cannot be regarded as relating to the indication of measures of interim protection, but as designed to obtain an interim judgment in favour of a part of the claim formulated in the Application above mentioned; That, consequently, the request under consideration is not covered by the terms of the provisions of the Statute and Rules cited therein.' Order of 21 November 1927, PCIJ Series A, No. 12, p. 10. See also Declaration of Judge Oda in the *LaGrand* case, ICJ Reports 1999, p. 19, para. 6.

[140] Sugihara, *Kokusai Shiho*, p. 285.

[141] J. G. Merrills, 'Interim Measures of Protection in the Recent Jurisprudence of the ICJ' (1995) 44 *ICLQ*, p. 100.

[142] *Arbitral Award of 31 July 1989* (Guinea-Bissau v. Senegal), Request for the Indication of Provisional Measures, Order of 2 March 1990, ICJ Reports 1990, p. 70, para. 26.

two views can be identified. According to one view, the Court does not have the power *proprio motu* to indicate any measures for protecting rights of the litigation parties that are not in dispute in the base before it.[143] According to another view (i.e. a less restrictive interpretation), however, the Court may indicate non-aggravation measures in the absence of linkage between the measures and the alleged rights in the principal request. The ICJ, in the 1996 *Cameroon/Nigeria* order, seemed to take the less restrictive interpretation, stating that:

> Considering that, *independently of the requests for the indication of provisional measures submitted by the Parties to preserve specific rights*, the Court possesses by virtue of Article 41 of the Statute the power to indicate provisional measures with a view to preventing the aggravation or extension of the dispute whenever it considers that circumstances so require.[144]

The less restrictive interpretation is echoed by Thirlway, stating that: '[T]he existence of a bar to the indication of preservative measures does not necessarily signify that the Court cannot indicate non-aggravation measure.'[145] Even so, non-aggravation measures are so general that further specification is required in order to effectively prevent the aggravation of disputes. As the Court itself pointed to, in all cases where it issued non-aggravation measures, other measures were also indicated.[146] Therefore, it can be said that normally non-aggravation measures are to be ordered only as an adjunct to other provisional measures to preserve the parties' rights.[147]

3.2.4 Urgency and Risk of Irreparable Prejudice

If the safeguard of the preservation of rights were not urgent, it would be acceptable to wait until such time as the international court would render the judgment. Thus urgency is at the heart of the provisional measures.[148] Indeed, the element of urgency has always been examined as an essential condition for provisional measures in the jurisprudence of the ICJ.[149] Urgency appears to have two meanings.[150]

First, urgency is needed at the procedural level. As provided in Article 74(1) of the Rules of Court, '[a] request for the indication of provisional measures shall have priority over all other cases'. Furthermore, '[t]he Court, if it is not sitting when the request is made, shall be convened forthwith for the purpose of proceeding to a decision on the request as a matter of urgency' pursuant to Article 74(2) of the Rules of Court.

---

[143] Merrills, 'Interim Measures', p. 123; P. Palchetti, 'The Power of the International Court of Justice to Indicate Provisional Measures to Prevent the Aggravation of a Dispute' (2008) 21 *LJIL*, pp. 631-2.

[144] Emphasis added. The *Cameroon/Nigeria* case, Provisional Measures, Order of 15 March 1996, ICJ Reports 1996, pp. 22-3, para. 41.

[145] Thirlway, *The Law and Procedure*, Vol. I, p. 951.

[146] The *Pulp Mills* case, Request for Provisional Measures, ICJ Reports 2007, p. 16, para. 49. See also Palchetti, 'The Power of the International Court of Justice', p. 635.

[147] See also Separate Opinion of Judge Ajibola in the *Cameroon/Nigeria* case, ICJ Reports 1996, p. 53.

[148] Sugihara, *Kokusai Shiho*, p. 279.

[149] S. Rosenne, *Provisional Measures in International Law: The International Court of Justice and the International Tribunal for the Law of the Sea* (Oxford University Press, 2005), p. 135.

[150] *Ibid.*, p. 136.

Second, urgency is at issue at the substantive level. In this regard, the ICJ in the *Passage through the Great Belt* case clearly stated that: 'Whereas provisional measures under Article 41 of the Statute are indicated "pending the final decision" of the Court on the merits of the case, and are therefore only justified if there is urgency in the sense that action prejudicial to the rights of either party is likely to be taken before such final decision is given.'[151]

In the ICJ jurisprudence, there is a clear trend that the Court examines the risk of irreparable prejudice and urgency at the same time.[152] By way of illustration, the ICJ, in *Certain Criminal Proceedings in France*, ruled that: '[T]here is at the present time no risk of irreparable prejudice, so as to justify the indication of provisional measures as a matter of urgency.'[153] Likewise, the Court, in the *Questions relating to the Obligation to Prosecute or Extradite* between Belgium and Senegal, ruled that: '[T]he power of the Court to indicate provisional measures will be exercised only if there is urgency, in the sense that there is a real and imminent risk that irreparable prejudice may be caused to the rights in dispute before the Court has given its final decision.'[154] This view is echoed by the Court in *Certain Activities Carried Out by Nicaragua in the Border Area* between Costa Rica and Nicaragua.[155] Here the risk of irreparable prejudice must be imminent.

While irreparable prejudice is context-specific,[156] there must be irreparable prejudice to the rights which are the subject of dispute in judicial proceedings.[157] Related to this, it is of particular interest to note that the loss of life was considered as irreparable damage to the rights of a State in the *Cameroon/Nigeria* order of 15 March 1996.[158] The ICJ, in the 2011 *Preah Vihear* order, also considered the loss of life and bodily injuries as an element of irreparable prejudice to the rights of Cambodia.[159] By considering 'the loss of life' and 'bodily injuries' as an element of irreparable prejudice to territorial sovereignty, it appears that the Court is inclined to indicate provisional measures for the protection of human life in a territorial dispute, provided that other conditions for such measures are fulfilled.

---

[151] ICJ Reports 1991, p. 17, para. 23. See also *Case Concerning Armed Activities on the Territory of the Congo* (Democratic Republic of the Congo v. Uganda), Provisional Measures, Order of 1 July 2000, p. 127, para. 39.

[152] Sugihara, *Kokusai Shiho*, p. 280; K. Oellers-Frahm, 'Article 41' in *A Commentary*, p. 1047.

[153] *Certain Criminal Proceedings in France* (Republic of the Congo v France), Request for the Indication of a Provisional Measure, Order of 17 June 2003, ICJ Reports 2003, p. 110, para. 35.

[154] *Case Concerning Questions relating to the Obligation to Prosecute or Extradite* (Belgium v. Senegal), ICJ Reports 2009, p. 152, para. 62.

[155] *Certain Activities Carried Out by Nicaragua in the Border Area* (Costa Rica v. Nicaragua), Provisional Measures, 8 March 2011, ICJ Reports 2011, p. 21, para. 64.

[156] Generally on this issue, Thirlway, *The Law and Procedure*, Vol. I, pp. 940–6; Vol. II, pp. 1794–9; Kolb, *The International Court of Justice*, pp. 628–30.

[157] *Aegean Sea Continental Shelf* (Greece v Turkey), Request for the indication of provisional measures, Order of 11 September 1976, p. 9, para. 25.

[158] *Land and Maritime Boundary between Cameroon and Nigeria* (Cameroon v. Nigeria: Equatorial Guinea intervening), Provisional Measures, Order of 15 March 1996, ICJ Reports 1996, p. 23, para. 42. This view was echoed by Judges Ajibola and Koroma. Separate Opinion of Judge Ajibola, *ibid.*, p. 53; Declaration of Judge Koroma, *ibid.*, p. 30.

[159] The *Temple of Preah Vihear* case (Request for Interpretation), Request for the Indication of Provisional Measures, ICJ Reports 2011, p. 551, para. 55.

3.3 Provisional Measures and the Ceasing of Execution of Individuals

The use of provisional measures to cease the execution of individuals is a debatable issue. This issue was raised in a series of cases before the Court. In the *Case Concerning the Vienna Convention on Consular Relations* between Paraguay and the United States of 1998, Paraguay claimed that in 1992 the authorities of the Commonwealth of Virginia arrested a Paraguayan national, Mr Angel Francisco Breard, without having been informed, as is required under Article 36(1)(b) of the 1963 Vienna Convention on Consular Relations of his rights under that provision.[160] Later on, the Virginia court sentenced Mr Breard to the death penalty and set an execution date of 14 April 1998.[161]

On 3 April 1998, Paraguay instituted proceedings against the United States on the basis of Article 36(1) of the ICJ Statute and Article I of the Optional Protocol concerning the Compulsory Settlement of Disputes to the Vienna Convention (hereafter the Optional Protocol).[162] On the same day, Paraguay requested that the Court indicate provisional measures to ensure that Mr Breard should not be executed pending the disposition of this case.[163] The ICJ considered that the execution of Mr Breard would render it impossible for the Court to order the relief that Paraguay sought and thus cause irreparable harm to the rights it claims.[164] It thus unanimously indicated that the United States should take all measures at its disposal to ensure that Mr Breard was not executed pending the final decision in these proceedings.[165]

The situation was more dramatic in the *LaGrand* case between Germany and the United States. According to Germany, in 1982, the authorities of the State of Arizona detained two German nationals, Karl and Walter LaGrand, and sentenced them to death without having been informed of their rights under Article 36(1)(b) of the Vienna Convention.[166] Karl LaGrand was executed on 24 February 1999 and the date of execution of Walter LaGrand was set for 3 March 1999. On 2 March 1999, Germany instituted proceedings against the United States on the basis of the optional clause and

---

[160] Text in: 596 *UNTS*, p. 261. Entered into force 19 March 1967. Article 36(1)(b) of the Vienna Convention stipulates that: 'With a view to facilitating the exercise of consular functions relating to nationals of the sending State: (b) if he so requests, the competent authorities of the receiving State shall, without delay, inform the consular post of the sending State if, within its consular district, a national of that State is arrested or committed to prison or to custody pending trial or is detained in any other manner. Any communication addressed to the consular post by the person arrested, in prison, custody or detention shall be forwarded by the said authorities without delay. The said authorities shall inform the person concerned without delay of his rights under this subparagraph.'

[161] *Case Concerning the Vienna Convention on Consular Relations* (Paraguay v. United States of America), Order of 9 April 1998, Request for the Indication of Provisional Measures, ICJ Reports 1998, p. 249, paras. 2-3.

[162] *Ibid.*, p. 249, para. 1. For the text of the Optional Protocol, see 596 *UNTS*, p. 487. Entered into force 19 March 1967. Article I of the Optional Protocol provides that: 'Disputes arising out of the interpretation or application of the Convention shall lie within the compulsory jurisdiction of the International Court of Justice and may accordingly be brought before the Court by a written application made by any party to the dispute being a Party to the present Protocol.'

[163] ICJ Reports 1998, p. 251, para. 9.

[164] *Ibid.*, p. 257, para. 37.

[165] *Ibid.*, p. 258, para. 41(I). However, Breard was executed at the state prison in Jarratt, Virginia. W. J. Aceves, 'Application of the Vienna Convention on Consular relations (Paraguay v. United States) Provisional Measures Order' (1998) 92 *AJIL*, p. 522.

[166] The *LaGrand* case, ICJ Reports 1999, p. 10, para. 2.

Article I of the Optional Protocol to the Vienna Convention and submitted the request for the urgent indication of provisional measures to cease the execution of Walter LaGrand.[167] The Court found that the circumstances required it to indicate provisional measures as a matter of the greatest urgency and without any other proceedings. It thus indicated that the United States should take all measures at its disposal to ensure that Walter LaGrand was not executed pending the final decision in these proceedings.[168] Two issues arise in the *LaGrand* case.

First, the Court, in the *LaGrand* case, proceeded without holding oral hearings in light of extreme urgency.[169] In consequence, the United States was not given an occasion to present its view. In this regard, some doubts were expressed by a member of the Court regarding whether the omission of an oral hearing was consistent with fundamental rules of the procedural equality of the parties.[170]

Second, as a general rule, provisional measures are indicated in order to preserve *rights of States* exposed to an imminent breach which is irreparable. In this regard, Judge Oda questioned whether the provisional measures indicated by the Court can be thought to concern the preservation of the rights of Germany under the Vienna Convention.[171] In this regard, the Court took the view that: 'Article 36, paragraph 1 [of the Vienna Convention on Consular Relations], creates individual rights, which, by virtue of Article 1 of the Optional Protocol, may be invoked in this Court by the national State of the detained person.'[172]

In subsequent cases, the ICJ continued to indicate provisional measures to cease execution of individuals. In the *Avena and Others* case where Mexico instituted proceedings against the United States on the basis of the optional clause and Article I of the Optional Protocol to the Vienna Convention, the ICJ ordered the United States to take all measures necessary to ensure that three Mexican nationals were not executed pending final judgment in these proceedings.[173] In the *Request for Interpretation of the Judgment of 31 March 2004 in the Case Concerning Avena and Other Mexican Nations*, the Court also indicated that the United States should take all measures necessary to ensure that five Mexican nationals were not executed pending the judgment on the request for interpretation submitted by Mexico.[174]

---

[167] *Ibid.*, p. 10, para. 1 and p. 12, paras. 8-9.
[168] *Ibid.*, p. 16, para. 29(I)(a). Yet, Walter LaGrand was eventually executed. The *LaGrand* case, Judgment of 27 June 2001, ICJ Reports 2001, p. 480, para. 38.
[169] ICJ Reports 1999, p. 14, para. 21.
[170] Separate Opinion of Judge Schwebel, *ibid.*, p. 21.
[171] Declaration of Judge Oda, *ibid.*, 19, para. 6. Judge Oda himself voted in favour of the majority opinion for humanitarian reasons with great hesitation. *Ibid.*, p. 18, para. 1 and p. 20, para. 7. See also Thirlway, *The Law and Procedure*, Vol. I, pp. 938-40.
[172] *LaGrand* (Germany v. United States of America), Judgment of 27 June 2001, ICJ Reports 2001, p. 494, para. 77.
[173] *Case Concerning Avena and Other Mexican Nationals* (Mexico v. United States), Request for the Indication of Provisional Measures, Order of 5 February 2003, pp. 91-2, para. 59(I)(a).
[174] *Request for Interpretation of the Judgment of 31 March 2004 in the Case Concerning Avena and Other Mexican Nations* (Mexico v. United States), Request for the Indication of Provisional Measures, Order of 16 July 2008, ICJ Reports 2008, p. 331, para. 80(II)(a). However, one of the Mexican nationals, José Ernesto Medellín Rojas, was executed in the State of Texas on 5 August 2008. Judgment of 19 January 2009, ICJ Reports 2009, p. 19, para. 52. In March 2005, the United States withdrew from the Optional Protocol to the Vienna Convention on Consular relations. J. R. Crook (ed.), 'Contemporary Practice of the United States Relating to International Law' (2005) 99 *AJIL*, p. 490.

3.4 Implementation of Provisional Measures

The question as to whether or not provisional measures are binding upon the parties to a case has been the subject of extensive debate.[175] The debate was eventually ended by the ICJ itself in the *LaGrand* case of 2001. In this case, the Court made an important statement:

> It follows from the object and purpose of the Statute, as well as from the terms of Article 41 when read in their context, that the power to indicate provisional measures entails that such measures should be binding, inas much as the power in question is based on the necessity, when the circumstances call for it, to safeguard, and to avoid prejudice to, the rights of the parties as determined by the final judgment of the Court. The contention that provisional measures indicated under Article 41 might not be binding would be contrary to the object and purpose of that Article.[176]

The binding nature of these measures is repeatedly confirmed by subsequent cases of the ICJ.[177]

Nonetheless, enforceability of provisional measures remains a matter for debate. It is doubtful whether Article 94(2) of the UN Charter is applicable to provisional measures since this provision refers only to a 'judgment' (i.e. final judgment).[178] A question thus arises as to how it is possible to ensure effective implementation of provisional measures. In this regard, it is of particular interest to note that the Court required the parties in dispute to provide information with regard to compliance with its provisional measures. In the *Burkina Faso/Mali* case, for instance, the Chamber of the Court called upon 'the Agents of the Parties to notify the Registrar without delay of any agreement concluded between their Governments within the scope of point 1 D above', namely, an agreement with regard to the terms of the troop withdrawal.[179] In the *Nicaragua* case, the Court decided to keep the matters covered by its order continuously under review.[180] In the *Georgia/Russia* case, the Court obliged each party to inform the Court as to its compliance with its provisional measures.[181] Likewise, the Court, in the *Avena* case, required the

---

[175] For a detailed analysis of this issue, see Thirlway, *The Law and Procedure*, Vol. I, pp. 956-68. See also Thirlway, *The International Court of Justice* (2016), pp. 149-53.

[176] The *LaGrand* case, Judgment of 27 June 2001, ICJ Reports 2001, p. 503, para. 102.

[177] See, for instance, the *Temple of Preah Vihear* case (Request for Interpretation), ICJ Reports 2011, p. 554, para. 67.

[178] Oellers-Frahm, 'Article 41', pp. 1068-9. See also Sztucki, *Interim Measures*, pp. 294-302; A. Tanzi, 'Problems of Enforcement of Decisions of the International Court of Justice and the Law of the United Nations' (1995) 6 *EJIL*, pp. 563-70; Mutlaq Al-Qahtani, 'The Role of the International Court of Justice in the Enforcement of Its Judicial Decisions' (2002) 15 *LJIL*, pp. 786-8; C. Schulte, *Compliance with Decisions of the International Court of Justice* (Oxford University Press, 2004), 60-2; G. Zyberi, 'Provisional Measures of the International Court of Justice in Armed Conflict Situations' (2010) 23 *LJIL*, pp. 575-7. On the other hand, Kolb supports the application of Article 94(2) of the UN Charter to Orders indicating provisional measures. Kolb, *The International Court of Justice*, p. 847. See also section 7.5 of this chapter.

[179] *Frontier Dispute* (Burkina Faso/Republic of Mali), Request for the indication of Provisional Measures, Order of 10 January 1986, ICJ Reports 1986, p. 12, para. 32(2).

[180] ICJ Reports 1984, p. 187, para. 41(4)(C). [181] ICJ Reports 2008, p. 399, para. 149(4)(D).

United States to inform it of the measures taken in implementation of its order indicating provisional measures.[182] The Court, in the 2011 *Temple of Preah Viher* case, decided the same provisional measures.[183] Requesting the parties to provide relevant information and continuous review seems to fall within the Court's *proprio motu* powers to indicate provisional measures.[184] The judicial supervision is noteworthy as an attempt to ensure effective implementation of provisional measures.

In the case of non-compliance with provisional measures by one of the disputing parties, the Court may take note of non-compliance with the measures in the merits phase. For instance, the Court in the *Costa Rica/Nicaragua* case clearly stated that: 'The judgment on the merits is the appropriate place for the Court to assess compliance with the provisional measures.'[185] In this case, the Court determined the breach of obligations under the 2011 order indicating provisional measures by Nicaragua.[186] Likewise the Court, in the *Application of the Genocide Convention* case between Bosnia and Herzegovina and Serbia and Montenegro, included in the operative clause of its judgment, by way of satisfaction, a declaration that the respondent (Serbia) had failed to comply with the Court's orders indicating provisional measures.[187] In the *LaGrand* case, it declared that by failing to take all measures at its disposal to ensure that Walter LaGrand was not executed pending the final decision, the United States breached the obligation incumbent upon it under the order indicating provisional measures of 3 March 1999.[188] However, it remains to be seen to what extent the risk of dishonourable record in the Court's judgment may deter non-compliance with provisional measures by the parties. Alternatively, the party which is affected by the ignoring of the provisional measures by the other party may request of the Court the indication of additional provisional measures.[189] It seems also possible to argue that the Court indicates *proprio motu* additional provisional measures to address the situation.

4 PRELIMINARY OBJECTIONS

4.1 Procedural Issues

According to Thirlway, a preliminary objection ('*exceptions préliminaires*' in French) is defined as 'a formal step by which a respondent raises a question that it contends should be dealt with separately, before any other issue in the proceedings is examined'.[190] Upon receipt by the Registry of a preliminary objection, the proceedings on

---

[182] ICJ Reports 2003, p. 92, para. 59, I(b).   [183] ICJ Reports 2011, p. 556, para. 69(C).
[184] See Articles 75(1) and 78 of the Rules of Court.
[185] *Certain Activities Carried Out by Nicaragua in the Border Area* (Costa Rica v. Nicaragua), Judgment, 16 December 2015, ICJ Reports 2015, para. 126.
[186] *Ibid.*, para. 129.
[187] *Application of the Convention on the Prevention and Punishment of the Crime of Genocide (Bosnia and Herzegovina v. Serbia and Montenegro)*, Judgment of 26 February 2007, ICJ Reports 2007, p. 236, para. 469; p. 238, para. 471(7).
[188] The *LaGrand* case (Germany v. USA), Judgment of 27 June 2001, ICJ Reports 2001, p. 508, para. 115; p. 516, para. 128(5).
[189] Zyberi, 'Provisional Measures of the International Court of Justice in Armed Conflict Situations', p. 576.
[190] Thirlway, *The International Court of Justice* (2016), p. 167.

the merits are to be suspended.[191] Under Article 79(1) of the Rules of Court, preliminary objections can be divided into three categories: (i) objection to jurisdiction, (ii) objection to admissibility and (iii) other objection. It is not infrequent that respondent States file a whole set of preliminary objections covering different categories at the same time.[192]

The Court's jurisdiction must normally be assessed on the date of the filing of the act instituting proceedings.[193] Objections to admissibility normally means that even if the Court has jurisdiction and the facts stated by the applicant State are assumed to be correct, nonetheless there are reasons why the Court should not proceed to an examination of the merits.[194] Examples of these objections include: the exhaustion of local remedies, hypothetical nature of the case, lack of interest in the subject matter, legal interest of a third State, and moot points. In practice, it is sometimes difficult to draw a strict distinction between objections on the grounds that the Court lacks jurisdiction and objections on the grounds of inadmissibility.[195]

Upon receipt by the Registry of a preliminary objection, the proceedings on the merits shall be suspended.[196] Concerning the procedure of preliminary objection, three elements merit particular note.

(i) *The party to a case*: Normally the preliminary objection is filed by the respondent State. Exceptionally, in the *Monetary Gold* case, the applicant State, Italy, submitted preliminary objections.[197]

(ii) *The timing of raising preliminary objections*: Under Article 79(1) of the Rules of Court, any objection by the respondent to the jurisdiction of the Court or to the admissibility of the application shall be made in writing as soon as possible, and not later than three months after the delivery of the memorial.

(iii) *The outcome*: The Court's decision regarding preliminary objections is rendered in the form of a judgment. In its judgment, the Court either upholds the objection, reject it, or declares that the objection does not possess an exclusively preliminary character. If the Court declares that it does not possess an exclusively preliminary character, the Court proceeds to hear the merits, while reserving the possibility to decide that the objection should be upheld. In practice, it may not always be easy to determine whether or not an objection is of 'an exclusively preliminary character'. The Court has a considerable discretion to determine whether or not an objection is of exclusively preliminary character.[198]

---

[191] Rules of Court, Article 79(5).
[192] Thirlway, *The International Court of Justice* (2016), pp. 169–70.
[193] *Application of the Convention on the Prevention and Punishment of the Crime of Genocide* (Bosnia and Herzegovina v. Serbia and Montenegro), Preliminary Objections, Judgment of 11 July 1996, ICJ Reports 1996, p. 613, para. 26; *Border and Transborder Armed Actions* (Nicaragua v. Honduras), Judgment of 20 December 1988, ICJ Reports 1988, p. 95, para. 66.
[194] The *Oil Platforms* case, ICJ Reports 2003, p. 177, para. 29.
[195] S. Oda, 'The International Court of Justice Viewed from the Bench 1976–1993' (1993) 244 *RCADI*, pp. 47–8.
[196] Article 79(3) of the Rules of Court.
[197] The *Monetary Gold* case will be discussed in section 4.2 of this chapter.
[198] Thirlway, *The International Court of Justice* (2016), p. 174.

Where multiple preliminary objections are filed, normally an objection to the jurisdiction of the Court is first dealt with by the Court. This order is not absolute, however. In fact, the Court, in the *Norwegian Loans* case, took the position that:

> The Court's competence is challenged on both grounds and the Court is free to base its decision on the ground which in its judgment is more direct and conclusive.[199]

Should there be the conclusive reason to uphold the preliminary objection concerning the admissibility of the particular case, there will be no need to examine each and every preliminary objection relating to the jurisdiction of the Court.[200] Although no comprehensive analysis of various preliminary objections can be made here, this is a convenient point to discuss two related issues. The first is the *Monetary Gold* rule and the second is the doctrine of highly political disputes.

4.2 The *Monetary Gold* Rule

The Court cannot decide upon legal rights of a third State which is not a party to the proceedings. This rule was underlined in the 1954 *Monetary Gold* case between Italy and France, the United Kingdom and the United States.[201] This case concerned the delivery of a quantity of monetary gold of the National Bank of Albania which was removed by the Germans from Rome in 1943 and recovered in Germany. Italy and Albania claimed their rights to the gold. On 25 April 1951, France, the United Kingdom and the United States – which has been entrusted to implement Part III of the 1946 Paris Agreement with regard to the restitution of monetary gold found in Germany or in third countries[202] – signed the Washington Agreement, by which they decided to submit to an arbitrator for his opinion the question whether the gold belonged to Albania or to Italy or to neither. The three governments also agreed that if the opinion of the arbitrator should be that Albania had established a claim to the gold in question, they would deliver the gold to the United Kingdom in partial satisfaction of the judgment in the *Corfu Channel* case, unless within ninety days either Albania or Italy made an application to the ICJ with regard to the monetary gold. The three governments accepted the jurisdiction of the Court for the purpose of the determination of such applications by Italy or by Albania or by both. In 1953, the arbitrator gave his opinion that the gold in question belonged to Albania.[203]

---

[199] *Certain Norwegian Loans* (France v. Norway), Judgment of 6 July 1957, ICJ Reports 1957, p. 25.

[200] *Interhandel* (Switzerland v. United States of America), Judgment of 21 March 1959, ICJ Reports 1959, p. 24.

[201] *Monetary Gold Removed from Rome in 1943* (Italy v. France, United Kingdom of Great Britain and Northern Ireland and United States of America), Judgment of 15 June 1954. Preliminary question, ICJ Reports 1954, p. 19. For the *Monetary Gold* rule, see also T. Thienel, 'Third States and the Jurisdiction of the International Court of Justice: The Monetary Gold Principle' (2014) 57 *GYIL*, pp. 321-52.

[202] France, the United Kingdom, the USA and Albania as well as other States are signatories of the Paris Agreement. Italy adhered to the provisions of Part III of the Agreement on 16 December 1947. ICJ Reports 1954, p. 25.   [203] *Ibid.*, p. 26.

Subsequently, the Italian Government, relying on the statement signed at Washington on 25 April 1951, instituted proceedings against France, the United Kingdom and the United States before the ICJ and claimed: (1) that the Governments of France, the United Kingdom and the United States should deliver to Italy any share of the monetary gold that might be due to Albania under Part III of the Paris Act in partial satisfaction for the damage caused to Italy by the Albanian law of 13 January 1945; (2) that Italy's right to receive the said share of monetary gold must have priority over the claim of the United Kingdom to receive the gold in partial satisfaction of the Judgment in the *Corfu Channel* case.[204] Albania, which has not accepted the jurisdiction of the Court, refrained from making any application to it. After filing her application, however, Italy posed a question as to the jurisdiction of the Court and requested the Court to adjudicate on the question of jurisdiction as a preliminary issue.[205]

While it was unusual that the applicant State subsequently challenge the jurisdiction of the Court, the Court examined this issue and unanimously found that in the absence of the consent of Albania, it was not authorised to adjudicate upon Italy's claim against Albania because Albania's legal interests formed 'the very subject-matter of the decision'. The key passage of the Court's decision bears quoting:

> In the present case, Albania's legal interests would not only be affected by a decision, but would form *the very subject-matter of the decision*. In such a case, the Statute cannot be regarded, by implication, as authorizing proceedings to be continued in the absence of Albania.[206]

The *dictum* of the Court was repeatedly confirmed in the ICJ jurisprudence. In the *Certain Phosphate Lands in Nauru* case between Nauru and Australia of 1992,[207] Australia gave rise to preliminary objections and contended that the claims of Nauru were inadmissible because any judgment on the question of breach of the Trusteeship Agreement would involve the responsibility of third States (i.e. the United Kingdom and New Zealand) that had not consented to the Court's jurisdiction in the present case.[208] However, the Court did not admit this objection, stating that:

> In the present case, the interests of New Zealand and the United Kingdom do not constitute the very subject-matter of the judgment to be rendered on the merits of Nauru's Application and the situation is in that respect different from that with which the Court had to deal in the *Monetary Gold* case.[209]

---

[204] *Ibid.*, p. 22.   [205] *Ibid.*, p. 27.   [206] Emphasis added. ICJ Reports 1954, p. 32.
[207] *Certain Phosphate Lands in Nauru*, ICJ Reports 1992, p. 240. This case concerned responsibility of Administering Authority made up of the Governments of Australia, New Zealand and the United Kingdom with regard to a Trusteeship over Nauru. *Ibid.*, p. 243, para. 5.
[208] *Ibid.*, p. 255, para. 39.   [209] *Ibid.*, p. 261, para. 55.

It thus found that the fact that New Zealand and the United Kingdom were not parties to the case was no bar to the proceedings brought by Nauru against Australia.[210]

The *Monetary Gold* rule was echoed in the *East Timor* case between Portugal and Australia of 1995.[211] In this case, the Court held that:

> [T]he very subject-matter of the Court's decision would necessarily be a determination whether, having regard to the circumstances in which Indonesia entered and remained in East Timor, it could or could not have acquired the power to enter into treaties on behalf of East Timor relating to the resources of its continental shelf. The Court could not make such a determination in the absence of the consent of Indonesia.[212]

It thus concluded that it cannot in the present case exercise its jurisdiction.[213]

However, care should be taken in noting that a third State concerned can prevent the judicial settlement simply by refraining from any action in accordance to this rule. Given that the essential task of the ICJ is to settle a dispute submitted to it, caution is needed in the application of the *Monetary Gold* rule.

4.3 Admissibility of Disputes Involving Highly Political Issues

Some argue that, due to its nature, highly political disputes are beyond the function of the Court as a judicial organ. Objections to the admissibility of a specific case on the basis of the doctrine of highly political disputes have been repeatedly filed in cases before the Court. In some cases, the admissibility of highly political disputes was also questioned by the members of the Court. For instance, Judge Gros, in the *Nuclear Tests* case, expressed his misgivings that:

> There is a certain tendency to submit essentially political conflicts to adjudication in the attempt to open a little door to judicial legislation and, if this tendency were to persist, it would result in the institution, on the international plane, of government by judges; such a notion is so opposed to the realities of the present international community that it would undermine the very foundations of jurisdiction.[214]

Furthermore, Judge Oda, in the *Nicaragua* case, argued that: '[I]t would in my view have been prudent for the Court, in the light of the merits of the present case, to find it a matter of judicial propriety not to proceed with a case so highly charged with issues central to the sensitive political relations of many States.'[215]

---

[210] *Ibid.*, p. 262, para. 57. However, Judge Jennings dissented the majority opinion in this matter. Dissenting Opinion of President Sir Robert Jennings, *ibid.*, pp. 301–2. See also Dissenting Opinion of Judge Ago, *ibid.*, p. 328; Dissenting Opinion of Judge Schwebel, *ibid.*, p. 342.

[211] *Case Concerning East Timor* (Portugal v. Australia), Judgment of 30 June 1995, ICJ Reports 1995, p. 90. This case concerns the infringement of the right of the people of East Timor to self-determination and to permanent sovereignty over its natural resources, and infringement of the rights of Portugal as the administering power by Australia.

[212] *Ibid.*, p. 102, para. 28.   [213] *Ibid.*, p. 106, para. 38.

[214] *Nuclear Tests* (Australia v. France), Separate Opinion of Judge Gros, ICJ Reports 1974, p. 297.

[215] Dissenting Opinion of Judge Oda in the *Nicaragua* case (Merits), ICJ Reports 1986, p. 220, para. 17. See also Dissenting Opinion of Judge Schwebel, *ibid.*, pp. 293–4, para. 69.

205 | International Court of Justice (II)

The Court has consistently rejected the objection to admissibility on the basis of the doctrine of highly political disputes. In the *Hostage* case, for instance, the Iranian Government argued, in its letter of 9 December 1979, that the Court cannot examine the American application divorced from 'the whole political dossier of the relations between Iran and the United States over the last 25 years'.[216] However, the Court did not admit Iran's claim, stating that:

> Yet never has the view been put forward before that, because a legal dispute submitted to the Court is only one aspect of a political dispute, the Court should decline to resolve for the parties the legal questions at issue between them. Nor can any basis for such a view of the Court's functions or jurisdiction be found in the Charter or the Statute of the Court; if the Court were, contrary to its settled jurisprudence, to adopt such a view, it would impose a far-reaching and unwarranted restriction upon the role of the Court in the peaceful solution of international disputes.[217]

Equally the doctrine of highly political disputes was clearly rejected by the Court in the *Nicaragua* case.[218]

Given that normally international disputes arise in actual political contexts and no objective criterion exists in order to judge the 'highly' political nature, the application of the doctrine of highly political disputes runs the risk of preventing the exercise of the Court's jurisdiction in many cases. As the Court rightly observed, international disputes are thought to be a mixture of political and legal issues and it is possible for the Court to deal only with legal issues, distinct from political issues. However, it must not be taken to mean that there is no limitation with the judicial function of the Court. In fact, the Court, in the *Northern Cameroons* case, recognised that: 'There are inherent limitations on the exercise of the judicial function which the Court, as a court of justice, can never ignore.'[219]

5 INTERVENTION UNDER ARTICLE 62 OF THE COURT'S STATUTE

5.1 General Considerations

Although international adjudication is bilateral by nature, an international judicial decision may affect rights and interests of a third State in the increasingly interdependent world. An issue thus arises how it is possible to safeguard rights and interests of a third State. In this regard, the ICJ Statute provides for two forms of intervention:

(i) intervention under Article 62 which concerns an interest of a legal nature of a third State which may be affected by the decision in the case
(ii) intervention under Article 63 which relates to the interpretation of a multilateral convention to which States other than those concerned in the case are parties.

---

[216] ICJ Reports 1980, p. 19, para. 35. [217] *Ibid.*, p. 20, para. 37.
[218] The *Nicaragua* case, Jurisdiction of the Court and Admissibility of the Application, Judgment of 26 November 1984, ICJ Reports 1984, p. 437, para. 101.
[219] *Northern Cameroons* (Cameroon v. United Kingdom), Judgment of 2 December 1963 Preliminary Objections, ICJ Reports 1963, p. 29.

An intervention under Article 62 is permissive, whilst one under Article 63 is considered an intervention as a right. This section will examine the intervention under Article 62.

The purpose of intervention under Article 62 is to protect the third State's interest of a legal nature that might be affected by a decision in an existing case already established between the parties to the case.[220] Two types of intervention should be distinguished under Article 62: non-party intervention and party intervention.[221] In the case of non-party intervention, a would-be intervener State seeks to intervene to the proceedings as a non-party and it confines itself to informing the Court of legal and factual contentions of the intervener with a view to safeguarding its legal interests that might be affected by the decision of the case.[222] In the *Jurisdictional Immunities of the State* case, the Court explicitly stated that: '[I]n so far as the object of Greece's intervention is to inform the Court of its interest of a legal nature which may be affected, this object accords with the function of intervention.'[223] In contrast, in the case of party intervention, the intervening State participates in the proceedings of a particular case as a full party.[224] The distinction is relevant when considering jurisdictional link between the would-be intervener and the original litigating parties. To date, only three requests, out of ten for intervention under Article 62, have been accepted by the Court (see Table 7.2). The intervention under Article 62 gives rise to three principal issues: (i) the concept of the interest of a legal nature, (ii) jurisdictional link between the would-be intervener and the original litigating parties and (iii) legal effect of the ICJ's judgment on an intervening State.

5.2 The Concept of an Interest of a Legal Nature

Under Article 62(1) of the ICJ Statute, '[s]hould a State consider that it has an interest of a legal nature which may be affected by the decision in the case, it may submit a request to the Court to be permitted to intervene'.[225] While the language of Article 62 precludes extra-legal interests, such as political, social, economic and factual interests, it must not

---

[220] *Land, Island and Maritime Frontier Dispute* (El Salvador/Honduras: Nicaragua intervening) Application by Nicaragua for Permission to Intervene, Judgment of 13 September 1990, ICJ Reports 1990, p. 133, para. 97.

[221] Thirlway, *The Law and Procedure*, Vol. II, p. 1840.

[222] The institution of non-party intervention – which was strongly advocated by Judge Oda – has developed through the ICJ Jurisprudence. See Dissenting Opinion of Judge Oda in *Case Concerning Sovereignty over Pulau Ligitan and Pulau Sipadan*, Judgment of 23 October 2001, ICJ Reports 2001, pp. 609–12, paras. 2–8. As for requests for non-party intervention, see, for instance, *Land and Maritime Boundary between Cameroon and Nigeria* (Cameroon v. Nigeria: Equatorial Guinea intervening), Order of 21 October 1999, Decision on intervention; fixing of time-limits: Written Statement and Written Observations, ICJ Reports 1999, p. 1032, para. 5; *Sovereignty over Pulau Ligitan and Pulau Sipadan* (hereafter the *Indonesia/Malaysia* case), Application by the Philippines for Permission to Intervene, Judgment of 23 October 2001, ICJ Reports 2001, pp. 580–1, para. 7; *Jurisdictional Immunities of the State* (Germany v. Italy), Application by the Hellenic Republic for Permission to Intervene, ICJ Reports 2011, pp. 502–3, para. 31.

[223] *Jurisdictional Immunities of the State* (Germany v. Italy), Application by the Hellenic Republic for Permission to Intervene, Order of 4 July 2011, ICJ Reports 2011, p. 502, para. 29. See also *Territorial and Maritime Dispute* (Nicaragua v. Colombia), Application to Intervene by Costa Rica, Judgment of 4 May 2011, ICJ Reports 2011, p. 360, para. 34.

[224] To this day, no State has been admitted to intervene as a party.

[225] See also Article 81(2) of the Rules of Court.

TABLE 7.2 REQUEST FOR INTERVENTION UNDER ARTICLE 62 OF THE ICJ STATUTE

Year	Case	Original Parties	Intervener	Result
1973	The *Nuclear Tests* cases	Australia and New Zealand/France	Fiji	Moot
1980	The *Tunisia/Libya* case	Tunisia/Libya	Malta	Rejected
1984	The *Libya/Malta* case	Libya/Malta	Italy	Rejected
1990	The *Land, Island and Maritime Frontier* Disputes	El Salvador/Honduras	Nicaragua	Admitted
1995	The *Nuclear Tests II* case	New Zealand/France	Several States in Pacific*	Rejected
1999	The *Cameroon/Nigeria* case	Cameroon/Nigeria	Equatorial Guinea	Admitted
2001	The *Sovereignty over Pulau Ligitan and Pulau Sipadan* case	Indonesia/Malaysia	Philippines	Rejected
2011	The *Nicaragua/Colombia* case	Nicaragua/Colombia	Costa Rica	Rejected
2011	The *Nicaragua/Colombia* case	Nicaragua/Colombia	Honduras	Rejected
2011	The *Germany/Italy* case	Germany/Italy	Greece	Admitted

* These States were: Australia, Samoa, Solomon Islands, the Marshall Islands and the Federated States of Micronesia. Request for an Examination of the Situation in Accordance with Paragraph 63 of the Court's Judgment of 20 December 1974 in the *Nuclear Tests* (New Zealand v. France) case, Order of 22 September 1995, Request for an examination of the situation – Request for the Indication of Provisional Measures, ICJ Reports 1995, p. 306, para. 67.

be taken to mean that an interest under Article 62 must be exclusively legal. In fact, legal and extra-legal interests may be intimately intertwined.

The existence of an interest of a legal nature is the key element of Article 62 intervention. According to the ICJ, '[i]t is for the State seeking to intervene to identify the interest of a legal nature which it considers may be affected by the decision in the case, and to show in what way that interest may be affected'.[226] However, it is for the Court to decide on the request to intervene, and to determine the limits and scope of such intervention in accordance with Article 62(2) of the Statute.[227]

Criteria for determining the existence of 'an interest of a legal nature' remain less clear and further development of the ICJ jurisprudence is needed to clarify the criteria.

---

[226] ICJ Reports 1990, p. 118, para. 61.
[227] *Territorial and Maritime Dispute* (Nicaragua v. Colombia), ICJ Reports 2011, Application to Intervene by Costa Rica, p. 358, para. 25. See also *Territorial and Maritime Dispute* (Nicaragua v. Colombia), Application to Intervene by Honduras, Judgment of 4 May 2011, ICJ Reports 2011, pp. 433–4, para. 35; Article 84(1) of the Rules of Court.

Tentatively five elements can be identified with a view to determining the existence of 'an interest of a legal nature'.

(i) To intervene as a non-party under Article 62, it is sufficient for the intervener to establish that its *interest*, not its rights, *may* be affected.[228] In this regard, the Chamber of the ICJ, in the *El Salvador/Honduras* case, held that the State seeking to intervene 'has only to show that *its interest* "may" be affected, not that it will or must be affected'.[229] According to the Court in the *Indonesia/Malaysia* case, 'the interest of a legal nature to be shown by a State seeking to intervene under Article 62 is not limited to the *dispositif* alone of a judgment. It may also relate to the reasons which constitute the necessary steps to the *dispositif*'.[230] In addition, 'a State which ... relies on an interest of a legal nature other than in the subject-matter of the case itself necessarily bears the burden of showing with a particular clarity the existence of the interest of a legal nature which it claims to have'.[231]

(ii) An interest of a legal nature must be concrete, not general or hypothetical.[232] By way of illustration, the Chamber of the Court, in the *El Salvador/Honduras* case, dismissed the request for intervention by Nicaragua because of the absence of any Nicaraguan interest liable to be directly affected by a decision relating to sovereignty over the islands in the Gulf of Fonseca.[233]

(iii) A third party's interest should not be the same kind as that of other States within the region. When requesting permission to intervene in the *Tunisia/Libya* case, Malta claimed that it had a 'specific and unique interest' in the proceedings by virtue of its geographical location vis-à-vis the two parties to the case.[234] However, the Court unanimously dismissed Malta's request partly because Malta's interest was of the same kind as that of other States within the region and Malta did not have an interest of a legal nature which might be affected by the decision.[235]

(iv) Intervention under Article 62 must not introduce a new dispute in the proceedings before the Court. An example in this matter was Italy's request for permission to intervene in the *Libya/Malta* case. In this case, Italy alleged that the areas of continental shelf to be delimited between the parties all belonged to one and the same region of the Central Mediterranean, and that Italy had a right over parts of the continental shelf in that region. The legal interest of Italy was not merely an 'interest' but constituted 'sovereign rights' over the appropriate areas of continental shelf.[236]

---

[228] *Territorial and Maritime Dispute* (Nicaragua v. Colombia), Application to Intervene by Costa Rica, ICJ Reports 2011, p. 358, para. 26; *Territorial and Maritime Dispute* (Nicaragua v. Colombia), Application to Intervene by Honduras, ICJ Reports 2011, p. 434, para. 37.
[229] Emphasis added. ICJ Reports 1990, p. 117, para. 61.
[230] ICJ Reports 2001, p. 596, para. 47.
[231] *Ibid.*, p. 598, para. 59.
[232] Kolb, *The International Court of Justice*, pp. 706–7.
[233] ICJ Reports 1990, p. 119, para. 66.
[234] *Continental Shelf* (Tunisia v. Libyan Arab Jamahiriya) (hereafter the *Tunisia/Libya* case), Application by Malta for Permission to Intervene, Judgment of 14 April 1981, ICJ Reports 1981, p. 9, para. 13.
[235] *Ibid*, p. 19, para. 33.
[236] *Continental Shelf* (Libyan Arab Jamahiriya v. Malta) (hereafter the *Libya/Malta* case), Application by Italy for Permission to Intervene, Judgment of 21 March 1984, ICJ Reports 1984, p. 11, para. 15. The original parties contested the permissibility of the intervention.

Italy's application to intervene was different from that of Malta in two respects. First, while Malta's objective was simply to submit its views, Italy would also attempt to defend its legal rights. Second, while Malta did not agree to be bound by the decision of the Court, Italy did.[237] However, Italy's request to intervene was rejected by eleven votes to five since, if Italy were permitted to intervene in the present proceedings, the Court would be called upon to determine a dispute, or some part of a dispute, between Italy and one or both of the principal parties.[238] Non-introduction of a new case was also confirmed by the ICJ in the *El Salvador/Honduras* case, stating that intervention under Article 62 'is not intended to enable a third State to tack on a new case ... '.[239]

(v) Intervention under Article 62 must not aim to ask the Court to prejudge the merits of the case. When requesting permission to intervene in the *Tunisia/Libya* case, Malta claimed that it had a 'specific and unique interest' in the proceedings by virtue of its geographical location vis-à-vis the two parties to the case.[240] However, the Court unanimously dismissed Malta's request. One of the reasons was that Malta's intervention would allow Malta to submit arguments to the Court on concrete issues forming an essential part of the case between Tunisia and Libya. According to the Court, however, it could lead to prejudging the merits of Malta's own claims against Tunisia and Libya in separate disputes with each of those States. The Court thus concluded that the Maltese request to intervene fell outside the scope of intervention under Article 62 of the Statute.[241]

5.3 Jurisdictional Link

In considering the jurisdictional link between the original parties and a would-be intervener State, distinction must be made between non-party intervention and party intervention. The jurisdictional link is not required in relation to non-party intervention. This point was confirmed by the Chamber of the ICJ in the *El Salvador/Honduras* case, stating that: '[T]he procedure of intervention is to ensure that a State with possibly affected interests may be permitted to intervene even though there is no jurisdictional link and it therefore cannot become a party.'[242] This view was echoed by the full Court in the *Jurisdictional Immunities of the State* case. In the words of the Court, 'it is not necessary to establish the existence of a basis of jurisdiction between the parties to the proceedings

---

[237] *Ibid.*, pp. 12–13, para. 17.
[238] *Ibid.*, pp. 19–20, paras. 30–1. However, Judge Jennings questioned the majority opinion. Dissenting Opinion of Judge Jennings, *ibid.*, p. 154, para. 19. See also Dissenting Opinion of Judge Sette-Camara, *ibid.*, p. 83, at para. 64; the dissenting opinion of Judge Ago, *ibid.*, pp. 125–6, para. 17. In the *Libya/Malta* case of 1985, the ICJ confined itself to areas where no claims by a third State existed. Judgment, ICJ Reports 1985, p. 26, para. 22.
[239] ICJ Reports 1990, pp. 133–4, para. 97.
[240] The *Tunisia/Libya* case, Application by Malta for Permission to Intervene, Judgment of 14 April 1981, ICJ Reports 1981, p. 9, para. 13. Malta did not intend to be bound by the decision of the Court. *Ibid.*, p. 10, para. 14. In addition, both of the original parties were opposed to Malta's application to intervene. *Ibid.*, pp. 10–12, paras. 15–18.
[241] *Ibid.*, pp. 18–20, paras. 31–7. In the *Tunisia/Libya* judgment of 1982, the Court refrained from drawing a delimitation line of the continental shelf in the area where Malta's rights may be involved. Thus the Court, to a certain extent, took Malta's interest into account.
[242] ICJ Reports 1990, p. 135, para. 100.

and the State which is seeking to intervene as a non-party'.[243] If a jurisdictional link is deemed at all times needed for intervention, the institution of intervention under Article 62 will die out and its purpose will be defeated.[244] In contrast, the jurisdictional linkage between the intervening State and original parties to the case is needed in the situation where the intervening State is to be a party to the case in order to formulate a claim.[245]

A related issue to be examined is whether or not consent of the original parties to the case is needed to permit an intervention under Article 62. According to the ICJ, the competence of the Court concerning intervention is not derived from the consent of the parties to the case, but from the consent given by them, in becoming parties to the Court's Statute, to the Court's exercise of its powers conferred by the Statute.[246] In the words of the Court, 'the opposition [to an intervention] of the parties to a case is, though very important, no more than one element to be taken into account by the Court'.[247]

5.4 Legal Effect of Judgments on an Intervener

The legal effect of the Court's judgments on an intervener under Article 62 differs according to the type of the intervention. In the case of party intervention, the decision of the Court is binding upon the intervening State as a party to the case. In the case of non-party intervention, however, the Court's decisions are not binding upon the intervening State.[248] In fact, the Chamber of the ICJ, in the *El Salvador/Honduras* case, held that: '[A] State permitted to intervene under Article 62 of the Statute, but which does not acquire the status of party to the case, is not bound by the Judgment in the proceedings in which it has intervened.'[249] Overall principal elements of intervention under Article 62 can be summarised as shown in Figure 7.2.

Finally, some mention must be made of the relationship between Articles 59 and 62 of the ICJ Statute. An issue is whether Article 59 of the ICJ Statute is adequate to protect the third State's legal interest. If Article 59 is enough to protect the third State's interests, it would do away entirely with any need for intervention under Article 62.[250] As will be

---

[243] ICJ Reports 2011, pp. 502–3, para. 31. See also the *Indonesia/Malaysia* case, Application to Intervene, Judgment, ICJ Reports 2001, p. 589, para. 35; *Territorial and Maritime Dispute* (Nicaragua v. Colombia), Application to Intervene by Costa Rica, ICJ Reports 2011, p. 361, para. 38.

[244] Oda, *The International Court of Justice*, p. 84.

[245] *Ibid.*, p. 83; Thirlway, *The Law and Procedure*, Vol. II, p. 1840; the *Indonesia/Malaysia* case, ICJ Reports 2001, p. 589, para. 35. *Territorial and Maritime Dispute* (Nicaragua v. Colombia), Application by Costa Rica for Permission to Intervene, ICJ Reports 2011, p. 361, para. 39. See also Separate Opinion of Judge Mbaye, *Continental Shelf* (Libyan Arab Jamahiriya v. Malta), Application by Italy for Permission to Intervene, ICJ Reports 1984, p. 42.

[246] ICJ Reports 1990, p. 133, para. 96.   [247] The *Libya/Malta* case, ICJ Reports 1984, p. 28, para. 46.

[248] Thirlway, *The International Court of Justice* (2016), p. 182. See also Thirlway, *The Law and Procedure*, Vol. I, p. 1068.

[249] *Land, Island and Maritime Frontier Dispute*, Judgment of 11 September 1992, ICJ Reports 1992, p. 609, para. 423. However, Judge Oda took the view that the decision of the Court should be binding upon the intervening State as a non-party to the case. Declaration of Judge Oda, *ibid.*, p. 620. See also Kolb, *The International Court of Justice*, p. 728.

[250] Dissenting Opinion of Judge Jennings in the *Libya/Malta* case, Application by Italy for Permission to Intervene, ICJ Reports 1984, pp. 159–60, para. 34; Kolb, *The International Court of Justice*, p. 713.

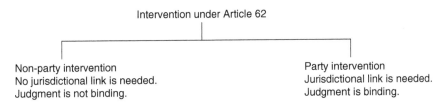

Figure 7.2 Intervention under Article 62 of the ICJ Statute

seen, the ICJ, in the *Cameroon/Nigeria* case, accepted that Article 59 may not sufficiently protect the third State's interests.[251] Accordingly, it can be considered that intervention under Article 62 is preventive by nature.[252]

6 THIRD STATE INTERVENTION UNDER ARTICLE 63 OF THE COURT'S STATUTE

The idea of intervention in cases involving the interpretation of multilateral treaties goes back to the 1899 and 1907 Hague Conventions for the Pacific Settlement of International Disputes.[253] This idea was incorporated into the Statute of the PCIJ in 1920 as Article 63 and it was inherited in the Statute of the ICJ as Article 63. To this date, there were four precedents concerning the intervention under Article 63 in the PCIJ and ICJ jurisprudence (see Table 7.3). Principal elements of intervention under Article 63 can be summarised as follows.

First, as explicitly stated in Article 63(2) of the ICJ Statute, every State so notified has the right to intervene under Article 63. However, this does not mean that intervention under Article 63 will be automatically admitted by the Court. It is for the Court to decide in each case whether or not the conditions for such intervention, laid down in Article 63, are fulfilled.[254] In fact, El Salvador's request to intervene under Article 63 in the *Nicaragua* case was declined by the Court.[255]

Second, the intervention under Article 63 must relate to the 'construction of a convention to which states other than those in the case are parties'.[256] Article 63(1) precludes bilateral treaties since no intervention under Article 63 can be envisaged if no other State is a party to the treaty.[257] Non-conventional instruments are precluded from the scope of

---

[251] *Land and Maritime Boundary between Cameroon and Nigeria* (Cameroon v Nigeria: Equatorial Guinea intervening), Judgment of 10 October 2002, ICJ Reports 2002, p. 421, para. 238. See also section 7.2 of this chapter.
[252] See Argument by P.-M. Dupuy, *Land and Maritime Boundary between Cameroon and Nigeria* (Cameroon v Nigeria: Equatorial Guinea intervening), Verbatim Record, CR 2002/21, p. 59, para. 16.
[253] Article 56 of the 1899 Convention; Article 84 of the 1907 Convention.
[254] Separate Opinion of Judge Ruda, Mosler, Ago, Sir Robert Jennings and de Lacharrière in *Military and Paramilitary Activities in and against Nicaragua* (Nicaragua v. United States of America), Declaration of Intervention of the Republic of El Salvador, ICJ Reports 1984, p. 219, para. 1.
[255] Order of 4 October 1984, *ibid.*, p. 216, para. 3.   [256] Article 63(1) of the ICJ Statute.
[257] Kolb, *The International Court of Justice*, p. 733.

TABLE 7.3 REQUEST FOR INTERVENTION UNDER ARTICLE 63 OF THE STATUTE OF THE PCIJ AND OF THE ICJ

Year	Case	Original parties to the case	Intervening State	Result
1923	SS Wimbledon	France, Great Britain, Italy, Japan v. Germany	Poland	Admitted
1950	Haya de la Torre	Colombia v. Peru	Cuba	Admitted
1984	Nicaragua	Nicaragua v. USA	El Salvador	Rejected
2013	Whaling in the Antarctic	Australia v. Japan	New Zealand	Admitted

Article 63. Also excluded is any treaty, whether bilateral or multilateral, to which neither the parties to the case nor the intending intervener were parties.

Third, the convention must be concerned with the principal subject of the proceedings before the Court. In this regard, it is adequate that its interpretation may be at issue, without knowing whether the Court will address the interpretation at a given stage.[258]

Fourth, intervention under Article 63 is limited to submitting observations on the construction of a convention to which States other than those concerned in the case are parties in question and does not allow the intervener to deal with any other aspect of the case before the Court.[259]

Fifth, in the case of intervention under Article 63, no jurisdictional link is apparently requested between the intervening State and the original litigant States. The third State may participate in the case but neither 'as a party' on an equal footing with the original litigant States, nor as an applicant or respondent or even as an independent claimant.[260]

Lastly, Article 63(2) of the ICJ Statute makes clear that if a State exercises its right to intervene as a party to a convention the interpretation of which is in question, 'the construction given by the judgment will be equally binding upon it'. As this provision only concerns 'the construction given by the judgment', the whole judgment is not binding upon the intervener.[261] Yet the scope of 'the construction given by the judgment' is not wholly unambiguous. There is no serious problem where the construction of a convention in question was given by the Court in the *dispositif* of the judgment. If this is not the case, interpretation of a convention which logically leads to the *dispositf* of the judgment is thought to be the construction of the convention under Article 63(2) of the ICJ Statute.[262]

---

[258] *Ibid.*, p. 734.
[259] *Whaling in the Antarctic* (Australia v. Japan), Declaration of Intervention of New Zealand, Order of 6 February 2013, ICJ Reports 2013, p. 9, para. 18.
[260] Oda, *The International Court of Justice*, p. 78.   [261] Kolb, *The International Court of Justice*, p. 741.
[262] Sugihara, *Kokusai Shiho*, p. 306.

7 JUDGMENT OF THE ICJ

7.1 *Res Judicata*

Under Article 59 of the ICJ Statute, '[t]he decision of the Court has no binding force except between the parties and in respect of that particular case'. The effect of this provision is to safeguard third States.[263] This provision also signifies that the finding of fact and the reasoning in law in former cases have no compelling force for the Court in later cases. However, the Court usually attempts to secure a sufficient degree of continuity and predictability of its jurisprudence. This holds particularly true of previous decisions of its own concerning its own procedure.[264]

The judgment is 'final and without appeal' under Article 60 of the Statute. Accordingly, the Court cannot give a provisional or conditional judgment even at the request of the parties.[265] From the combined effect of Articles 59 and 60, the judgment creates *res judicata*.[266] *Res judicata* means that the parties to a dispute cannot submit the same dispute before the Court and reopen the case that has already been decided in the earlier proceedings. In the words of the ICJ, 'the principle of *res judicata*, as reflected in Articles 59 and 60 of the Statute, is a general principle of law which protects, at the same time, the judicial function of a court or tribunal and the parties to a case which has led to a judgment that is final and without appeal'.[267] Three elements for identification of dispute must be noted: *persona* (person), *petitum* (claim) and *causa petendi* (the cause of the claims).[268] If the same dispute arose between different parties, for instance, the judgment of the dispute cannot be binding upon those parties.

In order to apply the principle of *res judicata*, the matter at issue must have been decided in the earlier proceedings.[269] Accordingly, it is necessary for the Court to determine whether and to what extent a matter in question has already been definitively settled.[270] The decision of the Court is contained in the operative clause of the judgment. However, the operative part and reasoning of the judgments are closely intertwined in the sense that the operative part of the judgment can be clarified referring to reasoning of the judgment. Thus there may be a need to determine the meaning of the operative clause by reference to the reasoning set out in the judgment in question in order to ascertain the scope of *res judicata*.[271]

---

[263] Thirlway, *The International Court of Justice*, pp. 133–9. See also section 7.2 of this chapter.
[264] Thirlway, *The International Court of Justice*, p. 138.
[265] Thirlway, *Ibid.*, p. 597.
[266] Separate Opinion of Judge Greenwood in *Question of the Delimitation of the Continental Shelf between Nicaragua and Colombia Beyond 200 Nautical Miles from the Nicaraguan Coast* (Nicaragua v. Colombia) (not yet reported), Preliminary Objection, 17 March 2016, para. 4.
[267] The 2016 *Nicaragua/Colombia* case, para. 58. See also *Case Concerning Application of the Convention on the Prevention and Punishment of the Crime of Genocide* (hereafter the *Bosnia* case) (Bosnia and Herzegovina v. Serbia and Montenegro), Judgment of 26 February 2007, ICJ Reports 2007, p. 90, para. 116.
[268] Dissenting Opinion of M. Anzilotti in *Interpretation of Judgments Nos. 7 and 8 (Factory at Chorzów)*, Judgment of 16 December 1927, PCIJ Series A, No. 13, p. 23.
[269] *Ibid.*, p. 95, para. 126. See also Separate Opinion of Judge Greenwood in the 2016 *Nicaragua/Colombia* case, Preliminary Objection, para. 4.
[270] The 2016 *Nicaragua/Colombia* case, para. 59.   [271] *Ibid.*, para. 61.

The application of the principle of *res judicata* has been at issue in various cases. One may take the *Corfu Channel* case as an example. After the judgment on the merits in the *Corfu Channel* case, which reserved for later consideration the question of compensation, Albania challenged the jurisdiction of the Court. In its written observations, the British Government pleaded that the matter was *res judicata*. No observations were filed by Albania, which took no further part in this stage of the proceedings. As a consequence, the issue of compensation came up for judgment by default. In its judgment of 15 December 1949, the Court accepted the plea of *res judicata* in emphatic terms:

> [T]he Albanian Government disputed the jurisdiction of the Court with regard to the assessment of damages. The Court may confine itself to stating that this jurisdiction was established by its Judgment of April 9th 1949; that, in accordance with the Statute (Article 60), which, for the settlement of the present dispute, is binding upon the Albanian Government, that Judgment is final and without appeal, and that therefore the matter is *res judicata*.[272]

More recently, the application of the principle of *res judicata* was considered in the 2016 *Nicaragua/Colombia* case. In the *dispositif* of the 2012 Judgment, the Court held that: '[S]ince Nicaragua, in the present proceedings, has not established that it has a continental margin that extends far enough to overlap with Colombia's 200-nautical-mile entitlement to the continental shelf, measured from Colombia's mainland coast, the Court is not in a position to delimit the continental shelf boundary between Nicaragua and Colombia, as requested by Nicaragua, even using the general formulation proposed by it.'[273] It thus found that it 'cannot uphold the Republic of Nicaragua's Claim contained in its final submission I(3)' with regard to a continental shelf boundary beyond 200 nautical miles.[274] Nonetheless, Nicaragua instituted new proceedings and asked the Court to declare the precise course of the maritime boundary between Nicaragua and Colombia in the areas of the continental shelf which appertain to each of them beyond the boundaries determined by the Court in its judgment of 19 November 2012.[275]

In this regard, Colombia raised a preliminary objection to the jurisdiction of the Court, arguing that the Court has already adjudicated on Nicaragua's request in its 2012 judgment and that the principle of *res judicata* bars the Court from examining Nicaragua's requests. However, the Court did not accept Colombia's objection. According to the Court, the judgment said nothing about the maritime areas located to the east of the line lying 200 nautical miles from the islands fringing the Nicaraguan coast, beyond which the Court did not continue its delimitation exercise, and to the west of the line lying 200 nautical miles from Colombia's mainland.[276] It thus concluded, by eight votes to eight

---

[272] *Corfu Channel* (United Kingdom of Great Britain and Northern Ireland v. Albania), Judgment of 15 December 1949, Assessment of the amount of compensation due from the People's Republic of Albania to the United Kingdom of Great Britain and Northern Ireland, ICJ Reports 1949, p. 248.
[273] ICJ Reports 2012(II), p. 669, para. 129. [274] *Ibid.*, p. 719, para. 251(3).
[275] The 2016 *Nicaragua/Colombia* case, para. 10. [276] *Ibid.*, para. 83.

and with the President's casting vote, that it was not precluded by the *res judicata* principle from ruling on the application submitted by Nicaragua on 16 September 2013.[277] As shown in the voting record, however, the opinions of the members of the Court were sharply divided in this matter.[278]

7.2 Effect of Article 59 of the ICJ Statute

After examining the principle of *res judicata*, the effect of Article 59 of the ICJ Statute must be discussed. A point at issue is whether or not rights and interests of third States can be adequately protected by Article 59. In this regard, the Court, in the *Cameroon/Nigeria* case, made an important statement:

> [I]n particular in the case of maritime delimitations where the maritime areas of several States are involved, the protection afforded by Article 59 of the Statute may not always be sufficient. In the present case, Article 59 may not sufficiently protect Equatorial Guinea or Sao Tome and Principle from the effects – even if only indirect – of a judgment affecting their legal rights. ... It follows that, in fixing the maritime boundary between Cameroon and Nigeria, the Court must ensure that it does not adopt any position which might affect the rights of Equatorial Guinea and Sao Tome and Principle.[279]

One cannot deny the possibility that the delimitation line drawn by the Court might affect legal rights and interests of third States creating a presumption of the finality of the boundary, regardless of the formalistic protection of Article 59. In this sense, the decision of the Court could change the status quo so creating a disadvantage to a non-party third State. In particular, the rights over the continental shelf exist *ipso facto* and *ab initio* and they are inherent rights. It is a right *erga omnes*. In such a case, as the Courts indicated, Article 59 may be insufficient to protect the rights of third States.

7.3 Interpretation of Judgments

7.3.1 Requirements for Interpretation

Some elements of obscurity which might be included in a judgment of the ICJ can deter its effective implementation. It would seem simple justice, therefore that a party to a dispute may ask the Court to provide an authoritative interpretation of its judgment. If there are too many requests for interpretation of judgments, however, the authority of *res judicata* is undermined and the implementation of the judgments will be delayed. Hence the procedure for interpretation of judgments of the Court creates particular sensitivity associated with a sound balance between the need to clarify the judgment and the finality of the judgment.

---

[277] *Ibid.*, para. 88; para. 126(1)(b).
[278] See Joint Dissenting Opinion of Vice-President Yusuf, Judges Cançado Trindade, Xue, Gaja, Bhandari, Robinson and Judge ad hoc Brower in the 2016 *Colombia/Nicaragua* case.
[279] ICJ Reports 2002, p. 421, para. 238.

As provided in Article 60 of the ICJ Statute, the interpretation of judgments is limited to clarifying 'the meaning or scope of the judgment'. A party or parties to a dispute cannot request the Court to adjudicate new issues or to change the content of the judgment since this would be contrary to the finality of the judgment. In the words of the ICJ:

> The real purpose of the request must be to obtain an interpretation of the judgment. This signifies that its object must be solely to obtain clarification of the meaning and the scope of what the Court has decided with binding force, and not to obtain an answer to questions not so decided. Any other construction of Article 60 of the Statute would nullify the provision of the article that the judgment is final and without appeal.[280]

Thus the binding character of the judgment must be respected, regardless of a request for interpretation. The decision of the Court on a request for interpretation is to be given in the form of judgment.[281] This judgment is merely declarative in its nature as it merely clarifies the meaning of the original judgment.

To date, a request for the interpretation of judgments has been filed in five cases (see Table 7.4).[282] The requirements for establishing jurisdiction over the request for interpretation and for accepting its admissibility have been specified through the jurisprudence of the ICJ. The principal requirements can be summarised as follows.[283]

First, as the ICJ stated in the *Request for Interpretation of the Judgment of 20 November 1950 in the Asylum Case,* 'it is necessary that there should exist a dispute as to the meaning or scope of the judgment'.[284] The existence of a dispute under Article 60 of the Statute does not require the same criteria to be fulfilled as those determining the existence of a dispute under Article 36(2) of the ICJ Statute.[285] According to the Court, it is not required that a dispute as to the meaning and scope of a judgment should have manifested itself in a formal way; it should be sufficient if the two governments have in fact shown themselves as holding opposite views in regard to the meaning or scope of a judgment of the Court.[286]

---

[280] *Request for Interpretation of the Judgment of 20 November 1950 in the Asylum Case* (Colombia v. Peru), Judgment of 27 November 1950, ICJ Reports 1950, p. 402. See also *Application for Revision and Interpretation of the Judgment of 24 February 1982 in the Case Concerning the Continental Shelf (Tunisia/Libyan Arab Jamahiriya)* (Tunisia v. Libyan Arab Jamahiriya), Judgment of 10 December 1985, ICJ Reports 1985, p. 223, para. 56.

[281] Article 100(2) of the Rules of Court.

[282] A. Zimmermann and T. Thienel, 'Article 60' in *A Commentary,* pp. 1476-8.

[283] The *Temple of Preah Vihear* case (Request for Interpretation), Judgment of 11 November 2013, ICJ Reports 2013, pp. 295-6, paras. 32-4.   [284] ICJ Reports 1950, p. 402.

[285] The *Temple of Preah Vihear* case (Request for the Indication of Provisional Measures), ICJ Reports 2011 (II), p. 542, para. 22.

[286] The *Temple of Preah Vihear* case (Request for Interpretation), ICJ Reports 2013, p. 296, para. 33. Related to this, it is to be noted that the French text of Article 60 of the ICJ Statute uses the term '*contestation*', not '*différend*'. The term '*contestation*' is wider in scope than the term '*différend*'. See *Request for Interpretation of the Judgment of 31 March 2004 in the Case Concerning Avena and Other Mexican Nationals* (Mexico v. United States of America), Request for the Indication of Provisional Measures, Order of 16 July 2008, ICJ Reports 2008, p. 325, para. 53. See also Thirlway, *The International Court of Justice* (2016), p. 190.

TABLE 7.4 REQUESTS FOR INTERPRETATION OF ICJ JUDGMENTS

Year of the Original Judgment	Year of a Request for interpretation	Cases
November 1950	November 1950	*Request for Interpretation of the Judgment of 20 November 1950 in the Asylum case* (Colombia v. Peru)
February 1982	July 1984	*Application for Revision and Interpretation of the Judgment of 24 February 1982 in the Case Concerning the Continental Shelf* (Tunisia/Libya)
June 1998	October 1998	*Request for Interpretation of the Judgment of 11 June 1998 in the Case Concerning the Land and Maritime Boundary between Cameroon and Nigeria* (Preliminary Objections)
March 2004	June 2004	*Request for Interpretation of the Judgment of 31 March 2004 in the Case Concerning Avena and Other Mexican Nationals* (Mexico v. United States of America)
June 1962	April 2011	*Request for Interpretation of the Judgment of 15 June 1962 in the Case Concerning the Temple of Preah Vihear* (Cambodia v. Thailand)

Second, a dispute within the meaning of Article 60 of the Statute must relate to the operative clause of the judgment in question and cannot concern the reasons for the judgment except in so far as these are inseparable from the operative clause.[287] A difference of opinion as to whether a particular point has or has not been decided with binding force constitutes a case which comes within the terms of Article 60 of the Statute.[288] However, parties to a dispute cannot request the Court to adjudicate new issues or to change the content of the judgment.

Third, the request for interpretation can be made at any time.[289] In the *Asylum* case, on the very day on which the judgment was delivered, Colombia requested an interpretation of the judgment.[290] By contrast, around fifty years passed before Cambodia requested the Court to interpret the Judgment which it delivered on 15 June 1962 in the case concerning the *Temple of Preah Vihear*.[291] As shown in the *Temple of Preah Vihear* case, later events could create problems in the implementation of the judgment. Further, caution is needed that a very tardy request may run the risk of being seen as an abuse of the process and contrary to good faith.[292]

---

[287] The *Temple of Preah Vihear* case (Request for Interpretation), Request for the Indication of Provisional Measures, ICJ Reports 2011, p. 542, para. 23.
[288] *Ibid.*, p. 544, para. 31.
[289] Kolb, *The International Court of Justice*, p. 781.
[290] ICJ Reports 1950, p. 396.
[291] Cambodia filed a request for interpretation on 28 April 2011. ICJ Reports 2013, p. 285, para. 1.
[292] Kolb, *The International Court of Justice*, pp. 781–2.

Fourth, it seems logical that the same judges who delivered the original judgment should interpret its meaning or scope. Yet, this becomes impossible if the original judges are no longer members of the Court. In the case of a delayed request for interpretation, it is inevitable that the Court will be composed differently from the time of the original judgment. Judges ad hoc who have participated in the initial proceedings are not entitled to participate in the proceedings of interpretation.[293]

Finally, the Court's jurisdiction on the basis of Article 60 of the Statute is not pre-conditioned by the existence of any other basis of jurisdiction as between the parties to the original case.[294] As suggested by the phrase of Article 60 'upon the request of any party', a party in dispute can unilaterally request interpretation of the judgment of the Court.[295] A unilateral request for interpretation of the judgment was at issue in the *Application for Revision and Interpretation of the Judgment concerning the Tunisia/Libya Case*. Article 3 of the Special Agreement provided that if an agreement on the delimitation line of the continental shelf is not reached within three months, the two parties shall together go back to the Court and request any explanations or clarification of the judgment. Libya argued that a joint request is a necessary condition to request the interpretation of the judgment under Article 3. However, the Court ruled that the jurisdiction of the Court to give an interpretation of judgment is a special jurisdiction deriving directly from Article 60 of the Statute; and that 'the Parties to this case, in becoming parties to the Statute of the Court, have consented to that jurisdiction without pre-condition'.[296] According to the Court, 'it is not lightly to be presumed that a State would renounce or fetter its right under Article 60 of the Statute to request an interpretation unilaterally'.[297] The Court thus concluded that the request made by Tunisia for interpretation in reliance on Article 60 of the ICJ Statute was not affected by Article 3 of the Special Agreement.[298]

7.4 Revision of Judgments

Where the validity of a judgment comes to be questioned on the basis of a newly discovered fact, the requirement of justice will call for a revision of the judgment. In this case, the *res judicata* of the judgment is to be reopened. A sharp tension thus arises between the finality of the judgment and the requirement of justice in individual case. In the ICJ jurisprudence, only a few cases exist in this matter. They are:

---

[293] *Ibid.*, p. 794.
[294] See, in particular, the *Temple of Preah Vihear* case (Request for Interpretation), Request for the Indication of Provisional Measures, ICJ Reports 2011, p. 542, para. 21; *Request for Interpretation of the Judgment of 31 March 2004 in the Case Concerning Avena and Other Mexican Nationals* (Mexico v. United States of America), Provisional Measures, Order of 16 July 2008, ICJ Reports 2008, p. 323, para. 44; Judgment, 19 January 2009, ICJ Reports 2009, p. 9, para. 15. See also, Kolb, *The International Court of Justice*, pp. 779-81.
[295] See also Article 98(2) of the Rules of Court.
[296] *Application for Revision and Interpretation of the Judgment of 24 February 1982 in the Case Concerning the Continental Shelf* (Tunisia/Libyan Arab Jamahiriya), Judgment of 10 December 1985, ICJ Reports 1985, p. 216, para. 43.   [297] *Ibid.*   [298] *Ibid.*

- *Application for Revision and Interpretation of the Judgment of 24 February 1982 in the Case Concerning the Continental Shelf* (Tunisia v. Libya)
- *Application for Revision of the Judgment of 11 July 1996 in the Case Concerning Application of the Genocide Convention* (Bosnia and Herzegovina v. Yugoslavia)
- *Application for Revision of the Judgment of 11 September 1992 in the Case Concerning the Land, Island and Maritime Frontier Dispute* (El Salvador v. Honduras: Nicaragua Intervening)
- *Application for revision of the Judgment delivered by the International Court of Justice (ICJ) on 23 May 2008 in the Case Concerning Sovereignty over Pedra Branca/Pulau Batu Puteh, Middle Rocks and South Ledge* (Malaysia/Singapore) (pending).

The Court declined the requests for revision in the *Tunisia/Libya*, *Bosnia and Herzegovina/Yugoslavia* and *El Salvador/Honduras* cases.

Revision is subject to requirements which are provided in the ICJ Statute and Rules of Court.[299] The requirements for revision can be summarised as follows:[300]

(i) The application should be based upon the 'discovery' of 'fact'.
(ii) The fact the discovery of which is relied on must be 'of such a nature as to be a decisive factor'.
(iii) The fact should have been 'unknown' to the Court and to the party claiming revision when the judgment was given.
(iv) Ignorance of this fact must not be 'due to negligence'.
(v) The application for revision must be 'made at latest within six months of the discovery of the new fact' and before ten years have elapsed from the date of the judgment.

These requirements call for three comments.

First, the burden of proof of the decisiveness of the fact rests on the State applying for revision.[301] The fact concerned must have existed prior to the deliberation of the judgment. Further, it must be unknown both to the Court and to the party seeking revision. However, it is not necessary that the alleged fact is known to the other litigating party.[302] Here the standard of negligence is at issue. In light of the exceptional character of revision proceedings reopening *res judicata*, arguably a high standard can be required.[303] The existence of such negligence was discussed in the Application for Revision and Interpretation of the Judgment concerning the *Tunisia/Libya* case. Tunisia claimed that there was no negligence for its part as its representatives have vainly

---

[299] See Article 61 of the ICJ Statute; Articles 99 and 100 of the Rules of Court.
[300] *Application for Revision of the Judgment of 11 July 1996 in the Case Concerning Application of the Convention on the Prevention and Punishment of the Crime of Genocide (Bosnia and Herzegovina v. Yugoslavia), Preliminary Objections* (Yugoslavia v. Bosnia and Herzegovina), Judgment of 3 February 2003, ICJ Reports 2003, pp. 11–12, para. 16; *Application for Revision of the Judgment of 11 September 1992 in the Case Concerning the Land, Island and Maritime Frontier Dispute* (El Salvador v. Honduras: Nicaragua Intervening), Judgment of 18 December 2003, ICJ Reports 2003, pp. 398–9, para. 19. For a detailed analysis of this issue, see Kolb, *The International Court of Justice*, pp. 807–19.
[301] *Ibid.*, p. 815; *A Commentary*, p. 1518.
[302] Kolb, *The International Court of Justice*, p. 816.
[303] *Ibid.*, p. 817; *A Commentary*, p. 1522.

requested their Libyan counterparts to communicate the coordinates of Concession No. 137.[304] However, Libya contended that while the coordinates of Concession No. 137 were never published, they were readily obtainable in Tripoli. According to Libya, it was also possible to obtain the information from the Libyan National Oil Corporation.[305] In this respect, the Court held that normal diligence would require that a State should first try to learn the exact coordinates of the other party's concession. According to the Court, it is to be expected that a State would not assert that such concession extended to its own area of continental shelf without knowing, or making efforts to discover, the exact limits of the concession. The Court thus concluded that one of the essential conditions for admissibility of a request for revision provided for in Article 61(1) of the Statute, namely ignorance of a new fact not due to negligence, was lacking in this case.[306]

Second, as noted, requests for revision are subject to two time limitations.[307] The first limitation is a relative time limit set out in Article 61(4) of the ICJ Statute, which requires a party to make the application for revision 'at latest within six months of the discovery of the new fact'. A party may discover a new fact at any time; it is only when a party discovered a new fact, the six-month timeframe begins to run. Since the determination of the date of discovery of the new fact is not always clear-cut, the determination of the six-month period may not be very clear. The second limitation is an absolute time limit of ten years. After the lapse of ten years from the date of the judgment, application for revision can no longer be made under Article 61(5) of the ICJ Statute. This limitation aims to secure legal certainty.

Third, revision of the judgment must be confined to points of *res judicata* of the original judgment. Revision is not a mechanism for modifying the original judgment in light of changing circumstances over time, but it concerns the accuracy of the judgment at the time it was delivered.[308]

The seisin of the Court can be either unilateral or joint. To this day, all applications for revision were unilaterally made by one of the litigating parties. A judgment on jurisdiction and admissibility can also be the subject of revision. In fact, the Court, in the *Application for Revision of the Judgment of 11 July 1996 in the Case Concerning Application of the Genocide Convention* between Bosnia and Herzegovina and Yugoslavia, accepted the applicability of Article 61 of the ICJ Statute to the judgment of 1996 with regard to preliminary objections.[309] Although the original judgment was not annulled by the application for revision, the original judgment will no longer be enforceable when a request for revision is accepted.[310]

Unlike interpretation cases, the proceedings for revision cases are divided into two separate stages: the stage of admissibility and that of the merits. The two-stage procedure is reflected in Article 61(2) of the ICJ Statute and Article 99(3) and (4) of the Rules of

---

[304] ICJ Reports 1985, p. 206, para. 26.   [305] *Ibid.*, para. 25.   [306] *Ibid.*, pp. 206–7, paras. 27–8.
[307] Kolb, *The International Court of Justice*, p. 818.   [308] *Ibid.*, p. 808.
[309] ICJ Reports 2003, p. 9, paras. 1 *et seq*. The ICJ eventually concluded that Yugoslavia's request for revision is inadmissible. *Ibid.*, p. 32, para. 73.
[310] Kolb, *The International Court of Justice*, p. 824.

Court.³¹¹ As provided in Article 100(2) of the Rules of Court, the decision of the Court or of the Chamber on a request for revision of a judgment is to be given in the form of a judgment. The judgment is definitive and has the force of *res judicata*.³¹²

7.5 Implementation of Judgments

Under Article 94(1) of the UN Charter, '[e]ach Member of the United Nations undertakes to comply with the decision of the International Court of Justice in any case to which it is a party'. This provision is closely linked to Article 59 of the ICJ Statute. Implementation rests primarily on the parties' spontaneous compliance with the judgment. In fact, the majority of judgments of the Court are normally implemented by the parties.³¹³ Nonetheless, a question arises where one of the parties in dispute refuses to implement the judgment of the Court.

The only provision respecting the implementation of a judgment of the Court is Article 94(2) of the UN Charter:

> 2. If any party to a case fails to perform the obligations incumbent upon it under a judgment rendered by the Court, the other party may have recourse to the Security Council, which may, if it deems necessary, make recommendations or decide upon measures to be taken to give effect to the judgment.

This provision calls for three comments.³¹⁴

First, the recourse to the Security Council under Article 94(2) is allowed only to the party to a case before the ICJ. It seems that third States may also apply to the Security Council under Chapter VI where the non-execution of the judgment might endanger the maintenance of international peace and security. In this case, however, a third State applying to the Security Council relies on Chapter VI, not Article 94(2). The Security Council can also be seised, or can seise itself on the basis of Chapter VII of the UN Charter, if the Council or a Member State considers that the failure to implement the judgment is a threat to international peace and security.³¹⁵

Second, the Security Council is not obliged to act but has a discretionary choice in three respects: (i) whether or not to take action, (ii) whether to recommend or decide and (iii) as to the exact content of the recommendations or decisions.³¹⁶ However, the Security Council cannot modify or substitute its own assessment of the merits for that of the ICJ since the judgment is final and unappealable under Article 59 of the ICJ Statute. As the ICJ Statute is an integral part of the UN Charter, it is apparent that the Security Council is bound by the Charter and the Statute.³¹⁷

---

[311] Emphasis added. In this regard, Kolb questioned the necessity of the two-stage procedure. Kolb, *The International Court of Justice*, pp. 823–4.
[312] *Ibid.*, p. 822.   [313] *Ibid.*, p. 831.   [314] *Ibid.*, pp. 833–5.   [315] *Ibid.*, p. 845.
[316] *Ibid.*, p. 849.   [317] *Ibid.*, pp. 851–2.

Third, Article 94(2) refers only to the non-execution of a 'judgment' (in French '*arrêt*'), whilst Article 94(1) refers to the 'decision' (in French '*décision*'). In this regard, an issue arises as to whether orders indicating provisional measures under Article 41 of the ICJ Statute fall within the scope of the 'judgment'. Given that provisional measures ordered by the ICJ are binding upon the parties, some argue that the procedure under Article 94(2) is also applicable to non-implementation of provisional measures.[318] This view has not yet been tested.

In reality, very little use has been made of this provision. A major difficulty in this regard is that recommendations or decisions rest on the political will of the Security Council. If the Security Council lacks the political will to deal with a disobedient party, it will be highly difficult for other States to enforce a judgment of the Court. In the *Nicaragua* case, for instance, the Security Council was unable to demand that the United States should comply with the duties cast upon by the Court's judgment because of the use of the United States veto,[319] while the UN General Assembly urgently called for full and immediate compliance with the Nicaragua judgment.[320]

Some constitutive instruments of international organisations allow their organs to take certain action if one of the Member States fails to implement a judgment of the Court. For instance, Article 33 of the Constitution of the International Labour Organisation (ILO) empowers the Governing Body to recommend to the General Conference such action as it may deem wise and expedient to secure compliance therewith.[321] Article 88 of the Constitution of the ICAO allows its Assembly to suspend the voting rights in the Assembly and in the Council of a member which has failed to comply with an arbitral award or with a judgment of the PCIJ (ICJ) to which it is a party.[322]

8 CONCLUSIONS

The above considerations reveal that procedural rules of the ICJ have been developed through the jurisprudence of the Court. The principal points discussed in this chapter can be summarised as follows:

(i) The distinction between *lex lata* and *lex ferenda* is a legal orthodoxy and this is repeatedly confirmed in the ICJ jurisprudence. Where an existing rule of customary law is being replaced by an emergent customary law, however, the mechanical application of *lex lata* encounters difficulty because the Court's decision may soon fall into desuetude. In this case, as shown in the *Fishery Jurisdiction* case, an element of *lex ferenda* can affect the *manner* of the interpretation and application of *lex lata*.

---

[318] *Ibid.*, pp. 847–8.
[319] Collier and Lowe, *The Settlement of Disputes*, p. 178.
[320] UN General Assembly, 41/31. Judgment of the International Court of Justice of 27 June 1986 concerning military and paramilitary activities in and against Nicaragua: need for immediate compliance, 3 November 1986.
[321] The electronic text is available at: www.ilo.org/public/english/bureau/leg/download/constitution.pdf.
[322] The electronic text is available at: www.mcgill.ca/files/iasl/chicago1944a.pdf; www.icao.int/publications/Documents/7300_orig.pdf.

(ii) Non-appearance creates challenges for both a respondent State and the ICJ since the non-appearance of a respondent State puts the applicant State and the Court in a difficult position owing to the lack of information. Given that the non-appearing State is likely to fail to implement the judgment of the Court, it also entails the risk of undermining the effectiveness of the judgment.

(iii) Article 79(1) of the Rules of Court recognise three kinds of preliminary objection: objection to the jurisdiction of the Court, to the admissibility of the application, and any other objection. If an objection is upheld, the case comes to an end. If the Court considers that the objection does not possess an exclusively preliminary character, the Court proceeds to hear the merits. The Court has a wide discretion to determine whether an objection is of exclusively preliminary character.

(iv) To indicate provisional measures, the following requirements must be fulfilled:

- *prima facie* jurisdiction
- plausible character of the alleged rights in the principal request
- link between the alleged rights and the measures requested
- urgency
- risk of irreparable prejudice.

Provisional measures indicated by the Court are increasingly diverse. Notably, provisional measures were repeatedly indicated by the Court to cease the execution of individuals. Further, the Court regarded the loss of life as irreparable damage to the rights of a State. The Court's practice appears to exemplify the impact of humanitarian consideration on procedural rules concerning provisional measures.

(v) In order to safeguard rights and interests of third States, two different forms of intervention are set out under the ICJ Statute. Intervention under Article 62 seeks to safeguard an interest of a legal nature of a third State which may be affected by the decision in the case, while intervention under Article 63 concerns the interpretation of a multilateral convention in question, to which States other than those concerned in the case are parties. Intervention under Article 62 of the ICJ Statute can be divided into two categories: intervention as a party and non-party intervention. In the case of non-party intervention under Article 62, no jurisdictional link is required between the would-be intervener and the original litigating parties. In the case of intervention as a party, however, such a linkage is needed. It is argued that a non-party intervener is not bound by the Court's decision, whilst the decision of the Court is binding upon an intervener as a party.

(vi) The judgment of the Court is binding upon the parties to a case and creates a *res judicata*. In consequence, the parties to a dispute cannot reopen the same dispute before the Court. The principle of *res judicata* is important to stabilise legal relations between the litigating parties. Where the validity of a judgment comes into question on the basis of a newly discovered fact, however, a litigating party may call for a revision of the judgment. As revision of the judgment is an exception to the principle of *res judicata*, it must be subject to requirements set out in the ICJ Statute and Rules of Court.

(vii) An evident weakness of the Court's judgments is that there is no effective mechanism for securing effective compliance with them. Indeed, the function of the

Security Council under Article 94(2) of the UN Charter is of only limited utility in practice.

FURTHER READING

Proceedings of the Court

S. A. Alexandrov, 'Non-Appearance before the International Court of Justice' (1995) 33 *Columbia Journal of Transnational Law*, pp. 41–72.

M. Benzing, 'Community Interests in the Procedure of International Courts and Tribunals' (2006) 5 *The Law and Practice of International Courts and Tribunals*, pp. 369–408.

J. G. Devaney, *Fact-Finding before the International Court of Justice* (Cambridge University Press, 2016).

G. Fitzmaurice, 'The Problem of the "Non-Appearing" Defendant Government' (1980) 51 *BYIL*, pp. 89–122.

M. Forteau, 'Les Techniques interprétative de la Court internationale de Justice' (2011) 115 *RGDIP*, pp. 399–416.

J. D. Fry, 'Non-Participation in the International Court of Justice Revisited: Change or Plus Ça Change?' (2010) 49 *Columbia Journal of Transnational Law*, pp. 35–74.

A. Riddell and B. Plant, *Evidence before the International Court of Justice* (London: British Institute of International and Comparative Law, 2009).

M. P. Scharf and M. Day, 'The International Court of Justice's Treatment of Circumstantial Evidence and Adverse Inferences' (2012) 13 *Chicago Journal of International Law*, pp. 123–51.

Y. Tanaka, 'Rethinking *Lex Ferenda* in International Adjudication' (2008) 51 *GYIL*, pp. 467–95.

H. Thirlway, *Non-Appearance before the International Court of Justice* (Cambridge University Press, 1985).

'The Drafting of ICJ Decisions: Some Personal Recollections and Observations' (2006) 5 *CJIL*, pp. 15–28.

Preliminary Objections

A. Coleman, 'The International Court of Justice and Highly Political Matters' (2003) 4 *Melbourne Journal of International Law*, pp. 29–75.

R. Higgings, 'Policy Considerations and the International Judicial Process' (1968) 17 *ICLQ*, pp. 58–84.

K. Oellers-Frahm, 'The Principle of Consent to International Jurisdiction: Is It Still Alive?: Observations on the Judgment on Preliminary Objections in the Case Concerning Application of the Convention on the Prevention and Punishment of the Crime of Genocide (Croatia v. Serbia)' (2010) 52 *GYIL*, pp. 487–524.

T. Sugihara, 'The Judicial Function of the International Court of Justice with Respect to Disputes Involving Highly Political Issues' in A. S. Muller *et al.* (eds.), *The International Court of Justice: Its Future Role after Fifty Years* (The Hague: Kluwer, 1997), pp. 117–38.

Provisional Measures

C. Dominicé, 'La Compétence *prima facie* de la Cour international de Justice aux fins d'indication de measures conservatoires' in N. Ando, E. McWhinney and R. Wolfrum (eds.), *Liber Amicorum Judge Shigeru Oda* (The Hague: Kluwer, 2002), pp. 383–95.

Y. Iwamoto (Lee), 'The Protection of Human Life through Provisional Measures Indicated by the International Court of Justice' (2002) 15 *LJIL*, pp. 345–66.

J. Kammerhofer, 'The Binding Nature of Provisional Measures of International Court of Justice: The "Settlement" of the Issue in the *LaGrand* Case' (2003) 16 *LJIL*, pp. 67–83.

B. Kempen and Zan He, 'The Practice of the International Court of Justice on Provisional Measures: The Recent Development' (2009) 69 *ZaöRV*, pp. 919–29.

R. Kolb, 'Note on New International Case-Law Concerning the Binding Character of Provisional Measures' (2005) 74 *NJIL*, pp. 117–29.

A. G. Koroma, 'Provisional Measures in Disputes Between African States before the International Court of Justice' in L. Boisson de Chazournes and V. Gowlland-Debbas (eds.), *The International Legal System in Quest of Equity and Universality, Liber Amicorum Georges Abi-Saab* (The Hague: Nijhoff, 2001), pp. 591–602.

J. G. Merrills, 'Interim Measures of Protection in the Recent Jurisprudence of the ICJ' (1995) 44 *ICLQ*, pp. 90–146.

A. Orakhelashvili, 'Questions of International Judicial Jurisdiction in the *LaGrand* Case' (2002) 15 *LJIL*, pp. 105–30.

P. Palchetti, 'The Power of the International Court of Justice to Indicate Provisional Measures to Prevent the Aggravation of a Dispute' (2008) 21 *LJIL*, pp. 623–42.

S. Rosenne, 'Provisional Measures and Prima Facie Jurisdiction Revisited' in N. Ando, E. McWhinney and R. Wolfrum (eds.), *Liber Amicorum Judge Shigeru Oda* (The Hague: Kluwer, 2002), pp. 515–44.

Provisional Measures in International Law: The International Court of Justice and the International Tribunal for the Law of the Sea (Oxford University Press, 2005).

J. Sztucki, *Interim Measures in the Hague Court* (Deventer: Kluwer, 1983).

Y. Tanaka, 'A New Phase of the *Temple of Preah Vihear* Case before the International Court of Justice: Reflections on the Indication of Provisional Measures of 18 July 2011' (2012) 11 *CJIL*, pp. 191–226.

I. Uchkunova, 'Provisional Measures before the International Court of Justice' (2013) 12 *The Law and Practice of International Courts and Tribunals*, pp. 391–430.

G. Zyberi, 'Provisional Measures of the International Court of Justice in Armed Conflict Situations' (2010) 23 *LJIL*, pp. 571–84.

Judgment

A. P. Liamzon, 'Jurisdiction and Compliance in Recent Decisions of the International Court of Justice' (2008) 18 *EJIL*, pp. 815–52.

A. V. Lowe, '*Res Judicata* and the Rule of Law in International Arbitration' (1996) 8 *African Journal of International and Comparative Law*, pp. 38–50.

C. Schulte, *Compliance with Decisions of the International Court of Justice* (Oxford University Press, 2004).

I. Scobbie, 'Res Judicata, Precedent and the International Court: A Preliminary Sketch' (1999) 20 *Australian Yearbook of International Law*, pp. 299–318.

Part II

International Dispute Settlement in Particular Fields

OUTLINE OF PART II

8   International Dispute Settlement in the UN Convention on the Law of the Sea   229
9   The WTO Dispute Settlement System   275
10   Peaceful Settlement of International Environmental Disputes   311
11   Peaceful Settlement of Disputes Involving Non-State Actors   334
12   The Quest for Peace in International Law   382

International Dispute Settlement in the UN Convention on the Law of the Sea

Main Issues

Generally, the effectiveness of mechanisms for the peaceful settlement of international disputes can be said to rely on a sound balance between voluntary and compulsory procedures. Thus the reconciliation of these elements should be an important issue when establishing mechanisms of international dispute settlement. The dispute settlement system in the LOSC provides a useful insight into this issue. This chapter will seek to examine the law and procedure of the dispute settlement system in the LOSC. In particular, the following issues will be discussed:[1]

(i) What are the principal features of the procedures of international dispute settlement in the LOSC?
(ii) What is the significance of the compulsory procedures for dispute settlement in the LOSC and what are their limitations?
(iii) What is the difference between the ICJ and ITLOS?
(iv) What is the role of arbitral tribunals under the LOSC in the settlement of disputes concerning marine affairs?
(v) Do the multiple judicial bodies set out in the LOSC create a fragmentation of international law?

1 INTRODUCTION

The ever-increasing use of the oceans necessitates international rules regulating various human activities at sea. The body of international rules that bind States and other subjects of international law in their marine affairs is called the international law of the sea. A global legal framework for governing the oceans was established by the LOSC, adopted in 1982.[2] The Convention that comprises 320 Articles and nine Annexes covers marine issues in a quasi-comprehensive manner. As the LOSC represents a complex balance of

---

[1] This chapter relies on the following study of the author with modifications and updates. Y. Tanaka, *The International Law of the Sea*, 2nd edn (Cambridge University Press, 2015), Chapter 13.
[2] 1833 *UNTS*, p. 3. Entered into force on 16 November 1994.

interests of various actors, however, international disputes are likely to arise with regard to its interpretation and application. Thus the establishment of the system of international dispute settlement is crucial in its implementation. The system of international dispute settlement under the Convention is characterised by three principal features.

The first noteworthy feature is that the dispute settlement system is set out as an integral part of the Convention. In this regard, the LOSC shows a clear contrast with the Optional Protocol Concerning Compulsory Settlement of Dispute, which was adopted as a distinct treaty at the First United Nations Conference on the Law of the Sea in 1958.[3] The built-in dispute settlement system, including the compulsory procedures, can be considered as an important tool for securing the integrity of the interpretation and application of the Convention.

The second noteworthy feature concerns the multiplicity of dispute settlement forums. As will be seen, the LOSC creates a flexible system whereby State Parties may choose one or more different procedures for compulsory settlement set out in Part XV of the Convention.

The third important feature pertains to the establishment of a new permanent judicial body: ITLOS. While ITLOS is largely modelled on the ICJ, it includes some new elements, such as a wide range of *locus standi* before the Tribunal.

Following the introduction, this chapter addresses the interlinkage between voluntary and compulsory procedures of international dispute settlement (section 2). It then examines compulsory procedures of international dispute settlement (section 3). Next, it moves on to examine the law and procedure of ITLOS (section 4) and the role of arbitration under the LOSC (section 5), respectively. Finally, conclusions are presented in section 6.

2 INTERLINKAGE BETWEEN VOLUNTARY AND COMPULSORY PROCEDURES OF INTERNATIONAL DISPUTE SETTLEMENT

2.1 The Interlinkage between Voluntary and Compulsory Procedures

Part XV of the LOSC, which is devoted to the dispute settlement procedures, consists of three sections:

- Section 1: General provisions and voluntary dispute settlement procedures
- Section 2: Compulsory procedures for dispute settlement
- Section 3: Limitations and optional exceptions to the compulsory procedures.

Rules on international dispute settlement are also provided in other parts of the Convention, such as Section 5 of Part XI concerning dispute settlement and advisory opinions by the Sea-Bed Disputes Chamber of ITLOS, Annex V (Conciliation), Annex VI (ITLOS), Annex VII (Arbitration) and Annex VIII (Special Arbitration).

Generally, the effectiveness of mechanisms of international dispute settlement relies on a sound balance between voluntary and compulsory procedure. In this regard, the LOSC establishes a two-tiered system. According to this system, as the first step, States Parties must

---

[3] 450 *UNTS*, 169. Entered into force 30 September 1962.

settle any dispute between them concerning the interpretation or application of the LOSC by peaceful means of their own choice.[4] It follows that peaceful settlement means chosen by the parties will prevail over dispute settlement procedures embodied in Part XV of the LOSC.[5] Where the disputing parties cannot settle a dispute through non-compulsory procedures, as the second step, that dispute must be settled in accordance with the compulsory procedures set out in Section 2 of Part XV. Three conditions must be fulfilled in order to set in motion the compulsory procedures: obligation to exchange views (Article 283), non-existence of a special agreement precluding the compulsory procedure of the LOSC (Article 281) and non-existence of an agreed procedure that entails a binding decision (Article 282).

2.1.1 Obligation to Exchange Views

Article 283 of the LOSC obliges the parties in dispute to proceed expeditiously to an exchange of views as a preliminary to any further steps. According to the Arbitral Tribunal in the *Chagos Marine Protected Area* case, Article 283 was intended to ensure that a State would not be taken entirely by surprise by the initiation of compulsory proceedings.[6] The obligation to exchange views under Article 283 was discussed in the 2001 *MOX Plant* case (provisional measures). In this case, the United Kingdom contended that the correspondence between Ireland and the United Kingdom did not amount to an exchange of views on the dispute under the LOSC and that its request for an exchange of views under Article 283 was not accepted by Ireland.[7] However, ITLOS did not accept the argument of the United Kingdom, stating that: '[A] State Party is not obliged to continue with an exchange of views when it concludes that the possibilities of reaching agreement have been exhausted.'[8] Furthermore, ITLOS, in the 2016 *M/V 'Norstar'* case, ruled that the absence of a response from one State Party to an attempt by another State Party to exchange views on the means of dispute settlement does not prevent the tribunal from finding that the requirements of Article 283 have been fulfilled.[9]

The interpretation of Article 283 was further elaborated by the Annex VII Arbitral Tribunal in the 2015 *Chagos Marine Protected Area* arbitration. In this case, the Tribunal took the following position:

> Article 283 thus requires the Parties to exchange views regarding the means for resolving their dispute; it does not require the Parties to in fact engage in negotiations or other forms of peaceful dispute resolution. As a matter of textual construction, the Tribunal considers that Article 283 cannot be understood as an obligation to negotiate the substance of the dispute.[10]

---

[4] LOSC, Articles 279 and 280.
[5] See LOSC, Articles 281 and 282.
[6] *Chagos Marine Protected Area* arbitration (Mauritius v. United Kingdom), Award of 18 March 2015, para. 382.
[7] The MOX Plant case (Provisional Measures) (Ireland v. United Kingdom) (2002) 41 ILM p. 413, paras. 56–7.
[8] *Ibid.*, p. 414, para. 60. The *dictum* was subsequently confirmed by ITLOS. See *Land Reclamation in and around the Straits of Johor* (Malaysia v. Singapore), Provisional Measures, Order of 8 October 2003, ITLOS Reports 2003, p. 10, para. 48; *ARA 'Libertad'* (Argentina v. Ghana), Provisional Measures, Order of 15 December 2012, ITLOS Reports 2012, p. 332, para. 71; the *M/V 'Norstar'* case (Panama v. Italy), Preliminary Objections, 4 November 2016, ITLOS Case No. 25, para. 216.
[9] *Ibid.*, para. 215.   [10] *Chagos Marine Protected Area*, para. 378.

This view was subsequently echoed by the Annex VII Arbitral Tribunal in the *'Arctic Sunrise'* arbitration[11] and the 2015 *Philippine/China* arbitration.[12]

2.1.2 Non-Existence of a Special Agreement Precluding the Compulsory Procedure of the LOSC

This requirement is provided in Article 281 of the Convention:

> 1. If the States Parties which are parties to a dispute concerning the interpretation or application of this Convention have agreed to seek settlement of the dispute by a peaceful means of their own choice, the procedures provided for in this Part apply only where no settlement has been reached by recourse to such means and the agreement between the parties does not exclude any further procedure.
> 2. If the parties have also agreed on a time limit, paragraph 1 applies only upon the expiration of that time limit.

As the Conciliation Committee observed in the 2016 *Timor-Leste/Australia case*, Article 281 forms part of a compromise on dispute settlement that was carefully negotiated at the UNCLOS III where some States favoured recourse to the compulsory settlement of disputes, while others sought to exclude it entirely from the LOSC.[13] This provision contains three requirements: (i) the disputing parties must have exhausted dispute settlement procedures on the basis of mutual agreement, (ii) that agreement does not exclude resort to the procedures provided in the LOSC and (iii) any agreed time limits have expired.[14] If one of the requirements has not been met, the procedures under Part XV of the LOSC do not apply. As will be discussed in section 6 of this chapter, the interpretation of the second requirement is not free from controversy.

In the *Timor-Leste/Australia* conciliation, an issue arose whether an 'agreement' under Article 281 means a legally binding agreement. Article 281 stands adjacent to Article 282 which contemplates formal and binding agreements. In this regard, the Conciliation Commission did not consider that the text of the LOSC would support significantly different meanings to the same terms appearing in two parallel articles. Neither did it consider that a reading of Article 281 that would permit a non-binding agreement to preclude the application of the compulsory dispute settlement provisions of Part XV would be consistent with the fact that Part XV of the Convention is itself a binding agreement. Hence the commission took the view that Article 281 requires a legally binding agreement.[15]

---

[11] The *'Arctic Sunrise'* arbitration (The Netherlands v. the Russian Federation), Award on Merits, 14 August 2015, p. 34, para. 151, available at: https://pca-cpa.org/en/cases. In this case, the exchange of views was brief and one-sided in the sense that Russia made no counter-proposal or accepted the proposal to arbitrate. Nonetheless, the Arbitral Tribunal considered that the requirement for an exchange of views set out in the LOSC was satisfied. *Ibid.*, pp. 35–6, paras. 154–6.

[12] PCA Case No. 2013–19, the *Philippine/China* arbitration (Jurisdiction and Admissibility), 29 October 2015, p. 115, para. 333, available at: https://pca-cpa.org/en/cases.

[13] A Conciliation Commission Constituted under Annex V to the 1982 United Nations Convention on the Law of the Sea between the Democratic Republic of Timor-Leste and the Commonwealth of Australia, Decision on Australia's Objections to Competence, 19 September 2016, para. 49, available at: https://pca-cpa.org/en/cases.

[14] The *Philippine/China* arbitration (Jurisdiction and Admissibility), p. 76, para. 195.

[15] The *Timor-Leste/Australia* conciliation, pp. 13–14, paras. 56–8.

2.1.3 Non-Existence of an Agreed Procedure that Entails a Binding Decision
Under Article 282 of the LOSC:

> If the States Parties which are parties to a dispute concerning the interpretation or application of this Convention have agreed, through a general, regional or bilateral agreement or otherwise, that such dispute shall, at the request of any party to the dispute, be submitted to a procedure that entails a binding decision, that procedure shall apply in lieu of the procedures provided for in this Part, unless the parties to the dispute otherwise agree.

The legal effect of Article 282 was tested in the 2001 *MOX Plant* case. In this case, the United Kingdom asserted that the main elements of the dispute submitted to the Annex VII Arbitral Tribunal were governed by the compulsory procedures for dispute settlement in the Convention for the Protection of the Marine Environment of the North-East Atlantic (OSPAR Convention) or the European Community (EC) Treaty or the Euratom Treaty and that the Arbitral Tribunal would not have jurisdiction.[16] On this issue, ITLOS considered that the dispute settlement procedures under the OSPAR Convention, the EC Treaty and the Euratom Treaty deal with disputes with regard to the interpretation and application of those agreements, and do not deal with disputes arising under the LOSC. Since the dispute before the Annex VII Arbitral Tribunal concerned the interpretation or application of the LOSC, only the dispute settlement procedure under that Convention was relevant to the dispute. The Tribunal thus concluded that for the purpose of determining prima facie jurisdiction of the Annex VII Arbitral Tribunal, Article 282 was not applicable to the dispute submitted to the Tribunal.[17]

Nonetheless, the Annex VII Arbitral Tribunal, in the *MOX Plant* case of 2003, took a different view in this matter.[18] According to the Tribunal, if the interpretation of the LOSC fell within the exclusive competence of the European Court of Justice, it would preclude the jurisdiction of the Tribunal entirely by virtue of Article 282 of the Convention. It follows that the determination of the Tribunal's jurisdiction relied essentially on the resolution of this question. In the view of the Arbitral Tribunal, the question is to be decided within the institutions of the European Community, particularly by the European Court of Justice. Furthermore, the European Commission has indicated that it is examining the question whether to institute proceedings under Article 226 of the European Community Treaty. Accordingly, 'bearing in mind considerations of mutual respect and comity', the Arbitral Tribunal decided that further proceedings on both jurisdiction and the merits in this arbitration would be suspended.[19] The arbitral award thus demonstrated that Article 282 may take effect to prevent recourse to compulsory procedures for dispute settlement under the LOSC.

A related issue that arises in this context concerns the interrelationship between the optional clause of the ICJ and Article 282. There appears to be little doubt that the optional clause under Article 36(2) of the Statute of the ICJ is 'a procedure that entails a

---

[16] The *MOX Plant* case (Provisional Measures), p. 412, paras. 43–4. [17] *Ibid.*, paras. 49–53.
[18] The *MOX Plant* case, Order No. 3, 24 June 2003. The order is available at: https://cpa-pca.org/en/cases.
[19] *Ibid.*, pp. 7–9, paras. 22–9.

binding decision' set out in Article 282. It would seem to follow that between two States which have accepted the optional clause, the jurisdiction of the ICJ prevails over procedures under Part XV of the LOSC by virtue of Article 282.[20]

The interrelationship between the optional clause of the ICJ and Article 282 was at issue in the 2016 *Somalia/Kenya* case (preliminary objections).[21] Article 282 provides that an agreement to submit a dispute to a specified procedure that applies in lieu of the compulsory procedures in Section 2 of Part XV may not only be contained in a 'general, regional or bilateral agreement' but may also be reached 'otherwise'. Here the Court considered that the phrase 'or otherwise' in Article 282 encompasses agreement to the jurisdiction of the Court resulting from optional clause declarations.[22] According to the Court, this interpretation can also be supported by *travaux préparatoires* of the LOSC.[23] Therefore, the Court concluded that under Article 282, the optional clause declarations of the parties constitute an agreement, reached 'otherwise', to settle in the Court disputes concerning interpretation or application of the LOSC.[24]

A more contentious issue concerned the effect of Kenya's reservation to the optional clause, which precludes disputes 'in regard to which the parties to the dispute have agreed or shall agree to have recourse to some other method or methods of settlement'. A point at issue is whether compulsory procedures under the LOSC can be regarded as other methods agreed by the parties and, thus, procedures under the Convention applies as *lex specialis*. In this regard, the ICJ took the view that: '[T]here is no indication in the *travaux préparatoires* of an intention to exclude from the scope of Article 282 the majority of optional clause declarations, i.e., those containing such reservations'; and that: 'Article 282 should therefore be interpreted so that an agreement to the Court's jurisdiction through optional clause declarations falls within the scope of that Article and applies "in lieu" of procedures provided for in Section 2 of Part XV, even when such declarations contain a reservation to the same effect as that of Kenya.'[25] Yet, the Court's reasoning on the basis of the *travaux préparatoires* seems to be weak.[26] Given that compulsory procedures under the LOSC provide alternative, more specialised, methods of dispute settlement, there appears to be some basis to argue that the parties agreed to apply the compulsory procedures under the LOSC as *lex specialis* by ratifying the Convention and that the compulsory procedures under the Convention would fall within the scope of Kenya's reservation.[27] In any case, while at a general

---

[20] This view was supported by commentators, including: A. Boyle, 'Problems of Compulsory Jurisdiction and the Settlement of Disputes Relating to Straddling Fish Stocks' (1999) 14 *IJMCL*, p. 7; P. Gautier, 'The Settlement of Disputes' in D. Attard, M. Fitzmaurice and N. Gutiérrez (eds.), *The IMLI Manual on International Maritime Law, Vol. I: The Law of the Sea* (Oxford University Press, 2014), p. 539; T. Treves, 'Conflicts between the International Tribunal for the Law of the Sea and the International Court of Justice' (1999) 31, *New York University Journal of International Law and Politics*, p. 812; P. C. Rao, 'Law of the Sea, Settlement of Disputes' in *Max Planck Encyclopaedia*, para. 11.
[21] Kenya and Somalia ratified the LOSC on 2 March and 24 July 1989, respectively.
[22] *Maritime Delimitation in the Indian Ocean* (Somalia v. Kenya), Preliminary Objections, Judgment of 2 February 2016, ICJ Reports 2016 (not yet reported), para. 128.
[23] *Ibid.*, paras. 127 and 129.   [24] *Ibid.*, para. 130.   [25] *Ibid.*, paras. 129–30.
[26] Dissenting Opinion of Judge Robinson, *ibid.*, para. 21.
[27] *Ibid.*, para. 31. See also presentation by Boyle, Verbatim Record, CR 2012/12, 21 September 2016, pp. 28–31, paras. 5–14.

level optional clause declarations are covered by Article 282, the effect of reservations to the declarations needs to be determined in a specific context.

2.2 Conciliation

The LOSC provides for two types of conciliation: voluntary conciliation and mandatory conciliation.[28] Voluntary conciliation is set out in Section 1 of Part XV. Under Article 284(1) of the Convention, a State Party which is a party to a dispute concerning the interpretation or application of this Convention may invite the other party or parties to submit the dispute to conciliation in accordance with the procedure under Annex V, Section 1, or another conciliation procedure. As this is a *voluntary* conciliation, consent of disputing parties is needed to submit the dispute to conciliation.[29] When a dispute has been submitted to conciliation, the proceedings may be terminated only in accordance with the agreed conciliation procedure, unless the parties otherwise agree pursuant to Article 284(4).

The procedure for voluntary conciliation is provided in Section 1 of Annex V of the LOSC in some detail. Under Article 3 of Annex V, the conciliation commission shall consist of five members. Two conciliators are appointed by each party and a fifth conciliator, who shall be chairperson, is appointed by the parties to the dispute. In case of disagreement between the parties, the UN Secretary-General shall make the necessary appointment. After examination of claims and objections by the parties, the commission makes proposals to the parties with a view to reaching an amicable settlement pursuant to Article 6 of Annex V. The commission is required to report within twelve months of its constitution. Its report shall record any agreements reached and, failing agreement, its conclusions on all questions of fact or law relevant to the matter in dispute and recommendations appropriate for an amicable settlement. The report is to be deposited with the UN Secretary-General and shall immediately be transmitted by him to the disputing parties. The report of the commission shall not be binding upon the parties.[30] The fees and expenses of the commission are to be borne by the parties to the dispute.[31]

Under Article 8 of Annex V, the conciliation proceedings are terminated when a settlement has been reached, when the parties have accepted or one party has rejected the recommendations of the report by written notification addressed to the UN Secretary-General or when a period of three months has expired from the date of transmission of the report to the parties. It follows that a dispute remains unsettled if one of the disputing parties has rejected the recommendations of the conciliation report. In this case, the dispute is to be transferred to the compulsory procedures for the settlement of dispute.

Section 2 of Annex V of the LOSC provides compulsory submission to conciliation procedure pursuant to Section 3 of Part XV. As we shall discuss next,[32] the compulsory conciliation procedure applies to the disputes which are exempted from compulsory procedures entailing binding decisions under Section 2, Part XV of the LOSC.

---

[28] Generally on this issue, see S. Yee, 'Conciliation and the 1982 UN Convention on the Law of the Sea' (2013) 44 *ODIL*, pp. 315–34.
[29] See, LSOC, Article 284(2) and (3).   [30] LOSC, Article 7 of Annex V.
[31] LOSC, Article 9 of Annex V.   [32] See section 3.2 of this chapter.

3 COMPULSORY PROCEDURES OF INTERNATIONAL DISPUTE SETTLEMENT

3.1 Multiplicity of Forums: Montreux Formula

3.1.1 Selection of a Forum

Where no settlement has been reached by recourse to Section 1 of Part XV, subject to Section 3, any dispute concerning the interpretation or application of the LOSC shall be submitted at the request of any party to the dispute to the court or tribunal having jurisdiction under Section 2.[33] Here the issue arises of which court or tribunal has jurisdiction over the dispute. In this regard, the LOSC provides the formula for flexibly choosing one or more of the four different forums for compulsory procedures.[34] This is called 'Montreux formula' because it was suggested by the Working Group's weekend meeting in Montreux at the 1975 Geneva session.[35] The four forums are:

- ITLOS
- ICJ
- an arbitral tribunal constituted in accordance with Annex VII
- a special arbitral tribunal constituted in accordance with Annex VIII.

While the ICJ and ITLOS are standing courts, arbitral tribunals under Annexes VII and VIII are to be established in an ad hoc manner.

The key issue in the Montreux formula concerns the selection of relevant forums of international dispute settlement. Under Article 287(1) of the LOSC, when signing, ratifying or acceding to the LOSC or at any time thereafter, a State is free to choose, by means of a written declaration, one or more of these four means for the settlement of disputes concerning the interpretation or application of the Convention.[36] If the parties to a dispute have accepted the same procedure for dispute settlement, it may be submitted only to that procedure, unless the parties otherwise agree under Article 287(4). If no declaration is made, a State Party shall be deemed to have accepted arbitration in accordance with Annex VII.[37] If the disputing parties have not accepted the same procedure for dispute settlement, it may be submitted only to arbitration in accordance with Annex VII, unless the parties otherwise agree pursuant to Article 287(5). In this sense, the Annex VII arbitration has residual jurisdiction. Since many States have made no declarations on the choice of dispute settlement means, the role of the Annex VII arbitral tribunal is particularly important.[38] The multiple forums call for three observations.

---

[33] LOSC, Article 286.   [34] LOSC, Article 287.
[35] A. O. Adede, *The System of Settlement of Disputes under the United Nations Convention on the Law of the Sea: A Drafting History and a Commentary* (Dordrecht: Nijhoff, 1987), p. 243; by the same writer, 'The Basic Structure of the Dispute Settlement Part of the Law of the Sea Convention' (1982) 11 *ODIL*, pp. 130–1.
[36] An updated list of choice of procedure under Article 287 is available at the website of UNDOALOS: www.un.org/Depts/los/settlement_of_disputes/choice_procedure.htm.
[37] LOSC, Article 287(3).   [38] See section 5.1 of this chapter.

First, where a State has chosen more than one forum, collaboration between the disputing States will be needed in order to identify a relevant forum even in the compulsory procedures. For instance, several States, such as Australia, Belgium, Estonia, Finland, Italy, Latvia, Oman and Spain, have chosen the ICJ and ITLOS without any order. If a dispute was raised between the two States, it would be necessary to exchange views to identify a relevant forum in accordance with Article 283(2) of the LOSC.

Second, in the event of a dispute as to whether a court or tribunal has jurisdiction, the matter shall be settled by a decision of that court or tribunal pursuant to Article 288(4) of the LSOC. In this regard, the LOSC provides a unique procedure for preliminary proceedings with a view to preventing abuse of the legal process. Under Article 294(1), a court or tribunal provided for in Article 287 to which an application is made in respect of a dispute referred to in Article 297 shall determine at the request of a party, or may determine *proprio motu*, whether the claim constitutes an abuse of legal process or whether *prima facie* it is well founded. If the court or tribunal determines that the claim constitutes an abuse of legal process or is *prima facie* unfounded, it shall take no further action in the case. This provision seeks to address the concerns expressed by some developing coastal States that they might be exposed to frequent legal actions by shipping States and would have to be involved in costly procedures in international courts and tribunals.[39] Preliminary proceedings must be distinguished from preliminary objections. In fact, Article 294(3) makes clear that nothing in this Article affects the right of any party to a dispute to make preliminary objections in accordance with the applicable rules of procedure.

Third, even if no declaration is made under Article 287 of the LOSC, ITLOS has compulsory jurisdiction over the request for the prompt release of vessels and crews[40] and the request for provisional measures,[41] unless the parties otherwise agree.

Fourth, as ITLOS observed in the *M/V 'Louisa'* case, 'in cases where States Parties have made declarations of differing scope under article 287 of the Convention, its jurisdiction exists only to the extent to which the substance of the declarations of the two parties to a dispute coincides'.[42] Related to this, ITLOS, in the *M/V 'Norstar'* case, took the view that the LOSC does not preclude a declaration limited to a particular dispute.[43]

3.2 Limitations and Exceptions to the Compulsory Procedures

The establishment of the compulsory procedure of international dispute settlement under the LOSC can be considered as a significant development in the law of the sea. Yet, the compulsory procedures are subject to limitations and optional exceptions provided in Articles 297 and 298, respectively (see Table 8.1).

---

[39] G. Jaenicke, 'Dispute Settlement under the Convention on the Law of the Sea' (1983) 43 *ZaöRV*, p. 817.
[40] LOSC, Article 292.   [41] LOSC, Article 290(5).
[42] The *M/V 'Louisa'* case (Saint Vincent and the Grenadines v. Kingdom of Spain), Judgment, 28 May 2013, ITLOS Reports 2013, p. 30, para. 81.
[43] The *M/V 'Norstar'* case, Preliminary Objections, para. 58.

TABLE 8.1 LIMITATIONS AND EXCEPTIONS TO THE COMPULSORY PROCEDURES

Automatic exceptions	Optional exceptions
(i) LOSC, Article 297(2)(a)	(i) Maritime delimitations, historic bays or title
The coastal State's rights or discretion or decision concerning marine scientific research in the EEZ/continental shelf	(ii) Disputes concerning military activities and law enforcement activities referred to under Article 297(2) and (3)
(ii) LOSC, Article 297(3)(a) Sovereign rights over the living resources in the EEZ	(iii) Disputes dealt with by the UN Security Council

3.2.1 Limitations to the Compulsory Procedures

Under Article 297(2), the compulsory procedures are subject to two important limitations. First, under Article 297(2)(a) of the LOSC, a coastal State shall not be obliged to accept the submission to such settlement of any dispute arising out of (i) the exercise by the coastal State of a right or discretion in accordance with Article 246 relating to marine scientific research in the EEZ and on the continental shelf, or (ii) a decision by the coastal State to order suspension or cessation of a research project in accordance with Article 253.

Second, under Article 297(3)(a), a coastal State shall not be obliged to accept the submission to such settlement of any dispute relating to its sovereign rights with respect to the *living resources* in the EEZ or their exercise, including its discretionary powers for determining the allowable catch, its harvesting capacity, the allocation of surpluses to other States and the terms and conditions established in its conservation and management laws and regulations. These limitations were introduced into the LOSC since fishing and marine scientific research in the EEZ raise particular sensitivities for coastal States, which have wide discretion on these subjects.

A dispute concerning the exercise of a coastal State's discretionary powers over marine scientific research in the EEZ is to be submitted, at the request of either party, to compulsory conciliation under Annex V, Section 2. However, the conciliation commission shall not call into question the exercise by a coastal State of its discretion to designate specific areas as referred to in LOSC Article 246(6), or of its discretion to withhold consent in accordance with LOSC Article 246(5).[44]

Where no settlement has been reached by recourse to Section 1 of Part XV, namely, non-compulsory procedures, a dispute relating to fisheries excluded from the compulsory settlement procedures shall be submitted to compulsory conciliation under Annex V, Section 2, at the request of any party to the dispute, when it is alleged that:

(i) a coastal State has manifestly failed to comply with its obligations to ensure through proper conservation and management measures that the maintenance of the living resources in the EEZ is not seriously endangered

---

[44] LOSC, Article 297(2)(b).

(ii) a coastal State has arbitrarily refused to determine, at the request of another State, the allowable catch and its capacity to harvest living resources with respect to stocks which that other State is interested in fishing

(iii) a coastal State has arbitrarily refused to allocate to any State, under Articles 62, 69 and 70 and under the terms and conditions established by the coastal State consistent with this Convention, the whole or part of the surplus it has declared to exist.[45]

It follows that fishing disputes which are exempted from the compulsory procedure by Article 297(3)(a) are not automatically submitted to the compulsory conciliation by Article 297(3)(b). The discretionary powers of a coastal State over fishing in the EEZ are also safeguarded by Article 297(c).[46] The report of the conciliation commission is not binding upon the disputing parties.[47] To date, no fishing disputes have been referred to compulsory conciliation.

The limitations to the compulsory procedures for dispute settlement raise at least two issues. The first issue relates to the categorisation of a dispute. Suppose that a dispute was raised with regard to a claim over an EEZ around a disputed island or rock and the exercise of a coastal State's jurisdiction over living resources within this EEZ.[48] If this dispute involves the exercise of sovereign rights with respect to living resources in the EEZ, the dispute will be exempted from the compulsory procedures by virtue of LOSC Article 297. If this is a dispute concerning entitlement to an EEZ under Part V and Article 121(3) of the LOSC, it is not excluded from compulsory procedures in the Convention. It follows that the scope of compulsory procedures may change according to the formulation of a dispute.[49] In any case, whether a particular dispute falls within the scope of LOSC Article 297 is not a matter to be unilaterally decided by the disputing State, but is an issue for the court or tribunal whose jurisdiction is in question.[50]

The second issue relates to the relevance of the distinction between disputes susceptible to the compulsory procedures and disputes which are exempted from them. A dispute concerning the management of fish stocks straddling the EEZ and the high seas is a case in point. As demonstrated in the *Fishery Jurisdiction* dispute between Spain and Canada,[51] a fisheries dispute may be raised with regard to fish stocks straddling the EEZ and the high seas. Whilst the question of high seas fisheries is subject to compulsory procedures for dispute settlement, the question of the management of fish stocks in the EEZ does not seem to be susceptible to the compulsory procedures. However, it makes little sense to separate the question concerning high seas fisheries from the viewpoint of the management of fish stocks in the adjacent EEZ.[52]

---

[45] LOSC, Article 297(3)(b).
[46] Article 297(c) provides that: 'In no case shall the conciliation commission substitute its discretion for that of the coastal State.'
[47] LOSC, Articles 7(2) and 14 of Annex V.
[48] The distinction between islands and rocks is important in the law of the sea since rocks only have the territorial sea and the contiguous zone, while islands can have the 200-nautical-mile exclusive economic zone. LOSC, Article 121.
[49] A. Boyle, 'Dispute Settlement and the Law of the Sea Convention: Problems of Fragmentation and Jurisdiction' (1997) 46 *ICLQ*, pp. 44–5.
[50] LOSC, Articles 288(4) and 294.
[51] *Fisheries Jurisdiction* (Spain v. Canada), Judgment of 4 December 1998, ICJ Reports 1998, p. 432.
[52] Boyle, 'Dispute Settlement', p. 43.

3.2.2 Optional Exceptions to the Compulsory Procedures

The compulsory procedures for dispute settlement under the LOSC may also be qualified by optional exceptions set out in Article 298 of the LOSC. Article 298 embodies a compromise between those States which favoured compulsory and binding dispute settlement procedures and other States which sought to exclude even non-binding dispute settlement procedures.[53] Under Article 298(1), when signing, ratifying or acceding to this Convention or at any time thereafter, a State may declare in writing that it does not accept any one or more of the compulsory procedures with respect to one or more of the following categories of disputes:

(i) disputes concerning the interpretation or application of Articles 15, 74 and 83 relating to maritime delimitations or those involving historic bays or title
(ii) disputes concerning military activities and disputes concerning law enforcement activities in regard to the exercise of sovereign rights or jurisdiction excluded from the jurisdiction of a court or tribunal under Article 297(2) or (3)[54]
(iii) disputes in respect of which the UN Security Council is exercising the functions assigned to it by the UN Charter, unless the Security Council decides to remove the matter from its agenda or calls upon the parties to settle it by the means provided for in the LOSC.

Under Article 298(4), a State Party which has made a declaration under paragraph 1 shall not be entitled to submit any dispute falling within the excepted category of disputes to any procedure in this Convention as against another State Party, without the consent of that party. Declarations and notices of withdrawal of declarations under Article 298 shall be deposited with the Secretary-General of the United Nations in accordance with Article 298(6). A new declaration, or the withdrawal of a declaration, does not in any way affect proceedings pending before a court or tribunal in accordance with this article, unless the parties otherwise agree, by virtue of Article 298(5). As stated in Article 299 of the LOSC, however, the disputing parties may submit a dispute in an excluded category to the compulsory procedures *by agreement*. Therefore, it can be said that the effect of Articles 297 and 298 is to prevent the unilateral submission of a dispute in an excluded category to the compulsory procedures.

While maritime delimitation disputes or those involving historic bays or title may be exempted from the compulsory procedures entailing binding decisions, nonetheless they are subject to the compulsory *conciliation* under Section 2, Annex V to the LOSC, when such a dispute arises subsequent to the entry into force of the LOSC and where no agreement within a reasonable period of time is reached in negotiations between the parties.

---

[53] The *Timor-Leste/Australia* conciliation, p. 16, para. 66.
[54] Thus, the disputes excluded from the compulsory procedures are: (i) disputes arising out of the exercise by the coastal State of a right or discretion with respect to marine scientific research in the exclusive economic zone and on the continental shelf (Articles 297(2)(a)(i) and 246); (ii) disputes arising out of a decision by a coastal State to order suspension or cessation of a marine scientific research project (Articles 297(2)(a)(ii) and 253); and (iii) disputes related to a coastal State's sovereign rights with respect to living resources in the exclusive economic zone or the exercise of such rights (Article 297(3)(a)). The *'Arctic Sunrise'* arbitration (The Netherlands v. the Russian Federation), Award on Jurisdiction, 26 November 2014, p. 15, para. 75, available at: https://pca-cpa.org/en/cases.

Yet, any dispute that necessarily involves the concurrent consideration of any unsettled dispute concerning sovereignty or other rights over continental or insular land territory shall be excluded from such submission.[55] The parties shall negotiate an agreement on the basis of the report of the conciliation commission. If these negotiations do not result in an agreement, the parties shall, by mutual consent, submit the question to one of the compulsory procedures provided for in Section 2 of Part XV, unless the parties otherwise agree.[56] However, this subparagraph does not apply to any sea boundary dispute finally settled by an arrangement between the parties, or to any such dispute which is to be settled in accordance with a bilateral or multilateral agreement binding upon those parties.[57]

The compulsory conciliation was, for the first time, triggered by the Democratic Republic of Timor-Leste pursuant to Article 298 and Annex V of the Convention. This case concerned the interpretation and application of Articles 74 and 83 of the LOSC for the delimitation of the EEZ and the continental shelf between Timor-Leste and Australia.[58] Although Australia raised objections to the competence of the Conciliation Commission, the latter decided that it had competence to deal with the case, in which two issues in particular arose.

The first issue is whether the unqualified reference to 'entry into force of this Convention' under Article 298(1)(a)(i) refers to the entry into force of the Convention as a whole on 16 November 1994 or to the entry into force of the Convention between the parties in dispute. On this issue, the commission took the view that the ordinary meaning of the unqualified phrase favours the former interpretation regarding entry into force of the Convention as a whole.[59]

The second issue concerns the starting point of the application of the twelve-month period. Article 7(1) of Annex V stipulates that: 'The commission shall report within 12 months of its constitution.' The question of interest here is whether the twelve-month period begins to run from the point of the constitution of the conciliation commission or run from the conciliation phase after deciding its competence. In this regard, the Conciliation Commission took the position that the deadline of the twelve-month period is properly understood to run only after a commission has addressed any objections that may be made. Accordingly, it concluded that the twelve-month period in Article 7 of Annex will begin to run as of the date of the decision on competence of the commission.[60]

3.2.3 Characterisation of an International Dispute: The Case of the *South China Sea* Arbitration (Jurisdiction and Admissibility)

It is a competent court that decides whether a dispute would fall within any of the categories of disputes exempted from the compulsory procedures under Article 298(1). When determining whether a dispute would fall within the scope of categories exempted from compulsory

---

[55] LOSC, Article 298(1)(a)(i).   [56] LOSC, Article 298(1)(a)(ii).
[57] LOSC, Article 298(1)(a)(iii).
[58] *Conciliation between the Democratic Republic of Timor-Leste and the Commonwealth of Australia*, Decision on Australia's Objections to Competence, 19 September 2016, para. 111, available at: https://cpa-pca.org/en/cases.
[59] The *Timor-Leste/Australia* conciliation, p. 19, para. 74.   [60] *Ibid.*, p. 30, paras. 109–10.

procedures, characterisation of the dispute becomes crucial. The issue of characterisation was vividly raised in the 2015 *South China Sea* arbitration (jurisdiction and admissibility).[61]

On 22 January 2013, the Republic of the Philippines instituted arbitration proceedings against the People's Republic of China in accordance with Articles 286 and 287 and Article 1 of Annex VII of the LOSC.[62] However, China maintained that the Annex VII Arbitral Tribunal had no jurisdiction to deal with this case. The Chinese view can be summarised in two points.[63] First, according to China, the essence of the subject matter of the arbitration concerns territorial sovereignty over several maritime features in the South China Sea. Nonetheless, a territorial dispute falls outside the scope of the LOSC. Second, even if the parties' dispute were concerned with the LOSC, the dispute would constitute an integral part of maritime delimitation between the two countries. However, maritime delimitation disputes are precluded from the compulsory procedures by virtue of the declaration filed by China in 2006.[64] In contrast, the Philippines claimed that none of its submissions require the Tribunal to express any view at all as to the extent of China's sovereignty over land territory, or that of any other State.[65] It also asserted that: 'The fact that resolution of delimitation issues may require the prior resolution of entitlement issue does not mean that entitlement issues are an integral part of the delimitation process itself.'[66]

In the Award on Jurisdiction of 29 October 2015, the Arbitral Tribunal took the position that it is entirely possible to approach the Philippines' submissions from the premise that China is correct in its assertion of sovereignty over Scarborough Shoal and the Spratlys. In fact, the Philippines expressly and repeatedly requested that the Tribunal refrain from ruling on sovereignty. Accordingly, the Tribunal did not consider that a territorial dispute is the appropriate characterisation of the Philippines' claims in the proceedings.[67] Furthermore, the Tribunal did not accept that the parties' dispute was properly characterised as a maritime delimitation dispute.[68] In this regard, it stressed that: '[A] dispute concerning the existence of an entitlement to maritime zones is distinct from a dispute concerning the delimitation of those zones in an area where the entitlement of parties overlap' since 'a dispute over claimed entitlement may exist even without overlap where – for instance – a State claims maritime zones in an area understood by other States to form part of the high seas or the Area for the purposes of the Convention'.[69] In conclusion, the Tribunal found that disputes concerning the interpretation and application of the LOSC exist in all of the Philippines' submissions.[70]

---

[61] PCA Case No. 2013-19, the *South China Sea* arbitration (Jurisdiction and Admissibility), 29 October 2015, available at: https://pca-cpa.org/en/cases. The members of the Arbitral Tribunal are: Judge Thomas A. Mensah, President, Judge Jean-Pierre Cot, Judge Stanislaw Pawlak, Professor Alfred Soons and Judge Rüdiger Wolfrum.

[62] The Philippines ratified the Convention on 8 May 1984, and China ratified it on 7 June 1996.

[63] The *South China Sea* arbitration (Jurisdiction and Admissibility), paras. 133–9. See also China's Position Paper, Parts II and IV, available at: www.fmprc.gov.cn/mfa_eng/zxxx_662805/t1217147.shtml.

[64] On 25 August 2006, China declared that: 'The Government of the People's Republic of China does not accept any of the procedures provided for in Section 2 of Part XV of the Convention with respect to all the categories of disputes referred to in paragraph 1(a) (b) and (c) of Art. 298 of the Convention.' See www.un.org/Depts/los/convention_agreements/convention_declarations.htm#China.

[65] Presentation by Sands, Hearing on Jurisdiction and Admissibility, Day 1, 7 July 2015, pp. 61–2.

[66] *Ibid.*, p. 46.

[67] The *South China Sea* arbitration (Jurisdiction and Admissibility), paras. 152–3.

[68] *Ibid.*, para. 155.   [69] *Ibid.*, para. 156.   [70] *Ibid.*, para. 178.

4 INTERNATIONAL TRIBUNAL FOR THE LAW OF THE SEA

4.1 The Structure of ITLOS

4.1.1 Members of ITLOS

ITLOS is a standing judicial body established in accordance with Annex VI to the LOSC (hereafter the ITLOS Statute).[71] Whereas the ICJ is the principal judicial organ of the United Nations,[72] ITLOS is not an organ of the United Nations.[73] The expenses of ITLOS are to be borne by the States Parties and by the International Sea-Bed Authority (hereafter the Authority).[74] The seat of ITLOS is in the Free and Hanseatic City of Hamburg in the Federal Republic of Germany.[75] Like the ICJ, the official languages of ITLOS are English and French.[76] The official inauguration of ITLOS took place on 18 October 1996.

ITLOS is a body composed of twenty-one independent members, elected from among persons enjoying the highest reputation for fairness and integrity and of recognised competence in the field of the law of the sea. The representation of the principal legal systems of the world and equitable geographical distribution shall be assured.[77] No two members of ITLOS may be nationals of the same State.[78] There shall be no fewer than three members from each geographical group as established by the UN General Assembly. The geographical distribution was decided by the Fifth Meeting of States Parties in 1996 and was rearranged by the Nineteenth Meeting in 2009. In accordance with the rearrangement, ITLOS shall have the following composition (see Table 8.2):[79]

(a) Five members of the Tribunal shall be from the Group of African States.
(b) Five members of the Tribunal shall be from the Group of Asian States.
(c) Three members of the Tribunal shall be from the Group of Eastern European States.
(d) Four members of the Tribunal shall be from the Group of Latin American and Caribbean States.
(e) Three members of the Tribunal shall be from the Group of Western European and other States.
(f) The remaining one member of the Tribunal shall be elected from among the Group of African States, the Group of Asian States and the Group of Western European and other States.

---

[71] LOSC, Article 287(1)(a).
[72] Article 92 of the UN Charter; ICJ Statute, Article 1.
[73] The general relations between ITLOS and the United Nations are regulated by the 1997 Agreement on Co-operation and Relationship between the United Nations and the International Tribunal for the Law of the Sea. Provisionally entered into force 18 December 1997; definitively entered into force March 1998. Text in: 2000 UNTS, p. 467. Under Article 1(1) of the Agreement, the United Nations recognises ITLOS as an autonomous international judicial body.
[74] ITLOS Statute, Article 19(1). The Authority is an international organisation which consists of all States Parties to the LSOC and it aims to organise and control activities in the deep sea-bed beyond national jurisdiction, i.e. the Area, on behalf of mankind as a whole under LOSC Article 153(1).
[75] ITLOS Statute, Article 1(2).
[76] Article 43 of the Rules of the International Tribunal for the Law of the Sea (hereafter ITLOS Rules).
[77] ITLOS Statute, Article 2.   [78] Ibid., Article 3(1).
[79] SPLOS/201, 26 June 2009, para. 1.

TABLE 8.2 CURRENT COMPOSITION OF THE MEMBERS OF ITLOS AND THE ICJ

	ITLOS	ICJ
Africa	5	3
Asia	5	3
Latin America and Caribbean States	4	2
Western European and other States	4	5
Eastern Europe	3	2
Total	21	15

The procedure for electing the members of ITLOS is provided in Article 4 of the ITLOS Statute. Each State Party may nominate not more than two persons having the qualifications prescribed in Article 2 of this Statute. The members of ITLOS are to be elected from the list of persons thus nominated. Elections are to be held at a meeting of the States Parties to the LOSC, and the members of ITLOS are to be elected by secret ballot. The persons elected to ITLOS shall be those nominees who obtain the largest number of votes and a two-thirds majority of the States Parties present and voting, provided that such majority includes a majority of the States Parties.[80] The members of ITLOS are elected for nine years and may be re-elected.[81] The President and Vice-President are elected for three years and they may be re-elected.[82] Under Article 7(1) of the ITLOS Statute:

> No member of the Tribunal may exercise any political or administrative function, or associate actively with or be financially interested in any of the operations of any enterprise concerned with the exploration for or exploitation of the resources of the sea or the sea-bed or other commercial use of the sea or the sea-bed.

This provision appears to signify that the members of ITLOS may engage in any other function which is not prohibited by this provision. This point represents a sharp contrast to Article 16(1) of the ICJ Statute, which prohibits members of the Court from exercising 'any political or administrative function' or engaging 'in any other occupation of a professional nature'.

The difference in status between the members of ITLOS and those of the ICJ is also reflected in their remuneration. While each member of the ICJ receives 'an annual salary' under Article 32(1) of the ITLOS Statute, the members of ITLOS receive 'an annual allowance' and, for each day on which he exercises his functions, 'a special allowance' in accordance with Article 18(1) of the ITLOS Statute. This system seems to

---

[80] The first election took place on 1 August 1996. For an examination in more detail of elections to ITLOS, see G. Eiriksson, *The International Tribunal for the Law of the Sea* (The Hague: Nijhoff, 2000), pp. 32 et seq.
[81] ITLOS Statute, Article 5(1).   [82] *Ibid.*, Article 12.

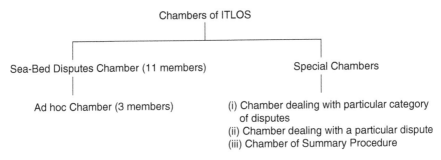

Figure 8.1 Chambers of ITLOS

suggest that members of ITLOS are not expected to be engaged on a full-time basis on the work of ITLOS, and judges are assumed to have some other sources of income.[83] When engaged on the business of ITLOS, its members are to enjoy diplomatic privileges and immunities by virtue of Article 10 of the ITLOS Statute. These privileges and immunities are defined in the 1997 Agreement on the Privileges and Immunities of ITLOS.[84]

Members of ITLOS of the nationality of any of the parties to a dispute shall retain their right to participate as members of the Tribunal. As with the ICJ, a judge ad hoc may be appointed by a party or parties to a dispute currently unrepresented in accordance with Article 17(2) and (3) of the ITLOS Statute. The provisions concerning national judges and judges ad hoc apply to the Sea-Bed Disputes Chamber and Special Chambers by virtue of Article 17(4) of the ITLOS Statute. Judges ad hoc shall fulfil the conditions required by Articles 2 (composition), 8 (conditions to participate in a particular case) and 11 (solemn declaration) of the ITLOS Statute.[85]

4.1.2 The Sea-Bed Disputes Chamber

ITLOS has multiple Chambers (see Figure 8.1). A Sea-Bed Disputes Chamber was established on 20 February 1997 in accordance with section 5, Part XI of the LOSC and Article 14 of the ITLOS Statute. The Sea-Bed Disputes Chamber is composed of eleven members, selected by a majority of the elected members of ITLOS from among them for a three-year term and may be selected for a second term.[86] As stated in Article 35(2) of the ITLOS Statute, the representation of the principal legal systems of the world and equitable geographical distribution must be assured in electing the Chamber.

The Chamber is empowered to form an ad hoc Chamber which is composed of three members in order to deal with particular disputes submitted to it under Article 188(b) of the LOSC. The establishment of this 'chamber of a chamber' can be considered as a result of compromise between States which supported the Sea-Bed Disputes Chamber as appropriate for dealing with disputes relating to Part XI of the LOSC

---

[83] Eiriksson, *The International Tribunal for the Law of the Sea*, p. 103.
[84] Entered into force on 30 December 2001. The text of the 1997 Agreement is available at: www.itlos.org/index.php?id=12&L=0.
[85] ITLOS Statute, Article 17(6). [86] *Ibid.*, Article 35(1) and (3).

and those which would have preferred arbitration. The composition of the ad hoc Chamber is to be determined by the Sea-Bed Disputes Chamber 'with the approval of the parties'.[87]

If the parties do not agree on the composition of an ad hoc Chamber, each party to the dispute is to appoint one member, and the third member is to be appointed by them in agreement. If they disagree, or if any party fails to make an appointment, the President of the Sea-Bed Disputes Chamber shall promptly make the appointment or appointment from among its members, 'after consultation with the parties'.[88] By emphasising the consent of the parties in the composition of the ad hoc Chamber, some argue that this Chamber is akin to a sort of 'arbitration within the Tribunal'.[89] The members of the ad hoc Chamber must not be in the service of, or nationals of, any of the parties to the dispute pursuant to Article 36(3) of the ITLOS Statute.

Under Article 187 of the LOSC, the Sea-Bed Disputes Chamber has jurisdiction over disputes with regard to activities in the area. Specifically the Sea-Bed Disputes Chamber exercises jurisdiction over disputes (i) between States; (ii) between a State and the Authority; (iii) between the parties to a contract, including States, a State enterprise, the Authority or the enterprise and natural or juridical persons; and (iv) between the Authority and a prospective contractor. It is noteworthy that the Sea-Bed Disputes Chamber is open to entities other than States, such as the Authority or the enterprise, State enterprises and natural or juridical persons.[90] Concerning the settlement of disputes between a State Party and the Authority, in particular, the Sea-Bed Disputes Chamber has jurisdiction to judge 'acts of the Authority alleged to be in excess of jurisdiction or a misuse of power'.[91] This power provides an insight into judicial review of acts of an international organisation.[92]

The Sea-Bed Disputes Chamber has no jurisdiction with regard to the exercise by the Authority of its discretionary powers. In no case shall it substitute its discretion for that of the Authority. Furthermore, the Chamber is not allowed to pronounce on the question of whether any rules and regulations of the Authority are in conformity with the LOSC, nor declare invalid any such rules and regulations.[93] A judgment given by the Sea-Bed Disputes Chamber is considered to be rendered by ITLOS.[94] The decisions of the Chamber shall be enforceable in the territories of the States Parties in the same manner as judgments or orders of the highest court of the State Party in whose territory the enforcement is sought by virtue of Article 39 of the ITLOS Statute. The Chamber is also empowered to give advisory opinions.[95]

---

[87] *Ibid.*, Article 36(1). [88] *Ibid.*, Article 36(2).
[89] R. Wolfrum, 'The Settlement of Disputes before the International Tribunal for the Law of the Sea: A Progressive Development of International Law or Relying on Traditional Mechanisms?' (2008) 51 *Japanese Yearbook of International Law*, pp. 161–2.
[90] See ITLOS Statute, Article 37. [91] LOSC, Article 187(b)(ii).
[92] See Chapter 11, section 5 of this book. [93] LOSC, Article 189.
[94] ITLOS Statute, Article 15(5). [95] See section 4.10.1 of this chapter.

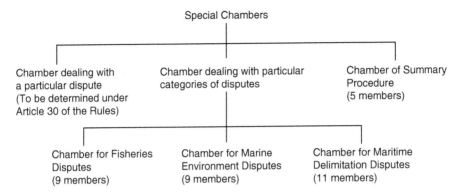

Figure 8.2 Special Chambers

4.1.3 Special Chambers

ITLOS may form three types of Special Chamber in accordance with Article 15 of the Statute of ITLOS:

- Chamber dealing with particular categories of disputes
- Chamber dealing with a particular dispute
- Chamber of Summary Procedure.

Furthermore, three Chambers are established to deal with particular categories of disputes (see Figure 8.2). A judge ad hoc may be appointed in Special Chambers pursuant to Article 17(4) of the ITLOS Statute. A judgment given by any of the Chambers is considered as rendered by ITLOS under Article 15(5) of the ITLOS Statute.

(i) *Chamber dealing with particular categories of disputes*: Under Article 15(1) of the ITLOS Statute, ITLOS may form this type of Chamber, composed of three or more of its selected members. In this case, it shall determine the particular category of disputes for which it is formed, the number of its members, the period for which they will serve, the date when they will enter upon their duties and the quorum for meetings. The members of the Chamber are selected by ITLOS upon the proposal of its President from among the members, having regard to any special knowledge or previous experience in relation to the category of disputes the Chamber deals with.[96] Accordingly, the expertise of members is secured in this type of Chamber. At present, three Chambers are formed: Chamber for Fisheries Disputes, Chamber for Marine Environmental Disputes and Chamber for Maritime Delimitation Disputes.[97]

(ii) *Chamber dealing with a particular dispute*: Under Article 15(2) of the ITLOS Statute, ITLOS is to form the Chamber if the parties so request. This is known as an ad hoc Chamber. Its composition is determined by ITLOS with the approval of the parties. A request for the formation of an ad hoc Chamber must be made within two months from the date of the

---

[96] ITLOS Rules, Article 29.
[97] See www.itlos.org/en/the-tribunal/chambers/.

institution of proceedings.[98] An ad hoc Chamber was formed in the 2000 *Swordfish Stocks* case between Chile and the European Community and the 2015 *Ghana/Côte d'Ivoire* case concerning maritime delimitation. Whilst the proceedings of the *Swordfish Stocks* case were discontinued, the Chamber in the *Ghana/Côte d'Ivoire* case prescribed provisional measures in 2015.[99]

(iii) *Chamber of Summary Procedure*: The establishment of this Chamber is mandatory and it is formed annually with a view to the speedy dispatch of business.[100] If the applicant has so requested in the application, the application shall be dealt with by the Chamber of Summary Procedure pursuant to Article 112 of the Rules of the Tribunal. The Chamber is composed of the President and the Vice-President of ITLOS, acting *ex officio*, and three other members. In addition, two members are to be selected to act as alternatives. The members and alternatives of the Chamber are to be selected by ITLOS upon the proposal of its President.[101]

4.2 Jurisdiction of ITLOS

Jurisdiction of ITLOS is provided in Article 288 of the LOSC and Articles 21 and 22 of the ITLOS Statute.

(i) *Jurisdiction ratione personae*: ITLOS is open to States Parties to the LOSC. It is also open to entities other than States Parties, but only as specifically provided for in the Convention.[102] In this regard, Article 20(2) of the ITLOS Statute holds that the Tribunal shall be open to entities other than States Parties in any case expressly provided for in Part XI or in any case submitted pursuant to any other agreement conferring jurisdiction on the Tribunal which is accepted by all the parties to that case. As noted, Article 37 of the ITLOS Statute makes clear that the Sea-Bed Disputes Chamber is to be open to the States Parties, the Authority and the other entities referred to in Part XI, Section 5. Such entities would comprise the enterprise, State enterprises and natural or juridical persons.[103] To this extent, ITLOS can be said to open up the possibility of potential parties other than States coming before the Tribunal.[104]

(ii) *Jurisdiction ratione materiae*: ITLOS has jurisdiction over any dispute concerning the interpretation and application of the LOSC, which is submitted to it in accordance with Part XV. It also has jurisdiction over any dispute concerning the interpretation and application of an international agreement related to the purposes of the LOSC, which is submitted to it in accordance with the agreement.[105] ITLOS also has the jurisdiction over all disputes and all applications submitted to it in accordance with the LOSC and all

---

[98] *Ibid.*, Article 30(1). Further, see R. Wolfrum, 'Ad Hoc Chambers' in H. N. Scheiber and Jin-Hyun Paik (eds.), *Regions, Institutions, and Law of the Sea: Studies in Ocean Governance* (Leiden: Nijhoff, 2013), pp. 37–45.
[99] *Dispute Concerning Delimitation of the Maritime Boundary between Ghana and Côte d'Ivoire in the Atlantic Ocean* (Ghana/Côte d'Ivoire), Case No. 23.
[100] ITLOS Statute, Article 15(3).   [101] ITLOS Rules, Article 28.
[102] LOSC, Article 291.   [103] *Ibid.*, Article 187.
[104] Wolfrum, 'The Settlement of Disputes before the International Tribunal for the Law of the Sea', pp. 143–5; Eiriksson, *The International Tribunal for the Law of the Sea*, p. 115.
[105] LOSC, Article 288.

matters specifically provided for in any other agreement which confers jurisdiction on the Tribunal.[106] If all the parties to a treaty or convention already in force and concerning the subject matter covered by this Convention so agree, any disputes concerning the interpretation or application of such treaty or convention may, in accordance with such agreement, be submitted to ITLOS.[107]

A contentious issue is whether or not an international court or tribunal under Part XV of the LOSC can determine a territorial dispute where it is a prerequisite to draw a maritime delimitation boundary. At present, there is a trend that territorial and maritime disputes are submitted to an international court in the same proceedings. It is likely that a maritime delimitation may require a decision concerning sovereignty over islands in dispute in the same proceedings. In this case, a difficult issue arises as to whether a court or tribunal under Article 287 would be expected to determine territorial issues.[108] Some argue that a tribunal, including ITLOS, may if necessary deal with both land and maritime disputes.[109] In this regard, Judge Wolfrum, a former President of ITLOS, clearly stated that:

> Issues of sovereignty or other rights over continental or insular land territory, which are closely linked or ancillary to maritime delimitation, concern the interpretation or application of the Convention and therefore fall within its scope.[110]

Where there is an agreement between the parties in dispute to settle territorial and marine disputes which are closely intertwined in the same proceedings, there may be some scope to argue that an international court or tribunal should not decline the request by the parties. Where such an agreement does not exist, however, the issue is more controversial. The *dictum* of the Annex VII Arbitral Tribunal in the *Chagos Marine Protected Area* arbitration provides an insight into this subject. According to the Arbitral Tribunal, where a dispute concerns the interpretation or application of the LOSC, the jurisdiction of a court or tribunal pursuant to Article 288(1) extends to making such findings of fact or ancillary determinations of law as are necessary to resolve the dispute presented to it; where the 'real issue in the case' and the 'object of the claim' do not relate to the interpretation or application of the Convention, however, an incidental connection between the dispute and some matter regulated by the Convention is insufficient to bring the dispute as a whole within the ambit of Article 288(1). According to the *dictum* of the

---

[106] ITLOS Statute, Article 21. [107] *Ibid.*, Article 22.
[108] Generally on this issue, see I. Buga, 'Territorial Sovereignty Issues in Maritime Disputes: A Jurisdictional Dilemma for Law of the Sea Tribunals' (2012) 27 *IJMCL*, pp. 59–95.
[109] Boyle, 'Dispute Settlement,' p. 49; Eiriksson, *The International Tribunal for the Law of the Sea*, p. 113; T. Treves, 'What Have the United Nations Convention and the International Tribunal for the Law of the Sea to Offer as Regards Maritime Delimitation Disputes?' in R. Lagoni and D. Vignes (eds.), *Maritime Delimitation* (Dordrecht: Nijhoff, 2006), p. 77.
[110] Statement by H. E. Judge Rüdiger Wolfrum, President of the International Law of the Sea, to the Informal Meeting of Legal Advisers of Ministries of Foreign Affairs, New York, 23 October 2006, p. 6 available at: www.itlos.org/index.php?id=49. See also Wolfrum, 'The Settlement of Disputes Before the International Tribunal for the Law of the Sea', p. 161.

Tribunal, disputes that are not genuinely ancillary to the interpretation and application of the LOSC, such as a pure land dispute, are to be precluded from jurisdiction of a court or tribunal under Article 288(1) of the Convention. Related to this, notably the Arbitral Tribunal held that:

> The Tribunal does not categorically exclude that in some instances a minor issue of territorial sovereignty could be ancillary to a dispute concerning the interpretation or application of the Convention.[111]

The *dictum* of the Tribunal does seem to imply that an arbitral tribunal can address a 'minor issue of territorial sovereignty' which is ancillary to the interpretation or application of the Convention could fall within the ambit of Article 288(1). By analogy, there appears to be some scope to argue that ITLOS can deal with a 'minor issue of territorial sovereignty' which is ancillary to the interpretation or application of the Convention.[112]

4.3 Applicable Law

Under Article 293(1) of the LOSC, '[a] court or tribunal having jurisdiction under this section shall apply this Convention [LOSC] and other rules of international law not incompatible with this Convention'. A court or tribunal, including ITLOS, may also decide a case *ex aequo et bono* if the parties so agree pursuant to Article 293(2). Furthermore, the Sea-Bed Disputes Chamber shall apply the rules, regulations and procedures of the Authority and the terms of contracts concerning activities in the area in accordance with Article 38 of the ITLOS Statute. A particular issue to be considered in this regard is whether or not ITLOS can determine disputes concerning rules of customary international law. This issue was raised in the *ARA 'Libertad'* case.[113]

Article 21 of Annex VI provides that: 'The jurisdiction of the Tribunal [ITLOS] comprises *all disputes and all applications* submitted to it in accordance with this Convention and all matters specifically provided for in any other agreement which confers jurisdiction on the Tribunal.'[114] Under this provision, the jurisdiction of the Tribunal is much less restricted than laid down in Article 288.[115] Further, under Article 293(1), '[a] court or tribunal having jurisdiction under this section shall apply this Convention and other rules of international law not incompatible with this Convention'. It can be argued that 'other rules of international law not incompatible with this Convention [LOSC]' include rules of customary international law. It seems to follow that a court or a tribunal referred to in Article 287 may decide matters of customary

---

[111] *Ibid.*, p. 90, paras. 220–1.
[112] Further, see Y. Tanaka, 'Reflections on the *Philippines/China* Arbitration: Award on Jurisdiction and Admissibility' (2016) 15 *The Law and Practice of International Courts and Tribunals*, pp. 311–19.
[113] Separate Opinion of Judge Wolfrum and Judge Cot in the *ARA 'Libertad'* case (Argentina v. Ghana), Case No. 20, Order of 15 December 2012, pp. 1–2, paras. 6–7.
[114] Emphasis added.
[115] Eiriksson, *The International Tribunal for the Law of the Sea*, p. 113.

international law.[116] In fact, ITLOS, in the *M/V 'Saiga' (No. 2)* case (Merits), applied 'international law' other than provisions of the LOSC, stating that:

> Although the Convention does not contain express provisions on the use of force in the arrest of ships, international law, which is applicable by virtue of article 293 of the Convention, requires that the use of force must be avoided as far as possible and, where force is unavoidable, it must not go beyond what is reasonable and necessary in the circumstances.[117]

The *dictum* was echoed by the Annex VII Arbitral Tribunal in the 2015 *'Arctic Sunrise'* arbitration.[118] In practice, it is not infrequent that international disputes concern rules of treaty law and customary law at the same time. In this case, it seems difficult and impractical for an international court to clearly distinguish issues concerning the interpretation and application of the LOSC from other issues relating to rules of customary international law which are not contained in the Convention and refrain from deciding on the customary law issues. Hence it may not be unreasonable to argue that in appropriate circumstances, a court or tribunal under LOSC Article 287 may exercise its jurisdiction over disputes respecting customary international law.[119]

4.4 Proceedings before ITLOS

As stated in Article 24 of the ITLOS Statute, disputes are submitted to ITLOS either by notification of a special agreement or by written application, addressed to the Registrar. In either case, the subject of the dispute and the parties shall be indicated. Article 54(2) of the ITLOS Rules requires that the application shall specify as far as possible the legal grounds upon which the jurisdiction of ITLOS is said to be based; it shall also specify the precise nature of the claim, together with a succinct statement of the facts and grounds on which the claim is based.

Like the ICJ, the issues of non-appearance of a party may arise in the proceedings before ITLOS.[120] In the 2013 *'Arctic Sunrise'* case between the Netherlands and the Russian Federation, the latter did not participate in the proceedings of provisional measures before ITLOS. In this regard, by referring to the ICJ jurisprudence case, ITLOS held that: '[T]he absence of a party or failure of a party to defend its case does not constitute a bar to the proceedings and does not preclude the Tribunal from prescribing provisional

---

[116] In this regard, Eiriksson, a former member of ITLOS, stated that: '[Q]uestions of customary international law and other questions outside the four corners of the Convention and other agreements would be addressed [by the Tribunal], were it necessary to reach a decision on the question raised'. *Ibid*. See also Boyle, 'Dispute Settlement', p. 49.

[117] The *M/V 'Saiga'* (No. 2) case (Saint Vincent and the Grenadines v. Guinea), Judgment of 1 July 1999 ITLOS case No.2, (1999) 38 ILM, p. 1355, para. 155.

[118] The *'Arctic Sunrise'* arbitration, Merits, p. 44, para. 191 and p. 46, paras. 197–8.

[119] See also *'Arctic Sunrise'* arbitration (Netherlands v. Russia), Award on the Merits of 14 August 2015, para. 198; para. 208; the *Duzgit Integrity* arbitration (Malta v. São Tomé and Príncipe), Award of 5 September 2016, para. 208.

[120] For problems with non-appearance, see also Chapter 7, section 2.3 of this book.

measures, provided that the parties have been given an opportunity of presenting their observations on the subject.'[121] At the same time, it stressed that: '[T]he non-appearing State is nevertheless a party to the proceedings.'[122] Accordingly, the non-appearing party is bound by the decision pursuant to Article 33 of the ITLOS Statute and there may be room for the view that the same applies to the order concerning provisional measures.[123]

4.5 Preliminary Objections

As stated in LOSC Article 288(4), in the event of a dispute as to whether a court or tribunal has jurisdiction, the matter is to be settled by decision of that court or tribunal. The procedure for preliminary objections is amplified by Article 97 of the ITLOS Rules. Under Article 97(1), any objection to the ITLOS's jurisdiction or to the admissibility of the application, or other objection the decision upon which is requested before any further proceedings on the merits must be made in writing within ninety days from the institution of proceedings. The preliminary objection must set out the facts and the law on which the objection is based, as well as the submissions in accordance with Article 97(2). As provided in Article 97(3), the submission of the preliminary objection suspends the proceedings on the merits. Finally, Article 97(6) makes clear that ITLOS gives its decision in the form of a judgment.

In relation to objections to admissibility in the proceedings of ITLOS, two particular issues may arise. The first issue relates to the nationality of claims. Any vessels could have crews or other persons who are not nationals of the flag State. Here an issue arises with regard to the relationship between the right of the State of nationality of the persons involved to exercise diplomatic protection and the right of flag State to seek redress.[124] In the 1999 *M/V 'Saiga' (No. 2)* case, Guinea claimed that Saint Vincent and the Grenadines was not competent to institute claims for damages in respect of natural and juridical persons who are not nationals of Saint Vincent and the Grenadines. However, ITLOS did not accept the Guinea's claim, stating that:

> The provisions referred to in the preceding paragraph [i.e. Articles 94, 106, 110(3), 111(8), 217, and 292] indicate that the Convention considers a ship as a unit, as regards the obligations of the flag State with respect to the ship and the right of a flag State to seek reparation for loss or damage caused to the ship by acts of other States and to institute proceedings under article 292 of the Convention.

Thus the ship, everything on it and every person involved or interested in its operations are treated as an entity linked to the flag State. The nationalities of these persons are not relevant.[125]

---

[121] The *'Arctic Sunrise'* case (Kingdom of the Netherlands v. Russian Federation), Provisional Measures, Case No. 22, Order of 22 November 2013, ITLOS Reports 2013, p. 242, para. 48. See also Article 28 of the ITLOS Statute and Article 9 of Annex VII to the LOSC.
[122] The *'Arctic Sunrise'* case, ITLOS Reports 2013, p. 242, para. 51.
[123] Joint Separate Opinion of Judge Wolfrum and Judge Kelly, *ibid.*, paras. 3-4; Separate Opinion of Judge Paik, paras. 4-6. See also the *'Arctic Sunrise'* arbitration, Merits, p. 2, para. 8.
[124] See also Article 18 of the ILC's Draft Articles on Diplomatic Protection.
[125] The *M/V 'Saiga' (No. 2)* case, p. 1347, para. 106.

The *dictum* in the *M/V 'Saiga' (No. 2)* judgment was echoed by ITLOS in the 2014 *M/V 'Virginia G'* case between Panama and Guinea-Bissau. In this case, Guinea-Bissau contended that there was no single person or entity related to the *M/V 'Virginia G'* which was of Panamanian nationality. It thus argued that the framework of diplomatic protection did not give Panama *locus standi* referring to claims of persons or entities that were not nationals of Panama. However, ITLOS found that: '[T]he *M/V 'Virginia G'* is to be considered as a unit and therefore the *M/V 'Virginia G'*, its crew and cargo on board as well as its owner and every person involved or interested in its operations are to be treated as an entity linked to the flag State.'[126] In the Tribunal's view, 'in accordance with international law, the exercise of diplomatic protection by a State in respect of its nationals is to be distinguished from claims made by a flag State for damage in respect of natural and juridical persons involved in the operation of a ship who are not nationals of that State'.[127] ITLOS thus rejected the objection raised by Guinea-Bissau. The view of ITLOS was echoed by the Annex VII Arbitral Tribunal in the 2015 *'Arctic Sunrise'* arbitration.[128]

The second issue concerns the applicability of the exhaustion of local remedies rule. Under Article 295 of the LOSC, any dispute between States Parties concerning the interpretation or application of the LOSC may be submitted to the compulsory procedures provided for in section 2, Part XV of the Convention only after local remedies have been exhausted where this is required by international law. The applicability of the exhaustion of local remedies was at issue in the *M/V 'Saiga' (No. 2)* case, where Guinea objected to the admissibility of the case because Saint Vincent and the Grenadines had failed to exhaust local remedies available in Guinea. In this case, ITLOS held that the rule on the exhaustion of local remedies did not apply because the claims advanced by Saint Vincent and the Grenadines all involved direct violations of the rights of that State.[129] The approach of the *M/V 'Saiga' (No. 2)* case was echoed by ITLOS in the *M/V 'Virginia G'* case. According to ITLOS, 'the exhaustion of local remedies rule does not apply where the claimant State is directly injured by the wrongful act of another State'.[130] When the claim contains elements of both injury to a State and injury to an individual, for the purpose of deciding the applicability of the exhaustion of local remedies rule, it is necessary to determine which element is preponderant.[131] In the *M/V 'Virginia G'* case, ITLOS ruled that the rule of exhaustion of local remedies did not apply to this case since the principal rights that Panama alleged had been violated by Guinea-Bissau were rights that belong to Panama under the LOSC.[132] Likewise ITLOS in the *M/V 'Norstar'* case considered that a violation of the right of Panama to enjoy freedom of navigation on the high seas is a right that belongs to Panama under Article 87 of the LOSC would amount to direct injury to Panama and that the claims for damage to the persons and entities with an interest in the ship or its cargo arises from the alleged injury to Panama. It thus concluded that the claims in respect of such damage were not subject to the rule of exhaustion of local remedies.[133]

---

[126] The *M/V 'Virginia G'* case (Panama v. Guinea-Bissau), ITLOS Case No. 19, 14 April 2014, ITLOS Reports 2014, p. 48, para. 127.
[127] *Ibid.*, para. 128.
[128] The *'Arctic Sunrise'* arbitration, Merits, pp. 39–40, paras. 170–2.
[129] The *M/V 'Saiga' (No. 2)* case, pp. 1344–6, paras. 89–102.
[130] The *M/V 'Virginia G'* case, p. 49, para. 153.   [131] *Ibid.*, p. 50, para. 157.
[132] *Ibid.*, paras. 157–60. Yet nine judges voted against this part of the judgment.
[133] The *M/V 'Norstar'* case, Preliminary Objections, paras. 270–1.

4.6 Provisional Measures

4.6.1 General Considerations

In order to ensure effectiveness of the judgment of a court, it is necessary to restrain either or both parties from aggravating the situation and to preserve the respective rights of the disputing parties pending the final decision of the court. Article 290(1) thus provides as follows:

> If a dispute has been duly submitted to a court or tribunal which considers that *prima facie* it has jurisdiction under this Part or Part XI, section 5, the court or tribunal may prescribe any provisional measures which it considers appropriate under the circumstances to preserve the respective rights of the parties to the dispute or to prevent serious harm to the marine environment, pending the final decision.

Article 25(1) of the ITLOS Statute makes clear that ITLOS and its Sea-Bed Disputes Chamber are empowered to prescribe provisional measures in accordance with Article 290. As stated in Article 25(2) of the ITLOS Statute, the Chamber of Summary Procedure shall prescribe provisional measures if ITLOS is not in session or a sufficient number of members is not available to constitute a quorum. Such provisional measures are subject to review or revision of ITLOS at the written request of a party within fifteen days of the prescription of the measures. ITLOS may also at any time decide *proprio motu* to review or revise the measures.[134] While there is no explicit provision in the ITLOS Statute, Special Chambers dealing with a particular category of disputes or a particular dispute may also prescribe provisional measures since such Chambers act as an organ of ITLOS.[135]

Under Article 290(5) of the LOSC, ITLOS or, with respect to activities in the area, the Sea-Bed Disputes Chamber have residual jurisdiction to prescribe provisional measures concerning a dispute that has been submitted to an arbitral tribunal, provided that two conditions are satisfied.[136] First, a request for provisional measures has been communicated by one of the disputing parties to the other party or parties, and they could not agree, within a period of two weeks after the request was made, on a court or tribunal to which the request has been submitted. Second, ITLOS concludes that *prima facie* the arbitral tribunal to which the dispute is being submitted on the merits would have jurisdiction over the merits of the dispute. Article 290 requires five brief observations.

First, Article 290(1) states that the court or tribunal may 'prescribe' provisional measures, whereas Article 41(1) of the ICJ Statute uses the term 'indicate'. Furthermore, Article 290(6) makes clear that: 'The parties to the dispute shall comply promptly with any provisional measures prescribed under this article.' These provisions signify that provisional measures prescribed by ITLOS are binding upon the disputing parties. Related to this, Article 95(1) of the ITLOS Rules obliges each party to inform ITLOS as soon as possible as to its compliance with any provisional measures the Tribunal has prescribed.

---

[134] ITLOS Rules, Article 91(2).
[135] Wolfrum, 'The Settlement of Disputes before the International Tribunal for the Law of the Sea', p. 153.
[136] T. A. Mensah, 'Provisional Measures in the International Law of the Sea (ITLOS)' (2002) 62 *ZaöRV*, p. 46.

Second, concerning the duration of the effect of provisional measures, Article 290(5) provides that once constituted, the arbitral tribunal to which the dispute has been submitted may modify, revoke or affirm those provisional measures. It would follow that where a dispute has been submitted to an arbitral tribunal, the provisional measures are to be binding pending a decision of the arbitral tribunal.[137] Where ITLOS considers a request for provisional measures under Article 290(1), these measures will be in force pending its own final decision.

Third, unlike Article 41(1) of the ICJ Statute, LOSC Article 290(1) refers to the prevention of 'serious harm to the marine environment'. Reference to the marine environmental protection, which is not directly linked to the interests of the disputing parties, as a justification for provisional measures appears to highlight the importance of the marine environmental protection as a community interest.[138]

Fourth, LOSC Article 290(3) makes clear that provisional measures may be prescribed, modified or revoked under this article only at the request of a party to the dispute and after the parties have been given an opportunity to be heard.[139] It follows that unlike the ICJ,[140] ITLOS does not possess the power, *proprio motu* (i.e. 'of its own motion'), to prescribe provisional measures and that there must be a request from a disputing party to prescribe provisional measures.

Fifth, ITLOS may prescribe provisional measures different in whole or in part from those requested. This is clear from Article 89(5) of the ITLOS Rules. In fact, it has exercised this power in all cases prescribing provisional measures.

Provisional measures occupy an important place in the ITLOS jurisprudence. To date, nine out of twenty-three cases submitted to ITLOS involved a request for the prescription of provisional measures and the Tribunal prescribed provisional measures in eight cases (see Table 8.3).

4.6.2 Requirements to Prescribe Provisional Measures

In the ICJ jurisprudence, five requirements must be satisfied for the Court to indicate provisional measures: *prima facie* jurisdiction, the plausible character of the alleged rights in the principal request, the link between the alleged rights and the measures requested, urgency and risk of irreparable prejudice.[141] While basically these requirements are also applied in the ITLOS jurisprudence concerning provisional measures, there are some differences between the ICJ and ITLOS jurisprudence in this matter.

(i) *Prima facie jurisdiction*: Under LOSC Article 290(1), it is necessary that the court or tribunal seised of a request for provisional measures has, *prima facie* (i.e. presumptively) jurisdiction under Part XV or Part XI, Section 5 of the LOSC. Unlike the ICJ, two cases

---

[137] In fact, ITLOS, in the *Southern Bluefin Tuna* cases, clearly stated that it prescribed the provisional measures 'pending a decision of the arbitral tribunal'. The *Southern Bluefin Tuna* cases, p. 1635, para. 90. According to Judge Treves, this expression should be read as meaning up to the moment in which a judgment on the merits has been rendered. Separate Opinion of Judge Treves, *ibid.*, p. 1644, para. 4. See also the *MOX Plant* case, p. 416, para. 89.
[138] Wolfrum, 'The Settlement of Disputes before the International Tribunal for the Law of the Sea', p. 155.
[139] See also ITLOS Statute, Article 25(2).   [140] Rules of Court, Article 75(1).
[141] See Chapter 7, section 3.2 of this book.

TABLE 8.3 LIST OF ITLOS CASES CONCERNING PROVISIONAL MEASURES

Year	Case	Outcome
1998	The *M/V SAIGA (No. 2)* case (Saint Vincent and the Grenadines v. **Guinea**)	Prescribed*
1999	The *Southern Bluefin Tuna* cases (**New Zealand** v. Japan; **Australia** v. Japan)	Prescribed*
2001	The *MOX Plant* case (**Ireland** v. United Kingdom)	Prescribed*
2003	The *Land Reclamation* case (**Malaysia** v. Singapore)	Prescribed*
2010	The *M/V 'Louisa'* case (**Saint Vincent and the Grenadines** v. Spain)	Not-prescribed
2012	The *ARA 'Libertad'* case (**Argentina** v. Ghana)	Prescribed*
2013	The *'Arctic Sunrise'* case (**The Netherlands** v. Russian Federation)	Prescribed*
2015	*Dispute concerning Delimitation of the Maritime Boundary* (Ghana v. **Côte D'Ivoire**)	Prescribed*
2015	The *'Enrica Lexie' Incident* (**Italy** v. India)	Prescribed*

Bold: the State which requested provisional measures.
* ITLOS prescribed measures different in whole or in part from those requested.

must be distinguished on this matter. First, where a dispute has been submitted to ITLOS and a party to the dispute requests the Tribunal to prescribe provisional measures, ITLOS has to verify its own *prima facie* jurisdiction. Second, pending the constitution of an arbitral tribunal, ITLOS or, with respect to activities in the Area, the Sea-Bed Disputes Chamber, may prescribe provisional measures in accordance with Article 290(5). In this case, ITLOS or the Sea-Bed Disputes Chamber is required to determine whether the arbitral tribunal to which a dispute is being submitted would have *prima facie* jurisdiction. Normally once an international court established *prima facie* jurisdiction at the request for provisional measures stage, the same body may be reasonably expected to entertain the merits of the case. Yet this has not always been the case.[142] Recently ITLOS in the *M/V 'Louisa'* case found that it had no jurisdiction to deal with the case,[143] although it had confirmed *prima facie* jurisdiction at the stage of the request for provisional measures.[144]

(ii) *The plausible character of the alleged rights in the principal request*:[145] This requirement was, for the first time in the ITLOS jurisprudence, discussed in the *Ghana/Côte d'Ivoire* case of 2015. According to the Special Chamber, while it need not concern itself with the competing claims of the parties, it needs to satisfy itself that the rights which Côte d'Ivoire claims on the merits and seeks to protect are at least plausible.[146] In this

---

[142] On this issue, see Y. Tanaka, 'A Note on the *M/V "Louisa"* Case' (2014) 45 *ODIL*, pp. 209–11.
[143] The *M/V 'Louisa'* case (Saint Vincent and the Grenadines v. Kingdom of Spain), Merits, Judgment of 28 May 2013, ITLOS Case No. 18, ITLOS Reports 2013, p. 46, para. 151 and p. 47, para. 160.
[144] The *M/V 'Louisa'* case (Saint Vincent and the Grenadines v. Kingdom of Spain), Provisional Measures, Order, 23 December 2010, ITLOS Reports 2008–2010, p. 69, para. 70.
[145] See Chapter 7, ITLOS Reports 2008-2010, p. 69, section 3.2.2 of this book.
[146] The *Ghana/Côte d'Ivoire* case, para. 58.

regard, the Special Chamber, in the *Ghana/Côte D'Ivoire* case, ruled that Côte d'Ivoire had presented enough material to show that the rights it seeks to protect in the disputed area are plausible.[147] Likewise, ITLOS in the 2015 *'Enrica Lexie' Incident* case considered that both parties have sufficiently demonstrated that the rights they seek to protect regarding the *'Enrica Lexie'* incident were plausible.[148] Yet, ITLOS and its Special Chamber provided no further precision with regard to the criterion for determining the plausibility of the claim of the disputing party.[149]

(iii) *Interlinkage between provisional measures and the application made*: As the prescription of provisional measures purports to preserve the rights which are in dispute, such measures must be ancillary to the main claim. Accordingly, provisional measures cannot be used to deal with issues which are not the subject of the main dispute and must not go beyond what is required to preserve the parties' respective rights in relation to the case.

(iv) *Urgency and a risk of irreparable prejudice*: Urgency is an essential requirement of the prescription of provisional measures.[150] LOSC Article 290(5) clarifies this condition, by providing that 'the urgency of situation so requires'. Article 89(4) of the ITLOS Rules also requires that a request for the prescription of provisional measures must indicate 'the urgency of the situation'. Where a dispute was submitted to ITLOS, the Tribunal examines the question as to whether urgency exists pending its own final decision. Where a dispute has been submitted to an arbitral tribunal, ITLOS is required to determine whether the urgency of the situation requires provisional measures pending the constitution of the arbitral tribunal pursuant to LOSC Article 290(5).[151] The requirement of urgency calls for three comments.

First, the ICJ jurisprudence shows that the situation of urgency is closely linked to an imminent risk of irreparable damage to rights of one or other of the parties.[152] However, the ITLOS jurisprudence seems to be inconsistent with regard to the standards of 'irreparable damage' in its reasoning.[153] In the 2002 *MOX Plant* case, ITLOS ruled that provisional measures may be prescribed 'if the Tribunal considered that the urgency of the situation so requires in the sense that action prejudicial to the rights of either party or causing serious harm to the marine environment is likely to be taken before the constitution of the Annex VII arbitral tribunal'.[154] ITLOS took a similar approach in the *Land Reclamation* case of 2003.[155] In the *ARA 'Libertad'* case, however, it did not directly

---

[147] *Ibid.*, para. 62.
[148] The *'Enrica Lexie' Incident* case (Italy v. India), Request for the prescription of provisional measures, Order of 24 August 2015, ITLOS Case No. 24, para. 85. On 15 February 2012, two Italian marines on board the *'Enrica Lexie'* flying the flag of Italy were arrested within the Indian contiguous zone because they allegedly shot and killed two persons on board a fishing vessel which was mistaken to be a pirate vessel. A dispute thus arose with regard to the exercise of criminal jurisdiction by India over the *'Enrica Lexie'* and the Italian marines in connection with the *'Enrica Lexie'* incident.
[149] See also Chapter 7, section 3.2.2 of this book.
[150] Separate Opinion of Judge Treves in the *Southern Bluefin Tuna* cases (Provisional Measures), p. 1644, para. 2.
[151] *Ibid.*, paras. 3–4.
[152] See Chapter 7, section 3.2.4 of this book.
[153] N. Klein, *Dispute Settlement in the UN Convention on the Law of the Sea* (Cambridge University Press, 2005), p. 78.
[154] The *MOX Plant* case, p. 414, para. 64.
[155] *Case Concerning Land Declamation by Singapore in and Around the Straits of Johor*, Provisional Measures, Order of 8 October 2003, ITLOS Case No. 12, ITLOS Reports 2003, p. 22, para. 72.

address the question as to how Ghana's action created irreparable prejudice to the right of Argentina, when accepting the urgency.[156]

Second, in some cases, ITLOS ordered provisional measures even where there was no situation of urgency. In the *MOX Plant* case, for instance, ITLOS prescribed provisional measures, even though it did not find that the urgency of the situation requires the prescription of the provisional measures requested by Ireland.[157] ITLOS, in the 2010 *M/V 'Louisa'* case between Saint Vincent and the Grenadines and Spain, focused on the question of whether or not there existed a real and imminent risk that irreparable prejudice would be caused to the rights of the parties, without directly referring to urgency.[158] The existence of urgency was the most contentious issue in the 2015 *'Enrica Lexie' Incident* case. Italy requested that the Tribunal order should state that, *inter alia*, India shall refrain from taking or enforcing any judicial or administrative measures against the two marines and from exercising any other form of jurisdiction over the *'Enrica Lexie' Incident* case.[159] While Italy contended that urgency was demonstrated by the fact that the exercise of jurisdiction by India was certain and ongoing,[160] India countered that there was absolutely no situation of urgency that justified the Tribunal issuing provisional measures.[161] Although ITLOS did not consider that Italy's requests was appropriate, it prescribed that Italy and India should both suspend all court proceedings and refrain from initiating new ones.[162] In its order, however, the Tribunal did not advance any satisfactory reason for urgency.[163]

Third, the concept of urgency is synonymous with imminence in the ICJ jurisprudence. However, the requirement of urgency needs different consideration in the context of conservation of marine living resources and marine environmental protection. In this regard, Judge Treves, in the *Southern Bluefin Tuna* cases, expressed an insightful view, stating that: 'The urgency concerns the stopping of a trend towards such collapse.'[164] Considering that the decline of fish stocks is a continuous process, as the learned Judge suggested, there appears to be a need to consider the question as to whether or not there is the urgency of situation which requires provisional measures to prevent *a trend* of decline toward a collapse of the fish stock. It must also be noted that since normally scientific uncertainty exists in conservation of these resources, 'prudence and caution' may be required when assessing the existence of urgency.[165] Hence the concept of urgency in the context of conservation of marine living resources is to be closely linked to the precautionary approach.[166] The same is true of the cumulative marine pollution, such as certain land-based marine pollution. In this case, the concept of urgency does not mean an imminent danger, but concerns the prevention of *a trend* of deterioration of the marine

---

[156] However, Judge Paik examined this issue. Declaration of Judge Paik in *ibid.*, pp. 2–3, paras. 5–7.
[157] The *MOX Plant* case, p. 415, para. 81.
[158] The *M/V 'Louisa'* case, Provisional Measures, p. 15, para. 72.
[159] The *'Enrica Lexie' Incident*, para. 29.
[160] *Ibid.*, para. 98.   [161] *Ibid.*, para. 101.   [162] *Ibid.*, para. 127; para. 141(1).
[163] See Declaration of Judge Kateka, *ibid.*, paras. 4–5.
[164] Separate Opinion of Judge Treves in the *Southern Bluefin Tuna* cases, p. 1645, para. 8.
[165] The *Southern Bluefin Tuna* cases, *ibid.*, p. 1634, para. 77.
[166] Separate Opinion of Judge Treves, *ibid.*, p. 1645, para. 8.

environment which may create serious harm in the future. Thus the concept of urgency in the context of conservation of marine living resources and marine environmental protection needs to be considered in a longer timeframe than an imminent risk.

4.6.3 Compliance with Provisional Measures

Finally, some consideration must be given to compliance with provisional measures. In approaching this issue, judicial supervision through ITLOS merits particular mention. Judicial supervision is a procedure which obliges the parties in dispute to submit a report concerning the implementation of these measures to the Tribunal. It is clearly enshrined in Article 95 of the Rules of ITLOS. Thus ITLOS, in its orders concerning provisional measures, has commonly required the disputing parties to submit the initial report to the Tribunal.

In the *Southern Bluefin Tuna* cases, for instance, ITLOS decided that each party shall submit the initial report referred to in Article 95(1) of the Rules not later than 6 October 1999.[167] Following the order, on 6 October 1999, Australia and New Zealand submitted a joint report. On the same day, Japan also submitted its report.[168] The obligation to submit the initial report was also ordered by ITLOS in the 2001 *MOX Plant* order.[169] As decided in the order, Ireland and the United Kingdom, by communications dated 17 December 2001, each submitted the initial report.[170] In this regard, the Annex VII Arbitral Tribunal, which dealt with the merits of the case, noted that it was consistent with the practice of ITLOS that each party should submit reports and information in compliance with the Tribunal's order.[171] The Arbitral Tribunal was also satisfied that since December 2001, there had been an increased measure of cooperation and consultation, as required by the ITLOS order.[172] The submission of a report was also ordered in the1998 *M/V 'Saiga' (No. 2)*[173] *Land Reclamation*,[174] *ARA 'Libertad'*,[175] *'Arctic Sunrise'*,[176] and *'Enrica Lexie' Incident* orders.[177]

When one of the disputing parties fails to comply with provisional measures prescribed by ITLOS, State responsibility arises with regard to that State. The responsibility of the State that failed to comply with these measures can be determined at the merits of the proceedings. The *'Arctic Sunrise'* case is an example. In this case, an issue was raised with regard to the failure of the Russian Federation to comply with provisional measures prescribed by ITLOS on 22 November 2013. In considering this issue, the Annex VII Arbitral Tribunal clearly stated that: 'The failure of a State to comply with provisional measures

---

[167] The *Southern Bluefin Tuna* cases, *ibid.*, p. 1636, para. 90(2).
[168] (1999) 3 *International Tribunal for the Law of the Sea Yearbook*, p. 51.
[169] The *MOX Plant* case, p. 416, para. 89(2).
[170] *Annual Report of the International Tribunal for the Law of the Sea for 2001*, 19 March 2002, SPLOS/74, p. 10, para. 50, available at: www.itlos.org/index.php?id=156; (2001) 5 *International Tribunal for the Law of the Sea Yearbook*, p. 54.
[171] The *MOX Plant* arbitration, p. 19, para. 68. [172] *Ibid.*, para. 66.
[173] The *M/V 'Saiga' (No. 2)* case, p. 1215.   [174] The *Land Reclamation* case, para. 106(3).
[175] The *ARA 'Libertad'* case, p. 23, para. 108.   [176] The *'Arctic Sunrise'* case, p. 24, para. 105(2).
[177] The *'Enrica Lexie' Incident*, para. 141(2).

prescribed by ITLOS is an internationally wrongful act.'[178] The Tribunal considered that Russia breached paragraphs (1) and (2) of the *dispositif* of the ITLOS order.[179]

4.7 Intervention

The ITLOS Statute provides two types of third-party intervention. First, Article 31 of the Statute deals with requests to intervene. Under Article 31(1), a State Party to the LOSC that has an interest of a legal nature which may be affected by the decision in any dispute, may submit a request to ITLOS to be permitted to intervene. If a request to intervene is granted, the decision of ITLOS in respect of the dispute is binding upon the intervening State Party in so far as it relates to matters in respect of which that State Party intervened.[180]

Second, Article 32 provides a right to intervene in the case of interpretation or application of the LOSC as well as other international agreements. Under Article 32(1), wherever the interpretation and application of the LOSC are in question, the Registrar notifies all States Parties forthwith. Whenever the interpretation or application of an international agreement is in question, the Registrar also notifies all the parties to the agreement pursuant to Article 32(2). In this case, every party has the right to intervene in the proceedings. If it uses this right, the interpretation given by the judgment will be equally binding upon it in accordance with Article 32(3).[181] To this day, there is no case concerning intervention in the ITLOS jurisprudence.

4.8 Prompt Release Procedure

4.8.1 General Considerations

According to the prompt release procedure set out in Article 292 of the LOSC, if a vessel is detained by a coastal State for a violation of its regulations with regard to, for instance, fisheries or marine pollution, the vessel shall be promptly released upon posting a bond or other financial security in order to protect the economic and humanitarian interests of the flag State. At the same time, it is necessary for the detaining State to ensure that the master or other relevant persons on the vessel will appear in its domestic courts. Thus, in the words of ITLOS, the prompt release procedure seeks to 'reconcile the interest of the flag State to have its vessel and its crew released promptly with the interest of the detaining State to secure appearance in its court of the Master and the payment of penalties'.[182] Prompt release cases occupy an important part of the ITLOS jurisprudence (see Table 8.4).

The jurisdiction of ITLOS under Article 292 is compulsory between all States Parties to the LOSC irrespective of whether they have accepted that jurisdiction under Article 287 of the Convention. The prompt release procedure is not incidental in nature but independent from any other proceedings in ITLOS.[183] This procedure is not a form of appeal against a

---

[178] The *'Arctic Sunrise'* arbitration, Merits, p. 84, para. 337.   [179] *Ibid.*, pp. 87–9, paras. 350–60.
[180] ITLOS Statute, Article 31(3). See also ITLOS Rules, Article 99.   [181] See also, *ibid.*, Article 100.
[182] The *'Monte Confurco'* case, Case No. 6, 18 December 2000, para. 71.
[183] The *M/V 'Saiga'* case, Case No. 1, 4 December 1997 (1998) 37 ILM, p. 370, para. 50.

TABLE 8.4 LIST OF PROMPT RELEASE CASES

1997	The *M/V 'Saiga'* case (Saint Vincent and the Grenadines v. Guinea)
2000	The *'Camouco'* case (Panama v. France)
2000	The *'Monte Confurco'* case (Seychelles v. France)
2001	The *Grand Prince* case (Belize v. France)
2001	The *Chaisiri Reefer 2* case (Panama v. Yemen) (removed from the list)
2002	The *Volga* case (Russian Federation v. Australia)
2004	The *'Juno Trader'* case (Saint Vincent and the Grenadines v. Guinea-Bissau)
2007	The *'Hoshinmaru'* case (Japan v. Russian Federation)
2007	The *'Tomimaru'* case (Japan v. Russian Federation)

decision of a national court.[184] The Tribunal can deal only with the question of release, without prejudice to the merits of the case before the appropriate domestic forum.

Under Article 292(2), '[t]he application for prompt release may be made only by or on behalf of the flag State of the vessel'. The phrase 'on behalf of the flag State' appears to suggest that applications could be made not only by a government official, including a consular or diplomatic agent, but also by a private person not part of the government of the flag State if that person is authorised to do so by the flag State. In either case, the detained vessel must be flying the flag of the applicant and, thus, the validity of the registration of a vessel is of particular importance.

4.8.2 Substantive Requirements

Under Article 292 of the LOSC, two substantive requirements exist. First, the prompt release procedure applies only to alleged violations of the provisions of the Convention on the prompt release of a vessel or its crew upon the posting of a reasonable bond or other financial security.[185] Views of commentators do not coincide as to which relevant provisions are subject to the prompt release procedure. ITLOS, in the *M/V 'Saiga' (No. 1)* case of 1997, pointed to three provisions that correspond expressly to the above description: Articles 73(2), 220(6) and (7), and, at least to a certain extent, 226(1)(c).[186] There may also be scope for considering that to some extent, the prompt release procedure applies to Articles 216, 218, 219, 220(2) and 226(1)(b).[187] To date, all prompt release disputes have concerned the violation of Article 73(2), which relates to enforcement of laws and regulations of the coastal State with respect to living resources. The fact seems to highlight the seriousness of illegal fishing.

---

[184] The *'Monte Confurco'* case, para. 72; the *'Hoshinmaru'* case, Prompt Release 6 August 2007, ITLOS Case No. 14, ITLOS Reports 2005-2008, p. 47, para. 89.
[185] LOSC, Article 292(1). [186] The *M/V 'Saiga' (No. 1)* case, p. 371, para. 52.
[187] Y. Tanaka, 'Prompt Release in the United Nations Convention on the Law of the Sea: Some Reflections on the ITLOS Jurisprudence' (2004) 51 *NILR*, pp. 241-6; R. Lagoni, 'The International Tribunal for the Law of the Sea: Establishment and "Prompt Release" Procedures' (1996) 11 *IJMCL*, pp. 153-8; D. H. Anderson, 'Investigation, Detention and Release of Foreign Vessels under the UN Convention on the Law of the Sea of 1982 and Other International Agreements' (1996) *IJMCL*, pp. 170-6.

Second, a vessel flying the flag of a State Party to the Convention and/or its crew must have been detained by the authorities of another State Party. As shown in the *'Camouco'*, *'Monte Confurco'* and *'Hoshinmaru'* cases, disputes may arise with regard to the legal situation of the crew of a vessel staying in the State which detained the vessel. Whilst the situation of a crew member must be judged on a case-by-case basis, a key factor may be the seizure of the crew member's passport by a coastal State authority. In the *'Camouco'* and *'Monte Confurco'* cases, ITLOS ordered the release of the master in accordance with Article 292(1) of the LOSC in light of the fact that the master's passport had been seized by the coastal State authorities.[188]

4.8.3 Procedural Requirements

The first procedural requirement for submitting a prompt release dispute to ITLOS is that the parties have failed to agree on submitting the case to a court or tribunal within ten days from the detention. Once the ten-day period has expired, the question of release may be brought before any court or tribunal accepted by the detaining State under Article 287, or such a question may be directly brought before ITLOS, unless the parties have agreed otherwise. The ten-day time limit ensures prompt action on this matter. At the same time, it allows the detaining State to release the detained vessel and/or its crew before the matter is brought before a court or tribunal.

The second procedural requirement is that the flag State has not decided to submit the application for prompt release to 'a court or tribunal accepted by the detaining State under Article 287'. Owing to the urgency of the prompt release procedure, it is hardly conceivable, in reality, that a flag State will bring a dispute relating to prompt release before an arbitral tribunal since it would run the risk of delaying the proceedings by the need to select arbitrators. For the same reason, it appears unlikely, if not impossible, that such a dispute will be submitted to the ICJ unless the Court adopts rules regarding prompt release proceedings.[189]

Third, Article 292(1) inserts another condition by reserving the case where the parties otherwise agree. This represents a fundamental principle of freedom of choice. Thus, if there is such an agreement, it is possible to extend the time limit for negotiation by agreement and not to use the prompt release procedure.[190]

However, the deposit of a bond or other financial security is not a requirement for invoking Article 292. This is clear from Article 111(2)(c) of the ITLOS Rules, which provides that the application 'shall specify the amount, nature and terms of the bond or other financial security that *may have been imposed* by the detaining State'.[191] ITLOS confirmed this view in the *M/V 'Saiga'* and the *'Camouco'* judgments.[192] Furthermore, it is generally recognised that the exhaustion of local remedies rule is not applicable to proceedings regarding prompt release.[193]

---

[188] The *'Camouco'* case, 7 February 2000, ITLOS Case No. 5 (2000) 39 *ILM*, p. 680, para. 71; the *'Monte Confurco'* case, para. 90.
[189] T. Treves, 'The Proceedings Concerning Prompt Release of Vessels and Crews before the International Tribunal for the Law of the Sea' (1996) 11 *IJMCL*, pp. 179–200, p. 188.
[190] Ibid.   [191] Emphasis added.
[192] The *M/V 'Saiga'* case, p. 375, para. 76; the *'Camouco'* case, p. 679, para. 63.
[193] M. H. Nordquist, S. Rosenne and L. B. Sohn (eds.), *United Nations Convention on the Law of the Sea 1982: A Commentary*, Vol. V (The Hague: Nijhoff, 1989), p. 81.

If a municipal court of the detaining State has already rendered a judgment, arguably it is no longer possible to bring the case before ITLOS. A leading case in this particular matter is the *'Tomimaru'* case between Japan and the Russian Federation. The arrested vessel flying the flag of Japan, the *'Tomimaru'*, was confiscated in accordance with a judgment of the Petropavlovsk-Kamchatsky City Court before the dispute was submitted to ITLOS. After the closure of the hearing before ITLOS, the Supreme Court of the Russian Federation dismissed the complaint concerning the review of the decision on the confiscation of the *'Tomimaru'*. ITLOS ruled that a decision to confiscate eliminates the provisional character of the detention of the vessel rendering the prompt release procedure without object.[194] Therefore, ITLOS concluded that the application of Japan no longer had any object.[195] At the same time, it stressed that confiscation of a fishing vessel must not be used in such a manner as to prevent the flag State from resorting to the prompt release procedure set out in the LOSC.[196]

4.8.4 Reasonable Bond

The reasonableness of the bonds to be posted is a crucial issue in the prompt release procedure. While a number of relevant factors need to be considered when determining the reasonableness of the bond, ITLOS, in the *'Camouco'* case, indicated four factors:[197]

(i) the gravity of the alleged offences
(ii) the penalties imposed or imposable under the laws of the detaining State
(iii) the value of the detained vessel[198]
(iv) the value of the cargo seized
(v) the amount of the bond imposed by the detaining State and its form.

The list was by no means complete. Nor did ITLOS lay down rigid rules on the exact weight to be attached to each factor.[199] In reality, the evaluation of those elements is not an easy task. For instance, the value of a vessel cannot always be easily determined. In fact, in the *'Camouco'*, *'Monte Confurco'* and *'Juno Trader'* cases, the parties differed on the value of the ship.[200] In the *'Hoshinmaru'* case, ITLOS did not take the value of the vessel into account in determining the amount of the bond. It would seem that there is a certain degree of inconsistency on this particular matter in the ITLOS jurisprudence.[201]

4.9 Judgment

All questions must be decided by a majority of the members of ITLOS. In the event of an equality of votes, the President or the member of ITLOS who acts in his place shall have a casting vote.[202] The quorum (i.e. the minimum number of judges required to

---

[194] The *'Tomimaru'* case, Prompt Release, 6 August 2007, ITLOS Case No. 15, ITLOS Reports 2005–2008, p. 96 para. 76.
[195] *Ibid.*, p. 98, para. 82.   [196] *Ibid.*, p. 96, paras. 75–6.
[197] The *'Camouco'* case, p. 679, para. 67.
[198] See also ITLOS Rules, Article 111(2)(b) and (c).
[199] The *'Monte Confurco'* case, para. 76.
[200] The *'Camouco'* case, p. 680, para. 69; the *'Monte Confurco'* case, para. 84; the *'Juno Trader'* case, Prompt Release, ITLOS Case No. 13, ITLOS Reports 2004, p. 42, para. 92.
[201] Declaration of Judge Kolodk in the *'Hoshinmaru'* case, p. 54.   [202] ITLOS Statute, Article 29.

constitute the tribunal) is eleven.[203] Like the ICJ, any member shall be entitled to deliver a separate opinion.[204] Article 33 of the ITLOS Statute holds that the decision of ITLOS is final and shall be complied with by all the parties to the dispute. The decision shall have no binding force except between the parties in respect of that particular case.[205] Unless otherwise decided by ITLOS, each party shall bear its own costs.[206]

In the case of the ICJ, if any party to a case fails to perform the obligations incumbent upon it under a judgment rendered by the Court, the other party may have recourse to the Security Council by virtue of Article 94 of the UN Charter. In this case, the Security Council may, if it deems necessary, make recommendations or decide upon measures to be taken to give effect to the judgment. Unlike the ICJ, there is no procedure to ensure the implementation of a judgment of ITLOS.

On the other hand, the LOSC contains provisions with regard to measures to be taken to implement a decision by the Sea-Bed Disputes Chamber. Where the Council of the Authority institutes proceedings on behalf of the Authority before the Sea-Bed Disputes Chamber, the Legal and Technical Commission of the Authority is entitled to make recommendations to the Council with respect to measures to be taken upon a decision by the Sea-Bed Disputes Chamber by virtue of Article 165(2)(j) of the LOSC. Pursuant to Article 162(2)(v), the Council is to notify the Assembly upon a decision by the Sea-Bed Disputes Chamber and make any recommendations which it may find appropriate with respect to measures to be taken. Furthermore, as noted, Article 39 of the ITLOS Statute requires that the decisions of the Chamber shall be enforceable in the territories of the States Parties in the same manner as judgments or orders of the highest court of the State Party in whose territory the enforcement is sought.

Under Article 33(3) of the ITLOS Statute, in the event of dispute as to the meaning or scope of *the decision*, ITLOS is to construe it upon the request of any party. Whilst the term 'the decision' appears to include both a judgment and an order, Article 126 of the ITLOS Rules makes clear that in the event of dispute as to the meaning or scope of *a judgment*, any party may make a request for its interpretation. Related to this, Article 127 of the ITLOS Rules provides for revision of the judgment. Under this provision, a request for revision of a judgment may be made only when it is based upon the discovery of some fact of such a nature as to be a decisive factor, which fact was unknown to ITLOS and also to the party requesting revision when the judgment was given. However, such ignorance must not be due to negligence. Such request must be made at the latest within six months of the discovery of the new fact and before the lapse of ten years from the date of the judgment.

4.10 Advisory Proceedings

Like the ICJ, ITLOS may also give advisory opinions. The advisory jurisdiction is exercised by the Sea-Bed Disputes Chamber as well as ITLOS as a full court.

---

[203] *Ibid.*, Article 13(1).   [204] *Ibid.*, Article 30(3).
[205] See also LOSC, Article 296.
[206] ITLOS Statute, Article 34. In order to assist developing States which are parties to a dispute before ITLOS, the International Tribunal for the Law of the Sea Trust Fund was established in 2000. The terms of reference of the Fund are annexed to UN General Assembly Resolution 55/7 of 30 October 2000 (Annex I).

4.10.1 The Advisory Jurisdiction of the Sea-Bed Disputes Chamber

The Assembly and the Council of the Authority is empowered to request an advisory opinion from the Sea-Bed Disputes Chamber. This means that the advisory jurisdiction is connected with the activities of the two principal organs of the Authority. The underlying reason for the advisory jurisdiction of the Sea-Bed Disputes Chamber is that the Authority may need to require the assistance of an independent and impartial judicial body in order to exercise its function properly.[207]

Under Article 159(10) of the LOSC, upon a written request addressed to the President and sponsored by at least one-quarter of the members of the Authority for an advisory opinion on the conformity with ITLOS of a proposal before the Assembly on any matter, the Assembly is to request the Sea-Bed Disputes Chamber to give an advisory opinion. The Council of the Authority is also allowed to request an advisory opinion from the Sea-Bed Disputes Chamber.[208] The key provision in relation to the advisory jurisdiction of the Sea-Bed Disputes Chamber is Article 191 of the LOSC. This provision contains three conditions to give an advisory opinion:

(i) there is a request from the Assembly or Council
(ii) the request concerns legal questions
(iii) these legal questions have arisen within the scope of the Assembly's or Council's activities.

Unlike Article 65(1) of the ICJ Statute which states that the Court 'may give' an advisory opinion, Article 191 provides that the Sea-Bed Disputes Chamber 'shall give' advisory opinions. In light of this difference, some argue that once the Sea-Bed Disputes Chamber has established its jurisdiction, it has no discretion to decline a request for an advisory opinion. Yet the Sea-Bed Disputes Chamber, in its first advisory opinion of 2011, did not pronounce the consequences of that difference.[209]

When exercising its functions relating to advisory opinions, the Sea-Bed Disputes Chamber shall consider whether the request for an advisory opinion relates to a legal question pending between two or more parties. When it so determines, Article 17 of the ITLOS Statute applies, as well as the provisions of these rules concerning the application of that article.[210] Any judge may attach a separate or dissenting opinion to the advisory opinion of the Chamber.[211] The advisory opinions of the Sea-Bed Disputes Chamber have no binding effect. On 1 February 2011, the Sea-Bed Disputes Chamber gave its first advisory opinion (i.e. *Responsibilities and Obligations of States Sponsoring Persons and Entities with Respect to Activities in the Area*).[212]

---

[207] *Responsibilities and Obligations of States Sponsoring Persons and Entities with Respect to Activities in the Area*, Case No. 17, 1 February 2011, para. 26.
[208] LOSC, Article 191.
[209] *Responsibilities and Obligations of States Sponsoring Persons*, paras. 47–8.
[210] ITLOS Rules, Article 130. Article 17 of the ITLOS Statute relates to nationality of members, including judges *ad hoc*.
[211] ITLOS Rules, Article 135(3).
[212] For a commentary on this opinion, see D. French, 'From the Depths: Rich Pickings of Principles of Sustainable Development and General International Law on the Ocean Floor – the Seabed Disputes Chamber's 2011 Advisory Opinion' (2011) 26 *IJMCL*, pp. 525–68; R. Rayfuse, 'Differentiating the Common? The Responsibilities and Obligations of States Sponsoring Deep Seabed Mining Activities in the Area' (2011) 54 *GYIL*, pp. 459–88; Y. Tanaka, 'Obligations and Liability of Sponsoring States Concerning Activities in the Area: Reflections on the ITLOS Advisory Opinion of 1 February 2011' (2013) 60 *NILR*, pp. 205–30.

4.10.2 The Advisory Jurisdiction of ITLOS Full Court

Unlike the Sea-Bed Disputes Chamber of ITLOS, the LOSC contains no explicit provision concerning the advisory jurisdiction of ITLOS as a full court. An issue thus arises whether the advisory jurisdiction is conferred to the full Tribunal under the LOSC. In the advisory opinion of 2015, ITLOS took the position that the legal basis of the advisory jurisdiction can be found in Article 21 of the ITLOS Statute, which provides that:

> The jurisdiction of the Tribunal comprises all disputes and all applications submitted to it in accordance with this Convention and all matters specifically provided for in any other agreement which confers jurisdiction on the Tribunal.

According to the Tribunal, the words all 'matters' should not be interpreted as covering only 'disputes' for, if that were to be the case, Article 21 would have used the word 'disputes'. Thus the words must mean something more than only 'disputes' and that something 'must include advisory opinions, if specifically provided for in "any other agreement which confers jurisdiction on the Tribunal"'.[213] In the Tribunal's view, 'the expression "all matters specifically provided for in any other agreement which confers jurisdiction on the Tribunal" does not by itself establish the advisory jurisdiction of the Tribunal', but 'it is the "other agreement" which confers such jurisdiction on the Tribunal'.[214]

Article 138 of the Rules of the Tribunal specifies three prerequisites for ITLOS to give an advisory opinion:[215]

(i) An international agreement related to the purposes of the Convention specifically provides for the submission to the Tribunal of a request for an advisory opinion.
(ii) The request must be transmitted to the Tribunal by a body authorised by or in accordance with the agreement mentioned above.
(iii) Such an opinion may be given on 'a legal question'.

These elements call for two comments.

First, under Article 131(1) of the Rules of the Tribunal, the request 'shall contain a precise statement of the question'[216] and it must be along with all documents likely to throw light upon the question.[217] To give an advisory opinion to highly abstract questions may entail the risk of affecting the rights and obligations of third States, without their consent. Furthermore, as explained above, the Sea-Bed Disputes Chamber is to deal with questions with regard to activities in the area. Accordingly, it appears logical to consider

---

[213] *Request for an Advisory Opinion Submitted by the Sub-Regional Fisheries Commission (SRFC)*, ITLOS Case No. 21, Advisory Opinion of 2 April 2015, para. 56, available at: www.itlos.org/cases/list-of-cases/case-no-21/. See also Gautier, 'The Settlement of Disputes', p. 565.

[214] The 2015 advisory opinion, para. 58. Yet the legal basis for the advisory jurisdiction of ITLOS as a full court is not free from controversy. In this regard, see Y. Tanaka, 'Reflections on the Advisory Jurisdiction of ITLOS as a Full Court: The ITLOS Advisory Opinion of 2015' (2015) 14 *The Law and Practice of International Courts and Tribunals*, pp. 321–33.

[215] The 2015 ITLOS advisory opinion, para. 60. See also T. M. Ndiaye, 'The Advisory Function of the International Tribunal for the Law of the Sea' (2010) 9 *CJIL*, pp. 585 *et seq.*

[216] Article 131(1) applies by virtue of Article 138(3) of the Rules of the Tribunal.

[217] Articles 131(1) and 138(3) of the Rules of the Tribunal.

that a legal question must be unrelated to such activities, though this condition is not expressly stated.

Second, the scope of a 'body' authorised by an international agreement to request an advisory opinion of ITLOS as a full court needs further clarification. In the case of the advisory Sea-Bed Disputes Chamber, only the Assembly and Council of the International Sea-Bed Authority are allowed to request an advisory opinion from the Chamber under Article 191 of the LOSC. Yet, there is no corresponding provision in the Rules of the Tribunal. It appears that the opinions of commentators are divided in this matter. According to the restrictive interpretation, 'a body' under Article 138 of the Rules of the Tribunal is limited to international organisations.[218] In contrast, according to the broad interpretation, any organ, entity, institution, organisation or State would be a 'body' within the meaning of Article 138(2) of the Rules of the Tribunal.[219] According to this interpretation, however, two States Parties to 'any other agreement which confers jurisdiction on the Tribunal' may request an advisory opinion from ITLOS touching on the provisions of the LOSC, whereas the parties to the LOSC cannot request an advisory opinion on the basis of the Convention.[220] This odd situation creates the risk that a small group of States can obtain some advantages in the detriment of the rights and interests of third States.[221] It might even encourage States to enter into new agreements, the sole purpose of which is to request for an advisory jurisdiction to the full Tribunal over a matter under another agreement that does not confer such jurisdiction.[222] In order to prevent the abuse of advisory opinions, arguably the scope of the body which is authorised to request an advisory opinion from the full Tribunal needs to be interpreted in a cautious and restrictive manner.[223]

Concerning the admissibility of a request for an advisory opinion, Article 138 of the Rules of the Tribunal, 'the Tribunal *may* give an advisory opinion'.[224] The language of this provision seems to suggest that the Tribunal has a discretionary power to refuse to give an advisory opinion.[225] By referring to the advisory opinion of the ICJ concerning

---

[218] This interpretation is supported by Judges Ndiaye and Treves. Ndiaye, 'The Advisory Function', p. 583; T. Treves, 'Advisory Opinion under the Law of the Sea Convention' in J. N. Moore and M. H. Nordquist (eds.), *Current Marine Environmental Issues and the International Tribunal for the Law of the Sea* (Leiden: Nijhoff, 2001), p. 92. See also Ki-Jun You, 'Advisory Opinions of the International Tribunal for the Law of the Sea: Article 138 of the Rules of the Tribunal, Revisited' (2008) 39 *ODIL*, pp. 364–5.

[219] P. Chandrasekhara Rao and P. Gautier (eds.), *The Rules of the International Tribunal for the Law of the Sea: A Commentary* (Leiden: Nijhoff, 2006), p. 394. The broad interpretation is echoed by Judges Wolfrum, Jesus and Registrar Gautier. Statement by Mr Rüdiger Wolfrum on Agenda Item 75(a), 28 November 2005, para. 16; Judge José Luis Jesus, President of the International Tribunal for the Law of the Sea, The Gilberto Amado Memorial Lecture held during the 61st Session of the International Law Commission, Geneva, 15 July 2009, pp. 9–10, available at: www.itlos.org/en/press-media/statements-of-the-president/statements-of-president-jesus/; Gautier, 'The Settlement of Disputes', pp. 565–6.

[220] Written statement of Australia, ITLOS Case No. 21, 28 November 2013, p. 11, para. 28; presentation by Mr Campbell, Verbatim Record, ITLOS/PV.14/C21/2, 3 September 2014, p. 18, available at: www.itlos.org/cases/list-of-cases/case-no-21/.

[221] Declaration of Judge Cot in the 2015 ITLOS advisory opinion, para. 9.

[222] Written statement of the United States of America, ITLOS Case No. 21, 27 November 2013, p. 12, para. 38.

[223] This interpretation is supported by Judges Ndiaye and Treves. Ndiaye, 'The Advisory Function', p. 583; Treves, 'Advisory Opinion under the Law of the Sea Convention', p. 92. See also Ki-Jun You, 'Advisory Opinions of the International Tribunal for the Law of the Sea: Article 138 of the Rules of the Tribunal, Revisited' (2008) 39 *ODIL*, pp. 364–5; Tanaka, 'Reflections on the Advisory Jurisdiction', pp. 336–8.

[224] Emphasis added.

[225] The 2015 ITLOS advisory opinion, para. 71.

Legality of the Threat or Use of Nuclear Weapons,[226] however, ITLOS held that: 'It is well settled that a request for an advisory opinion should not in principle be refused except for "compelling reasons".'[227]

5 ARBITRATION UNDER THE LOSC

5.1 Annex VII Arbitral Tribunal under the LOSC

A noteworthy feature of dispute settlement under the LOSC concerns the activation of an arbitral tribunal constituted in accordance with Annex VII of the LOSC. As shown in Table 8.5, an increasing number of disputes is submitted to an Annex VII arbitral tribunal. Subject to the provisions of Part XV, any party to a dispute may submit the dispute to the arbitral procedure provided for in this annex by written notification addressed to the other party or parties to the dispute.[228] A list of arbitrators is to be drawn up and maintained by the UN Secretary-General. Every State Party shall be entitled to nominate four arbitrators, each of whom shall be a person experienced in maritime affairs and enjoying the highest reputation for fairness, competence and integrity. The names of the persons so nominated shall constitute the list.[229] The arbitral tribunal consists of five members. Each party is to appoint one member to be chosen preferably from the list of arbitrators set out in Article 2 of Annex VII. The other three members are to be appointed by agreement between the parties preferably from the list. The parties to the dispute are to appoint the president of the arbitral tribunal from among those three members. If, within sixty days of receipt of the notification referred to in Article 1 of this annex, the parties are unable to reach agreement on the appointment of one or more of the members of the tribunal to be appointed by agreement, or on the appointment of the president, the President of ITLOS is to make the necessary appointments in accordance with Article 3(e) of Annex VII.

The arbitral tribunal has jurisdiction over any dispute concerning the interpretation or application of this Convention which is submitted to it in accordance with Part XV. It also has jurisdiction over any dispute concerning the interpretation or application of an international agreement related to the purposes of this Convention which is submitted to it in accordance with the agreement.[230] It shall apply the LOSC and other rules of international law not incompatible with this Convention. It also has the power to decide a case *ex aequo et bono*, if the parties so agree.[231]

5.2 Annex VIII Special Arbitral Tribunal

The special arbitral tribunal constituted under Annex VIII consists of five members, and they are experts in the fields of fisheries, protection and preservation of the marine environment, marine scientific research, and navigation, including pollution from vessels and by dumping. Accordingly, special arbitrators do not need to be lawyers. The jurisdiction of a special arbitral tribunal is restricted to disputes in the four special fields.[232] It is

---

[226] *Legality of the Threat or Use of Nuclear Weapons*, ICJ Reports 1996, p. 235, para. 14.
[227] The 2015 ITLOS advisory opinion, para. 71.
[228] Article 1 of Annex VII of the LOSC.   [229] Article 2(1) of Annex VII of the LOSC.
[230] Article 288(1) and (2) of the LOSC.
[231] Article 293 of the LOSC.   [232] Articles 1 and 2 of Annex VIII.

TABLE 8.5 ARBITRATION UNDER ANNEX VII OF THE LOSC

1998	The *M/V 'Saiga'* arbitration (discontinued in 1998)
2000	The *Southern Bluefin Tuna* arbitration (Australia and New Zealand v. Japan) (jurisdiction and admissibility)
2003	The *MOX Plant* arbitration (Ireland v. UK) (suspension of proceedings on jurisdiction and merits and request for further provisional measures) (case withdrawn 2008)
2005	The *Land Reclamation by Singapore in and around the Straits of Johor* arbitration (Malaysia v. Singapore) (case settled in 2005)
2006	The *Barbados/Trinidad and Tobago* arbitration (Barbados v. Trinidad and Tobago)
2007	The *Guyana/Suriname* arbitration (Guyana v. Suriname)
2009	The *Bangladesh/Myanmar* arbitration (discontinued in 2009)
2011	The *M/V 'Virginia G'* arbitration (Panama v. Guinea-Bissau, transferred to ITLOS 2011)
2013	The *ARA 'Libertad'* arbitration (Argentina v. Ghana, terminated in 2013)
2014	The *Bay of Bengal Maritime Boundary* arbitration (Bangladesh v. India)
2014	The *Atlando-Scandian Herring* case (Denmark in respect of the Faroe Islands v. The European Union, terminated in 2014)
2014	The *'Arctic Sunrise'* arbitration (Netherlands v. Russia)
2015	The *Chagos Marine Protected Area* arbitration (Mauritius v. United Kingdom)
2016	The *South China Sea* arbitration (Philippines v. People's Republic of China)
2016	The *Duzgit Integrity* arbitration (Malta v. São Tomé and Principe)
	The *'Enrica Lexie' Incident* arbitration (Italy v. India, pending)
	Dispute Concerning Coastal State Rights in the Black Sea, Sea of Azov, and Kerch Strait (Ukraine v. The Russian Federation, pending)

relevant to note that a special arbitral tribunal under Annex VIII is empowered to carry out an inquiry in accordance with the agreement between the parties to a dispute. The findings of fact of such a tribunal are considered as conclusive as between the parties.[233] The fact-finding of a special arbitral tribunal seems to provide an interesting example of 'binding inquiry'. If all the disputing parties so request, the special arbitral tribunal may formulate non-binding recommendations for a review by the parties of the questions giving rise to the dispute.[234] In this case, it appears that the function of such a tribunal is akin to conciliation.

6 FRAGMENTATION OF INTERNATIONAL LAW

As explained earlier, the LOSC created new judicial organs. Thus this is a convenient point to discuss the issues of fragmentation of international law arising from the proliferation of international courts and tribunals. It is argued that the proliferation of judicial organs may entail the risk of creating fragmentation of international

---

[233] Article 5(1) and (2) of Annex VIII. [234] Article 5(3) of Annex VIII.

law.[235] Indeed, when establishing ITLOS, a concern was voiced that the creation of a new tribunal specialised in law of the sea disputes would run the risk of separating the development of the law of the sea from the general rules of international law.[236] In considering this issue, an interesting example is provided by the interpretation of Article 281 of the LOSC.[237]

The legal effect of Article 281 was tested in the 1999 *Southern Bluefin Tuna* cases between Australia and New Zealand on the one hand and Japan on the other hand. A pivotal issue was whether or not Article 16 of the 1993 Convention for the Conservation of Southern Bluefin Tuna (hereafter the 1993 Convention) precludes the application of compulsory procedures in the LOSC. Japan contended that recourse to the arbitral tribunal was excluded because the 1993 Convention provides for a dispute settlement procedure. However, Australia and New Zealand denied the claim of Japan since the 1993 Convention does not provide for a compulsory dispute settlement procedure entailing a binding decision as required under Article 282 of the LOSC.[238] ITLOS was not persuaded by Japan's argument. According to ITLOS, the fact that the 1993 Convention applies between the parties 'does not preclude recourse to the procedures in Part XV, section 2, of the Convention on the Law of the Sea'.[239] It thus held that the requirements for invoking those procedures had been fulfilled and that the arbitral tribunal would *prima facie* have jurisdiction over the disputes.[240]

However, the view of ITLOS was not echoed by the Annex VII Arbitral Tribunal at the merits stage. Article 16 does not expressly exclude the applicability of any procedure, including the compulsory procedures of section 2 of Part XV of the LOSC. In the view of the Arbitral Tribunal, however, 'the absence of an express exclusion of any procedure in Article 16 is not decisive' since the dispute is not referable to adjudication by the ICJ or ITLOS or to arbitration 'at the request of any party to the dispute' under Article 16 of the 1993 Convention.[241] The Arbitral Tribunal also pointed out that the wording of Article 16(1) and (2) has its essential origins in the terms of Article XI of the Antarctic Treaty. According to the Arbitral Tribunal, 'it is obvious that these provisions are meant to exclude compulsory jurisdiction'.[242] It thus concluded that Article 16 of the 1993 Convention excludes any further procedure within the contemplation of Article 281(1) of the LOSC[243] and that the Annex VII Tribunal lacked jurisdiction to entertain the merits of the dispute.[244] Thus two different interpretations were taken by ITLOS and the Annex VII Arbitral Tribunal.[245]

---

[235] Generally on this issue, see in particular, *Fragmentation of International Law: Difficulties Arising from the Diversification and Expansion of International Law, Report of the Study Group of the International Law Commission Finalised by Martti Koskenniemi*, A/CN.4/L.682, 13 April 2006; R. Higgins, 'The ICJ, the ECJ, and the Integrity of International Law' (2003) 52 *ICLQ*, pp. 1–20; by the same writer, 'A Babel of Judicial Voices? Ruminations from the Bench' (2006) 55 *ICLQ*, pp. 791–804.
[236] S. Oda, 'Dispute Settlement Prospects in the Law of the Sea' (1995) 44 *ICLQ*, p. 864.
[237] See also Chapter 8, section 2.1 of this book.
[238] *Southern Bluefin Tuna* cases (New Zealand v. Japan; Australia v. Japan), Provisional Measures, ITLOS Case No. 3 and 4, Order of 27 August 1999 (1999) 38 *ILM*, pp. 1632–3, paras. 53–4.
[239] *Ibid.*, p. 1633, para. 55.   [240] *Ibid.*, paras. 61–2.
[241] *Southern Bluefin Tuna* award, 4 August 2000, 23 *RIAA*, p. 43, para. 57.
[242] *Ibid.*, p. 44, para. 58.   [243] *Ibid.*, para. 59.   [244] *Ibid.*, p. 46, para. 65.
[245] The interpretation of Article 281 by the Arbitral Tribunal was challenged by one of its members, Judge Keith. Separate Opinion of Justice Sir Kenneth Keith in *Southern Bluefin Tuna* award, *ibid.*, pp. 53–5, paras. 18–22.

The interpretation of Article 281 was discussed in the 2015 *South China Sea* arbitration (jurisdiction and admissibility) again. A pivotal issue in this case was whether an explicit exclusion is required to preclude the application of the Part XV dispute settlement procedures. While the Philippines argued that the intent to exclude further procedures under the LOSC must be evident from the terms of the agreement itself, China considered an explicit exclusion unnecessary and it subscribed to the majority view of the Annex VII Tribunal in the *Southern Bluefin Tuna* cases. Notably, the Annex VII Arbitral Tribunal departed from the broad interpretation taken in the *Southern Bluefin Tuna* arbitration, stating that: '[T]he better view is that Article 281 requires some clear statement of exclusion of further procedures.'[246] The Tribunal thus explicitly supported the views of ITLOS in its order of 1999 as well as the separate opinion of Judge Keith in the 2000 *Southern Bluefin Tuna* award.[247] This would entail a decision not to accord precedential effect to the *Southern Bluefin Tuna* arbitral award. It appears that the different interpretation with regard to Article 281 of the LOSC exemplifies a real possibility of the fragmentation of international law.

As shown in the above example, one cannot completely deny the risk that the fragmentation of international law exists in international jurisprudence. However, there appears to be some scope for considering the question of whether the risk derives from the proliferation of international courts and tribunals alone. Although unity of international law can be easily exaggerated,[248] total harmony of interpretation of rules of international law cannot be secured in the international legal system which lacks a centralised authority to exercise legislative, executive and judicial functions. Fragmentation can be regarded as an inherent limitation with a decentralised and unhierarchical legal system and it is not a novel phenomenon in international law. As Higgins observed, it is conceivable that harmonisation of interpretation of rules of international law is left to the wisdom of international judges.[249]

7 CONCLUSIONS

Overall it can be said that the LOSC created a unique system of international dispute settlement. Principal points of the system can be summarised as follows:

(i) Multiple forms of judicial settlement are set out in Part XV of the Convention. This is a unique mechanism that seeks to strike a balance between compulsory procedures and the flexibility of the selection of an appropriate forum on the basis of the consent of the disputing parties.

(ii) The establishment of the compulsory procedures for dispute settlement is a key step forward. Nonetheless, two important categories of disputes – namely, fisheries and

---

[246] PCA Case No. 2013-19, the *South China Sea* arbitration (Jurisdiction and Admissibility), 29 October 2015, pp. 86-7, para. 223.
[247] *Ibid.*, p. 87, para. 223.
[248] H. Thirlway, 'The Proliferation of International Judicial Organs and the Formation of International Law' in W. P. Here (ed.), *International Law and the Hague's 750th Anniversary* (The Hague: T. M. C. Asser Press, 1999), pp. 434-5.
[249] See also Higgins, 'A Babel of Judicial Voices?', p. 804.

marine scientific research in the EEZ – are exempted from the compulsory procedures for dispute settlement. Furthermore, certain categories of disputes – those concerning maritime delimitations or those involving historic bays or title, those concerning military activities and those in respect of which the UN Security Council is exercising its functions – may also be exempt from such procedures. It may have to be admitted that the automatic limitations and optional exceptions weaken the compulsory procedures for dispute settlement. Furthermore, as typically demonstrated in the *South China Sea* arbitration, characterisation of an international dispute constitutes a crucial issue when determining whether that dispute would fall within the category excluded from the compulsory procedure.

(iii) ITLOS is a permanent judicial organ and comprises a variety of Chambers. Notably, with regard to particular disputes, ITLOS is open to a broad range of entities other than States. The wide scope of *locus standi* of ITLOS seems to reflect the diversity of actors involved in marine affairs.

(iv) The jurisprudence of ITLOS and Annex VII arbitral tribunals has a valuable role in the identification, clarification and formulation of rules of the law of the sea. Moreover, advisory opinions of the Sea-Bed Disputes Chamber and ITLOS can be considered as important tools to clarify relevant rules of the law of the sea. The accumulation of the jurisprudence will also contribute to the development of procedural rules governing the dispute settlement system under the LOSC.

(v) As shown in the interpretation of Article 281, one cannot completely deny the risk that different judicial organs may take different views on the interpretation of the same rule. In this sense, it may have to be admitted that the risk of the fragmentation of international law exists in international jurisprudence. Even so, it can be observed that ITLOS has endeavoured to secure consistency with the jurisprudence of the ICJ as well as the development of the rules of international law in general. Thus it would be wrong to lay too great an emphasis on the risk of the fragmentation of international law in ITLOS jurisprudence.

FURTHER READING

General

As there are many studies on the dispute settlement system under the LOSC, only publications after 2000 will be listed here.

R. Churchill, 'Trends in Dispute Settlement in the Law of the Sea: Towards the Increasing Availability of Compulsory Means' in D. French, M. Saul and N. D. White (eds.), *International Law and Dispute Settlement: New Problems and Techniques* (Oxford and Portland: Oregon, Hart Publishing, 2010), pp. 143–71.

P. Gautier, 'The Settlement of Disputes' in D. J. Attard, M. Fitzmaurice and N. A. Martínex Gutiérrez (eds.), *The IMLI Manual on International Maritime Law, Vol. I: The Law of the Sea* (Oxford University Press, 2014), pp. 533–76.

I. V. Karaman, *Dispute Resolution in the Law of the Sea* (Leiden: Nijhoff, 2012).

N. Klein, *Dispute Settlement in the UN Convention on the Law of the Sea* (Cambridge University Press, 2005).

'Expansions and Restrictions in the UNCLOS Dispute Settlement Regime: Lessons from Recent Decisions'(2016) 15 *CJIL*, pp. 403–15.

D. König (ed.), 'Symposium to Mark the Tenth Anniversary of ITLOS: the Jurisprudence of the International Tribunal of the Law of the Sea: Assessment and Prospects' (2007) 22 *IJMCL*, pp. 347 *et seq*.

B. H. Oxman, 'Courts and Tribunals: The ICJ, ITLOS, and Arbitral Tribunals' in D. R. Rothwell et al. (eds.), *The Oxford Handbook of the Law of the Sea* (Oxford University Press, 2015), pp. 394–415.

ITLOS

P. Chandrasekhara Rao, 'ITLOS: The First Six Years' (2002) 6 *Max Planck Yearbook of United Nations Law*, pp. 183–300.

P. Chandrasekhara Rao and P. Gautier (eds.), *The Rules of the International Tribunal for the Law of the Sea: A Commentary* (Leiden: Nijhoff, 2006).

G. Eiriksson, *The International Tribunal for the Law of the Sea* (The Hague: Nijhoff, 2000).

M. G. García-Revillo, *The Contentious and Advisory Jurisdiction of the International Tribunal for the Law of the Sea* (Leiden: Nijhoff, 2015).

M. Kamto, 'Regard sur la jurisprudence du Tribunal international du droit de la mer depuis son entrée en fonctionnement (1997–2004)' (2005) 109 *RGDIP*, pp. 769–828.

M. M. Marsit, *Le Tribunal du droit de la mer: présentation et texts officiels* (Paris: Pedone, 1999).

T. M. Ndiaye, 'Proceedings on the Merits Before the International Tribunal for the Law of the Sea' (2008) 48 *Indian Journal of International Law*, pp. 169–87.

T. Treves, 'The Law of the Sea Tribunal: Its Status and Scope of Jurisdiction after November 16 1994' (1995) 55 *ZaöRV*, pp. 421–51.

R. Wolfrum, 'The Settlement of Disputes before the International Tribunal for the Law of the Sea: A Progressive Development of International Law or Relying on Traditional Mechanisms?' (2008) 51 *Japanese Yearbook of International Law*, pp. 140–63.

Provisional Measures

P. Gautier, 'Mesures conservatoire, préjudice irréparable et protection de l'environnement' in *Liber amicorum Jean-Pierre Cot: Le procès international* (Brussels: Bruyant, 2009), pp. 131–54.

J-G. Mahinga, 'Les Procedures en prescription de measures conservatoires devant le Tribunal international du droit de la mer' (2004) 9 *Annauire du droit de la mer*, pp. 65–113.

T. A. Mensah, 'Provisional Measures in the International Law of the Sea (ITLOS)' (2002) 62 *ZaöRV*, pp. 43–54.

F. Orrego Vocuña, 'The International Tribunal for the Law of the Sea and Provisional Measures: Settled Issues and Pending Problems' (2007) 22 *IJMCL*, pp. 451–62.

S. Rosenne, *Provisional Measures in International Law: The International Court of Justice and the International Tribunal for the Law of the Sea* (Oxford University Press, 2005).

Y. Tanaka, 'Juridical Insights into the Protection of Community Interests through Provisional Measures: Reflections on the ITLOS Jurisprudence' (2014) 14 *The Global Community Yearbook of International Law and Jurisprudence*, pp. 249–73.

T. Treves, 'Les Mesures conservatoires au Tribunal de droit de la mer et à la Cour internationale de justice : Contribution au dialogue entre cours et tribunaux internationaux' in *Liber amicorum Jean- Pierre Cot : Le procès international* (Brussels: Bruyant, 2009), pp. 341–8.

P. Weckel, 'Les Premières Applications de l'article 290 de la Convention sur le droit de la mer relative à la prescription de mesures conservatoires' (2005) 109 *RGDIP*, pp. 829–58.

R. Wolfrum, 'Provisional Measures of the International Tribunal for the Law of the Sea' in P. C. Rao and R. Khan (eds.), *The International Tribunal for the Law of the Sea* (The Hague: Kluwer, 2001), pp. 173–86.

Advisory Opinions

M. Lando, 'The Advisory Jurisdiction of the International Tribunal for the Law of the Sea: Comments on the Request for an Advisory Opinion Submitted by the Sub-Regional Fisheries Commission' (2016) 29 *LJIL*, pp. 441-61.

Tafsir Malick Ndiaye, 'The Advisory Function of the International Tribunal for the Law of the Sea' (2010) 9(3) *CJIL*, pp. 565-87.

Y. Tanaka, 'Reflections on the Advisory Jurisdiction of ITLOS as a Full Court: The ITLOS Advisory Opinion of 2015' (2015) 14 *The Law and Practice of International Courts and Tribunals*, pp. 318-39.

T. Treves, 'Advisory Opinions Under the Law of the Sea Convention' in M. H. Nordquist and J. N. Moore (eds.), *Current Marine Environmental Issues and the International Tribunal for the Law of the Sea* (The Hague: Nijhoff, 2001), pp. 81-93.

Ki-Jun You, 'Advisory Opinions of the International Tribunal for the Law of the Sea: Article 138 of the Rules of the Tribunal, Revisited' (2008) 39 *ODIL*, pp. 360-71.

Prompt Release

For an overview of the prompt release procedure, the following articles are of particular interest.

T. A. Mensah, 'The Tribunal and the Prompt Release of Vessels' (2007) 22 *IJMCL*, pp. 425-50.

Y. Tanaka, 'Prompt Release in the United Nations Convention on the Law of the Sea: Some Reflections on the ITLOS Jurisprudence' (2004) 51 *NILR*, pp. 237-71.

T. Treves, 'The Proceedings Concerning Prompt Release of Vessels and Crews before the International Tribunal for the Law of the Sea' (1996) 11 *IJMCL*, pp. 179-200.

M. White, 'Prompt Release Cases in ITLOS' in T. M. Ndiaye, R. Wolfrum and C. Kojima (eds.), *Law of the Sea, Environmental Law and Settlement of Disputes: Liber Amicorum Judge Thomas A. Mensah* (Leiden: Nijhoff, 2007), pp. 1025-52.

The *South China Sea* Arbitration (Jurisdiction and Admissibility)

K. Parlett, 'Jurisdiction of the Arbitral Tribunal in Philippines v. China under UNCLOS and in the Absence of China' (2016) 110 *American Journal of International Law Unbound*, pp. 266-72.

P. S. Rao, 'The South China Sea Arbitration (The Philippines v. China): Assessment of the Award on Jurisdiction and Admissibility' (2016) 15 *Chinese Journal of International Law*, pp. 265-307.

A. D. Sofaer, 'The Philippine Law of the Sea Action against China: Relearning the Limits of International Adjudication' (2016) 15 *CJIL*, pp. 393-402.

S. Talmon, 'The South China Sea Arbitration: Observations on the Award on Jurisdiction and Admissibility' (2016) 15 *CJIL*, pp. 309-91.

Y. Tanaka, 'Reflections on the *Philippines/China* Arbitration: Award on Jurisdiction and Admissibility' (2016) 15 *The Law and Practice of International Courts and Tribunals*, pp. 305-25.

C. Whomersley, 'The South China Sea: The Award of the Tribunal in the Case Brought by Philippines against China – A Critique' (2016) 15 *CJIL*, pp. 239-64.

The WTO Dispute Settlement System

Main Issues

The WTO dispute settlement system is characterised by some particular features, such as the 'reverse consensus' decision-making procedure, appellate review procedure and surveillance of the implementation of recommendations and rulings. Owing to its unique features, the dispute settlement system of the WTO provides a useful insight into development of the international law of peaceful settlement of international disputes. This chapter will seek to examine the key issues of the WTO dispute settlement system. In particular, the following issues will be discussed:

(i) What are the principal features of the WTO dispute settlement system?
(ii) What is the role of consultations in the WTO dispute settlement system?
(iii) What are the procedures of a panel and the Appellate Body?
(iv) How is it possible to secure the effective implementation of recommendations and ruling of WTO panels and the Appellate Body?
(v) What is the role of arbitration and how is it integrated into the WTO dispute settlement system?
(vi) What is the position of developing Members in the WTO dispute settlement system?

1 INTRODUCTION

1.1 International Dispute Settlement in GATT

In the blueprint for the post-war international order, economic development was considered as a prerequisite to establish international peace. Before the end of World War II, the United States already advanced the view that economic development on the basis of international free trade would provide an important mechanism for achieving world peace.[1] In the 1941 Atlantic Charter, Franklin Roosevelt, the President of the United States, and Winston Churchill, the Prime Minister of the United Kingdom, stated that all of the nations of the world must come to the abandonment of the use of force to establish peace and that they would endeavour to further the enjoyment by all States of access to the trade and to the raw materials of the world which are needed for their economic

---

[1] A. Narlikar, *The World Trade Organisation: A Very Short Introduction* (Oxford University Press, 2005), p. 10.

prosperity.[2] Furthermore, Article VII of the 1942 Anglo-American Mutual Aid Agreement provided that in return for aid furnished by the United States to the United Kingdom, the two governments took agreed action directed to the expansion of 'production, employment, and the exchange and consumption of goods, which are the material foundations of the liberty and welfare of all peoples; to the elimination of all forms of discriminatory treatment in international commerce, and to the reduction of tariffs and other trade barriers'.[3] The Atlantic Charter and Anglo-American Mutual Aid Agreement reflected the Allies' post-war plans on the basis of the two goals of 'freedom, non-discrimination, and multilateralism' and 'economic recovery and full employment through expansionism'.[4] Subsequently the idea of the interlinkage between economic development and world peace was reflected in the UN Charter,[5] stating in Article 55 that '[w]ith a view to the creation of conditions of stability and well-being which are necessary for peaceful and friendly relations among nations', the United Nations shall promote:

a. higher standards of living, full employment, and conditions of economic and social progress and development.

After World War II, the framework for international economic relations was established particularly by three pillars: the International Monetary Fund, the World Bank and the General Agreement on Tariffs and Trade (GATT). Originally the GATT, created in 1947, was to serve as an interim agreement for the liberalisation of tariffs until the International Trade Organisation (ITO) was formed. The ITO never came into existence, however. As a consequence, the GATT continued to provide the basis for the international trading system for forty-seven years.

If economic development can be thought to be a prerequisite for world peace, peaceful settlement of international trade disputes should be an issue of considerable importance in international relations. Yet, the 1947 GATT contains only a few provisions on this subject, including Article XXII that calls for mandatory consultations and Article XXIII concerning submission of issues to the GATT contracting parties.[6] Since these articles provide only general rules and procedures with regard to the settlement of disputes, the dispute settlement procedures of the GATT have had to evolve over time through practice.[7]

In the early years of the GATT, investigation and reports on individual cases were transferred to the 'working parties' consisting of the interested representatives of States, always including the parties in dispute. The working parties then examined questions

---

[2] Atlantic Charter, 14 August 1941, available at: http://avalon.law.yale.edu/wwii/atlantic.asp.
[3] The text is available at: http://avalon.law.yale.edu/wwii/angam42.asp.
[4] K. Yago, Y. Asai and M. Itoh (eds.), *History of the IMF: Organisation, Policy, and Market* (Heidelberg: Springer, 2015), p. 5.
[5] Further, see J. Toye and R. Toye, *The UN and Global Political Economy: Trade, Finance, and Development* (Indiana University Press, 2004), pp. 17 et seq.
[6] The contracting parties acting jointly as provided for in Article XXV are designated as the contracting parties. See Article XXV(1).
[7] N. Saiki, 'WTO Rules and Procedures for the Settlement of Disputes – Their Formation: A Practitioner's View' in M. K. Young and Y. Iwasawa (eds.), *Trilateral Perspectives on International Legal Issues: Relevance of Domestic Law and Policy* (New York: Transnational Publishers, 1996), p. 404.

and issued a report recording various views of the States. In the 1940s and early 1950s, working parties were often set up for the settlement of disputes referred to under Article XXIII:2. After the introduction of the panel system in 1953, however, the panel procedure became a preferred method of dispute settlement under Article XXIII:2.[8]

Even though the creation of panels was thought to be a significant development in the dispute settlement procedures of the GATT,[9] a serious shortcoming of the panel procedure was that it relied on 'positive consensus' of the contracting parties. According to this system, any contracting party, including the parties to the dispute, could block the establishment of a panel or the subsequent adoption of the panel report. The problem associated with blockage of adoption of panel reports became more serious over time and the dispute settlement procedure of the GATT became incapable of handling controversial cases because one of the disputing parties was likely to block adoption of the panel report. Even if a panel report could be adopted, mechanisms for surveillance of the implementation of decisions remained weak.[10] Furthermore, since rules and procedures of the GATT dispute settlement were scattered in several instruments, including Tokyo Round Codes of 1979, the dispute settlement procedures entailed the risk of forum shopping.[11]

1.2 Principal Features of the WTO Dispute Settlement System

In contrast, the WTO, created in 1995 after the end of the Uruguay Round (1986-94),[12] is equipped with a significantly stronger procedure of international dispute settlement. The WTO is an international organisation and has legal personality under Article XIII:1 of the WTO Agreement. The WTO has four objectives relating to economic development: the increase of standards of living, the attainment of full employment, the growth of real income and effective demand, and the expansion of production of, and trade in, goods and services. Further to this, sustainable development, environmental protection and the needs of developing countries are highlighted in the Preamble.[13] At present, the WTO has 162 Members, accounting for about 95 per cent of world trade.[14] The agreements and associated legal instruments included in Annexes 1, 2 and 3 are integral parts of the WTO

---

[8] Y. Iwasawa, 'Settlement of Disputes Concerning the WTO Agreement: Various Means Other than Panel Procedures' in M. K. Young and Y. Iwasawa (eds.), *Trilateral Perspectives on International Legal Issues: Relevance of Domestic Law and Policy* (New York: Transnational Publishers, 1996), p. 387.

[9] Saiki, 'WTO Rules and Procedures', p. 404.

[10] For shortcomings of the GATT dispute settlement, see A. T. Guzman and J. H. B. Pauwelyn, *International Trade Law*, 2nd edn (Wolters: Kluwer, 2012), p. 129; Narlikar, *The World Trade Organisation*, pp. 86-9; J. G. Merrills, *International Dispute Settlement*, 6th edn (Cambridge University Press, 2017), pp. 207-8; P. Van den Bossche and W. Zdouc, *The Law and Policy of the World Trade Organization: Text, Cases and Materials*, 3rd edn (Cambridge University Press, 2013), pp. 159-60; P.-T. Stoll, 'World Trade Organization, Dispute Settlement' in *Max Planck Encyclopaedia*, para. 3.

[11] Saiki, 'WTO Rules and Procedures', p. 406; E.-U. Petersmann, 'The Dispute Settlement System of the World Trade Organisation and Evolution of the GATT Dispute Settlement System Since 1948' (1994) 31 *Common Market Law Review*, p. 1203.

[12] The Agreement Establishing the World Trade Organisation (hereafter the WTO Agreement). The WTO came into existence on 1 January 1995. The text is available at: www.wto.org/English/docs_e/legal_e/04-wto.pdf. For the institutional structure, mandate and functions of the WTO in general, see Van den Bossche and Zdouc, *The Law and Policy*, pp. 74 et seq.

[13] Preamble to the WTO Agreement; Van den Bossche and Zdouc, *The Law and Policy*, p. 85.

[14] See www.wto.org/english/thewto_e/whatis_e/tif_e/org6_e.htm.

Agreement, binding on all Members.[15] While Annex 1A includes the General Agreement on Tariffs and Trade 1994 as specified in Annex 1A (hereinafter GATT 1994), it is legally distinct from the 1947 GATT.[16]

The dispute settlement system of the WTO is set out in Annex 2 to the WTO Agreement, titled 'the Understanding on Rules and Procedures Governing the Settlement of Disputes' (hereafter the DSU).[17] Notably, the DSU clearly recognises that: 'The dispute settlement system of the WTO is a central element in providing security and predictability to the multilateral trading system.'[18]

Under Article 3(7) of the DSU, '[t]he aim of the dispute settlement mechanism is to secure a positive solution to a dispute' and, in the absence of a mutually agreed solution, 'the first objective of the dispute settlement mechanism is usually to secure the withdrawal of the measures concerned if these are found to be inconsistent with the provisions of any of the covered agreements'. Related to this, Article 3(2) of the DSU makes clear that the system contributes to achieve three purposes which are intimately interlinked:

(i) to provide security and predictability to the multilateral trading system
(ii) to preserve the rights and obligations of Members under the covered agreements
(iii) to clarify the existing provisions of those agreements.

The new dispute settlement system of the WTO is characterised particularly by six features:[19]

(i) In contrast to the GATT, the DSU establishes a single unified dispute settlement system across all WTO agreements.[20]
(ii) Unlike the GATT, which relied on the principle of 'positive consensus', the WTO dispute settlement system works on the principle of 'reverse consensus'. This means that unless the Dispute Settlement Body (DSB) decides by consensus not to allow the establishment of a panel, the panel is to be established. Likewise, a report by a panel or the Appellate Body also requires consensus to be rejected. In consequence, the establishment of WTO panels and subsequent adoption of panel and Appellate Body reports can be said to be quasi-automatic. The 'reverse consensus' can be said to give compulsory jurisdiction to the WTO panels. The compulsory jurisdiction of WTO panels sharply contrasts with the jurisdiction of the ICJ which rests on the consent of the parties in dispute.
(iii) The jurisdiction of the WTO dispute settlement system is exclusive.[21] In this regard, Article 23 of the DSU precludes the use of other forums for the settlement of disputes arising under the covered agreements.[22]

---

[15] Article 2(2) of the WTO Agreement.
[16] Article 2(4) of the WTO Agreement. GATT 1994 comprises the provisions in the 1947 GATT as rectified, amended or modified by the terms of legal instruments which have entered into force before the date of entry into force of the WTO Agreement. GATT 1994, para. 1, available at: www.wto.org/english/docs_e/legal_e/06-gatt_e.htm.
[17] The text is available at: www.wto.org/english/docs_e/legal_e/28-dsu.pdf.   [18] DSU, Article 3(2).
[19] Narlikar, *The World Trade Organisation*, pp. 86–8; Van den Bossche and Zdouc, *The Law and Policy*, pp. 179 *et seq.*
[20] See also DSU, Article 1(1).
[21] Van den Bossche and Zdouc, *The Law and Policy*, p. 161; WTO, *A Handbook on the WTO Dispute Settlement System* (Cambridge University Press, 2004), p. 8.
[22] The covered agreements include: the WTO Agreement, Multilateral Agreements on Trade in Goods, General Agreement on Trade in Services, Agreement on Trade-Related Aspects of Intellectual Property Rights and the DSU.

279 The WTO Dispute Settlement System

(iv) The DSU provides procedure of appellate review. The appellate review organ is the Appellate Body and its task is to hear appeals from panel cases. Given that normally judgments of international courts and tribunals are final and no appeal is accepted, the appellate review in the WTO merits particular note.[23]

(v) The DSU provides for improved surveillance mechanisms for the implementation of rulings and recommendations of WTO panels. This is a unique feature that is unknown to the ICJ.[24]

(vi) Each stage of dispute settlement in the WTO is managed within strict timeframes. The strict timeframes can contribute to expedite the dispute settlement process and enhance predictability of dispute settlement.[25] The timeframe also contrasts with the ICJ where litigation often continues over several years.

Since 1995, more than 500 requests had already been referred to the WTO dispute settlement system.[26] The figure demonstrates that this is a highly active mechanism of international dispute settlement. Since a full discussion of the WTO falls outside the scope of this book, this chapter has only the modest aim of examining the key issues of the WTO dispute settlement system in turn: basic elements for the WTO dispute settlement system (section 2), consultation (section 3), good offices, conciliation and mediation (section 4), panel proceedings (section 5), appellate review (section 6), legal effect of reports of WTO panels and Appellate Body (section 7), implementation of rulings and recommendation (section 8), legal nature of the panel procedure (section 9), arbitration (section 10) and developing States in dispute settlement process (section 11). Finally, conclusions are presented (section 12).

2 BASIC ELEMENTS OF THE WTO DISPUTE SETTLEMENT SYSTEM

2.1 General Considerations

In broad terms, the process of dispute settlement in the WTO can be divided into four steps:[27]

Step I: Consultation
Step II: Panel procedures
Step III: Appellate procedures
Step IV: Implementation and enforcement of the recommendations and ruling of the panel and/or the Appellate Body, as adopted by the DSB.

As a general rule, the period from the date of establishment of the panel by the DSB until the date the DSB considers the panel or appellate report for adoption is within

---

[23] See section 6 of this chapter.   [24] See section 8 of this chapter.
[25] As will be seen, however, most panel proceedings exceed the prescribed periods in practice. Peter Van den Bossche and D. Prévost, *Essentials of WTO Law* (Cambridge University Press, 2016), p. 290.
[26] A chronological list of WTO dispute cases is available at: www.wto.org/english/tratop_e/dispu_e/dispu_status_e.htm. The electronic text of reports of WTO panels and the Appellate Body can be searched via: www.wto.org/english/tratop_e/dispu_e/dispu_e.htm#disputes.
[27] Van den Bossche and Zdouc, *The Law and Policy*, p. 244. A detailed flow chart of dispute settlement process is available at: www.wto.org/english/tratop_e/dispu_e/disp_settlement_cbt_e/c6s1p1_e.htm.

nine months where the panel report is not appealed, or *twelve months where the report is appealed*.[28] In practice, however, the panel process often exceeds this time limit.[29] Although, as a general rule, the proceedings of the appellate review shall not exceed sixty days from the date a party to the dispute formally notifies its decision to appeal to the date the Appellate Body circulates its report,[30] the Appellate Body also frequently failed to keep the time limit.[31] If this is the case, a complainant State suffers continued economic harm if the challenged measures are indeed contrary to WTO law.[32]

The DSU contains detailed rules with regard to the dispute settlement process of the WTO. Before examining each step of the process, it is necessary to discuss some basic elements of the WTO dispute settlement system, namely, (i) the role of the DSB, (ii) *locus standi*, (iii) causes of action and (iv) applicable law.

2.2 The Dispute Settlement Body

First of all, the role of the DSB in the WTO dispute settlement system merits mention. Under Article 1(1) of the DSU, the rules and procedures of the DSU are to apply to:

- disputes brought pursuant to the consultation and dispute settlement provisions of the agreements listed in Appendix 1 to this Understanding (the covered agreements)
- consultation and the settlement of disputes between Members concerning their rights and obligations under the WTO Agreement and of the DSU taken in isolation or in combination with any other covered agreement.

These rules and procedures and the consultation and dispute settlement provisions of the covered agreements are administered by the DSB established under Article 2(1) of the DSU.

The DSB is a political organ constituted by all Member governments of the WTO. The DSB has the authority to establish panels, adopt panel and Appellate Body reports, maintain surveillance of implementation of ruling and recommendations, and authorise suspension of concessions and other obligations under the covered agreements.[33] At the same time, the DSB is required to inform the relevant WTO Councils and Committees of any developments in disputes related to provisions of the respective covered agreements.[34] Thus the DSB can be regarded as the central organ governing the dispute settlement system of the WTO as a whole. It is unique that adjudicative organs are subject to control of a political organ. As will be discussed, however, key decisions – namely, establishment of panels, adoption of panel and Appellate Body reports, and authorisation of retaliation – are taken by 'reverse consensus'. In consequence, the DSB's political influence on the judicial process remains modest.

---

[28] DSU, Article 20.   [29] Van den Bossche and Zdouc, *The Law and Policy*, p. 247.
[30] DSU, Article 17(5).   [31] Van den Bossche and Zdouc, *The Law and Policy*, p. 248.
[32] WTO, *A Handbook*, p. 117.   [33] Article 2(1) of the DSU.   [34] Article 2(2) of the DSU.

2.3 Access to the Dispute Settlement System of the WTO

The second issue relates to access to the WTO dispute settlement system. Since the WTO dispute settlement system aims to settle disputes among WTO Members, only WTO Members are entitled to have access to the dispute settlement system. Individuals, international organisations, NGOs or industry associations are not entitled to have recourse to the WTO dispute settlement system.[35] However, it would be wrong to consider that the position of private economic actors is of no relevance to the WTO dispute settlement system.[36] In fact, private parties may facilitate their *indirect* access to the process of the WTO dispute settlement by persuading a WTO Member to espouse their case, even though they have no direct access to it.[37]

Furthermore, attention must be paid to the use of *amicus curiae* ('friend of the court') briefs.[38] *Amicus curiae* briefs provide an avenue for any interested third party to the dispute to make its views known. The use of *amicus curiae* briefs is permissible on the ground that panels have the right to seek information and technical advice from any individual or body which it deems appropriate under Article 13(1) of the DSU. Such information is also needed to make an objective assessment of the matter.[39] According to this mechanism, individuals, companies, organisations and other Members may submit written briefs to WTO panels and the Appellate Body. Such written briefs are referred to as *amicus curiae* briefs. Even though the DSU contains no rule concerning *amicus curiae*, the Appellate Body in *US – Shrimp* took the view that panels have the authority to accept and consider *amicus curiae* briefs.[40] Furthermore, the Appellate Body, in *US – Lead and Bismuth II*, stated that under Article 17(9) of the DSU, 'the Appellate Body has broad authority to adopt procedural rules which do not conflict with any rules and procedures in the DSU or the covered agreements'.[41] Therefore, 'as long as we act consistently with the provisions of the DSU and the covered agreements, we have the legal authority to decide whether or not to accept and consider any information that we believe is pertinent and useful in an appeal'.[42]

However, care must be taken in noting that *amicus curiae* briefs in the WTO dispute settlement system are not a right of individuals and organisations and that panels and

---

[35] See Appellate Body Report, *United States – Import Prohibition of Certain Shrimp and Shrimp Products*, WT/DS58/AB/R, adopted 6 November 1998, para. 101.
[36] Panel Report, *United States – Sections 301–310 of the Trade Act 1974*, WT/DS152/R, adopted 27 January 2000, para. 7.73.
[37] T. J. Schoenbaum, 'WTO Dispute Settlement: Praise and Suggestions for Reform' (1998) 47 *ICLQ*, p. 654. See also Van den Bossche and Zdouc, *The Law and Policy*, pp. 177–8.
[38] For *amicus curiae* in the WTO dispute settlement system, see Van den Bossche and Zdouc, *The Law and Policy*, pp. 263 *et seq*.; WTO, *A Handbook*, pp. 98–100; Guzman and Pauwelyn, *International Trade Law*, pp. 168 *et seq*.; L. Boisson de Chazournes and M. M. Mbengue, 'The Amici Curiae and the WTO Dispute Settlement System: The Doors are Open' (2003) 2 *The Law and Practice of International Courts and Tribunals*, pp. 205–48; S. P. Subedt, 'The WTO Dispute Settlement Mechanism as a New Technique for Settling Disputes in International Law' in D. French, M. Saul and N. D. White (eds.), *International Law and Dispute Settlement: New Problems and Techniques* (Oxford: Hart Publishing, 2010), pp. 183–5.
[39] DSU, Article 11.
[40] Appellate Body Report, *United States – Import Prohibition of Certain Shrimp and Shrimp Products*, WT/DS58/AB/R, adopted 6 November 1998, para. 106; para. 110.
[41] Appellate Body Report, *United States – Imposition of Countervailing Duties on Certain Hot-Rolled Lead and Bismuth Carbon Steel Products Originating in the United Kingdom*, WT/DS138/AB/R, adopted 7 June 2000, para. 39.   [42] *Ibid.*

the Appellate Body have no legal duty to accept or consider unsolicited *amicus curiae* briefs submitted by individuals or organisations not Members of the WTO.[43] If *amicus curiae* briefs are submitted by WTO Members, there is no obligation for panels and the Appellate Body to consider them. In this regard, the Appellate Body, in *EU – Sardines*, clearly stated that: '[A]cceptance of any *amicus curiae* brief is a matter of discretion, which we must exercise on a case-by-case basis.'[44] Only when WTO Members become third parties to the dispute are panels and the Appellate Body obliged to consider their submissions in their rulings.

2.4 Causes of Action

The third issue concerns causes of action. The key provision in this regard is Article XXIII(1) of GATT 1994:[45]

> 1. If any contracting party should consider that any benefit accruing to it directly or indirectly under this Agreement is being nullified or impaired or that the attainment of any objective of the Agreement is being impeded as the result of
>
>   (a) the failure of another contracting party to carry out its obligations under this Agreement, or
>   (b) the application by another contracting party of any measure, whether or not it conflicts with the provisions of this Agreement, or
>   (c) the existence of any other situation the contracting party may, with a view to the satisfactory adjustment of the matter, make written representations or proposals to the other contracting party or parties which it considers to be concerned. Any contracting party thus approached shall give sympathetic consideration to the representations or proposals made to it.

This provision specifies two types of causes of action: (i) nullification and impairment of benefits and (ii) impedance of the attainment of an objective of the Agreement. It further provides for three types of complaint:

(a) 'violation' complaints
(b) 'non-violation complaints'
(c) 'situation' complaints.[46]

---

[43] *Ibid.*, p. 15, para. 41. In addition, the Appellate Body in *EC – Asbestos* adopted an additional procedure for *amicus curiae* for the purposes of this appeal only. Appellate Body Report, *European Communities – Measures Affecting Asbestos and Products Containing Asbestos*, WT/DS135/AB/R, adopted 5 April 2001, paras. 51-2.

[44] Appellate Body Report, *European Communities – Trade Description of Sardines*, WT/DS231/AB/R, adopted 23 October 2002, para. 167.

[45] While each covered agreement contains dispute settlement provisions, many of these provisions simply refer to Articles XXII and XXIII of GATT 1994. WTO, *A Handbook*, pp. 28-9.

[46] In accordance with Article XXIII(3) of the GATS, however, situation complaints are not possible in disputes arising under the GATS. Pursuant to Article 64(2) and (3) of the Agreement on Trade-Related Aspects of Intellectual Property Rights (TRIPS Agreement) and successive ministerial decisions, non-violation complaints and situation complaints are currently not possible in disputes arising under the TRIPS Agreement. Van den Bossche and Zdouc, *The Law and Policy*, p. 174, footnote 96.

It follows that there are six different types of causes of action which set in motion the dispute settlement system of the WTO, namely, types (i)-(a), (i)-(b), (i)-(c), (ii)-(a), (ii)-(b) and (ii)-(c).[47]

In relation to (b) 'non-violation complaints' and (c) 'situation' complaints, the breach of the covered agreements is not in issue. In this sense, the scope of the WTO dispute settlement system is broader than that of international adjudication that is confined to adjudicating only violations of relevant rules of international law.[48] It is notable that a Member of the WTO is allowed to bring a complaint on the ground that an objective of the WTO is being impeded, even if that Member has suffered no direct injury. In this regard, some argue that the WTO dispute settlement system can be thought to be an example of *actio popularis*.[49] In practice, however, most complaints pertain to an alleged nullification or impairment of benefits. To date, there have been no successful non-violation complains under the DSU and no situation complaint has ever been adjusted.[50] Therefore, the impediment of an object of the agreement lacks practical relevance as a cause of action. It follows that three out of six causes of action identified above have no practical relevance.

While literally understood, the 'situation complaint' could cover any situation whatsoever, few complaints were brought to the WTO on the basis of GATT Article XXIII(1)(c) and none of them resulted in a panel report.[51] Most complaints concern the nullification of a benefit as the result of another Member's breach of its obligations (type (i)-(a)).[52] This type of complaint (type (i)-(a)) is also pursued as a result of another Member's measure. When the complainant demonstrates that there is an infringement of the obligations assumed under a covered agreement, the action is considered *prima facie* to constitute a case of nullification or impairment.[53] In no case to date has the respondent been successful in rebutting the presumption of nullification or impairment. Therefore, it is doubtful whether this presumption is rebuttable.[54] Thus, in the case of type (i)-(a) complaint, the element of violation plays a much more important role than the element of nullification or impairment of a benefit.[55]

Complaints on the basis of nullification of a benefit as a result of another Member's measure (type (i)-(b)) are far less frequent.[56] No presumption applies in this type of complaint.[57] Rather, Article 26(1)(a) of the DSU requires the complaining party to 'present a detailed justification in support of any complaint relating to a measure which does not conflict with the relevant covered agreement'. To this day, there have been only a few non-violation complaints and none of the non-violation complaints

---

[47] Y. Iwasawa, 'WTO Dispute Settlement as Judicial Supervision' (2002) *Journal of International Economic Law*, p. 294.
[48] WTO, *A Handbook*, p. 30.   [49] Iwasawa, 'WTO Dispute Settlement', p. 294.
[50] Van den Bossche and Prévost, *Essentials of WTO Law*, p. 268.
[51] WTO, *A Handbook*, pp. 30–1.
[52] *Ibid*. See also Iwasawa, 'WTO Dispute Settlement', p. 294.
[53] DSU Article 3(8).
[54] Van den Bossche and Zdouc, *The Law and Policy*, pp. 174–5.
[55] WTO, *A Handbook*, p. 31.   [56] *Ibid*.
[57] *Ibid*., p. 33.

brought to the WTO has been successful.[58] In this regard, by referring to the panel report in *Japan – Film*,[59] the Appellate Body in *EC – Asbestos* considered that the remedy in Article XXIII:1(b) 'should be approached with caution and should remain an exceptional remedy'.[60] Further, there has not been any adjudication of situation complaints.[61] In summary, mainly violation complaints (type (i)-(a)) are of practical importance in the WTO dispute settlement system. Accordingly, with regard to causes of action, the difference between the WTO dispute settlement system and other international adjudication systems is thin.[62]

2.5 Applicable Law

Finally, some mention must be made of applicable law in the WTO dispute settlement system. Unlike Article 38(1) of the ICJ Statute, the DSU contains no explicit provision concerning applicable law.[63] However, it can be reasonably considered that relevant provisions of covered agreements apply to the disputes. This point is confirmed in light of Articles 3(2), 7(1) and 11 of the DSU.

The WTO agreements contain no explicit provisions concerning the relationship between WTO rules and the other rules of international law.[64] In this regard, it is of particular interest to note that the Appellate Body often applies the rules of the Vienna Convention on the Law of Treaties as rules of customary international law. In *US – Gasoline*, for instance, the Appellate Body took the view that the general rule of interpretation set out in Article 31(1) of the Vienna Convention 'has attained the status of a rule of customary or general international law'.[65] As such, it forms part of the 'customary rules of interpretation of public international law' which the Appellate Body has been directed to apply in seeking to clarify the provisions of GATT 1994 and the other covered agreements of the WTO Agreement. According to the Appellate Body, '[t]hat direction reflects a measure of recognition that the *General Agreement* is not to be read in clinical isolation from public international law'.[66] The Appellate Body's view in *US – Gasoline* was echoed by the Appellate Body report in *Japan – Taxes on Alcoholic Beverages*.[67] It further expressed the view that Article 32 of the Vienna Convention, dealing with the role of supplementary means of interpretation, has also attained the status of a rule of customary international

---

[58] Van den Bossche and Zdouc, *The Law and Policy*, p. 175.
[59] Panel Report, *Japan – Measures Affecting Consumer Photographic Film and Paper*, WT/DS44/R, adopted 22 April 1998, para. 10.36.
[60] Appellate Body Report, *European Communities – Measures Affecting Asbestos and Asbestos-Containing Products*, WT/DS135/AB/R, adopted 5 April 2001, para. 186.
[61] Van den Bossche and Zdouc, *The Law and Policy*, p. 175.
[62] Ibid.
[63] Generally on this issue, see J. Pauwelyn, *Conflict of Norms in Public International Law: How WTO Law Relates to Other Rules of International Law* (Cambridge University Press, 2003), pp. 456 *et seq.*; J. Cameron and K. Gray, 'Principles of International Law in the WTO Dispute Settlement Body' (2001) 50 *ICLQ*, pp. 248–98.
[64] Subedt, 'The WTO Dispute Settlement Mechanism', pp. 185–6.
[65] Appellate Body Report, *United States – Standards for Reformulated and Conventional Gasoline*, WT/DS2/AB/R, adopted 20 May 1996, p. 17 (electronic text).
[66] Ibid.
[67] Appellate Body Report, *Japan – Taxes on Alcoholic Beverages*, WT/DS8/AB/R, WT/DS10/AB/R, WT/DS11/AB/R, adopted 1 November 1996, p. 10 (electronic text).

law.[68] In addition, the Panel, in *US – Anti-Dumping and Countervailing Duties (China)*, took the position that it is well settled in WTO law that the principles codified in Articles 31–33 of the Vienna Convention are such customary rules.[69]

Even though treaties other than covered agreements or non-WTO treaties are inapplicable to WTO disputes, they may be taken into account as a supplementary means of interpretation of these agreements.[70] In *EC – Measures Affecting the Importation of Certain Poultry Products*, for instance, the Appellate Body stated that the Oilseeds Agreement may serve as a supplementary means of interpretation of the Schedule of Concessions of the EC pursuant to Article 32 of the Vienna Convention, although it did not consider the Oilseeds Agreement as a covered agreement within the meaning of Articles 1 and 2 of the DSU.[71] At the same time, it must be noted that the panel and Appellate Body cannot add to or diminish the rights and obligations provided in the covered agreements.[72]

In relation to this, Article 31(3)(c) of the Vienna Convention merits particular attention. This provision provides that:[73]

> There shall be taken into account, together with the context:
>
> ...
>
> (c) any relevant rules of international law applicable in the relations between the parties.

On the basis of this provision, there may be some scope to argue that where appropriate, treaties other than covered agreements or rules of customary international law and general principles of international law should be taken into account in the interpretation of covered agreements. In this regard, the Panel in *EC – Approval and Marketing of Biotech Products* noted that:

> Article 31(3)(c) [of the Vienna Convention] directly speaks to the issue of the relevance of other rules of international law to the interpretation of a treaty. In considering the provisions of Article 31(3)(c), we note, initially, that it refers to 'rules of international law'. Textually, this reference seems sufficiently broad to encompass all generally accepted sources of public international law, that is to say, (i) international conventions (treaties), (ii) international custom (customary international law), and (iii) the recognized general principles of law.[74]

---

[68] *Ibid.*
[69] Panel Report, *United States – Definitive Anti-Dumping and Countervailing Duties on Certain Products from China*, WT/DS379/R, adopted 25 March 2011, as modified by Appellate Body Report WT/DS379/AB/R, para. 7.1.
[70] See also Article 31(3)(c) of the Vienna Convention.
[71] Appellate Body Report, *European Communities – Measures Affecting the Importation of Certain Poultry Products*, WT/DS69/AB/R, adopted 23 July 1998, paras. 79–83.
[72] DSU, Article 19(2).
[73] For an analysis of Article 31(3)(c) of the Vienna Convention in the context of the WTO dispute settlement, see Pauwelyn, *Conflict of Norms*, pp. 264–74; *Fragmentation of International Law: Difficulties arising from the Diversification and Expansion of International Law: Report of the Study Group of the International Law Commission Finalised by Martti Koskenniemi*, A/CN.4/L.682, 13 April 2006, pp. 223–8, paras. 443–50.
[74] Panel Reports, *European Communities – Measures Affecting the Approval and Marketing of Biotech Products*, WT/DS291/R, Add.1 to Add.9 and Corr.1/WT/DS292/R, Add.1 to Add.9 and Corr.1/WT/DS293/R, Add.1 to Add.9 and Corr.1, adopted 21 November 2006, para. 7.67.

Furthermore, by referring to the principle of good faith and the doctrine of abuse of right, the Appellate Body in *US – Shrimp* stated that: '[O]ur task here is to interpret the language of the chapeau [of Article XX of the GATT 1994], seeking additional interpretative guidance, as appropriate from the general principles of international law.'[75] Related to this, it made, for the first time, clear reference to Article 31(3)(c) of the Vienna Convention, albeit in a footnote only.[76] Since then, the rules of the Vienna Convention concerning interpretation, including Article 31(3)(c), have been repeatedly referred to in the WTO dispute settlement process.[77]

Here an issue arises with regard to the meaning of the term 'the parties' in Article 31(3)(c). This issue relates to the question whether the term 'the parties' in Article 31(3)(c) refers to *all* WTO Members, or rather to a subset of Members, such as the parties *to the dispute*. The Appellate Body in *EC and Certain Member States – Large Civil Aircraft* took a nuanced view in this matter. On the one hand, the Appellate Body noted that caution must be exercised in drawing up an international agreement to which not all WTO Members are party since the purpose of treaty interpretation is to establish the common intention of the parties to the treaty. On the other hand, the Appellate Body held that Article 31(3)(c) of the Vienna Convention provides the 'principle of systemic integration' that seeks to ensure that international obligations are interpreted by reference to their normative environment in a manner that gives 'coherence and meaningfulness' to the process of legal interpretation. The Appellate Body thus stated that:

> In a multilateral context such as the WTO, when recourse is had to a non-WTO rule for the purposes of interpreting provisions of the WTO agreements, a delicate balance must be struck between, on the one hand, taking due account of an individual WTO Member's international obligations and, on the other hand, ensuring a consistent and harmonious approach to the interpretation of WTO law among all WTO Members.[78]

3 CONSULTATION

The first step that triggers the WTO dispute settlement system is consultation. WTO dispute settlement proceedings are always to start with consultation between the parties in dispute.[79] In this regard, Article 3(7) of the DSU stresses that: 'A solution mutually acceptable to the parties to a dispute and consistent with the covered agreements is clearly to be preferred.'[80] Under Article 4(1) of the DSU, 'Members affirm their resolve to

---

[75] Appellate Body Report, *United States – Import Prohibition of Certain Shrimp and Shrimp Products*, WT/DS58/AB/R, adopted 6 November 1998, para. 158.
[76] *Ibid.*, footnote 157.
[77] Van den Bossche and Zdouc, *The Law and Policy*, pp. 187 et seq.
[78] Appellate Body Report, *European Communities and Certain Member States – Measures Affecting Trade in Large Civil Aircraft*, WT/DS316/AB/R, adopted 1 June 2011, para. 845.
[79] Van den Bossche and Prévost, *Essentials of WTO Law*, p. 276.
[80] See also Iwasawa, 'Settlement of Disputes', p. 380.

287 The WTO Dispute Settlement System

strengthen and improve the effectiveness of the consultation procedures employed by Members.' Therefore, much weight is given to the settlement of disputes through consultation.[81] Rules concerning consultation are set out in Article 4 of the DSU in some detail. Here two points can be made.

The first point concerns the strict timeframe set out with regard to the consultation process. Under Article 4(3), if a request for consultation is made pursuant to a covered agreement, the Member to which the request is made shall reply to the request within ten days after the date of its receipt and shall enter into consultation in good faith within a period of no more than thirty days after the date of receipt of the request. As suggested in the term 'shall', consultation under the DSU is mandatory. If the Member does not respond or does not enter into consultation within the time limits stated above, the Member that requested consultation may proceed directly to request the establishment of a panel.[82] Where a dispute could not be settled by consultation within sixty days after the date of receipt of the request for consultation, the complaining party may request the establishment of a panel in accordance with Article 4(7).[83] Accordingly, consultation constitutes a condition to the establishment of a panel. However, it is not suggested that the establishment of a panel must be requested on expiry of sixty days. The deadline seeks to prevent further delays to triggering panel proceedings in cases of fruitless and endless consultations. Members often continue consultations for longer period of time than sixty days in an effort to resolve the dispute amicably.[84]

The second point relates to the role of the DSB in the consultation process. Consultations shall be confidential, and without prejudice to the rights of any Member in any further proceedings.[85] Under DSU Article 4(4), however, all such requests for consultation shall be notified to the DSB and the relevant councils and committees by the Member which requests consultations. Mutually agreed solutions to matters formally raised under the consultation and dispute settlement provisions of the covered agreements are required to be notified to the DSB and the relevant councils and committees in accordance with DSU Article 3(6). These requirements of notification contribute to placing bilateral consultations under the control of the WTO.[86]

Consultation can continue during the panel proceedings.[87] In this regard, DSU Article 11 requires panels to give the parties in dispute to 'adequate opportunity to develop a mutually satisfactory solution'. In fact, a mutually agreed solution was reached in many cases, even though the dispute was already before a panel.[88] In this case, 'the

---

[81] Van den Bossche and Prévost, *Essentials of WTO Law*, p. 262.
[82] Van den Bossche and Zdouc, *The Law and Policy*, p. 271.
[83] Article 4(8) goes on to provide that in cases of urgency, including those which concern perishable goods, members shall enter into consultation within a period of no more than ten days after the date of receipt of the request; and that if the consultation has failed to settle the dispute within a period of twenty days after the date of receipt of the request, the complaining party may request the establishment of a panel.
[84] WTO, *A Handbook*, p. 47.   [85] DSU, Article 4(6).
[86] Merrills, *International Dispute Settlement*, p. 209.
[87] Van den Bossche and Zdouc, *The Law and Policy*, p. 274.   [88] *Ibid.*

report of the panel shall be confined to a brief description of the case and to reporting that a solution has been reached' under Article 12(7) of the DSU. All in all, consultations can be said to have a prominent role to play in the WTO dispute settlement system.[89]

4 GOOD OFFICES, CONCILIATION AND MEDIATION

Before examining panel proceedings, some consideration must be given to good offices, conciliation and mediation in the WTO dispute settlement system. The DSU contains a single article (i.e. Article 5) with regard to good offices, conciliation and mediation together. As provided in Article 5(1), good offices, conciliation and mediation are voluntary procedures. Procedures for good offices, conciliation and mediation may be requested at any time by any party to a dispute.[90] Under Article 5(6) of the DSU, the Director-General may, acting in an *ex officio* capacity, offer good offices, conciliation or mediation with a view to assisting Members to settle a dispute. Where a dispute involving a least-developed country Member could not be settled in a satisfactory manner in the course of consultations, Article 24(2) of the DSU requires the Director-General or the Chairman of the DSB to offer, upon the request by that Member country, their good offices, conciliation and mediation before a request for a panel is made. In order to exercise good offices, conciliation and mediation, such offer must be accepted by the disputing parties. Proceedings involving good offices, conciliation and mediation shall be confidential and without prejudice to the rights of either party in any further proceedings under these procedures.[91]

When good offices, conciliation or mediation are entered into within sixty days after the date of receipt of a request for consultations, the complaining party must allow a period of sixty days after the date of receipt of the request for consultations before requesting the establishment of a panel. If the parties to the dispute jointly consider that the good offices, conciliation or mediation process has failed to settle the dispute, however, the complaining party may request the establishment of a panel during the sixty-day period.[92] Procedures for good offices, conciliation or mediation may continue while the panel process proceeds, if the parties to a dispute so agree.[93]

In contrast to the LOSC which contains detailed provisions concerning conciliation,[94] the DSU provides no procedures for exercising conciliation. In this sense, conciliation under the DSU is less institutionalised comparing it to conciliation in the LOSC.

---

[89] According to the WTO, by January 2008, only around 136 of the nearly 369 cases had reached the full panel process. The data is indicated at the homepage of the WTO. Understanding the WTO: Settling Disputes, A Unique Contribution, www.wto.org/english/thewto_e/whatis_e/tif_e/disp1_e.htm. Further, see W. Alschner, 'Amicable Settlements of WTO Disputes: Bilateral Solutions in a Multilateral System' (2014) 13 *World Trade Review*, pp. 66–7, 73–5.
[90] DSU, Article 5(3).   [91] DSU, Article 5(2).   [92] DSU, Article 5(4).
[93] DSU, Article 5(5).
[94] See Chapter 8, section 2.2 of this book.

5 PANEL PROCEEDINGS

5.1 The Establishment of a Panel

The second step to be taken is panel proceedings. Panels are ad hoc bodies established with a view to adjudicating a particular dispute.[95] A panel can be established in the following cases:

(i) If the Member does not respond within ten days after the date of receipt of the request for consultations, or does not enter into consultations within a period of no more than thirty days, or a period otherwise mutually agreed, after the date of receipt of the request for consultations, the Member that requested the holding of consultations may proceed directly to request the establishment of a panel.[96]
(ii) If consultations fail to settle the dispute within sixty days of the request for consultations, the complaining party may request the establishment of a panel to rule on the dispute.[97]
(iii) If the consulting parties jointly consider that consultations have failed to settle the dispute, the complaining party may request a panel during the sixty-day period.[98]

The request for the establishment of a panel must be made in writing. It must indicate whether consultations were held, identify the specific measures at issue and provide a brief summary of the legal basis of the complaint sufficient to present the problem clearly.[99] If the complaining party so requests, a panel is to be established at the latest at the DSB meeting following that at which the request first appears as an item on the DSB's agenda, 'unless at that meeting the DSB decides by consensus not to establish a panel' in accordance with DSU Article 6(1). In the first meeting in which such a request is made, the decision is taken by normal consensus and, thus, the responding party can block the creation of a panel once. In practice, the respondent often rejects establishing the panel at the first DSB meeting. At the second DSB meeting where the request is on the agenda, however, the establishment of the panel can no longer be blocked unless there is a consensus against it.[100] In light of the reverse consensus procedure, the panel is to be virtually automatically established. Therefore, it can be said that the WTO panels have compulsory jurisdiction and that a WTO Member has a right to a panel.[101] The compulsory jurisdiction of a WTO panel sharply contrasts with the ICJ whose jurisdiction rests on the consent of the parties in dispute. In addition, the exhaustion of local remedies is not required in the panel proceedings.

---

[95] Van den Bossche and Prévost, *Essentials of WTO Law*, p. 271.
[96] DSU, Article 4(3). [97] DSU, Article 4(7). [98] *Ibid*. [99] DSU, Article 6(2).
[100] See Van den Bossche and Zdouc, *The Law and Policy*, p. 276; WTO, *Understanding the WTO: Settling Disputes, A Unique Contribution*, available at: www.wto.org/english/thewto_e/whatis_e/tif_e/disp1_e.htm. See also WTO, *Dispute Settlement System Training Module*, Chapter 6, 6.3, 'The Panel Stage', available at: www.wto.org/english/tratop_e/dispu_e/disp_settlement_cbt_e/c6s3p1_e.htm.
[101] Stoll, 'World Trade Organization', para. 14; Subedt, 'The WTO Dispute Settlement Mechanism', p. 179; Y. Iwasawa, 'Third Parties Before International Tribunals: The ICJ and the WTO' in N. Ando, E. McWhinney and R. Wolfrum (eds.), *Liber Amicorum Judge Shigeru Oda* (The Hague: Kluwer, 2002), p. 873.

Where more than one Member requests the establishment of a panel related to the same matter, a single panel may be established.[102] If more than one panel is established to examine the complaints related to the same matter, to the greatest extent possible the same persons shall serve as panellists on each of the separate panels.[103] If one of the parties to the dispute so requests, the panel is to submit separate reports on the dispute concerned.[104] *US – Steel Safeguards* is a case in point. In this case, the United States requested that the Panel submit eight separate reports. The Panel thus decided 'to issue its Reports in the form of a single document constituting eight Panel Reports'.[105] Similarly, a single panel was established in *EC – Bananas*, but it issued separate reports.[106]

5.2 Composition and terms of Reference of Panels

Once a panel is established, its composition and terms of reference must be determined. Panels shall be composed of three panellists, but may be composed of five panellists if the parties agree.[107] Under Article 8(1) of the DSU, panels shall be composed of well-qualified governmental and/or non-governmental individuals. To assist in the selection of panellists, the Secretariat maintains an indicative list of well-qualified governmental and non-governmental individuals from which panellists may be drawn as appropriate.[108] In accordance with Article 8(6) of the DSU, the Secretariat is to propose nominations for the panel to the parties to the dispute. The parties to the dispute shall not oppose nominations except for compelling reasons. In reality, however, parties often reject the nominations proposed by the Secretariat and the composition of the panel may take several weeks.[109]

If there is no agreement on the panellists within twenty days after the date of the establishment of a panel, either party may request that the Director-General determine the composition of the panel pursuant to Article 8(7). In practice, it has become more common for the Director-General to appoint panels.[110] In the event that a dispute was raised between a developed country Member and a developing country Member, the panel shall, if the latter so requests, include at least one panellist from a developing country Member in accordance with Article 8(10).

As discussed in the previous chapters,[111] independence and impartiality of international judges are of central importance in international adjudication and the same can be held true of the WTO panels. In this regard, Article 8(2) of the DSU requires that panel

---

[102] DSU, Article 9(1).   [103] DSU, Article 9(3).   [104] DSU, Article 9(2).
[105] Panel Reports, *United States – Definitive Safeguard Measures on Imports of Certain Steel Products*, WT/DS248/R, Corr.1/WT/DS249/R, Corr.1/WT/DS251/R, Corr.1/WT/DS252/R, Corr.1/WT/DS253/R, Corr.1/WT/DS254/R, Corr.1/WT/DS258/R, Corr.1/WT/DS259/R and Corr.1, adopted 10 December 2003, para. 10.725. See also Note by the Secretariat, *ibid.*; www.wto.org/english/tratop_e/dispu_e/cases_e/ds248_e.htm.
[106] Panel Reports, *European Communities – Regime for the Importation, Sale and Distribution of Bananas*, WT/DS27/R/ECU *(Ecuador)*/WT/DS27/R/GTM, WT/DS27/R/HND *(Guatemala and Honduras)*/WT/DS27/R/MEX *(Mexico)*/WT/DS27/R/USA *(US)*, adopted 25 September 1997, as modified by Appellate Body Report WT/DS27/AB/R, DSR 1997:II, p. 695 to DSR 1997:III, p. 1085.
[107] DSU, Article 8(5).   [108] DSU, Article 8(4).
[109] Van den Bossche and Zdouc, *The Law and Policy*, pp. 215–16.
[110] Guzman and Pauwelyn, *International Trade Law*, p. 133.
[111] See Chapter 5, section 3.2 and Chapter 6, section 3.2 of this book.

members should be selected with a view to ensuring the independence of the members, a sufficiently diverse background and a wide spectrum of experience. Article 8(9) further stresses that:

> Panellists shall serve in their individual capacities and not as government representatives, nor as representatives of any organisation. Members shall therefore not give them instructions nor seek to influence them as individuals with regard to matters before a panel.

Under Article 8(3) of the DSU, citizens of Members whose governments are parties to the dispute or third parties as defined in Article 10(2) cannot serve on a panel concerned with that dispute, unless the parties to the dispute agree otherwise.[112] This system shows a clear contrast with the ICJ and ITLOS which allow the participation of national judges in the proceedings.

The requirements of independence and impartiality are also stressed in the Rules of Conduct.[113] Section II of the Rules of Conduct explicitly states that each person covered by these rules (i.e. panellists, arbitrators and experts) shall be independent and impartial. Furthermore, each person covered by these rules is expected to 'disclose the existence or development of any interest, relationship or matter that that person could reasonably be expected to know and that is likely to affect, or give rise to justifiable doubts as to, that person's independence or impartiality'.[114]

Unless the parties to the dispute agree otherwise within twenty days from the establishment of the panel, the standard terms of reference apply in accordance with Article 7 of the DSU. The panel's standard terms of reference are to examine the claims and measures identified in the 'request for the establishment of a panel'. If the applicant requests the establishment of a panel with other than standard terms of reference, however, the proposed text of special terms of reference must be included in the written request.[115]

5.3 Scope of Jurisdiction of WTO panels

The jurisdiction of WTO panels is limited to claims under WTO-covered agreements. This is clear from Article 1(1) of the DSU, providing that the DSU applies to disputes brought pursuant to the consultation and dispute settlement provisions of the agreements listed in DSU Appendix 1. Article 3(2) also stipulates that the dispute settlement system of the WTO 'serves to preserve the rights and obligations of Members under the *covered agreements*'.[116] Accordingly, a WTO panel has no jurisdiction to rule on claims under WTO rules other than those included in WTO-covered agreements, such as the ministerial decisions and

---

[112] In some cases, parties in dispute agreed that a national of one of the parties became a panellist. Van den Bossche and Zdouc, *The Law and Policy*, p. 215.
[113] WTO, Rules of Conduct for the Understanding on Rules and Procedures Concerning the Settlement of Disputes, adopted on 3 December 1996. Text in: (1997) 36 *ILM*, p. 477. The electronic text is available at: www.wto.org/english/tratop_e/dispu_e/rc_e.htm.
[114] *Ibid.*, Section III, para. 1.   [115] DSU, Article 6(2).   [116] Emphasis added.

declarations that are part of the final Act, but not of the WTO Agreement. Nor does it have jurisdiction to deal with claims of violation of non-WTO rules, such as environmental or human rights conventions or rules of customary international law.[117] As noted, the panel cannot add to or diminish the rights and obligations provided in the covered agreement.[118] This means that WTO panels may not engage in 'gap-filling' or 'rule-making', but they may only clarify the meaning of relevant provisions of the covered agreements.

However, an issue may arise to what extent WTO panels and the Appellate Body have jurisdiction to decide legal issues not directly relating to a covered agreement. Under Article 11 of the DSU:

> [A] panel should make an objective assessment of the matter before it, including an objective assessment of the facts of the case and the applicability of and conformity with the relevant covered agreements, and make such other findings as will assist the DSB in making the recommendations or in giving the rulings provided for in the covered agreements.

On the basis of this provision, some argue that the jurisdiction of WTO panels and the Appellate Body should be interpreted broadly so that they can decide all issues necessary to settle a dispute.[119] In any case WTO panels have the jurisdiction to determine jurisdictional matters in accordance with the principle of *la compétence de la compétence*. This point was confirmed by the Appellate Body in *US – Anti-Dumping Act of 1916*, stating that 'it is a widely accepted rule that an international tribunal is entitled to consider the issue of its own jurisdiction on its own initiative, and to satisfy itself that it has jurisdiction in any case that comes before it'.[120]

5.4 Panel Procedure

The panel procedure can be divided into three main stages: (i) panel examination, (ii) interim review and (iii) issuance of a final report.[121]

5.4.1 Panel Examination

Each party to the dispute is to deposit its written submissions with the Secretariat for immediate transmission to the panel and to the other party or parties to the dispute. The complaining party submits its first submission in advance of the responding party's first submission unless the panel decides otherwise.[122] All written submissions to the panel must be treated as confidential, but they must be available to the parties to the dispute.

---

[117] J. Pauwelyn, *Conflict of Norms in Public International Law: How WTO Law Relates to Other Rules of International Law* (Cambridge University Press, 2003), p. 444.
[118] DSU, Article 19(2). The same applies to the Appellate Body.
[119] Schoenbaum, 'WTO Dispute Settlement', pp. 652–3.
[120] Appellate Body Report, *United States – Anti-Dumping Act of 1916*, WT/DS136/AB/R, WT/DS162/AB/R, adopted 26 September 2000, footnote 30.
[121] For a more detailed explanation of the panel proceedings, see WTO, www.wto.org/english/tratop_e/dispu_e/disp_settlement_cbt_e/c6s3p1_e.htm; WTO, *A Handbook*, pp. 47 *et seq.*; Van den Bossche and Zdouc, *The Law and Policy*, pp. 274 *et seq.* See also Guzman and Pauwelyn, *International Trade Law*, pp. 132 *et seq.*
[122] DSU, Article 12(6).

The parties may disclose their own submission to the public. However, Members must treat as confidential information submitted by another Member to the panel which that Member has designated as confidential.[123] After the exchange of the first written submissions, the panel convenes the first meeting with parties. The meeting is not public.[124] After the first panel meeting, the parties simultaneously exchange written rebuttals, called the second written submissions. After receiving the parties' second submissions, the second meeting with parties is to be convened.

A third party having a substantial interest in a matter before a panel and having notified its interest to the DSB is allowed to have an opportunity to be heard by the panel and to make written submissions to the panel. These submissions are also to be given to the parties to the dispute and shall be reflected in the panel report.[125] Third parties are entitled to receive only the first written submissions of the parties by virtue of Article 10(3) of the DSU. Although the term 'intervention' is not used in the DSU, in essence, this mechanism is thought to correspond to third-party intervention in the ICJ. The mechanism is widely used in the dispute settlement system of the WTO. In *EC – Bananas*, for instance, the complaining parties were five States and some twenty-five States intervened as third parties.[126] The liberal practice of third-party intervention in the WTO is contrasted with the restrictive practice of the ICJ.[127]

5.4.2 Interim Review Stage

After the oral hearings are concluded, the panel moves to the stage of internal deliberations. Panel deliberations are confidential and the reports of panels are drafted without the presence of the parties to the dispute pursuant to Article 14(1) and (2) of the DSU. Under Article 18(1) of the DSU, *ex parte* communications with the panel concerning matters under consideration by the panel are prohibited.[128] Following the consideration of rebuttal submissions and oral arguments, the panel is to issue the descriptive (factual and argument) sections of its draft report to the parties to the dispute. Within a period of time set by the panel, the parties are required to submit their comments in writing.[129] Following the expiration of the set period of time for receipt of comments from the parties to the dispute, the panel is to issue an interim report to the parties, including both the descriptive sections and the panel's findings and conclusions. The interim report is a complete report that contains the revised descriptive part, the findings, the conclusions and the recommendations, even though it is not yet final.[130] The interim report is confidential,

---

[123] DSU, Article 18(2). See also Van den Bossche and Prévost, *Essentials of WTO Law*, pp. 290–2.
[124] Para. 2, Appendix 3 of Working Procedures provides that: 'The panel shall meet in closed session.' If both parties to the dispute agree, however, panel and the Appellate Body hearings can be public.
[125] DSU, Article 10(2). Generally on this issue, Iwasawa, 'Third Parties', p. 871; Iwasawa, 'Settlement of Disputes', pp. 296 *et seq.*
[126] Complainants were: Ecuador; Guatemala; Honduras; Mexico; United States. Third parties were: Belize, Cameroon, Canada, Colombia, Costa Rica, Dominica, Dominican Republic, Ghana, Grenada, India, Jamaica, Japan, Mauritius, Nicaragua, Panama, the Philippines, Saint Lucia, Saint Vincent and the Grenadines, Senegal, Suriname, Venezuela, Bolivarian Republic of, Côte d'Ivoire, Brazil and Madagascar.
[127] Iwasawa, 'Third Parties', p. 888. See also Chapter 7, sections 6 and 7 of this book.
[128] The same applies to the Appellate Body.
[129] DSU, Article 15(1).   [130] WTO, *A Handbook*, p. 58.

but one or more of the parties often leak its content to the press.[131] A party is allowed to submit a written request for the panel to review precise aspects of the interim report prior to circulation of the final report to the Members.[132] Normally the party's comments relate to technical errors or unclear drafting, not the findings themselves. According to the WTO Secretariat, the interim review is the last opportunity for the parties to rectify any factual mistake in the panel report.[133] Interim review is a unique feature which is not seen in judicial settlement, such as the ICJ and ITLOS.[134] The findings of the final panel report shall include a summary and a discussion of the arguments made at the interim review stage.[135] This will contribute to enhance the transparency of the review process.

5.4.3 Issuance of the Final Report

If no comments are received from any party within the comment period, the interim report shall be considered the final panel report.[136] The findings of the final panel report must include a discussion of the arguments made at the interim review stage.[137] In so doing, the transparency of the review process can be enhanced. As a general rule, the panel shall issue its report to the parties to the dispute within six months. In cases of emergency, it shall aim to issue its report within three months.[138] When the panel considers that it cannot issue its report within six months, or within three months in cases of urgency, it shall inform the DSB in writing of the reasons for the delay together with an estimate of the period within which it will issue its report. In no case *should* the period from the establishment of the panel to the circulation of the report to the Members exceed nine months.[139] As noted earlier, however, panels regularly exceed the nine-month period.[140] Where a settlement of the matter among the parties to the dispute has been found, the report of the panel is to be confined to a brief description of the case and to reporting that a solution has been reached. Where the parties to the dispute have failed to develop a mutually satisfactory solution, however, the panel submits its findings in the form of a written report to the DSB.[141]

A final report of the panel is circulated to the general WTO membership.[142] It is first issued to the parties in dispute and, then, translated into two other WTO official languages. After that, it is circulated to all WTO Members. On the same day that a report is circulated to WTO Members, it becomes a public document and published on the WTO website.[143] Members having objections to a panel report give written reasons to explain their objections for circulation at least ten days prior to the DSB meeting at which the

---

[131] *Ibid.* [132] DSU, Article 15(2).
[133] WTO, *A Handbook*, p. 59.
[134] Van den Bossche and Zdouc, *The Law and Policy*, pp. 281–2.
[135] DSU, Article 15(3). See also Van den Bossche and Zdouc, *The Law and Policy*, p. 281.
[136] DSU, Article 15(2).   [137] DSU, Article 15(3).   [138] DSU, Article 12(8).
[139] DSU, Article 12(9). Thus there is more flexibility with regard to the time limits for panels than for the Appellate Body.
[140] Van den Bossche and Zdouc, *The Law and Policy*, p. 247; WTO, *A Handbook*, p. 59.
[141] DSU, Article 12(7).   [142] DSU, Article 15(2).   [143] See also WTO, *A Handbook*, p. 59.

panel report will be considered.[144] Under Article 16(3) of the DSU, the parties to a dispute have the right to participate fully in the consideration of the panel report by the DSB, and their views are fully recorded. Within sixty days after the date of circulation of a panel report to the Members, however, the report must be adopted at a DSB meeting, unless a party to the dispute formally notifies the DSB of its decision to appeal or the DSB decides by consensus not to adopt the report.[145] Accordingly, one single Member insisting on adoption is adequate to secure the adoption of the report and the losing party cannot block the adoption of report.[146] The adoption of the panel reports becomes quasi-automatic owing to the 'reverse consensus'. The panel report becomes binding only when the DSB has adopted it.[147] If a party has notified its decision to appeal, however, the report by the panel shall not be considered for adoption by the DSB until after completion of the appeal.[148] According to statistics of the WTO, between 1995 and 2014, 201 panel reports were adopted and 136 panel reports, or 68 per cent, were appealed.[149]

6 APPELLATE REVIEW

Given that panel reports are almost automatically adopted by the DSB, the parties in dispute can no longer block the adoption of the reports. Thus a mechanism for appellate review is of particular importance for the Members of the WTO. In fact, comparatively, many panel reports are appealed in practice. The appellate review process is governed by Article 17 of the DSU and Working Procedures for Appellate Review.[150] Under Article 17(4), only parties to the dispute, not third parties, may appeal a panel report to the Appellate Body.[151] Either side can appeal a panel's ruling or sometimes both sides do appeal since either party in the dispute may disagree with the panel's conclusions.[152]

The Appellate Body is a standing organ established by the DSB and it is composed of seven persons, three of whom shall serve on any one case.[153] Persons to serve on the Appellate Body are appointed by the DSB for a four-year term, and each person may be reappointed only once.[154] The members of the Appellate Body are persons of recognised authority with demonstrated expertise in law, international trade and the subject matter of the covered agreement generally. In light of the importance of the independence and impartiality of the members of the Appellate Body, Article 17(3) of the DSU provides that

---

[144] DSU, Article 16(2).   [145] DSU, Article 16(4).
[146] Guzman and Pauwelyn, *International Trade Law*, p. 135.
[147] WTO, *A Handbook*, p. 61; Van den Bossche and Prévost, *Essentials of WTO Law*, p. 281.
[148] DSU, Article 16(4).
[149] WTO, Dispute Settlement: Statistics Table 2, at www.wto.org/english/tratop_e/dispu_e/stats_e.htm.
[150] The Working Procedures for Appellate Review is available at: www.wto.org/english/tratop_e/dispu_e/ab_e .htm#20. For a detailed explanation on the Appellate Review process, see Van Den Bossche and Zdouc, *The Law and Policy*, pp. 283 *et seq.*; WTO, www.wto.org/english/tratop_e/dispu_e/disp_settlement_cbt_e/ c6s5p1_e.htm.
[151] Third parties which have notified the DSB of a substantial interest in the matter may also make written submission to the Appellate Body and be given an opportunity to be heard by the Body (Article 17(4) of the DSU).
[152] WTO, *A Handbook*, p. 64.   [153] DSU, Article 17(1).   [154] DSU, Article 17(2).

they shall be unaffiliated with any government and shall not participate in the consideration of any disputes that would create a direct or indirect conflict of interest.[155] Under the same provision, the Appellate Body membership must also be broadly representative of membership in the WTO.

An appeal is limited to issues of law covered in the panel report and legal interpretations developed by the panel.[156] An appeal cannot address the facts on which the panel report is based by re-examining existing evidence or examining new factual evidence.[157] However, it is possible for the Appellate Body to review whether a panel has made an objective assessment of the facts as required under Article 11 of the DSU.[158] As explained earlier,[159] as a general rule, the proceedings of the appellate review shall not exceed sixty days from the date a party to the dispute formally notifies its decision to appeal to the date the Appellate Body circulates its report. In no case shall the proceedings exceed ninety days.[160] In recent years, however, it appears that the ninety-day period is no longer feasible because of the extreme workload and limited resources of the Appellate Body and the complexity of the cases.

The proceedings of the Appellate Body are confidential.[161] An Appellate Body's report must be adopted by the DSB and unconditionally accepted by the parties to the dispute unless the DSB decides by consensus not to adopt the Appellate Body report within thirty days following its circulation to the Members.[162] In other words, the reports are adopted by reverse consensus. Unlike the panel procedure, there is no interim review in the procedure of the Appellate Body.

Where a panel or the Appellate Body concludes that a measure is inconsistent with a covered agreement, the Member concerned is to be recommended to bring the measure into conformity with that agreement. The panel or Appellate Body is also empowered to suggest ways in which the Member concerned could implement the recommendations.[163]

7 LEGAL EFFECT OF REPORTS OF WTO PANELS AND THE APPELLATE BODY

The DSU contains no explicit provision with regard to the legal effect of the panel or appellate report. Under Article 17(4) of the DSU, once an appellate report was adopted by the DSB, the parties to the dispute must unconditionally accept the report. Further, Article 22(1) of the DSU stresses that compensation and the suspension of concessions or other obligations are *temporary* measures available in the event that the recommendations and rulings are not implemented within a reasonable period of time. This provision does seem to suggest that the recommendations and ruling must be implemented. In the case of *non-violation* complaints, the complaining party is under no obligation to withdraw a measure

---

[155] See also Rules of Conduct, Section II, para. 1.   [156] DSU, Article 17(6).
[157] WTO, *A Handbook*, p. 66; Van den Bossche and Zdouc, *The Law and Policy*, pp. 236 et seq.
[158] *Ibid.*, p. 237; Van den Bossche and Prévost, *Essentials of WTO Law*, p. 282.
[159] See section 2.1 of this chapter.   [160] DSU, Article 17(5).
[161] DSU, Article 17(10).   [162] DSU, Article 17(14).   [163] DSU, Article 19(1).

which has been found to nullify or impair benefits under, or impede the attainment of objectives of, the relevant covered agreement without violation thereof.[164] It seems to follow that in the case of violation complaints, the complaining party is obliged to withdraw the measure in question. In light of these provisions, one can argue that the conclusions and recommendations contained in a report of a panel and the Appellate Body are binding upon the parties after the DSB has adopted the report.[165]

Like the ICJ, the principle of binding precedents does not apply to the panel procedure.[166] In fact, the Appellant Body, in the *Japan – Taxes on Alcoholic Beverages* case, stated that adopted panel reports 'are not binding, except with respect to resolving the particular dispute between the parties to that dispute'.[167] The language seems to be parallel to Article 59 of the ICJ Statute.[168] In the same case, however, the Appellant Body went on to add that:

> Adopted panel reports are an important part of the GATT *acquis*. They are often considered by subsequent panels. They create legitimate expectations among WTO Members, and, therefore, should be taken into account where they are relevant to any dispute.[169]

This view was echoed by the Appellant Body, in *United States – Final Anti-Dumping Measures on Stainless Steel from Mexico*:

> It is well settled that Appellate Body reports are not binding, except with respect to resolving the particular dispute between the parties. This, however, does not mean that subsequent panels are free to disregard the legal interpretations and the *ratio decidendi* contained in previous Appellate Body reports that have been adopted by the DSB.[170]

In this regard, the Appellant Body's view deserves quoting in full:

> Dispute settlement practice demonstrates that WTO Members attach significance to reasoning provided in previous panel and Appellate Body reports. Adopted panel and Appellate Body reports are often cited by parties in support of legal arguments in dispute settlement proceedings, and are relied upon by panels and the Appellate Body in subsequent

---

[164] DSU, Article 26(1)(b).
[165] WTO, *A Handbook*, pp. 88–9. This view is also supported by writers, including: Iwasawa, 'WTO Dispute Settlement', pp. 289–90; Iwasawa, 'Third Parties', pp. 873–4; J. H. Jackson, 'International Law Status of WTO Dispute Settlement Reports: Obligation to Comply or Option to "Buy Out"' (2004) 98 *AJIL*, pp. 115–17; J. Pauwelyn, 'Enforcement and Countermeasures in the WTO: Rules are Rules–Toward a More Collective Approach' (2000) 94 *AJIL*, p. 5; Stoll, 'World Trade Organisation', para. 67.
[166] Iwasawa, 'WTO Dispute Settlement', p. 290.
[167] Appellate Body Report, *Japan – Taxes on Alcoholic Beverages*, WT/DS8/AB/R, WT/DS10/AB/R, WT/DS11/AB/R, adopted 1 November 1996, p. 14 (electronic text).
[168] *Ibid.*, footnote 30 of the Report.   [169] *Ibid.*, p. 14.
[170] Footnotes omitted. Appellate Body Report, *United States – Final Anti-Dumping Measures on Stainless Steel from Mexico*, WT/DS344/AB/R, adopted 20 May 2008, para. 158.

disputes. In addition, when enacting or modifying laws and national regulations pertaining to international trade matters, WTO Members take into account the legal interpretation of the covered agreements developed in adopted panel and Appellate Body reports. Thus, the legal interpretation embodied in adopted panel and Appellate Body reports becomes part and parcel of the *acquis* of the WTO dispute settlement system. Ensuring 'security and predictability' in the dispute settlement system, as contemplated in Article 3.2 of the DSU, implies that, absent cogent reasons, an adjudicatory body will resolve the same legal question in the same way in a subsequent case.[171]

8 IMPLEMENTATION OF RULINGS AND RECOMMENDATIONS

8.1 Remedies for Breach of WTO Law

Under the DSU, there are three types of remedies for breach of WTO law:[172]

- the withdrawal or modification of the WTO-inconsistent measures
- compensation
- suspension of concessions or other obligations (retaliation).

As provided in Article 3(7) of the DSU, the principal remedy for breach of WTO law is the withdrawal of the WTO-inconsistent measures; the other two types of remedies (i.e. compensation and retaliation) are only temporary. The withdrawal of these measures should be 'immediate'.[173] In this regard, Article 21(1) of the DSU stresses that: 'Prompt compliance with recommendations or rulings of the DSB is essential in order to ensure effective resolution of disputes to the benefit of all Members.' In the view of the arbitrator in *Chile – Taxes on Alcoholic Beverages*, 'prompt' compliance is, in principle, 'immediate' compliance.[174]

The Member concerned is obliged to inform the DSB of its intentions in respect of implementation of the recommendations and rulings of the DSB at a DSB meeting held within thirty days after the date of adoption of the panel or Appellate Body report. If it is impracticable to comply immediately with the recommendations and rulings, the Member concerned shall have a reasonable period of time in which to do so.[175] The reasonable period of time may be agreed by the parties within forty-five days of the date of adoption of the recommendations and rulings or, if they cannot agree, it is determined by arbitration within ninety days after the date of adoption of the recommendations and rulings.[176]

---

[171] *Ibid.*, para. 160.
[172] Further, see Van den Bossche and Zdouc, *The Law and Policy*, pp. 194 *et seq.*
[173] Article 3(7) provides that: 'The provision of compensation should be resorted to only if the *immediate withdrawal* of the measure is impracticable ... ' (Emphasis added).
[174] Award of the Arbitrator, *Chile – Taxes on Alcoholic Beverages*, Arbitration under Article 21.3(c) of the Understanding on Rules and Procedures Governing the Settlement of Disputes, WT/DS87/15, WT/DS110/14, 23 May 2000, para. 38.
[175] DSU, Article 21(3). [176] *Ibid.*

As the arbitrator observed in *Chile – Taxes on Alcoholic Beverages*, it may be said that a certain element of flexibility in respect of time is built into the notion of compliance with the recommendations and rulings of the DSB.[177] Where there is disagreement as to the existence of, or consistency with, a covered agreement of measures taken to comply with the recommendations and rulings, such dispute is to be resolved through the normal dispute settlement procedures of the DSU including, wherever possible, resort to the original panel. In this case, the panel shall circulate its report within ninety days after the date of referral of the matter to it.[178] When the panel considers that it cannot provide its report within this timeframe, it must inform the DSB in writing of the reasons for the delay together with an estimate of the period within which it will submit its report.[179]

The implementation of adopted recommendations or rulings is kept under surveillance of the DSB.[180] This can be considered as an important political inducement to comply.[181] Under Article 21(6) of the DSU, the issue of implementation of the recommendations or rulings may be raised at the DSB by any Member at any time following their adoption. As a general rule, the issue of implementation of the recommendations or rulings is to be placed on the agenda of the DSB meeting after six months following the date of establishment of the reasonable period of time pursuant to Article 21(3) and shall remain on the DSB's agenda until the issue is resolved.

8.2 Compensation and Retaliation

In the event that the recommendations and rulings are not implemented within a reasonable period of time, as noted, two *temporary* measures can be taken: compensation and the suspension of concessions or other obligations. The latter is referred to as countermeasures or retaliation.

8.2.1 Compensation

Compensation is voluntary and, if granted, shall be consistent with the covered agreements.[182] If the Member concerned fails to achieve full compliance by the end of the reasonable period of time, upon request, such Member is obliged to enter into negotiations with any party having invoked the dispute settlement procedures with a view to developing mutually acceptable compensation.[183] Compensation does not mean monetary payment, but, rather, offering a benefit, such as a tariff reduction or market access.[184] Compensation under Article 22 of the DSU is forward-looking in the sense that it concerns only damages that will be suffered in the future. In other words, compensation is

---

[177] Award of the Arbitrator, *Chile – Taxes on Alcoholic Beverages*, Arbitration under Article 21.3(c) of the Understanding on Rules and Procedures Governing the Settlement of Disputes, WT/DS87/15, WT/DS110/14, 23 May 2000, para. 38.
[178] DSU, Article 21(5).
[179] *Ibid*. Yet the average duration of an Article 21(5) compliance procedure is said to be 246 days. Van den Bossche and Zdouc, *The Law and Policy*, p. 293.
[180] DSU, Article 21(6). See also Article 21(3).
[181] Pauwelyn, 'Enforcement and Countermeasures', p. 337.
[182] DSU, Article 22(1).   [183] DSU, Article 22(2).   [184] WTO, *A Handbook*, p. 80.

only prospective.[185] Furthermore, compensation is to be offered to the winning party as well as to all WTO Members.[186] As compensation is subject to the agreement of the law-breaker, it is difficult to obtain. Therefore, compensation is a rare event in reality.[187]

8.2.2 Retaliation

If no satisfactory compensation has been agreed within twenty days after the date of expiry of the reasonable period of time, any party having invoked the dispute settlement procedures may request authorisation from the DSB to suspend the application to the Member concerned of concessions or other obligations under the covered agreements.[188] When there has been non-compliance and no compensation has been agreed, the complainant may request the DSB to authorise the suspension of concessions or other obligations. In such a situation, the DSB, upon request, must grant authorisation to suspend concessions or other obligations within thirty days of the expiry of the reasonable period of time unless the DSB decides by consensus to reject the request.[189] Owing to the reverse consensus, the approval by the DSB is quasi-automatic. However, if the Member concerned objects to the level of suspension proposed, or claims that the principles and procedures set forth in Article 22(3) have not been followed, the matter is to be referred to arbitration. Concessions or other obligations shall not be suspended during the course of the arbitration.[190]

Since countermeasures entail the raising of trade barriers, they are thought to be 'trade destructive' and they entail the risk of damaging not only the economy of the non-complying Member but also of the Member applying the retaliatory measures. Thus the DSB sets out certain requirements. First, in principle the sanctions should be imposed in the same sector as that in which the violation or other nullification or impairment was found.[191] Second, if that party considers that it is not practicable or effective to suspend concessions or other obligations with respect to the same sector(s), it may seek to suspend concessions or other obligations in other sectors under the same agreement.[192] Third, if that party considers that it is not practicable or effective to suspend concessions or other obligations with respect to other sectors under the same agreement, and that the circumstances are serious enough, it may seek to suspend concessions or other obligations under another covered agreement.[193] The suspension of concessions in other sectors or under another agreement is often called 'cross-retaliation'. Given that the bilateral trade relationship may be asymmetrical, the suspension in the same sector or under the

---

[185] Van den Bossche and Zdouc, *The Law and Policy*, p. 200; Van den Bossche and Prévost, *Essentials of WTO Law*, p. 287.
[186] Pauwelyn, 'Enforcement and Countermeasures', p. 337. In fact, an important obligation in the covered agreements is that of 'most favoured nation' treatment which requires that any advantage offered to any country be offered immediately and unconditionally to all other WTO Members.
[187] Stoll, 'World Trade Organization', para. 48; Pauwelyn, 'Enforcement and Countermeasures', pp. 337 and 345. An example of compensation is provided by the *Japan – Alcoholic Beverages II* case. Van den Bossche and Zdouc, *The Law and Policy*, p. 200.
[188] DSU, Article 22(2).   [189] DSU, Article 22(6).   [190] DSU, Article 22(6).
[191] DSU, Article 22(3)(a).
[192] DSU, Article 22(3)(b). This is called 'cross-sector retaliation'.
[193] DSU, Article 22(3)(c). This is called 'cross-agreement retaliation'.

same agreement may be ineffective. Hence, some argue that for developing States, the 'cross-retaliation' can be a feasible tool that could lead to improved compliance by developed States.[194] In any case it must be remembered that retaliation is the last resort and that it is the exception, not the rule.[195]

The level of the suspension of concessions or other obligations authorised by the DSB must be equivalent to the level of the nullification or impairment.[196] As the arbitrator stated in *EC – Bananas III* of 1999, the suspension is not punitive by nature.[197] Punitive countermeasures will be contrary to the objective set out in Article 22(1) of the DSU (i.e. securing full implementation of DSB's recommendations and rulings). Thus the requirement of equivalence of the level of the nullification or impairment is of central importance. If the Member concerned objects to the level of suspension proposed or claims that inappropriate measures have been imposed, the matter is to be referred to arbitration.[198] Here arbitration, which is usually carried out by the original panel,[199] performs an important role to secure the requirement of equivalence of countermeasures. Concessions or other obligations shall not be suspended during the course of the arbitration by virtue of Article 22(6). If a covered agreement prohibits such suspension, the DSB shall not authorise suspension of concessions or other obligations.[200] The suspension of obligations is prospective, not retroactive. In other words, it covers only the period after the DSB has granted authorisation.[201] In light of their objective to achieve implementation, there appears to be a general sense that suspension may be applied until inconsistent measures have been removed, or a mutually satisfactory solution has been agreed.[202]

8.2.3 Difficulties with Retaliation

In practice, the application of countermeasures is not free from difficulty. First, countermeasures in the WTO are of a bilateral nature in the sense that they can be taken only by the complaining parties. Yet, it would be difficult or even counterproductive for weaker Member States to take countermeasures against stronger Members, such as the United States. A direct negative effect of retaliation for economically weaker Members is the damage that these measures cause to their own economies. There is also a risk for developing States that countermeasures may provoke counter-retaliation in other fields than WTO, such as economic aid. Hence it is questionable whether countermeasures would be a realistic option to the weaker Members.[203]

---

[194] Further, Lucas Eduardo F. A. Spadano, 'Cross-Agreement Retaliation in the WTO Dispute Settlement System: An Important Enforcement Mechanism for Developing Countries?' (2008) 7 *World Trade Review*, pp. 511–45.
[195] DSU, Article 3(7); WTO, *A Handbook*, p. 82.
[196] DSU, Article 22(4).
[197] Decision by the Arbitrators, *European Communities – Regime for the Importation, Sale and Distribution of Bananas – Recourse to Arbitration by the European Communities under Article 22.6 of the DSU*, WT/DS27/ARB, 9 April 1999, p. 34, para. 6.3.
[198] DSU, Article 22(6).
[199] Van den Bossche and Zdouc, *The Law and Policy*, p. 292.
[200] DSU, Article 22(5).   [201] WTO, *A Handbook*, p. 82.
[202] Merrills, *International Dispute Settlement*, p. 224.
[203] Pauwelyn, 'Enforcement and Countermeasures', p. 338.

Second, countermeasures imply the raising of trade barriers by the winning party vis-à-vis the losing party. Yet, these measures may threaten the progress of trade liberalisation and free trade principles. Thus it is not surprising that parties have often refrained from resorting to the suspension of concessions in practice.[204]

Third, as noted, countermeasures must not exceed the level of the nullification or impairment. In some cases, however, the equivalent level is hard to determine. One may take national legislation which is contrary to WTO agreements as an example. According to the Appellate Body, it is firmly established that dispute settlement proceedings may be brought based on the alleged inconsistency of a Member's legislation as such with that Member's obligations.[205] In this regard, an issue arises whether the other Member can suspend obligations in order to adopt an equivalent legislation (i.e. a mirror legislation) to the illicit national legislation of its opponent. This issue relates to the question whether a WTO Member can suspend 'qualitatively equivalent' obligations. It appears that arbitration, in *US – 1916 Act (EC)*, did not *a priori* deny the possibility of the suspension of 'qualitatively equivalent' obligation.[206] However, arbitrators went on to add that an equivalent legislation does not automatically mean the equivalency of the level of the nullification or impairment and that 'it is necessary to determine how the actual suspension resulting from such "qualitative equivalence" would be *applied*'.[207]

A related issue that arises in this regard is whether 'nullification or impairment of benefits' that is used to determine the level of retaliation is limited to trade losses or includes all the economic harm or adverse effects resulting from the WTO-inconsistent measure. On this issue, the arbitrator acting under Article 22(6) of the DSU, in *US – COOL*, took the view that the 'benefit' that is nullified or impaired is limited to trade benefits and, thus, other economic harm that results from the violation of WTO law cannot be addressed through retaliation.[208]

8.2.4 Problem with Delay of Compliance

In most cases, compliance occurs without the need for retaliation.[209] In some cases, however, problems associated with delay of compliance arise.[210] An illustrative example is provided by *EC – Hormones*.[211] The report of the Appellate Body of this case was

---

[204] *Ibid.*, p. 337; Stoll, 'World Trade Organization', para. 46; N. Horlick, 'Problems with the Compliance Structure of the WTO Dispute Resolution Process' in D. L. M. Kennedy and J. D. Southwick (eds.), *The Political Economy of International Trade Law: Essays in Honour of Robert E. Hudec* (Cambridge University Press, 2002), p. 641.
[205] Appellate Body Report, *US – Anti-Dumping Act of 1916*, WT/DS136/AB/R, WT/DS162/AB/R, adopted 26 September 2000, para. 75.
[206] Decision by Arbitration, *United States – Anti-Dumping Act of 1916, Original Complaint by the European Communities – Recourse to Arbitration by the United States under Article 22.6 of the DSU*, WT/DS136/ARB, 24 February 2004, para. 5.21.
[207] *Ibid.* Emphasis original.
[208] Decisions by the Arbitrator, *United States – Certain Country of Origin Labelling (COOL) Requirements – Recourse to Article 22.6 of the DSU the United States*, WT/DS384/ARB and Add.1 / WT/DS386/ARB and Add.1, circulated to WTO Members 7 December 2015, paras. 5.11–5.27.
[209] According to Van den Bossche and Prévost, '[i]n 85 percent of all disputes in which a WTO-inconsistent measures must be amended or withdrawn, the respondent complies with the recommendations and the rulings of the DSB'. Van den Bossche and Prévost, *Essentials of WTO Law*, p. 289.
[210] Horlick, 'Problem with Compliance Structure', pp. 637 *et seq.*; Merrills, *International Dispute Settlement*, p. 224.
[211] For a chronological summary of the dispute, see www.wto.org/english/tratop_e/dispu_e/cases_e/ds26_e.htm.

adopted at the meeting of the DSB on 13 February 1998.[212] On 8 April 1998, however, the European Communities requested that the 'reasonable period of time' be determined by binding arbitration under Article 21(3)(c). In May 1998, the arbitrator decided that a reasonable period of time in this case would be fifteen months from the date of adoption of the Appellate Body and Panel Reports by the DSB – that is, fifteen months from 13 February 1998.[213] It followed that the deadline would be 13 May 1999. At the end of the deadline, however, the European Communities had still not brought its beef import ban into compliance.

In return, on 3 June 1999, the United States requested authorisation to suspend tariff concessions pursuant to Article 22(2). In response, the European Communities requested arbitration on the level of suspension of concessions requested by the United States in conformity with Article 22(6). On 12 July 1999, the arbitrators determined that the level of nullification or impairment suffered by the United States in this matter was US$116.8 million per year.[214] On 26 July 1999, the DSB thus authorised the suspension of concessions to the European Communities by the United States in accordance with the arbitral award. All in all, it was after more than seventeen months when the retaliatory tariffs authorised against the European Communities finally came into effect. The entire range of delay tactics is problematic because, even if a government lost the case, it may be a market winner owing to the effects of its temporary unfair competitive advantage in the present fast-paced market.[215]

9 LEGAL NATURE OF THE WTO PANEL PROCEDURE

Given that a WTO panel is established on an ad hoc basis, it is arguable that the panel procedures are akin to arbitration. Unlike arbitration, however, the panel procedures and applicable law are predetermined by the DSU. Furthermore, as explained earlier, a standing organ (i.e. the Appellate Body) may ultimately deal with the case. These features do seem to suggest that the WTO panel procedures are more akin to judicial settlement.[216]

At the same time, it must be noted that panels are required to consult regularly with the parties to the dispute and give them adequate opportunity to develop a mutually satisfactory solution. Indeed, as explained already, the panel is required to issue the descriptive (factual and argument) sections of its draft report to the parties to the dispute and the parties are entitled to submit their comments in writing in accordance with Article 15(1) of the DSU. At the stage of an interim report, a party may submit a written request for the panel to review precise aspects of the report prior to circulation of the final report to the

---

[212] Appellate Body Report, *EC Measures Concerning Meat and Meat Products (Hormones)*, WT/DS26/13, WT/DS48/11, adopted 13 February 1998.

[213] Award of the Arbitrator, *EC Measures Concerning Meat and Meat Products (Hormones)*, Arbitration under Article 21.3(c) of the Understanding on Rules and Procedures Governing the Settlement of Disputes, WT/DS26/15, WT/DS48/13, 29 May 1998, p. 20, para. 48.

[214] Decision by the Arbitrators, *European Communities – Measures Concerning Meat and Meat Products (Hormones), Original Complaint by the United States – Recourse to Arbitration by the European Communities under Article 22.6 of the DSU*, WT/DS26/ARB, 12 July 1999, p. 17, para. 83.

[215] Horlick, 'Problem with Compliance Structure', p. 640. Further, see W. J. Davey, 'Compliance Problems in WTO Dispute Settlement' (2009) 42 *Cornell International Law Journal*, pp. 119–28.

[216] Iwasawa, 'WTO Dispute Settlement', p. 290; Iwasawa, 'Third Parties', p. 875.

Members under Article 15(2).[217] Here one can find an element of conciliation. It is also to be noted that a report of a panel and/or the Appellate Body is subject to adoption by the DSB – that is, a political organ of the WTO – even though political influence of the DSB on the outcome of dispute settlement are almost non-existent due to reverse consensus decision-making in the DSB. All in all, it seems reasonable to consider that panel proceedings in the WTO are regarded as a *sui generis* system of dispute settlement which has a mixed character of judicial settlement and conciliation.[218]

10 ARBITRATION

Arbitration and panel procedures are two distinct processes and, thus, the DSU contains a separate article concerning arbitration. Article 25(1) of the DSU recognises that expeditious arbitration within the WTO as an alternative means of dispute settlement can facilitate the solution of certain disputes that concern issues that are clearly defined by both parties. In this regard, it is to be noted that arbitration is not exclusively autonomous but is integrated into the WTO system in three ways.

First, agreements to resort to arbitration shall be notified to all Members sufficiently in advance of the actual commencement of the arbitration process in accordance with Article 25(2) of the DSU.

Second, when the arbitral award is rendered, it shall be notified to the DSB and the council or committee of any relevant agreement where any Member may raise any point relating thereto.[219] This procedure is important since arbitral awards may affect the interpretation of the WTO Agreement.

Third, the DSB is involved in the implementation of arbitral awards. In this regard, Article 25(4) of the DSU provides that Articles 21 and 22 apply *mutatis mutandis* to arbitration awards. The DSB thus plays the same role with regard to the implementation of arbitral awards and panel reports.

Under Article 25(2) of the DSU, resort to arbitration is subject to mutual agreement of the parties which shall agree on the procedures to be followed. It follows that arbitration under Article 25 is voluntary. However, arbitration is mandatory with regard to disputes concerning retaliation which may arise at the implementation stage under Article 22 of the DSU and the 'reasonable period of time' granted to the respondent for implementation under Article 21(3)(c) of the DSU.[220]

As stated in Article 22(7) of the DSU, arbitrators under Article 22(6) cannot examine 'the nature of the concessions or other obligations to be suspended but shall determine whether the level of such suspension is equivalent to the level of nullification or impairment'. In addition, they do not have jurisdiction to deal with a matter concerning non-WTO rules, such as the compatibility of the proposed suspension with other rules

---

[217] Normally the review concerns technical errors, not the findings themselves. According to the WTO Secretariat, the interim review is the last opportunity for the parties to rectify any factual mistake in the panel report. WTO, *A Handbook*, p. 59.
[218] Iwasawa, 'WTO Dispute Settlement', p. 291.
[219] DSU, Article 25(3).
[220] See also WTO, *A Handbook*, p. 25.

of international law.[221] Thus the jurisdiction of arbitrators with regard to retaliation is limited to determining the following matters:

(i) the level of retaliation as called for in Article 22(4)
(ii) compliance with principles and procedures set out in Article 22(3)
(iii) the permissibility of the proposed suspension.[222]

As the DSU contains no provisions respecting relevant procedures for arbitration, arbitral procedures, such as the selection of the arbitrators,[223] the procedure to be followed and the applicable law, must be arranged by the parties in dispute. Unlike panel or Appellate Body reports, an arbitration award is not adopted by the DSB.[224] Under Article 22(7) of the DSU, the parties shall accept the arbitrator's decision as final and the parties concerned shall not seek a second arbitration. Unlike the panel proceedings, the protection of the interests of third parties is limited in an arbitration process. Under Article 25(3) of the DSU, however, other Members may become party to an arbitration proceeding upon the agreement of the parties which have agreed to have recourse to arbitration. The parties to the proceeding shall agree to abide by the arbitration award.

So far, arbitration under Article 25 as an alternative to the panel and Appellate Body procedure has never been used. By contrast, arbitration under Article 21(3)(c) concerning the reasonable period of time for implementation and arbitration under Article 22(6) on the level of retaliation has been used several times.[225]

11 THE WTO DISPUTE SETTLEMENT SYSTEM AND DEVELOPING STATES

A criticism that may arise with regard to the WTO dispute settlement system is that developing States are marginalised in the system. This issue must be examined from a dual viewpoint, namely, institutional and practical viewpoints.[226]

11.1 Consideration of Developing States in the DSU

Notably, the DSU pays particular attention to the interest of developing States at the stages of consultation, panel proceedings and the implementation in five respects.

First, at the consultation stage, Article 4(10) of the DSU requires that: 'During consultations Members should give special attention to the particular problems and interests of developing country Members.' Where consultation involves a measure taken by

---

[221] Pauwelyn, *Conflict of Norms*, pp. 446–7.
[222] *Ibid.*, p. 446. See also DSU, Article 22(5) and (7).
[223] To date, arbitrations under Article 21(3)(c) of the DSU have been conducted by current or former Appellate Body Members acting in an individual capacity. *Appellate Body Annual Report for 2013*, p. 10.
[224] Van den Bossche and Zdouc, *The Law and Policy*, p. 292.
[225] See www.wto.org/english/tratop_e/dispu_e/disp_settlement_cbt_e/c8s2p1_e.htm; www.wto.org/english/tratop_e/dispu_e/arbitrations_e.htm; WTO, *A Handbook*, p. 96.
[226] There is a large body of literature on this subject. For a recent study, see for instance, K. M. W. Mitchell, 'Developing Country Success in WTO Disputes' (2013) 47 *Journal of World Trade*, pp. 77–104; K. Zeng, 'Legal Capacity and Developing Country Performance in the Panel Stage of the WTO Dispute Settlement System' (2013) 47 *Journal of World Trade*, pp. 187–214. See also WTO, *A Handbook*, pp. 109–15; Van den Bossche and Zdouc, *The Law and Policy*, pp. 299–302.

a developing country Member, Article 12(10) of the DSU allows the parties to agree to extend the periods established in Article 4(7) and (8).

Second, in panel proceedings, Article 8(10) of the DSU requires that at least one panellist from a developing country must be included in a panel to deal with a dispute between a developed country Member and a developing country Member, if the latter so requests. When examining a complaint against a developing country Member, the panel must accord sufficient time for the developing country Member to prepare and present its argumentation pursuant to Article 12(10) of the DSU. Where one or more of the parties is a developing country Member, the panel's report must explicitly indicate the form in which account has been taken of relevant provisions on differential and more-favourable treatment for developing country Members that form part of the covered agreements which have been raised by the developing country Member in the course of the dispute settlement procedures.[227]

Third, at the implementation stage, Article 21(2) of the DSU requires that particular attention should be paid to matters affecting the interests of developing country Members with respect to measures which have been subject to dispute settlement. If the matter is one which has been raised by a developing country Member, the DSB is required to consider what further action it might take which would be appropriate to the circumstances in accordance with Article 21(7). Furthermore, if the case is one brought by a developing country Member, Article 21(8) obliges the DSB to take into account not only the trade coverage of measures complained of, but also their impact on the economy of developing country Members concerned in considering what appropriate action might be taken.

Fourth, the WTO Secretariat is required to provide additional legal advice and assistance in respect of dispute settlement to developing country Members. In this regard, Article 27(2) of the DSU requires the Secretariat to make available a qualified legal expert from the WTO technical cooperation services to any developing country Member which so requests. This expert is to assist the developing country Member in a manner ensuring the continued impartiality of the Secretariat.

Fifth, Article 24 of the DSU provides 'special procedures involving least-developed country members'. Under Article 24(1):

> At all stages of the determination of the causes of a dispute and of dispute settlement procedures involving a least-developed country Member, particular consideration shall be given to the special situation of least-developed country Members. In this regard, Members shall exercise due restraint in raising matters under these procedures involving a least-developed country Member. If nullification or impairment is found to result from a measure taken by a least-developed country Member, complaining parties shall exercise due restraint in asking for compensation or seeking authorization to suspend the application of concessions or other obligations pursuant to these procedures.

Article 24(2) further requires the Director-General or the Chairman of the DSB to offer, upon request by a least-developed country Member, their good offices, conciliation and

---

[227] DSU, Article 12(11).

mediation with a view to assisting the parties to settle the dispute, before a request for a panel is made, where a satisfactory solution has not been found in the course of consultations concerning cases involving a least-developed country.

11.2 Practice of Developing States

According to statistics,[228] the United States and the European Union constitute two major complaining parties in the WTO. The total number of complaining parties between 1995 and 2013 is 502. In this period, 106 cases were initiated by the United States and 90 cases were brought by the European Union. During the same period, thirty-three complaints were brought by Canada, while nineteen complaints were brought by Japan. The Republic of Korea brought sixteen complaints. In addition, twenty-five complaints were brought by other developed States.[229] In broad terms, around 57.6 per cent of complaints were brought by developed States.

Recently, however, developing States have tended to bring complaints in almost equal numbers as developed States.[230] In fact, between 2010 and 2013, the total number of complaints brought by Brazil, China, India, Mexico and other developing States was thirty-nine out of seventy-two, or 54 per cent.[231] Even so, a striking fact is that least-developed States brought only one complaint between 1995 and 2013.[232]

A major obstacle for developing States, in particular least-developed States, is the high cost of litigation.[233] For example, lawyers for Kodak and Fuji in the *Japan – Photographic Film* case were said to charge their clients fees in excess of $10 million dollars.[234] The high costs would over-burden developing States, in particular, least-developed States. Furthermore, the lack of human resources, including experienced lawyers, prevents developing and least-developed States from using the WTO dispute settlement system. In this regard, Article 27(2) of the DSU realises that there may be a need to provide additional legal advice and assistance in respect of dispute settlement to developing country Members when the Secretariat assists Members in respect of dispute settlement at their request. To this end, the Secretariat is required to make available a qualified legal expert from the WTO technical cooperation services to any developing country Member which so requests.

An attempt to assist developing countries is the establishment of the Advisory Centre on WTO Law (ACWL), created in Geneva in 2001. The Agreement Establishing the Advisory Centre on WTO Law recognised, in its preamble, that developing countries, in particular the least developed among them, and the countries with economies in transition have

---

[228] K. Leitner and S. Lester, 'WTO Dispute Settlement 1995–2013: A Statistical Analysis' (2014) 17 *Journal of International Economic Law*, pp. 191–201.
[229] *Ibid.*, p. 193.
[230] See also J. T. Fried, '2013 in WTO Dispute Settlement', Figure 11, available at: www.wto.org/english/tratop_e/dispu_e/jfried_13_e.htm.
[231] Leitner and Lester, 'WTO Dispute Settlement 1995–2013', p. 193.
[232] *Ibid*.
[233] Narlikar, *The World Trade Organisation*, p. 96.
[234] G. Shaffer, 'How to Make the WTO Dispute Settlement System Work for Developing Countries: Some Proactive Developing Country Strategies' in G. Shaffer, V. Mosoti and A. Qureshi, *Towards a Development-Supportive Dispute Settlement System in the WTO*, ICTSD Resource Paper No. 5, March 2003, p. 16, available at: http://ictsd.org/downloads/2008/06/dsu_2003.pdf.

limited expertise in WTO law and the management of complex trade disputes and their ability to acquire such expertise is subject to severe financial and institutional constraints.[235] The ACWL thus aims to provide legal training, support and advice on WTO law and dispute settlement procedures to developing countries, in particular to the least developed among them, and to countries with economies in transition.[236] The ACWL has been very successful in providing support in all stages of WTO dispute settlement at discounted rates at varying levels that depend on the level of economic development and on whether they are members of the Centre. Furthermore, the ACWL provides free of charge legal advice on substantive and procedural aspects of WTO law.[237] To date, it has provided support in some forty-nine WTO dispute settlement proceedings.[238]

12 CONCLUSIONS

The matters considered in this chapter can be summarised as follows:

(i) The dispute settlement system of the WTO is unique, particularly in four respects:
- strict timeframes for different stages of the dispute settlement process
- compulsory jurisdiction of WTO panels and the Appellate Body on the basis of the principle of negative consensus
- the establishment of the appeal procedure
- institutionalised surveillance of the implementation of recommendations and ruling.

(ii) The compulsory jurisdiction of WTO panels and the Appellate Body presents a major difference between the WTO dispute settlement system and other international courts, including the ICJ. Since reverse consensus applies to the adoption of reports of the panels and the Appellate Body, the adoption of reports of panels and the Appellate Body is quasi-automatic. The reports adopted by the panels and the Appellate Body are binding upon the parties to a dispute. In this sense, the WTO panel procedure seems to be more akin to judicial settlement. However, it also has some elements of conciliation. Therefore, it is argued that WTO panel proceedings can be considered as a *sui generis* system of dispute settlement mixing elements of both adjudication and conciliation.

(iii) Under the dispute settlement system of the WTO, the implementation of adopted recommendations or rulings is supervised by the DSB. Suspension of concessions or other obligations is authorised by the DSB by reverse consensus.[239] Given that international courts and tribunals lack effective mechanisms for securing the implementation of their decisions, the institutionalised mechanism for securing the implementation of recommendations or ruling in the WTO is noteworthy. Even so, as demonstrated in the *EC – Hormones* case, there is a concern with regard to delay of compliance.

---

[235] Agreement Establishing the ACWL, available at: https://verdragenbank.overheid.nl/en/Verdrag/Details/009244/009244_Gewaarmerkt_0.pdf.
[236] *Ibid.*, Article 2(1).
[237] WTO, *A Handbook*, pp. 114–15.
[238] See www.acwl.ch/wto-disputes/.
[239] DSU, Article 22(6).

(iv) Generally, the dispute settlement system of the WTO can be said to contribute to the strengthening of the rule-based world trading system. Yet, complaints by least-developed States remain exceptional, even though the number of complaints brought by developing States is increasing. Whether the system is helpful for the least-developed States needs further consideration. In reality, high costs and lack of human resources are a matter of particular concern for developing States, in particular, least-developed States. Thus providing support to developing countries, including least-developed countries, should be an important issue in order that the dispute settlement procedures of the WTO can be a truly useful system for all Members.

FURTHER READING

There are many books and articles concerning the WTO dispute settlement system. Here only monographs published after 2000 will be listed.

R. Becroft, *The Standard of Review in WTO Dispute Settlement: Critique and Development* (Cheltenham: Edward Elgar Publishing, 2012).

Y. Bonzon, *Public Participation and Legitimacy in the WTO* (Cambridge University Press, 2014).

P. Van den Bossche and W. Zdouc, *The Law and Policy of the World Trade Organization: Text, Cases and Materials*, 3rd edn (Cambridge University Press, 2013), Chapter 3.

C. P. Bown and J. Pauwelyn (eds.), *The Law, Economics and Politics of Retaliation in WTO Dispute Settlement* (Cambridge University Press, 2010).

G. Cook, *A Digest of WTO Jurisprudence on Public International Law Concepts and Principles* (Cambridge University Press, 2015).

C. L. Davis, *Why Adjudicate? Enforcing Trade Rules in the WTO* (Princeton: Princeton University Press, 2012).

M. Foltea, *International Organizations in WTO Dispute Settlement: How Much Institutional Sensitivity?* (Cambridge University Press, 2012).

P. Gallagher, *Guide to Dispute Settlement* (London: Kluwer, 2002).

M. T. Grando, *Evidence, Proof, and Fact-Finding in WTO Dispute Settlement* (Cambridge University Press, 2009).

A. T. Guzman and J. H. B. Pauwelyn, *International Trade Law*, 2nd edn (Alphen aan den Rijn: Wolters Kluwer, 2012), Chapter 5.

M. Martin, *WTO Dispute Settlement Understanding and Development* (Leiden: Nijhoff, 2013).

A. D. Mitchell, *Legal Principles in WTO Disputes* (Cambridge University Press, 2008).

M. Molinuevo, *Protecting Investment in Service: Investor–State Arbitration versus WTO Dispute Settlement* (Alphen aan den Rijn: Kluwer Law International, 2012).

D. Palmeter and P. C. Mavroidis, *Dispute Settlement in the World Trade Organisation: Practice and Procedure*, 2nd edn (Cambridge University Press, 2004).

G. Sacerdoti, A. Yanovich and J. Bohanes (eds.), *The WTO at Ten: The Contribution of the Dispute Settlement System* (Cambridge University Press, 2006).

S. Shadikhodjaev, *Retaliation in the WTO Dispute Settlement System* (Alphen aan den Rijn: Kluwer, 2009).

G. C. Shaffer and R. Meléndez-Ortiz (eds.), *Dispute Settlement at the WTO: The Developing Country Experience* (Cambridge University Press, 2014).

G. Verhoosel, *National Treatment and WTO Dispute Settlement: Adjudicating the Boundaries of Regulatory Autonomy* (Oxford: Hart Publishing, 2002).

F. Weiss (ed.), *Improving WTO Dispute Settlement Procedures: Issues and Lessons from the Practice of Other International Courts and Tribunals* (London: Cameron May, 2000).

WTO, *A Handbook on the WTO Dispute Settlement System* (Cambridge University Press, 2004).

WTO, *WTO Dispute Settlement: One-Page Case Summaries, 1995–2011* (Geneva: WTO, 2012).

WTO, *Dispute Settlement System Training Module,* available at: www.wto.org/english/tratop_e/dispu_e/disp_settlement_cbt_e/signin_e.htm.

The following website is also useful: www.wto.org/english/thewto_e/whatis_e/tif_e/disp1_e.htm.

WTO Secretariat, *The WTO Dispute Settlement Procedures: A Collection of the Relevant Legal Texts*, 3rd edn (Cambridge University Press, 2012).

R. Yerxa and B. Wilson (eds.), *Key Issues in WTO Dispute Settlement* (Cambridge University Press, 2005).

10

Peaceful Settlement of International Environmental Disputes

Main Issues

International disputes concerning environmental protection arise in various contexts of international relations. As there is no single judicial body specialised for the settlement of international environmental disputes, the issues of environmental protection are to be addressed by multiple judicial bodies, such as the ICJ, ITLOS and WTO panels, if these disputes cannot be resolved by diplomatic means. Furthermore, to protect the environment effectively, it is necessary to secure compliance with the obligations provided in environmental treaties. In this regard, non-compliance procedures set out in multilateral environmental treaties are crucial as an alternative dispute resolution. This chapter will seek to examine the following issues:

(i) What are the principal features of peaceful settlement of international disputes concerning environmental protection?
(ii) What is the role of international adjudication in the peaceful settlement of international environmental disputes and what are its limitations?
(iii) What is the role of the Treaty Commission in the peaceful settlement of international environmental disputes?
(iv) What is the difference between the non-compliance procedures and traditional means of international dispute settlement?

1 INTRODUCTION

International disputes concerning environmental protection are arising in multiple contexts, such as the regulation of trans-frontier air pollution, the use of international watercourses, the regulation of marine pollution, the exploration and exploitation of natural resources, and international trade and commerce. In light of the diversity of issues relating to environmental protection, it is difficult and even illusory to define an 'international environmental dispute'.[1] For the purposes of this chapter, an environmental dispute is broadly understood as a dispute which includes an environmental aspect.

---

[1] A. Boyle and J. Harrison, 'Judicial Settlement of International Environmental Disputes: Current Problems' (2013) 4 *Journal of International Dispute Settlement*, pp. 247–50.

In light of the increasing importance of environmental protection, including protection of natural resources and biological diversity, disputes will more frequently arise with regard to the interpretation and application of relevant rules of international law on this subject. Hence the peaceful settlement of international environmental disputes should be a crucial issue in international law. Following the introduction, this chapter analyses the role of international courts and tribunals in the settlement of international environmental disputes (section 2). It then examines the role of fact-finding commissions established in environmental treaties (section 3). Furthermore, this chapter moves on to address non-compliance procedures set out in multiple environmental treaties (section 4), before offering conclusions (section 5).

2 INTERNATIONAL ADJUDICATION AND THE SETTLEMENT OF INTERNATIONAL ENVIRONMENTAL DISPUTES

2.1 General Considerations

It is generally considered that the role of litigation remains modest in the settlement of environmental disputes. Given that the settlement of international environmental disputes can be influenced not only by economic, political and social elements but also by scientific and technological elements,[2] it is understandable that the preference of States is for flexible solutions through negotiation.[3] In fact, international adjudication encounters considerable challenges in the peaceful settlement of international environmental disputes.[4]

First, more often than not, it is difficult to prove causality between a certain activity and the environmental damage suffered. For instance, persistent organic pollutants (POPs) that have a negative impact on human health tend to concentrate in colder parts of the globe, such as the South and North Poles. Yet, it is difficult to precisely determine their origin. Thus an injured State encounters considerable challenges when invoking the responsibility of a specific State for the damage suffered.[5]

Second, environmental pollution, such as pollution of international watercourses and trans-frontier air pollution, can be caused by activities of multiple States. Here shared responsibility may arise.[6] According to an orthodox approach, a dispute involving

---

[2] N. Klein, 'Settlement of International Environmental Disputes' in M. Fitzmaurice, D. M. Ong and P. Merkouris (eds.), *Research Handbook on International Environmental Law* (Cheltenham: Edward Elgar, 2011), p. 384.
[3] P. Birnie, A. Boyle and C. Redgwell, *International Law and Environment* (Oxford University Press, 2009), p. 252; M. A. Fitzmaurice, 'International Protection of the Environment' (2001) 293 *RCADI*, p. 352; Klein, 'Settlement of International Environmental Disputes', p. 386.
[4] Klein, 'Settlement of International Environmental Disputes', pp. 386-9.
[5] G. Loibl, 'Environmental Law and Non-Compliance Procedures: Issues of State Responsibility' in M. Fitzmaurice and D. Sarooshi (eds.), *Issues of State Responsibility before International Judicial Institutions* (Oxford: Hart Publishing, 2004), p. 203.
[6] According to Nollkaemper and Jacobs, shared responsibility arises in two distinct situations in international law. First, shared responsibility arises in the situation where cumulative pollution was caused by the conducts of multiple States but there is no direct linkage between the actions of these States. This is the case of cumulative shared responsibility. The second is shared responsibility arising out of joint or concerted action. A. Nollkaemper and D. Jacobs, 'Shared Responsibility in International Law: A Conceptual Framework' (2013) 34 *Michigan Journal of International Law*, pp. 368-9. See also, A. Nollkaemper and I. Plakokefalos (eds.), *Principles of Shared Responsibility in International Law: An Appraisal of the State of the Art* (Cambridge University Press, 2014), pp. 9-10; J. Crawford, *State Responsibility: General Part* (Cambridge University Press, 2013), p. 333.

plural States' responsibility is to be divided into several bilateral disputes between an injured State and responsible States. As the ICJ stated in the *Certain Phosphate Lands in Nauru* case,[7] it is true that a State responsible for an internationally wrongful act cannot escape from its own responsibility on the pretext that other States were jointly involved in the act. Where a third State's legal interests form the very subject matter of the decision, however, an international court cannot exercise its jurisdiction over the dispute in light of the *Monetary Gold* rule or the indispensable party principle.[8] If the responsibility of one of the States concerned could be established by an international court, the question remains how reparation is to be allocated between multiple responsible States.[9] Where environmental pollution caused by activities of multiple States is cumulative by nature, it is not easy to establish the cause and effect relationship concerning environmental damage.

Third, as the ICJ stated in the *Gabčíkovo-Nagymarous Project* case, environmental damage is often irreversible.[10] Hence determination of State responsibility by an international court after damage has occurred contains an inherent limitation. Furthermore, failure by a State to comply with treaty obligations concerning environmental protection by developing States may often result from inadequate financial, technological and human resources. If this is the case, international adjudication will not resolve the fundamental question of non-compliance.

Nonetheless, it is not suggested that international adjudication has no valuable role to play in the peaceful settlement of international environmental disputes. Since environmental issues arise in connection to various international disputes, these issues are actually discussed in multiple judicial forums. For instance, conservation measures of natural resources may create a dispute with regard to compliance or compatibility with WTO agreements. In this case, WTO panels and Appellant Bodies will have jurisdiction over the issues.[11] An often cited example in this regard is provided by *US - Shrimp*.[12] This case concerned the legality of a ban imposed by the United States on the importation of

---

[7] *Certain Phosphate Lands in Nauru* (Nauru v. Australia), Preliminary Objections, ICJ Reports 1992, pp. 258–9, para. 48.

[8] *Monetary Gold Removed from Rome in 1943* (Italy v. France, United Kingdom of Great Britain and Northern Ireland and United States of America), Preliminary Question, ICJ Reports 1954, p. 27. See also Chapter 7, section 4.2 of this book.

[9] J. D. Fry, 'Attribution of Responsibility' in A. Nollkaemper and I. Plakokefalos (eds.), *Principles of Shared Responsibility in International Law: An Appraisal of the State of the Art* (Cambridge University Press, 2014), p. 129; P. A. Nollkaemper and I. Plakokefalos, 'Conclusions: Beyond the ILC Legacy', *ibid.*, pp. 350–1.

[10] *Gabčíkovo-Nagymaros Project* (Hungary/Slovakia), Judgment of 25 September 1997, ICJ Reports 1997, p. 78, para. 140. The ILC also stressed the importance of prevention. Draft Articles on Prevention of Transboundary Harm from Hazardous Activities (2001) II (Part 2) *Yearbook of the International Law Commission*, General Commentary, p. 148, para. 2.

[11] Birnie, Boyle and Redgwell, *International Law and Environment*, p. 261. Generally, see J. Gomula, 'Environmental Disputes in the WTO' in M. Fitzmaurice, D. M. Ong and P. Merkouris (eds.), *Research Handbook on International Environmental Law* (Cheltenham: Edward Elgar Publishing, 2011), pp. 401–25.

[12] In this case, the Appellate Body ruled that: '[A]lthough the measure of the United States in dispute in this appeal serves an environmental objective that is recognized as legitimate under paragraph (g) of Article XX of the GATT 1994, this measure has been applied by the United States in a manner which constitutes arbitrary and unjustifiable discrimination between Members of the WTO, contrary to the requirements of the chapeau of Article XX.' *United States – Import Prohibition of Certain Shrimp and Shrimp Products*, WT/DS58/AB/R, 12 October 1998, para. 186.

certain shrimp and shrimp products to protect sea turtles. As illustrated by *US – Shrimp*, trade and environmental issues can be referred to the WTO dispute settlement system, even though the WTO is not a forum for the settlement of international environmental disputes.[13] Environmental issues are also discussed in the ICJ, ITLOS and arbitral tribunals. Hence the role of international courts and tribunals in the settlement of international environmental disputes needs reconsideration. In this regard, three issues merit discussion: (i) the role of arbitration, (ii) provisional measures and (iii) *locus standi* on the basis of the breach of obligations *erga omnes partes*.

2.2 The Role of Arbitration in the Settlement of International Environmental Disputes

2.2.1 Advantages of Arbitration

As discussed in Chapter 5, arbitration can be viewed as a flexible means of international dispute settlement in four respects: composition of arbitral tribunals, applicable law, procedure and publicity.[14] Flexibility of arbitration is relevant in the peaceful settlement of international environmental disputes. For instance, where appropriate, the parties in dispute can freely appoint scientists or other experts as arbitrator. In the *Indus Waters Kishenganga* arbitration,[15] one of the arbitrators was an expert in hydrology. A special arbitral tribunal constituted under Annex VIII of the LOSC consists of five experts in the fields of (i) fisheries, (ii) protection and preservation of the marine environment, (iii) marine scientific research or (iv) navigation, including pollution from vessels and by dumping. Given that the settlement of environmental disputes may necessitate consideration of scientific and technical elements, flexibility of applicable law and procedure may also be an advantage of arbitration.[16]

In fact, quite a few environmental disputes were settled by arbitration and some of them, such as the *Bering Sea Fur Seal* (1893), *Trail Smelter* (1935/41) and *Lac Lanoux* arbitrations (1957), are of historical importance. Within recent decades, Annex VII arbitral tribunals under the LOSC have been invoked on many occasions. Furthermore, some disputes were submitted to arbitration with the PCA in accordance with a specific treaty. Examples include: the *OSPAR* arbitration between Ireland and the United Kingdom (2003),[17] the *Iron Rhine* arbitration between Belgium and the Netherlands (2005)[18] and the *Indus Waters Kishenganga* arbitration between Pakistan and India (2013). It appears that arbitration has potential utility in the settlement of international environmental disputes.[19]

---

[13] Birnie, Boyle and Redgwell, *International Law and Environment*, p. 262.
[14] Chapter 5, section 1.
[15] *Indus Waters Kishenganga* arbitration (Pakistan v. India), Partial Award, 18 February 2013, Final Award, 20 December 2013, available at: https://pca-cpa.org/en/cases.
[16] See also Chapter 5, section 4.3.
[17] PCA, *Dispute concerning Access to Information under Article 9 of the OSPAR Convention* (Ireland v. United Kingdom), available at: https://pca-cpa.org/en/cases.
[18] *The Arbitration Regarding the Iron Rhine ('Ijzeren Rijn') Railway* (Bergium v. the Netherlands), available at: https://pca-cpa.org/en/cases.
[19] P. Sands *et al.*, *Principles of International Environmental Law*, 3rd edn (Cambridge University Press, 2012), p. 170.

2.2.2 The *South China Sea* Arbitration

In a particular context of marine environmental protection, the role of the Annex VII Arbitral Tribunal under the LOSC merits mention. An eminent example is provided by the 2016 *South China Sea* arbitration (Merits).[20] In this case, the Philippines claimed to the effect that China breached obligations under the LOSC to protect and preserve the marine environment surrounding certain maritime features in the South China Sea.[21] The Tribunal held that China breached its obligations under Articles 192 and 194(5) of the LOSC, to take necessary measures to protect and preserve the marine environment, with respect to the harvesting of endangered species from the fragile ecosystems at Scarborough Shoal and Second Thomas Shoal.[22] It also considered that China's artificial island-building activities on the seven reefs in the Spratly Islands had caused devastating and long-lasting damage to the marine environment. The Tribunal accordingly found that through its construction activities, China had breached its obligations under Articles 192, 194(1) and (5).[23] At the same time, it ruled that China had not fulfilled its duties under Articles 123 and 206 of the LOSC concerning cooperation of States in semi-enclosed seas and environmental impact assessment, respectively.[24]

What is of particular interest in the *South China Sea* arbitration is the use of experts. Scientific evidence is a key element in the settlement of international environmental disputes. More often than not, parties in dispute present competing scientific data. Evaluation of such data creates a considerable challenge to international courts and tribunals. Hence the use of experts merits discussion in the settlement of environmental disputes involving issues of science. In the *South China Sea* arbitration, the Tribunal sought an independent opinion on the environmental impact of China's construction activities by appointing three experts on coral reef ecology.[25]

The appointment of tribunal experts is provided in Article 24 of the Rules of Procedure.[26] Under Article 24(1):

> After seeking the views of the Parties, the Arbitral Tribunal may appoint one or more independent experts. That expert may be called upon to report on specific issues and in the manner to be determined by the Arbitral Tribunal. A copy of the expert's terms of reference, established by the Arbitral Tribunal, shall be communicated to the Parties.

Article 24(2) further requires that: 'Any expert shall, in principle before accepting appointment, submit to the Arbitral Tribunal and to the Parties a description of his or

---

[20] PCA Case No. 2013-19, the *South China Sea* arbitration (Merits), Judgment of 12 July 2016, available at: https://pcacases.com/web/view/7. See also Y. Tanaka, 'The South China Sea Arbitration (Merits, 12 July 2016): Environmental Obligations under the UN Convention on the Law of the Sea' (2017) *RECIEL* (forthcoming).
[21] The *South China Sea* arbitration (Merits), para. 112.
[22] Ibid., para. 964. See also paras. 992-3.
[23] Ibid., para. 983 and para. 993.
[24] Ibid., para. 986 and para. 991. See also para. 993.
[25] Ibid., para. 821.
[26] Article 24 was inspired by Article 29 of the 2013 UNCITRAL Arbitration Rules. M. M. Mbengue, 'The South China Sea Arbitration: Innovations in Marine Environmental Fact-Finding and Due Diligence Obligations' (2016) 110 *American Journal of International Law Unbound*, p. 287.

her qualifications and a statement of his or her impartiality and independence.' Under the same provision, the parties are to inform the Arbitral Tribunal whether they have any objections as to the expert's qualifications, impartiality or independence and the Arbitral Tribunal is to decide promptly whether to accept any such objections. After an expert's appointment, a party may object to the expert's qualifications, impartiality or independence only if the objection is for reasons of which the party becomes aware after the appointment has been made. It is important to note that Article 24 provides a procedure to secure independence and impartiality of expert appointed by the tribunal.

At the same time, Article 24(3) of the Rules of Procedure places an obligation upon the parties to 'give the expert any relevant information or produce for his or her inspection any relevant documents or goods that he or she may require of them'. Under the same provision, the parties are also obliged to 'afford the expert all reasonable facilities in the event that the expert's terms of reference contemplate a visit to the localities to which the case relates'. These obligations contribute to facilitating the investigation of the experts and credibility of its report. Overall, it can be observed that comparatively detailed rules embodied in Article 24 go well beyond a simple rule provided in Article 50 of the ICJ Statute.[27]

The Tribunal, in its arbitral award, widely referred to the expert reports. In examining adverse effects of harvesting giant clams, for instance, the Ferse Report and McManus Report provided important evidence for the Arbitral Tribunal.[28] It also relied on the Ferse Report when examining the impacts of China's construction activities on the coral reefs.[29] The wide use of experts in the *South China Sea* arbitration contrasted with the practice of the ICJ which is reluctant to appoint an expert in its proceedings.[30] The *South China Sea* arbitration provides an insight into the role of experts in the settlement of disputes involving scientific and technical aspects.

2.2.3 The Protocol on Environmental Protection to the Antarctic Treaty

This is a convenient point to mention the 1991 Protocol on Environmental Protection to the Antarctic Treaty.[31] Apart from the LOSC, this is the only instrument which sets out a comprehensive system of the settlement of environmental disputes.[32] The system rests on the voluntary and compulsory procedures.

(i) *Voluntary procedure*: Under Article 18 of the Protocol, if a dispute arises concerning the interpretation or application of this Protocol, the parties to the dispute are obliged, at the request of any one of them, to consult among themselves as soon as possible with a view to having the dispute resolved by negotiation, inquiry, mediation, conciliation, arbitration, judicial settlement or other peaceful means to which the parties to the dispute agree.

---

[27] *Ibid*. Article 50 of the ICJ Statute stipulates that: 'The Court may, at any time, entrust any individual, body, bureau, commission, or other organization that it may select, with the task of carrying out an enquiry or giving an expert opinion.'
[28] The *South China Sea* arbitration (merits), paras. 957–8.
[29] *Ibid*., paras. 978–83.
[30] See Chapter 7, section 2.1.4. See also Mbengue, 'The South China Sea Arbitration', pp. 287–9.
[31] Entered into force 1998. The electronic text is available at: www.ats.aq/documents/recatt/att006_e.pdf.
[32] Birnie, Boyle and Redgwell, *International Law and Environment*, p. 260.

(ii) *Compulsory procedure*: If the parties have not agreed on a means for resolving certain categories of disputes set out in Article 20(1)[33] within twelve months of the request for consultation pursuant to Article 18, the dispute is to be referred, at the request of any party to the dispute, for settlement in accordance with the procedure determined by Article 19(4) and (5). In this regard, the choice of dispute settlement procedure is set out under Article 19. In accordance with the procedure, each party, when signing, ratifying, accepting, approving or acceding to this Protocol, or at any time thereafter, may choose, by written declaration, one or both of the following means for the settlement of disputes: the International Court of Justice and the Arbitral Tribunal.[34] If the parties to a dispute have accepted the same means for the settlement of a dispute, the dispute may be submitted only to that procedure, unless the parties otherwise agree.[35] If the parties to a dispute have not accepted the same means for the settlement of a dispute, or if they have both accepted both means, the dispute may be submitted only to the Arbitral Tribunal, unless the parties otherwise agree.[36] A party which has not made a declaration under paragraph 1 of Article 19 or in respect of which a declaration is no longer in force shall be deemed to have accepted the competence of the arbitral tribunal.[37] The mechanism of the choice of dispute settlement procedure of the Protocol is essentially parallel to the LOSC.

Under Article 20(2), however, the Arbitral Tribunal shall not be competent to decide or rule upon any matter within the scope of Article IV of the Antarctic Treaty. Article IV of the Antarctic Treaty concerns a renunciation of previously asserted rights of or claims to territorial sovereignty in Antarctica by contracting parties. In addition, nothing in this Protocol shall be interpreted as conferring competence or jurisdiction on the ICJ or any other tribunal established for the purpose of settling disputes between parties to decide or otherwise rule upon any matter within the scope of Article IV of the Antarctic Treaty.

The Schedule to the Protocol contains detailed rules concerning arbitration. Under Article 2(1) of the Schedule, each party is entitled to designate up to three arbitrators. Each arbitrator shall be experienced in Antarctic affairs and have thorough knowledge of international law. The Arbitral Tribunal decides disputes by applying the provisions of the Protocol and other applicable rules and principles of international law that are not incompatible with such provisions. It may also decide, *ex aequo et bono*, a dispute, if the parties to the dispute so agree.[38] The award is final and binding on the parties to the dispute and on any party which intervened in the proceedings under Article 11(3). The arbitral procedure under the Protocol presents two unique features.

The first noteworthy feature relates to two types of provisional measures provided in the Schedule: provisional measures under Article 6(1)(a) and those measures under Article 6(1)(b) of the Schedule. Where it considers that *prima facie* it has jurisdiction under the

---

[33] These are disputes concerning the interpretation or application of Article 7, 8, or 15 or any Annex and, to a limited extent, Article 13. Article 7 provides prohibition of mineral resource activities. Article 8 sets out an obligation of environmental impact assessment. Article 15 relates to emergency response action. Article 13 provides compliance with the Protocol.
[34] Article 19(1) of the Protocol.   [35] Article 19(4) of the Protocol.
[36] Article 19(5) of the Protocol.   [37] Article 19(3) of the Protocol.
[38] Article 10 of the Schedule.

Protocol, the Arbitral Tribunal may, at the request of any party to a dispute, *indicate* such provisional measures as it considers necessary to preserve the respective rights of the parties to the dispute pursuant to Article 6(1)(a). The Arbitral Tribunal may also *prescribe* any provisional measures which it considers appropriate under the circumstances to prevent serious harm to the Antarctic environment or dependent or associated ecosystems by virtue of Article 6(1)(b). Only provisional measures under Article 6(1)(b) are binding upon the parties.[39]

The second noteworthy feature pertains to a third-party intervention. Under Article 7 of the Schedule, any party which believes it has a legal interest, whether general or individual, which may be substantially affected by the award of an Arbitral Tribunal, may intervene in the proceedings, unless the Arbitral Tribunal decides otherwise. This provision seems to be broad enough to allow any party to the Protocol to intervene.[40]

2.3 The Role of Provisional Measures in Environmental Protection

The next issue to be examined concerns the role of provisional measures in environmental protection. The ITLOS jurisprudence provides an important insight into this subject.[41] One may take the 2001 *MOX Plant* case as an example. The central issue in this case concerned the breach of obligations to prevent radioactive marine pollution in the Irish Sea from the MOX plant in Sellafield, United Kingdom. Ireland alleged that the United Kingdom had breached its obligation under Article 206 of the LOSC with regard to the authorisation of the MOX plant, including by failing to assess the potential effects of the operation of the MOX plant on the marine environment of the Irish Sea.[42] Ireland thus requested that the Tribunal order, *inter alia*, that the United Kingdom immediately suspend the authorisation of the MOX plant dated 3 October 2001 and that the United Kingdom immediately stop movements into or out of the waters over which it has sovereignty or exercises sovereign rights of any radioactive substances.[43]

Even though ITLOS declined to order the requested measures, it unanimously ordered that Ireland and the United Kingdom should cooperate and should, for this purpose, enter into consultations forthwith in order to:

(a) exchange further information with regard to possible consequences for the Irish Sea arising out of the commissioning of the MOX plant;
(b) monitor risks or the effects of the operation of the MOX plant for the Irish Sea;
(c) devise, as appropriate, measures to prevent pollution of the marine environment which might result from the operation of the MOX plant.[44]

---

[39] Article 6(2) of the Schedule.
[40] Birnie, Boyle and Redgwell, *International Law and Environment*, p. 261.
[41] This section relies on the research results of the following article by the author: Y. Tanaka, 'Juridical Insights into the Protection of Community Interests through Provisional Measures: Reflections on the ITLOS Jurisprudence' (2014) 14 *The Global Community Yearbook of International Law and Jurisprudence*, pp. 249–73.
[42] The *MOX Plant* case (Ireland v. United Kingdom), Provisional Measures, ITLOS Case No. 10, Order of 3 Dec. 2001, 41 ILM 405 (2002), p. 409, para. 26.
[43] *Ibid.*, p. 410, para. 29(1) and (2).   [44] *Ibid.*, p. 416, para. 89(1).

The *MOX Plant* order has proven that provisional measures can be used as a judicial procedure to oblige the disputing parties to carry out a joint monitoring of the marine environment. Given that radioactive materials or wastes may be transported beyond the Irish Sea by currents and contaminate other parts of the oceans, joint monitoring can be viewed as an important devise to protect not only the Irish Sea but also other parts of the oceans. A joint monitoring is also useful with a view to facilitating international cooperation between parties in dispute.[45] By ordering the joint monitoring, ITLOS can be said to perform a facilitative function.[46]

Another example in this matter is provided by the 2003 *Land Reclamation* case.[47] In this case, ITLOS ordered, *inter alia*, that Malaysia and Singapore shall enter into consultations forthwith in order to establish promptly a group of independent experts with the mandate to conduct a study to determine the effects of Singapore's land reclamation and to exchange, on a regular basis, information on, and assess risks or effects of, Singapore's land reclamation works.[48] The effect of provisional measures ordered by the Tribunal seems to be equivalent to effectuate a joint environmental impact assessment.[49] The ITLOS order seems to suggest that provisional measures can be used as a judicial tool to enforce the obligation to carry out an environmental impact assessment,[50] which is fundamental to any regulatory system which seeks to identify environmental risk and integrates environmental concerns into the decision-making process with regard to future projects.[51]

Provisional measures can also contribute to the conservation of marine living resources. The best example in this matter is the 1999 *Southern Bluefin Tuna* cases between Australia and New Zealand, on the one hand, and Japan, on the other hand. A pivotal issue of the dispute was whether Japan had breached its obligations in relation to the conservation and management of the Southern Bluefin Tuna stock particularly by carrying out unilateral experimental fishing. In its order of 1999, ITLOS ordered provisional measures, *inter alia*, that: Australia, Japan and New Zealand should resume negotiations without delay with a view to reaching agreement on measures for the conservation and management of Southern Bluefin Tuna and that Australia, Japan and New Zealand should make further efforts to reach agreement with other States and fishing entities engaged in fishing for Southern Bluefin Tuna, with a view to ensuring conservation and promoting the objective

---

[45] In this regard, ITLOS stressed that: '[T]he duty to cooperate is a fundamental principle in the prevention of pollution of the marine environment under Part XII of the Convention and general international law ... '. The *MOX Plant* case, p. 415, para. 82.
[46] N. Klein, *Dispute Settlement in the UN Convention on the Law of the Sea* (Cambridge University Press, 2005), pp. 83–4.
[47] ITLOS, *Case Concerning Land Reclamation by Singapore in and around the Straits of Johor* (Malaysia v. Singapore) (hereafter the *Land Reclamation* case), Provisional Measures, Case No. 12, Order of 8 October 2013, ITLOS Reports 2003, p. 10.
[48] *Ibid.*, p. 27, para. 106(1).
[49] The 1991 Convention on Environmental Impact Assessment in a Transboundary Context (the Espoo Convention) defines EIA as 'a national procedure for evaluating the likely impact of a proposed activity on the environment' (Article 1(vi)). Entered into force 10 September 1997. The text is available at: www.unece.org/env/eia/about/eia_text.html.
[50] A. Boyle, 'Developments in the International Law of Environmental Impact Assessments and their Relation to the Espoo Convention' (2011) 20(3) *RECIEL*, p. 229.
[51] Birnie, Boyle and Redgwell, *International Law and the Environment*, p. 165.

of optimum utilization of the stock.[52] These measures would facilitate the settlement of the dispute through negotiations. The interlinkage between provisional measures and negotiation merits particular attention. All in all, one can argue that the provisional measures prescribed by ITLOS can afford a significant judicial tool to protect the marine environment.

2.4 *Locus Standi* on the Basis of the Breach of Obligations *Erga Omnes Partes*

A breach of environmental obligations may affect rights of all contracting parties to a treaty or members of the international community as a whole. Here an issue arises with regard to *locus standi* (i.e. title to sue) in the settlement of environmental disputes. A key concept in this regard is obligations *erga omnes* and *erga omnes partes*. The concept of obligations *erga omnes* was given currency by the ICJ in the *Barcelona Traction* case.[53] Subsequently, Article 1 of the 2005 Resolution of the *Institut de droit international* specifies two types of obligations: an obligation *erga omnes* (Article 1(a)) and an obligation *erga omnes partes* (Article 1(b)) as follows:

> (a) an obligation under general international law that a State owes in any given case to the international community, in view of its common values and its concern for compliance, so that a breach of that obligation enables all States to take action; or
> (b) an obligation under a multilateral treaty that a State Party to the treaty owes in any given case to all the other States Parties to the same treaty, in view of their common values and concern for compliance, so that a breach of that obligation enables all these States to take action.[54]

The question of interest here is whether or not a State Party to a treaty concerning conservation of marine living resources can submit a dispute involving the alleged breach of treaty obligations by another State Party to an international court or tribunal, even though no damage occurred to the applicant State. The 2014 *Whaling in the Antarctic* case provides an insight into this subject.[55]

A central issue in this case was whether JARPA II, Japan's scientific whaling programme, can be regarded as scientific research under Article VIII of the 1946 International Convention for the Regulation of Whaling. In this regard, it is important to note that the applicant State (i.e. Australia) suffered no damage from Japan's scientific whaling. According to Counsel for Australia, 'Australia is seeking to uphold its collective interest, an interest it shares with all other parties.'[56] Thus Australia submitted the dispute to the ICJ on the basis of the alleged breach of obligations *erga omnes*

---

[52] The *Southern Bluefin Tuna* cases (New Zealand v. Japan; Australia v. Japan), Provisional Measures, Case Nos. 3 and 4, Order of 27 August 1999 (1999) 38 ILM, p. 1635, para. 90.
[53] *Barcelona Traction, Light and Power Company, Limited* (Belgium v. Spain) (New Application: 1962), Judgment of 5 February 1970, Second Phase, ICJ Reports 1970, p. 32, para. 33.
[54] *Institut de droit international*, Resolution: Obligation *Erga Omnes* in International Law, Krakow Session 2005, available at: www.idi-iil.org/app/uploads/2017/06/2005_kra_01_en.pdf. For a detailed analysis of the concept of *erga omnes*, see, in particular, M. Ragazzi, *The Concept of International Obligations 'Era Omnes'* (reprint, Oxford: Clarendon Press, 2002); C. J. Tams, *Enforcing Obligations 'Era Omnes' in International Law* (Cambridge University Press, 2005).
[55] *Whaling in the Antarctic* (Australia v. Japan: new Zealand Intervening), Judgment of 31 March 2014, ICJ Reports 2014, p. 226.
[56] *Whaling in the Antarctic*, Presentation by Burmester, Verbatim Record, CR 2013/18, 9 July 2013, p. 28, para. 19. See also presentation by Boisson de Chazournes, *ibid.*, pp. 33–4, paras. 18–20.

partes by Japan.[57] Notably, the ICJ accepted the *locus standi* of Australia in this case. It would seem to follow that the Court accepted *locus standi* on the basis of obligation *erga omnes partes*, even though the Court did not explicitly refer to the obligation.[58]

It appears that the *Whaling in the Antarctic* judgment is in line with the 2012 *Belgium/Senegal* judgment.[59] The ICJ, in the *Belgium/Senegal* case, held that any State Party to the 1984 UN Convention against Torture may invoke the responsibility of another State Party with a view to ascertaining the alleged failure to comply with its obligation *erga omnes partes*. It thus concluded that Belgium, as a State Party to the Convention against Torture, had standing to invoke the responsibility of Senegal for the alleged breaches of its obligations before the ICJ under Articles 6(2) and 7(1) of the Convention.[60] It must also be recalled that under Article 48(1) of the ILC Draft Articles on State Responsibility,[61] not directly injured States are entitled to invoke the responsibility of another State if the obligation *erga omnes partes* or obligation *erga omnes* is breached by that State.[62] Although further accumulation of case law is needed to draw more general conclusions, the *Belgium/Senegal* and *Whaling in the Antarctic* cases appear to hint at the direction that the ICJ would accept *locus standi* on the basis of the alleged breach of obligations *erga omnes partes*, if it can establish its jurisdiction. If this is the case, the ICJ would assume the role of advocate of the international community in the protection of a common interest reflected in treaties.

3 FACT-FINDING BY TREATY COMMISSION

Since international environmental disputes often involve technical and factual aspects, the expert fact-finding is crucial in the settlement of these disputes. This is particularly true in the settlement of international water disputes. In fact, fact-finding procedures are enshrined in treaties concerning the management of water resources.[63]

An illustrative example in this matter is the fact-finding procedures established by the 1909 Boundary Water Treaty between the United States and Canada.[64] The first paragraph of Article IX of the treaty holds that:

> The High Contracting Parties further agree that any other questions or matters of difference arising between them involving the rights, obligations, or interests of either in relation to the other or to the inhabitants of the other, along the common frontier between the United

---

[57] M. Fitzmaurice, *Whaling and International Law* (Cambridge University Press, 2015), pp. 109–10.
[58] It is to be noted that Japan did not dispute *locus standi* of Australia in the *Whaling in the Antarctic* case.
[59] Fitzmaurice, *Whaling and International Law*, p. 110.
[60] *Questions relating to the Obligation to Prosecute or Extradite* (Belgium v. Senegal), ICJ Reports 2012, paras. 69–70. See also Separate Opinion of Judge Cançado Trindade, *ibid.*, pp. 527–9, paras. 104–8.
[61] This instrument is available at: http://legal.un.org/ilc/texts/instruments/english/commentaries/9_6_2001.pdf.
[62] Following Kawasaki, these states which are not directly injured can be called 'not directly injured States' in the sense that they do not personally suffer any kind of damage, material or moral, although their subjective rights are considered to have been infringed. K. Kawasaki, 'The "Injured State" in the International Law of State Responsibility' (2000) 28 *Hitotsubashi Journal of Law and Politics*, p. 22.
[63] E. B. Weiss, *International Law for a Water-Source World* (Leiden: Nijhoff, 2013), pp. 135–8.
[64] Treaty between the United States and Great Britain relating to Boundary Waters, and Questions arising between the United States and Canada. Entered into force 5 May 1910. The electronic text is also available at: www.ijc.org/rel/agree/water.html#text.

> States and the Dominion of Canada, shall be referred from time to time to the International Joint Commission for examination and report, whenever either the Government of the United States or the Government of the Dominion of Canada shall request that such questions or matters of difference be so referred.

The International Joint Commission is authorised in each case so referred to examine into and report upon the facts and circumstances of the particular questions and matters referred, together with such conclusions and recommendations as may be appropriate, subject to the terms of the reference in accordance with this provision. The Commission is to make a joint report to both governments in all cases in which all or a majority of the Commissioners agree. In case of disagreement the minority may make a joint report to both governments, or separate reports to their respective governments. In case the Commission is evenly divided upon any question or matter referred to it for report, separate reports shall be made by the Commissioners on each side to their own government.[65] Although, as stated in Article IX, the report is not legally binding,[66] it is usually followed. The reference of a dispute over water quality in the Great Lakes led to the Canada-United States Great Lakes Water Agreement in 1972.[67]

Another noteworthy example is the fact-finding procedure in the 1993 North American Agreement on Environmental Cooperation.[68] Articles 14 and 15 of the agreement provide a unique process for any NGO or person residing or established in Canada, Mexico or the United States to make assertion that a party is failing to effectively enforce its environmental law. This is called the Submission on Enforcement Matters (SEM) process.[69] The SEM process results in a detailed factual record concerning enforcement matters.[70]

Furthermore, some mention must be made of the mandatory procedure for inquiry set out in the 1997 United Nations Convention on the Law of the Non-Navigational Uses of International Watercourses.[71] Under Article 33(3):

> Subject to the operation of paragraph 10, if after six months from the time of the request for negotiations referred to in paragraph 2, the parties concerned have not been able to settle their dispute through negotiation or any other means referred to in paragraph 2, the dispute shall be submitted, at the request of any of the parties to the dispute, to impartial fact-finding in accordance with paragraphs 4 to 9, unless the parties otherwise agree.

---

[65] The fourth paragraph of Article IX.
[66] The third paragraph of Article IX provides that: 'Such reports of the Commission shall not be regarded as decisions of the questions or matters so submitted either on the facts of the law, and shall in no way have the character of an arbitral award.'
[67] Weiss, *International Law for a Water-Source World*, p. 136.
[68] Entered into force 1 January 1994. Text in: (1993) 32 *ILM*, p. 1480.
[69] For an outline of the SEM process, see *Guidelines for Submissions on Enforcement Matters under Articles 14 and 15 of the North American Agreement on Environmental Cooperation*, available at: www3.cec.org/islandora/en/item/10838-guidelines-submissions-enforcement-matters-under-articles-14-and-15-north-en.pdf.
[70] The complete list of submissions, factual records, and active files can be found at: www.cec.org/sem-submissions/all-submissions.
[71] Entered into force 17 August 2014. The electronic text is available at: http://legal.un.org/ilc/texts/instruments/english/conventions/8_3_1997.pdf; https://treaties.un.org/doc/Publication/UNTS/No%20Volume/52106/Part/I-52106-0800000280025697.pdf. See also Weiss, *International Law for a Water-Source World*, p. 138.

A fact-finding commission, which is composed of three members, is to be established in accordance with Article 33(4) and (5). Under Article 33(4), a fact-finding commission is composed of one member nominated by each party concerned and in addition a member not having the nationality of any of the parties concerned chosen by the nominated members who shall serve as chairman. The parties concerned are obliged to provide the commission with such information as it may require and, on request, to permit the commission to have access to their respective territory and to inspect any facilities, plant, equipment, construction or natural feature relevant for the purpose of its inquiry pursuant to Article 33(7). Under Article 33(8), the commission shall adopt its report by a majority vote and submit a report to the parties concerned setting forth its findings and the reasons therefor and such recommendations as it deems appropriate for an 'equitable solution' of the dispute. The parties concerned shall consider it in good faith. By recommending an equitable solution, the power of the commission seems to go beyond a fact-finding function.

4 NON-COMPLIANCE PROCEDURES

4.1 General Considerations

To protect the environment effectively, there is a need to secure compliance with obligations provided in environmental treaties. In this regard, non-compliance procedures set out in multilateral environmental treaties deserve serious consideration. Non-compliance procedures are a mechanism to prevent the breach of environmental treaties.[72] The origin of non-compliance procedures can be found in the 1987 Montreal Protocol on Substances that Deplete the Ozone Layer (hereafter the Montreal Protocol).[73] Since then, these procedures have been set out in many multilateral environmental treaties. Non-compliance procedures are characterised by four principal features.[74]

The first noteworthy feature is the non-confrontational character. Failure by a State to comply with treaty obligations may be attributable to certain technical or financial difficulties. Thus non-compliance procedures aim to encourage States to comply with treaty obligations by providing technical and financial assistance, not to determine the breach of treaty obligations. In this regard, the Procedures and Mechanisms on Compliance under the Cartagena Protocol on Biosafety state that: 'The compliance procedures and mechanisms shall be simple, facilitative, non-adversarial and cooperative in

---

[72] The term 'compliance procedures' is also used in international instruments. In this chapter, the terms 'non-compliance procedures' and 'compliance procedures' are used interchangeably. In this regard, see G. Loibl, 'Compliance Procedures and Mechanisms' in M. Fitzmaurice, D. M. Ong and P. Merkouris (eds.), *Research Handbook on International Environmental Law* (Cheltenham: Edward Elgar Publishing, 2011), p. 429. The United Nations Environment Programme (UNEP) defines 'compliance' as: 'the fulfilment by the contracting parties of their obligations under a multilateral environmental agreement and any amendments to the multilateral environmental agreement'. UNEP Guidelines on Compliance with and Enforcement of Multilateral Environmental Agreements, Section C, para. 9(a), available at: www.unep.org/delc/Portals/119/UNEP.Guidelines.on.Compliance.MEA.pdf.

[73] P.-M. Dupuy and J. E. Viñuales, *International Environmental Law* (Cambridge University Press, 2015), p. 285. Text in: 1522 *UNTS*, p. 3. Entered into force 1 January 1989.

[74] See also Loibl, 'Compliance Procedures and Mechanisms', p. 427.

nature.'[75] Thus non-compliance procedures are designed to provide a 'softer' mechanism to address non-compliance than that furnished by international adjudication.[76]

Second, non-compliance procedures are preventive and future-oriented by nature.[77] In this regard, the contracting parties to the Basel Convention make clear that the mechanisms of non-compliance procedure of the Convention shall be non-confrontational and preventive in nature.[78]

Third, unlike arbitration and judicial settlement, non-compliance procedures are not consent-based. As will be seen, non-compliance procedures can be invoked by one or more parties regarding another party's implementation of treaty obligations. These procedures may also be triggered by a treaty organ, such as the secretary. Furthermore, the existence of an 'injured State' is not needed to invoke non-compliance procedures since they do not aim to determine responsibility of the defaulting State.[79]

Fourth, non-compliance procedures seek to safeguard common interests of the parties to environmental treaties, while international adjudication aims to determine the responsibility of a respondent State in dispute and obtain reparation for an applicant State. Provided that, from a broad perspective, global environmental protection can be regarded as common interests of the international community as a whole, it may be said that non-compliance procedures under multilateral environmental treaties contribute to safeguarding common interests of the international community.[80]

All in all, non-compliance procedures can be viewed as a non-adversarial and assistance-oriented procedure. Most non-compliance procedures can be understood as a form of dispute avoidance or alternative dispute resolution in the sense that these procedures seek to avoid binding third-party procedures.[81]

Generally, the creation of non-compliance procedures relies on a specific treaty provision. On the basis of the provision, a specific mechanism and procedure of non-compliance is to be set out by decisions of treaty bodies.[82] By way of example, Article 8 of the Montreal Protocol requires the parties, at their first meeting, to approve procedures and institutional mechanisms for determining non-compliance with the provisions of this Protocol and for treatment of parties found to be in non-compliance. Following this provision, the non-compliance procedure of the Montreal Protocol was adopted in 1992

---

[75] Establishment of procedures and mechanisms on compliance under the Cartagena Protocol on Biosafety COP-MOP Decisions BS-I/7, 23–27 February 2004, Annex Procedures and Mechanisms on Compliance under the Cartagena Protocol on Biosafety (hereafter Cartagena compliance procedures), para. 2, available at: www.cbd.int/decisions/mop/?m=mop-01. See also Conf. 14.3. CITES Compliance Procedures, 15 June 2007, Annex, para. 4. Text in: (2007) 14 *ILM*, pp. 1178–82.

[76] M. A. Fitzmaurice and C. Redgwell, 'Environmental Non-Compliance Procedures and International Law' (2000) 31 *Netherlands Yearbook of International Law*, p. 39.

[77] Loibl, 'Compliance Procedures and Mechanisms', p. 439.

[78] Decision VI/12 Establishment of a Mechanism for Promoting Implementation and Compliance (hereafter Basel compliance procedures), UNEP/CHW.6/40. 10 February 2003, Appendix, para. 2. For an outline of the Basel compliance procedures, see A. Shibata, 'The Basel Compliance Mechanism' (2003) 12 *RECIEL*, pp. 183–98.

[79] Fitzmaurice and Redgwell, 'Environmental Non-Compliance Procedures', p. 41.

[80] Y. Matsui, *International Law of the Environment: Its Fundamental Principles* (in Japanese) (Tokyo: Toshindo, 2010), p. 329.

[81] Birnie, Boyle and Redgwell, *International Law and Environment*, p. 245.

[82] Dupuy and Viñuales, *International Environmental Law*, p. 287; Loibl, 'Compliance Procedures and Mechanisms', pp. 427–8.

and amended in 1998.[83] To name but a few, the same is equally true of non-compliance procedures under the Kyoto Protocol,[84] Biosafety Protocol,[85] Water and Health Protocol[86] and the Aarhus Convention.[87] Some other treaties, such as the Ramsar Convention,[88] the CITES[89] and the Basel Convention,[90] established non-compliance procedures without an explicit legal basis.

The existence of a legal basis is important when determining the binding nature of the decision resulting from the non-compliance procedures.[91] Some treaties empower the Meeting of the Parties (MOP) or Conference of the Parties (COP) to adopt binding decisions. For instance, Article 2(9)(d) of the Montreal Protocol provides that the decisions shall be binding on all parties. In contrast, Article 15 of the Aarhus Convention makes clear that the non-compliance procedure is non-judicial and consultative nature. Where the treaty does not allow the MOP or COP to adopt binding decisions or remains mute on this matter, it seems reasonable to consider that the decisions resulting from non-compliance procedures will be non-binding. Even so, normative effects of such decisions cannot be underestimated in practice.[92]

4.2 Triggering Non-Compliance Procedures

Triggering mechanism of non-compliance procedures varies according to treaties.[93] In broad terms, triggering mechanisms of these procedures can be divided into two categories: self-triggering and triggering by a third party.

In the case of self-triggering, a State that will be unable to comply with treaty obligations submits to the Secretariat of a treaty its particular circumstances that the State considers to be the cause of its non-compliance. In this case, non-compliance procedures are to be triggered prior to failure of compliance with treaty obligations or a dispute with regard to

---

[83] Non-Compliance Procedure (hereafter Montreal non-compliance procedures), Decision IV/5, 25 November 1992, UNEP/OzL.Pro.4/15, Annex IV, amended by Decision X/10, the Report of the Tenth Meeting of the Parties 3 December 1998, UNEP/OzL.Pro.10/9, available at: http://ozone.unep.org/Meeting_Documents/mop/10mop/10mop-9e.shtml. The text of the amended procedure is available in Annex II of the Report, *ibid*. See also Vienna Convention for the Protection of the Ozone Layer. Text in: 1513*UNTS*, p. 293. Entered into force 22 September 1988.

[84] Article 18. Text in: (1998) 37 *ILM*, p. 22. Entered into force 16 February 2005. See also Procedure and Mechanisms relating to Compliance under the Kyoto Protocol (hereafter Kyoto compliance procedures), Decision 27/CMP.1, 30 March 2006, FCC/KP/CMP/2005/8/Add.3, Annex.

[85] Article 34, 2000 Cartagena Protocol on Biosafety to the Convention on Biological Diversity. Text in: 2226 *UNTS*, p. 208. Entered into force 11 September 2003.

[86] Article 15, 1999 Protocol on Water and Health to the 1992 Convention on the Protection and Use of Transboundary Watercourses and International Lakes. Text in: 2331 *UNTS*, p. 202. Entered into force 4 August 2005.

[87] Article 15, 1998 Convention on Access to Information, Public Participation in Decision-making and Access to Justice in Environmental Matters. Text in: 2161 *UNTS*, p. 447. Entered into force 30 October 2001.

[88] 1971 Convention on Wetlands of International Importance especially as Waterfowl Habitat. Text in: 996 *UNTS*, p. 245. Entered into force 17 February 1976. See also Recommendation 4.7 Mechanisms for improved application of the Ramsar Convention, Annex 1, Monitoring Procedure, REC. C.4.7, 1990.

[89] 1973 Washington Convention on International Trade in Endangered Species of Wild Fauna and Flora. Text in: 993 *UNTS*, p. 243. Entered into force 1 July 1975.

[90] 1989 Basel Convention on the Control of Transboundary Movements of Hazardous Wastes and their Disposal. Text in: 1673 *UNTS*, p. 57. Entered into force 5 May 1992.

[91] Dupuy and Viñuales. *International Environmental Law*, p. 287.

[92] *Ibid.*, p. 288.

[93] Generally on this issue, see Loibl, 'Compliance Procedures and Mechanisms', pp. 431–4.

compliance actually arises. Under the Montreal non-compliance procedures, for instance, where a party concludes that it is unable to comply fully with its obligations under the Protocol, it may address to the Secretariat a submission in writing, explaining, in particular, the specific circumstances that it considers to be the case of its non-compliance. The Secretariat is to transmit such submission to the Implementation Committee which shall consider it as soon as practicable.[94] The self-triggering mechanism is an important feature which distinguishes non-compliance procedures from international adjudication.

With regard to triggering by a third party, four modes exist: triggering by (i) other State Parties, (ii) a secretariat, (iii) the Compliance Committee and (iv) the public. Triggering by other parties (i.e. party-to-party trigger), is widely provided in various non-compliance procedures. Under the Montreal non-compliance procedures, for example, if one or more parties have reservations regarding another party's implementation of its obligations under the Protocol, those concerns may be addressed in writing to the Secretariat. Such a submission must be supported by corroborating information.[95] Further, the Montreal non-compliance procedures provide that where the Secretariat becomes aware of possible non-compliance by any party with its obligations under the Protocol, it may request the party concerned to furnish necessary information about the matter. If there is no response from the party concerned within three months, the Secretariat is to include the matter in its report to the MOP under Article 12(c) of the Protocol and inform the Implementation Committee.[96]

The Espoo compliance procedures provide 'committee initiative'. Under the initiative, where the Implementation Committee becomes aware of possible non-compliance by a party with its obligations, it may request the party concerned to furnish necessary information about the matter. The Implementation Committee is to consider the matter as soon as possible in the light of any reply that the party may provide.[97] Similarly, referrals by the Secretariat and the Implementation Committee are provided in the LTAP non-compliance procedures.[98] The secretariat trigger is also provided in the Basel compliance procedures.[99]

Referral by the public remains exceptional.[100] The Aarhus compliance procedures are an example. In addition to the three actors, the Aarhus compliance procedures allow the public to bring communications with regard to compliance with the Convention.[101] The communication

---

[94] Montreal non-compliance procedures, para. 4.   [95] *Ibid.*, para. 1.
[96] *Ibid.*, para. 3.
[97] Economic Commission for Europe, Structure and Functions of the Implementation Committee and Procedures for Review of Compliance (hereafter the Espoo compliance procedures), para. 6, available at: www.unece.org/fileadmin/DAM/env/eia/documents/ImplementationCommittee/2014_Structure_and_functions/Implementation_Committee_structure_functions_procedures_rules.e_2014.pdf.
[98] Decision 2012/25 On Improving the Functioning of the Implementation Committee, ECE/EB.AIR/113/Add.1, Annex Implementation Committee, Its Structure and Functions and Procedures for Review (hereafter LTAP compliance procedures), para. 5bis.
[99] Basel compliance procedures, para. 9. In the last few years, however, the inclusion of a secretariat trigger was rejected by a majority of parties under some environmental treaties since it would undermine the objectivity and impartiality of the secretariat. Loibl, 'Compliance Procedures and Mechanisms', p. 432.
[100] *Ibid.*, pp. 432–3.
[101] Economic and Social Council, Decision I/7, Review of Compliance, ECE/MP.PP/2/Add.8, 2 April 2004, Annex Structure and Functions of the Compliance Committee and Procedures for the Review of Compliance (hereafter the Aarhus compliance procedures), para. 18. For an outline of the Aarhus compliance procedures, see J. Jendrośka, 'Aarhus Convention Compliance Committee: Origins, Status and Activities' (2011) 8(4) *Journal for European Environmental and Planning Law*, pp. 301–4.

is to be addressed to the Compliance Committee and it must consider any such communication unless it determines that the communication is: (a) anonymous, (b) an abuse of the right to make such communications, (c) manifestly unreasonable and (d) incompatible with the provisions of this decision or with the Convention.[102] The Compliance Committee must bring any communications submitted to it from the public to the attention of the party alleged to be in non-compliance.[103] A party must subsequently submit to the Committee written explanations or statements clarifying the matter and describing any response that it may have made.[104] Communications from the public are also allowed in the non-compliance procedures under the Water and Health Protocol.[105]

4.3 Composition of Organs of Non-Compliance Procedures

While the composition of organs to supervise compliance with treaty obligations varies according to each treaty, in a broad perspective, two principal types can be identified: organs composed of representatives of States (type I) and organs consisting of independent experts (type II).[106] The first type can be divided into two groups: organs composed of representatives of all State Parties (type I-A) and organs composed of representatives of selected States (type I-B).

An example of type I-A is provided by the OSPAR Commission. This was established by the 1992 Convention for the Protection of the Marine Environment of the North-East Atlantic (OSPAR Convention) and is composed of all contracting parties to the Convention.[107] In accordance with Article 23 of the Convention, the OSPAR Commission is to 'assess' non-compliance with the Convention by plural States with regard to marine pollution.

As for an example of type I-B, the Implementation Committee of the Montreal Protocol consists of ten parties elected by the MOP for two years based on equitable geographical distribution.[108] The Implementation Committee of the Convention on Environmental Impact Assessment in a Transboundary Context (the Espoo Convention) consists of eight parties.[109] The Implementation Committee of the 1979 Convention on Long-Range Transboundary Air Pollution consists of nine parties to the Convention each elected for a term of two years.[110] In any case this type of committee can be viewed as a political organ.

An example of type II is the Compliance Committee of the Aarhus Convention. It consists of eight members who shall serve in their personal capacity. They are persons of high moral character and recognised competence in the fields to which the Convention relates,

---

[102] Aarhus compliance procedures, para. 20.   [103] *Ibid.*, para. 22.   [104] *Ibid.*, para. 23.
[105] Decision I/2 Review of Compliance, Annex Compliance Procedure (hereafter Water compliance procedure), ECE/MP.WH/2/Add.3 EUR/06/5069385/1/Add.3, 3 July 2007, para. 16.
[106] Dupuy and Viñuales, *International Environmental Law*, p. 290.
[107] Convention for the Protection of the Marine Environment of the North-East Atlantic, Paris, 22 September 1992, in force 25 March 1998, 2354 *UNTS*, p. 67.
[108] Montreal non-compliance procedures, para. 5.
[109] Espoo compliance procedures, para. 1(a). Parties are elected for two terms. Term(s) means the period that begins at the end of one MOP and ends at the end of the next MOP. *Ibid.*, para. 1(b) and (d).
[110] LTAP compliance procedures, para. 1. The Implementation Committee was established by the Executive Body in 1997. www.unece.org/fileadmin/DAM/env/documents/2012/EB/Decision_2012_25.pdf.

including persons having legal expertise.[111] The members of the committee are elected by the meeting of the parties by consensus or, failing consensus, by secret ballot.[112] Another example is the committee established by the Basel Convention. It consists of fifteen members elected by the COP.[113] Members of the committee must have expertise relating to the subject matter of the Convention in areas including scientific, technical, socio-economic and/or legal fields and they serve objectively and in the best interest of the Convention.[114] The Compliance Committee under the Water and Health Protocol consists of nine members, who shall serve in their personal capacity and objectivity. The members are experts in the fields to which the Protocol relates.[115]

4.4 Functions of the Compliance/Implementation Committee

While the functions of the Compliance or Implementation Committee vary according to treaties, normally non-judicial and consultative measures can be taken. By way of example, a committee for administering the mechanism for promoting implementation and compliance of the Basel Convention is empowered to provide a party with advice, non-binding recommendations and information relating to, *inter alia*: establishing and/or strengthening its domestic/regional regulatory regimes, facilitation of assistance in particular to developing countries and countries with economies in transition, elaborating voluntary compliance action plans and any follow-up arrangements.[116]

Relevant measures under the Aarhus Convention are taken by the MOP upon consideration of a report and recommendations of the Compliance Committee. As explained earlier, under the Aarhus Convention, one or more members of the public is allowed to bring communications concerning party's compliance with the Convention. In this case, the MOP may make recommendations to the party concerned on specific measures to address the matter raised by the member of the public.[117]

In this regard, it is notable that the MOP of the Aarhus Convention is empowered to issue a declaration of non-compliance and suspend the special rights and privileges accorded to the party concerned under the Convention.[118] Similarly, the MOP of the Montreal Protocol is allowed to suspend 'specific rights and privileges under the Protocol, whether or not subject to time limits, including those concerned with industrial rationalization, production, consumption, trade, transfer of technology, financial mechanism and institutional arrangements'.[119] Where a party's compliance matter is unresolved and persistent and the party is showing no intention to achieve compliance, the Standing Committee of CITES may decide to recommend the suspension of commercial or all trade in specimens of one or more

---

[111] Aarhus compliance procedures, paras. 1–2.   [112] *Ibid.*, para. 7.
[113] Basel compliance procedures, para. 3.   [114] *Ibid.*, para. 5.
[115] Water compliance procedure, paras. 4-5.
[116] Basel compliance procedures, para. 19.
[117] Aarhus compliance procedures, para. 37(d).
[118] *Ibid.*, para. 37(e) and (g).
[119] Annex V Indicative list of measures that might be taken by a Meeting of the Parties in respect of non-compliance with the Protocol, 25 November 1992, UNEP/OzL.Pro.4/15, available at: http://ozone.unep.org/Meeting_Documents/mop/04mop/MOP_4.shtml.

CITES-listed species.[120] Upon consideration of the report and any recommendations of the Compliance Committee, the MOP under the Water and Health Protocol can also suspend the special rights and privileges accorded to the party concerned.[121]

A related issue concerns the interlinkage between reporting obligations and non-compliance procedures. As compliance with treaties is primarily assessed on the basis of information provided by contracting parties, reporting can be thought to be a prerequisite for non-compliance procedures.[122] Thus, normally environmental treaties provide an obligation to report at regular intervals. An illustrative example is provided by the OSPAR Convention. Article 22 of the Convention obliges the contracting parties to report to the OSPAR Commission at regular intervals on:

(a) the legal, regulatory or other measures taken by them for the implementation of the provisions of the Convention and of decisions and recommendations adopted thereunder, including in particular measures taken to prevent and punish conduct in contravention of those provisions;
(b) the effectiveness of the measures referred to in subparagraph (a) of this Article;
(c) problems encountered in the implementation of the provisions referred to in subparagraph (a) of this Article.

On the basis of the periodical reports, the OSPAR Commission is to assess compliance with the OSPAR Convention. When appropriate, it also decides upon and calls for steps to bring about full compliance with the Convention, and decisions adopted thereunder, and promote the implementation of recommendations, including measures to assist a contracting party to carry out its obligations.

Obviously the effectiveness of reporting systems relies on the accuracy of data and diligence of the reporting authorities.[123] Notably, some committees are empowered to gather information on their own. For instance, the Compliance Committee of the Aarhus Convention may undertake, with the consent of any party concerned, information-gathering in the territory of that party.[124] The same is equally true of the Basel compliance procedures[125] and the Water compliance procedures.[126] Information-gathering can be viewed as an important tool to supervise compliance with treaty obligations by the parties.

4.5 Relationship between Non-Compliance Procedures and Dispute Settlement Procedures

Multilateral environmental treaties continue to provide traditional dispute settlement procedures, while creating non-compliance procedures. The question of interest here concerns the relationship between non-compliance procedures and dispute settlement

---

[120] CITES compliance procedures, para. 30.   [121] Water compliance procedures, para. 35(f).
[122] Fitzmaurice and Redgwell, 'Environmental Non-Compliance Procedures', p. 42; Loibl, 'Compliance Procedures and Mechanisms', p. 427.
[123] Further, see Y. Tanaka, 'Reflections on Reporting Systems in Treaties Concerning the Protection of the Marine Environment' (2009) 40 *Ocean Development and International Law*, pp. 157 *et seq.*
[124] Aarhus compliance procedures, para. 25(b).   [125] Basel compliance procedures, para. 22(d).
[126] Water compliance procedures, para. 23(b).

procedures.[127] In this regard, normally these treaties provide that non-compliance procedures shall be without prejudice to dispute settlement procedures. For example, the Aarhus compliance procedures state that: '[T]he present compliance procedure shall be without prejudice to article 16 of the Convention on the settlement of disputes.'[128] The 'non-prejudice' clause is equally provided in the Alpine compliance mechanism,[129] Basel compliance procedures,[130] the Espoo compliance procedures,[131] the LTAP compliance procedures,[132] the Kyoto compliance procedures,[133] and the Montreal compliance procedures.[134] Related to this, it may be relevant to note that the MOP under the Montreal Protocol endorsed the conclusion of the Ad Hoc Working Group of Legal Experts that the judicial and arbitral settlement of disputes provided for in Article 11 of the Vienna Convention for the Protection of Ozone Layer and the Non-Compliance Procedure pursuant to Article 8 of the Montreal Protocol were two distinct and separate procedures.[135] Overall non-compliance procedures and dispute settlement procedures can be considered as separate procedures and the two procedures coexist without prejudicing each other.[136]

However, the 'non-prejudice' clause itself does not serve to clarify the relationship between non-compliance procedures and dispute settlement procedures.[137] In practice, the parallel existence of the two types of procedures may create difficult legal issues. For instance, is it possible to set in motion non-compliance procedures, while negotiations are ongoing? In the situation where there is an agreement to recourse to arbitration or judicial settlement, is it possible to invoke non-compliance procedures? Where a matter was referred to arbitration or judicial settlement, although non-compliance procedures had been set in motion, what is the relationship between the two procedures?

It seems that the relationship between non-compliance procedures and dispute settlement procedures may vary according to the means of dispute settlement being invoked.[138] In so far as negotiation, good offices and mediation are concerned, simultaneous recourse to non-compliance procedures will not create a serious legal problem.[139] Yet, the parallel recourse to non-compliance and legal means of dispute settlement, arbitration or judicial settlement creates a more difficult legal question. In this regard, some argue that when the Compliance or Implementation Committee is acting as a facilitator in a dispute to bring it to an amicable solution, it is not in conflict with a dispute

---

[127] Generally on this issue, see Fitzmaurice and Redgwell, 'Environmental Non-Compliance Procedures', pp. 43–52; Fitzmaurice, 'International Protection of the Environment', pp. 351–62.
[128] Aarhus compliance procedures, para. 38.   [129] Alpine compliance procedures, para. 4.4.
[130] Basel compliance procedures, para. 27.   [131] Espoo compliance procedures, para. 14.
[132] LTAP compliance procedures, para. 12.   [133] Kyoto compliance procedures, XVI.
[134] Montreal compliance procedures, Preamble.
[135] Decision III/2: Non-compliance procedure, para. (a)(vi), available at: http://ozone.unep.org/Meeting_Documents/impcom/MOP_decisions_on_NCP.pdf.
[136] Shibata, 'The Basel Compliance Mechanism', p. 196.
[137] Loibl, 'Compliance Procedures and Mechanisms', p. 438; Fitzmaurice and Redgwell, 'Environmental Non-Compliance Procedures', p. 44.
[138] Ibid., p. 49.   [139] Ibid., pp. 49–50.

under consideration by a court or tribunal and should even be encouraged.[140] When a party has recourse to arbitration or judicial settlement, however, the matter becomes *sub judice* and it would be inappropriate to allow the Compliance or Implementation Committee to continue its proceedings to the stage that *de facto* determines a party's non-compliance. In such a case, the proceedings within the Committee should be suspended, but not necessarily terminated.[141] In any case, since there is no general rule in this matter, this question should be resolved by the contracting parties of each environmental treaty.

The Espoo compliance procedures may provide an insight into this issue. Paragraph 15 of the Espoo compliance procedures provides that where a matter is being considered under an inquiry procedure under Article 3(7) of the Espoo Convention, that matter may not be the subject of a submission under this decision. Paragraph 15 applied to the Bystroe Canal Project.[142] On 26 May 2004, Romania made a submission to the Implementation Committee with regard to Ukraine's compliance with its obligation under the Espoo Convention with respect to the Danube–Black Sea Deep-Water Navigation Canal in the Ukrainian Sector of the Danube Delta (the Bystroe Canal Project). On 19 August 2004, Romania also requested the establishment of an inquiry commission under Article 3(7) of the Convention in this matter. Noting paragraph 15, the Implementation Committee decided that it was not in a position to consider the submission of Romania.[143] The Inquiry Commission completed its work on 10 July 2006 and took the view that the project was likely to have a significant adverse transboundary impact on the environment. Thus, on 23 January 2007, Romania made a second submission with regard to the Bystroe Canal Project. In this regard, the Implementation Committee agreed that the second submission by Romania superseded Romania's first submission, which was considered closed. It thus agreed to consider the second submission.[144] The Committee eventually found that Ukraine did not comply fully with Article 2(2) of the Convention because it did not provide sufficiently clearly in its regulatory framework the relevant information with regard to proper implementation of the Espoo Convention.[145] This instance appears to show that the Implementation Committee may *de facto* determine non-compliance with treaty obligations by a party.[146] Even though this is not a judicial decision, a sensitive issue will arise when the Committee's view differs from an arbitral award or decision of an international court.

---

[140] M. Koskenniemi, 'Breach of Treaty or Non-Compliance? Reflections on the Enforcement of the Montreal Protocol' (1992) 3 *Yearbook of International Environmental Law*, p. 159.

[141] *Ibid.*

[142] Loibl, 'Compliance Procedures and Mechanisms', p. 439.

[143] Economic and Social Council, Review of the Work Done by the Working Group on Environmental Impact Assessment and Adoption of Decisions, Findings and Recommendations further to a Submission by Romania Regarding Ukraine (EIA/IC/S/1). ECE/MP/EIA/2008/6, 27 February 2008, paras. 1–3; Economic and Social Council, Report of the Sixth Meeting of the Implementation Committee, MP.EIA/WG.1/2005/3, 1 February 2005, para. 14.

[144] ECE/MP/EIA/2008/6, paras. 4–8.   [145] *Ibid.*, para. 60.

[146] Between 2004 and 2011, the Compliance Committee of the Aarhus Convention also confirmed non-compliance of a party in sixteen out of some fifty-eight cases. A. Andrusevych, T. Alge and C. Konrad (eds.), *Case Law of the Aarhus Convention Compliance Committee (2004–2011)*, 2nd edn (Lviv: RACSE, 2011), pp. 200–5.

5 CONCLUSIONS

As environmental disputes may arise in various contexts, these disputes must be settled by applying multiple means of international dispute settlement. The consideration on this subject can be summarised in four points:

(i) Generally, the role of international adjudication remains comparatively modest in the settlement of environmental disputes. However, this does not mean that international courts and tribunals have no valuable role to play in this field. In particular, the role of arbitration in the settlement of environmental disputes merits particular note owing to its flexibility. It is also notable that the ITLOS makes strong commitments in the protection of the marine environment by prescribing various provisional measures.

(ii) Non-adjudicative procedures perform a crucial role in the settlement of environmental disputes. In this regard, two procedures merit particular note: fact-finding by Treaty Commission and non-compliance procedures. Fact-finding by Treaty Commission can perform an important function by clarifying technical and factual aspects of environmental disputes. It can also provide a basis for an equitable solution with regard to the use of water resources.

(iii) Non-compliance procedures are a mechanism to prevent breach of obligations provided in treaties. These procedures are characterised by four features:

- their non-confrontational nature
- their preventive nature
- their non-consent-based nature
- the safeguarding of common interests of the parties to environmental treaties.

As non-compliance procedures seek to avoid binding third-party procedures, they can be considered as a form of dispute avoidance or alternative dispute resolution.

(iv) While triggering mechanisms vary according to treaties, non-compliance procedures can be triggered by a State that will be unable to comply with treaty obligations and a third party (i.e. other State Parties, a secretariat, the Compliance Committee or the public). The self-triggering mechanism is a unique feature which distinguishes non-compliance procedures from international adjudication. Generally, non-compliance procedures and dispute settlement procedures can be regarded as separate procedures and the two procedures coexist without prejudicing each other. Yet, a parallel use of non-compliance procedures and dispute settlement procedures needs further consideration.

FURTHER READING

A. Boyle and J. Harrison, 'Judicial Settlement of International Environmental Disputes: Current Problems' (2013) 4 *Journal of International Dispute Settlement*, pp. 245–76.

M. A. Fitzmaurice, 'The International Court of Justice and Environmental Disputes' in D. French, M. Saul and N. D. White (eds.), *International Law and Dispute Settlement: New Problems and Techniques* (Oxford: Hart Publishing, 2010), pp. 17–56.

C. E. Foster, *Science and the Precautionary Principle in International Courts and Tribunals: Expert Evidence, Burden of Proof and Finality* (Cambridge University Press, 2011).

N. Klein, 'Settlement of International Environmental Disputes' in M. Fitzmaurice, D. M. Ong and P. Merkouris (eds.), *Research Handbook on International Environmental Law* (Cheltenham: Edward Elgar Publishing, 2011), pp. 379–400.

J. Pauwelyn, 'Judicial Mechanisms: Is There a Need for a World Environment Court?' in W. B. Chambers and J. F. Green (eds.), *Reforming International Environmental Governance: From Institutional Limits to Innovative Reforms* (Tokyo: United Nations University Press, 2005), pp. 150–77.

C. P. R. Romano, 'International Dispute Settlement' in D. Bodansky, J. Brunnée and H. Hey (eds.), *The Oxford Handbook of International Environmental Law* (Oxford University Press, 2007), pp. 1036–56.

T. Stephens, *International Courts and Environmental Protection* (Cambridge University Press, 2009).

'The Settlement of Disputes in International Environmental Law' in S. Alam *et al.* (eds.), *Routledge Handbook of International Environmental Law* (London: Routledge, 2015), pp. 175–87.

11

Peaceful Settlement of Disputes Involving Non-State Actors

Main Issue

Peaceful settlement of disputes between two parties of which at least one party is a non-State actor is an increasingly important issue in international law. The settlement of these disputes necessitates particular procedures. As such procedures are diverse, this chapter will focus on some prototypical examples in this matter: the role of the United Nations in internal armed conflicts, intra-State arbitration, the International Centre for the Settlement of Investment Disputes (ICSID), the Iran–United States Claims Tribunal, the United Nations Compensation Commission, judicial review by the ICJ, the UN internal justice system and the World Bank Inspection Panel. In particular, the following issues will be examined:

(i) What is the role of the United Nations in the settlement of intra-State disputes?
(ii) What is the role of arbitration in the settlement of intra-State disputes?
(iii) What are the law and procedures of the ICSID and the Iran–United States Claims Tribunal?
(iv) What are the principal features of the United Nations Compensation Commission?
(v) Is it possible for the International Court of Justice to review the validity of UN Security Council resolutions?
(vi) What is the role of the World Bank Inspection Panel?

1 INTRODUCTION

In light of increasing activities of non-State actors in international relations, growing attention is paid to the peaceful settlement of disputes between two parties of which at least one party is a non-State actor. As discussed in Chapter 1, section 3.4, four types of international disputes involving non-State actors can be identified:

(i) intra-State disputes
(ii) disputes between the State and juridical/natural persons
(iii) disputes between an international organisation and its Member States
(iv) disputes between an international organisation and individuals.

Relevant procedures of the settlement of international disputes involving non-State actors considerably differ according to the nature of disputes. Thus this chapter has only the modest aim of examining some prototypical examples concerning the settlement of the four types of disputes.

Following the Introduction, this chapter examines the role of the United Nations and arbitration in the settlement of intra-State disputes (section 2). Next, it addresses mixed arbitration with specific focus on the ICSID and the Iran–United States Claims Tribunal (section 3). This chapter then discusses the United Nations Compensation Commission (UNCC) (section 4). It moves on to examine the potential of judicial review of UN Security Council resolutions by the ICJ (section 5). Finally it discusses the UN justice system and the World Bank Inspection Panel (section 6), before offering conclusions (section 7).

2 PEACEFUL SETTLEMENT OF INTRA-STATE DISPUTES

2.1 The Role of the United Nations in the Settlement of Intra-State Disputes

2.1.1 General Considerations

Intra-State disputes can be characterised by two principal features. The first noteworthy feature concerns diversity of actors. While intra-State disputes are often accompanied with internal armed conflicts, these conflicts are fought not only by regular armies but also by militias and armed civilians with little discipline and with ill-defined chains of command. Civilians are the main victims and often the main targets.[1] The second noteworthy feature pertains to the collapse of State institutions, especially the police and judiciary institutions. More often than not, not only are the functions of government suspended, its assets are destroyed or looted and experienced officials are killed or flee the country.[2] Given that intra-State disputes involving internal armed conflicts often destroy governmental institutions and society itself, it is difficult to restore society by the government of the State concerned alone. Hence the involvement of a third party, such as the United Nations, becomes crucial. In this regard, it is of particular interest to note that in *An Agenda for Peace*, UN Secretary-General Boutros Boutros-Ghali advocated a comprehensive approach comprising the four elements: preventive diplomacy, peacekeeping, peacemaking and post-conflict peacebuilding.[3] Generally, the four areas for action can be thought to correspond to different phases of intra-State disputes:

Phase I   Prevention of intra-State disputes (preventive diplomacy)[4]
Phase II Prevention of escalation of disputes (peacekeeping operation)
Phase III Resolution of disputes (peacemaking)[5]
Phase IV Re-establishment of governmental institutions and society (peacebuilding).

---

[1] *Supplement to an Agenda for Peace: Position Paper of the Secretary-General on the Occasion of the Fiftieth Anniversary of the United Nations*, A/50/60-S/1995/1, 25 January 1995, para. 12.
[2] *Ibid.*, para. 13.
[3] Boutros Boutros-Ghali, *An Agenda for Peace*, 2nd edn (New York: United Nations, 1995), pp. 45–6, paras. 20–1.
[4] See Chapter 4, section 4.1.2 of this book.
[5] See Chapter 4 of this book.

In practice, the four areas for action are not always taken in chronological order from preventive diplomacy (phase I) to post-conflict peacebuilding (phase IV). Where a new armed conflict takes place in the process of post-conflict peacebuilding, for instance, a new peacekeeping operation may be needed to prevent escalation of the conflict. Peacebuilding can also be an important element to prevent disputes in the future. Hence it must be stressed that these four areas for action are not mutually exclusive but integrally interlinked.

2.1.2 Interlinkage of Peacekeeping and Peacebuilding

In considering the comprehensive approach, particular attention must be paid to the interlinkage between peacekeeping and peacebuilding. Peacekeeping is the deployment of a United Nations presence in the field, hitherto with the consent of all the parties concerned, normally involving United Nations military and/or police personnel and frequently civilians as well. Peacekeeping is a technique that expands the possibilities for both the prevention of conflict and the making of peace.[6] It is generally considered that the UN peacekeeping operations were given currency by the UN Emergency Force in the Suez (UNEF I).[7] Traditionally peacekeeping is carried out in accordance with three core principles:[8]

- consent of the State(s) on whose territory operations are carried out
- minimal use of force
- impartiality.

First, under the principle of consent, peacekeeping must be deployed with the consent of the State on whose territory operations are carried out. This principle is of central importance to respect territorial sovereignty of the State where such operations are conducted.[9]

Second, in accordance with the principle of minimal use of force, peacekeepers cannot use force beyond self-defence. In this regard, UN Secretary-General Dag Hammarskjold's final report on UNEF I, called the *Summary Study*, made clear that: '[M]en engaged in the operation may never take the initiative in the use of armed force ... The basic element involved is clearly the prohibition against any initiative in the use of armed force.'[10]

Third, under the principle of impartiality, force cannot be used in favour, or to the detriment of, one of the parties in dispute. The *Summary Study* stressed that: '[T]he United Nations personnel cannot be permitted in any sense to be a party to internal conflicts.'[11] The principle of impartiality creates particular sensitivity associated with the composition

---

[6] Boutros-Ghali, *An Agenda for Peace*, p. 45, para. 20. See also Chapter 4, section 4.1.4 of this book.
[7] P. I. Labuda, 'Peacekeeping and Peace Enforcement' in *Max Planck Encyclopaedia*, para. 8.
[8] *Ibid.*, para. 3. See also UN General Assembly, *Report of the Secretary-General: Summary Study of the Experience Derived from the Establishment and Operation of the Force* (hereafter *Summary Study*), UN Doc A/3943, 9 October 1958; United Nations, *United Nations Peacekeeping Operations: Principles and Guidelines* (New York: United Nations Department of Peacekeeping Operations, Department of Field Support, 2008), pp. 31–5.
[9] *Summary Study*, p. 28, para. 155.   [10] *Ibid.*, p. 31, para. 179.   [11] *Ibid.*, p. 29, para. 166.

of peacekeeping operation units. In this regard, the *Summary Study* specified two principles: not to include units from any of the permanent members of the Security Council and not to include units from any country which, because of its geographical position or for other reasons, might be considered as possibly having a special interest in the situation which has called for the operation.[12]

In 1995, UN Secretary-General Boutros Boutros-Ghali, in his report titled *Supplement to an Agenda for Peace*, affirmed that the three principles are essential to the success of peacekeeping.[13] The core functions of traditional peacekeeping are limited to a variety of non-enforcement functions, such as:

- the supervision of a ceasefire, or a peace agreement
- monitoring and reporting on developments in conflict areas
- acting as a buffer or a temporary interposition force between rival factions.

The ultimate goal of traditional peacekeeping is to provide a measure of stability and security in a conflict zone. In summary, traditional peacekeeping can be regarded as a temporary, confidence-building measure.[14]

The vital role of UN peacekeeping in helping disputing parties to end hostilities is acknowledged in the international community.[15] However, traditional peacekeeping mostly had a ceasefire-monitoring mandate without direct peacebuilding responsibilities. As a consequence, a peacekeeping force may simply freeze a situation without addressing structural causes of disputes in question.[16] In response, the Security Council and the General Assembly's Special Committee on Peace-keeping Operations have each recognised and acknowledged the importance of peacebuilding as integral to the success of peacekeeping operations.[17]

The United Nations defines 'peacebuilding' as 'a complex, long-term process of creating the necessary conditions for sustainable peace'.[18] Peacebuilding seeks to address the deep-rooted, the structural causes of internal disputes. In so doing, it contributes to prevention of future disputes. Peacebuilding comprises a wide range of activities, such as: disarming the previously warring parties, the custody and destruction of weapons, the restoration of order, repatriating refugees, training support for security personnel, monitoring elections, reforming governmental institutions, protection of human rights and promotion of political participation.[19]

As various types of actors involve a peacebuilding project simultaneously at different levels and in different fields, coordination of activities becomes a challenging task. A response is the establishment of the Peacebuilding Commission in 2005. The Peacebuilding Commission is an intergovernmental advisory body created by the UN

---

[12] *Ibid.*, p. 29, para. 160. [13] *Supplement to an Agenda for Peace*, para. 33.
[14] Labuda, 'Peacekeeping', paras. 3 and 26.
[15] UN General Assembly, 60/1, *2005 World Summit Outcome*, 24 October 2005, p. 23, para. 92.
[16] C. Gray, *International Law and the Use of Force*, 3rd edn (Oxford University Press, 2008), p. 263.
[17] *The Brahimi Report*, p. 3, paras. 17–18 and p. 6, para. 35.
[18] United Nations, *United Nations Peacekeeping Operations*, p. 18.
[19] Boutros-Ghali, *An Agenda for Peace*, p. 61, para. 55.

Assembly Resolution 60/180 of 20 December 2005 and was confirmed by the Security Council in its identical Resolution 1645 of 20 December 2005.[20] It has three mandates:[21]

(a) to bring together all relevant actors to marshal resources and to advise on and propose integrated strategies for post-conflict peacebuilding and recovery
(b) to focus attention on the reconstruction and institution-building efforts necessary for recovery from conflict and to support the development of integrated strategies in order to lay the foundation for sustainable development
(c) to provide recommendations and information to improve the coordination of all relevant actors within and outside the United Nations, to develop best practices, to help to ensure predictable financing for early recovery activities and to extend the period of attention given by the international community to post-conflict recovery.

The Commission operates through its standing Organisational Committee that is composed of five groups of members: (a) seven members of the UN Security Council; (b) seven members of the Economic and Social Council; (c) five top providers of assessed contributions to United Nations budgets and of voluntary contributions to United Nations funds, programmes and agencies; (d) five top providers of military personnel and civilian police to United Nations missions that are not among those selected in (a), (b) or (c) above; and (e) seven additional members elected according to rules and procedures decided by the General Assembly.[22] The Commission also operates through country-specific meetings, upon invitation of the Organizational Committee.[23] At present, six countries (i.e. Burundi, Sierra Leone, Guinea-Bissau, Central African Republic, Guinea and Liberia) are on the agenda of the Commission's country-specific meetings.[24] The Commission's work is assisted by the Peacebuilding Support Office.[25] In October 2006, a Peacebuilding Fund (PBF) for post-conflict peacebuilding initiatives was established by the UN Secretary-General with a view to addressing immediate needs in countries emerging from conflict at a time when sufficient resources are not available from other funding mechanisms. The PBF is currently supporting more than 120 projects in twenty-five countries.[26]

2.1.3 Transitional Justice

The 2012 Declaration on the Rule of Law stressed that: '[J]ustice, including transitional justice, is a fundamental building block of sustainable peace in countries in conflict and post-conflict situations.'[27] As the Declaration stated, transitional justice is a key concept in consolidating peace in post-conflict situations. Although there is no uniform

---

[20] UN General Assembly Resolution, *The Peacebuilding Commission*, A/RES/60/180, 20 December 2005, para. 1; UN Security Council Resolution, S/RES/1645 (2005), para. 1. Entered into existence in June 2006. For an outline of the Peacebuilding Commission, see F. Baetens and K. Kohoutek, 'United Nations Peacebuilding Commission' in *Max Planck Encyclopaedia*.
[21] A/RES/60/180, para. 2.   [22] *Ibid.*, para. 4.   [23] *Ibid.*, para. 7.
[24] The United Nations Peacebuilding Commissions, Country-Specific Configurations, available at: www.un.org/en/peacebuilding/countryconfig.shtml.
[25] See www.un.org/en/peacebuilding/pbso/.
[26] See www.unpbf.org/.
[27] UN General Assembly Resolution, 67/1. *Declaration of the High-level Meeting of the General Assembly on the Rule of Law at the National and International Level*, A/RES/67/1, 30 November 2012, para. 18.

definition of transitional justice, the 2004 Report of the UN Secretary-General defines this concept as:

> the full range of processes and mechanisms associated with a society's attempts to come to terms with a legacy of large-scale past abuses, in order to ensure accountability, serve justice and achieve reconciliation. These may include both judicial and non-judicial mechanisms, with differing levels of international involvement (or none at all) and individual prosecutions, reparations, truth-seeking, institutional reform, vetting and dismissals, or a combination thereof.[28]

While the concept of transitional justice is composite in nature, it includes, *inter alia*, the following elements:[29]

(i) criminal prosecutions (i.e. judicial investigations of those responsible for human rights violations)
(ii) truth commissions
(iii) reparations programmes, namely State-sponsored initiatives that help repair the material and moral damages of past abuse and are the most victim-centred justice mechanism available and may facilitate reconciliation and confidence in the State
(iv) institutional reform, including vetting,[30] that seeks to transform the military, police, judiciary and related State institutions from instruments of repression and corruption into instruments of public service and integrity
(v) memorialisation efforts, including museums and memorials that preserve public memory of the victims and raise moral consciousness about past abuse
(vi) amnesties, namely immunity in law from either criminal or civil legal consequence, or from both, for wrongs committed in the past in a political context.

As noted, transitional justice comprises both judicial and non-judicial institutions. Concerning judicial institutions, a variety of institutional models has emerged. They include:[31]

(i) a permanent criminal court: the International Criminal Court
(ii) ad hoc international criminal tribunals established by the Security Council: International Criminal Tribunal for the Former Yugoslavia and International Criminal Tribunal for Rwanda
(iii) a mixed tribunal for Sierra Leone, established as a treaty-based court

---

[28] UN Security Council, *The Rule of Law and Transitional Justice in Conflict and Post-Conflict Societies, Report of the UN Secretary-General*, S/2004/616, 23 August 2004, p. 4, para. 8.
[29] International Centre for Transitional Justice, 'What Is Transitional Justice?', p. 1, available at: http://legal.un.org/avl/pdf/ls/Van-Zyl_RecReading1_.pdf; T. Sato, 'Transitional Justice, Peacebuilding, and International Law: What Role Is Played by the UN in Post-Conflict Peacebuilding?' (2012) 110 *The Journal of International Law and Diplomacy*, pp. 596–7.
[30] Vetting refers to processes for screening public employees or candidates for public employment to determine if their prior conduct warrants their exclusion from public institutions. Sato, 'Transitional Justice', p. 597, footnote 30.
[31] UN Security Council, *The Rule of Law and Transitional Justice*, p. 13, para. 38; Sato, 'Transitional Justice', pp. 598–9.

(iv) a mixed tribunal for Cambodia, proposed under a national law specially promulgated in accordance with a treaty
(v) a mixed tribunal in the form of a Special Chamber in the State Court of Bosnia and Herzegovina
(vi) a panel with exclusive jurisdiction over serious criminal offences in Timor-Leste, established by the United Nations Transitional Administration in East Timor
(vii) the use of international judges and prosecutors in the courts of Kosovo, pursuant to regulations of the United Nations Interim Administration Mission in Kosovo
(viii) the Commission for the Investigation of Illegal Groups and Clandestine Security Organizations in Guatemala, to be established by agreement between the United Nations and Guatemala.

As the 2004 Report of the UN Secretary-General aptly observed, criminal trials are crucial in transitional contexts since they can provide a direct form of accountability for perpetrators and ensure a measure of justice for victims. Furthermore, they can contribute to greater public confidence in the State's ability and willingness to enforce the law.[32] International criminal tribunals will also help national reconciliation.[33]

As for non-judicial institutions, the role of truth commissions merits particular mention. A truth commission refers to a variety of official or quasi-official, temporary and non-judicial bodies which seek to collect information concerning the facts of a prior conflict and attendant human rights violations in a given country during a specific time period.[34] Truth commissions essentially aim to construct the truth and to achieve reconciliation between former enemies by allowing the truth to come to the surface so as to enable the wounds to heal.[35] In recent times, truth commissions have been increasingly established in the process of post-conflict resolution.[36] Whilst truth commissions are most commonly established by national government, they may also be established under auspices of the United Nations or regional organisations. The Commission on the Truth for El Salvador, which was sponsored by the United Nations and staffed entirely by non-nationals, is a well-known example in this matter.[37] The 2004 Report of the UN Secretary-General recognised that truth commissions can positively complement criminal tribunals.[38] Overall the 2012 Declaration on the Rule of Law stressed the importance of

---

[32] UN Security Council, *The Rule of Law and Transitional Justice*, p. 13, para. 39.
[33] When discussing the establishment of the International Criminal Tribunal for Rwanda at the meeting of the UN Security Council, many delegates referred to the role of the Tribunal in national reconciliation. See Statement by the delegates of Argentina, Spain, Nigeria, Rwanda and Oman at the 3453rd Meeting, 8 November 1994, S/PV.3453, pp. 8, 10, 12–17.
[34] UN Security Council, *The Rule of Law and Transitional Justice*, p. 17, para. 50; Anne-Marine La Rosa and X. Philippe, 'Transitional Justice' in V. Chetail (ed.), *Post-Conflict Peacebuilding: A Lexicon* (Oxford University Press, 2009), p. 372; J. Bercovitch and R. Jackson, *Conflict Resolution in the Twenty-First Century: Principles, Methods, and Approaches* (University of Michigan Press, 2009), p. 155.
[35] A. O'Shea, 'Truth and Reconciliation Commission' in *Max Planck Encyclopaedia*, para. 41.
[36] Examples include: Argentina, Bolivia, Brazil, Canada, the Central African Republic, Chad, Chile, the Democratic Republic of Congo, East Timor, Ecuador, El Salvador, Fiji, Germany, Ghana, Grenada, Guatemala, Haiti, Indonesia, Morocco, Nepal, Nigeria, Panama, Paraguay, Peru, the Philippines, Serbia and Montenegro, Sierra Leone, South Africa, South Korea, Sri Lanka, Uganda, Uruguay and Zimbabwe. O'Shea, 'Truth and Reconciliation Commission', para. 6. See also the United States Institute of Peace's Truth Commissions Digital Collection, www.usip.org/publications/truth-commission-digital-collection.
[37] Bercovitch and Jackson, *Conflict Resolution*, pp. 155–6.
[38] UN Security Council, *The Rule of Law and Transitional Justice*, p. 9, para. 26.

a comprehensive approach to transitional justice incorporating the full range of judicial and non-judicial measures.[39]

2.1.4 Main Challenges

The settlement of intra-State disputes and post-conflict peacebuilding encounter several challenges in practice. Five challenges merit in particular highlighting.

The first challenge concerns a difficulty associated with peacekeeping operations in internal armed conflicts. As intra-State disputes are often complicated because of the involvement of multiple actors, it is difficult to implement the three core principles in internal armed conflicts. Experience demonstrates that peacekeeping operations were less successful when one or other of the principles could not be respected. The difficulty was exemplified by the failure of UNPROFOR in Yugoslavia and UNOSOM II (United Nations Operation in Somalia II) in Somalia. In a series of resolutions, most of which were adopted under Chapter VII, UNPROFOR was given increasingly expanded mandates, including the use of force to secure the delivery of humanitarian aid, to enforce no-fly zones and to protect the safe haven. Yet, Member States were not willing to provide enough troops that were necessary for UNPROFOR to carry out its mandates. In the end, enforcement action under Chapter VII was taken by NATO air forces.[40]

UNOSOM II was the first UN peacekeeping operation that was created under Chapter VII of the UN Charter with functions that went beyond traditional peacekeeping operations.[41] UNOSOM II was given one of the broadest authorisations to take enforcement measures which included all necessary measures to establish the effective authority of UNOSOM II throughout Somalia, including securing the investigation and arrest of those responsible for attacks against the personnel of UNOSOM II and detention for prosecution, trial and punishment.[42] Yet, UNOSOM II was involved in conflict with one of the warring factions and proved unable to carry out its mandate in the absence of an effective ceasefire.[43] UNOSOM II was eventually withdrawn from Somalia in early March 1995.[44]

In both cases, peacekeeping operations were given mandates that required the use of force and, in consequence, could not comply with the principles of host State consent, impartiality and the non-use of force.[45] In this regard, the UN Secretary-General Boutros Boutros-Ghali stressed that:

> In reality, nothing is more dangerous for a peace-keeping operation than to ask it to use force when its existing composition, armament, logistic support and deployment deny it the capacity to do so.[46]

---

[39] UN General Assembly Resolution, 67/1, para. 21.
[40] C. Gray, 'The Use of Force and the International Legal Order' in M. D. Evans, *International Law*, 4th edn (Oxford University Press, 2014), p. 642; Gray, *International Law and the Use of Force*, pp. 282–6.
[41] UN Security Council Resolution 814 (1993), S/RES/814 (1993), 26 March 1993.
[42] UN Security Council Resolution 837 (1993), S/RES/837 (1993), 6 June 1993, para. 5.
[43] Gray, *International Law and the Use of Force*, pp. 286–9.
[44] Further, see www.un.org/en/peacekeeping/missions/past/unosom2backgr2.html.
[45] *Supplement to an Agenda for Peace*, para. 35.
[46] *Ibid*. Further, see S. Sheeran, 'The Use of Force in United Nations Peacekeeping Operations' in M. Weller (eds.), *The Oxford Handbook of the Use of Force in International Law* (Oxford University Press, 2015), pp. 347–74.

Second, transitional justice is not free from challenges with regard to its application. For instance, ethical dilemmas may arise between the universal values attached to human rights and humanitarian law and local traditions and customs. There is also the risk that pursuing justice may endanger the peace process. The application of transitional justice in the process of peacebuilding gives rise to a difficult question concerning the relationship between peace and justice.[47]

Third, the management of natural resources in post-conflict peacebuilding ('environmental peacebuilding') is a challenging task.[48] As natural resources are often intertwined in intra-State disputes,[49] the management of these resources is crucial in post-conflict peacebuilding. Here particular attention must be devoted to water resources. Since water resources and infrastructure often become strategic targets during armed conflict, recovery of water infrastructure presents significant challenges for meeting basic human needs and protecting public health in post-conflict situations.[50] Clean water is also essential for peacebuilding actors, including UN peacekeepers. Yet, meeting water requirements can be a major challenge for UN peacekeeping operations in desert or semi-desert environments.[51]

Fourth, gender in peacebuilding must be examined. The vast majority of people affected by armed conflict are civilians, including women and children. Accordingly, there is a need to incorporate a gender perspective into peacekeeping operations and peacebuilding.[52] In this regard, the UN Security Council Resolution 1325 of 2000 reaffirmed 'the important role of women in the prevention and resolution of conflicts and in peace-building' and stressed 'the importance of their equal participation and full involvement in all efforts for the maintenance and promotion of peace and security, and the need to increase their role in decision-making with regard to conflict prevention and resolution'.[53] Subsequently, the Report of the Secretary-General on Women, Peace and Security was issued in 2002.[54] In this report, the UN Secretary-General submitted, *inter alia*, the following proposals to the Security Council:

- to explicitly integrate gender perspectives into the terms of reference of Security Council missions to countries and regions in conflict

---

[47] Bercovitch and Jackson, *Conflict Resolution*, pp. 160–5.
[48] See http://environmentalpeacebuilding.org/.
[49] Natural resources are also closely linked to inter-State disputes in practice. On this issue, see M. Pertile, 'The Changing Environment and Emerging Resources Conflicts' in M. Weller (ed.), *The Oxford Handbook of the Use of Force in International Law* (Oxford University Press, 2015), pp. 1077–94.
[50] J. Troell and E. Weinthal, 'Shoring Up Peace: Water and Post-Conflict Peacebuilding' in E. Weinthal, J. Troell and M. Nakayama (eds.), *Water and Post-Conflict Peacebuilding* (London: Earthscan, 2014), p. 7.
[51] UNEP, *Greening the Blue Helmets: Environment, Natural resources and UN Peacekeeping Operations*, Policy Paper No. 3 (Nairobi, 2012), p. 24, available at: http://postconflict.unep.ch/publications/UNEP_greening_blue_helmets.pdf.
[52] O. Ramsbotham, T. Woodhouse and H. Miall, *Contemporary Conflict Resolution: The Prevention, Management and Transformation of Deadly Conflicts*, 3rd edn (Cambridge: Polity, 2011), pp. 305 *et seq.*
[53] UN Security Council Resolution 1325(2000), S/RES/1325(2000), 31 October 2000, preambular para. 5. See also, *Women, Peace and Security, Study Submitted by the Secretary-General Pursuant to Security Council Resolution 1325 (2000)* (New York: United Nations, 2002), available at: www.un.org/womenwatch/daw/public/eWPS.pdf.
[54] UN Security Council, *Report of the Secretary-General on Women, Peace and Security*, S/2002/1154, 16 October 2002.

- to ensure full involvement of women in negotiations of peace agreements at national and international levels
- to incorporate gender perspectives explicitly into mandates of all peacekeeping missions.[55]

The important role of women in the prevention and resolution of conflicts and in peacebuilding was further stressed by the 2005 World Summit Outcome.[56] In February 2016, the Global Acceleration Instrument (GAI) for Women, Peace and Security and Humanitarian Action was established to enhance women's engagement in peace and security and/or humanitarian action.[57]

Finally but not least, further consideration must be given to vulnerable economic conditions of less developed countries. More often than not, countries which need peacebuilding are States that are marginalised in a global economic system. The structures of poverty and relative deprivation may lead to internal or international conflicts. Here a difficult question arises as to how it is possible to address the problem with poverty and relative deprivation in countries that lie on the periphery of the global economic system.[58] This is a fundamental question associated with the global economic system.

2.2 Intra-State Arbitration: The *Abyei* Arbitration

2.2.1 The Course of the Litigation

Normally international courts and tribunals have no jurisdiction to adjudicate intra-State disputes between the government and a non-State entity, such as 'rebel' or secessionist movements. Accordingly, the role of legal means remains limited in the settlement of intra-State disputes. However, a notable exception is provided by the *Abyei* arbitration. This arbitration concerned a dispute between the Government of Sudan and the Sudan People's Liberation Movement/Army (SPLM/A), the principal armed force of the Southern Sudanese.[59] The Abyei area is located between the north and south of Sudan and is an important region owing to the existence of significant oil reserves.[60] The *Abyei* arbitration forms part of the settlement of a long-running dispute between the Northern and Southern Sudanese. The arbitration concerns a boundary delimitation of the Abyei area.[61]

In 1899, Sudan was colonized by the Anglo-Egyptian Condominium Government. After withdrawal of the colonising powers in 1954, Sudan descended into the first civil war between the north and south.[62] Although the Addis Ababa Agreement was concluded to end the war in 1972, Sudan descended into a second civil war in 1983. The Abyei area

---

[55] *Ibid.*, Actions 7, 9 and 10, respectively.
[56] UN General Assembly, 60/1. *2005 World Summit Outcome*, 24 October 2005, pp. 26–7, para. 116. See also UN Security Council Resolution 2242(2015), S/RES/2242(2015), 13 October 2015.
[57] In February 2016, the Global Acceleration Instrument (GAI) for Women, Peace and Security and Humanitarian Action was established to enhance women's engagement in peace and security and/or humanitarian action. See http://mptf.undp.org/factsheet/fund/GAI00.
[58] Bercovitch and Jackson, *Conflict Resolution*, p. 180.
[59] *Abey Arbitration* (The Government of Sudan v. the Sudan People's Liberation Movement/Army), 22 July 2009, available at: https://pca-cpa.org/en/cases.
[60] It is estimated that between 2005 and 2007, three major oilfields in the Abyei area yielded US$1.8 billion in revenues. *Abyei Arbitration*, p. 36, para. 104.
[61] *Ibid.*, p. 37, paras. 108 *et seq.*
[62] Sudan obtained independence on 1 January 1956.

was said to be at the geographical centre of the civil war. The second civil war endured for some two decades and, on 20 July 2002, the belligerent parties signed the Machakos Protocol outlining the framework of a peace agreement. Furthermore, in May 2004, the parties reached agreement on the Protocol on the Resolution of Abyei Conflict (the Abyei Protocol). The Protocol provided, *inter alia*, for the administration of the Abyei area during the interim period and for a referendum in which the residents of Abyei would choose whether the region would become part of Southern Sudan or remain with the North. Section 1.1.2 of the Abyei Protocol defined the Abyei area as 'the area of the nine Ngok Dinka chiefdoms transferred to Kordofan in 1905'.[63] Since the parties to the Comprehensive Peace Agreement could not agree on the limits of the Abyei area, they decided to establish the Abyei Boundaries Commission (ABC) to define and demarcate the Abyei area. In addition, on 9 January 2005, the parties signed the Comprehensive Peace Agreement (CPA) that reconfirmed multiple instruments previously agreed upon.

On 20 June 2005, the ABC Experts completed their deliberations and, on 14 July 2005, the ABC Experts' Report was presented to the Sudanese Presidency. The scope of the Abyei area was defined by the 'Final and Binding Decision' of the ABC Experts' Report. Nonetheless, disagreement was raised between the parties as to whether the ABC Experts had exceeded their mandate. After an outbreak of local fighting, on 8 June 2008, the parties signed the Abyei Road Map which provided, *inter alia*, for the referral of the Abyei dispute to arbitration. Thus, on 7 July 2008, the parties signed the arbitration agreement.[64]

Under Article 1.1 of the arbitration agreement, the parties agreed to refer their dispute to final and binding arbitration under the arbitration agreement and the PCA Optional Rules for Arbitrating Disputes between Two Parties of Which Only One is a State (the PCA State/non-State actor Rules).[65] Under Article 5 of the arbitration agreement, the parties agreed that the Tribunal should be composed of five arbitrators.[66] Under Article 2 of the arbitration agreement, the Arbitral Tribunal was to determine first whether or not the ABC Experts had exceeded their mandate. If the Tribunal determined that the ABC Experts exceeded their mandate, it should proceed to define (i.e. delimit) on the map the boundaries of the area of the nine Ngok Dinka chiefdoms transferred to Kordofan in 1905, based on the submissions of the parties.

The Tribunal gave the arbitral award on 22 July 2009. In its award, the Tribunal considered that reasonableness can be regarded as the applicable standard for reviewing the interpretation and implementation of the ABC Experts' mandate. Thus, in the view of the Tribunal, it 'must confine itself to determining whether the ABC Experts' interpretation of their mandate was reasonable'.[67] By applying the review standard, the Tribunal ruled that the Experts' reasoning was insufficient with regard to the northern, eastern and western boundaries of the Abyei area, while the reasoning was sufficient with respect to the southern boundary of the area. It thus redrew the northern, eastern and western boundaries of

---

[63] *Abyei Arbitration*, p. 32, para. 95.

[64] Arbitration agreement between the Government of Sudan and the Sudan People's Liberation Movement/Army on Delimiting Abyei Area, 7 July 2008, available at: https://pcacases.com/web/view/92.

[65] *Ibid.*, p. 1, para. 3. For the choice of procedural rules, see B. Daly, 'The Abyei Arbitration: Procedural Aspects of an Intra-State Border Arbitration' (2010) 23 *LJIL*, pp. 804-8.

[66] *Abyei Arbitration*, p. 2, para. 7. The members of the Arbitral Tribunal were: P.-M. Dupuy (Presiding Arbitrator), A. Al-Khasawneh, G. Hafner, W. M. Reisman and S. M. Schwebel.

[67] *Ibid.*, p. 175, para. 496.

the Abyei area.[68] As a consequence, the Abyei area was reduced from the 18,559 square kilometres in the ABC Experts Report to 10,459 square kilometres.[69]

2.2.2 Principal Features of the *Abyei* Arbitration

The *Abyei* arbitration presents some unique features. The first noteworthy feature concerns the transparency of the proceedings.[70] The parties in the *Abyei* arbitration agreed that the oral pleadings of the Tribunal must be open to the media.[71] Thus, the oral pleadings were broadcast via a live webcast for interested members of the public.[72] Under Article 9(3) of the Agreement, the Tribunal and the parties were to make public the award as of the same day of its rendering. The ceremony for the rendering of the arbitral award was webstreamed live on the website of the PCA. The award was made public through the PCA website immediately after the ceremony.[73] In this particular case, one of the underlying reasons for these strong guarantees of transparency of the arbitral proceedings seems to have been to enhance legitimacy and confidence-building by bringing the process of justice closer to the people who are directly affected by the arbitral award.[74]

The second noteworthy feature pertains to the fast-track procedure.[75] The formation of the Arbitral Tribunal was completed on 27 October 2008 and the arbitral award was rendered on 22 July 2009. It seems that the unprecedented expediency of the *Abyei* arbitration was needed to prevent hostile outbreaks and resolve the highly sensitive dispute as soon as possible. Indeed, it was remarkable that no outbreaks of hostilities took place during the arbitral proceedings. At the same time, the fast-track procedure also demonstrates flexibility of arbitration to meet political and other contextual needs of the disputing parties.[76]

Third, application of international law as part of the applicable law is worth noting. Under Article 3 of the arbitration agreement, the Tribunal was to apply the provisions of the Comprehensive Peace Agreement, particularly the Abyei Protocol and the Abyei Appendix, the Interim National Constitution of the Republic of Sudan, and general principles of law and practices as the Tribunal may determine to be relevant. However, the Tribunal stressed that:

> [T]here is a widely shared understanding that reference to 'general principles of law' within the context of boundary disputes includes general principles of international law. This is especially true in the case of intra-State disputes, where municipal law does not typically make provision for such matters.[77]

---

[68] *Ibid.*, p. 267, paras. 770 *et seq.*
[69] P. von Muhlendahl, 'International Tribunal Redraws Boundareis of Sudanese Abyei Region: A Chance for Peace?' *The Hague Justice Portal*, p. 6, available at: www.haguejusticeportal.net/index.php?id=11256. See also *Abyei Arbitration*, Appendix 2.
[70] F. Baetens and R. Yotova, 'The Abyei Arbitration: A Model Procedure for Intra-State Dispute Settlement in Resource-Rich Conflict Areas?' (2011) 3 *Goettingen Journal of International Law*, pp. 434–5; Daly, 'The Abyei Arbitration', pp. 819–20.
[71] Article 8(6) of the arbitration agreement. Written pleadings of the arbitration are also public.
[72] *Abyei Arbitration*, p. 21, para. 80.
[73] PCA, Press Release: Arbitral Tribunal to Render Final Award, 14 July 2009.
[74] Baetens and Yotova, 'The Abyei Arbitration', p. 435.
[75] *Ibid.*, pp. 432–4; Daly, 'The Abyei Arbitration', pp. 817–19.
[76] Baetens and Yotova, 'The Abyei Arbitration', p. 433.
[77] *Abyei Arbitration*, p. 155, para. 430.

It is also to be noted that the parties selected arbitrators with expertise and experience in public international law.[78]

The award was accepted by the disputing parties in a joint statement they issued on the same day the award was rendered.[79] As demonstrated by the *Abyei* arbitration, arbitration can be cautiously viewed as a useful means of resolving intra-State disputes owing to its flexibility with regard to *locus standi* and procedures.[80] As arbitration leads to a binding award, the parties can expect to settle legal aspects of a particular dispute with certainty. It is also important to note that the *Abyei* arbitration forms part of the peace process across Sudan's north/south division.[81] To provide an arbitration clause in a peace agreement seems to be useful with a view to securing peaceful settlement of disputes concerning the interpretation or implementation of the peace agreement.[82]

3 MIXED ARBITRATION

3.1 The International Centre for the Settlement of Investment Disputes (ICSID)

3.1.1 General Considerations

In addition to inter-State arbitration and intra-State arbitration, another type of arbitration exists: mixed arbitration. Mixed arbitration which combines features of both public and private international arbitration is a particular procedure of the settlement of disputes between States and juridical/natural persons. In broad terms, two principal types of mixed arbitration merit discussion.

The first type is mixed arbitration for the settlement of investment disputes between the State and investors. The International Centre for the Settlement of Investment Disputes (ICSID or the Centre) is a case in point.

The second type is mixed arbitration that is created as part of a peace process between hostile States. The Iran-United States Claims Tribunal is an example. This type of arbitration involves normalisation of international relations between parties in dispute.

Before examining the Iran-United States Claims Tribunal, it would be appropriate to outline ICSID. ICSID was created by the 1965 Convention on the Settlement of Investment Disputes between States and Nations of other States (ICSID Convention).[83] As provided in

---

[78] *Ibid.*, p. 145, para. 407; p. 156, para. 433.
[79] Joint Statement by the National Congress Party and the Sudan People's Liberation Movement Announcing Their Firm Commitment to Implement the Abyei Arbitration Decision, available at: www.southsudanembassydc.org/PressRelease_Archivedetails.asp?artId=5D58. See also Paul von Muhlendahl, 'International Tribunal Redraws Boundaries of Sudanese Abyei Region' (2009) 4 *Hague Justice Journal*, p. 232; Baetens and Yotova, 'The Abyei Arbitration', p. 443; W. J. Miles and D. Mallett, 'The Abyei Arbitration and the Use of Arbitration to Resolve Inter-State and Intra-State Conflicts' (2010) 1 *Journal of International Dispute Settlement*, p. 323.
[80] *Ibid.*, p. 324.
[81] C. G. Lathrop, 'Government of Sudan v. Sudan People's Liberation Movement/Army ("Abyei Arbitration"), Arbitral Tribunal, July 22, 2009' (2010) 104 *AJIL*, p. 73.
[82] Miles and Mallett, 'The Abyei Arbitration', p. 334.
[83] Entered into force 14 October 1966. Text in: 575 *UNTS*, p. 159; C. J. Tams and A. Tzanakopoulos (eds.), *The Settlement of International Disputes: Basic Documents* (Oxford: Hart Publishing, 2012) (hereafter *Basic Documents*), p. 421. For a commentary of the ICSID Convention, see C. Schreuer *et al.* (ed.), *The ICSID Convention: A Commentary*, 2nd edn (Cambridge University Press, 2009). As of 2016, 152 States had become parties to the ICSID Convention.

347 Settlement of Disputes Involving Non-State Actors

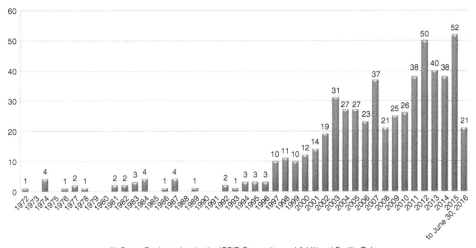

Figure 11.1 Total number of ICSID cases registered, by calendar year

Source: *ICSID Caseload – Statistics*, Issue 2016-2, p. 7.

Article 1(2) of the Convention, the purpose of ICSID is to provide facilities for conciliation and arbitration of investment disputes between Contracting States and nationals of other Contracting States in accordance with the ICSID Convention. The Centre consists of an Administrative Council and a Secretariat.[84] It sits at the principal office of the World Bank.[85] The official languages of the Centre are English, French and Spanish.[86] In addition, on 27 September 1978, the ICSID Additional Facility was created in order to offer arbitration, conciliation and fact-finding for certain disputes that fall outside the scope of the ICSID Convention.[87] The ICSID Additional Facility Rules have been amended twice and the current Rules came into force on 10 April 2006.[88] The volume of cases handled by ICSID is increasing with time. According to statistics, as of 30 June 2016, ICSID had registered 570 cases under the ICSID Convention and Additional Facility Rules (see Figure 11.1).[89]

3.1.2 Composition of the Arbitral Tribunal

ICSID itself does not conciliate or arbitrate investment disputes. Rather, the settlement of these disputes is carried out by either conciliation commissions or arbitral tribunals which are constituted on an ad hoc basis for each specific dispute. To this end, ICSID

---

[84] The ICSID Convention, Article 3.
[85] *Ibid.*, Article 2.
[86] Administrative and Financial Regulations, Article 34(1).
[87] See https://icsid.worldbank.org/apps/ICSIDWEB/icsiddocs/Pages/ICSID-Additional-Facility-Rules.aspx; See also R. Mackenzie *et al.*, *Manual of International Courts and Tribunals* (Oxford University Press, 2010), p. 127.
[88] Rules Governing the Additional Facility for the Administration of Proceedings by the Secretariat of the International Centre for Settlement of Investment Disputes. Text in: Tams and Tzanakopoulos, *Basic Documents*, p. 455.
[89] *ICSID Caseload – Statistics*, Issue 2016-2, p. 7, available at: https://icsid.worldbank.org/en/Pages/resources/ICSID-Caseload-Statistics.aspx.

maintains a Panel of Conciliators and a Panel of Arbitrators.[90] Under Article 14(1), '[p]ersons designated to serve on the Panels shall be persons of high moral character and recognised competence in the fields of law, commerce, industry or finance, who may be relied upon to exercise independent judgment'. The Panel of Conciliators and the Panel of Arbitrators shall each consist of qualified persons.[91] Each Contracting State may designate to each Panel four persons, while the Chairman of ICSID may designate ten persons to each panel.[92] Panel members are to serve for renewable periods of six years.[93] Members of conciliation commissions and arbitral tribunals may be appointed from the Panels or from outside them.[94]

The most often chosen method is arbitration by a tribunal of three arbitrators, while conciliation is rarely used.[95] In fact, arbitration cases under the ICSID Convention constitute 89.5 per cent of cases registered under the Convention and arbitration cases under Additional Facilities constitute 8.8 per cent. In total, arbitration cases constitute 98.3 per cent, while conciliation cases remain merely 1.7 per cent of cases registered under the ICSID Convention and Additional Facilities.[96] The arbitral tribunal under the ICSID Convention consists of a sole arbitrator or any uneven number of arbitrators appointed as the parties shall agree. If the parties cannot agree on this matter, the tribunal is to consist of three arbitrators, one arbitrator appointed by each party and the third, who is to be the president of the tribunal, appointed by agreement of the parties.[97]

Related to this, the disqualification of arbitrators must be examined.[98] Under Article 57 of the ICSID Convention, a party may propose to a tribunal the disqualification of any of its members on account of any fact indicating a manifest lack of the qualities required by paragraph (1) of Article 14 of the Convention.[99] The decision on any proposal to disqualify an arbitrator is to be taken by the other members of the tribunal. Where those members are equally divided, or in the case of a proposal to disqualify a sole conciliator or arbitrator, or a majority of the arbitrators, the Chairman of ICSID Administrative Council is to take that decision.[100] In reality, the increasing number of challenges have been initiated at ICSID. The most usual ground for arbitrator challenges relates to an alleged absence of impartiality or independence.[101] The increased challenges to arbitrator appointment seem to highlight the importance of impartiality and independence of the arbitrator.[102]

---

[90] The ICSID Convention, Article 3. See also Article 12.
[91] *Ibid.*, Article 12.   [92] *Ibid.*, Article 13.   [93] *Ibid.*, Article 15(1).
[94] *Ibid.* Articles 31 and 40.
[95] C. Schreuer, 'International Centre for Settlement of Investment Disputes (ICSID)' (hereafter ICSID) in *Max Planck Encyclopaedia*, para. 23.
[96] *ICSID Caseload – Statistics*, Issue 2016-2, p. 8.
[97] The ICSID Convention, Article 37(2)(b).
[98] Generally on this issue, see B. S. Vasani and S. A. Palmer, 'Challenge and Disqualification of Arbitrators at ICSID: A New Dawn?' (2015) 30 *ICSID Review*, pp. 194–216.
[99] See also Rule 9 of Rules of Procedure for Arbitration Proceedings (Arbitration Rules).
[100] The ICSID Convention, Article 58. The President of the World Bank is to be *ex officio* Chairman of the Administrative Council. *Ibid.*, Article 5.
[101] M. Kinnear, 'Challenge of Arbitrators at ICSID: An Overview' (2014) 108 *Proceedings of the Annual Meeting, American Society of International Law*, p. 414.
[102] See also Chapter 5, section 3.2 of this book.

3.1.3 Jurisdiction

Under Article 25(1) of the ICSID Convention:

> The jurisdiction of the Centre shall extend to any legal dispute arising directly out of an investment, between a Contracting State (or any constituent subdivision or agency of a Contracting State designated to the Centre by that State) and a national of another Contracting State, which the parties to the dispute consent in writing to submit to the Centre. When the parties have given their consent, no party may withdraw its consent unilaterally.

This provision needs further explanation.

(i) *Ratione personae*: The jurisdiction of the Centre is limited to a Contracting State and a national of another Contracting State. The term a 'national of another Contracting State' comprises both natural and juridical persons.[103] Proceedings under the ICSID Convention are always mixed in the sense that ICSID deals with between Contracting States on the one hand and natural or juridical persons on the other hand.[104] As noted, the Additional Facility Rules expanded the application of ICSID's facilities so as to include disputes which are not within the jurisdiction of the Centre. Thus, a State and a national of another State may agree to use the Additional Facility, even if one of the States concerned (i.e. the State Party to the dispute or the State of nationality of the private party) is not a party to the ICSID Convention.[105] Prior to initiating proceedings, however, the agreement of the parties to accept the jurisdiction of the Additional Facility must be approved by the Secretary-General.[106]

(ii) *Ratione materiae*: The jurisdiction of the Centre is limited to 'any legal dispute arising directly out of an investment'. Although the concept of 'investment' is not defined in the ICSID Convention, many bilateral and multilateral investment treaties contain definition of 'investment'.[107] As provided in Article 25(1) of the ICSID Convention, separate consent in writing by the parties is needed to establish the jurisdiction of the Centre.[108] Many bilateral investment treaties and regional multilateral treaties, such as the 1992 North American Free Trade Agreement (NAFTA),[109] contain clauses offering access to ICSID to the nationals of one of the parties to the treaty against the other party to the treaty.[110] Once consent to ICSID arbitration has been given, any other remedy is to be excluded. It follows that unless otherwise agreed, no domestic courts are available for the settlement of disputes that have been submitted to the Centre.[111]

---

[103] The ICSID Convention, Article 25(2). [104] Schreuer, 'ICSID', para. 26.
[105] Additional Facility Rules, Article 2. [106] *Ibid.*, Article 4. See also Mackenzie *et al.*, *Manual*, pp. 135-6.
[107] Schreuer, 'ICSID', para. 25; Mackenzie *et al.*, *Manual*, p. 136.
[108] Schreuer, 'ICSID', para. 28. [109] Text in: (1993) 32 *ILM*, p. 289. Entered into force 1 January 1994.
[110] Schreuer, 'ICSID', para. 29. [111] *Ibid.*, para. 35; The ICSID Convention, Article 26.

(iii) *Ratione temporis*: The ICSID Convention and the Additional Facility Rules contain no time limits for the submission of disputes to ICSID. This matter is governed by the parties' consent.[112]

(iv) *Provisional measures*: Under Article 47 of the ICSID Convention, the arbitral tribunal may recommend any provisional measures which should be taken to preserve the respective rights of either party.[113] At any time during the proceeding, a party may request that provisional measures for the preservation of its rights be recommended by the tribunal. Accordingly, a party is allowed to make a request before constitution of the tribunal. In this case, the Secretary-General of the ICSID Secretariat is to fix time limits for the parties to present observations on the request, so that the request and observations may be considered by the arbitral tribunal promptly upon its constitution.[114] The arbitral tribunal may also recommend provisional measures on its own initiative or recommend measures other than those specified in a request. It may at any time modify or revoke its recommendations.[115] The term 'recommend' appears to deny the binding force of provisional measures. Nonetheless, ICSID tribunals have advocated the binding nature of these measures.[116] In the *Tokios Tokelės v. Ukraine* case, the Arbitral Tribunal clearly accepted the binding force of provisional measures, stating that:

> It is to be recalled that, according to a well-established principle laid down by the jurisprudence of the ICSID tribunals, provisional measures 'recommended' by an ICSID tribunal are legally compulsory; they are in effect 'ordered' by the tribunal, and the parties are under a legal obligation to comply with them.[117]

Furthermore, in *City Oriente Limited v. Ecuador*, the Arbitral Tribunal ruled that: '[A] failure to comply with orders given to respondents by the Tribunal in accordance with Article 47 of the Convention will entail a violation of Article 26 thereof, and engage Respondents' liability.'[118] On the other hand, ICSID has no advisory jurisdiction under the Convention.[119]

3.1.4 Applicable Law

Under Article 42(1) of the ICSID Convention, the Arbitral Tribunal is to decide a dispute in accordance with such rules of law as may be agreed by the parties.[120] In the absence of such agreement, the Tribunal shall apply the law of the Contracting State Party to the dispute and such rules of international law as may be applicable. Thus the applicable law comprises both municipal and international law. Interestingly, a finding of *non liquet* is prohibited

---

[112] Mackenzie *et al.*, *Manual*, pp. 137–8.
[113] See also Arbitration Rules, Rule 39(1).
[114] *Ibid.*, Rule 39(5).   [115] *Ibid.*, Rule 39(3).
[116] Further, 'Article 47' in Schreuer *et al.* (eds.), *The ICSID Convention*, pp. 764–5.
[117] *Tokios Tokelės v. Ukraine* (ICSID Case No. ARB/02/18), Order No. 1, 1 July 2003, para. 4.
[118] *City Oriente Limited v. Republic of Ecuador and Empresa Estatal Petróleos del Ecuador (Petroecuador)* (ICSID Case No. ARB/06/21), 19 November 2007, para. 53.
[119] Mackenzie *et al.*, *Manual*, p. 138.
[120] By way of example, Article 1131(1) of NAFTA refers exclusively to international law.

under Article 42(2). The Tribunal is also empowered to decide a dispute *ex aequo et bono* if the parties so agree by virtue of Article 42(3).

3.1.5 The Award

Under Article 53(1) of the ICSID Convention, the award is binding on the parties and shall not be subject to any appeal or to any other remedy except those provided for in this Convention. Accordingly, the arbitral award rendered under the ICSID Convention is not subject to any kind of domestic courts of the Contracting States.[121] Related to this, Article 54(1) of the ICSID Convention makes clear that:

> Each Contracting State shall recognise an award rendered pursuant to this Convention as binding and enforce the pecuniary obligations imposed by that award within its territories as if it were a final judgment of a court in that State.

Under Article 54(3) of the Convention, '[e]xecution of the award shall be governed by the laws concerning the execution of judgments in force in the State in whose territories such execution is sought'. At the same time, Article 55 of the Convention provides that:

> Nothing in Article 54 shall be construed as derogating from the law in force in any Contracting State relating to immunity of that State or of any foreign State from execution.

Here there is the risk that the award is not executed due to immunity from execution. In fact, arbitral tribunals under the ICSID Convention do not have the power to order execution of their own awards. Nor does the Convention enjoin the courts of States Parties to the Convention to enforce ICSID awards if this would be contrary to their law governing the immunity from execution of judgments and arbitral awards. Accordingly, a State whose courts refuse to execute an ICSID award for reasons of State immunity is not in violation of Article 54. As a commentary observed, Article 55 'may be seen as the Achilles' heel of the Convention'.[122] In the case of non-compliance of the award, a possible solution may be recourse to diplomatic protection. Related to this, Article 27(1) of the ICSID Convention stipulates that no Contracting State shall give diplomatic protection, 'unless such other Contracting State shall have failed to abide by and comply with the award rendered in such dispute'. The language of the provision seems to suggest that the right of diplomatic protection will revive in case of non-compliance with the award.[123]

When any dispute arises with regard to the meaning or scope of an award, either party may request interpretation of the award by an application in writing addressed to the Secretary-General.[124] Likewise, either party may also request revision of the award on the

---

[121] Schreuer, 'ICSID', para. 69.
[122] Schreuer et al., *The ICSID Convention*, p. 1154.   [123] *Ibid.*, p. 426.
[124] The ICSID Convention, Article 50.

ground of discovery of some fact of such a nature as decisively to affect the award in accordance with Article 51(1) of the ICSID Convention.

Under Article 52 of the Convention, either party may request annulment of the award to an ad hoc committee of three persons. The grounds for annulment are listed exclusively in Article 52(1) of the Convention. They are:

(a) that the Tribunal was not properly constituted,
(b) that the Tribunal has manifestly exceeded its powers,
(c) that there was corruption on the part of a member of the Tribunal,
(d) that there has been a serious departure from a fundamental rule of procedure, or
(e) that the award has failed to state the reasons on which it is based.

In practice, however, annulment of the award remains rather rare.[125]

3.2 The Iran–United States Claims Tribunal

3.2.1 General Considerations

The Iran–United States Claims Tribunal was established as one part of normalisation of international relations between Iran and the United States on the basis of the 1981 Algiers Accords (General Declaration) as part of the solution to the Tehran hostage crisis between the two States, mediated by the Algerian Government.[126]

The Iran-US Claims Tribunal is governed by the Claims Settlement Declaration, which forms part of the Algiers Accords.[127] As stated in Article I of the Declaration, the Tribunal is the 'binding third-party arbitration'. It sits in The Hague.[128] Under Article III(1) of the Claims Settlement Declaration, the Tribunal consists of nine members or such larger multiple of three as Iran and the United States may agree are necessary to conduct its business expeditiously. Each government appoints one-third of the members and the members so appointed shall, by mutual agreement, select the remaining third of the members and appoint one of the latter category to be the president of the Tribunal. In principle, members of the Tribunal are to be appointed and the Tribunal is to conduct its business in accordance with the arbitration rules of the United Nations Commission on International Trade Law (UNCITRAL).[129] Rules of Procedures are set out in Tribunal Rules of Procedure of 3 May 1983.[130]

---

[125] From 2011, the number of decisions annulling the award in part or in full remains only three. *ICSID Caseload – Statistics*, Issue 2016-2, p. 17. See also Mackenzie *et al.*, *Manual*, pp. 147–8; J. G. Merrills, *International Dispute Settlement*, 6th edn (Cambridge University Press, 2017), p. 117.

[126] Declaration of the Government of the Democratic and Popular Republic of Algeria (General Declaration) (1981) 20 *ILM*, p. 224; Tams and Tzanakopoulos, *Basic Documents*, p. 93. See also D. L. Jones, 'The Iran-United States Claims Tribunal: Private Rights and State Responsibility' (1984) 24 *Virginia Journal of International Law*, p. 269.

[127] Declaration of the Government of the Democratic and Popular Republic of Algeria Concerning the Settlement of Claims by the Government of the United States of America and the Government of the Islamic Republic of Iran (the Claims Settlement Declaration) (1981) 20 *ILM*, p. 224; Tams and Tzanakopoulos, *Basic Documents*, p. 766.

[128] The Claims Settlement Declaration, Article VI(1).

[129] *Ibid.*, Article III(2).

[130] The document was reproduced in Tams and Tzanakopoulos, *Basic Documents*, p. 768.

353 Settlement of Disputes Involving Non-State Actors

The mixed character of the Iran-US Claims Tribunal is reflected in two aspects of the Tribunal's function.[131] First, the Tribunal deals with dispute between the two governments (i.e. Iran and the United States) and disputes between a private party on the one hand and a government. Second, it involves the interpretation and application of international law and municipal law as well as general principles of law. The mixed character was pronounced by the Tribunal as follows:

> While this Tribunal is clearly an international tribunal established by treaty and while some of its cases involve disputes between the two Governments and involve the interpretation and application of public international law, most disputes (including all of those brought by dual nationals) involve a private party on one side and a Government or Government-controlled entity on the other, and many involve primarily issues of municipal law and general principles of law.[132]

3.2.2 Jurisdiction of the Tribunal

The scope of the Tribunal's jurisdiction is specified by the Algiers Declarations as follows.[133]

(i) *Ratione personae*: *Locus standi* of the Tribunal is limited to nationals of Iran and nationals of the United States and to each government. A national of Iran may only claim against the United States Government and a US national may only claim against the Iranian Government.[134] It is noteworthy that States and private persons are given equal judicial status before the Tribunal.[135] In this context, an issue arises with regard to the Tribunal's jurisdiction over claims brought by dual Iran-United States nationals. The Tribunal took the position that it had jurisdiction over claims against Iran by dual Iran-United States nationals when the 'dominant and effective nationality' of the claimant at the relevant time was that of the United States.[136]

(ii) *Ratione temporis*: The Tribunal's jurisdiction is limited to claims that arose prior to 19 January 1981, that were outstanding on that date and that were filed with the Tribunal within one year from that date (i.e. 19 January 1982).[137] Accordingly, the number of the claims is finite. In total, some 3,816 claims were said to be filed.[138]

(iii) *Ratione materiae*: The Tribunal has jurisdiction over claims of nationals that arise out of debt, contracts, expropriations or other measures affecting property rights and any counterclaim that arises out of the same contract, transaction or occurrence that constitutes

---

[131] Further, see Jones, 'The Iran-United States Claims Tribunal', pp. 259–85.
[132] Iran-United States Claims Tribunal, Decision in Case No. A/18, 6 April 1984 (1984) 23 *ILM*, p. 498.
[133] C. Pinto, 'Iran-United States Claims Tribunal' in *Max Planck Encyclopaedia*, paras. 28–35.
[134] Claims of less than US$ 250,000 were to be presented by the claimants' government. The Claims Settlement Declaration, Article III(3).
[135] J. Collier and V. Lowe, *The Settlement of Disputes in International Law: Institutions and Procedures* (Oxford University Press, 1999), p. 77.
[136] Iran-United States Claims Tribunal, Case No. A/18, 6 April 1984 (1984) 23 *ILM*, p. 501. The Tribunal went to add that: 'In cases where the Tribunal finds jurisdiction based upon a dominant and effective nationality of the claimant, the other nationality may remain relevant to the merits of the claim.' *Ibid.*, p. 502.
[137] The Claims Settlement Declaration, Articles II(1) and III(4).
[138] Pinto, 'Iran-United States Claims Tribunal', para. 45.

the subject matter of the national's claim.[139] It also has jurisdiction over official claims of the United States and Iran against each other arising out of contractual arrangements between them for the purchase and sale of goods and services and any dispute as to the interpretation or performance of any provision of the General Declaration.[140] However, the following categories of claims were excluded from the Tribunal's jurisdiction:

(a) the seizure of the fifty-two United States nationals on 4 November 1979
(b) their subsequent detention
(c) injury to United States property or property of the United States nationals within the United States Embassy compound in Tehran after 3 November 1979
(d) injury to the United States nationals or their property as a result of popular movements in the course of the Islamic Revolution in Iran which were not an act of the Government of Iran[141]
(e) claims arising out of the actions of the United States in response to the conduct described in Paragraph 11 of the General Declaration
(f) claims arising under a binding contract between the parties specifically providing that any disputes thereunder shall be within the sole jurisdiction of the competent Iranian courts in response to the Majlis position[142]
(g) late-filed claims.

3.2.3 Applicable Law

The Tribunal is empowered to apply both rules of public international law and those of private law.[143] The Tribunal has a wide discretion as to the choice of the applicable law that comprises both international law and private law.[144] Furthermore, the Tribunal can decide *ex aequo et bono* only if the arbitrating parties have expressly and in writing authorised it to do so.[145] In principle, all awards and other decisions are to be made available to the public in accordance with Article 32(5) of the Tribunal Rules.

3.2.4 Implementation of Awards of the Tribunal

Under Article IV(1) of the Claims Settlement Declaration, all decisions and awards of the Tribunal shall be final and binding. To implement the awards of the Tribunal, Iran agreed to establish a Security Account of US$1 billion with a view to be used for the sole purpose of securing the payment of, and paying, claims against Iran in accordance with the Claims Settlement Agreement.[146] Whenever the balance in the Security Account has fallen below US$500 million, Iran is obliged to promptly make new deposits sufficient to maintain a minimum balance of US$500 million in the Account.[147] In so doing, the payment to claimants of the United States against Iran is to be secured.

---

[139] The Claims Settlement Declaration, Article II(1).   [140] *Ibid.*, Article II(2) and (3).
[141] General Declaration, para. 11.   [142] The Claims Settlement Declaration, Article II(1).
[143] The Claims Settlement Declaration, Article V.
[144] Collier and Lowe, *The Settlement of Disputes*, p. 82; Pinto, 'Iran-United States Claims Tribunal', paras. 42–3.
[145] Tribunal Rules of Procedure, Article 33(2).
[146] General Declaration, para. 7.   [147] *Ibid.*

However, there is no comparable mechanism for securing awards in favour of Iranian claimants against the United States. Thus, in Case A/21, Iran contended that the United States was obligated to satisfy awards rendered by the Tribunal in favour of Iran against nationals of the United States. According to Iran, Algiers Declarations establish a 'reciprocal system of commitments' that obligates the United States to pay awards if its nationals fail to do so.[148] Even though the Tribunal did not accept Iran's contention, it held that: '[T]he Algiers Declarations impose upon the United States a duty to implement the Algiers Declarations in good faith so as to ensure that the jurisdiction and authority of the tribunal are respected';[149] and that: 'It is therefore incumbent on each State Party to provide some procedure or mechanism whereby enforcement may be obtained within its national jurisdiction, and to ensure that the successful Party has access thereto.'[150]

In summary, the Iran-United States Claims Tribunal differs from ICSID in three respects. First, unlike the ICSID, *locus standi* of the Iran-United States Claims Tribunal is strictly limited to Iran and United States nationals and the two governments. Second, unlike the ICSID, the role of the Iran-United States Claims Tribunal is only temporal. Third and importantly, the Iran-United States Claims Tribunal constituted a part of the peace process to normalise the Iran-United States relationship, while ICSID can be regarded as one part of the mechanism for promoting economic development.

4 UNITED NATIONS COMPENSATION COMMISSION

4.1 Outline of the UNCC

4.1.1 Background

Compensation for losses and damages from armed conflicts constitutes an important issue in the process of restoring peace. In approaching this issue, the United Nations Compensation Commission (UNCC) merits discussion since it performed a fact-finding function to examine claims submitted not only by States but also by non-State actors, such as international organisations, corporations and individuals.[151]

The UNCC was established in 1991 as a subsidiary organ of the UN Security Council after Iraq's unlawful invasion of Kuwait.[152] In this regard, UN Security Council Resolution 687 of 1991 reaffirmed that Iraq was 'liable under international law for any direct loss, damage, including environmental damage and the depletion of natural resources, or injury to foreign Governments, nationals and corporations, as a result of Iraq's unlawful invasion and occupation of Kuwait'.[153] It then decided to create a fund to pay compensation for claims that fall within paragraph 16 of the Resolution and to establish a

---

[148] Iran-United States Claims Tribunal, Decision in Case No. A/21, 4 May 1987 (1987) 26 *ILM*, p. 1594, para. 2 and p. 1595, para. 4.   [149] *Ibid.*, p. 1598, para. 14.   [150] *Ibid.*, p. 1598, para. 15.
[151] For an outline of the UNCC, see its homepage: www.uncc.ch/home. See also P. Sands *et al.*, *Principles of International Environmental Law*, 3rd edn (Cambridge University Press, 2012), pp. 720-5.
[152] UN Security Council Resolution 692(1991) of 20 May 1991, para. 3. For the background of the UNCC, see V. Heiskanen, 'The United Nations Compensation Commission' (2002) 296 *RCADI*, pp. 265-9.
[153] Resolution 687 (1991), S/RES/687 (1991), 8 April 1991, para. 16.

Commission that will administer the fund.[154] It thus directed the UN Secretary-General to develop and present to the Security Council for decision recommendations for the fund to meet the requirement for the payment of claims.[155] Following the resolution, the Report of the Secretary-General was submitted on 2 May 1991.[156] It stressed that:

> The Commission is not a court or an arbitral tribunal before which the parties appear; it is a political organ that performs an essentially fact-finding function of examining claims, verifying their validity, evaluating losses, assessing payments and resolving disputed claims. It is only in this last respect that a quasi-judicial function may be involved.[157]

As stated in the above passage, the primary task of the UNCC was to process claims and pay compensation for losses and damage suffered by individuals, corporations, governments and international organisations as a direct result of Iraq's invasion of Kuwait.[158] Compensation to be paid by Iraq was drawn from the United Nations Compensation Fund which received 5 per cent of the revenue generated from the export of Iraqi petroleum and petroleum products.[159] The fixing of the percentage in this regard would permit Iraq to carry out its obligation to give compensation to successful claimants without the risk of serious detrimental effects on its economy.[160]

4.1.2 The Structure of the UNCC

The UNCC comprised a Governing Council, panels of Commissioners and a Secretariat.[161] The Geneva-based Secretariat, headed by the Executive Secretary, provided administrative, technical and legal support to the Governing Council and the panels of Commissioners. Under Article 14 of the Provisional Rules,[162] the Secretariat was also empowered to make a preliminary assessment of the claims received in order to determine whether they meet the formal requirements established by the Governing Council.

The Governing Council consisted of fifteen Member States each representing the membership of the UN Security Council at any given time. The Governing Council was the political decision-making organ and it had the responsibility to set the policy of the Commission within the framework of relevant UN Security Council resolutions. Unlike the UN Security Council, there was no veto power at the Governing Council.[163]

---

[154] *Ibid.*, para. 18.   [155] *Ibid.*, para. 19.
[156] Report of the Secretary-General Pursuant to Paragraph 19 of Security Council Resolution 687 (1991), S/22559, 2 May 1991 (hereafter the 1991 Secretary-General Report).
[157] *Ibid.*, p. 7, para. 20.
[158] T. A. Mensah, 'United Nations Compensation Commission (UNCC)' in *Max Planck Encyclopaedia*, para. 21.
[159] UN Security Council Resolution 1483 (2003), S/RES 1483 (2003), 22 May 2003, para. 21.
[160] L. Boisson de Chazournes and D. Campanelli, 'The United Nations Compensation Commission: Time for an Assessment?' in A. Fischer-Lescano *et al.* (eds.), *Peace in Liberty: Festschrift fur Michael Bothe zum 70. Geburtstag* (Barden-Barden: Nomos, 2008), p. 16.
[161] Part I of the 1991 Secretary-General Report. Further, see Boisson de Chazournes and Campanelli, 'The United Nations Compensation Commission', pp. 7-9; Heiskanen, 'The United Nations Compensation Commission', pp. 270-5; Mensah, 'United Nations Compensation Commission (UNCC)', paras. 9-18; www.uncc.ch/who-we-are.
[162] Provisional Rules for Claims Procedure, S/AC.26/1992/10, 26 June 1992.
[163] Boisson de Chazournes and Campanelli, 'The United Nations Compensation Commission', p. 7.

The Commissioners, who were independent experts of law and other disciplines,[164] performed three functions:

- determining whether the damages were suffered as a direct result of Iraq's invasion and occupation of Kuwait
- assessing the value of losses suffered by claimants
- recommending compensation in reports to the Governing Council.

The Commissioners worked in panels of three members and altogether nineteen panels of Commissioners were established to review different categories of claims. Under Article 31, the Commission was directed to apply 'Security Council Resolution 687 (1991) and other relevant Security Council resolutions, the criteria established by the Governing Council for particular categories of claims, and any pertinent decisions of the Governing Council' and, where necessary, 'other relevant rules of international law'. The determination made by the panels of Commissioners was to be submitted to the Governing Council in the form of a 'report and recommendations'. The Commissioners had no formal decision-making powers; it had only recommendatory powers towards the Governing Council. Under Article 40(1) of the Provisional Rules, the amounts recommended by the panels of Commissioners were subject to approval by the Governing Council and the Council could review the amounts recommended and, where appropriate, increase or reduce them.[165] The interplay between the political organ (i.e. the Governing Council) and fact-finding organ (i.e. the panels of Commissioners) can be said to be original.[166] The Commissioners completed their work in June 2005.

4.1.3 Principal Features of the UNCC

The UNCC presents some unique features. The first noteworthy feature concerns a wide circle of subjects that are eligible to claim for damage. Claims to the Commission may be submitted by States, international organisations, corporations and individuals. Notably, eligible claimants included not only private persons but also States.[167] In fact, nearly one hundred governments submitted claims for their nationals, corporations and/or themselves. In addition, thirteen offices of three international organisations (i.e. the United Nations Development Programme (UNDP), the United Nations High Commissioner for Refugees (UNHCR) and the United Nations Relief and Works Agency for Palestine Refugees in the Near East (UNRWA)) submitted claims for individuals who were not in a position to have their claims filed by governments.[168]

The second feature relates to multiple categories of damage covered. In this regard, the UNCC accepted for filing six categories (A–F) of claims.[169] Category A was for individuals

---

[164] Under Article 19(2), commissioners were experts in fields such as finance, law, accounting, insurance, environmental damage assessment, oil, trade and engineering.
[165] Some criticised that the mechanism lacked independence from political influence. See F. L. Kirgis, Jr, 'The Security Council's First Fifty Years' (1995) 89 *AJIL*, p. 525.
[166] Boisson de Chazournes and Campanelli, 'The United Nations Compensation Commission', p. 8.
[167] *Ibid.*, p. 9.   [168] See www.uncc.ch/claims.
[169] Further, see Mensah, 'United Nations Compensation Commission (UNCC)', paras. 28–47; Boisson de Chazournes and Campanelli, 'The United Nations Compensation Commission', p. 10; www.uncc.ch/claims. In 2004, the Governing Council decided that the Council would not consider or accept any further requests for the late filing of claim in any claims' category. See Decision 219, S/AC.26/Dec. 219 (2004).

who had to leave Kuwait or Iraq during the invasion. Category B concerned claims for serious personal injury and/or death of an immediate family member. Category C related to individual claims for less than US$100,000 for various losses. Category D concerned individual claims for more than US$100,000 for various losses. Category E was for claims of corporations, other private legal entities and public sector enterprises. This category was further divided into four subcategories: E1 concerning claims made by the oil sector; E2 concerning claims made by non-Kuwaiti corporations that did not fall into any other subcategory of category E; E3 relating to claims of non-Kuwaiti corporations belonging to the field of construction and engineering, excluding corporations of the oil sector; and E4 concerning claims of Kuwaiti corporations, excluding claims of oil corporations. Finally, category F related to claims filed by governments and international organisations. This category was further organised in four subcategories: F1 concerning claims or losses suffered by State and international organisations; F2 relating to claims of Jordan and Saudi Arabia; F3 dealing with claims filed by Kuwait, excluding environmental claims; and F4 concerning claims for environmental damage. In addition, a mixed subcategory E/F concerned claims with regard to export guarantee and insurance submitted both under categories E and F. Overall the six categories can be divided into three categories in accordance with eligible claimants: claims of individuals (categories A, B, C and D), claims by corporations (category E) and claims from governments and international organisations (category F).

The third noteworthy feature pertains to differentiated evidence requirement according to urgency of claims.[170] The claims before the UNCC can be divided into two principal groups: urgent and non-urgent claims. Urgent claims contained categories A, B and C that were given priority over other categories. Evidentiary requirements for urgent claims were lower than those required for non-urgent claims. For categories A and B, the claimants were required to provide simple documentation of the fact and date of departure from Iraq/Kuwait or date of injury.[171] For category C, claims were required to be documented by appropriate evidence of the circumstances and amount of the claimed loss.[172] As a consequence, urgent claims benefited from a simplified evidence requirement. On the other hand, claims in categories D, E and F were to be supported by documentary and other appropriate evidence sufficient to demonstrate the circumstances and amount of the claimed loss.[173]

4.2 The UNCC and Claims for Environmental Damage

'The environment has always been a silent casualty of conflict.'[174] As the United Nations Environment Programme (UNEP) aptly stated, armed conflicts are a source of serious threats to the environment. Environmental damage by armed conflicts was exemplified by the 1991 Gulf War, during which Kuwait's oil wells were set on fire and millions of tonnes of crude oil were discharged into waterways. Generally, armed conflicts have adverse impacts on

---

[170] Boisson de Chazournes and Campanelli, 'The United Nations Compensation Commission', pp. 10–12; www.uncc.ch/claims-processing.
[171] Article 35(2)(a) and (b) of the Provisional Rules for Claims Procedure.
[172] Article 35(2)(c) of the Provisional Rules for Claims Procedure.
[173] Article 35(3) of the Provisional Rules for Claims Procedure.
[174] UNEP, *From Conflict to Peacebuilding: The Role of Natural Resources and the Environment* (Nairobi: UNEP, 2009), p. 15.

the environment in three ways. The first is direct impacts that are caused by the physical destruction of ecosystems and wildlife or the release of polluting and hazardous substances into the natural environment during conflict. The second is indirect impacts that result from the coping strategies used by local and displaced populations to survive the socio-economic disruption and loss of basic services caused by conflict. The third is institutional impacts that are caused by a disruption of various State institutions leading to the collapse of positive environmental practices.[175] Thus Principle 24 of the Rio Declaration stated that:

> Warfare is inherently destructive of sustainable development. States shall therefore respect international law providing protection for the environment in times of armed conflict and cooperate in its further development, as necessary.

It is beyond serious argument that a party to the conflict which violates relevant rules of international humanitarian law is liable to compensation.[176] When environmental damage was caused by a party to the armed conflict, however, a difficult issue arises as to how it is possible to demand compensation. Even though a dispute concerning compensation for the breach of international humanitarian law can be referred to the ICJ, this is only exceptional.[177] It is also to be noted that *locus standi* before the Court is limited to States.

It was remarkable that the UNCC accepted claims for damages to the environment. In paragraph 35 of the Decision 7 of 1992, the Governing Council decided that payments would be available with respect to direct environmental damage and the depletion of natural resources as a result of Iraq's unlawful invasion and occupation of Kuwait. This would include losses or expenses resulting from:

(a) Abatement and prevention of environmental damage, including expenses directly relating to fighting oil fires and stemming the flow of oil in coastal and international waters;
(b) Reasonable measures already taken to clean and restore the environment or future measures which can be documented as reasonably necessary to clean and restore the environment;
(c) Reasonable monitoring and assessment of the environmental damage for the purposes of evaluating and abating the harm and restoring the environment;
(d) Reasonable monitoring of public health and performing medical screenings for the purposes of investigation and combating increased health risks as a result of the environmental damage; and
(e) Depletion of or damage to natural resources.[178]

---

[175] *Ibid*. See also P.-M. Dupuy and J. E. Viñuales, *International Environmental Law* (Cambridge University Press, 2015), pp. 339 *et seq*.
[176] Article 91 of the Protocol Additional to the Geneva Conventions of 12 August 1949, and relating to the Protection of Victims of International Armed Conflicts (Protocol I), 8 June 1977.
[177] An example is *Case Concerning Armed Activities on the Territory of the Congo* (Democratic Republic of the Congo v. Uganda), Judgment of 19 December 2005, ICJ Reports 2005, p. 168.
[178] Decision taken by the Governing Council of the United Nations Compensation Commission During Its Third Session, at the 18th Meeting, held on 28 November 1991, as revised at the 24th Meeting held on 16 March 1992, S/AC.26/1991/7/Rev.1, 17 March 1991, pp. 7–8, para. 35.

A Panel of the Commission took the view that paragraph 35 of Governing Council Decision 7 did not give an exhaustive list of the activities and events that can give rise to compensable losses or expenses, but provided guidance in this matter.[179]

It is of particular interest to note that monitoring and assessment costs were listed as an independent head of liability. Compensation for the costs of monitoring and assessment would not be unreasonable since, for a claimant, monitoring and assessment would be needed to develop evidence to establish whether environmental damage has occurred and to quantify the extent of the resulting loss.[180] A monitoring and assessment activity could also be beneficial in alleviating the concerns of claimants regarding potential risks of damage and help to avoid unnecessary and wasteful measures to deal with non-existent or negligible risks. The Panel thus considered that: '[T]he possibility that a monitoring and assessment activity might not establish conclusively that environmental damage has been caused is not necessarily a valid reason for rejecting a claim for expenses resulting from that activity.'[181] Notably, compensation for the costs of monitoring and assessment is not merely to compensate the claimants for injury suffered but rather to safeguard a community interest of restoring the environment.[182]

Claims for damage to the environment are called category F4 claims. Category F4 claims can be divided into two groups. The first group comprised claims for environmental damage and the depletion of natural resources in the Persian Gulf region, including those resulting from oil-well fires and the discharge of oil into the sea. The second group comprised claims for costs incurred by governments outside of the region in providing assistance to countries that were directly affected by environmental damage, such as the alleviation of the damage caused by the oil-well fires and the prevention and clean up of pollution.[183] Category F claims could be filed only by governments and international organisations. According to the UNCC, the Commission received approximately 170 F4 claims seeking a total of approximately US$85 billion in compensation.[184]

Precisely speaking, the environmental damage concerned arose from Iraq's unlawful invasion and occupation of Kuwait, not from the breach of rules of international humanitarian law applicable to environmental protection during armed conflict. In other words, Iraq's obligation to pay compensation for environmental damage derived from the breach of the *jus ad bellum* (i.e. Article 2(4) of the UN Charter), not from any breach of the *jus in bello*.[185] Accordingly, the UNCC cannot be viewed as an example of compensation for

---

[179] Report and Recommendations made by the Panel of Commissioners Concerning the Second Instalment of 'F4' Claims, S/AC.26/2002/26, 3 October 2002, para. 22.

[180] Report and Recommendations made by the Panel of Commissioners Concerning the Second Instalment of 'F4' Claims, S/AC.26/2001/16, 22 June 2001, p. 13, paras. 29–30.

[181] *Ibid.*, p. 14, para. 32. See also O. Elias, 'The UN Compensation Commission and Liability for the Costs of Monitoring and Assessment of Environmental Damage' in M. Fitzmaurice and D. Sarooshi (eds.), *Issues of State Responsibility before International Judicial Institutions* (Oxford: Hart, 2004), pp. 226–8.

[182] Elias, 'The UN Compensation Commission and Liability for the Costs of Monitoring and Assessment of Environmental Damage', p. 235.

[183] www.uncc.ch/category-f.

[184] www.uncc.ch/claims.

[185] Y. Dinstein, 'Protection of the Environment in International Armed Conflict' (2001) 5 *Max Planck Yearbook of United Nations Law*, p. 548; L. Low and D. Hodgkinson, 'Compensation for Wartime Environmental Damage: Challenges to International Law After the Gulf War' (1994–5) 35 *Virginia Journal of International Law*, p. 456; M. N. Schmitt, 'Green War: An Assessment of the Environmental Law of International Armed Conflict' (1997) 22 *Yale Journal of International Law*, p. 92.

violation of environmental obligation during armed conflict. Even so, the UNCC sheds some light on the valuation of claims for environmental damage. Four points can be made here.

The first point relates to a duty to mitigate environmental damage.[186] In this regard, the F4 Panel stressed that:

> [E]ach claimant has a duty to mitigate environmental damage to the extent possible and reasonable in the circumstances. Indeed, in the view of the Panel, that duty is a necessary consequence of the common concern for the protection and conservation of the environment, and entails *obligations towards the international community* and future generations.[187]

The above passage seems to suggest that a duty to mitigate environmental damage can be viewed as an obligation *erga omnes*. Furthermore, the explicit reference to future generations implies that the obligation is inter-temporal by nature.

The second point pertains to valuation of environmental damage. Notably the F4 Panel accepted compensation for damage to natural resources without commercial value.[188] In fact, when valuating environmental damage, the Panel accepted 'habitat equivalency analysis' (HEA) as an appropriate method for determining the nature and extent of compensatory restoration that is necessary to compensate for the loss of ecological services that were provided by the resources before they were damaged.[189]

The third point concerns reimbursement of mutual assistance costs. In its second report, the Panel stated that: '[E]xpenses resulting from assistance rendered to countries in the Persian Gulf region to respond to environmental damage, or threat of damage to the environment or public health, qualify for compensation pursuant to Security Council Resolution 687 (1991) and Governing Council decision 7.'[190] It is noteworthy that the Panel accepted the reimbursement of mutual assistance costs that can be characterised as 'environmental solidarity costs'.[191] In fact, the UNCC received claims from six States for reimbursement of costs that they had incurred in assisting Gulf countries and recommended compensation in the amount of some US$8.3 million.[192]

---

[186] P. H. Sand, 'Compensation for Environmental Damage from the 1991 Gulf War' (2005) 35(6) *Environmental Policy and Law*, p. 246.

[187] Emphasis added. United Nations Compensation Commission Governing Council, Report and Recommendations made by the Panel of Commissioners Concerning the Third Instalment of 'F4' Claims, S/AC.26/2003/31, 18 December 2003, p. 13, para. 42.

[188] United Nations Compensation Commission Governing Council, Report and Recommendations made by the Panel of Commissioners Concerning the Third Instalment of 'F4' Claims, S/AC.26/2005/10, 30 June 2005, p. 19, paras. 57–8.

[189] *Ibid.*, p. 100, para. 606; p. 74, para. 424. See also pp. 64–5, paras. 353–66; Sand, 'Compensation for Environmental Damage', p. 247; Sands *et al.*, *Principles of International Environmental Law*, p. 724.

[190] United Nations Compensation Commission Governing Council, Report and Recommendations made by the Panel of Commissioners Concerning the Third Instalment of 'F4' Claims, S/AC.26/2002/26, 3 October 2002, p. 11, para. 34.

[191] Sands *et al.*, *Principles of International Environmental Law*, p. 723; Sand, 'Compensation for Environmental Damage', p. 246.

[192] *Ibid.* Further, see S/AC.26/2002/26, p. 48, para. 347.

Finally, in 2005, the Guidelines for the Follow-up Programme for Environmental Awards were adopted by the Governing Council.[193] The Follow-up Programme aimed to ensure that the F4 award funds were spent in a transparent and appropriate manner on conducting the Environmental Projects. In 2011, the Government Council adopted a further decision concerning the fulfilment of the Follow-up Programme for Environmental Awards.[194] It can be considered that claims for environmental damage reflect community interests concerning environmental protection that are beyond the claimants' individual interests.[195]

5 SETTLEMENT OF DISPUTES BETWEEN AN INTERNATIONAL ORGANISATION AND ITS MEMBER STATES: JUDICIAL REVIEW

5.1 General Considerations

Even though it is not frequent, a dispute may arise between an international organisation and its Member States. As explained in Chapter 8, the ITLOS Sea-Bed Disputes Chamber is empowered to deal with a dispute between the International Sea-Bed Authority and a State Party.[196] However, an international organisation cannot be a party to proceedings before the ICJ. Thus a dispute between an international organisation, particularly the United Nations, and its Member States cannot be settled through contentious procedure of the Court. A possible solution may be to request an advisory opinion to the Court.[197] By way of illustration, the 1946 Convention on the Privileges and Immunities of the United Nations provides that:

> If a difference arises between the United Nations on the one hand and a Member on the other hand, a request shall be made for an advisory opinion on any legal question involved in accordance with Article 96 of the Charter and Article 65 of the Statute of the Court. The opinion given by the Court shall be accepted as decisive by the parties.[198]

As the non-binding character of an advisory opinion is not affected, no legal obstacles would arise with regard to the conclusion of a treaty of this kind.[199]

---

[193] United Nations Compensation Commission Governing Council, Decision Concerning Follow-up Programme for Environmental Claims Awards Taken by the Governing Council of the United Nations Compensation Commission at its 150th Meeting, on 8 December 2005, S/AC.26/Dec.258 (2005). See also Sands et al., *Principles of International Environmental Law*, p. 724.
[194] United Nations Compensation Commission Governing Council, Decision Concerning the Fulfilment of the Follow-up Programme for Environmental Awards Taken by the Governing Council of the United Nations Compensation Commission at its 176th Meeting, on 7 April 2011, S/AC.26/Dec.269 (2011), 7 April 2011.
[195] Sand, 'Compensation for Environmental Damage', p. 248.
[196] See Chapter 8, section 4.1.2 of this book.
[197] For advisory opinion, see Chapter 6, section 6 of this book.
[198] Article VIII, section 30. Text in: 1 *UNTS*, p. 15. Entered into force 17 September 1946.
[199] H. Thirlway, *The International Court of Justice* (Oxford University Press, 2016), p. 140. See also Chapter 6, section 6.4 of this book.

363 Settlement of Disputes Involving Non-State Actors

However, a more controversial issue is whether the ICJ can review the legality of resolutions of the organs of the United Nations, in particular, the Security Council.[200] As will be seen next, this issue sparked extensive debates particularly in the *Lockerbie* case.

5.2 The *Lockerbie* Case

The *Lockerbie* case related to the explosion of Pan Am flight 103 above the small town of Lockerbie in Scotland, killing 270 people, on 21 December 1988. In a joint declaration made on 27 November 1991, the United States and the United Kingdom asked Libya to surrender the suspects for trial, to accept responsibility for the actions of its officials, to reveal all information and evidence available to Libya and to pay compensation. During the Security Council's debate over what was to become Resolution 731, the United Kingdom and the United States had mentioned the possibility of pressing for sanctions against Libya, should it fail to comply with the terms of the resolution. This threat prompted Libya, on 3 March 1992, to institute two parallel proceedings before the ICJ against the United Kingdom and the United States, respectively, for having breached the Convention for the Suppression of Unlawful Acts against the Safety of Civil Aviation of 1971 (the Montreal Convention). In this regard, Libya invoked Article 14 of that Convention as a jurisdictional basis.

In its application, Libya asked the Court to adjudicate and declare that it had fully complied with all of its obligations under the Montreal Convention; that the United Kingdom and the United States had breached and continued to breach their legal obligations to Libya under Articles 5(2)(3), 7, 8(3) and 11 of that Convention;[201] and that the respondent States should desist from such violations and from using or threatening the use of force against Libya.[202] While, on the same day, the Libyan Government, acting under Article 41 of the ICJ Statute, requested the latter to indicate provisional measures,[203] the United Kingdom and the United States asked the Court to reject the applicant's request for provisional measures.

On 31 March 1992, three days after the oral hearings of the ICJ devoted to the Libyan request for provisional measures, but prior to any decision thereon, the UN Security Council adopted Resolution 748 determining that Libya failed to respond fully and effectively to Resolution 731. In this resolution, the Security Council, acting under Chapter VII of the Charter, decided that Libya must forthwith comply with Resolution 731 and commit itself to cease definitively all forms of terrorism; and that, starting

---

[200] Generally on this issue, see R. Kolb, *The International Court of Justice* (Oxford: Hart Publishing 2013), pp. 879 *et seq.*

[201] Article 5(2) of the Montreal Convention asks the Contracting States to take such measures as may be necessary to establish jurisdiction over alleged offenders found on their territory, unless they choose to extradite them. Article 7 of the Convention attributes jurisdiction to the State on whose territory the alleged offenders are found and adds that the territorial State shall have to proceed against the latter if it does not extradite them.

[202] *Questions of Interpretation and Application of the 1971 Montreal Convention arising from the Aerial Incident at Lockerbie* (Libyan Arab Jamahiriya v. United Kingdom) (Libyan Arab Jamahiriya v. USA) (hereafter the *Lockerbie* case), Order of 14 April 1992, ICJ Reports 1992, pp. 6–7, para. 7; pp. 117–18, para. 7.

[203] *Ibid.*, p. 8, para. 11; p. 119, para. 11.

from 15 April 1992, all States must take non-military sanctions by establishing an aerial embargo against Libya and by reducing the number of Libyan Diplomatic personnel on their territories.[204]

Noting that both Libya and the United States, as Members of the United Nations, are obliged to accept and carry out the decisions of the Security Council in accordance with Article 25 of the Charter, the majority opinion of the ICJ considered that 'prima facie this obligation extends to the decision contained in Resolution 748 (1992)'. It follows that 'in accordance with Article 103 of the Charter, the obligations of the parties in that respect prevail over their obligations under any other international agreement, including the Montreal Convention'.[205] In its orders of 14 April 1992, the Court thus found, by eleven votes to five, that the circumstances of the case are not such as to require the exercise of its power under Article 41 of the Statute to indicate provisional measures.[206]

The issue of its power to review the legality of the Security Council resolution was not examined by the Court in its order of 1992. While the ICJ, in its judgment of 1998, rejected preliminary objections of the respondents and upheld its jurisdiction,[207] it did not deal with the matter relating to the judicial review of the Security Council resolution.[208] As will be seen below, however, some members of the Court addressed judicial review.

5.3 Discussion

Some judges denied the Court's power to review the Security Council resolution. Judge Jennings stated that: 'The Court is not a revising body, it may not substitute its own discretion of that of the Security Council; nor would it in my view be a suitable body for doing that; nor is the forensic adversarial system suited to the making of political decisions.'[209] This view was further amplified by Judge Schwebel. In this regard, the learned judge highlighted, *inter alia*, three points.

First, '[t]he texts of the Charter of the United Nations and of the Statute of the Court furnish no shred of support for a conclusion that the Court possesses a power of judicial review in general, or a power to supervene the decisions of the Security Council in particular'.[210]

---

[204] UN Security Council Resolution 748, 31 March 1992.
[205] The *Lockerbie* case, ICJ Reports 1992, p. 15, para. 39; p. 126, para. 42.
[206] *Ibid.*, p. 15, para. 43; p. 127, para. 46.
[207] The *Lockerbie* case, Judgment of 27 February 1998, ICJ Reports 1998, pp. 30-1, para. 53; pp. 135-6, para. 53.
[208] After the ICJ judgment, Libya agreed on surrendering the suspects for proceedings in Camp Zeist (the Netherlands) under Scottish law before a Scottish Court. On 31 January 2001, the Scottish court at Camp Zeist sentenced Abdelbaset Ali Mohmed Al Megrahi to life imprisonment, whilst the second suspect, Al Amin Khalifa Fhimah, was acquitted. Although the judgment did not include compensation for the families of the victims, Libya declared its readiness to pay US$2.7 billion as compensation. A. L. Palulus and A. Dienelt, 'Lockerbie Cases (Libyan Arab Jamahiriya v. United Kingdom and United States of America)' in *Max Planck Encyclopaedia*, para. 21. See also J. P. Grant, 'Lockerbie Trial' in *Max Planck Encyclopaedia*.
[209] Dissenting Opinion of Judge Jennings in the *Lockerbie* case (Libya v. United Kingdom), Preliminary Objections, Judgment of 27 February 1998, ICJ Reports 1998, p. 111.
[210] Dissenting Opinion of Judge Schwebel, *ibid.*, pp. 75 and 166.

365 Settlement of Disputes Involving Non-State Actors

Second, at the San Francisco Conference, Belgium proposed that a State Party to a dispute which considered its rights under international law to have been infringed by a Council's recommendation or decision be permitted to request an advisory opinion from the Permanent Court of International Justice. However, this proposal was opposed by Great Powers Sponsors of the Conference and Belgium eventually withdrew its proposal.[211]

Third, the Court's judgment cannot bind the Security Council by the terms of Article 59 of the ICJ Statute.[212]

In many legal systems, review functions are entrusted to the very organ which is entitled to act.[213] In fact, the ICJ, in its advisory opinion of 1962, stated that:

> In the legal systems of States, there is often some procedure for determining the validity of even a legislative or governmental act, but no analogous procedure is to be found in the structure of the United Nations. Proposals made during the drafting of the Charter to place the ultimate authority to interpret the Charter in the International Court of Justice were not accepted.[214]

Likewise the Court, in its advisory opinion of 1971, clearly stated that: 'Undoubtedly, the Court does not possess powers of judicial review or appeal in respect of the decisions taken by the United Nations organs concerned.'[215] According to this view, the legality of the action of the UN Security Council is to be secured on self-censorship by the organ itself, not by the ICJ.

However, some members of the Court in the *Lockerbie* case took a more nuanced view. For instance, Judge Shahabuddeen argued that 'The validity of the resolution, though contested by Libya, has, *at this stage*, to be presumed.'[216] Judge Bedjaoui expressed the view that: '[T]he exercise of this possible jurisdiction would be premature *at the present stage* of a request for the indication of provisional measures, all that needs to be borne in mind is that the Court has not been seised of this vast dispute, brought before the Security Council.'[217] These statements seem to preserve the Court's power to review the legality of the resolution when dealing with the merits.

If the UN Security Council's power is unlimited, there will be no scope for judicial review. In order to review the validity of resolutions of the Council, there must be some limitations with the power of the Security Council. In this regard, the Appeals Chamber

---

[211] *Ibid.*, pp. 77–9 and 169–70. The opposing States were: the Soviet Union, the United States, France and the United Kingdom.

[212] *Ibid.*, pp. 80–1 and 171–2.

[213] L. Caflisch, 'Is the International Court Entitled to Review Security Council Resolutions Adopted under Chapter VII of the United Nations Charter?' in N. Al-Nauimi and R. Meese (eds.), *International Legal Issues Arising under the United Nations Decade of International Law* (The Hague: Kluwer, 1995), p. 655; Dissenting Opinion of Judge Schwebel, ICJ Reports 1998, pp. 76 and 167.

[214] *Certain Expenses of the United Nations (Article 17, paragraph 2, of the Charter)*, Advisory Opinion of 20 July 1962, ICJ Reports 1962, p. 168.

[215] *Legal Consequences for States of the Continued Presence of South Africa in Namibia (South West Africa) notwithstanding Security Council Resolution 276*, Advisory Opinion of 21 June 1971, ICJ Reports 1971, p. 45.

[216] Emphasis added. Separate Opinion of Judge Shahabuddeen, ICJ Reports 1992, pp. 28 and 140.

[217] Emphasis added. Dissenting Opinion of Judge Bedjaoui, *ibid.*, p. 41, para. 18; p. 151, para. 18.

of the International Criminal Tribunal for the former Yugoslavia (ICTY) in the *Tadic* case clearly stated that:

> The Security Council is an organ of an international organization, established by a treaty which serves as a constitutional framework for that organization. The Security Council is thus subjected to certain constitutional limitations, however broad its powers under the constitution may be. Those powers cannot, in any case, go beyond the limits of the jurisdiction of the Organisation at large, not to mention other specific limitations or those which may derive from the internal division of power within the Organisation.[218]

There are good reasons to argue that the UN Security Council must comply with principles of international law, such as the principle of good faith and the prohibition of abuse of rights.[219] In fact, measures set out in Security Council resolutions are required to comply with principles of the protection of human rights, humanitarian law and *jus cogens*. In this regard, the European Court of Human Rights, in the *Al-Jedda* case, considered that: '[T]here must be a presumption that the Security Council does not intend to impose any obligation on Member States to breach fundamental principles of human rights.'[220] Furthermore, the Swiss Federal Court, in the *Nada* case, accepted that the obligation to implement the Security Council's decisions was limited by norms of *jus cogens*.[221] As Judge ad hoc Lauterpacht stated in the *Crime of Genocide* case, the possibility that a Security Council resolution might inadvertently or in an unforeseen manner lead to a violation of *jus cogens* or human rights cannot be excluded.[222] If this is the case, there appears to be some scope for arguing that the ICJ has some power to examine the legality of Security Council resolutions, even though it cannot substitute its discretion for that of the Security Council.[223] In fact, the Court, in its advisory opinions, interpreted United Nations resolutions and examined their validity.[224] Yet, a drawback of judicial review may be that many States against which Chapter VII measures

---

[218] *Prosecutor v. Dusko Tadic a/k/a 'DULE'*, ICTY, Decision on the Defence Motion for Interlocutory Appeal on Jurisdiction, 2 October 1995, para. 28.

[219] V. Gowlland-Debbas, 'The Relationship between the International Court of Justice and the Security Council in the Light of the Lockerbie Case' (1994) 88 *AJIL*, p. 663. See also V. Gowlland-Debbas, 'Security Council Enforcement Action and Issues of State responsibility' (1994) 43 *ICLQ*, pp. 90–4.

[220] *Case of Al-Jedda v. The United Kingdom*, Application No. 27021/08, Judgment, 7 July 2011, para. 102.

[221] European Court of Human Rights, Grand Chamber, *Case of Nada v. Switzerland*, Application No. 10593/08, Judgment, 12 September 2012, para. 46; *Youssef Nada v. State Secretariat for Economic Affairs and Federal Department of Economic Affairs*, Administrative Appeal Judgment, Case No. 1A 45/2007; ILDC 461(CH 2007); BGE 133 II 450, 14 November 2007, para. 7 cited in *Oxford Reports on International Law in Domestic Courts*. However, the Swiss Federal Supreme Court considered that the Security Council was bound by *jus cogens* only. This view invited criticisms from a commentator because it imputed an enormous abundance of power to the Security Council. Analysis by Markus Lanter, *ibid.*, para. 3.

[222] Separate Opinion of Judge ad hoc Lauterpacht in *Application of the Convention on the Prevention and Punishment of the Crime of Genocide* (Bosnia and Herzegovina v. Serbia and Montenegro), Further Requests for the Indication of Provisional Measures, Order of 13 September 1993, ICJ Reports 1993, p. 441, para. 102.

[223] See, *ibid.*, p. 439, para. 99.

[224] See for instance, the *Certain Expenses* case, ICJ Reports 1962, pp. 179–80; the *Namibia* case, ICJ Reports 1971, p. 53, para. 115. See also Gowlland-Debbas, 'The Relationship', p. 669; by the same writer, 'Security Council', pp. 94 *et seq.*

are directed would henceforth be in a position to block these measures.[225] It must also be noted that the decisions of the Court cannot bind the Security Council. In any case it is inconceivable that the Court will lightly choose to pronounce the Security Council resolutions invalid.[226]

6 INTERNATIONAL ORGANISATIONS AND INDIVIDUALS

At present, the importance of international organisations in international relations cannot be overestimated. At the same time, the proliferation of these organisations creates at least two issues of dispute settlement. The first issue concerns the settlement of disputes between an international organisation and its staff, while the second issue pertains to remedies for individuals affected by projects financed by a multilateral financial institution. After a brief outline of the UN internal justice system, in particular, this section addresses the second issue.

6.1 UN Internal Justice System

Disputes between an international organisation and its staff can be regarded as internal disputes within the organisation. These disputes are to be settled in accordance with internal procedures of the organisation concerned. In the case of the United Nations, the new system of administration of justice became operational on 1 July 2009.[227] This is a two-tier judicial system on the basis of the United Nations Dispute Tribunal (UNDT) and the United Nations Appeals Tribunal (UNAT).[228] The new system is coordinated by the Office of Administration of Justice.[229]

The UNDT is the first instance court. It is composed of three full-time judges and two part-time judges.[230] It has jurisdiction to render judgment on appeals against administrative decisions taken by UN-related entities.[231] Normally cases before the UNDT are to be considered by a single judge.[232] The judgments and orders of the Dispute Tribunal shall be binding upon the parties, but are subject to appeal in accordance with the Statute of the UNAT.[233]

---

[225] Caflisch, 'Is the International Court Entitled to Review Security Council Resolutions', p. 662.
[226] Gowlland-Debbas, 'The Relationship', p. 670.
[227] The new system was established in 2007 by the UN General Assembly. See UN General Assembly Resolution, A/RES/61/261, 4 April 2007, para. 4.
[228] See www.un.org/en/oaj/. Further, see L. Otis and E. H. Reiter, 'The Reform of the United Nations Administration of Justice System: the United Nations Appeals Tribunal after One Year' (2011) 10 *The Law and Practice of International Courts and Tribunals*, pp. 405–28; A. Megzari, *The Internal Justice of the United Nations: A Critical History 1945–2015* (Leiden: Brill, 2015).
[229] See www.un.org/en/oaj/unjs/office.shtml. OAJ was established by the UN General Assembly. UN General Assembly Resolution, A/RES/62/228 of 22 December 2007, para. 10.
[230] Article 4(1) of the Statute of the United Nations Dispute Tribunal, available at: www.un.org/en/oaj/files/undt/basic/2008-12-24-undt-statute.pdf.
[231] The list of the entities is available at: www.un.org/en/oaj/dispute/jurisdiction.shtml. See also Article 2 of the Statute of the UNDT.
[232] Article 10(9) of the Statute of the UNDT.   [233] *Ibid.*, Article 11(3).

The UNAT is an appellate court to review appeals against judgments rendered by the UNDT. The UNAT shall be composed of seven judges[234] and exercise its function in New York.[235]

Normally cases before the UNAT are to be reviewed by a panel of three judges and shall be decided by a majority vote.[236] The Appeals Tribunal shall be competent to hear and pass judgment on an appeal filed against a judgment rendered by the UNDT in which it is asserted that the Dispute Tribunal has:

(a) Exceeded its jurisdiction or competence,
(b) Failed to exercise jurisdiction vested in it,
(c) Erred on a question of law,
(d) Committed an error in procedure, such as to affect the decision of the case, or
(e) Erred on a question of fact, resulting in a manifestly unreasonable decision.[237]

The judgments of the Appeals Tribunal shall be final and without appeal.[238]

Concerning the new system, the UNAT, in its Judgment No. 2010-UNAT-084, stated that:

The Dispute Tribunal and Appeals Tribunal established under the new system of administration of justice are a marked improvement on the earlier system on account of their independence, transparency, and professionalism.[239]

Since the judgments of the former Administrative Tribunal are not treated by the new tribunals as binding precedent, new jurisprudence will develop over time through the new system of justice.[240]

6.2 Inspection Panel of the World Bank

6.2.1 Remedies for Individuals

Projects financed by a multilateral financial institution can affect not only the borrowing States but also individuals and local communities in the States. Since international organisations rarely grant standing to individuals, however, it is impossible for individuals to bring a claim against an international organisation where conflicting assertions or interpretations on the issues of the facts and law were raised between the international organisation and individuals. Apart from international human rights tribunals, normally individuals do not have any standing before international courts and tribunals. Furthermore, one cannot easily expect that a borrowing State would seek redress for wrongs resulting from a financed project that affected individuals.[241] An issue thus arises

---

[234] Article 3(1) of the Statute of the United Nations Appeals Tribunal, available at: www.un.org/en/oaj/files/unat/basic/2012-04-11-statute.pdf.
[235] Ibid., Article 4(1).   [236] Ibid., Article 10(1).   [237] Ibid., Article 2(1).
[238] Ibid., Article 10(6).   [239] Judgment No. 2010-UNAT-084, 27 October 2010, para. 37.   [240] Ibid.
[241] Y. Wong and B. Mayer, 'The World Bank's Inspection Panel: A Tool for Accountability?' (2015) 6 *The World Bank Legal Review*, pp. 498-9.

with regard to redress for individuals affected by activities of a multilateral financial institution. In approaching this issue, the inspection procedure set out at multilateral development banks deserves serious consideration.

The inspection procedure aims to provide independent review of the activities of these banks and international remedies for non-State actors. It was, for the first time, created at the World Bank and subsequently similar procedures were established at other multilateral financial institutions, such as the Inter-American Development Bank, the International Finance Corporation, the Multilateral Investment Guarantee Agency, the Asian Development Bank, the European Bank for Reconstruction and Development and the African Development Bank.[242] Although these procedures have their own particularities, they commonly aim to provide redress or solution in response to complaints from project-affected people and to enhance accountability.[243] Since a detailed examination of each and every procedure is beyond the scope of this chapter, this section focuses on the World Bank Inspection Panel as an example since this is the pioneering mechanism in this matter.[244]

6.2.2 Outline of the Panel Procedure

In the late 1980s and early 1990s, widespread concern and protest were voiced from civil society and project-affected communities with regard to the social and environmental impacts of Bank-financed operations.[245] A central criticism was that the Bank failed to comply with its own policy commitments to prevent adverse social and environmental impacts. A 'development disaster' arising from non-compliance with Bank policies was exemplified by the Bank's funding of the Sardar Sarovar Dam project on the Narmada River in India that required the resettlement of some 120,000 people and caused devastating human and environmental consequences. The review of this project, known as the 1992 Morse Commission report, found the failure of the World Bank to comply with Bank policies.[246] Furthermore, the internal report compiled by Bank Vice President Willi

---

[242] E. Hey, 'The World Bank Inspection Panel and the Development of International Law' in N. Boschiero et al. (eds.), *International Courts and the Development of International Law* (The Hague: T. M. C. Asser Press, 2013), pp. 731–2. The relevant websites of the international financial institutions are available at: http://ewebapps.worldbank.org/apps/ip/Pages/Related%20Organizations.aspx.

[243] P. L. Lallas, 'Citizen-Driven Accountability: The Inspection Panel and Other Independent Accountability Mechanisms' (2013) *ASIL Proceedings*, pp. 313–14.

[244] For a detailed outline of the Inspection Panel, see The Inspection Panel at the World Bank: Operating Procedures April 2014 (hereafter the 2014 Operating Procedures), available at: http://ewebapps.worldbank.org/apps/ip/Pages/Panel-Mandate.aspx. The Inspection Panel, *Accountability at the World Bank: The Inspection Panel at 15 Years* (Washington DC: The World Bank, 2009). In addition, the term 'World Bank' refers to the International Bank for Reconstruction and Development (IBARD) and the International Development Association (IDA).

[245] For the background of the creation of the Inspection Panel, see *Accountability at the World Bank*, pp. 3–5; Wong and Mayer, 'The World Bank's Inspection Panel', pp. 496–7; Lallas, 'Citizen-Driven Accountability', pp. 309–10.

[246] B. Morse and T. R. Berger, *Sardar Sarovar: Report of the Independent Review* (Ottawa: Resource Futures International, 1992). See also T. R. Berger, 'The World Bank's Independent Review of India's Sardar Sarovar Projects' (1993) 9 *American University International Law Review*, pp. 33–48.

Wapenhans in 1992 criticised the Bank's 'culture of approval' to develop as many project as possible without giving adequate consideration to social and environmental impacts.[247] Moreover, the 1992 Rio Summit called for expanded participation of the public, including women and indigenous people, transparency and access to justice.[248]

Against that background, the Inspection Panel was established in September 1993 as an independent accountability mechanism of the World Bank[249] and became operational on 1 August 1994. The Panel, which is located within the World Bank's headquarters in Washington DC, consists of three members of different nationalities from Bank member countries.[250] The members of the Panel are appointed by the Board of Executive Director for a fixed five-year term which is non-renewable.[251] The Panel members are assisted by a permanent Executive Secretariat, headed by an Executive Secretary, and internationally recognised expert consultants.[252] The Inspection Panel is designed to be an independent and impartial body.[253] In fact, the Panel maintains complete and independent control over its budget and resource decisions in the discharge of its function.[254] Furthermore, the Resolution contains several elements for securing impartiality. For instance, members of the Panel are to be selected 'on the basis of their ability to deal with thoroughly and fairly with the requests brought to them ... '.[255] Under paragraph 5 of the resolution, Executive Directors, Alternates, Advisors and staff members of the Bank Group may not serve on the Panel until two years have elapsed since the end of their service in the Bank Group. Furthermore, a Panel member is to be disqualified from participation in the hearing and investigation of any request related to a matter in which he/she has a personal interest or had significant involvement in any capacity.[256] In addition, members of the Panel may not be employed by the World Bank Group following the end of their service on the Panel.[257]

The Panel is essentially regarded as an impartial fact-finding body,[258] and its primary purpose is to determine whether the World Bank is complying with its own policies and procedures in order to make the Bank more accountable to people affected by Bank-financed projects. Here 'accountability' becomes the key concept. According to the Inspection Panel:

> Accountability is by the World Bank (*by whom*) to affected people (*to whom*) on the question of whether the Bank is complying with its own operational policies and procedures (*the standard*). This type of accountability is distinct from, and complementary to, 'top-down' forms of accountability, such as evaluations initiated by the organisation itself.[259]

---

[247] *Accountability at the World Bank*, p. 4.
[248] See Principles 10, 20 and 22 of the Rio Declaration.
[249] Resolution No. IBRD 93-10, Resolution No. IDA 93-6, 'The World Bank Inspection Panel', 22 September 1993 (hereafter the Resolution).
[250] The Resolution, para. 2.
[251] *Ibid.*, para. 3; the 2014 Operating Procedures, para. 7.
[252] *Ibid.*, para. 8; *Accountability at the World Bank*, p. 15.
[253] The Panel's independence is stressed by para. 1 of the Resolution.
[254] *Accountability at the World Bank*, p. 19.
[255] The Resolution, para. 4; the 2014 Operating Procedures, para. 7.
[256] The Resolution, para. 6.
[257] The 2014 Operating Procedures, para. 7.
[258] See http://ewebapps.worldbank.org/apps/ip/Pages/AboutUs.aspx.
[259] *Accountability at the World Bank*, p. 6.

Settlement of Disputes Involving Non-State Actors

This type of accountability is sometimes called citizen-led or 'bottom-up' accountability. Given that traditionally it has been generally understood that an international organisation needs to be accountable only to its Member States, the citizen-led accountability can be said to introduce a new concept of accountability in an international organisation.[260] According to the Inspection Panel, it performs a dual function:

- to provide a forum for people to seek recourse for harm which they believe results from Bank-supported operations
- to provide an independent and impartial assessment of claims about harm and related non-compliance with Bank policies as a check-and-balance for the Board and other concerned stakeholders.[261]

In broad terms, the Panel process can be divided into four steps (see Figure 11.2).[262]

(i) *Phase I: Receipt of a request and registration of the request.* An affected party in the territory of the borrower which is not a single individual may present requests for

Phase I: Receipt of a request and decision on registration
An initial review
Request for additional information (if necessary)
A notice of registration
↓
Phase II: Eligibility
Management response (MR, 21 days)
Panel's field visit (if necessary)
Submission of the Panel's Report to the Board (21 days from MR)
Board decision on Panel recommendation
↓
Phase III: Investigation
Submission of the final Investigation Report to the Board and Management
↓
Phase IV: Action following an investigation
Submission of the Management Report and Recommendation (MRR) to the Board (6 weeks)
Board's meeting and decision
Public disclosure of the Investigation report and the MRR (2 weeks after the Board meeting)
A return visit to meet with the Requesters

Figure 11.2 The Panel process

---

[260] L. Boisson de Chazournes, 'The World Bank Inspection Panel: About Public Participation and Dispute Settlement' in T. Treves *et al.* (eds.), *Civil Society, International Courts and Dispute Settlement* (The Hague: T. M. C. Asser Press, 2005), p. 195.
[261] The 2014 Operating Procedures, para. 2. See also *Accountability at the World Bank*, pp. 6–7.
[262] The Panel process is outlined in the 2014 Operating Procedures in some detail. See also Wong and Mayer, 'The World Bank's Inspection Panel', pp. 502 *et seq.*

inspection to the Panel.[263] Those who submit a Request are referred to as 'Requesters'.[264] Requesters are:[265]

- two or more people with common interests and concerns who claim that they have been or are likely to be adversely affected by a Bank-financed operation
- a duly appointed local representative acting on behalf of affected people
- in exceptional cases, a non-local representative[266]
- an Executive Director of the Bank in special cases of serious alleged violations of the Bank's policies and procedures
- the Executive Directors acting as a Board.

Requests for inspection must be in writing and state all relevant facts, including the harm suffered by or threatened to an affected party or parties by the alleged action or omission of the Bank.[267] According to the 2014 Operating Procedures, a Request for Inspection should contain four elements: a description of harm, a description of the Bank-financed project, actions or omissions of the Bank and steps taken or efforts made to bring the issue to the attention of Bank staff.[268]

However, Panel procedures do not require the Request to cite specific Bank policies since locally affected people and Requesters may not have access to information about Bank policies.[269] In fact, the 1999 Clarification of the Board's Second Review of the Inspection Panel (the 1991 Clarification) merely requires that: 'The request does assert in substance that a serious violation by the Bank of its operational policies and procedures has or is likely to have a material adverse effect on the requester.'[270] Requests may be submitted in the Requesters' local language, while the working language of the Panel is English.[271] Within fifteen business days of receipt of the Request, the Panel decides whether: (a) to ask for additional information from Requesters; (b) to issue a Notice of Registration; or (c) to find the Request not to be admissible.[272] In some recent cases, the Panel favoured an approach supporting early solutions via consultations between the Management and the Requesters before the registration of the Request.[273] The new approach to support

---

[263] The Resolution, para. 12. See also, 'How to File a Request for Inspection to the World Bank Inspection Panel, General Guidelines' available at: http://ewebapps.worldbank.org/apps/ip/Documents/Guidelines_How%20to%20File_for_web.pdf.
[264] The 2014 Operating Procedures, para. 1.   [265] *Ibid.*, para. 10.
[266] A request for inspection concerning the China Western Poverty Reduction Project was submitted by the International Campaign for Tibet, a US-based NGO, acting in representational capacity for people who are living in the project area. Request for Inspection, 18 June 1999.
[267] The Resolution, para. 16.
[268] The 2014 Operating Procedures, para. 12.
[269] *Ibid.* See also *Accountability at the World Bank*, p. 23.
[270] The 1999 Clarification of the Board's Second Review of the Inspection Panel, para. 9(b), available at: http://ewebapps.worldbank.org/apps/ip/Pages/Panel-Mandate.aspx. See also The Resolution, paras. 12–14.
[271] The 2014 Operating Procedures, para. 15.
[272] *Ibid.*, para. 26.
[273] Wong and Mayer, 'The World Bank's Inspection Panel', p. 506. For instance, the Inspection Panel did not register Case 90, Nepal: Enhanced Vocational Education and Training Project, owing to the quick action taken by the Management. Nepal: Enhanced Vocational Education and Training Project (P104015), Notice of Non-registration, IPN REQUEST RQ 13/08, 30 October 2013.

early solutions in the Inspection Panel process was introduced in Annex 1 of the 2014 Operating Procedures.

(ii) *Phase II: Confirmation of technical eligibility.* Once the Panel has registered a Request for Inspection, the Panel sends a Notice of Registration to the Requesters, the Board, the Management and the Borrower.[274] The Bank Management is required to provide the Panel with evidence that it has complied, or intends to comply, with the Bank's relevant policies and procedures within twenty-one business days from the date of registration.[275] Within twenty-one days of receiving the response of the Management, the Panel is to decide whether to recommend an investigation to the Board.[276] The Panel's recommendation is called 'Report and Recommendation'.[277] A task of the Panel in this regard is to confirm the eligibility of the request in accordance with eligibility criteria set out in the 1999 Clarification.[278] To this end, normally a Panel team conducts a field visit to the project area.[279] The Panel may decide not to recommend an investigation even if it confirms that the technical eligibility criteria for an investigation are met.[280] By way of example, the Panel did not recommend an investigation with regard to the Red Sea-Dead Sea Water Conveyance Study Programme that involved the cooperation of Israel, Jordan, the West Bank and Gaza, owing to 'the unique and special circumstances surrounding this unprecedented regional collaborative effort'.[281] In any case the Panel's Recommendation is to be submitted to the Board for approval.[282]

(iii) *Phase III: Investigation.* Once an investigation is approved, the Panel enters the investigation phase. Two central issues are to be addressed by the Panel: non-compliance by the Bank with its own policies and the issue of harm to affected people or the environment.[283] The Panel's research consists of desk research and field research. While desk research focuses on the written documents concerning the project, field research is conducted mainly during the Panel's visit to the country where the project is being implemented.[284] The focus of the Panel's investigation is on the Bank Management as a whole and, thus, the Panel does not investigate individual staff members within the Bank.[285] After completing the research, the Panel is to submit its report to the Executive Directors and the President.[286] The Panel's report to the Board is to focus on whether there is a serious Bank failure to observe its operational policies and procedures with respect to project design, appraisal and/or implementation and include all relevant facts that are needed to understand fully the context and basis for the Panel's findings and conclusions.[287] However, the Panel does not directly engage in mediation, nor does

---

[274] The 2014 Operating Procedures, paras. 28 and 32.
[275] The Resolution, para. 18; the 2014 Operating Procedures, paras. 33-5.
[276] The Resolution, para. 19; the 2014 Operating Procedures, para. 36.   [277] *Ibid.*
[278] The 1999 Clarification, para. 9; the 2014 Operating Procedures, para. 39.
[279] *Ibid.*, para. 37.   [280] *Ibid.*, para. 41.
[281] Case 76. The Inspection Panel, *Report and Recommendation: Red Sea-Dead Sea Water Conveyance Study Programme*, 15 February 2012, p. 20, para. 92. Wong and Mayer, 'The World Bank's Inspection Panel', pp. 505-6.
[282] The 2014 Operating Procedures, para. 48.
[283] *Accountability at the World Bank*, p. 10. See also the 2014 Operating Procedures, para. 63.
[284] *Accountability at the World Bank*, pp. 30-1.   [285] *Ibid.*, pp. 16-17.
[286] The Resolution, para. 22.   [287] The 1999 Clarification, para. 13

it provide recommendations for remedial actions to be taken by Management or the Borrower.[288] All decisions of the Panel on procedural matters, its recommendations to the Board on whether to proceed with the investigation of a Request, and its findings reported to the Board must be reached by consensus.[289] The report is not binding. The final Investigation Report is submitted to the Board and conveyed to Management via the President.[290]

(iv) *Phase IV: Action following an investigation.* Within six weeks from receiving the Panel's findings, Management is required to submit to the Board the 'Management Report and Recommendation in Response to the Inspection Panel Investigation Report' (MRR). The MRR normally includes proposed actions in response to the Panel's findings.[291] Here a distinction is made between remedial efforts that Management can take on its own to address Bank failure and a plan of action agreed between the Borrower and the Bank to improve project implementation.[292] The Board meets to consider the Panel's Investigation Report and the MRR and decides whether to approve the plans of action that Management may have included in its Report. Within two weeks after the Board meeting, the Bank makes the Investigation Report and the MRR publicly available. At this time, the Panel promptly informs the Requesters of the actions approved by the Board.[293] The Panel also contacts the Requesters to convey and explain the results of the Panel process. This may involve a return visit to meet with the Requesters.[294]

6.2.3 Commentary

It is important that the Panel process opens up a channel for individuals to bring complaints with regard to alleged misconduct of an international organisation. In this sense, the Inspection Panel can be thought of as a nexus connecting people with the decision-making process within the Bank.[295] Furthermore, the Inspection Panel may identify, in its report, non-compliance with policies on the protection of environmental protection and indigenous peoples. In the China Western Poverty Reduction Project, for instance, the Inspection Panel found that there had been non-compliance with the policies on environmental assessment,[296] pest management[297] and conservation of natural habitats.[298] It also identified the breach of policies on indigenous people and involuntarily resettled

---

[288] The 2014 Operating Procedures, para. 4.
[289] The Resolution, para. 24; the 2014 Operating Procedures, para. 9.   [290] *Ibid.*, para. 65.
[291] *Ibid.*, paras. 67–8; the Resolution, para. 23.
[292] The 2014 Operating Procedures, para. 68.
[293] *Ibid.*, paras. 71–2.   [294] *Ibid.*, para. 75.
[295] Boisson de Chazournes, 'The World Bank Inspection Panel', p. 192; L. Boisson de Chazournes, 'Access to Justice: The World Bank Inspection Panel' in G. Alfredsson *et al.* (eds.), *International Human Rights Monitoring Mechanisms: Essays in Honour of Jakob Th. Moller* (The Hague: Nijhoff, 2009), p. 519.
[296] The Inspection Panel Investigation Report, China: Western Poverty Reduction Project (Credit No. 3255-CHA and Loan No. 4501-CHA), 28 April 2000, paras. 81 and 237.
[297] *Ibid.*, para. 244.   [298] *Ibid.*, para. 254.

persons.[299] Therefore, there may be some scope to argue that the Inspection Panel actually performs a quasi-judicial function in practice.[300]

The World Bank Inspection Panel has received some 104 requests in more than twenty years of operation. This figure appears to be relatively few compared with the number of projects approved by the Bank. In this regard, some obstacles are identified by commentators. For instance, it is said that many people affected by Bank projects remain unaware of the availability of the Panel in reality. Since finance from the Bank can be easily blended with State-financed project, it may be less easy for civil society actors to realise that the project in question receives financial support from the Bank.[301] Furthermore, linguistic and cultural barriers can be obstacles to recourse to the Panel. In some borrowing States, filing a claim against a public authority may entail the serious risk of reprisal.[302] Moreover, it cannot pass unnoticed that there are some procedural limitations with the Panel process.

First, as explained earlier, the decision on the question whether an investigation should take place is eventually that of the Board of Executive Directors. Appropriate remedial measures are also subject to the decision of the Board. Accordingly, there is no guarantee that the Panel's recommendation on investigation is always approved by the Board. By way of example, the process concerning case 7, *Argentina/Paraguay: Yacretá Hydroelectric Project*, became highly politicised and the Board eventually refused to approve the Panel's recommendation for an investigation.[303]

Second, no appeal mechanism exists in the Panel process. As a consequence, where the Panel's report or action plans could not adequately respond to Requesters' concerns, there appears to be little for the Requesters to do.

Third, as the task of the Panel is limited to fact-finding, the Panel cannot determine reparation that many actual or potential requesters expect. Furthermore, the Panel is not empowered to enforce the Management action plan. The Board can request the Panel to take on a follow-up role. Absent a request by the Board, however, the Panel Resolution and the 1999 Clarification are generally understood not to create a standing monitoring role for the Panel concerning implementation of the Management action plan. In this regard, a concern is voiced from affected people and civil society that the Panel remains weak in monitoring and checking the effectiveness of the Management action plan.[304]

A further issue to be considered concerns the scope of jurisdiction of the Inspection Panel. As noted, the Inspection Panel is not a judicial body, nor is it a mechanism for determining responsibility of international organisations and/or borrower States.[305] In

---

[299] *Ibid.*, paras. 280, 293, 340 and 408. See also A. G. Gualtieri, 'The Environmental Accountability of the World Bank to Non-State Actors: Insights from the Inspection Panel' (2002) 72 *BYIL*, pp. 241–2.
[300] Further, A. N. Fourie, 'The World Bank Inspection Panel's Normative Potential: A Critical Assessment, and A Restatement' (2012) 59 *NILR*, pp. 206 *et seq.*; A. Orakhelashvili, 'The World Bank Inspection Panel in Context: Institutional Aspects of the Accountability of International Organisations' (2005) 2 *International Organizations Law Review*, pp. 84 *et seq.*
[301] Wong and Mayer, 'The World Bank's Inspection Panel', p. 507.
[302] *Ibid.*, pp. 508–9.   [303] *Ibid.*, p. 512.
[304] *Accountability at the World Bank*, pp. 44–5; Wong and Mayer, 'The World Bank's Inspection Panel', p. 514; E. Nurmukhametova, 'Problems in Connection with the Efficiency of the World Bank Inspection Panel' (2006) 10 *Max Planck Yearbook of United Nations Law*, p. 420.
[305] Boisson de Chazournes, 'The World Bank Inspection Panel', p. 199.

some cases, however, the Inspection Panel ventured to examine legal issues in international law. In the Investigation Report on the *Chad–Cameroon Petroleum and Pipeline Project*, for instance, the Inspection Panel took the view that:

> It is not within the Panel's mandate to assess the status of governance and human rights in Chad in general or in isolation, and the Panel acknowledges that there are several institutions (including UN bodies) specifically in charge of this subject. However, the Panel felt obliged to examine whether the issues of proper governance or human rights violations in Chad were such as to impede the implementation of the Project in a manner compatible with the Bank's policies.[306]

The Inspection Panel, in the *Honduras: Land Administration Project*, expressed its concern that the Bank did not adequately consider whether the proposed Project plan and its implementation would be consistent with ILO Convention No. 169 concerning indigenous and tribal peoples.[307] Furthermore, in the *Albania: Power Sector Generation and Restructuring Project*, compliance with the Aarhus Convention was at issue. In this regard, the Aarhus Committee had already concluded that Albania had failed to comply with the requirements for public participation under the Convention. On the basis of the finding, the Panel found that Management did not ensure that the Project preparation activities complied with the consultation and public participation requirements of the Aarhus Convention.[308] Yet, whether the Inspection Panel, which is not a legal body, and its members are not always international lawyers, could be relevant to determine non-compliance with treaty obligations needs careful consideration.

7 CONCLUSIONS

Owing to the increasing activities of non-State actors in international relations, peaceful settlement of international disputes involving non-State actors should be a crucial issue in international law. The considerations in this chapter can be summarised as follows:

(i) The peaceful settlement of intra-state disputes requires a comprehensive approach that comprises preventive diplomacy, peacekeeping, peacemaking and post-conflict peacebuilding. In particular, post-conflict peacebuilding is crucial to address the deep-rooted, structural causes of internal disputes. In this regard, it is argued that transitional justice constitutes a key element in post-conflict peacebuilding.

---

[306] Footnotes omitted. The Inspection Panel Investigation Report, Chad–Cameroon Petroleum and Pipeline Project (Loan No. 4558-CD); Petroleum Sector Management Capacity Building Project (Credit No. 3373-CD); and Management of the Petroleum Economy (Credit No. 3316-CD), 17 July 2002, pp. 62-3, para. 215.
[307] The Inspection Panel, Investigation Report Honduras: Land Administration Project (IDA Credit 3858-HO), Report No. 39933-HN, 12 June 2007, p. 72, para. 258.
[308] The Inspection Panel, Investigation Report Albania: Power Sector Generation and Restructuring Project (IDA Credit No. 3872-ALB), Report No. 49504-AL, 7 August 2009, p. 79, paras. 330-2.

(ii) Since *locus standi* before international courts and tribunals is in principle limited to the State, international adjudication is of only modest utility in the settlement of intra-State disputes between the government and a non-State entity. As demonstrated by the *Abyei* arbitration, however, arbitration can perform a valuable role in the settlement of intra-State disputes owing to its flexibility of rules of procedure with regard to, *inter alia, locus standi*, transparency of the proceedings and the timeframe.
(iii) Mixed arbitration is relevant to the settlement of disputes between States on the one hand and natural and juridical persons on the other hand. In this regard, at present, investment arbitration that seeks to settle investor–State investment disputes attracts growing attention. It must also be stressed that as demonstrated by the Iran–United States Claims Tribunal, mixed arbitration can perform a valuable role in the normalisation of the relationship between two hostile States. In this sense, it can contribute to restoring peace in international relations.
(iv) The settlement of disputes between States and individuals is needed in post-conflict situations. A noteworthy example is provided by the UNCC. It is argued that the Commission is characterised by some unique features:

- a dual structure combined with separate political and fact-finding organs
- a wide range of eligible claimants
- sophisticated categorisation of claims
- differentiated evidence requirement according to urgency of claims
- claims for environmental damage, including the costs incurred by States for monitoring and assessing the environmental damage.

As demonstrated by the UNCC, compensation under the control of the United Nations can be thought to provide better assurances as to the effectiveness of the compensation process.
(v) A dispute between an international organisation and its Member States may be raised with regard to the validity of the UN Security Council resolutions. In this regard, an issue arises as to whether the ICJ is competent to judicially review the resolutions. Although, to date, no clear answer has been given by the Court, as a matter of theory at least, there appear to be no decisive reasons to prevent judicial review by the Court.
(vi) When considering the relationship between an international organisation and individuals, two issues arise. The first issue pertains to the settlement of disputes between an international organisation and its staff. Since these disputes are essentially internal disputes within the organisation, they are to be settled in accordance with internal procedures of the organisation concerned. The second issue concerns remedies for individuals affected by projects financed by a multilateral financial institution. The World Bank Inspection Panel provides an important mechanism to secure that affected people can bring complaints with regard to alleged misconduct of the Bank. Unlike the traditional concept of accountability to Member States, the Panel process introduces a new concept of citizen-led accountability in an international organisation. Nonetheless, the number of requests remains comparatively few and further efforts must be made to overcome external obstacles, including unawareness of the Panel process and linguistic/cultural barriers, and internal obstacles arising from non-approval by the Board and the lack of appeal mechanism.

FURTHER READING

Peacekeeping, Peacebuilding and Transitional Justice

A. J. Bellamy, P. D. Williams and S. Griffin, *Understanding Peacekeeping*, 2nd edn (Cambridge: Polity Press, 2010).

V. Chetail (ed.), *Post-Conflict Peacebuilding: A Lexicon* (Oxford University Press, 2009).

D. Dam-de Jong, *International Law and Governance of Natural Resources in Conflict and Post-Conflict Situations* (Cambridge University Press, 2015).

J. Elster, *Closing the Books: Transitional Justice in Historical Perspective* (Cambridge University Press, 2004).

D. Higashi, *Challenges of Constructing Legitimacy in Peacebuilding: Afghanistan, Iraq, Sierra Leone, and East Timor* (London: Routledge, 2015).

B. Kondoch (ed.), *International Peacekeeping* (Aldershot: Ashgate, 2007).

H. Nasu, *International Law on Peacekeeping: A Study of Article 40 of the UN Charter* (Leiden: Nijhoff, 2009).

N. Roht-Arriaza and J. Mariezcurrena (eds.), *Transitional Justice in the Twenty-First Century: Beyond Truth Versus Justice* (Cambridge University Press, 2006).

T. Sato, 'Transitional Justice, Peacebuilding, and International Law: What Role Is Played by the UN in Post-Conflict Peacebuilding?' (2012) 110 *The Journal of International Law and Diplomacy*, pp. 588–620.

O. Simić (ed.), *An Introduction to Transitional Justice* (New York: Routledge, 2017).

J. Sloan, *The Militarisation of Peacekeeping in the Twenty-First Century* (Oxford: Hart Publishing, 2011).

C. Stahn and J. K. Kleffner (eds.), *Jus Post Bellum: Towards a Law of Transition from Conflict to Peace* (The Hague: T. M. C. Asser Press, 2008).

R. G. Teitel, *Transitional Justice* (Oxford University Press, 2000).

G. Verdirame, *The UN and Human Rights: Who Guards the Guardians?* (Cambridge University Press, 2011).

See also *The International Journal of Transitional Justice* from 2007.

The *Abyei* Arbitration

F. Baetens and R. Yotova, 'The Abyei Arbitration: A Model Procedure for Intra-State Dispute Settlement in Resource-Rich Conflict Areas?' (2011) 3 *Goettingen Journal of International Law*, pp. 417–46.

B. Daly, 'The Abyei Arbitration: Procedural Aspects of an Intra-State Border Arbitration' (2010) 23 *LJIL*, pp. 801–23.

B. W. Daly and G. Schofield, 'Abyei Arbitration' in *Max Planck Encyclopaedia*.

C. G. Lathrop, 'Government of Sudan v. Sudan People's Liberation Movement/Army ("Abyei Arbitration"), Arbitral Tribunal, July 22, 2009' (2010) 104 *AJIL*, pp. 66–73.

J. McKay, 'The Permanent Court of Arbitration and the Sudanese Peace Process: Legal Issues from the Abyei Arbitration in Reviewing the Mandate of an Ad Hoc Body' (2009) 16 *Australian International Law Journal*, pp. 233–9.

W. J. Miles and D. Mallett, 'The Abyei Arbitration and the Use of Arbitration to Resolve Inter-State and Intra-State Conflicts' (2010) 1 *Journal of International Dispute Settlement*, pp. 313–40.

P. von Muhlendahl, 'International Tribunal Redraws Boundareis of Sudanese Abyei Region: A Chance for Peace?' *The Hague Justice Portal*, pp. 1–10, available at: www.haguejusticeportal.net/index.php?id=11256.

ICSID

As there are many studies on ICSID, only some recent monographs will be listed here.

R. D. Bishop and S. M. Marchili, *Annulment under the ICSID Convention* (Oxford University Press, 2012).

N. J. Calamita, D. C. Earnest and M. Burgstaller, *The Future of ICSID and the Place of Investment Treaties in International Law* (London: British Institute of International and Comparative Law, 2013).

H. E. Kjos, *Applicable Law in Investor–State Arbitration: The Interplay between National and International Law* (Oxford University Press, 2013).

A. R. Parra, *The History of ICSID* (Oxford University Press, 2012).

L. Reed, J. Paulsson and N. Rawding, *Guide to ICSID Arbitration*, 2nd edn (Alphen aan den Rijn: Wolters Kluwer, 2010).

C. H. Schreuer et al., *The ICSID Convention: A Commentary*, 2nd edn (Cambridge University Press, 2009).

T. H. Webster, *Handbook of Investment Arbitration: Commentary, Precedents and Models for ICSID Arbitration* (London: Sweet and Maxwell, 2012).

Iran–United States Claims Tribunal

C. N. Brower and J. D. Brueschke, *The Iran–United States Claims Tribunal* (The Hague: Nijhoff, 1998).

D. D. Caron and J. R. Crook (eds.), *The Iran–United States Claims Tribunal and the Process of International Claims Resolution* (New York: Transnational Publishers, 2000).

C. R. Drahozal and C. S. Gibson (eds.), *The Iran-U.S. Claims Tribunal at 25: The Cases Everyone Needs to Know for Investor–State & International Arbitration* (Oxford University Press, 2007).

The United Nations Compensation Committee

L. Boisson de Chazournes and D. Campanelli, 'The United Nations Compensation Commission: Time for an Assessment?' in A. Fischer-Lescano et al., *Peace in Liberty: Festschrift fur Michael Bothe zum 70. Geburtstag* (Baden-Baden: Nomos, 2008), pp. 3–17.

D. Campanelli, 'The United Nations Compensation Commission (UNCC): Reflections on its Judicial Character' (2005) 4 *The Law and Practice of International Courts and Tribunals*, pp. 107–39.

D. D. Caron, 'The United Nations Compensation Commission for Claims Arising Out of the 1991 Gulf War: the "Arising Prior to" Decision' (2005) 14 *Journal of Transnational Law and Policy*, pp. 309–34.

J. J. Chung, 'The United Nations Compensation Commission and the Balancing of Rights between Individual Claimants and the Government of Iraq' (2005) 10 *UCLA Journal of International Law and Foreign Affairs*, pp. 141–78.

Y. Dinstein, 'Protection of the Environment in International Armed Conflict' (2001) 5 *Max Planck Yearbook of United Nations Law*, pp. 523–49.

O. Elias, 'The UN Compensation Commission and Liability for the Costs of Monitoring and Assessment of Environmental Damage' in M. Fitzmaurice and D. Sarooshi (eds.), *Issues of State Responsibility before International Judicial Institutions* (Oxford: Hart Publishing, 2004), pp. 219–36.

T. J. Feighery, 'The United Nations Compensation Commission' in C. Giorgetti (ed.), *The Rules, Practice, and Jurisprudence of International Courts and Tribunals* (Leiden: Nijhoff, 2012), pp. 515–43.

T. J. Feighery, C. S. Gibson and T. M. Rajah (eds.), *War Reparations and the UN Compensation Commission: Designing Compensation after Conflict* (Oxford University Press, 2015).

A. Gattini, 'The UN Compensation Commission: Old Rules, New Procedures on War Reparations' (2002) 13 *EJIL*, pp. 161–81.

V. Heiskanen, 'The United Nations Compensation Commission' (2002) 296 *RCADI*, pp. 255–397.

H. Van Houtte, H. Das and B. Delmartino, 'The United Nations Compensation Commission' in P. de Greiff (ed.), *The Handbook of Reparation* (Oxford University Press, 2008), pp. 321–89.

M. Kazazi, 'Environmental Damage in the Practice of the UN Compensation Committee' in M. Bowman and A. Boyle (eds.), *Environmental Damage in International and Comparative Law* (Oxford University Press, 2002), pp. 111–31.

F. E. McGovern, 'Dispute System Design: The United Nations Compensation Commission' (2009) 14 *Harvard Negotiation Law Review*, pp. 171–94.

R. Rayfuse, *War and the Environment: New Approaches to Protecting the Environment in Relation to Armed Conflict* (Leiden: Nijhoff, 2014).

P. H. Sand, 'Compensation for Environmental Damage from the 1991 Gulf War' (2005) 35(6) *Environmental Policy and Law*, pp. 244–9.

L. A. Taylor, 'The United Nations Compensation Committee' in C. Ferstman, M. Goetz and A. Stephens (eds.), *Reparations for Victims of Genocide, War Crimes and Crimes against Humanity: Systems in Place and Systems in the Making* (Leiden: Nijhoff, 2009), pp. 197–241.

Judicial Review

D. Akande, 'The International Court of Justice and the Security Council: Is There Room for Judicial Control of Decisions of the Political Organs of the United Nations?' (1997) 46 *ICLQ*, pp. 309–43.

J. E. Alvarez, 'Judging the Security Council' (1996) 90 *AJIL*, pp. 1–39.

M. Bedjaoui, *The New World Order and the Security Council: Testing the Legality of Its Acts* (The Hague: Kluwer Interantional, 1995).

L. Caflisch, 'Is the International Court Entitled to Review Security Council Resolutions Adopted under Chapter VII of the United Nations Charter?' in N. Al-Nauimi and R. Meese (eds.), *International Legal Issues Arising under the United Nations Decade of International Law* (The Hague: Kluwer, 1995), pp. 633–62.

K. R. Cronin-Furman, 'The International Court of Justice and the United Nations Security Council: Rethinking a Complicated Relationship' (2006) 106 *Colombia Law Review*, pp. 435–63.

D. D'Angelo, 'The "Check" on International Peace and Security Maintenance: The International Court of Justice and Judicial Review of Security Council Resolutions' (1999–2000) 23 *Suffolk Transnational Law Review*, pp. 561–93.

T. M. Franck, 'The "Powers of Appreciation": Who is the Ultimate Guardian of UN Legality?' (1992) 86 *AJIL*, pp. 519–23.

V. Gowlland-Debbas, 'The Relationship between the International Court of Justice and the Security Council in the Light of the Lockerbie Case' (1994) 88 *AJIL*, pp. 643–77.

'Security Council Enforcement Action and Issues of State Responsibility' (1994) 43 *ICLQ*, pp. 55–98.

B. Graefrath, 'Leave to the Court What Belongs to the Court: The Libyan Case' (1993) 4 *EJIL*, pp. 184–205.

B. Martenczuk, 'The Security Council, the International Court and Judicial Review: What Lessons from Lockerbie?' (1999) 10 *EJIL*, pp. 517–47.

I. Petculescu, 'The Review of the United Nations Security Council Decisions by the International Court of Justice' (2005) 52 *NILR*, pp. 167–95.
M. Plachta, 'The Lockerbie Case: The Role of the Security Council in Enforcing the Principle Aut Dedere Aut Judicare' (2001) 12 *EJIL*, pp. 125–40.
A. Reinisch, 'Should Judges Second-Guess the UN Security Council?'(2009) 6 *International Organisations Law Review*, pp. 257–91.
W. M. Reisman, 'The Constitutional Crisis in the United Nations' (1993) 87 *AJIL*, pp. 83–100.
K. Robert, 'Second-Guessing the Security Council: The International Court of Justice and Its Power of Judicial Review' (1993) 7 *Pace International Law Review*, pp. 281–327.
G. R. Watson, 'Constitutionalism, Judicial Review and the World Court' (1993) 34 *Harvard International Law Journal*, pp. 1–45.

The World Bank Inspection Panel

L. Boisson de Chazournes, 'The World Bank Inspection Panel: About Public Participation and Dispute Settlement' in T. Treves *et al.* (eds.), *Civil Society, International Courts and Dispute Settlement* (The Hague: T. M. C. Asser Press, 2005), pp. 187–203.
  'Access to Justice: The World Bank Inspection Panel' in G. Alfredsson *et al.* (eds.) *International Human Rights Monitoring Mechanisms: Essays in Honour of Jakob Th. Moller* (The Hague: Nijhoff, 2009), pp. 513–20.
  'Les Panels d'Inspection' in SFDI, *Colloque de Lyon: Droit international et développement* (Paris: Pedone, 2015), pp. 111–20.
A. N. Fourie, 'The World Bank Inspection Panel's Normative Potential: A Critical Assessment, and a Restatement' (2012) 59 *NILR*, pp. 199–234.
E. Hey, 'The World Bank Inspection Panel and the Development of International Law' in N. Boschiero *et al.* (eds.), *International Courts and the Development of International Law* (The Hague: T. M. C. Asser Press, 2013), pp. 727–38.
The Inspection Panel, *Accountability at the World Bank: The Inspection Panel at 15 Years* (Washington DC: The World Bank, 2009).
K. Lukas, 'The Inspection Panel of the World Bank: An Effective Extrajudicial Complaint Mechanism?' (2015) 6 *The World Bank Legal Review*, pp. 531–44.
E. Nurmukhametova, 'Problems in Connection with the Efficiency of the World Bank Inspection Panel' (2006) 10 *Max Planck Yearbook of United Nations Law*, pp. 397–421.
A. Orakhelashvili, 'The World Bank Inspection Panel in Context: Institutional Aspects of the Accountability of International Organisations' (2005) 2 *International Organisations Law Review*, pp. 57–102.
Y. Wong and B. Mayer, 'The World Bank's Inspection Panel: A Tool for Accountability?' (2015) 6 *The World Bank Legal Review*, pp. 495–530.

12

The Quest for Peace in International Law

Main Issues

In a narrow sense, sustainable peace in the international community means absence of armed conflicts and disputes endangering international peace and security. While the peaceful settlement of international disputes is a prerequisite to achieve sustainable peace in a narrow sense, it is not sufficient to achieve this goal. Sustainable peace in a narrow sense relies on the interlinkage of three elements: peaceful settlement of international disputes, the prohibition of the threat or use of force secured by an international security system, and disarmament. The three pillars can be regarded as essential conditions for peace. The role of the peaceful settlement of international disputes in international relations must be examined in connection to the other two elements. Focusing on the interlinkage of the three pillars, this chapter will seek to consider the role of the peaceful settlement of international disputes in a broad context. In particular, the following issues will be discussed:

(i) What is the interrelationship between peaceful settlement of international disputes, the prohibition of the use or threat of force and disarmament?
(ii) What are the problems associated with the interaction of the three elements?
(iii) How is it possible to strengthen the interlinkage of the three elements to achieve sustainable peace?

1 INTRODUCTION

'Peace' is an elusive concept and it is difficult to define it *a priori* in abstract. The Preamble of the UN Charter appears to contain two categories of components of peace. The first category relates to components necessary to maintain peace in a narrow sense which means absence of armed conflicts and disputes endangering international peace and security. This category includes two elements that are closely interlinked: the prohibition of armed force and the maintenance of international peace and security. The second category of components is those necessary to achieve peace in a broad sense which refers to the situation where human rights are adequately protected and all people can promote economic and social progress.[1] These components embodied in the Preamble include: the protection of 'fundamental human rights', promotion of social progress and better standards of life in larger freedom, and the promotion of the economic and social advancement of all peoples. Given that a healthy environment provides a foundation for all life, it is also necessary to add the protection of the environment as a component of peace in a broad sense. In summary, it can be said that peace in a broad sense relies essentially on the interlinkage between the three elements: human rights, the environment and sustainable development.[2] In any case peace must be sustainable to promote the benefits of the present and future generations.

While the peaceful settlement of international disputes is a prerequisite to maintain peace in a narrow sense, it is not sufficient to achieve this goal. In fact, the effectiveness of peaceful settlement of international disputes rests on two other elements: the principle of non-use of force and disarmament. The peaceful settlement of international disputes is closely linked to the principle of non-use of force in a dual sense. First, the international dispute settlement system cannot be truly effective, unless the resort to the use of force is prohibited. In this sense, the effectiveness of the international dispute settlement system can be said to rely on the prohibition of the threat or use of force. Second, as explained earlier,[3] the principle of non-use of force was established in international law reflected in the UN Charter. However, the UN Charter does not prohibit all types of use of force. What is prohibited in the UN Charter is the *illegal* use of force. Accordingly, the distinction between legal and illegal use of force is crucial in international law. In practice, the illegal use of force emerges as the breach of the obligation of peaceful settlement of international law. In other words, illegal use of force means the use of force which is contrary to the obligation of peaceful settlement of international disputes. Thus the establishment of procedures of international dispute settlement is a prerequisite to determine the legality of use of force. Here the peaceful settlement of international disputes and the principle of non-use of force are intimately intertwined.

The effectiveness of the principle of non-use of force must be secured by an international security system. In the UN Charter, the collective security provides for the international security system. The collective security system rests ultimately on military sanction in accordance with the UN Charter. If there is a great military risk, however, it would be difficult to trigger the collective security system. Accordingly, disarmament is crucial to effectuate the system. Furthermore, ever-increasing modern arms will undermine the effectiveness of the peaceful settlement of international disputes by increasing the risk of armed conflicts. Hence disarmament is also needed to enhance the effectiveness of international dispute settlement. One can thus argue that disarmament is a prerequisite for the collective security system and the peaceful settlement of international disputes.

---

[1] It is common knowledge that Johan Galtung distinguished two types of peace – namely, negative peace which means absence of personal violence and positive peace which refers to absence of structural violence. J. Galtung, 'Violence, Peace, and Peace Research' (1969) 6 *Journal of Peace Research*, p. 183.

[2] In 2015, the 2030 Agenda for Sustainable Development was adopted by the UN General Assembly. The Agenda specified seventeen goals and 169 targets for sustainable development. UN General Assembly, 70/1. *Transforming Our World: The 2030 Agenda for Sustainable Development*, A/RES/70/1, 25 September 2015.

[3] See Chapter 1, section 2.

In summary, the three elements (i.e. peaceful settlement of international disputes, the non-use of force secured by the collective security system and disarmament) can be considered as essential conditions for sustainable peace in a narrow sense. The three elements can be called a 'triad for peace'. According to Claude, Jr, the essence of the interrelationship between the three elements can be summarised as follows:

> Whereas pacific settlement proposes to leave states with nothing to fight about, and collective security proposes to confront aggressors with too much to fight against, disarmament proposes to deprive nations of anything to fight with.[4]

The idea of the linkage of the three elements can be traced back to the 1919 Covenant of the League of Nations (hereafter the League Covenant).[5] Since World War I created enormous human loss and economic and social damage to the world, it was hardly surprising that the creation of an international organisation for the maintenance of international peace and security became a crucial issue after World War I. Thus the League of Nations attempted to establish international peace and security on the basis of three pillars – namely, peaceful settlement of international disputes, collective security associated with the outlawry of war and disarmament. In so doing, the League of Nations presented a prototype of the peacemaking machinery on the basis of the three pillars. Even though the League of Nations failed to prevent World War II, this does not directly mean that the approach of the League of Nations was irrelevant. The idea of interlinkage of the three pillars seems to deserve reconsideration in a contemporary context of international relations.

Against that background, this chapter examines the role of the peaceful settlement of international disputes in a broad context focusing on the interaction of the three pillars for sustainable peace in a narrow sense. It first examines the interlinkage between international dispute settlement and the prohibition of the threat or use of force (section 2). It then discusses the interlinkage between international dispute settlement and disarmament (section 3). Finally, a perspective is briefly suggested (section 4).

2 INTERLINKAGE BETWEEN INTERNATIONAL DISPUTE SETTLEMENT AND THE PROHIBITION OF THE THREAT OR USE OF FORCE

2.1 The League of Nations

While the movement toward the prohibition of war commenced in the early twentieth century, it was the League of Nations that took a crucial step toward outlawry of war. The Preamble of the League Covenant declared that the High Contracting Parties agree to this Covenant '[i]n order to promote international co-operation and to achieve international

---

[4] Inis L. Claude, Jr, *Swords into Plowshares: The Problems and Progress of International Organization*, 4th edn (New York: Random House, 1984), p. 287.
[5] Entered into force 10 January 1920. The electronic text is available at: http://avalon.law.yale.edu/20th_century/leagcov.asp.

peace and security by the acceptance of obligation not to resort to war'. To effectuate the prohibition of war, the League of Nations adopted the collective security system, stating in Article 11(1) of the Covenant that:

> Any war or threat of war, whether immediately affecting any of the Members of the League or not, is hereby declared a matter of concern to the whole League, and the League shall take any action that may be deemed wise and effectual to safeguard the peace of nations.

However, the mechanism of the League Covenant remained weak in some respects.

First, Article 12(1) of the Covenant provided two obligations to restrict the free right to resort to war: (i) if there should arise between the members of the League any dispute likely to lead to a rupture, they would submit the matter either to arbitration or to judicial settlement or to inquiry by the Council; and (ii) they agreed in no case to resort to war until three months after the award by the arbitrators or the judicial decision, or the report by the Council. Here the prohibition of war was integrally linked to the procedures of peaceful settlement of international disputes. Nevertheless, 'three months after the award by the arbitrators or the judicial decision, or the report by the Council', the Member States could resort to war, subject to Articles 13(4), 15(6) and (10) of the League Covenant.

Second, under Article 13(4) of the League Covenant, '[t]he Members of the League agree that they will carry out in full good faith any award or decision that may be rendered, and that they will not resort to war against a Member of the League which complies therewith'. In other words, League members could resort to war in the case where a Member State did not comply with the arbitral award or decision.

Third, under Article 15(1) of the League Covenant, if any dispute likely to lead to a rupture between members of the League was not submitted to arbitration in accordance with Article 13, the members were required to submit the matter to the Council. Under Article 15(6), '[i]f a report by the Council is unanimously agreed to by the members thereof other than the Representatives of one or more of the parties to the dispute, the Members of the League agree that they will not go to war with any party to the dispute which complies with the recommendation of the report'. To this extent, the free right to resort to war was restricted. Under Article 15(7), however, if the Council failed to reach a report which was unanimously agreed to by the members thereof, other than the Representatives of one or more of the parties to the dispute, the members of the League had the right eventually to resort to war.

In summary, the League Covenant did not completely preclude the possibility of war between Member States of the League. Nor did it prohibit the resort to force short of war. This qualification induced States to resort to de facto war by claiming that it was short of war and that there was no breach of the provisions of the Covenant of the League of Nations.

Moreover, it cannot pass unnoticed that the dispute settlement procedures in the League Covenant contained some weaknesses. As noted, Article 12(1) of the Covenant obliged the Members of the League to submit any dispute which was likely to lead to a rupture between them either to arbitration or to judicial settlement or to inquiry by the Council. Article 13(1) of the Covenant further required the members of the League to submit the whole subject matter to arbitration whenever any dispute should arise between them which they recognised as suitable for submission to arbitration or judicial settlement and which could not be satisfactorily settled by diplomacy. Article 13(2) then specified four categories of disputes that were relevant to judicial settlement: disputes as to the interpretation of a treaty, as to any question of international law, as to the existence of any fact which if established would constitute a breach of any international obligation, or as to the extent and nature of the reparation to be made for any such breach. Nonetheless, whether a dispute would be suitable for the submission to judicial settlement was determined by the parties in dispute. By considering a dispute as being unsuitable for judicial settlement, they could easily escape from the obligation set out in this provision. Furthermore, the word 'generally' suggests the existence of exceptions. Accordingly, it was possible for the members of the League to exclude the obligation to refer to judicial means, by making a dispute an exception in its discretion.

Subsequently the League of Nations attempted to further advance a system to regulate war. The League's effort resulted in the 1924 Protocol for the Pacific Settlement of International Disputes (Geneva Protocol).[6] The main object of the Protocol was to introduce such amendments into the Covenant of the League of Nations so that the Covenant would supply means for securing the peaceful settlement of all international disputes and that States would be enabled to effect a reduction of their armaments pursuant to Article 8 of the League Covenant.[7] In its Preamble, the Geneva Protocol declared that a war of aggression constituted an international crime. It then stressed the need to facilitate the complete application of the system provided in the Covenant of the League of Nations for the pacific settlement of disputes between States. It also highlighted the need to reduce national armaments to the lowest point consistent with national safety and the enforcement by common action of international obligations.[8] Thus the three elements for peace (i.e. prohibition of war (use of force), peaceful settlement of international disputes and disarmament) were reflected in the Geneva Protocol.

Under Article 3, the signatory States agreed to undertake to recognise as compulsory, *ipso facto* and without special agreement, the jurisdiction of the Permanent Court of International Justice in the cases covered by Article 36(2) of the Statute of the Court. The Geneva Protocol also provided for compulsory arbitration in accordance with Article 4. Article 10 then declared that: 'Every State which resorts to war in violation of the undertakings contained in the Covenant or in the present Protocol is an aggressor.' Furthermore, under Article 2, the signatory States agreed 'in no case to resort to war either with one another or against a State which, if the occasion arises, accepts all the obligations hereinafter set out, except in case of resistance to acts of aggression or when acting in agreement with the Council or the Assembly of the League of Nations in accordance with the provisions of the Covenant and of the present Protocol'. It is of particular interest to note that the Protocol consolidated the

---

[6] See Articles 2, 3 and 4. The electronic text is available at: www.cfr.org/treaties/protocol-pacific-settlement-international-disputes-geneva-protocol/p22306. Generally on the Geneva Protocol, see H. Shinohara, *US International Lawyers in the Interwar Years: A Forgotten Crusade* (Cambridge University Press, 2012), pp. 71–4; J. F. Williams, 'The Geneva Protocol of 1924 for the Pacific Settlement of International Disputes' (1924) 3 *Journal of the British Institute of International Affairs*, pp. 288–304.
[7] Williams, 'The Geneva Protocol of 1924 for the Pacific Settlement of International Disputes', p. 288.
[8] See also Article 7 of the Geneva Protocol.

linkage between the regulation of war and procedures of peaceful settlement of international disputes. Yet, the Geneva Protocol never entered into force.[9]

While the League of Nations failed to effectuate the Geneva Protocol, a movement for the outlawry of war never ceased. In April 1927, France proposed an anti-war treaty with the United States and the latter made a counter-proposal for a multilateral treaty to renounce war. Thus the Kellog-Briand Pact was signed in Paris on 27 August 1928.[10] The 1928 Pact contains only three provisions.[11] Under Article I, the High Contracting Parties declared that: '[T]hey condemn recourse to war for the solution of international controversies, and renounce it, as an instrument of national policy in their relations with one another.' Under Article II, the High Contracting Parties agreed that: '[T]he settlement or solution of all disputes or conflicts of whatever nature or of whatever origin they may be, which may arise among them, shall never be sought except by pacific means.' Here one can find the interlinkage between the prohibition of war and the peaceful settlement of international disputes. Nonetheless, the effectiveness of the 1928 Pact remained questionable. In particular, the lack of a definition of self-defence was thought to be a serious flaw of the Pact.[12] Furthermore, the Pact contained no specific procedure of international dispute settlement. More fundamentally, it was uncertain whether and to what extent the contracting parties to the Pact honoured the value and spirit reflected in the Pact in their interpretations and applications of it.[13]

2.2 The United Nations

2.2.1 General Considerations

After World War II, the principle of non-use of force was clearly declared in Article 2(4) of the UN Charter. Notably, this provision refers to the phrase 'the threat or use of force', not the term 'war'. As already mentioned in Chapter 1,[14] the interlinkage between the prohibition of the use of force and peaceful settlement of international disputes can be found in Article 2(3) and (4) of the UN Charter. The linkage between the two elements can also be seen in the 1947 Inter-American Treaty of Reciprocal Assistance[15] and the 1948 American Treaty on Pacific Settlement.[16] Furthermore, the ICJ in the 1986 *Nicaragua* case (Merits) regarded the principle of peaceful settlement of international disputes as 'complementary to the principles of a prohibitive nature', such as the principle of the prohibition on the threat or use of force or the principle of non-intervention.[17] However, the interlinkage

---

[9] Shinohara, *US International Lawyers in the Interwar Years*, p. 74; N. Schrijver, 'The Ban on the Use of Force in the UN Charter' in M. Weller et al. (eds.), *The Oxford Handbook of the Use of Force* (Oxford University Press, 2015), p. 468.
[10] The text is available at: http://avalon.law.yale.edu/20th_century/kbpact.asp. Entered into force 24 July 1929.
[11] Shinohara, *US International Lawyers in the Interwar Years*, p. 77.
[12] C. G. Fenwick, 'War as an Instrument of National Policy' (1928) 22 *AJIL*, pp. 827–8. See also Shinohara, *US International Lawyers in the Interwar Years*, pp. 77–83.
[13] Shinohara, *US International Lawyers in the Interwar Years*, p. 83. See also p. 90.
[14] See Chapter 1, section 2 of this book.
[15] Articles 1 and 2. The text of the treaty is available at: http://avalon.law.yale.edu/20th_century/decad061.asp.
[16] Article I. Text in: (1949) 30 *UNTS*, p. 83.
[17] ICJ Reports 1986, p. 145, para. 290.

between the prohibition of the use of force and peaceful settlement of international disputes is compromised by two major problems: malfunction of the collective security system and absence of mechanism for peaceful change.

2.2.2 Malfunction of the Collective Security System

The collective security system is at the heart of the maintenance of international security under the UN Charter. This system can be defined as 'a system, regional or global, in which each state in the system accepts that the security of one is the concern of all, and agrees to join in a collective response to threats to, and breaches of, the peace'.[18] Under this system, a lawbreaker must expect to face collective action of all States in defence of international law. In simple terms, 'one for all and all for one' is the watchword of the collective security.[19]

The collective security system in the United Nations is to be triggered by the Security Council's determination under Article 39 of the UN Charter. In accordance with this provision, the Council is to determine the existence of any threat to the peace, breach of the peace or act of aggression. It then makes recommendations, or decides what measures shall be taken in accordance with Articles 41 and 42, to maintain or restore international peace and security. Article 41 provides non-military measures. Should the Security Council consider that measures provided for in Article 41 would be inadequate or have proved to be inadequate, it may take military action, such as demonstrations, blockade, and other operations by air, sea or land forces of members of the United Nations by virtue of Article 42. To effectuate Article 42, all members of the United Nations must undertake to make available to the Security Council armed forces, assistance and facilities in accordance with a special agreement or agreements. To this date, however, no agreement has been concluded on this matter. It is unlikely that the original scheme of Chapter VII of the UN Charter will function in the near future. As an alternative solution, there is a trend that the Security Council will authorise Member States to use force under Chapter VII. At present, it is generally agreed that the Security Council can authorise Member States to take military enforcement action, even though the precise legal basis for this method in the Charter is not clear.[20]

In order to effectuate a collective security system, *inter alia*, five requirements need to be fulfilled:[21]

(i) the prohibition of illegal use of force
(ii) universality of membership
(iii) the premise of indivisible peace
(iv) effective machinery for sanctions
(v) relative equality of power.

---

[18] V. Lowe et al. (eds.), *The United Nations Security Council and War: The Evolution of Thought and Practice Since 1945* (Oxford University Press, 2008), p. 13.
[19] H. J. Morgenthau, *Politics Among Nations: The Struggle for Power and Peace*, 7th edn (Boston: McGraw-Hill, 2006), p. 435.
[20] C. Gray, *International Law and the Use of Force*, 3rd edn (Oxford University Press, 2008), p. 328.
[21] T. Sato, *The Law of International Organization* (in Japanese) (Tokyo: Yuhikaku, 2005), pp. 290–2. See also Claude, Jr, *Swords into Plowshares*, pp. 250–61.

As discussed in Chapter 4, the UN Security Council cannot impose any sanctions upon permanent members of the Security Council because of the veto.[22] It would also be difficult to impose sanctions to allied States of one of the permanent members of the Council against their will, while military action can be taken against non-allied States. This is a double standard. Thus it is hard to consider that requirement (iv) is fulfilled. Furthermore, in light of the practice of the Security Council, along with the absence of special agreements under Article 43 of the UN Charter, it is open to doubt whether the premise of indivisible peace exists in the international community.

More fundamentally, the collective security system rests essentially on the idea of the maintenance of international security by military forces. If the United Nations could take military action under Chapter VII of the UN Charter, such action will create armed conflicts between States and impose considerable damage and risk upon States participating in the action. Given that a significant inequality of power exists in the international community, it is unrealistic to require small countries to participate in military operations against a big power to the detriment of their nationals. For the above reasons, there are serious doubts whether the collective security system under the UN Charter can function effectively.

2.2.3 Inadequate Mechanism of Peaceful Change

Traditionally war was a device to bring about change of the status quo as a primitive way of self-help.[23] In order to eliminate 'war' or illicit use of force from the realm of international law, there is a need to create machinery for peaceful change that can be a substitute for war.[24] Yet, peaceful change creates a sharp tension between change and stability of a legal order.

A procedure of peaceful change was provided in Article 19 of the Covenant of the League of Nations. This provision allowed the Assembly to advise the reconsideration by members of the League of treaties which have become inapplicable and the consideration of international conditions whose continuance might endanger the peace of the world. Nonetheless, this provision turned out to be a dead letter.[25]

Under the UN Charter, a key provision in this matter is Article 14:

> Subject to the provisions of Article 12, the General Assembly may recommend measures for the peaceful adjustment of any situation, regardless of origin, which it deems likely to impair the general welfare or friendly relations among nations, including situations resulting from a violation of the provisions of the present Charter setting forth the Purposes and Principles of the United Nations.[26]

---

[22] The veto is discussed in Chapter 4, section 2.3 of this book.
[23] J. L. Kunz, 'The Problem of Revision in International Law ("Peaceful Change")' (1939) 33 *AJIL*, p. 33.
[24] J. L. Brierly, 'International Law and Resort to Armed Force' (1930-2) 4 *Cambridge Law Journal*, p. 318; J. L. Kunz, 'The Law of Nations, Static and Dynamic' (1933) 27 *AJIL*, p. 635.
[25] H. Owada, 'Peaceful Change' in *Max Planck Encyclopaedia*, para. 14.
[26] For the difference between Article 19 of the League Covenant and Article 14 of the UN Charter, see B. Simma *et al.* (eds.), *The Charter of the United Nations: A Commentary* (hereafter *A Commentary*), 3rd edn, Vol. I (Oxford University Press, 2012), p. 557.

According to the ICJ, 'the word "measures" implies some kind of action, and the only limitation which Article 14 imposes on the General Assembly is the restriction found in Article 12, namely, that the Assembly should not recommend measures while the Security Council is dealing with the same matter unless the Council requests it to do so'.[27] However, the opportunities for the General Assembly to act on the basis of Article 14 seem to be rather limited,[28] since, under the UN Charter, the Security Council is given the primary role in the field of international dispute settlement.[29] Furthermore, as 'recommendations' by the General Assembly are non-binding by nature, they lack enforceability. In reality, peaceful change appears to be mostly controlled by the political will of powerful States.[30]

3 INTERLINKAGE BETWEEN DISARMAMENT AND PEACEFUL SETTLEMENT OF INTERNATIONAL DISPUTES

As noted, disarmament is a prerequisite to effectuate the principle of non-use of force and peaceful settlement of international disputes.[31] An obligation of disarmament was explicitly enshrined in Article 8(1) of the League Covenant:

> The Members of the League recognise that the maintenance of peace requires the reduction of national armaments to the lowest point consistent with national safety and the enforcement by common action of international obligations.

However, the results achieved in the field of disarmament during the League era were very modest. Efforts on disarmament by the League of Nations were supplemented by such extra-League negotiations as those at the Washington Conference of 1921–1922 and the London Naval Conference of 1930. Unfortunately the ultimate failure of the League's efforts in the field of disarmament was exemplified by the outbreak of World War II.[32]

The UN Charter gives three separate bodies a role in international disarmament efforts: the General Assembly,[33] the Security Council[34] and the Military Staff Committee.[35] Since the UN Charter was drafted when World War II was still in progress, planning a disarmament system might have seemed ill timed.[36] Even so, the General Assembly has

---

[27] *Certain Expenses of the United Nations (Article 17, paragraph 2, of the Charter)*, Advisory Opinion of 20 July 1962, ICJ Reports 1962, p. 163.
[28] *A Commentary*, p. 559.   [29] See Articles 33–8 of the UN Charter.   [30] *A Commentary*, p. 566.
[31] Morgenthau defined 'disarmament' as 'the reduction or elimination of certain or all armaments for the purpose of ending the armaments race'. Strictly speaking, disarmament is distinct from arms control, which is concerned with regulating the armaments race for the purpose of creating measure of military stability. Morgenthau, *Politics Among Nations*, p. 403. However, presently the concept of arms control covers a wide range of measures and the distinction between arms control and disarmament is less clear. See J. Goldblat, *Arms Control: A Guide to Negotiations and Agreements*, 2nd edn (London: Sage, 2002), p. 3; A. Loets, 'Arms Control' in *Max Planck Encyclopaedia*, para. 2.
[32] Claude, Jr, *Swords into Plowshares*, p. 295.
[33] Article 11(1).   [34] Article 26.   [35] Article 47(1).   [36] Goldblat, *Arms Control*, p. 33.

been particularly active in the field of international disarmament.[37] Indeed, as early as 1954, the General Assembly, in its Resolution 808(IX)A of 4 November 1954, called for a convention on nuclear disarmament and has repeated this call in many subsequent resolutions.[38]

While there were some developments in the context of disarmament and arms control after World War II, disarmament of nuclear weapons encounters considerable challenges. As at June 2017, there are around 14,900 nuclear warheads in the world.[39] While nuclear weapon tests were partially prohibited by the Partial Test Ban Treaty,[40] the 1996 Comprehensive Nuclear Test Ban Treaty has not yet entered into force.[41] Three nuclear power States (i.e. India, Israel and Pakistan) have not yet ratified the 1968 Treaty on the Non-Proliferation of Nuclear Weapons (NPT).[42] In addition, the Democratic People's Republic of Korea gave its notice of withdrawal from the NPT in 1993 and 2003.[43] On the other hand, remarkably the Treaty on the Prohibition of Nuclear Weapons, a legally binding instrument to prohibit nuclear weapons, leading towards their total elimination, was adopted on 7 July 2017.[44]

Generally, success or failure of disarmament rests on the answers that can be given to at least two fundamental questions. The first question relates to the ratio among the armaments of different States and the second question concerns the standards according to which different types and quantities of armaments are to be allocated to different States within the agreed ratio. To answer these questions, there is a need to evaluate the power of a State in comparison with the power of other States and the military needs of relevant States. However, it is highly difficult, if not impossible, to objectively evaluate these matters since they involve the actual and anticipated security policies of States.[45] This is a fundamental obstacle to promoting disarmament.

In reality, it is uncommon that disputes concerning the breach of obligations concerning disarmament and arms control are submitted to an international court. However, it is not suggested that judicial organs have no role to play in this field. A remarkable example is the ICJ's advisory opinion on the *Legality of the Threat or Use of Nuclear Weapons*. Even though, as a judicial body, the ICJ does not directly involve the process of disarmament and arms control, it may be possible for the Court to identify the obligation of

---

[37] *Obligations concerning Negotiations relating to Cessation of the Nuclear Arms Race and to Nuclear Disarmament* (Marshall Islands v United Kingdom), Judgment of 5 October 2016, Preliminary objections (not yet reported), para. 15. [38] *Ibid*.
[39] Nagasaki University Research Centre for Nuclear Weapons Abolition, www.recna.nagasaki-u.ac.jp/recna/en-nuclear/worlds-nuclear-warheads-count.
[40] Treaty Banning Nuclear Weapon Tests in the Atmosphere, in Outer Space and Under Water. The electronic text is available at: http://disarmament.un.org/treaties/t/test_ban/text. Entered into force 10 October 1963.
[41] The electronic text is available at: http://disarmament.un.org/treaties/t/ctbt/text.
[42] Text in 729 *UNTS*, p. 161. Entered into force 5 March 1970.
[43] IAEA, Fact Sheet on DPRK Nuclear Safeguards, available at: www.iaea.org/newscenter/focus/dprk/fact-sheet-on-dprk-nuclear-safeguards. See also F.K. Kirgis, 'North Korea's Withdrawal from the Nuclear Nonproliferation Treaty' (2003) 8 *Insights*, available at: www.asil.org/insights/volume/8/issue/2/north-koreas-withdrawal-nuclear-nonproliferation-treaty.
[44] See www.un.org/disarmament/ptnw/.
[45] Morgenthau, *Politics among Nations*, pp. 408–17.

disarmament. In fact, the ICJ, in the advisory opinion on *the Legality of the Threat or Use of Nuclear Weapons*, observed that:

> In the long run, international law, and with it the stability of the international order which it is intended to govern, are bound to suffer from the continuing difference of views with regard to the legal status of weapons as deadly as nuclear weapons. It is consequently important to put an end to this state of affairs: the long-promised complete nuclear disarmament appears to be the most appropriate means of achieving that result.[46]

It then unanimously held that:

> There exists an obligation to pursue in good faith and bring to a conclusion negotiations leading to nuclear disarmament in all its aspects under strict and effective international control.[47]

The Court's statement is noteworthy since it explicitly accepted the existence of an obligation to promote nuclear disarmament.

Another notable example is the *Nuclear Disarmament* cases between the Marshall Islands on the one hand and India, Pakistan and the United Kingdom on the other hand. On 24 April 2014, the Marshall Islands instituted proceedings against the nine nuclear-armed States before the ICJ.[48] Apart from India, Pakistan and the United Kingdom, however, no States accepted the jurisdiction of the Court. Thus the Court was only seised of three cases against India, Pakistan and the United Kingdom. In its application, the Marshall Islands requested the Court to adjudge and declare, *inter alia*, that the three States had violated and continued to violate their international obligations under Article VI of the NPT and/or customary international law. In all three cases, however, the ICJ dismissed a case on the ground that no dispute existed between the applicant and the respondent prior to the filing of the application instituting proceedings.[49] Unfortunately the Court seemed to miss an important opportunity to determine the alleged breach of the obligation to promote nuclear disarmament incumbent upon nuclear powers.

4 LOOKING AHEAD

Overall it can be observed that disarmament, in particular, nuclear disarmament, is very slow to progress. This means that one of the foundations for peace remains highly fragile. At the same time, it can be observed that the requirements to effectuate the collective security system are not yet fulfilled. States will not disarm until collective security has clearly shown that it merits confidence. Here the problem of

---

[46] *Legality of the Threat or Use of Nuclear Weapons*, Advisory Opinion of 8 July 1996, ICJ Reports 1996, p. 263, para. 98.
[47] *Ibid.*, p. 267, para. 105(2)(F).
[48] The nuclear-armed States are: the United States, United Kingdom, France, Russia, China, India, Pakistan, Israel and North Korea.
[49] See Chapter 1, section 3.2 of this book.

circularity arises.[50] Furthermore, the ineffectiveness of the collective security system and slow progress of disarmament weaken the peaceful settlement of international disputes. While the three components for peace must be supported together at the same time, the ineffectiveness of one element deters the progress of the other two elements in reality. It can be said that this is a fundamental problem that impedes sustainable peace in the international community. Here a difficult but crucial question arises as to how it is possible to strengthen the interlinkage between the three pillars. While no definitive answer can be given here, four points can be made.

First, the role of judicial organs, in particular, the ICJ, in consolidating the principle of non-use of force should not be underestimated. Even though some pronounced the death of Article 2(4) of the UN Charter because of widely diverging State practice and the ineffectiveness of the collective security system,[51] the ICJ has never alluded to the possibility that the principle of non-use of force might have lost its legal validity.[52] Instead, it declared that: 'The prohibition against the use of force is a cornerstone of the United Nations Charter.'[53] Given that the principle of non-use of force is being discarded even as a fig leaf,[54] the role of the Court in consolidating the vulnerable principle is crucial.

Second, the role of the ICJ's provisional measures in armed conflict situations merits highlighting. The Court has indicated provisional measures in several cases involving armed conflicts or the use of force. In a broad perspective, these measures can be divided into four categories:

(i) provisional measures to refrain from any action which might aggravate the dispute before the Court (non-aggravation measures)
(ii) provisional measures to cease hostile activities (negative measures)
(iii) provisional measures to take specific action, including the withdrawal of troops (positive measures)
(iv) provisional measures to secure evidence and provide information with regard to the implementation of provisional measures (securing evidence measures).[55]

In armed conflict situations, 'non-aggravation measures' were indicated by the Court in the *Nicaragua*,[56] *Burkina Faso/Mali*,[57] *Cameroon/Nigeria*,[58] *Congo/Uganda*,[59] *Costa Rica/*

---

[50] Claude, Jr, *Swords into Plowshares*, pp. 259–60 and 293.
[51] T. M. Franck, 'Who Killed Article 2(4)' (1970) 64 *AJIL*, p. 809.
[52] C. Kreß, 'The International Court of Justice and the "Principle of Non-Use of Force"' in M. Weller (ed.), *The Oxford Handbook of the Use of Force in International Law* (Oxford University Press, 2015), p. 570.
[53] *Armed Activities on the Territory of the Congo* (Democratic Republic of the Congo v Uganda), Judgment of 19 December 2005, ICJ Reports 2005, p. 223, para. 148.
[54] See Separate Opinion of Judge Simma in the *Oil Platforms* case, ICJ Reports 2003, p. 328, para. 6.
[55] P. Palchetti, 'The Power of the International Court of Justice to Indicate Provisional Measures to Prevent the Aggravation of a Dispute' (2008) 21 *LJIL*, pp. 623–42; Y. Tanaka, 'A New Phase of the Temple of Preah Vihear Dispute before the International Court of Justice: Reflections on the Indication of Provisional Measures of 18 July 2011' (2012) 11 *CJIL*, pp. 193 and 207–10.
[56] *Military and Paramilitary Activities in and against Nicaragua* (Nicaragua v USA), Provisional Measures, Order of 10 May 1984, ICJ Reports 1984, p. 187, para. 41(3).
[57] *Case Concerning the Frontier Dispute* (Burkina Faso v Mali), Provisional Measures, Order of 10 January 1986, ICJ Reports 1986, pp. 11–12, para. 32(1)(A).
[58] *Land and Maritime Boundary between Cameroon and Nigeria* (Cameroon v Nigeria: Equatorial Guinea intervening), Provisional Measures, Order of 15 March 1996, ICJ Reports 1996, p. 24, para. 49(1).
[59] *Armed Activities on the Territory of the Congo* (Democratic Republic of the Congo v Uganda), Provisional Measures, Order of 1 July 2000, ICJ Reports 2000, p. 129, para. 47(1).

Nicaragua[60] and *Temple of Preah Vihear* cases.[61] Non-aggravation measures are particularly warranted in armed conflict situations, whilst the relevance of these measures is not limited to cases involving use of force.[62] As for the second category of provisional measures, the ICJ, in the *Nicaragua* case, unanimously indicated that: 'The United States of America should immediately cease and refrain from any action restricting, blocking or endangering access to or from Nicaraguan ports, and, in particular, the laying of mines.'[63] A variation of this type of measure was indicated by the Court in the *Burkina Faso/Mali*,[64] *Cameroon/Nigeria*,[65] *Costa Rica/Nicaragua*[66] and *Crime of Genocide* cases.[67] A third category of provisional measures seeks to require both parties to take positive action. In this regard, it is of particular interest to note that the Court, in the 2011 *Temple of Preah Vihear* order, established the provisional demilitarised zone. It indicated provisional measures that require both parties to immediately withdraw their military personnel currently present in the provisional demilitarised zone.[68] Further to this, the Court required Cambodia and Thailand to allow the observers appointed by ASEAN to have access to the provisional demilitarised zone.[69] A fourth category of provisional measures aims to securing evidence in the dispute before the Court. In the *Burkina Faso/Mali* case, for instance, the Chamber of the Court required both parties to 'refrain from any act likely to impede the gathering of evidence material to the present case'.[70] Likewise, the Court, in its order in the *Cameroon/Nigeria* case, indicated that: 'Both Parties should take all necessary steps to conserve evidence relevant to the present case within the disputed area.'[71] As explained earlier, provisional measures indicated by the Court have binding effect.[72] Accordingly, so far as the litigating parties before the Court are concerned, the ICJ's provisional measures would have the same legal effect as that of a Security Council resolution under Chapter VII of the UN Charter.[73] Hence the Court can contribute to effectuating the principle of non-use of force through the indication of provisional measures.

Third, as the ICJ stated in the *Nicaragua* case, 'the Court has never shied away from a case brought before it merely because it had political implications or because it involved serious elements of the use of force'.[74] In fact, the Court has given judgment on the merits

---

[60] *Certain Activities carried out by Nicaragua in the Border Area* (Costa Rica v Nicaragua), Provisional Measures, Order of 8 March 2011, ICJ Reports 2011, p. 27, para. 86(3).
[61] *Request for Interpretation of the Judgment of 15 June 1962 in the Case Concerning the Temple of Preah Vihear* (Cambodia v Thailand), Provisional Measures, Order of 18 July 2011, ICJ Reports 2011, p. 555, para. 69(B)(4).
[62] Palchetti, 'The Power of the International Court of Justice', p. 628.
[63] ICJ Reports 1984, p. 187, para. 41(B)(1).   [64] ICJ Reports 1986, p. 12, para. 32(1)(A).
[65] ICJ Reports 1996, 24, para. 49(2) and (3).   [66] ICJ Reports 2011, para. 86(1).
[67] *Application of the Convention on the Prevention and Punishment of the Crime of Genocide*, Provisional Measures, Order of 8 April 1993, ICJ Reports 1993, 24, para. 52(A)(2).
[68] ICJ Reports 2011, p. 555, para. 69(B)(1).
[69] *Ibid.*, para. 69(B)(3).   [70] ICJ Reports 1986, p. 12, para. 32(1)(B).
[71] ICJ Reports 1996, p. 25, para. 49(4).
[72] The *LaGrand* case (Germany v USA), Provisional Measures, Order of 3 March 1999, ICJ Reports 2001, p. 506, para. 109. See also Chapter 7, section 3.4 of this book.
[73] K. Oellers-Frahm, 'Article 41' in A. Zimmermann, C. Tomuschat and K. Oellers-Frahm (eds.), *The Statute of the International Court of Justice: A Commentary*, 2nd edn (Oxford University Press, 2006), p. 1069.
[74] ICJ Reports 1984, p. 435, para. 96.

in four cases involving the use of force: *Corfu Channel*,[75] *Nicaragua*, *Oil Platforms*[76] and *DRC v Uganda*.[77] Two advisory opinions (i.e. the *Nuclear Weapons* opinion and the *Wall* opinion)[78] have also addressed the legality of the use of force. As shown in the *Guyana/Suriname* arbitration, where appropriate, an arbitral tribunal can also determine the issues regarding the use of force.[79] The determination of the illegality of the use of force by an impartial third party can be an important step when applying the principle of non-use of force to a particular case.

Fourth, to prevent international disputes, there is a need to address the deep-rooted and the structural causes of these disputes. This is particularly true in the prevention of intra-State disputes. In this regard, post-conflict peacebuilding through the United Nations is of particular importance in restoring peace and preventing further disputes in a State or a region. It can also directly or indirectly contribute to preventing use of force and to promoting disarmament. Despite several challenges,[80] it appears that the role of the United Nations, in conjunction with cooperation with other international organisations and NGOs, continues to be crucial in post-conflict peacebuilding.

FURTHER READING

J. D. Fry, *Legal Resolution of Nuclear Non-Proliferation Disputes* (Cambridge University Press, 2013).

C. Gray, 'The International Court of Justice and the Use of Force' in C. J. Tams and J. Sloan (eds.), *The Development of International Law by the International Court of Justice* (Oxford University Press, 2013), pp. 237–61.

V. Koutroulis, 'The Prohibition of the Use of Force in Arbitrations and Fact-finding Reports' in M. Weller (ed.), *The Oxford Handbook of the Use of Force in International Law* (Oxford University Press, 2015), pp. 605–26.

C. Kreß, 'The International Court of Justice and the "Principle of Non-Use of force"' in M. Weller (ed.), *The Oxford Handbook of the Use of Force in International Law* (Oxford University Press, 2015), pp. 561–604.

H. Shinohara, *US International Lawyers in the Interwar Years: A Forgotten Crusade* (Cambridge University Press, 2012).

M. Wählisch, 'Peace Settlements and the Prohibition of the Use of Force' in M. Weller (ed.), *The Oxford Handbook of the Use of Force in International Law* (Oxford University Press, 2015), pp. 962–87.

A. M. Weisburd, 'Use of Force: Justiciability and Admissibility' in M. Weller (ed.), *The Oxford Handbook of the Use of Force in International Law* (Oxford University Press, 2015), pp. 329–46.

---

[75] *Corfu Channel* (United Kingdom v Albania), Judgment of 9 April 1949, Merits, ICJ Reports 1949, p. 4.
[76] *Oil Platforms* (Islamic Republic of Iran v United States of America), Judgment of 6 November 2003, ICJ Reports 2003, p. 161.
[77] *Armed Activities on the Territory of the Congo* (Democratic Republic of the Congo v Uganda), Judgment of 19 December 2005, ICJ Reports 2005, p. 168.
[78] *Legal Consequences of the Construction of a Wall in the Occupied Palestinian Territory*, Advisory Opinion of 9 July 2004, ICJ Reports 2004, p. 136.
[79] *Guyana/Suriname* arbitral award, 17 September 2007, 30 *RIAA*, p. 126, para. 445.
[80] See Chapter 11, section 2.1.4 of this book.

Index

Additional Facility (ICSID) 347
adjudicative means of dispute settlement 23
Annan, Kofi 89, 92, 94
Antarctic Treaty arbitration 317
applicable law
  ICSID 350
  inter-State arbitration 106, 117
  Iran-United States Claims Tribunal 354
  judicial settlement 106
arbitration
  environmental disputes. *see* international environmental disputes
  ICSID 346
  inquiry close to being 61
  inter-State. *see* inter-State arbitration
  intra-State, example 343
  Iran-United States Claims Tribunal 352
  as 'litigation in conditions of privacy' 118
  LOSC/UNCLOS. *see* United Nations Convention on the Law of the Sea
  mixed arbitration 343
armed conflicts
  environmental damage. *see* United Nations, Compensation Commission (UNCC)
  ICJ provisional measures 393
  non-aggravation measures 393
  peacekeeping challenges in internal armed conflicts 341

Ban Ki-moon 82
Boutros-Ghali, Boutros 18, 89, 93, 96, 99, 335, 337
burden of proof in ICJ proceedings 182

capital punishment, provisional measures against 197
co-deployment by UN and regional organisations 99
collective security
  ineffectiveness 388
  League of Nations 384
  and non-use of force 383
compensation
  environmental damage. *see* United Nations

WTO Dispute Settlement System 299
compétence de la compétence 142
compromissory clause (*clause compromissoire*)
  arbitration under 115
  negotiation under 30
compulsory procedure
  Antarctic Treaty arbitration 317
  ITLOS dispute settlement 230
conciliation
  bilateral treaties 69
  commissions 67
  compulsory 65
  conditions for 66
  current study focus 52
  early version 69
  functions 65, 70
  inquiry distinguished 52
  League of Nations 70
  limitations 69
  as means of dispute settlement 28
  numbers of conciliation proceedings 69
  optional 65
  process 53, 67
  summary overview 70
  types 65
  UNCLOS 235
  usefulness 70
conflicts and disputes distinguished 9
consultation between UN and regional organisations 99
contentious cases. *see* International Court of Justice, contentious cases
cooperation between UN and regional organisations 98
criminal law
  provisional measures against death penalty 197
  transitional justice 339

death penalty, provisional measures against 197
developing States
  economic difficulties during peacebuilding process 343
  WTO and 305, 309, 343
diplomacy

diplomatic methods of dispute settlement 20
diplomatic support between UN and regional
    organisations and arrangements 99
preventive diplomacy 89
disarmament
    conditions 391
    disputes as to breach of obligations 391
    future 392
    and international dispute settlement 390
    League of Nations 390
    nuclear weapons 391, 392
    and sustainable peace 383
    UN bodies 390
disputations and negotiation distinguished 30
dispute settlement. *see* international dispute settlement
disputes and conflicts distinguished 9
Dogger Bank inquiry (1904) 56
domestic law. *see* municipal law; States
dynamic means of dispute settlement 22

economy
    developing States and peacebuilding process 343
    dispute settlement. *see* WTO Dispute Settlement System
environment. *see* international environmental disputes;
        United Nations, Compensation Commission
        (UNCC)
erga omnes partes obligations, *locus standi* and 320
ex aequo et bono principle 176
exchanges of views, negotiation distinguished 31
execution (death penalty), provisional measures against
    197

fact-finding. *see* inquiry
force. *see* use of force
forum prorogatum 144

GATT. *see* WTO Dispute Settlement System
gender issues in peacebuilding process 342
good faith, negotiation in 37
good offices
    current study focus 28
    functions 44
    general considerations 43
    limitations 49
    as means of dispute settlement 21
    mediation distinguished 29
    process 43
    summary overview 50
    UN Secretary-General 78
    UN Security Council 78

Hague Convention 1907, inquiries under 57
Hammarskjöld, Dag 89, 91, 92, 95, 97, 100
highly political cases 169, 204

ICJ. *see* International Court of Justice
ICSID. *see* International Centre for the Settlement of
    Investment Disputes
individuals
    disputes with international organisations 19, 367
    disputes with States 18

mediation by 49
provisional measures against death penalty 197
inquiry
    close to being arbitration 61
    commissions of 54, 56, 61
    conciliation distinguished 52
    current study focus 52
    definition 53
    examples
        Dogger Bank inquiry (1904) 56
        inquiries under 1907 Hague Convention 57
        KE007 incident 62
        Letelier and Moffitt Inquiry (1991) 60
        Malaysia Airlines flight NM17 64
        Mavi Marmara incident 63
        Red Crusader incident (1961) 59
    fact-finding 52
    functions 53
    General Assembly fact-finding 85
    by individuals 55
    international environmental disputes 321
    by international organisation 62, 64
    as means of dispute settlement 22
    outcome 62
    process 54
    summary overview 70
    UN Secretary-General 80
    UN Security Council 79
    World Bank 370, 375
internal armed conflicts, peacekeeping challenges in 341
international adjudication
    international environmental disputes 312
    and international organisations 100
    negotiation and
        before adjudication 32
        during adjudication 32
        following adjudication 33, 34, 35
International Centre for the Settlement of Investment
        Disputes
    Additional Facility 347
    applicable law 350
    arbitral tribunals 347
    awards 351
    establishment 346
    jurisdiction
        provisional measures 350
        ratione materiae 349
        ratione personae 349
        ratione temporis 350
        scope 349
    mixed arbitration. *see* ICSID mixed arbitration
    purpose 346
International Court of Justice
    ad hoc Chamber
        cases 140
        composition 141
        establishment 139
        members 139
        procedure 140
    advisory opinions

International Court of Justice (cont.)
   admissibility of request 167, 168, 169
   conditions 164
   definition 163
   effect 170
   governing instruments 164
   number 164
   procedure 164, 166
   request 84, 87, 167
   summary overview 172
  applicable law
   ex aequo et bono 176
   ICJ Statute provision 175
   lex lata and lex ferenda 176, 222
  authority 130
  Chamber of Summary Procedure 139
  chambers 139
  contentious cases
   burden of proof 182
   counter-claims 180
   Decisions of the Court 184
   equality of parties 181
   experts 183, 184
   non ultra petita (not beyond what is asked for) principle 185
   non-appearance of party 187, 223
   official language of proceedings 178
   oral proceedings 181
   outline of procedure 178
   process of proceedings 180
   under special agreement 180
   standard of proof 182
   written proceedings 180
  establishment 129
  global general jurisdiction 130
  governing instruments 130
  highly political cases 169, 204
  importance 129
  independence and impartiality 129
  intervention under Article 62 ICJ Statute
   general considerations 205
   interest of a legal nature, concept of 206
   jurisdictional link between original parties and intervener State 209
   legal effect of judgments on intervener 210
  intervention under Article 63 ICJ Statute 211
  judges
   ad hoc 137
   election 132
   independence and impartiality 134
   national judges 137
   President 133
  judgments
   effect of Article 59 ICJ Statute 215
   implementation 221
   interpretation 215, 216
   res judicata 213
   revision 218
   use of force 394
  jurisdiction
   advisory jurisdiction 163
   compétence de la compétence 142
   compromissory clause 144
   forum prorogatum 144
   global general jurisdiction 130
   optional clause declarations 147, 148, 161, 162, 163
   optional clause reservations 149, 151, 152, 154, 156, 157, 160, 172
   prima facie jurisdiction, provisional measures 191
   special agreement 142
   States consent 141
   summary overview 171
  Lockerbie case 363
  and non-use of force 393
  organisation 132
  parallel proceedings 84
  parties
   equality 181
   only States may be 131
   third-party intervention 205
  pending cases 130
  Practice Directions 131
  precedent 130
  preliminary objections
   admissibility of disputes involving highly political issues 204
   Monetary Gold rule 202
   procedural issues 200
   summary overview 223
  President 133
  principal UN judicial organ 129
  procedure
   advisory opinions 164, 166
   contentious cases 178
   current study focus 175
   summary overview 222
  provisional measures
   armed conflicts 393
   cease of execution of individuals 197
   implementation 199
   purpose 190
   requirements to indicate 191, 193, 194, 195, 196
   summary overview 223
  ratione materiae reservations 154
  ratione personae reservations 151
  Registry 141
  Rules 130
  special agreement
   contentious cases 180
   jurisdiction 142
  Special Chamber 139
  States access 131
  Statute 129, 130
  summary overview 171
  and sustainable peace 393
  third-party intervention 205
  UN General Assembly referral 87
  UN Security Council referral 84
  workload 130
international courts
  fragmentation of international law 269
  judgments. see judgments and orders

Index

international dispute settlement
  adjudicative/quasi-adjudicative means 23
  balance of stability and change in international law 4
  classification of means 19
  consent-based nature 24
  current study focus 3
  disarmament and 390
  disputes and conflicts distinguished 9
  distinction between legal (static) and non-legal (dynamic) disputes 14
  dual model 20
  dynamic means of 22
  as essential function of law 3
  evolutionary nature 24
  features 24
  flexibility 24
  GATT/WTO. see WTO Dispute Settlement System
  international law. see international dispute settlement in international law 3
  inter-State. see inter-State dispute settlement
  LOSC/UNCLOS. see United Nations Convention on the Law of the Sea
  methods 21
  need for effective mechanisms for peaceful resolution 5
  new means 23
  non-adjudicative means 23
  non-hierarchical nature 24
  obligation for peaceful settlement 5
  and prohibition of threat or use of force
    League of Nations 384
    United Nations
  single model 19
  static means of 22
  structural causes of disputes 395
  summary overview 25
  and sustainable peace 383
  system 19
  theoretical foundation 1
  United Nations 73. see United Nations
  WTO. see WTO Dispute Settlement System
international disputes
  decentralised system of international law 4
  definition 8
  distinction between legal (static) and non-legal (dynamic) disputes 14
  diversity 17
  identification of
    case study on 12
    criteria for 9
  need for effective mechanisms for peaceful resolution 5
  non-State actors. see non-State actors
  obligation for peaceful settlement 5
international environmental disputes
  arbitration
    advantages 314
    experts 315
    Protocol on Environmental Protection to the Antarctic Treaty
      arbitration rules 317
      compulsory procedure 317
      provisional measures 317
      third party intervention 318
      voluntary procedure 316
    UNCLOS 315
  causality, proving of 312
  current study focus 311
  definition 311
  fact-finding 321
  importance 312
  international adjudication 312
  litigation, role of 312
  locus standi and obligations *erga omnes partes* 320
  multiple judicial fora 313
  negotiation, preference for 312
  non-compliance procedures
    activation
      self-triggering 325
      third party 326
    assistance oriented 324
    composition of supervisory bodies 327
    dispute settlement procedures in relation 329
    legal basis 325
    need for effective mechanisms for 323
    non-adversarial 324
    non-confrontational character 323
    'non-prejudice' clause 330
    not consent-based 324
    preventive purpose 324
    provision 324
    safeguarding of common interests of treaty parties 324
    specific measures 328
  provisional measures 318
  shared responsibility 312
  State responsibility, limitations on 313
  summary overview 332
international law
  balance of stability and change in 4
  decentralised system of 4
  dispute settlement in 3
  expansion 29
  international disputes in 3, 8
  interpretation and application of rules of international law 3
  municipal law. see municipal law
  negotiation in 29
  rules of, interpretation and application of 3
  traditional focus on inter-State dispute settlement 17
  treaties. see treaties
  UNCLOS and fragmentation of 269
international law of the sea
  definition 229
  ITLOS. see International Tribunal of the Law of the Sea
  LOSC/UNCLOS. see United Nations Convention on the Law of the Sea
international organisations
  disputes with individuals 19, 367
  disputes with member States 18, 362
  and international adjudication 100
  regional organisations

international organisations (cont.)
  limitations 101
  preventive diplomacy 90
  and UN. see United Nations
international relations. see diplomacy
international trade disputes. see WTO Dispute Settlement System
International Tribunal of the Law of the Sea
  advisory jurisdiction
    admissibility of request 267
    conditions 266
    provision 266
  applicable law 250
  Chamber of Summary Procedure 248
  chambers dealing with particular categories of disputes 247
  chambers dealing with particular disputes 247
  compulsory dispute settlement
    characterisation of dispute 241
    conciliation 235
    conditions for commencement 231
    forum selection, Montreux formula 236
    and ICJ optional clause 233
    limitations 238
    link with voluntary procedures 230
    multiplicity of forums 236
    no agreed procedure entailing binding decision 233
    no special agreement precluding 232
    obligation to exchange views 231
    optional exceptions 240
  conciliation
    compulsory 235
    voluntary 235
  establishment 230, 243
  fragmentation of international law 269
  international dispute settlement
    two-tiered system 230
    UNCLOS provisions 230
  intervention by third parties 260
  judgments 263
  jurisdiction
    maritime delimitation 249
    optional clause declarations 233
    ratione materiae 248
    ratione personae 248
  living resources, sovereign rights over 238
  marine scientific research 238
  members
    composition 243
    election 244
    national judges and judges ad hoc 245
    remuneration 244
  preliminary objections
    to admissibility 252
    to applicability of exhaustion of local remedies rule 253
    procedure 252
  proceedings
    non-appearance of party 251
    submission of dispute 251
  prompt release procedure

    applicability 261
    cases 261
    jurisdiction 260
    procedural requirements 262
    purpose 260
    reasonableness of bonds to be posted 263
    request 261
    substantive requirements
  provisional measures
    compliance 259
    conditions 255
    link with application made 257
    number of cases 255
    plausible character of alleged rights in principal request 256
    prescribing of 254
    prima facie jurisdiction 255
    provision for 254
    risk of irreparable prejudice 257
    urgency 257
  Sea-Bed Disputes Chamber. see Sea-Bed Disputes Chamber (ITLOS)
  special chambers 247
  structure 243
  summary overview 272
  third party intervention 260
  voluntary dispute settlement
    conciliation 235
    link with compulsory procedures 230
international tribunals
  fragmentation of international law 269
  ITLOS. see International Tribunal of the Law of the Sea
  judgments. see judgments and orders
inter-State arbitration
  applicable law 106, 117
  arbitrators
    disagreement over appointment 109
    independence and impartiality 111
  awards
    denial of validity 119
    implementation 119
    interpretation 125
    nullity 120, 121
    under bilateral treaty 114
  binding force 105
  commencement 114
  composition of arbitral tribunals 105
  under compromissory clause (*clause compromissoire*) 115
  confidentiality 106
  current study focus 105, 128
  development 107
  intervention by third States 118
  judicial settlement distinguished 105
  jurisdiction 116
  objective 105
  Permanent Court of Arbitration 108
  procedure 106
  process 114
  under special agreement (*compromis*) 115
  speed 107

summary overview 126
inter-State dispute settlement
  traditional international law focus on 17
intervention by third parties. *see* third party intervention
intra-State disputes. *see* States
Iran-United States Claims Tribunal
  applicable law 354
  awards 354
  Claims Settlement Declaration 352
  establishment 352
  function 353
  jurisdiction
    excluded claims 354
    ratione materiae 353
    ratione personae 353
    ratione temporis 353
    scope 353
  mixed arbitration 352
Iraq and UNCC. *see* United Nations, Compensation Commission (UNCC)
irreparable prejudice, risk of 196
ITLOS. *see* International Tribunal of the Law of the Sea

joint operations between UN and regional organisations 99
judgments and orders
  negotiation as to 33, 34
  orders for negotiation 30
judicial settlement
  applicable law 106
  arbitration speediness 107
  inter-State arbitration distinguished 105
  procedure 106
juridical persons. *see* individuals
jurisdiction
  concurrent between UN and regional organisations 99
  ICJ. *see* International Court of Justice
  ICSID 349
  inter-State arbitration 116
  Iran-United States Claims Tribunal
  ITLOS. *see* International Tribunal of the Law of the Sea
  Sea-Bed Disputes Chamber 246
  WTO. *see* WTO Dispute Settlement System

KE007 incident 62
Kuwait and UNCC. *see* United Nations, Compensation Commission (UNCC)

law of the sea
  definition 229
  ITLOS. *see* International Tribunal of the Law of the Sea
  LOSC/UNCLOS. *see* United Nations Convention on the Law of the Sea
League of Nations
  conciliation 70
  disarmament 390
  distinction between legal and political disputes 14
  equivalence of Assembly and Council 87
  peaceful change procedure 389
  and Permanent Court of International Justice 129, 149
  prohibition of threat or use of force 384
  and sustainable peace 384
legal methods of dispute settlement 21
Letelier and Moffitt Inquiry (1991) 60
lex lata and *lex ferenda* 176, 222
Lie, Trygve 92
litigation
  arbitration as 'litigation in conditions of privacy' 118
  cost 307
  international environmental disputes 312
  prelusion by ICJ Statute optional clause reservations 151, 161, 163
Lockerbie case
  background 363
  discussion 364
locus standi and obligations *erga omnes partes* 320
LOSC. *see* United Nations Convention on the Law of the Sea

Malaysia Airlines flight MH17 64
marine living resources, sovereign rights over 238
maritime law
  definition 229
  ITLOS. *see* International Tribunal of the Law of the Sea
  LOSC/UNCLOS. *see* United Nations Convention on the Law of the Sea
maritime scientific research 238
Mavi Marmara incident 63
mediation
  conditions for effectiveness 45
  general considerations 45
  good offices distinguished 29
  limitations 49
  as means of dispute settlement 21
  by non-State actors 48
  practice 47
  process 46
  by States 47
  summary overview 50
  UN Guidelines 29
  UN Mediation Support Unit 48
mixed arbitration 343
Monetary Gold rule 202
municipal law
  dispute settlement in 3
  interpretation and application of international law rules 3

national law. *see* municipal law; States
natural persons. *see* individuals
natural resources, management during peacebuilding process 342
negotiation
  concept 30
  distinction from protests or disputations 30
  and exchanges of views 31
  forms of 31
  good faith 37
  and international adjudication 31
  international court or tribunal order for 30

negotiation (cont.)
  in international law 29
  international law basis 29
  as means of dispute settlement 21
  obligation 37
  outcome 41
  precondition 31
  relevance to treaty subject-matter 30
  single model of dispute settlement 19
  summary overview 50
  time-frame 40
  treaty obligation for 30
  UN Security Council 78
  warnings distinguished 31
  willingness 30
non ultra petita (not beyond what is asked for) principle 185
non-adjudicative means of dispute settlement 23
non-aggravation measures as to armed conflicts 393
non-State actors
  current study focus 334
  intra-State disputes
    diversity of disputes 335
    features 335
    peacekeeping and peacebuilding in relation 336
    third-party intervention, need for 335
    UN approach 335
  mediation by 48
  preventive diplomacy 90
  summary overview 376
  types of disputes involving 17, 334

orders. *see* judgments and orders

peace. *see* sustainable peace
peaceful settlement
  international disputes. *see* international dispute settlement
  international environmental disputes. *see* international environmental disputes
peacekeeping and peacebuilding. *see* United Nations
Pérez de Cuéllar, Javier 48, 93
Permanent Court of Arbitration
  activities 108
  establishment 108
  reform 109
Permanent Court of International Justice 129, 149
persons. *see* individuals
preventive diplomacy 89
proof and ICJ proceedings 182
protests and negotiation distinguished 30
provisional measures
  armed conflicts 393
  ICJ. *see* International Court of Justice
  ICSID 350
  international environmental disputes 318
  ITLOS. *see* International Tribunal of the Law of the Sea

quasi-adjudicative means of dispute settlement 23

ratione materiae
  ICJ 154
  ICSID 349
  Iran-United States Claims Tribunal 353
  ITLOS 248
ratione personae
  ICJ 151
  ICSID 349
  Iran-United States Claims Tribunal 353
  ITLOS 248
ratione temporis
  ICJ 152
  ICSID 350
  Iran-United States Claims Tribunal 353
Red Crusader incident (1961) 59
regional organisations. *see* international organisations
res judicata 213
rules of international law
  balance of stability and change in international law 4
  interpretation and application of 3

Sea-Bed Disputes Chamber (ITLOS)
  ad hoc Chamber 245
  advisory jurisdiction
    conditions 265
    discretion over 265
    exercise 265
    purpose 265
    request 265
  discretion over requests 265
  establishment 245
  jurisdiction 246
  members 245
  summary overview 272
settlement of disputes. *see* dispute settlement
special agreement (*compromis*) for arbitration 115
standard of proof in ICJ proceedings 182
States
  access to International Court of Justice 131
  developing States and WTO 305, 309
  disputes with international organisations 18, 362
  disputes with natural/juridical persons 18
  disputes with non-State actors. *see* non-State actors
  internal armed conflicts 18
  intra-State disputes
    arbitration, example of 343
    structural causes of disputes 395
  mediation by 47
  preventive diplomacy 90
static means of dispute settlement 22
sustainable peace
  conditions 384
  current study focus 382
  definition of peace 382
  disarmament and 383
  future 392
  ICJ role 393
  non-aggravation measures 393
  non-use of force, principle of 383, 387

peaceful change procedure 389
and peaceful settlement of international disputes 383
prohibition of threat or use of force
   League of Nations 384
   United Nations
structural causes of disputes 395

third-party intervention
   Antarctic Treaty arbitration 318
   ICJ 205
   intra-State disputes 335
   ITLOS 260
time
   negotiation timescale 40
   ratione temporis
      ICJ 152
      ICSID 350
      Iran-United States Claims Tribunal 353
   WTO strict time-frames 279, 287
trade disputes. see WTO Dispute Settlement System
transitional justice
   challenges 342
   definition 338
   elements 339
   importance 338
   judicial institutions 339
   non-judicial institutions 340
   truth commissions 340
treaties
   conciliation provisions 69
   inter-State arbitration under 114
   negotiation under 30
   obligation for negotiation 37
truth commissions in transitional justice process 340

UNCLOS. see United Nations Convention on the Law of the Sea
United Nations
   Appeals Tribunal (UNAT) 368
   collective security system 388, 392
   Compensation Commission (UNCC)
      access 357
      claims for environmental damage
         acceptance 359
         armed conflicts 358
         category 360
         duty to mitigate environmental damage 361
         Follow-up Programme for Environmental Awards 362
         legal basis 360
         liability to compensate 359
         monitoring and assessment costs 360
         reimbursement of mutual assistance costs 361
         valuation of environmental damage 361
      Commissioners 357
      differentiated evidence requirement 358
      establishment 355
      fact-finding function 355
      function 356
      Governing Council 356

      multiple categories of damage covered 357
      non-urgent claims 358
      panels 357
      structure 356
      urgent claims 358
   disarmament 390
   dispute settlement
      current study focus 73
      summary overview 102
      UN as global forum 73
   Dispute Tribunal (UNDT) 367
   General Assembly
      decisions 86
      disarmament 390
      discussions 85
      dispute settlement role 102
      fact-finding 85
      functions 85
      reference to International Court of Justice 87
      resolutions 86
      Security Council predominance 87
      submission of dispute 85
      submission of dispute to Security Council 75
      support for Secretary-General 97
   as global forum 73
   ICJ. see International Court of Justice
   internal justice system 367
   intervention in intra-State disputes
      approach to 335
      challenges 341
      peacekeeping and peacebuilding in relation 336
      transitional justice 338
      UN role 335
   Lockerbie case 363
   Mediation Support Unit 48
   negotiation guidelines 29
   non-use of force, principle of 387
   peacebuilding
      definition 337
      economic difficulties of developing States 343
      gender issues 342
      management of natural resources 342
      Peacebuilding Commission 337
      peacekeeping in relation 336, 337
      transitional justice 338
   peaceful change procedure 389
   peacekeeping
      challenges in internal armed conflicts 341
      consent principle 336
      definition 336
      functions 337
      goal 337
      impartiality principle 336
      minimal use of force, principle of 336
      peacebuilding in relation 336, 337
      principles 336
   prohibition of threat or use of force
   and regional organisations and arrangements
      co-deployment 99
      concurrent jurisdiction 99

404 Index

United Nations (cont.)
    consultation 99
    cooperation 98
    diplomatic support 99
    joint operations 99
    operational support 99
    summary overview 102
    Secretary-General
        dispute settlement role 88, 102
        fact-finding 90
        good offices 78, 92
        independence 95, 102
        inquiry and investigation 80
        list of Secretary-Generals 89
        mediation 48, 92
        peacekeeping operations 91, 93
        preventive diplomacy 89
        reliance on Member States support 96
        ruling of disputes 94
        submission of dispute to Security Council 75, 88
    Security Council
        calling for negotiations 78
        decision to examine dispute 76
        determination of specific measures 76
        disarmament 390
        dispute settlement procedure 74
        dispute settlement role 102
        disqualification from voting 82
        good offices 78
        inquiry and investigation 79
        and International Court of Justice 84
        non-procedural matters 81
        parallel proceedings 84
        predominance over General Assembly 87
        submission of dispute 74, 75
        support for Secretary-General 97
        and UNCLOS dispute settlement 240
        use of veto 80
    UNCLOS. *see* United Nations Convention on the Law of the Sea
    use of force
        non-use, principle of 387
        prohibition
United Nations Convention on the Law of the Sea
    arbitration
        Annex VII arbitral tribunal 268, 315
        Annex VIII arbitral tribunal 268
    current study focus 229
    fragmentation of international law 269
    international dispute settlement
        flexibility 230
        integral part of the Convention 230
        ITLOS. *see* International Tribunal of the Law of the Sea
    and international law of the sea 229
    summary overview 271
urgency of ICJ provisional measures 196
use of force
    ICJ judgments 394
    non-use, principle of 383, 387, 393
    prohibition of

voluntary procedures
    Antarctic Treaty arbitration 316
    ITLOS conciliation 235
    ITLOS dispute settlement 230

warnings and negotiation distinguished 31
women's issues in peacebuilding process 342
World Bank
    Inspection Panel
        accountability function 370
        fact-finding function 370, 375
        jurisdiction 375
        number of requests 375
        panel procedure
            appeal mechanism 375
            establishment 369
            limitations 375
            need for 369
            process 371
            quasi-judicial function 374
            remedies for individuals 368
    mediation by 49
WTO Dispute Settlement System
    access 281
    appellate review
        compulsory jurisdiction 308
        legal effect 296
        process 295
        provision 279
    applicable law 284
    arbitration 304
    causes of action 282
    compensation 299
    compliance delay 302
    compulsory jurisdiction 308
    conciliation 288
    consultations
        DSB role 287
        during panel proceedings 287
        requirement 286
        strict time-frames 287
    countermeasures 300
    current study focus 275
    developing States
        consideration of 305
        practice 307
        summary overview 309
    Dispute Settlement Body (DSB)
        consultations 287
        role 280
    exclusive jurisdiction 278
    features 278, 308
    GATT international dispute settlement
        and economic development goal 275
        panel system 277
        peaceful settlement of international trade disputes 276
        working parties 276
    good offices 288
    implementation of rulings and recommendations
        compensation 299

countermeasures/retaliation 300
delay of compliance 302
remedies for breach of WTO law 298
retaliation difficulties 301
summary overview 308
suspension of concessions or other obligations 300
jurisdiction
  appellate review 308
  panel proceedings 291, 308
mediation 288
'non-violation complaints' 282
panel proceedings
  composition and terms of reference 290
  consultations during 287
  establishment 289
  final report 294
  independence and impartiality 290
  interim review stage 293
  jurisdiction and scope 291
  legal effect 296
  legal nature of panel procedure 303
  panel examination 292
process 279
remedies for breach of WTO law 298
requests 279
retaliation 300
retaliation difficulties 301
reverse consensus principle 278
'situation' complaints 282
strict time-frames 279, 287
summary overview 308
surveillance mechanisms 279
suspension of concessions or other obligations 300
unified system 278
'violation' complaints 282
in WTO Agreement 278
  WTO establishment and objectives 277

For EU product safety concerns, contact us at Calle de José Abascal, 56–1°, 28003 Madrid, Spain or eugpsr@cambridge.org.

www.ingramcontent.com/pod-product-compliance
Ingram Content Group UK Ltd.
Pitfield, Milton Keynes, MK11 3LW, UK
UKHW030655060825
461487UK00011B/949